ECONOMIC SYSTEMS

ECONOMIC SYSTEMS
Analysis
and Comparison

Vaclav Holesovsky
Professor of Economics
University of Massachusetts

McGraw-Hill Book Company

New York   St. Louis   San Francisco   Auckland   Bogotá   Düsseldorf
Johannesburg   London   Madrid   Mexico   Montreal   New Delhi
Panama   Paris   São Paulo   Singapore   Sydney   Tokyo   Toronto

ECONOMIC SYSTEMS: Analysis and Comparison

2 3 4 5 6 7 8 9 0 FGRFGR 7 8 3 2 1 0 9 8

This book was set in Times Roman by National ShareGraphics, Inc. The editors were J. S. Dietrich and Joseph F. Murphy; the cover was designed by Jack Ellis; the production supervisor was Charles Hess. The drawings were done by Danmark & Michaels, Inc.
Fairfield Graphics was printer and binder.

Library of Congress Cataloging in Publication Data

Holesovsky, Vaclav.
    Economic systems.

    Includes bibliographies.
    1. Comparative economics. I. Title.
HB90.H64   330   76–44409
ISBN 0–07–029557–3

28,781

Contents

Preface

Of all the high-sounding phrases coupling two words, "continuity and change" is the one that has always fascinated me most. It makes me think of the same life material being forever molded into new forms; the old being preserved behind the backs of innovators; the new being born from what seemed to be an outdated and outlived tradition. It makes me think of reality putting constraints on the flight of fancy, and the same reality forever creating fresh opportunities for the new to take shape.

Another fascinating thing to me has been the participation of human consciousness and will in that universal objective process of change in continuity. It implies the possibility of change that does not just happen but is wrought to suit our human and humane purposes. In other words, the possibility of progress.

By way of keynoting this volume, let those two thoughts be the twin notes signaling the key in which I planned to compose it.

As for my thanking all those who helped this text come into being, the list of persons named can, in the nature of the case, represent only a fraction. There is Mrs. Jeannie Cashman, who patiently typed and ran off on the departmental duplicator an incredible number of chapter drafts, and Mrs. Carolyne Gouin, who meticulously typed the final manuscript. There is also David Ledgere, last in a series of students who helped me with their legs and ingenuity to take care of library errands, checking references, xeroxing, clipping, and filing.

Several generations of students, from 1972 on, who took the course on comparative economic systems at the University of Massachusetts in Amherst helped me greatly to road test the aforementioned chapter drafts, uncovering errors and reacting to obscurities and infelicities, as well as, generously, to clarities and felicities. They have earned the kind of acknowledgment that goes to professional reviewers and editorial assistants.

From among my colleagues at U Mass with whom I had the good opportunity to exchange views and whose brains I have been picking over the years let me name Arthur Wright, Solomon Barkin, and George Treyz. While absolving them of all responsibility for any deformation their ideas might have suffered in my hands, I should like them to enjoy as our common property any that may have turned out to their liking.

I also wish to mention here, and give it special emphasis, the intellectual stimulation I had received years before this undertaking was conceived from my Paris friend and early mentor in Marxian thought, George Veltruský. And another grateful thought goes to the Czech economists Jaroslav Krejčí, now at the University of Lancaster (England), and Jaroslav Habr, who helped me switch to economics.

To all the named and the many unnamed ones, my sincere thanks.

Vaclav Holesovsky

The Field:
An Orientation Session

It is the business of economists to help the society know what it is doing, to understand the choices, benefits, and risks it confronts.

James Tobin

In contrast to pure theory, the study of economic systems has all the attractiveness that comes from closeness to the live, changing, problem-ridden real world. In contrast to the parochialism of courses which mistake the American economy for the world and today for eternity, a comparative study of systems holds the promise of broad horizons and new alternatives. However, for every point in its favor there is a host of questions as to the appropriate approach to the subject matter.

This opening chapter has been styled in the vein of a preface and introduction all rolled into one, with the idea of letting the reader, student and instructor alike, in on some of the difficulties which have troubled this area of economics, as well as the preparation of this book. It is a peek into the kitchen before the meal is served in the dining room.

One becomes particularly sensitive to the problematic side of the comparative-systems field if one ventures off the beaten path, as the author of this text often did. His main ambition was to get away from a country-by-country account of national economies, and to be as systematic about economic systems as one can, without falling into pedantry. To call the work that resulted a "treatise" would be going too far, but it is not a rehash, in a new verbal garb, of the conventional consensus either. Let us go over the major doubts which had to be resolved, though rarely without a residual feeling that rejected solutions might have done better. Fortunately, doubts or no doubts, there is the practical necessity which commands us to settle on one definite arrangement and then hope for the best.

National Economies or Economic Systems?

Every concrete national economy operates within its own formal framework of institutions and rules of organized economic behavior, i.e., it has its own specific economic system. However, we are not interested in the economic story of individual countries as such. We would then be in the field of economic *area studies*, and not in comparative *systems* analysis. Our task is to filter out the formal, systemic aspects from the concrete and substantive content of the given country's economic life. More than that: We want to see the specific economic system of a country only as an exhibit illustrating a general type of which it is an example, or as a composite model made up of several general types living in symbiotic coexistence. The Dutch economy with its *polders*, tulips, and oil refineries is of secondary importance to us; we want it for its blend of private business organization and governmental planning, and we treat it as a case of regulated market capitalism in general.

On the other hand, general types of economic systems cannot help being abstractions from observed specific, national cases. What use are they if not to help us, in turn, see individual countries more sharply through the grid of analytic concepts? Therefore, comparative analysis of systems cannot avoid speaking of Japan, Italy, the Soviet Union, even though it presents them under a special angle, and not as full-blown, lifelike portraits.

The "special angle" is always the "systemic angle": questions of organization, information signals, incentives, methods of allocation, and so on. If we occasionally mention some features having to do, say, with natural-resource endowment or psychological traits of the population, it is only to point out their interaction with the systemic characteristics. In short, we shall differentiate throughout between (1) general model types of economic systems, (2) specific economic systems of each given country, and (3) a country's national economy in all its concreteness. Emphasis will always be on the first two.

Case-by-Case or Trait-by-Trait?

The next troublesome issue is a formal problem of exposition. How should the material be presented? The subject matter seems to be pulling in two different directions: on the one hand, economic systems can be compared by passing them in review one after another, putting each system on display in its entirety; on the other hand, one can select a single systemic aspect, one after another, and follow it through each time, as it appears under conditions of different systems. In terms of Figure 1-1, exposition following the vertical arrangement of material amounts to the case-by-case method. Horizontal arrangement proceeds according to the principle of comparing systems trait by trait.

Either of these methods is, in its own way, useful as well as awkward. One severe critic of the trait-by-trait approach broke a lance for the case-by-case approach, in a private communication, as follows:

> The problem for each system is a general equilibrium problem: the specification of major participants in the economic system and each of their behavioral equations and identification of the mechanisms which coordinate their separate behavior. (When equilibrium is not attained, that approach identifies the culprit or culprits in the system.) . . . To understand the role of the firm in a particular system you need to know how the firm behaves—what is given for the firm, what choices are open to the firm, how its success is judged, and what incentives it has to succeed—and to know this you need to know the role of the state and the roles of households as consumers and as suppliers of services. . . . From an analytic point of view, each system as a whole needs to be studied.

The trouble with this traditional approach is that it greatly weakens the element

Figure 1-1 Alternative methods of exposition in comparing economic systems.

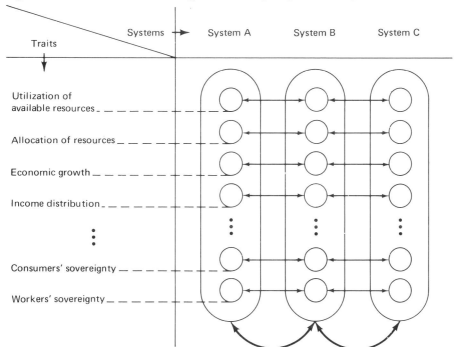

Horizontally: Select an aspect and compare its variations as they appear in different economic systems. Vertically: Give a comprehensive account of each economic system in terms of all the aspects, and then compare one system with the others.

of comparison. The material falls apart into single self-contained case studies, and stays segregated in such compartments. To make comparisons, findings about individual traits have to be stored in a memory freeze and retrieved when they are met again in the study of the next system, by which time they will have lost their freshness.

The trait-by-trait approach sounds much more lively. It promises to keep the comparatist element astir, as it spotlights the variations of a given trait in different systemic contexts, while holding them all before one's eyes simultaneously. Nevertheless, there is a danger: the image of the organic unity of individual systems may become excessively fragmented. By jumping from one system to another, with only one trait in mind at a time, the student never gets a chance to see any of them as a whole. Obviously, some compromise solution is needed, in the sense indicated by George N. Halm:

> . . . After a description of the essential features of each system has been given, it is then possible to use the horizontal method of studying the variations of a problem as it appears in different surroundings of competing economic systems.[1]

To reduce the risks of fragmentation, we decided to provide a few thumbnail sketches of important economic systems in Chapters 3 and 4, and to conduct the trait-by-trait comparisons by defining the traits quite broadly. If need be, the case-by-case treatment can easily be reconstructed by following the suggestions in the appendix to this chapter, or with the help of the index. In any case, the reader should be ready for many cross-references and frequent leafing through the book from one portion to another. It is also advisable to use, as a supplement, a selection of paperback monographs on the economies of a sample of countries, or a companion reader.

How Rigorous a Classification?

There has been a growing dissatisfaction, over the years, with the loose stereotyping of economic systems as "capitalism," "socialism" (presumably democratic), and "communism" (presumably despotic). A parallel classification of systems according to the prevalence of "tradition," "market," and "plan" has also become quite stale. In this text, the task of classification of economic systems is taken very seriously, in the conviction that understanding the nature of different systems is reflected in the adequacy of the schemes of classification.[2]

---

[1] George N. Halm, *Economic Systems: A Comparative Analysis*, 3d ed., Holt, Rinehart and Winston, New York, 1968, pp. 5–6.

[2] See the charming passage which might have served as a motto of this section were it not so long:

"Many dry river beds in central Arizona are filled with pebbles and rock fragments of infinite variety, resulting from earthcrust disturbances centuries ago. Once in such a spot I watched a little girl playing with attractive specimens selected from the millions of stones around her. She made little piles, first of all the white pebbles, then the red pebbles, the black pebbles, the multi-colored pebbles. But many were left which were of no dominant color. So she started again; she put the sharp-cornered pebbles in one pile and the round pebbles in another. Then she tried putting all the longish stones in one pile, the flat ones in a second pile, the chunky ones in a third pile. But this didn't work either, and by this time she was tired of playing and went into the house.

Questions of classification fall into the competence of a special field called taxonomy. They usually occupy the subbasement of the edifice of economics and suffer the insult of being treated as a matter of "mere terminology." One has the impression of scholars always being in a hurry to pin some name—any name—on a given phenomenon in order to get down to the really interesting questions of substantive research. However, in the comparative analysis of systems, classification happens to be part of the substantive research. To sort out systems according to types is not just a matter of the convenient labeling of diversity. It is part of the work of conceptualization and mental reconstruction of observed economies in the form of general models. Taxonomic questions have been too often treated lightly, with the consequence of a serious confusion between scientific notions and ideological mystifications.

The confusion is greatest in the approach to systems which go by the name of "socialism," and in the manner in which they are being contrasted with the capitalist system. The most significant departure of this text from tradition lies precisely in its refusal to accept customary labels as guides for classification of systems. Concretely, the fact that a political regime declares its economic system to be "socialism" is not regarded as sufficient reason for nodding obligingly and doing the same. If more exact analysis should reveal an essential similarity between such a system and capitalism in general, then the socialist label will be rejected without apologies. What may appear as an innovation is actually a return to the old distinction between ideology and scientific understanding, between self-serving label and substance. To paraphrase Lenin (who, in his turn, was paraphrasing Marx): Can anything more "shallow" be imagined than this judgment of an economic system based on nothing more than what the representatives of that system say about themselves?[3]

This revision of approach to classification and terminology has been long overdue, considering what amount of confusion in political attitudes and policies it could have spared humanity ever since 1917. The case for such a revision has been fully argued elsewhere,[4] and it is presented concisely in Chapter 3 and other dispersed sections of this book. Initially, it may rub many users of this text the wrong way. However, the aim here is not to convert anyone to a particular doctrinal creed but to deal openly with the argument on analytic grounds. The rule which applies is the one the author has used with his students: "I don't care

"Of course the little girl had no objective purpose in her classification; she merely was trying to comply with some inner demand for order which, like hope, seems to spring early as well as eternal in the human breast. Perhaps, too, she was attempting to gain some understanding of these little pieces of the universe by discovering classes in which individual specimens had membership. She was using common-sense methods to do this, and she was having the same difficulties which a more sophisticated person using scientific knowledge would have had. She knew nothing about mineralogy, or she might have sorted out the quartz, the obsidian, the calcite, the granite, the conglomerate; but she would still have been overwhelmed by the complexity of her task." (Karl Menninger et al., *The Vital Balance*, Viking, New York, 1967, pp. 9–10.)

[3] See V. I. Lenin, "What Is to Be Done," in *Collected Works*, Lawrence and Wishart, London, 1961, vol. 5, p. 357.

[4] See Vaclav Holesovsky, "Revision of the Taxonomy of 'Socialism': A Radical Proposal," *The Association for Comparative Economic Studies (ACES) Bulletin*, vol. 15, Winter 1974, pp. 19–40.

whether you change your convictions or not; what I ask of you is to grasp the argument intellectually and to be able to explain how it differs from alternative views." Besides, what is more enjoyable for the instructor, and more instructive for the student, than to pick a quarrel, here and there, with the textbook?

Can Values Serve Objectivity and Objectivity Serve Values?

There was a time when most social scientists in the academic world took pride in keeping their value judgments a closely guarded secret. Publicly they insisted on dispensing only what they thought was a strictly objective analysis of facts. Today, there is a good deal less opposition toward value judgments in social sciences. The insight has gained ground that values, consciously or unconsciously held, and perception of facts are subtly linked, even in science. Scholars have realized more and more that the problem of objective truth in social sciences cannot be properly dealt with by trying to separate neatly value orientation from a presumably detached presentation and interpretation of facts. (A posture of studied detachment is in itself an expression of a value judgment![5]) However, the pendulum may have swung too far in the opposite direction; from a corrective insight about how values and factual analysis interact, some have swiftly moved to the position that they could, in good conscience, turn the classroom into a propaganda forum.

The issue is particularly acute in the study of economic systems. Critique and defense of existing systems, and advocacy of alternatives or of the status quo, are the lifeblood of controversy between economists of different persuasions. The field is shot through with value-laden assumptions and beliefs. How does one proceed if one neither is inclined to play the professional uncommitted neutralist nor particularly relishes the strident decibels of partisanship?

Since there is no way of escaping one's value-determined point of view, there is only one honest and pedagogically sound solution: to become aware of one's values; to make the values explicit; and to show students how a particular interpretation of facts is related to the point of view of the instructor. Only then can students inspect, for themselves, how knowledge and understanding spring from both the intellectual and moral sources of scholarship, and make up their own minds.

As to the author's confession of values, his basic orientation is that of a democratic socialist, but one who finds what passes for contemporary socialist theory and practice sadly wanting and in need of profound rethinking. This means absence of commitment to any existing model or doctrine, and at the same time an attitude of social critique. Is there a danger of bias in adopting such an

---

[5] A fair sample of works dealing with this issue might include the following: Karl Mannheim, *Ideology and Utopia*, Harcourt, Brace, New York, 1936; Gunnar Myrdal, *Value in Social Theory*, Harper, New York, 1958; Alvin W. Gouldner, "Anti-Minotaur: The Myth of a Value-Free Sociology," *Social Problems*, nos. 9–10, Winter 1962, pp. 199–213. The work which has often been used as a theoretical underpinning for attacks against the claims of mainstream economics is Thomas S. Kuhn's *The Structure of Scientific Revolutions*, 2d ed., The University of Chicago Press, Chicago, 1970.

outspoken point of view? We do not believe so. Commitment to this kind of attitude demands verifiable facts. It has no use for distorting or excluding any evidence, if this is what bias means. Without scrupulous attention to facts, value judgment would become prejudice. In their turn, value orientation and moral involvement, openly acknowledged, sharpen our sense of observation. They help us notice things which we would miss if we tried to turn ourselves into instruments recording facts in a cool and detached manner.

To try for a perfect formulation of the problem of values, truth, and objectivity could get us far into the philosophical depths of the theory of knowledge. Let us stop here and conclude with the quotation of one of the better statements on the topic of value judgments and objectivity:

> The two are by no means synonymous. Objectivity has to do with freedom from bias in assessing facts, that is, events describable in empirically directly verifiable assertions. A value orientation has to do with preferences in the *selection* of questions to be posed and consequently of facts to be assessed. To claim a value-free orientation is to maintain that "all facts are created equal." If this were so, then a science would either have to take into account all facts (which is manifestly impossible) or to make a random selection (which is senseless).[6]

How Much Theory?

Comparative analysis of economic systems is necessarily grounded in empirical research. However, no self-respecting practitioner wishes to stop at describing how different institutional arrangements work, or how they evolved, blow by blow, in various countries through time. One keeps reaching out for theory, for at least three reasons. The natural urge is to cast the discussion in some unifying conceptual framework. Then, in dealing with the comparative evaluation of different systems and their performance, there is a need for theoretically defined criteria and standards. Finally, as a crowning enterprise, one wishes to reconstruct in one's mind a theoretical model of how systemic structures develop in the long run. One wants to use theory to look into the future.

The aspiration to be professionally respectable (i.e., theory-minded) may clash with the interest of students who want to know what life is like under different systems, and what makes them tick. Undergraduates, and graduate students as well, regularly revive when they hear stories and anecdotes used for illustration. It is not easy to convince them that theoretical treatment, by presenting intellectual challenges, is higher-order entertainment, too. The students' demand for touches of color and candid shots from the factories, shops, and offices of France, Russia, Britain, and Japan should, we believe, be met by the instructor or by supplementary readings. The intention here is to slant the text, in a measured way, toward emphasis upon the theoretical scaffolding.

As far as the conceptual framework is concerned, a good deal of effort has been made in the recent past to clarify what we mean by the systemic aspects of

---

[6] A. Rapoport, "Methodology in the Physical, Biological, and Social Sciences," in E. O. Attinger (ed.), *Global Systems Dynamics*, S. Karger, Basel, Switzerland, 1970, pp. 20–22.

real economies, what are the constituent parts of an economic system, and how they are to be separated from those aspects of real economies which are not the "system," as well as from noneconomic aspects of the social structure. Professors John M. Montias, Tjalling Koopmans, Egon Neuberger, Leonid Hurwicz, and Thomas Marshak are some of the names that come to mind as major scholarly contributors to the conceptual dissection of the social and economic phenomena. Their ideas are used in Chapter 2, in combination with an attempt at saying a few useful things about how the parts and partial aspects hang together and how they interact. This attempt at synthesis is of Marxian-structuralist inspiration.

Theory as systematizer, theory as provider of a conceptual framework, continues to play that role in Chapters 3, 4, and 6, where classification of economic systems from various points of view is the dominant theme.

Theory as a source for the formulation of performance criteria enters the picture starting with Chapter 5. The criteria gravitate around the notion of social-welfare maximization, but, in contrast to theoretical welfare economics, the concern is with finding usable empirical data and statistics that would make the criteria practically relevant.

Theoretical performance criteria and pieces of standard economic analysis are brought to bear eclectically upon the empirical material throughout Chapters 7 to 17, as the need arises. The input-output framework is used rather heavily in the discussion of the coordination problem under market capitalism, Soviet-type systems, and indicative planning (particularly of the French variety). It is the author's conviction that input-output accounting provides much deeper and more comprehensive insights into a major set of interdependencies that hold economic systems together than are possible with partial demand-and-supply analysis or the two-dimensional device of the production-possibilities frontier. Since most students are likely to encounter the input-output concepts for the first time, enough space is devoted (in Chapter 7) to their initiation.

The level of students' preparation for an elective course of this kind is altogether a thorny problem. Most teachers of comparative economic systems will agree that the prerequisite of elementary economics, though essential, is far from guaranteeing an adequate preparation. The course often attracts students from other disciplines than economics and business, such as political science, anthropology, and even a sprinkling of engineers, natural scientists, and nurses eager to find out more about the wide world we live in. Comparative study of economic systems thus necessarily becomes also an occasion for the review or relearning of basic economics.

To meet this need, the text has to provide enough discussion of theoretical reference points to anchor the discussion of the empirical material. But, again, there is a danger. It is easy to let oneself be drawn into extensive explanations of theory which threaten to swallow up pages and pages of the text and hours of lecture time. There is no better way out than to ask students to keep their textbooks on basic economics on their bedside tables. In any case, as in other courses with a heterogeneous student population, with every individual bringing a different background and degree of training in economics, students must expect a

certain amount of frustration due to the need for catching-up work or, on the contrary, due to being bored by what they find redundant.

As for the role of theory in the "crowning enterprise" mentioned earlier, reference is to Chapter 18, which deals with the change and succession of economic systems in historical perspective. It links up with those portions of Chapter 2 which try to elucidate how the interaction of component aspects of economic systems and society at large produces historical change. To define the limits and possibilities of conscious human intervention in this process of change is the most challenging assignment of all.

The long-term dynamics of economic structures constitutes a sadly neglected line of inquiry, which is why both historic retrospectives and futurologist predictions are the field's weak spot. We tend to scoff at Marx's ambition to discover the "laws of motion" of capitalism, but in that respect we have little to offer ourselves. Keynes's little overquoted phrase "In the long run we are all dead" had a most nefarious effect on the attitudes of economists. We may be dead, but our grandchildren and their grandchildren may not be, and they ought to matter to us.

The portion of theory which is deliberately omitted, though for some reason it usually figures in the traditional curriculum of the field, is a comprehensive exposition of Marx's economic labor theory of value. There are, of course, aspects of Marx's theorizing which are highly relevant to the analysis of economic systems, and these are organically incorporated into the text wherever appropriate. However, the labor theory of value as such is not one of them. As important as it may be, and although it is, in a deep sense, indissolubly linked to those of Marx's categories which are directly relevant to the analysis of economic systems, it belongs properly in the history of economic doctrines or in a special monograph where it can receive adequate treatment.

By virtue of tradition, one is used to expect the exposition of Marx's doctrines preceding the discussion of Soviet-type and other so-called socialist economies. This custom has obviously arisen in deference to such countries' claim that they were the executors of Marx's ideas. However, a close study of the economic systems in question finds very little correspondence between Marx's general pronouncements on the character and organizational aspects of socialism or communism and the realities which are supposed to be their embodiment. There is nothing surprising about that, since these systems are not "socialist" or "communist" in Marx's original sense. One usually stops wondering as soon as one puts aside the official claims, concerning the socialist character of such systems, and sees them for what they are: a public-relations matter. In any case, research concerning the so-called socialist economies has to be conducted with the help of the ordinary tools of economic analysis or those of organization theory. It is symptomatic that, after traditional introductory passages on Marx, authors leave them behind like unclaimed baggage as soon as they get down to concrete exposition of the systems in question.

However, it is never too late to break a bad habit. Therefore, the present text purposely takes special care to maintain a strict separation between Marx's conceptions of the postcapitalist systems and present-day realities of Soviet-type economies and analogous systems.

How Much Trespassing?

Our field is famous for poorly defined boundaries. What used to be said about the subject matter of economics in general—"Economics is what economists do"—is even more appropriate to the study of economic systems. There has been a good deal of variation in the selection of topics in the texts and courses on "comparative economic systems." It is hard to defend teachers in the field against the accusation of not knowing how to limit themselves. However, the fault may not be so much with the teachers as with the nature of the field.

Wherever boundaries are fluid, there appears a tendency toward expansion or invasion. In this case, it is our field which is, actually or potentially, expansionist. It has an impressive appetite for topics to be covered. This has its reasons. By virtue of its comparatist assignment, there is no economic system, past or present, close or distant, real or imagined, which might not be included. This raises the issue of the proper delimitation of our subject matter with respect to other specialized fields of economics and to neighboring social sciences.

As for other specialized fields of economics, there is no real danger of swallowing them up in their entirety. They are too big for that. The appropriate simile might be to view our field as placed at the intersection of the other specialized fields, with easy access to their individual workshops. From each of them—industrial organization, labor relations, foreign trade, macroeconomics, agricultural economics, and especially area studies—enough is borrowed to make intelligent cross-national comparisons possible. The study of systems has then the extra task of doing a synthesizing job: to show how these special aspects of economies are integrated, in their variants, into the respective economic systems as a whole.

With respect to other social sciences, comparative study of economic systems has the privilege of acting as a kind of two-way intercom. It is *the* interdisciplinary part of economics and thus calls for a certain acquaintance with the fields of anthropology, sociology, political science, etc. The gain to economics is a certain amount of cross-ventilation which helps remove the stale odors of smugness, the delusion of methodological superiority.

A particular aspect of the academic division of labor is the tradition according to which comparative systems deal mainly with the dominant economies of the contemporary scene, while anthropology deals with "primitive economies," economic history with past economic systems, and economics of development with the less developed systems in the process of industrialization. There is a gentlemen's agreement with respect to this splitting up—or cartelization—of the territory.[7] We shall adhere to it, within reason, and with certain exceptions (such as China or Cuba), without feeling any compunctions about encroaching upon the other specialties if we find it useful to make a point in our exposition, follow-

---

[7] See the tabular presentation in George Dalton (ed.), *Economic Development and Social Change*, The Natural History Press, Garden City, N.Y., 1971, pp. 196–197.

ing Professor Peter Wiles's credo: "If . . . I have trespassed beyond the borders of economics, I make no apology: such borders, like international ones, exist only to be trampled upon."[8]

In one sense, our field is part of economic history, namely, of its contemporary, open-ended portion. One quickly becomes aware of this fact when one realizes how fast the findings in comparative study of economic systems become obsolete. By the time this text reaches its readers, many of its statements will no longer reflect up-to-date realities. They will refer to a past which, even if recent, is a past. This deficiency afflicts all fields which try to encompass the contemporary scene, but it can be put to an advantage: It can serve as a perfect occasion for the training of students in the art of gathering the latest bibliographical references and as a source of topics for term papers updating the dated story of the book.

*   *   *

All comparative studies which take us beyond the confines of our own society have a special kind of ethics and intellectual value of their own. They cut the ground from under narrow-mindedness and self-righteousness which go with never leaving one's hometown, physically or intellectually. At the same time, provided they are honest, such studies are apt to make us immune against illusions that the grass on the other side of the fence is bound to be greener, an attitude which is nothing but provincialism in reverse.

Mobility gives rise to comparisons. Comparison is a source of insight and understanding. It kills static certitudes of isolation; it breeds abilities of relative orientation. Relativism leads to rationality. Wasn't travel always considered broadening? Comparative studies are a substitute for travel. They make it harder both for uncritical self-congratulations and for naïve admiration of the unknown and the exotic to hold sway. They make us skeptical. They also make us sensitive to the possibilites of new options.

As readers settle down to the detailed and sometimes plodding study of the material, may they keep in the back of their minds that they are participating in the search of humanity for such options: for ways of forging its own (better) future. Also, let them have fun.

APPENDIX TO CHAPTER 1: Suggestions for Using the Text

For the purposes of a one-semester course in comparative economic systems the present text surely covers too much territory, unless the instructor knows how to proceed at a very fast clip without losing the students. Hence, it has to some extent the character of a menu. In most cases, a decision will have to be made as to which topics should be studied thoroughly and which skimmed or skipped. The selection will depend on the instructors' idea of the proper design of the course, or their scholarly interests and predilections. We assume a bimodal distri-

---

[8] P. J. Wiles, *Communist International Economics*, Basil Blackwell, Oxford, 1968, p. vii.

bution of instructors—some leaning more toward the empirical study of contemporary systems, others preferring a model-theoretical slant.

The book has not been written as a collection of self-contained modules that can be freely assembled into different combinations to suit individual tastes. It has been conceived as an organic whole. Certain leading ideas are being developed throughout the entire text, and later sections build on earlier ones. Nevertheless, with a slight effort it is possible to sort out chapters and topics so as to satisfy the needs of either of the two major types of course design.

Recommended to All Users   Fundamental to all discussion of specific models and illustrative cases are those chapters which deal with the classification of economic systems, i.e.,

Chapter 3 (models by type of ownership) and
Chapter 4 (models by mode of allocation).

Chapter 2, dealing with conceptualization, will ordinarily have little charm for users with weak interest in macrosociological theory and interdisciplinary cross-referencing with other social sciences outside economics. It may also be a shade too abstract for students who like to stick to down-to-earth facts and do not wish to be bothered by broad theoretical-analytic problems. However, even they might be encouraged at least to skim the chapter, especially the first half of it, which is more oriented toward economics proper. Similarly, Chapter 5 (on performance criteria) should also be skimmed by everyone.

Chapter 6 (on normative economic systems) is essential for discussing intelligently the topic of socialism as an objective of various social and political movements.

For the Empirically Minded Comparors   Those who wish to concentrate on contrasting economic systems of the contemporary scene will have to piece together relevant sections of the book into their own thematic blocks and in a sequence different from the one in which they are presented.

The market-capitalist systems might best be treated starting with Chapter 8, accompanied by flashbacks to Chapter 5 (sections dealing with the rational price system, profit maximization, competition, and monopoly). Then, Chapter 7 is needed to prepare the theoretical background for the comparison of individual case histories country by country, as well as for the study of Soviet-type economies.

The general exposition of planning under Soviet-type systems is given in Chapter 9. It is a matter of convenience whether this should be postponed for treatment after the survey of market-capitalist systems country by country or inserted as a major contrasting general model right after the general discussion of the market-capitalist model in Chapter 8.

Material for the study of individual-country systems can be gathered using the detailed references under the appropriate country titles in the index.

For the Theoretically Oriented   A course slanted in the general theoretical direction, i.e., toward the study of systemic models, will have to be anchored, in addition to Chapters 3 and 4, in the following chapters:

 2   Conceptualization
 5   Performance criteria
16   Consumers' sovereignty
 6   Normative systems
 7   Coordination in theory
 8   Market capitalism
 9   Soviet-type planning

The study of Vanek's "participatory economy" may be combined with the section on the Yugoslav firm in Chapter 17, or with all of Chapter 17.

A study of Marx's approach to the analysis of systems will combine latter sections of Chapters 2 and 6, as well as the last three sections of Chapter 3, starting with "Corporate Capitalism."

Optional for Either Design   Depending on available time and interests of the instructor and/or students, there is a choice among several major topics treated from a comparative perspective. Questions of industrial organization are treated in Chapter 13, agricultural organization in Chapter 14, international trade relations in Chapter 15, and labor relations in Chapter 17. (Chapter 17 is also organically related to issues of socialism as an objective of social and political movements.) Chapter 18 supplies food for thought concerning the future of economic systems.

Chapter 2

Conceptualization: What Is an "Economic System"?

As the strong man exults in his physical ability, delighting in such exercises as call his muscles into action, so glories the analyst in that moral activity which disentangles.

Edgar Allan Poe

The purpose of this chapter is to put the reader into the proper analytic frame of mind. We shall work out a number of concepts for our think toolkit and suggest certain useful approaches to the analysis of social phenomena in general. This is not to say that the vocabulary developed here will be used slavishly throughout the rest of the book. Occasionally, yes. But the main point is to use this rather abstract survey of ideas as a stimulant for an intellectually subtle perception of economies and their systems. It should be more a matter of mentally absorbing and digesting these ideas. Afterward, they should be kept in the background, called upon when the need arises, but not unpacked at every stop.

Let us first agree on a preliminary definition of the word "system," though intuitively we know, of course, what it means. Formally, it refers to any set of objects which together form a functioning whole, as well as to the relationships between these objects or their characteristics which link them up into that whole. The objects are to be understood very broadly, not necessarily as material things.

An economic system's objects are people, their institutions, their resources and productive assets, their wealth of consumables, their skills, and others. As for the characteristics which tie these objects together into an economic system, we shall be better able to answer that after having considered the question of the next subtitle.

WHERE IS THE ECONOMIC SYSTEM LOCATED?

We are presumably all sophisticated enough to know that the question refers to the "social space." However, knowing that has not saved anybody yet from being misled by the spatial metaphor into looking for the economic system in some particular corner or area in the literal sense of the word. Unwittingly, one tends to imagine systems to exist "somewhere": the system of religious values to dwell in churches; the political system in the legislative chambers, government offices, and smoke-filled rooms of party conventions; and the economic system in factories, banks, and supermarkets. To guard against such misplaced concreteness, one needs only to bring to mind what "economic" really means.

The adjective "economic" refers to one particular aspect of human behavior. All human activities—and we mean all—involve the use of some resources: material assets, persons' aptitudes, and time. All human activities also involve choice between alternative courses of action and their combinations. Choice involves the consideration of available alternatives from the point of view of the intended purpose, i.e., the benefit value of the outcome, and the associated costs. Thus, activities appear as economic if the accompanying allocation of resources is considered from the point of view of costs and benefits.

If that is the case, then there exists no special class of activities that are strictly economic, and other classes that are strictly political, artistic, educational, religious, play-centered, and so on. Every activity has its resource-allocation and cost-benefit side. Therefore, every activity has its economic angle, besides having plenty of other characteristics. The anthropologist Robbins Burling put it very aptly: ". . . Economics deals not with a type but rather with an aspect of behavior. This economic view of society becomes one way, or if one prefers, one model for looking at society."[1] This is also why a number of economists (Gary Becker, Mancur Olson, etc.) could break out of the old-fashioned confines of economics and aim formal tools of economic analysis at such seemingly outlandish topics as leisure activities, marriage, bureaucratic behavior, clubs, universities, crime, boredom, and many more.

The answer to our question is contained in the conclusion which follows from the meaning of "economic," and it should not come as a surprise after what we said. If every activity has its economic aspect, then "economy" is coextensive with society, and the "economic system," too, spreads out across the social space. Its location is the entire span of the social system of which it is an aspect—a subsystem.

[1] Robbins Burling in *American Anthropologist*, vol. 64, 1962, p. 817.

The aspect character of the economic universe deserves some further elaboration. Every social fact may be looked upon as a compound of its various aspects. Take such an eminently economic fact as work. Its economic function consists in the allocation of labor services to some desirable end. But it can also be studied as a physiological fact. It has its moral aspect (duty? vocation?); emotional aspect (drudgery? fun?); psychological aspect (matter of sublimation? of inner compulsion?); a religious side (punishment for sins? a way to "laud the Lord"? religiously neutral?); a legal side (subject of contract? matter of coercion?); and an aesthetic side (pleasure to watch? a "lousy job"?). However, it is none of these exclusively. Each aspect is freely brought to the fore by virtue of the interest of the observer, while the others are kept out of the field of vision. If we take as a contrary example some noneconomic fact, such as political leadership or artistic creation, on reflection we discover the economic function clinging to it, too: some allocation of resources ("sacrifice") in view of some desired satisfactions ("benefits") is always present.

What shall we do, then, with the instinctive tendency to see some behavior and institutions as primarily economic, others as primarily political, religious, etc.? Is there something to the impression that, after all, the economic function somehow predominates in the activity of business firms and is absent or secondary in what we do at home, in politics, or on the playground? There is nothing to it. It is an illusion due to the fact that business firms do their cost-benefit calculations very explicitly and conspicuously, with prices and money and bookkeeping. Elsewhere they tend to be done implicitly, perhaps imprecisely, and even unconsciously, but they are not absent for that. If economists occupied themselves for ages almost exclusively with production and distribution involving the business-enterprise sector, this is just a reflection of a stage, albeit a long one, in the historic development of scientific interests in the field. Lately (during the last fifteen to twenty years), the scope of interests has been expanding and expanding, but in the public mind economics still ends at the gates of the marketplace.

In that case, when we study economic systems, we should practice what we preach and cover the economic-system side of all activities, including those which fall outside the business sector. Why don't we? The reasons are strictly practical. There just has not been enough empirical and comparative work done on the economics of household activities and the public sector under various economic systems. Therefore, not counting occasional references to some outstanding issues of the nonmarket area, the scope of the book remains, in this respect, regrettably old-fashioned. It is narrower than we would wish it to be.

WHAT IS AN "ECONOMIC SYSTEM"?

Let us now return to the preliminary definition of the economic system given above, and work at it further. The key notions in that definition were interconnected objects, the relationships between them and between their characteristics. Let us first examine what the constituent objects are, and to get rid of the material-thing connotation, from here on, let us call them very generally *elements* of the system.

There are four major classes of elements which constitute an economic system: resources, participants, process elements, and institutions. There is no special difficulty in sorting out into these "boxes" all the basic familiar concepts one encounters in discussing things economic. Only the process elements will require a somewhat extended discussion.

Resources

These include, first of all, portions of the nature-given environment, selected by people as suitable for their purposes. These are the raw *natural resources*—land, in the old parlance, though they include also water, air, gravity, as well as physical, chemical, and biological properties of inorganic and organic things. Processed natural resources become *materials* and *fixed producer durables*, i.e., "tools" in the broadest sense, not just plows or machine tools but also structures, means of transportation and communication, computers, books, records of information, etc. The stock of money and other assets of social use belong here too. Finally, there is *labor*—the so-called human capital: a reservoir of physical and mental services, a stock of capacity to work, skills, and accumulated knowledge attached to human beings.

Technology is an element which is often set apart, though it is incorporated in the human and manufactured productive assets enumerated before. It is made up of the qualitative characteristics of producer goods and the stock of technical knowledge. "Production functions" used in economic analysis are an expression of technology stored in the area of knowledge.

Entrepreneurship—the creative organizing activity which provides the spark and combines and integrates resources into actual activities—is merely a special skill, embodied usually (but not necessarily) in a specific category of human resources. If it is singled out as "entrepreneur," it is usually set against the other resource elements considered as "factors of production" or "economic inputs."

Participants

These are naturally people. They may be considered as individuals, but it is more useful to think of them as aggregated into groups or units organized for definite purposes. (Some of these may, of course, remain one-person units.) Also, one and the same individual will, as a rule, appear in different participating groups, simultaneously or in succession. We all play different roles as members of a consuming household, citizens, producers (workers, entrepreneurs, hobbyists, or governmental agents), etc.

The standard way is to subdivide participants of the economic system into *firms* (mainly transforming inputs into outputs), *households* (mainly transforming outputs into final satisfaction, i.e., consuming, plus supplying human resources), and the *government* (transforming inputs into outputs which have the character of public or collective goods). This is acceptable provided we keep in mind a qualifying thought. If we choose to subdivide participants differently, into *producing units* and *final-use units*, each of the two will contain firms, households, and the government. Households, too, are producers: transformation of outputs into final satisfactions entails a good deal of latter-stage processing (everyday housework, house maintenance, shopping, assembling of purchased items, child rearing). Firms and government, at their end, also serve as framework for final uses, though admittedly in a minor way: Christmas parties, business lunches, etc. However, government may be viewed wholly as a collective agent of households, organized to process inputs into outputs satisfying society's collective needs ("public consumption"), such as administration, judicial order, traffic safety, defense, health control, etc. In other words, the same way as households have to cook purchased ingredients to make meals, the government has to buy, install, and run traffic signals to produce road safety. In such a view, government would be treated like analogous units created voluntarily by members of households, who also "tax" themselves, voluntarily, for specific collective-consumption purposes: private car pools, clubs, trade unions, bird-watching associations, educational institutions, etc.

There is a trace of artificiality in this interpretation of the government as a voluntary association. Some readers may feel it more strongly than others. This is because it abstracts from the authority and power aspect. Government is a specialized organ of society, but its role is ambiguous. Is it its servant? Partner? Master? A mixture of all three? The problem, which we shall not pursue here, points to an extremely important aspect of the relationship between participants in general: that of hierarchy. However, before we discuss that, one other essential attribute of participants needs to be mentioned.

Goals and Preferences   Every participating unit has its own objectives it wishes to attain through its participation in the economic process. These are the system's ultimate purpose: satisfaction of wants, needs, desires. We call them neutrally "preferences." We think of them as being arranged in a scale, where ordinarily "more" means "better." At the same time, we take into account possibilities of attaining a given level of satisfaction within that scale through different combinations of sources. For instance, less of one item may be compensated for by more of another, keeping the degree of satisfaction unchanged. This is the kingdom of indifference curves, consumption trade-offs, and preference maps familiar from elementary price theory. In the preference sets of participants there is a natural place for other than material assets, too: psychic satisfactions derived from alternative activities (e.g., jobs), income-distribution patterns, characteristics of the economic system itself, and various "states of the world" in general.

Participating units made up of larger sets of individuals are also thought of as having their own goals and preferences. These are not necessarily formed by summing up (aggregating) the preferences of participating individuals; they are not "reducible" to them. They may be of an entirely different order. Thus, the objective of a firm (to maximize profits, to grow, to keep its share of the market) may have nothing to do, directly, with the private objectives of its employees or other interested parties. We deal with such issues by viewing some of the individual participants (e.g., "capitalists" or managers) as representatives, agents, or spokesmen of such supraindividual objectives. Sometimes these representatives can even be interpreted as giving voice to some kind of impersonal objectives of the system, having to do with the way it works as an impersonal mechanism. This is how Marx consistently interpreted the role of the capitalist as capitalist, keeping it analytically separated from the capitalist's private preferences as a person:

> Only as personified capital is the capitalist respectable. As such, he shares with the miser the passion for wealth as wealth. But that which in the miser is a mere idiosyncrasy, is, in the capitalist, the effect of the social mechanism, of which he is but one of the wheels. . . . So far . . . as his actions are a mere function of capital—endowed as capital is, in his person, with consciousness and a will—his own private consumption is a robbery perpetrated on accumulation. . . . [2]

Neil W. Chamberlain deals with the same issue from the point of view of the modern art of management, as a "process by which differing views of individuals in an organization are compromised into a more or less compatible set of policies and practices."[3]

In the case of government's activities, the problem of synthesizing individual preferences appears even more strongly, inasmuch as individual preferences may be totally incompatible, and hence cannot be harmoniously compromised. In that case, power relations provide a "solution": preferences of some individuals or groups are suppressed or ignored, in any case frustrated, in favor of the preferences of others.[4] The others may be the majority or the group in power itself, even if not a majority. Where divergences between conflicting sets of preferences appear particularly striking, it may be useful to express them in words. Thus, under conditions of Soviet-type planning, it has become customary to speak of "planners' preferences" as opposed to preferences of the population (to be kept in mind for Chapter 16 on consumers' sovereignty).

Hierarchy between Participants   Hierarchy arises from the fact that participating units are engaged in constant decision making. Decision making is subject to division of labor, as much as the production process itself. Decision making can be split up and arranged into a structure going from the most general to the most specific. At the most general level are decisions on "policy," "strategy," "overall objectives." At the most specific are decisions such as "oil that joint," "tighten that screw," "calm that irate customer tactfully." Decisions can be also fragmented along functional lines: decisions on finances, investment, marketing, production, public relations, etc. The point to be made here is that all partial decisions in a set are complementary, but they may also be a source of superiority and subordination. As far as decision making is concerned, individual participants within a unit, or participating units between them, may fall into a hierarchical pattern. They rank higher or lower. They issue orders or they obey. They form tiers.

The most obvious example of hierarchy within participating units is the authority pyramid in early old-style patriarchal firms or under the Soviet princi-

---

[2] K. Marx, *Capital*, International Publishers, New York, 1967, vol. I, p. 592.

[3] Neil W. Chamberlain, *Private and Public Planning*, McGraw-Hill, New York, 1965, p. 7. See also his *A General Theory of Economic Process*, Harper & Row, New York, 1955.

[4] This is the simple meaning, or implication, of Kenneth Arrow's theorem on the impossibility of a "social welfare function."

ple of "one-man management" (*edinonachalie*) with the enterprise director on top. However, households, too, have internal hierarchies ("authoritarian family"), though within both firms and households the patterns of distribution of authority tend to be more complex than the image of a one-way chain of command suggests. Hierarchies are also present in relations within multidivisional corporations (between headquarters, individual divisions, and their plants) or within conglomerates (between the holding company, or its equivalent, and the member companies or subsidiaries).

However, the most interesting issues concern hierarchies between production or consumption units and a class of units of which government is the most obvious example. Here, the notion of logical subdivision of the decision-making process into component phases is not so useful any more. The issues are better grasped by thinking of some participating units making decisions which constrain, or "frame" the decisions of the subordinate units. They formulate the general rules of conduct. They provide the "codes of behavior" and watch over their being followed. This type of hierarchy is established between the enterprise sector and a segment of the government, namely, those units of government which have the legislative function (or administrative prerogatives) and the judicial function: congress or parliament, food and drug administration in the United States, antitrust organs, zoning boards, licensing organs, and courts. The household sector is also subject to this kind of hierarchy. Certain categories of consumption may require licensing (e.g., use of automobiles), and certain modes of "consumption" may be prohibited or imposed (use of matches for the annihilation of one's property, nude bathing, garbage disposal, littering). Koopmans and Montias call this particular tier the "ruling organizations."[5] Such participating units may also be created by production units voluntarily. Professional associations may assume the function of licensing (e.g., the Barbers' Examination Board), setting fees (e.g., lawyers' bar associations), or otherwise regulating the decisions of members.

These "framework functions" of ruling organizations must be distinguished from actual participation of governmental units in operational decisions of the production sector. If the government imposes production quotas, issues export licenses, fixes or controls prices and wages, controls the supply of money and credit, administers rationing, or affects distribution of income through taxes, it effectively shares in the decisions of the subordinate units. In the extreme, it takes over the management entirely. In all such cases we have an interpenetration of government and enterprises in decision making. One speaks of "government interference." Or one speaks of the "state as entrepreneur." In the case of Soviet-type centrally administered economies, there is no clear dividing line between managerial decisions of the enterprise sector and those of governmental administrative units, up to the State Planning Commission and the Council of Ministers.

Participating units may also have their decision making constrained or framed by rules agreed upon with other units which are not in any hierarchical

---

[5] Tjalling C. Koopmans and John Michael Montias, "On the Description and Comparison of Economic Systems," in Alexander Eckstein (ed.), *Comparisons of Economic Systems: Theoretical and Methodological Approaches*, University of California Press, Berkeley, 1971, p. 54.

sense above them. Thus, labor unions conclude collective agreements with the management of firms, resulting in certain rules of conduct. Relationships of this type are better described as involving "bargaining organizations" than "ruling organizations." Various interest groups exercise an influence upon decision making in essentially the same way, e.g., consumer-interest groups, environmentalists, churches, etc. However, the process is much more diffuse and conduct rules are not binding. It amounts to "moral suasion."

Centralization and Decentralization   The phenomenon of hierarchy raises a further issue of great significance for the analysis of economic systems, that of centralization and decentralization. The terms sound simple, their meaning obvious, but as soon as we try to formulate precisely how they differ, we discover a tantalizing degree of complexity.[6] Therefore, no rigorous and exhaustive treatment will be given here, only a few pointers.

An economic system would be completely centralized if all decisions, from the most general to the most minute, emanated from only one participating unit, the *center*. All other participating units would be only executing them, passively and obediently: the case of the perfect economic dictatorship. In this form it surely cannot be found anywhere in the world. Omnipotence requires omniscience, and absolute centralized knowledge may be safely excluded from the realm of the possible. This makes it necessary for the center to try and organize all the decisions into higher ones (broader in scope) and lower ones (more specific), in such a way that a set of lower ones is always implied by the next higher one. If this can be done, the top decisions can be then delegated for execution via lower-level decisions, down a vertical pyramid of authority. We may call this arrangement decentralization, but it is a decentralization within the scope of a central authority. It amounts to a disaggregation of the central command.

Is this true decentralization? True decentralization presumably means that a participating unit, in dealing with (responding to) other participating units, does not have to take into account any decisions coming down some vertical chain of authority. The relations are all in the horizontal direction, between equals, from one unit to another unit, at the same level of authority and power. In that case, they are autonomous, the opposite of subordinate. It is clear that all real economic systems contain a blend of centralized and decentralized structures of authority. For instance, firms that deal "laterally" with their suppliers and customers, i.e., in a decentralized fashion, may be internally organized as tightly centralized units.

However, there is a class of vertical relationships for which the notion of centralization is not suitable, even though it resembles them in outer form. Centralization in the earlier sense implies that the decisions of the center are one with the will of the center. How do we deal with cases where a set of participating units bands together and charges one other unit with certain tasks to be performed "centrally"? (For instance, farmers may create a central cooperative

---

[6] See Leonid Hurwicz, "Centralization and Decentralization in Economic Processes," in Alexander Eckstein (ed.), *Comparison of Economic Systems: Theoretical and Methodological Approaches*, University of California Press, Berkeley, 1971, pp. 79–102.

charged with selling or purchasing; a bank may become a central deposit bank and clearinghouse for others; a chamber of commerce does market research for its members; in an idealized model of workers' management, employees may choose their own chief executive.) Certain operations lend themselves naturally to being performed centrally (or at some intermediate tiers or nodes) on behalf of other units. Or they may be too costly to be performed by each of them going it alone. The difference is that, in this case, decisions get delegated "upward." Authority (or authorization) flows from the periphery to the center, even though in the process of execution, decisions of the center may technically reach the participants from the opposite direction, i.e., "from above." Since "centraliza-tion" has its meaning fixed for authority emanating from the center, we propose to refer to this other kind of centralism as *articulation of decision making*. The interpretation of government as faithful agent of society would be the prime example.

Process Elements

Up to now we have discussed elements constituting economic systems from a static point of view, as if presenting the cast of characters. We now come to the category of elements needed for describing economic systems in action. These elements are not objects or things, as resources and participants are, but aspects and results of activities in which the system's participants are engaged. We shall first list them and then construct a very general schematic model of the system's functioning.

The process elements form a logical sequence. The list starts with *information* which underlies *decisions*. Decisions are followed by their *implementation*, i.e., the use of real inputs, and their transformation into various *outcomes*. Among out-comes we count not only outputs in the narrow sense, but also income distribu-tion, price changes, inventory accumulation, degree of unemployment, environ-mental disruption, new inventions and discoveries, and ultimately the level of satisfactions, the state of "social welfare," which includes the impact upon the social structure and its various noneconomic aspects.

To use the language proposed by adherents of systems analysis (which is a special theoretical school in scientific methodology), we may define the function of the economic system as follows: It serves to transform a given state (or condi-tion) of the system to another state. This is exactly what is entailed in the path which leads from information via decisions and their implementation to out-comes. But there is more. Since the elements of the economic system are simulta-neously parts of other systems which constitute society (culture, values, social relations, etc.), the economic function transforms also the state of society in general. This is what Marx had in mind when he spoke repeatedly of the econom-ic process as a "process of the material reproduction of society." (He was a systems analyst before systems analysis was invented.)

The interaction of the process elements will be best explained with the help of Figure 2-1. To make circular diagrams of this kind speak their message, one has only to find the logical beginning and follow through from there. The strategic

23

Figure 2-1 Process elements of an economic system in action.

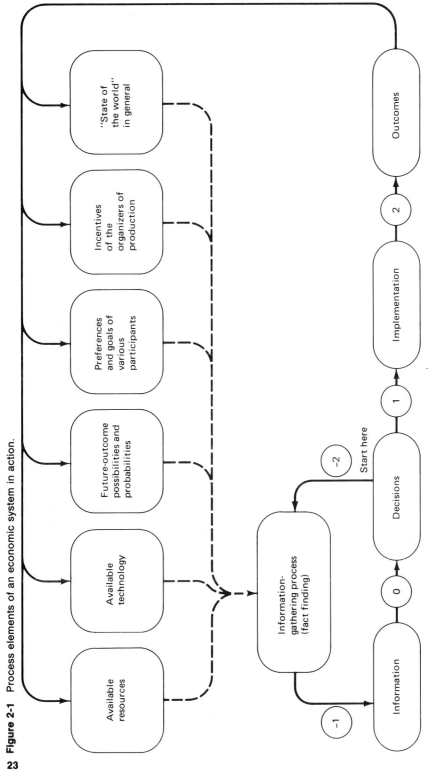

origin of the movement is decisions. However, decisions have to be based on information. Therefore, as a preliminary stage, decisions have to concern allocation of resources to the gathering of information. Information is the preliminary outcome which serves as "input" into decisions leading to other outcomes than information ("outcomes proper"). This is why this preliminary stage is represented by arrows numbered -2, -1, and zero.

Let us pause here to consider what the information is about. It concerns the given "state of the world," in particular of the nonprocess elements of the economic system: available resources including technology (which are partly remnants of past outcomes of economic processes); goals of the participants (which include preferences of final users, "ruling" and "bargaining organizations," as well as preferences of decision makers in the production process, i.e., their "motivation"); attainable possibilities; incentive systems (i.e., systems of rewards and sanctions which lead decision makers to choose among possibilities by modifying the pursuit of their own private preferences); the response mechanism of the economic system to decisions ("how it works"). One might think of adding the state of the noneconomic environment (legal norms, cultural values), but, upon reflection, one will find it covered by the goals and preferences of all the participants taken together. (The broken-line arrows represent connections which are not part of the process circuit.)

Once information is fed into the decision-making process and decisions are formed (as "plans"), they are passed on to the implementing stage (arrow 1).[7] The implementing stage draws upon available resources—indeed, it is synonymous with what we usually call "allocation of resources." Participants who implement the "plans" may be other than those who decided on them, but the decision maker and the one who does the implementing may also be the same person or participating unit. The implementation stage ends in some results—the outcomes—characterized earlier.

The process circuit is easily applied to the active functioning of any participant in the system. It is natural to visualize it, first, as a description of the production process, whether it is undertaken by enterprises, households, or governmental units. However, it applies just as well to households and government in their role as consumers ("final users"): they, too, require information as input, they have to make decisions, allocate resources to implement them (e.g., in shopping), and face the outcomes (e.g., actually attained states of satisfaction).

The outcomes may correspond to the original plans (expectations are fulfilled), but more often they will more or less diverge (expectations are exceeded or disappointed). In that case, outcomes generate new information which will be taken into account at the next round of decision making. A process of learning is involved: there is a feedback loop leading from outcomes back to information and the decision stage, leading to revisions, corrections, and adjustments of the past course of action.

However, the feedback loops are much more numerous and complex than

---

[7] This takes place via another flow of information which consists of "signals" containing invitation to action (instructions, commands, offers, bids). Information preceding decisions is of a different, fact-finding sort. There, the decision maker acts as a passive or active recipient of information messages.

that. We said earlier that the economic function transforms the state of society in general. In terms of Figure 2-1, this translates in outcomes affecting goals and preferences of participants, their notion of attainable possibilities, and altogether the "state of the noneconomic environment." This is particularly so in the case of outcomes which have a strong qualitative content: economic processes resulting in output of cultural goods (books, movies, media production) or output of political services (leadership, articulation of the political will, legislation, representation). The changed state of society generates new information which then returns into the process circuit.

Institutions

By "institutions" (in the sense of elements of the economic system) we mean certain *stabilized patterns of relationships* which tie the participants together, or particular *forms and patterns of the process elements in action.* "Institutions" in this sense are analytic abstractions. Needless to say, they must not be confused with the buildings (such as offices, factories, or stock and commodity exchanges) in which some of these stabilized patterns of behavior occur. Market is an economic institution in that sense: stabilized patterns of buying or selling. Slavery is an institution: behavior of human beings such that one class is treated as property of another class. Private property is an institution: it stabilizes the access to the use of certain objects and narrows it down to specified individuals while excluding the rest. Examples of other institutions are wage labor; lending and borrowing; gift; taxation; charity. Ownership patterns, as well as various forms of obtaining information, and responding to it in allocating resources, are the institutions which will be discussed at length in Chapters 3 and 4.

Behavior patterns become stabilized ("institutionalized") through repetition reflecting their advantageous character to at least some of the participants. They become routine. Their stability is reinforced by social sanctions of approval and disapproval and belief systems which make historic institutions appear as "natural." The ultimate reinforcement takes place through legal codes and legal sanctions, e.g., legal enforcement of private contracts, legally imposed duty to work and prohibition to become an entrepreneur under communist systems, etc. Destabilization of institutions occurs through contrary phenomena, usually initiated by participants who are not happy with them.

* * *

What use is this formalization of the various elements of the economic system? It may look like an intellectual toy and, on the face of it, not add much to what we know about the economic system anyway. It is true that it does not add anything to our substantive knowledge—it does not tell us anything about the concrete ways in which economic systems coordinate the decisions of individual participants and integrate them into the economic process as a whole. However, the value of formalization is in making precise and explicit what we intuitively know. It is the spadework of scientific thinking. It enables us to go about describing objects and analyzing their problems in an orderly, systematic way. To be analytic means to be methodical rather than haphazard, and formal conceptualization is the first step.

ECONOMIC SYSTEM AND THE SOCIAL STRUCTURE

We are now turning to the big picture. Somewhere in the beginning we mentioned in passing that the economic system is a subsystem of the complete social system of society and is coextensive with it, inasmuch as the economic side is only one aspect of all social behavior. What remains to be examined is how the economic subsystem and the other subsystems of society hang together, what is the nature of their interdependence, how they interact, and how they produce change.

To talk of social subsystems means slicing up social reality mentally according to some consistent rule. In real life, social facts, concrete social behavior, are a seamless web. Humans are many things at once. They are physical and biological creatures before they are social animals. To maintain themselves—and develop qualitatively—they depend on activities called work. In the process, they communicate with each other, accumulate knowledge, and develop rules of conduct. They develop distinctions between what is to be considered right and wrong— they become moral creatures. They consolidate some of the desirable rules of conduct by expressing and enforcing them as law. They develop ways of organizing their collective interests, resolving conflicts, regulating power relations, and translating interests into laws—they develop the sphere of politics. They form beliefs about the meaning of their existence and create ideologies. They create objects charged with aesthetic values and develop art.

There is no need to continue this enumeration. We are merely repeating here in a general way what we pointed out earlier about the social fact of "work." We said it was a compound of its various characteristics. We may repeat that for every other fact of social behavior, and emphasize the simultaneous presence of all such partial aspects in every concrete fact. The purpose of enumerating these various aspects or characteristics is to show that they furnish a consistent rule, or principle, for slicing up social reality, analytically, into subsystems.

Every such partial characteristic may become the basis for establishing in our mind a corresponding sphere, i.e., subsystem which has its own special function with respect to the whole. It is as if we decided to turn every social fact around, with one chosen facet pointing toward our eyesight. We would then study them from that special angle: it would thereby become part of that particular sphere (i.e., subsystem), but only for the purpose of analysis. In reality, it would retain all the other characteristics, except that they would be kept out of focus.

Social sciences have been at a loss in trying to find the right word for these partial ways of viewing society. We just referred to them as "spheres." Traditionally, one is used to talking about "planes" or "levels" of social reality: at the "ideological level"; at the "political level"; on the "economic plane"; on the "legal plane." The trouble with all these expressions is that they have spatial connotations. That is why the term "subsystems" is so attractive, despite its sounding like technical jargon. At least it does not make you think of the structure of the social system in terms of strata, as if it were a chocolate seven-layer cake. In particular, it makes it easier to think about all the multiple interdependencies between partial aspects, their interaction, their interpenetration, and their concrete unity.

There are also other ways of analytic slicing of society where such difficulties with complexity do not arise. If we proceed to divide up a social system into individuals, families, tribes, and the population, we analyze its structure not by aspects but from the point of view of its components. Each of these components is also a subsystem, but they exist within each other like nested flowerpots. It is a matter of aggregating units into larger and larger components, until we arrive at the whole. In other cases, we merely sum up the components (if they are mutually exclusive), e.g., when we study the social structure as made up of social classes or professional categories, or age groups. We need to distinguish, therefore, between the *functional structure* of the social system (from the point of view of its "aspects" or "spheres"), and its composition, i.e., *structure by components*, obtained by partitioning the participants of the system in various ways. (Here we are dealing with the functional structure.)

INTEGRATION OF SUBSYSTEMS

How shall we visualize the interdependence of the subsystems? We start with the notion of their *integration* into the functioning social whole. When we say that subsystems are integrated, we mean that, in some sense, they are matched. They correspond to each other, they support each other's functioning, they imply each other. Together they form a social order. (See Figure 2-2.) We intuitively rebel against the idea that a social system could be pieced together from an arbitrarily chosen set of characteristics. The sociologist Talcott Parsons expresses these ideas through his concept of social equilibrium.[8] The anthropologist Manning Nash coins the expressions "normative coherence" and "functional fit."[9] Marx is, of course, full of references to the organic tie between various subsystems of the social structure. He says, for example, "Don Quixote long ago paid the penalty for wrongly imagining that knight errantry was compatible with all economic forms of society."[10] And "Social relations are closely bound up with productive forces. . . . The handmill gives you society with the feudal lord; the steam-mill, society with the industrial capitalist. The same men who establish their social relations in conformity with their material productivity, produce also principles, ideas and categories, in conformity with their social relations."[11]

The series of examples from the literature of social sciences, especially anthropology, is endless. There is Max Weber's famous thesis on the relevance of religious values to the operational characteristics of the capitalist economic system.[12] One can palpably observe the "functional fit" in action when a foreign element is introduced into a social system in relative equilibrium.

The classic example concerns the introduction of steel axes by well-meaning missionaries into a stone-age society of Australian aborigines. Before their introduction, social values, roles, and customs of the tribe were structured around the

[8] See, for example, Talcott Parsons and Neil J. Smelser, *Economy and Society*, Free Press, Glencoe, Ill., 1956, or Talcott Parsons, *The Structure of Social Action*, McGraw-Hill, New York, 1937.

[9] Manning Nash, *Primitive and Peasant Economic Systems*, Chandler, San Francisco, 1966, pp. 90–97.

[10] K. Marx, *Capital*, vol. I, pp. 82f.

[11] K. Marx, *The Poverty of Philosophy*, International Publishers, New York, 1963, p. 109.

[12] Max Weber, *The Protestant Ethic and the Spirit of Capitalism*, G. Allen, London, 1948. Also R. H. Tawney, *Religion and the Rise of Capitalism*, Harcourt, Brace, New York, 1952.

Figure 2-2 Schematic presentation of social subsystems and their interdependence.

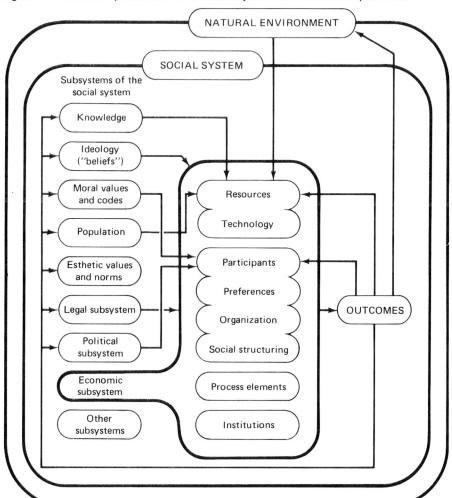

laborious and solemn provision of material for the stone tools from a distant place, the tool fabrication, and the rules of their use. In all this, males of the tribe had a prominent place. Once the women could have any number of steel axes from the mission for the asking, the men lost an obviously vital function, fell apart morally, started to drink, and the social fabric of the tribe disintegrated.[13]

A similar fate befell some American Indians after they had been deprived of the traditional base of their economic existence—the buffalo.[14] On the other

---

[13] R. L. Sharp, "Steel Axes for Stone-Age Australians," *Human Organization*, vol. II, 1952, pp. 17–22.

[14] See Erik Erikson's study of the American Sioux in his *Childhood and Society*, Norton, New York, chap. 3, pp. 114–165.

hand, it was the introduction of the horse and the gun which "created" the economic system of the Great Plains Indians in the first place.

The correspondence between different subsystems is subtle and goes very deep. Thus, the subjective perception of time will vary between agricultural and industrial societies. In agriculture it is intimately linked to the organic processes of growth, physiological needs of livestock, and seasons. In industrial societies, it becomes a homogeneous flow mechanically subdivided into precise units. There ticks in our mind the mechanical rhythm of machinery, but also the internalized need for punctuality under conditions of cooperative work in collectives.

Japan is in some respects a veritable laboratory for the study of adjustment of cultural patterns and the economic system. For instance, it has been observed that in Japanese industrial firms one finds a very weak emphasis on personal responsibility and performance-related incentives. There is no piece-rate wage system to speak of, and profits do not play the same role for the evaluation of managers as in Western companies. Everett Hagen, among many others, has traced these features to the psychological subsystem of the society which abhors shaming an individual for personal mistakes. The feeling of individual integrity depends vitally on the approval by the group and their support. In contrast, Western concepts of sin and guilt, unknown in that form to the Japanese, fit the notion of personal accountability, sanctions, and incentives.[15]

One more important illustration of "coherence" is the relation of the character of the legal system to the character of the economic systems. Two key notions in law concern the difference between administrative, "statutory law" (which provides the legal framework for superior units handing down decisions to the subordinate units) and "contractual law" (which provides general rules for voluntary agreements between parties). It is immediately obvious that decentralized systems require a well-developed system of contractual law to function. Under centralized systems, administrative law predominates. However, one could also say that, for contractual law to be effective, it has to rest on well-ingrained habits of reliability that go with contracts.[16]

[15] See E. Hagen, "The Internal Functioning of Capitalist Organizations," *Journal of Economic History*, vol. 30, 1970, pp. 222–239. The same author pursued the idea of systemic interdependence under economic development in his book *On the Theory of Social Change*, Dorsey, Homewood, Ill., 1962.

[16] Alexander Gerschenkron notes the weakness of contractual morality as one of the obstacles to private capitalist accumulation, and need for government financing, in czarist Russia: "The scarcity of capital in Russia was such that no banking system could conceivably succeed in attracting sufficient funds to finance a large-scale industrialization; the standards of honesty in business were so disastrously low, the general distrust of the public so great, that no bank could have hoped to attract even such small capital funds as were available, and no bank could have successfully engaged in long-term credit policies in an economy where fraudulent bankruptcy had been almost elevated to the rank of a general business practice." *Economic Backwardness in Historical Perspective*, Praeger, New York, 1965, pp. 19–20.

BADLY MATCHED SUBSYSTEMS, ADJUSTMENT, AND THE DYNAMICS OF CHANGE

Stating that subsystems are integrated amounts to saying that "everything depends on everything else." This, however, leaves the structure of their relationships undefined. Our mental image of the system still resembles a messed-up bundle of threads: the links between one subsystem and the others point in all directions. How does one, then, define the structure of these relationships? By establishing the *direction of influence* from one subsystem to another, at least in a major way.

Before we get to the heart of the issue, let us ask ourselves, just on the basis of common-sense experience, whether the "functional fit" is always perfect. It most certainly is not. If we think back to the example of time perception, machine technology, and punctuality needed for synchronizing individual activities in a work team, it may occur to us that there is a certain incongruity with respect to the physiological subsystem. Physiology has its own rhythm, and it is not the same as that of the machine. To some extent, adjustment is possible: relief workers at an assembly line step in for those who have to absent themselves; a woman employee may take a day off when she has her period. But there is a residue where the "human factor" takes its toll: for instance, judging by television commercials, contemporary humanity is haunted by the problem of "regularity"; allowances for paid sick leave may be woefully inadequate; some people develop a time neurosis. Obviously, there is functional maladjustment between the subsystems in question.

If we now try to formalize the structure of these relationships by trying to establish the direction of influence (or "determination"), it will undoubtedly run from the technology subsystem to the time perception and to the effects upon the physiological subsystem. In other words, the technology element is the determining one. This does not mean that technology can entirely disregard physiology. For instance, fatigue and need for recuperation put limits to the length of the working day. However, putting limits to a force is not quite the same thing as mutual functional adjustment.[17]

Let us now deal with instances where functional maladjustment arises in consequence of changes within some particular subsystem. The primordial origin of such localized changes is usually hard to pin down. An invention, a shift in moral values, a change of political rule may be the result of a confluence of circumstances—"accidents"—throughout the social system, which escape precise observation. When we know little about the causation of a given change, we treat it as spontaneous or autonomous. If an autonomous change occurs, and there is no automatic adjustment in other subsystems, an incongruity appears. The social system experiences friction, stress, tension.

The question is: "Will such an autonomous change necessarily force adjust-

---

[17] The call for a "humanistic technology" on the part of some radical economists amounts to a demand to reverse the direction of determination: technology ought to adjust to the needs of the human subsystem.

ments in the other subsystems?" This is couched in very general terms, but the specific issues that are really on our minds are: "How is it that change occurs in economic systems? Do they change inexorably on their own? Is it possible to change them, or at least influence them, through action in other subsystems? Are revolutions possible? And if so, in what sense?" The analytic model we are developing here is a stepping-stone to these and similar questions, to be taken up again in Chapters 6 and 18.

In principle, autonomous change can make its appearance anywhere. For instance, fads in tastes or ideas suddenly appear, unasked, and disappear again, without taking proper leave. More seriously: every subsystem seems to have deep down its own logic of autonomous development. A hundred years ago we might have called it "laws." Art forms develop according to their own logic, so do legal thinking, science, political forms and events, and so on. However, the tendency indicated by their autonomous logic of development may not be able to assert itself successfully because of the influence of the "environment," i.e., the state of the other subsystems.

The developmental logic of a plant, dictated by its genetic program, is to grow and spread. Whether it actually will depends on the state of its environment. If water supply dries up, the plant may languish and die. On the other hand, its roots may change the consistency of the soil, draw water from below, and conserve it for the rest of the environment. Biological systems offer some instructive analogies for our purpose. The problem for the plant is which effect will be stronger. Our uneducated guess is that the exogenous supply of sufficient amounts of water will be, as a rule, decisive.

Social scientists, too, have been trying to find out which subsystems in society are, as a rule, the decisive ones. There is a strong suspicion that changes in certain subsystems are more powerful than in others, as far as their overall determining effect on the social system is concerned.

The Marxian Structuralist Model

Marx's famous hypothesis was that the structure of social relations in the economic subsystem (and their changes) exerts a more powerful pressure upon the subsystems of law, opinion, politics, and ideology than the other way around. Furthermore, the structure of social relations in the economic sphere is more powerfully shaped by developments in the subsystem of production technology and its corollary, productivity of labor. Such was, in Marx's view, the hierarchy in the relative power of influence exerted by the subsystems of technology ("forces of production"), social structure ("production relations"), and the other subsystems. Hence his grouping of the first two under the term of "base," and the rest (law, politics, beliefs, etc.) under the term of a derivative "superstructure."

The Simple Version When one hears of Marx's "economic determinism," reference is usually to this simple scheme of "directed adjustment" between subsystems. In Marx's major work it comes out considerably modified, as we shall presently indicate. However, because of its wide currency, every student of economic systems ought to be acquainted with the preliminary, big-brushstrokes version of the model in its original wording:

> In the social production of their life, men enter into definite relations that are indispensable and independent of their will, relations of production which correspond to a definite stage of development of their material productive forces. The sum total of these relations of production constitutes the economic structure of society, the real foundation, on which rises a legal and political superstructure and to which correspond definite forms of social consciousness. The mode of production of material life conditions the social, political and intellectual life in general. It is not the consciousness of men that determines their being, but, on the contrary, their social being that determines their consciousness. At a certain stage of their development, the material productive forces of society come in conflict with the existing relations of production, or—what is but a legal expression for the same thing—with the property relations within which they have been at work hitherto. From forms of development of the productive forces these relations turn into their fetters. Then begins an epoch of social revolution. With the change of the economic foundation the entire immense superstructure is more or less rapidly transformed. In considering such transformations a distinction should always be made between the material transformation of the economic conditions of production, which can be determined with the precision of natural science, and the legal, political, religious, aesthetic or philosophic—in short, ideological forms in which men become conscious of this conflict and fight it out.[18]

The reader should have no difficulty in recognizing the correspondence between Marx's idiom and the terminology we have used so far.

The Sophisticated Version   In analyzing the dynamics of the capitalist system in *Das Kapital* (Capital), and also in widely dispersed passages in other writings, Marx uses a model which is considerably more complex. However, it is left implicit. We miss an explicit theoretical summary that might be placed side by side with the above-quoted passage for comparison. It needs to be reconstructed from Marx's treatment of concrete matters.

In what respects did Marx modify his earlier version? One can discern several major innovations: emphasis on feedback effects; the notion of limiting and permissive circumstances with respect to change; the notion of leads and lags of partial changes with respect to their "equilibrium adjustment"; and the active, instrumental role of politics and law. None of these expressions will be found in Marx's writings, but we shall briefly illustrate each of them to demonstrate that the concepts are there. In doing that, we shall be further elaborating a conception of systemic change which we believe to be generally useful and valid, independently of Marx's specific theories.

Feedback Effects   The progress of production technology does not unilaterally determine the social structure of the economic system (its "class structure"). There are feedback effects in the opposite direction. Thus, the capitalist structure of the firm gives rise to "discoveries" of new technologies; the firm's economic

---

[18] K. Marx, preface to *A Contribution to the Critique of Political Economy* (1859), in Robert C. Tucker (ed.), *The Marx-Engels Reader*, Norton, New York, 1972, pp. 4–5.

expansion (in terms of the firm's "value") leads to the development of large-scale machinery and mass-production techniques; struggles for a shorter work day lead to more capital-intensive processes and increased labor productivity.

Limiting and Permissive Circumstances   Change in the social structure of the economic system (in particular the emergence of capitalism) is not a simple consequence of technological factors alone. The state of other subsystems may create obstacles or put insurmountable limits to the change in the social structure of production: legislation fixing output quotas to artisan entrepreneurs; absence of labor mobility (as under serfdom or slavery); absence of entrepreneurial values (as among nobility). On the other hand, change in any of these subsystems will not, by itself, allow technology to "produce" capitalist relations. Thus, availability of a mobile labor force is only a permissive factor—necessary, but not sufficient. Furthermore, an established economic system may find its built-in tendencies blocked by the state of other subsystems: moral revulsion against employment of child labor put a stop to this capitalist practice; moral condemnation of slavery (among other influences) abolished that economic system.

We may generalize: Autonomous changes in particular subsystems (or absence of change) limit the possibilities of unfettered change in other subsystems, or else open up new possibilities to such change, i.e., act permissively.

Leads and Lags in the Process of Change   To understand this part, we have to postulate, abstractly, that every autonomous change in a particular subsystem has a tendency to force adjustments in the other subsystems so as to transform the entire social system "in the image" of the change that gave the original impulse. The delay of this transformation makes the impulse appear as *leading*, the adjustment in the other subsystems as *lagging*. However, the delay may be infinitely long; i.e., the initial tendency becomes frustrated, because of inertia (stability) of the other subsystems or effects of other autonomous changes intervening in the meantime.

The formal framework is useful for comprehending the recurrent phenomenon of failures to introduce changes by deliberate action. Social and economic history is littered with defeated revolutions, frustrated reform movements, abortive legislation. "Socialism" has been "introduced" innumerable times, to make observers sigh again and again—*Plus ça change, plus c'est la même chose*, "the more it changes, the more it is the same old thing." The underlying assumption of every new generation of social reformers and inventors of the perfect formula is that the "opinion subsystem" is decisive.

On the other hand, there are successful changes produced by deliberate action. This means, in the language of "leads" and "lags," that the delay between an autonomous change in the ideological, political, or legal subsystems and the adjustments in the subsystem aimed at by the action are relatively short. We say that "the time was ripe." In the Marxian language, the enabling or permissive "maturity of conditions" was there.

Instrumental Role of Politics and Law   In the simple version of Marx's model, law is derivative: it is patterned after the social structure of the economic system, it is an epiphenomenon, it follows and never precedes. As late as 1875, sixteen years after the formulation quoted earlier, Marx returns to this conception: "Right can never be higher than the economic structure of society and its cultural development conditioned thereby."[19]

However, in the model underlying the text of *Das Kapital*, the legal subsystem appears in a different light. In the first place, law does, of course, tend to codify the social relations of participants in the economic system and all that these practically entail. However, preferences of the dominant groups in the hierarchy of the social structure in the economy are not necessarily the only ones that determine the legislative process. The economic system is not the only subsystem of society whose interests converge upon the formulation of laws via the political process. Hence the possibility that laws may become the expression of preferences held by other subgroups of the social structure (ethnic groups, women, political and religious groups, etc.) or some compromise thereof. Insofar as law is enforced by the "power subsystem" of the state, it is capable of modifying the behavior of the members of society, including that of the private participants in the economic system, in particular the dominant agents, or representatives, of its tendencies.

It is in this spirit that Marx treats law and the political process as instrumentalities for obtaining feasible changes in the economic system. Indeed, on occasion, Marx sees the political and legal subsystems as the medium through which society as such is able to exercise control over the economic system. Thus, he characterizes British protective factory legislation as "that first conscious and methodical reaction of society against the spontaneously developed form of the process of production."[20] In a narrower sense, the working class could and should strive, in Marx's view, for favorable legislation. This would transpose labor's conflicts with the representatives of the economic system from the social-relations subsystem (struggles at the workshops and factory level) to the political and legislative subsystems, and thereby make the assertion of labor interests ("preferences") more effective. This, incidentally, is why Marx kept emphasizing the stake workers had in political democracy.

The relation of the sphere of law to the other subsystems offers also a good example of how the intrinsic character of one subsystem can generate autonomous change affecting other areas. Modern law has been dominated by two major principles: the requirement of inner consistency between legal norms (lower norms being derived from higher ones, and not contradicting each other) and universal applicability ("equality before law"). These are the intrinsic features of the legal subsystem. In the practical application of law it may easily happen that the two principles lead to unexpected consequences by revealing hidden practical implications of a given piece of legislation.

Thus, the legal notion of contract—the basic form of transactions in the system of market capitalism—implies equality between parties. Without equality there would not be contract but coercion by the more powerful. Now, in the case

---

[19] K. Marx, *Critique of the Gotha Program*, reprinted in ibid., p. 388.

[20] K. Marx, *Capital*, vol. I, p. 480. (Unlike Kenneth Arrow, Marx apparently assumed the possibility of a "social-welfare function" of some sort.)

of the labor contract, wage earners could not, in the earlier days, match the bargaining power of employers. Thus, the need arose to correct the imbalance by tilting the scale in favor of the wage earners. Such is the legal justification of all sorts of measures which, on the face of it, "favor labor" and lead to changes in the relations between participants in the economic subsystem. Marx noted these connections by stating:

Figure 2-3 Structure of the social system according to the Marxian model.

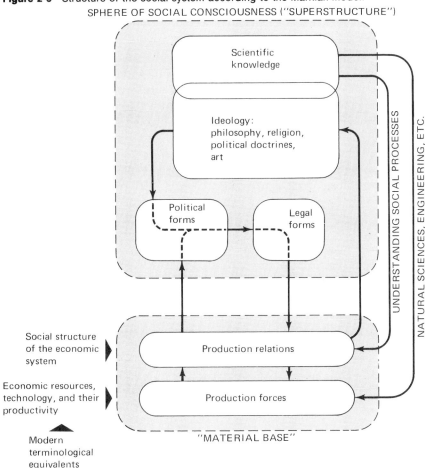

Marx was not always consistent in his use of the term "ideology," and did not deal explicitly with the place of scientific knowledge in the total system. The area in the diagram where "scientific knowledge" overlaps with "ideology" indicates the following two ideas: on the one hand, scientific understanding may contain elements of ideological beliefs; on the other hand, ideological beliefs may contain elements of knowledge adequate to facts. Where "ideology" does not overlap, it corresponds to Marx's notion of "false consciousness." (However, art and esthetics have a special place among the "ideological forms" because the issue of "adequacy of knowledge" does not apply.)

The revolution effected by machinery in the juridical relations between the buyer and the seller of labour-power, causing the transaction as a whole to lose the appearance of a contract between free persons, afforded the English Parliament an excuse, founded on juridical principles, for the interference of the state with factories.[21]

This, by the way, shows further how sophisticated Marx's model became, compared to the simple version which held that "the executive of the modern State is but a committee for managing the common affairs of the whole bourgeoisie."[22]

In place of a recapitulation of the Marxian structuralist model we have provided its schematic representation, which captures the major relationships between the subsystems, in Figure 2-3.

*   *   *

This concludes our survey of the analytic tools and approaches relevant to the study of economic systems. One more idea occurs to us—it has been in the back of our mind throughout the last section: "How does scientific knowledge, which is a subsystem in its own right, fit into the structure of the social system as a whole?"

It may be helpful to return to Figure 2-1 and situate scientific knowledge in that scheme. Scientific knowledge is clearly part of the information set. It is the outcome of decisions and allocation of resources in the preliminary circuit indicated by arrows -2, -1, and zero. Example: Decision on a research project $\rightarrow$ work of a scholar or research team at a university $\rightarrow$ findings, or a theory. This outcome can then be used in making decisions whose purpose is to obtain some desired outcomes which concern the general state of the economic system. Example: Insights of Keynesian theories are used by the government to make policy decisions and implement them via policy instruments in order to achieve full employment.

Scientific knowledge is clearly not a passive reflection of reality. It is an active element of the system, and a continuous source of autonomous impulses toward change, opening up new options in the permissive sense discussed earlier. Whether they will be taken up in reality depends on other subsystems, particularly the political one. In any case, the study we are engaged in here is part of that preliminary circuit: not only for the sake of contemplating how things are, but also with the perspective on how they change and might be changed.

BIBLIOGRAPHY*

Eckstein, Alexander (ed.): *Comparison of Economic Systems*, University of California Press, Berkeley, 1971, esp. contributions by Tjalling C. Koopmans and John Michael Montias (pp. 27–28), Leonid Hurwicz (pp. 79–102), Benjamin Ward (pp. 103–134), and Morris Bornstein (pp. 339–355).

[21] Ibid., p. 397.
[22] K. Marx, *The Communist Manifesto*, reprinted in R. C. Tucker (ed.), op. cit., p. 337.
*The entries in each chapter's bibliography are arranged in the order of appearance of corresponding topics in the chapter.

Neuberger, Egon, and William Duffy: *Comparative Economic Systems: A Decision-making Approach*, Allyn and Bacon, Boston, 1976, esp. chaps. 1–6.

Silverman, David: *The Theory of Organizations*, Heinemann, London, 1970.

Commons, John R.: *Legal Foundations of Capitalism*, Macmillan, New York, 1924.

Parsons, Talcott, and Neil J. Smelser: *Economy and Society*, Free Press, New York, 1956.

Smelser, Neil J.: *The Sociology of Economic Life*, Prentice-Hall, Englewood Cliffs, N.J., 1963.

Nash, Manning: *Primitive and Peasant Economic Systems*, Chandler, San Francisco, 1966, esp. chaps. 2 and 5.

Cortes, Fernando, Adam Przeworski, and John Sprague: *Systems Analysis for Social Scientists*, Wiley, New York, 1974.

Meehan, Eugene J.: *Explanation in Social Sciences: A Systems Paradigm*, Dorsey, Homewood, Ill., 1968.

Sutherland, John W.: *A General Systems Philosophy for the Social and Behavioral Sciences*, George Braziller, Inc., New York, 1973.

Swingewood, Alan: *Marx and Modern Social Theory*, Wiley, New York, 1975.

Chapter 3

Classification of Economic Systems by Type of Ownership

No classification can be any better than the classifier's knowledge and understanding of the observations he is classifying.

Karl Menninger

Biology found its grand master of taxonomy in the eighteenth-century Swedish scientist Linnaeus, who sorted out into clear classification categories the vegetable and animal kingdoms, and on the side minerals as well. The study of economic systems has been, and still is, waiting for its Linnaeus. The classification scheme to be offered in this chapter does not pretend to accomplish more than part of the spadework, but not a bit less either. It takes its inspiration from Marx's approach to the problem and seeks to bypass and go beyond most of the traditional and widely accepted conventions.

It also is supposed to serve as a practical aid for easier orientation in the socioeconomic universe. What a good classification ought to do for us is to be a guide in methodically identifying similarities and differences between objects. Similarities between objects tie them into common categories. Differences between objects send them scurrying into different categories, and bound these off against each other. Categories then become a shorthand, an easy frame of reference: we know what to expect when a concrete animal can be referred to as "mammal" and do not have to go each time through lengthy explanations. Methodical differentiation of objects by their attributes is also able to guard against our being misled by chance similarities or superficial differences. A successful classification, if it is not only good in itself but also finds a wide enough acceptance, can enormously reduce the social cost of misunderstandings and do away with sterile controversies. It clarifies.

THE ISSUES IN GENERAL

What Is Classification?

"Methodical differentiation"—what does that mean? Classification—ever since Aristotle—has been assumed to reproduce the actual, objectively existing structure of reality. Real objects have many different attributes, or characteristics, which can be identified and singled out as "aspect categories" in terms of which the objects can be described. Now, some attributes are common to many objects, others are common only to few, and still others are utterly unique to one concrete and impossible-to-duplicate individual or thing. Thus, attributes can be arranged as a hierarchy of decreasing order of generality, going from the universal to the most specific ones. This insight forms the basis of any general classification.

In the age of computers it is possible to explain the process of classification by describing the preparation of computer punch cards for a classification program. There is one punch card for every single object of the set to be classified. We have a list of characteristics obtained through careful observation and examination of the objects. Every individual object may receive on its punch card a "yes" hole if it has a given characteristic, and a "no" hole if it does not, in the appropriate spot on the card designated for that characteristic. Or if an aspect exists in more than two variant characteristics, a hole will be punched for that variant in which it appears in the given individual.

A computer program is then designed to instruct the computer to sort out the objects into a succession of groups according to the following rule: "Subdivide all objects into groups, and each group into subgroups, defined by characteristics so chosen that, at each step, the groups obtained by subdivision comprise all the individuals of the broader group before its subdivision." This rule makes the classification exhaustive, which is what *general* classification should be. It also prevents overlapping of subdivisions, which makes for clear either-or decisions as to where a specific object fits in. The groups, or categories, obtained in this manner, form what mathematicians call "nested sets." The diagram in Figure 3-1 shows why they are called that.

To illustrate, these are the principles on the basis of which the animal kingdom is classified: first into monocellular and multicellular, the multicellular into organless tissue animals (sponges) and animals with organs, etc., etc., down to chordates, chordates into vertebrates and nonvertebrates, vertebrates into mammals, fishes, birds, reptiles, and amphibians, mammals into further orders, then into families, families into genera, these into species, and further into subspecies.

Figure 3-1 Classification categories presented as "nested sets."

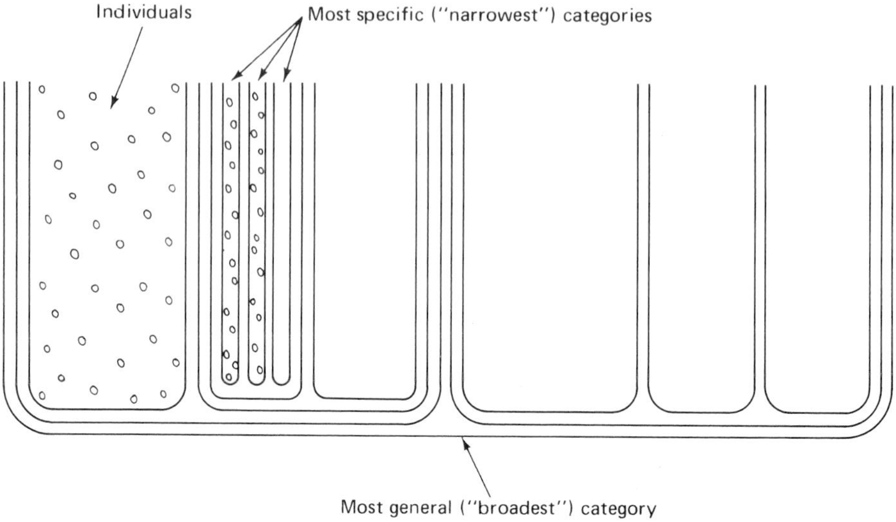

Individuals   Most specific ("narrowest") categories

Most general ("broadest") category

A concrete individual, say your own empirically observable dog Snoopy, can be fitted to all the relevant successive abstract categories containing each other, all the way from beagles to multicellulars.[1]

The Two Classification Criteria

In the study of economic systems, any classifiers worth their salt should aspire to setting up an analogous structure of categories—not a small task. To start with, they can fall back on two different sets of time-honored criteria which supply the basis of classification of economic systems: ownership of means of production and modes of allocating resources.

The ownership criterion provides descriptive characteristics that have to do with the *patterns according to which various kinds of decision-making powers are distributed among the participants in the economic system.* The crudest of the crude characteristics concern the question of who holds the ownership title to material production assets, a private person or a public agency. The resulting traditional classification of economic systems into those of private ownership and public ownership is equally crude and calls for substantial revision.

The mode-of-allocation criterion supplies characteristics which describe economic systems from the point of view of *how the process elements—information, incentives, and decisions—are constituted and how they are related to each other, in order to integrate the participants into institutionalized patterns of coherent economic activities.* As with the ownership criterion, the traditional subdivision into market

---

[1] In the children's game called Twenty Questions, one asks which abstract classification category the guessed object belongs to. Through a series of successive questions one tries to go down the categories, from the more general to the less general ones, until one reaches a category narrow enough to make it fairly certain what the unknown specific object might be. It is nothing but taxonomy turned into a source of fun.

systems and systems of direct allocation (via custom or plan) is neither strikingly subtle nor precise. It will be examined in Chapter 4.

What Is Ownership?

"Ownership of means of production," that forever recurrent simple phrase, hides a complexity of issues which need to be taken apart and displayed in clear daylight.

"Ownership" refers to the authority of making decisions related to the use of the objects of ownership. This authority may be exercised by specific individuals, or groups, in which case other individuals and groups are excluded from it. These patterns of inclusion and exclusion from the exercise of decision making are then at the base of all social patterns of ownership.

If the exercise of ownership is socially accepted (either by voluntary consensus or by force), in other words, if it is sanctioned and protected, it becomes a "right." It has long been realized that the right of ownership is actually a "bundle of rights," i.e., of several particular aspects of using the object of ownership. Customarily one distinguishes the following:

1 *Custody rights*, i.e., authority to make decisions associated with the actual utilization of the owned asset. This is what is meant by "possession," real "control," or "management" of the asset.

2 *Usufruct rights*, i.e., authority to claim the appropriation of new assets resulting from the utilization of the object of ownership (such as value added in production), either directly in the form of real products or in the form of income (wages, interest, rent, or profit).

3 *Alienation*, in the sense of transferring the ownership through sale or bequest to another subject.

4 *Destruction*, which needs no comment.

These are the *substantive ownership rights*, the real, *practical content of ownership*, its exercise.

If these rights are codified by law, they become expressed formally in a legal title of ownership. We then speak of *formal (legal, titular, or nominal) ownership*, which then may appear as the fountainhead of the substantive rights. In reality, formal ownership has historically grown out of the exercise of substantive ownership functions. It has become its confirmation. Effective settlement of land originally led to the right to the land and the legal ownership title. The simplest example of this sequence is in the phrase "Finders—keepers," whereupon, by virtue of statutes of limitations, or law of the sea, keepers become legal owners.

The distinction between the legal ownership title and the exercise of substantive ownership rights is of far-reaching importance. So is the subdivision of substantive ownership into the component rights, especially the first two, custody and usufruct rights. We can sense at this point already that many different ownership patterns may arise if the seemingly natural unity between the legal title and the substantive functions is destroyed (e.g., if the titular owner delegates the substantive functions to other subjects) or if several distinct agents divide up the substantive functions among themselves in different combinations and degrees. In Chapter 2 we mentioned government and other participants sharing in the decision making of firms, i.e., in the custody rights. We may add now the case of seeing usufruct rights split between employees (distributed profits) and the government (taxes). Let us keep in mind this kind of variation in who is the titular owner, who exercises which portion of the substantive ownership rights, and who puts constraints upon their exercise. It will be essential to our proper understanding of the major ownership models on today's scene.

Analysis of ownership patterns is further complicated by the fact that property rights extend not only over means of production in the sense of material production assets. Labor, too, is an object of property rights.[2] Labor can be owned outright, as if it were another material asset, which is what one understands by the expression "human chattel" in the system of slavery. At the other extreme, one may be the subject and at the same time object of ownership rights with respect to the labor power one represents: one is one's own free master, one is a sovereign producer. In between, there are types of arrangements according to which labor is not an object of outright legal ownership, as under slavery, but where subjects other than the workers have some substantive rights to their utilization or to the appropriation of the usufruct, or its part, resulting from their work.

The modalities encountered in this last category may be vastly different. Thus, forced labor under the regime of concentration camps is, legally, not the object of ownership of the agents in charge who fully control its utilization and appropriation of the usufruct. This has the consequences that the controlling agents are under no such constraints to moderate the utilization of forced labor as the slave owners who are limited, as a minimum, by the concern for the slaves as their property.[3] In the case of serfs under feudalism, labor is not an object of ownership in the modern sense either. Substantive "property rights" of the feudal lord with respect to his subjects consist in the claim to a portion of their working time or of the usufruct, and in their enforced immobility (see below).

For our purposes, the most important shading which falls between the concept of labor as sovereign worker and labor as object of property rights of other agents is that of modern *wage labor*. Here, labor is formally not object of

---

[2] "Labor" may be used in a broad and narrow sense. In the most general sense it covers all labor force—human beings in their role of engaging in productive activities ("labor services").

Entrepreneurship is a special function of a special category of "labor." It is a type of "labor service" which consists in initiating and organizing the production process in its fundamental aspects: its foundation, content, scope, and direction. *Management* is another specialized function consisting in the more or less routine implementation of the entrepreneurial decisions. *Entrepreneurship and management* together refer to decisions making up the exercise of substantive ownership rights. If entrepreneurship and management are exercised by a specialized segment of "labor," then we oppose them conceptually to "labor" or "labor force" in the narrow sense, i.e., in the function of implementing entrepreneurial and managerial decisions ("taking orders").

In the classification scheme the term "labor" is used in the narrow sense.

[3] This analytic consideration is needed to put into proper perspective the popular habit of equating the condition of forced labor with that of slavery, as if slavery were the ultimate degree of exploitation.

anyone's property rights. Workers have the legally acknowledged right to dispose of their own capacity to work as they wish, and in that sense they are free. However, to make meaningful use of this freedom, they need access to material production assets, i.e., to the complementary inputs without which productive activity cannot take place. Under the system of wage labor, property rights to material assets are vested in members of another social group, the "capitalists." Workers are able to gain access to these material assets only if they surrender their otherwise empty custody right with respect to their capacity to work and place it, temporarily, at the disposal of the capitalist employer. They do so in the form of a contract whereby, in exchange for surrendering the right to control their work activity, the workers receive the right to a portion of the resulting usufruct, a wage. These institutional arrangements are what constitute wage labor.

In developing the precise notion of wage labor, we have also indirectly thrown light back on the notion of *sovereign workers* who are fully their own masters. To qualify for that status, it is clearly necessary for the workforce to have unobstructed access to material production assets, i.e., to own them effectively. What we have here is *fusion of ownership control of material assets with the workforce controlling the supply of its own labor services*. These two sets of controls may be united in the hands of an individual, as in the case of a Robinson Crusoe, an independent peasant, artisan, tradesman, and any other person "running" an owner-operated production unit; or in the hands of a collective, as in the case of a pure producers' cooperative or in a hypothetical system of socialism.

In pinpointing these relationships we have brought out the fact that the ownership status of labor broadly implies whether labor is excluded from the exercise of substantive ownership rights with respect to material assets, or whether it is included. This aspect of social distribution of ownership rights among members of society establishes a still further basis for distinguishing economic systems according to the basic ownership patterns. By now we are also ready to examine the full classification scheme.

The Classification Scheme

To appreciate the scheme presented in Table 3-1, it would be nice if the student came to it equipped with some notion of the economic systems which are being classified. To a degree he does, of course, But fuller understanding can come only from the study of Chapters 6 through 18, and other sources. The student may then wish to consult it again, in order to *really* profit. As a stopgap, we shall follow the explanation of Table 3-1 with a handful of selected case descriptions. This should make the classification scheme more meaty and at the same time provide sketches of systems to be filled in with color and detail as we proceed.

The scheme follows the principles explained at the outset and in Figure 3-1 except that it is much less elaborate than classifications in natural sciences. Characteristics establishing the classification categories, from the bigger "bowls" to the smaller and smaller ones, are marked on the left. Note that the last subdivi-

Table 3-1 Classification system of economic systems by type of ownership (a tryout set).

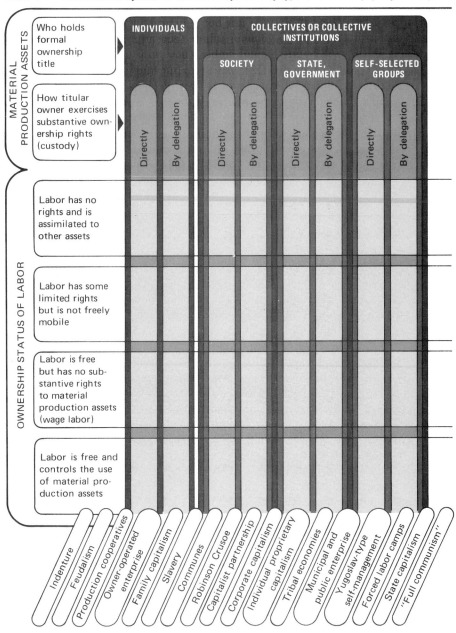

sions (according to the ownership status of labor) are arranged to cut across the next-to-the-last subdivisions horizontally. Otherwise, each space marked "directly" or "by delegation" would have to be split vertically into four labor-status subdivisions—a graphic monstrosity.

The first tier of the classification establishes the two broadest categories according to the identity of the subject of the formal (legal) ownership title to material productive assets: Is it an individual person or an aggregate of individuals, i.e., a social collective?

At the next tier, the identity of the titular owner is specified further. The category of collective ownership is broken down into three subcategories, according to whether the subject of collective titular ownership is a self-selected group (as in a business partnership), the government (or some segment thereof), or society as a whole.

At the third tier from the left, we abandon the characteristic of titular ownership, and we switch to the characteristic of substantive ownership rights or, more precisely, of the effective exercise of the custodial function: Is it exercised directly by the subject of titular ownership, or is it delegated to agents designated or hired for the purpose?

Finally, at the fourth tier, we introduce the characteristic of the status of labor which defines the patterns in which substantive ownership rights with respect to labor and material assets are distributed among social classes.

Patterns of distribution of usufruct rights have been ignored. The possible claimants are so many that we would be led into the kingdom of multidimensional diagrams, where we do not wish to tread. Besides, the variations are not of the sort that would establish other classes of economic systems than those we already have. Patterns of usufruct rights are more a matter of cross-classification: of quantitative proportions according to which various claimants in *any* system dip into the usufruct emerging from productive utilization of material and human assets. The claimants may be the titular owners of material assets, their effective custodians (managers), labor, government, other institutions, and members of households in other roles than suppliers of labor services.

The objects to be fitted into this framework are selected *models* of the more important historical and contemporary economic systems. In other words, they are not yet the concrete, empirically observable individual specimens existing (or having existed) in time and space. Of course, the models must have been obtained by observation from real systems of experience, by abstracting from all characteristics which are not in the scheme. These other characteristics will naturally have to be brought in when we study the systems concretely. The scheme just provides a general orientation. It does not pretend to say everything.

It does not say, for instance, that the models do not necessarily refer to national economies as a whole but only to their segments organized, as far as ownership is concerned, according to the particular model. National economies are, as a rule, composites of different ownership models. Even though one model may predominate, it coexists with others. Feudalism contained, in its interstices, independent owner-operated production units of peasants and artisans, as well as emerging capitalist traders. What we call "capitalist economies" contain segments organized on precapitalist, noncapitalist, and even embryonic postcapitalist ownership models. We can hardly avoid referring to particular national systems as "feudal," "capitalist," and so on, but we should never lose from sight the secondary ingredients, overshadowed by what is conspicuously dominant.

In Table 3-1, the specific models have been left floating outside the scheme to give readers a chance to try their hand at identifying systems characteristics and test for themselves how the scheme works. The models are listed in no particular order underneath the table. You take a case and ask where it fits, going down the scale of the four classification characteristics. Table 3-2 shows the proposed solution. There may be questions raised as to whether a slot is appropriate for this or that model, especially if the ownership arrangements are of some complexity, e.g., in the Yugoslav model of ownership rights and functions (see Chapter 17). There is always a duck-billed platypus around to cause headaches for the taxonomist. Such ambiguous instances do not invalidate the scheme. It is the scheme that helps us see why certain cases are hard to classify, and understand them. It helps us formulate fuzziness clearly.

Before we take up the series of vignettes of selected ownership models, two more general remarks are in order. One concerns the difference between "classification" and "typology." The other defines the relationship between a "general classification" and other classifications for ad hoc purposes.

What Is "Typology"?

It may happen that some objects we want to put in order seem each a medley of hopelessly knotted characteristics. One then looks naturally for some easy way out rather than attempting, off the bat, to construct a neat hierarchy of taxonomic categories. So one picks a few individual objects which seem well developed and strikingly different from others in view of the cluster of characteristics they possess; one calls them representative "types," and ranges other objects around each of them on the basis of prima facie similarity.[4]

This is quite often a workable way of organizing diversity. It may not be up to the standards of perfection of the taxonomist's trade, but there is the consoling thought that it is serviceable, as scientists like to say, "for heuristic purposes"[5] — if it is. One can say many useful things by using typological concepts such as "Soviet-type economies" or "Western-type market capitalism," and we do not think for a moment of rejecting that usage ourselves. However, we had better watch out not to be misled by superficial similarities into grouping together disparate objects or segregating things that belong together. We might get wrong answers to certain important questions.

Speaking, for instance, of "Soviet-type economies" is like speaking of "dog-type creatures" when we really mean "mammals." If we then meet a dolphin or a bat, we are in danger of keeping them out of the family of mammals because they do not look at all like "dog-type creatures." Chances are we shall lump the dolphin together with "cod-type creatures" and the bat with creatures typed, as, say, "robinlike." The reason for such taxonomic miscasting is that with the type "dog" a random set of nonessential similarities creep in which are entirely out of logical order; i.e., they ignore the hierarchic ranking of characteristics required for a general classification.

---

[4] See footnote 2 in Chap. 1.
[5] "Heuristic" refers to the pragmatic role of concepts in guiding research, suggesting ideas, etc., in a not necessarily systematic or formally neat way.

Table 3-2 Classification system of economic systems by type of ownership.

MATERIAL PRODUCTION ASSETS		INDIVIDUALS		COLLECTIVES OR COLLECTIVE INSTITUTIONS					
				SOCIETY		STATE GOVERNMENT		SELF-SELECTED GROUPS	
Who holds formal ownership title									
How titular owner exercises substantive ownership rights (custody)		Directly	By delegation	Directly	By delegation	Directly	By delegation	Directly	By delegation
OWNERSHIP STATUS OF LABOR	Labor has no rights and is assimilated to other assets	Slavery	"Absentee ownership"						
	Labor has some limited rights but is not freely mobile	Feudalism / Indenture	"Absentee ownership"			Forced labor camps			
	Labor is free but has no substantive rights to material production assets (wage labor)	Individual proprietary capitalism	"Absentee ownership"			Municipal & public enterprise	State capitalism	Family capitalism / Capitalist partnership	Corporate capitalism
	Labor is free and controls the use of material production assets	Robinson Crusoe / Owner-operated enterprise		Tribal economies / "Full communism"	Yugoslav-type self-management			Communes	Production cooperatives

47

In the study of economic systems this happens all the time. Thus, the case of individual private property is chosen as a type standing for capitalism, which then leads to grouping under "capitalism" any system of owner-operated production units just because they are privately owned! On the other hand, all ownership models from which private individual ownership is absent are mechanically grouped under "socialism" just because absence of private ownership is among the characteristics of socialism by any definition. We shall return to this issue more thoroughly below.

What Is an Ad Hoc Classification?

By that term we mean any single-purpose classification of a set of objects based on a one-dimensional criterion. Thus, animals may be reclassified according to their habitat, methods of locomotion, orientation systems, etc. Individuals belonging to different categories of the general classification may then easily hobnob with each other in the new ad hoc categories: "ocean fauna" will include fish, mammals, insects, spiders, protozoa, etc.

Why is this kind of classification different from the general one? It appears that an ad hoc classification does not call for any elaborate system of categories in which every lower one would be subsumed under all the higher ones. Classification boxes at more or less one "level of discourse" are all that is needed. The example of classifying animals by habitat makes it clear: we have desert, aquatic, marsh, tropical-forest, high-mountain animal groups, all side by side. A parallel classification of economic systems might be by technology used: fruit gathering and hunting; handicrafts; machinery-using systems. One might also classify economic systems by geographic areas, by level of economic development, or by concomitant political systems. There may emerge highly interesting correlations, or lack of correlation, e.g., between ownership patterns and the character of political regimes, or among ownership patterns, level of development, and technology.

Economic systems are sometimes discussed loosely in terms of such ad hoc categories. One hears of "industrial economic systems," of the "technetronic age" (Zbigniew Brzezinski), the "postindustrial system" (Daniel Bell); advanced and primitive systems; fascist economic systems; etc. Sometimes the intention seems to be to supersede and obliterate by these expressions traditional distinctions such as between "capitalism" and "socialism." While it makes sense to use any of these terms when the context is appropriate, to take them for basic classification categories would be decidedly amateurish.

SELECTED CASES

The following capsule characterizations of a few economic ownership models should bring the classification scheme of Table 3-2 to life. The core sections are those arguing the case of conceptual continuity between the system of corporate capitalist ownership and state capitalism. However, on account of the frequent, and often indiscriminate use of the terms "feudal" and "feudalism" in reference to certain features of contemporary systems, we shall first devote space to putting down their precise meaning.

Feudalism or the Manorial System

At the origin of the concept are medieval forms of land tenure and status of agricultural population which took shape, between the seventh and tenth centuries, in Western Europe. They prevailed over large areas of the Continent, in many local variants, for a number of centuries, though slowly the economic impact of emerging towns made for a transformation—one speaks of decay and decomposition—of the feudal system. Exactly when feudalism ended we cannot tell. It faded away. Its decomposition was an extremely protracted and uneven process.

In Western Europe feudalism developed and disappeared through a confluence of historical circumstances. In Russia, it was largely created "from above," by means of czars' successive decrees, remolding the previous system of free peasantry, between 1550 and 1650. (It was also ended by decree in 1861.) It is Western European feudalism that usually serves as the primary historical referent of the feudal model. However, certain historic systems elsewhere—in Japan especially—have been sufficiently similar to make the term applicable without risking the reproach of loose usage.

The essential features defining feudalism are two. (1) Titular "ownership" of land is vested in members of a class of feudal lords (suzerains, nobles, church dignitaries, or institutions, such as monasteries of religious orders). These lords form a hierarchy, starting with a king on top, his vassals, and vassals' vassals of successively lower ranks. The word "ownership" appears in quotation marks because, originally, feudal land tenure did not have the same meaning as modern unencumbered private property. Land was "held" by a given lord as a grant ("fief") on the part of his superior in the feudal hierarchy and was encumbered by obligations of loyalty, payment of tribute, and service, especially military service. The superior did not relinquish his title to the land when he passed it on to his vassal and could reclaim it under certain conditions. Nonetheless, direct exercise of custody and usufruct rights did eventually transform the feudal title into permanent hereditary ownership.

(2) At the bottom of the hierarchy is labor that actually cultivates the land. These are bondsmen (serfs), who receive from the lord an allotment of land for their own use, encumbered by the obligation to provide service or pay a tribute to the lord. The lord usually keeps a portion of his fief for his own exploitation. It is mainly on this "domain" (or *demesne*) that the serfs perform their due labor services (*corvée*). The tribute has the form of turning over to the lord a portion of their harvest, assets, or family inheritance or, in later stages, of a money tax.

Serfs are not free. In what way does their unfreedom differ from that of a slave? In legal terms the slave is similar to a material asset, a thing, with no rights whatsoever. Serfs have a legal personality: they can be subjects with *some* rights. However, the economic pattern of ownership rights is of greater interest to us. Under slavery, custody (i.e., direct supervision of the slaves' economic utilization, their maintenance and reproduction) as well as usufruct rights is jointly exercised by the slave owner, even if through the intermediary of other supervisors. Under feudalism, serfs receive the custody of their land allotment, as well as the responsibility for their maintenance and reproduction—they have the right to a family. The lord retains only a portion of the usufruct rights which amounts, economically speaking, to the feudal type of "taxation," to a tax in kind, in labor, and later in money.

Seemingly a formality, this change in ownership arrangements produced a revolution in the structure of motivation and incentives, making it worth the tillers' while to raise their productivity above that of the slave, who could not care less. However, for the lord to continue to benefit, it was necessary for him to use his legislative and police powers to immobilize the serfs, to tie them to his land.

Once we have specified the feudal ownership model, our task at hand is over. There remain many interesting questions as to the origins and local variants of feudalism which cannot be answered here. Let us merely note the relationship between the system's ideological self-image and the power structure which held the economic system together. It may serve as a paradigm for understanding many a present-day system. The stylized self-interpretation of feudalism postulated a mutuality of functions—the lord providing protection and paternal care, the serfs material sustenance. This may have had some foundation in the early facts. While serfdom came about largely through changes in the status of slaves, an important tributary consisted in free peasants voluntarily seeking to become subjects of a lord (through "infeodation"), for the sake of having a protector against looters and robbers of the Dark Ages. Nonetheless, military power of the lord, needed to protect his charges, was equally good for oppressing them. With progressive internal pacification of European lands the need for police protection waned and there remained the unilateral use and abuse of naked power on the part of the feudal military class of lords.

Is it legitimate to speak of feudalism when a system does not display all the basic characteristics of classic feudalism? Obviously, large-scale landownership alone, without powers of taxation and territorial prerogatives of government, without legally established prohibition of free mobility of human resources, does not answer the description. Simple levying of tributes, e.g., by a privileged group of chieftains in the context of tribal economies, does not constitute feudalism. Speaking of the Soviet collective-farm peasant who until 1974–1975 was legally bound to the kolkhoz where he was born, Peter Wiles was inspired to use the feudal term *adscriptus glebae*, i.e., "bound to the soil."[6] There is no objection to speaking of single "feudal features" as long as we do not mistake them for fullfledged feudalism.

Owner-operated Units of Independent Producers

Free private farmers, artisans in their workshops, physicians in their private practices, any "self-employed" in the terminology of the U.S. Internal Revenue Service, are examples of this ownership model.

---

[6] Peter Wiles, *The Political Economy of Communism*, Harvard, Cambridge, Mass., 1962, p. 110.

The decomposition of feudalism mentioned above consisted mainly in the transformation of the feudal land allotments worked by the serfs into free hereditary holdings of independent peasants. Tenant farmers are representative of an intermediate model, between serfs and freeholders. Tenants do not own the land. They lease it from landlord-owners against a specified rent payment or share in the crop (sharecropping or *métayage*). Beyond that, they have no obligations to the owners. They are not legally forced to enter the contracts, but neither are the landlords forced to renew them. As the renewal becomes quasi-automatic and the rental fee lighter, to the point of disappearance, tenants become freeholders. This was one of the economic accomplishments of the French Revolution, which did not "abolish feudalism" but only its successor, the heavy-duty tenancy system.

As the illustrations suggest, the system of independent producers is not limited to agriculture. It exists wherever ownership of material factors of production is in the hands of individuals using their own labor. The important negative attribute of this model in its pure state is the *absence of any hired labor*: all work is done by the heads of the production unit (which is attached to, or coextensive with their households) and their families. If they become master artisans who train apprentices and employ journeymen, or merchants who operate with the help of hired employees, the purity of the model is marred. It is true that the status of journeymen has been interpreted as something between a family member and a hired hand on the way to the status of a master. Still, the element of wage labor, together with manifestations of class conflicts typical for capitalism (journeymen's defense organizations, strikes, rebellions), forces us to mark *systems of independent producers employing labor* as a transitional variant between independent producers pure and simple and *proprietary capitalism*.

Individual Proprietary Capitalism

If the system of independent producers precludes employment of wage labor, individual proprietary capitalism presupposes it. It is its definitional characteristic, as of capitalism in general.[7]

One might say the difference in the ownership pattern is strictly a matter of change in scale of productive operations. The scale of producer durables and complementary material inputs is so great that owners are physically incapable of supplying the corresponding necessary volume of labor themselves. They have to turn to others willing to work for them for a wage. However, they can do that only if such persons are available—a condition which cannot be taken for granted because its fulfillment depends on many historical, demographic, and sociological circumstances (see Chapter 4). But assuming there are human resources available for hire, the corollary is a social polarization of ownership rights and

[7] Nonspecialists and amateurs sometimes think that the term "capitalism" is derived from the fact of capital-using technology, "capital" in the sense of material producer durables. They do not see the point why "capitalism" should be distinguished from other economic systems that use producer durables—"Why, Robinson Crusoe is also a capitalist!" They need to be told that nomenclature of economic systems is based on social ownership patterns with respect to production assets, not on the character of production technology.

functions between two groups: the titular ownership of material production assets, entrepreneurial decisions, and management at one pole, and naked labor force (in the narrow sense), without sufficient productive equipment, at the other. Whereas in the system of independent producers there was fusion of all these functions in one person, in capitalism they are separated between "capitalists" (and those employed to help them perform their functions), and hired "wage labor."

Such is the essence of the capitalist class structure. There is, as ever, technological complementarity between the functions of all participants in the system, but by social organization they are kept separated. They can be joined only if the workers succeed in clearing the obstacle of concluding a labor contract with the "capitalists" in their role as employers.

It is clear from this explicit treatment of the elementary ownership pattern defining capitalism that a definition in terms of private property is painfully inadequate and misleading. "Private property" characterizes just as much the systems of slavery and owner-operated units of independent producers as proprietary capitalism. On the other hand, as we shall see, the fundamental features of capitalism may be preserved in systems from which individual private property has completely disappeared.

Gratuitous lumping of independent producers with capitalist owners and entrepreneurs leads to subsuming erroneously the former under the latter. Such theoretical confusion can have seriously destructive economic consequences if, for instance, it dominates the thinking of a presumably anticapitalist revolutionary government. Anticapitalist policies may then actually hit a sector which has nothing to do with capitalism, except for the nonessential feature of private ownership.

The most notable culprit here was the Soviet government during the nineteen-twenties. Unsure of the political support of the peasantry and, at the end of the decade, bent on collectivization, the Communist party waged an increasingly fierce struggle against independent peasants. The doctrinal cloak was a struggle against "capitalism in the countryside." In a parallel process of extermination, private individual producers, tolerated by the New Economic Policy after 1921, were reduced to insignificant numbers. This policy of eliminating private handicrafts, services, and trade was reproduced after World War II, in faithful imitation of the Soviet precedent, in all countries under Soviet domination.

Corporate Capitalism

Subdivisions of the broad category of capitalism turn on the question of who is the subject of titular ownership. The titular owners (or owner) are usually the persons (or the group, or agency) that supply the bulk of the initial investible funds necessary to start and run a capitalist firm. This establishes their ownership and serves then as ground for claiming a portion of the usufruct, namely, net revenue. Individual proprietors of enterprises of which they are the bosses, who put up their own money to buy durable equipment and inputs, and to hire labor, are the prototype of capitalist organization. Here, the individual capitalist is investor, entrepreneur, and manager all rolled into one.

From here on, the capitalist pattern undergoes a series of mutations. They concern arrangements at the pole of titular ownership, entrepreneurship, and management, but they do not touch the status of the workforce as hired wage labor.

The individual capitalist may join other individuals and become a partner in a capitalist partnership. The title of the firm bearing his name grows an appendix, such as "and Co." or, if the partner is a relative, "and Son" or "Bros." In those cases, one speaks sometimes of "family capitalism."

As the scale of operations expands, the group of owners may delegate some of their functions to salaried employees; this gives rise to "management" as a specialized group. At the same time, there are changes in the methods of raising investible funds, either in order to found new firms or to supplement old funds in existing firms. The initiators offer the public-at-large the possibility of becoming investors by buying shares in the firm. By the same token, investors become co-owners in title, to the extent of their financial participation, with the prospect of participating also in the usufruct—of receiving a dividend, i.e., the distributed part of net revenue. Thus, the capitalist corporation is born.

Under the corporate ownership pattern, the structure of relationships at the capitalist pole can become incredibly complex compared to the individual-boss prototype, and also compared to the basic corporate floor plan. The basic scheme is still relatively simple: the titular owner is the mass of individual stockholders; this collective exercises its sovereignty as owner through the general meeting of stockholders; the stockholders' meeting elects the members of the board of directors, an executive organ of the corporation, who, in turn, appoint the top management personnel. (Sometimes, instead of a single board of directors, there is a two-tier structure of a supervisory body and an executive committee.) This scheme presents the corporation, as far as ownership is concerned, "as the republic in miniature," where shareholders are the electorate and the board of directors together with management are the executive branch.

Against the backdrop of sociological realities, the formal scheme appears as a legal fiction. The realities referred to are the familiar set of observations described usually as "divorce of ownership from control." In our terms, of all the substantive ownership rights the titular owners, the stockholders, retain for all practical purposes only a conditional usufruct right to a dividend—if it is declared by the board of directors. All other substantive rights are exercised by the directors and other managerial executives.

The two men usually credited with drawing attention to this discrepancy between legal fiction and the actual state of affairs are Adolf A. Berle, Jr., and Gardiner C. Means, authors of the 1932 book *Modern Corporation and Private Property*. It has since become a commonplace, dramatized in 1944 by James Burnham's *Managerial Revolution* and by John K. Galbraith's renaming management "technostructure" in *The New Industrial State*. Actually, the issue was clearly formulated as early as 1864–1867 by Karl Marx, who himself referred to observations made more than thirty years earlier by A. Ure to the effect that "it is not the industrial capitalists, but the industrial managers who are the 'soul of our industrial system.' "[8]

In his treatment of the corporate form of ownership, Marx made the distinction between the "money capitalist" (whom we would call the investor) and the "functioning capitalist" performing the "work of supervision," i.e., control (whom we call the entrepreneur-manager). The pertinent passages, which are relatively little known and rarely get the honor of being quoted, show incidentally how far removed Marx was from a simplistic identification of capitalism with private property, to wit:

> The capitalist mode of production has brought matters to a point where the work of supervision entirely divorced from the ownership of capital, is always readily obtainable. It has, therefore, come to be useless for the capitalist to perform it himself. An orchestra conductor need not own the instruments of his orchestra. . . . [9]

And a few paragraphs later:

> . . . Since, on the one hand, the mere owner of capital, the money-capitalist, has to face the functioning capitalist . . . , the mere manager who has no title whatever to the capital . . . performs all the real functions pertaining to the functioning capitalist as such, only the functionary remains and the capitalist disappears as superfluous from the production.[10]

Nonetheless, the complexity of real social relationships behind the threadbare legal fiction goes further.

First of all, there is usually an overlap between the sets of stockholders and entrepreneur-managers. On the one hand, large concentrations of a small fraction of total shares in the hands of a few stockholders make such individuals stand out from the anonymous mass. It gives them clout in the stockholders' meetings and the selection of the executive personnel, and a stake in the affairs of the corporation. On the other hand, executives receive part of their renumeration in the form of stock of the company ("stock options"), which tends to partly fuse ownership and control again.

Further, the corporation acquires its own legal personality. As such, it can become, as an institution, the subject of ownership rights beyond its original confines, through acquisitions, mergers, and establishment of new firms (see Chapter 13). Indeed, a legal personality may be created, in the form of a corporation, a "holding company," just for the purpose of serving as pivot of ownership rights with respect to corporations engaged in actual productive operations.

Finally, the exercise of substantive ownership rights is never absolute. "Corporate power" does not mean ability to make totally arbitrary decisions. Exercise of custody always takes place within the network of multiple constraints. Man-

---

[8] Karl Marx, *Capital*, vol. III, p. 386.
[9] Ibid.
[10] Ibid., p. 388.

agement operates within the constraints of objective demand (which can be manipulated only up to a point—see Chapter 16) and of technological input requirements enforced by cost competition. It has to take into account the interests of stockholders in dividends and the market value of their shares because this influences the cost and supply of additional investible funds. The state comes to regulate corporate decision making to protect the stockholding public against fraud and the community-at-large against untoward repercussions upon environment, employment, etc.

Some economists would wish to see corporate behavior squeezed back into the mold of the legal fiction. Thus, Milton Friedman maintains that "a corporate executive is an employe of the owners of the business. He has the direct responsibility to his employers. That responsibility is to conduct the business in accordance with their desires, which generally will be to make as much money as possible. . . . "[11] Authors of "radical" tendency in economics and social sciences tend to equate the concentration of decision making in the hands of corporate managerial bureaucracy with the increase of their power to shape the content of those decisions without regard to social constraints.

An increasingly prevalent approach tries to take into account the fact that corporate decision making takes place at the intersection of many partial group interests—employees, customers, local and central state authorities, lenders, general social climate, etc. These groups are called the corporate firm's "constituencies." The task of management is understood to be reconciliation and coordination of their partially conflicting interests in view of the attainment of the economic objectives of the firm. In contrast with the image of autocratic wielders of corporate power, we encounter thought-provoking perceptions such as that of Harlan Cleveland, for whom "the result of bigness is actually a diffusion of the decision-making and decision-influencing process far beyond the wildest dreams of those . . . who wanted to keep power diffused by keeping the units of society small."[12] The last word on these questions has not yet been spoken. They touch obviously upon one of the major open issues in the study of contemporary economic systems; we shall come back to them on a number of later occasions.

State Capitalism

At issue is how to classify economic systems which have the following characteristics: the workforce has the status of hired wage labor; custodial functions are exercised by a distinct social group of decision makers appointed by the state and its agencies; leaving wages aside, usufruct is "appropriated" (not necessarily for consumption purposes) by the managerial and governmental bureaucracy.

The presence of hired wage labor, which implies a workforce devoid of substantive ownership rights with respect to material productive assets, points to the general class of capitalism. The supply of investible funds comes, proximately at least, from the state agencies, and so does the selection of the entrepreneurial-

[11] Milton Friedman, *The New York Times Magazine*, Sept. 13, 1970.
[12] Harlan Cleveland, "Dinosaurs and Personal Freedom," *Saturday Review*, Feb. 28, 1959, p. 12.

managerial personnel. When investible funds were supplied by an individual whose titular ownership was based on the supply of these funds, and who exercised effective control in the sense of substantive ownership (whether personally or through hirelings), we talked of the "species" of individual proprietary capitalism. If for the individual proprietor we substitute throughout the agency of the state, we have another parallel "species," that of state capitalism.

Confusion may arise because of the way in which titular ownership is formulated by law. Sometimes the legal formula unashamedly makes the government, or the state, the titular owner. In other cases, the legal formula says the ownership belongs to the "nation," the "people," "workers," or "society." In the first instance, one speaks of "public enterprises" or "state enterprises." The conversion from private ownership (individual or corporate) may be called *étatisation*, to use a French word for want of an English equivalent. In the second instance, the term is "nationalized" or "socialized"—industry, sector, or the entire economy.

The last verbal formulas are supposed to convey the meaning that, whoever makes the actual decisions falling under substantive ownership rights, does so in the name and interest of the titular owner—nation, people, or society. Whether this claim corresponds to social realities can be decided only by examining the social realities. These find usually a more faithful expression in the fine print of specific legislation concerning the rights of management, state agencies, the workforce, and the citizenry, than in the preambles of laws or solemn articles of state constitutions. But even specific legislation may be misleading. Fortunately, from the examination of corporate-capitalist ownership we are used by now to the need of distinguishing between legal fiction and underlying realities. Ideological fictions couched in the terminology of "socialism" are merely one extra layer which needs to be pierced.

Analytic continuity between the corporate paradigm and that of state capitalism becomes evident with the help of the following formulation. Under corporate capitalism, the titular owners, the stockholders, were degraded to the status of creditors of the firm, with a conditional right to usufruct in the form of dividends and ability to sell their claim (share) for cash. Under state capitalism, the process of degradation of the titular owners is carried one step further. Their property "share" takes the form of general legal declaration as to social ownership, but there are no specific claims they have or could enforce. Whether and how they benefit by their ownership beyond their claims as wage earners depend entirely on the wisdom and goodwill of the state-capitalist management.

The political character of the state is obviously of great importance, as it determines the character of decisions made by the caretakers of state capitalism. At least two boxes are needed for its subdivision into subspecies. State-capitalist firms run under national democratic auspices are equivalent, as far as ownership is concerned, to capitalist corporations minus the stockholders, but otherwise are exposed to similar objective social and economic constraints. (Nothing essential is changed if the political organ is local government or a municipality.) State capitalism operating under despotic political structures is relieved by them of much of the pressure of social constraints; this enables it to cater more fully to demands dictated by the interests of the group in power. Examples of the first subspecies can be drawn from any public-enterprise sector in Western capitalist economies (see Chapter 13); the second subspecies is represented mainly by Soviet-type economies in the Soviet Union, Eastern Europe, China, and Cuba.[13] Underdeveloped countries launching their industrialization programs in the framework of state-run enterprises are thereby also adopting the state-capitalist ownership model.

Marx took note of such enterprises, founded and run by the state, at the beginnings of capitalist industrialization, but only in an auxiliary role, on the basis of historical experience known to him.[14] A full elimination of private ownership he foresaw only in the later stages of capitalism. The capitalist corporation represented to him "the abolition of capital as private property within the framework of capitalist production itself."[15] It was to be the vanishing point of a process of change in ownership relation: "In the last instance [capitalist mode of production] aims at the expropriation of the means of production from all individuals."[16] Or, speaking of the fusion of individual capitals into ever larger units, he wrote: "In a given society the limit would be reached only when the entire social capital was united in the hands of either a single capitalist or a single capitalist company."[17] It was left to Friedrich Engels to dot the *i* and say: "The more productive forces [the state] takes over, placing them under its ownership, the more does it turn into a true integral capitalist, the more citizens does it exploit. Workers remain wage earners, proletarians. The capitalist relationship is not abolished; rather, it is pushed to the extreme."[18]

Production Cooperatives, Communes, Socialism

With the production cooperatives, we revert to the system of owner-operated production units, except for the fact that the "independent producer" is not an individual but a social group: members of the cooperative.

This difference in numbers poses subtle problems for analysis of this ownership model. As long as entrepreneurial and managerial functions remain a highly specialized activity, not accessible to people without proper schooling and training, the titular owners of a cooperative have little choice but to entrust the substantive controls of the enterprise to professional managers. This creates a highly ambiguous situation. Executive managers are employees of members of the cooperative. However, in the daily run of the production process, cooperative mem-

---

[13] Fascist regimes did not develop a special pattern of ownership, nor did they adopt the state-capitalist model, except marginally. They took over the existing mixed ownership structures of individual proprietary and corporate capitalism, the latter dominated by powerful family dynasties of individual entrepreneurs, such as the Krupps in Germany or Mitsui in Japan.

[14] "On the continent of Europe, after Colbert's example, the process was much simplified. The primitive industrial capital, here, came in part directly out of the state treasury." (K. Marx, *Capital*, vol. I, p. 757.)

[15] Ibid., vol. III, p. 436.

[16] Ibid., p. 439.

[17] Ibid., vol. I, p. 627.

[18] F. Engels, "Anti-Dühring," in *Marx-Engels Werke*, vol. 20, Dietz Verlag, Berlin, 1968, p. 260 (our translation).

bers must submit to the authority of managers as if they were *their* employees. It is mainly with respect to usufruct rights—disposition of net revenue—that members assert their ownership status again.

In jotting down remarks for later analysis of transitional ownership models, Marx dealt with these paradoxes as follows: "In a cooperative factory the antagonistic nature of the labor of supervision disappears, because the manager is paid by the labourers instead of representing capital counterposed to them."[19] This is simple and straightforward, but also, by Marx's own standards, somewhat superficial. One realizes that when one gets to ponder, a little later, the complexity of another formulation: "The antithesis between capital and labour is overcome within [cooperative factories], if at first only by way of making the associated labourers into their own capitalist, i.e., by enabling them to use the means of production for the employment of their own labour."[20]

The inner contradictions of the production cooperative can presumably be solved only in the course of further economic development, as many variables of the system change in value and character. Among them, one has to assume an intellectual and cultural level such that performance of technically different functions, including management, would not mean social differentiation into a hierarchy of class power. Marx considered both the corporate and the cooperative ownership model to be an open-ended framework for such a development: "The capitalist stock companies, as much as the cooperative factories, should be considered transitional forms from the capitalist mode of production to the associated one."[21] The contradictions inherent in the cooperative form of ownership can be studied empirically in the example of the Yugoslav firm, which is a variant of a producer cooperative. Its employees are not owners of the firm. Formally, the nation is, and employees receive the custody and usufruct rights in trust, exercising them through so-called workers' councils. However, the contradictions are fully apparent, as we shall see in detail in Chapter 17, though the situation is complicated by the authoritarian political environment and the still low level of economic development.

Where there is *complete fusion of titular ownership, authority to make entrepreneurial and managerial decisions, and implementation of these decisions, and all are exercised by a hierarchically undifferentiated group of producers*, we may speak properly of a commune. As a special ownership model, a *commune* is a cooperative rid of its contradictions, especially of all traces of wage labor. Sometimes, one thinks of communes in terms of a still wider fusion, in the same framework, between productive activities and social life in general. Isolated experiments with communal organization have been made by like-minded individuals of the utopian socialist persuasion (see Chapter 6), but the only durable example—or its closest approximation—seems to be the organization of the Israeli kibbutz (see Chapter 14).

"Associated mode of production," mentioned in the last quoted passage by

[19] K. Marx, *Capital*, vol. III, p. 387.
[20] Ibid., p. 440.
[21] Ibid.

Marx, was his way of referring to *socialism*. The rigorous logic of our classification scheme does not permit this notion of socialism to be fitted anywhere else but in the same slot as the commune in the definition given in the preceding paragraph. By the same token, there is no room in that slot for ownership models of contemporary experience which go under the label of "socialism" but display real characteristics of capitalism, in particular the presence of wage labor and all it implies for the social distribution pattern of ownership rights. This is the reason why we have classified all such systems routinely as state capitalism.

There is one distinction between the ownership model of a commune and socialism. The commune model refers to a single production unit. Socialism refers to an extension of the commune model to the economy as a whole, where one must assume an articulation and coordination of individual communal units with communelike organization of decision making at the level of society and economy as a whole. Such practical arrangements of social ownership relations can be reduced, philosophically, to the notion that the human subjects of decision making are identical with its objects.

The reader surely realizes the wide gap, nay, incompatibility of the popular and well-nigh universal usage of terms like "socialism" and "capitalism" with the concepts developed here. This discrepancy is regrettable, but it is the necessary price one has to pay if one prefers analytic precision to helter-skelter tagging. The price consists in mustering the courage of appearing to be out of step with the rest of the world. However, if the eel called itself a snake and the whale a fish, and everyone echoed them without protest—would that be a reason to go along?

BIBLIOGRAPHY

Furubotn, Eirik, and Svetozar Pejovich: "Property Rights and Economic Theory: A Survey of Recent Literature," *Journal of Economic Literature*, vol. 10, no. 4, December 1972, pp. 1137–1162.

———— (eds.): *The Economics of Property Rights*, Ballinger, Cambridge, Mass., 1974.

Wiles, P. J. D.: *The Political Economy of Communism*, Harvard, Cambridge, Mass., 1962, chaps 1 and 2.

Pryor, Frederic L.: *Property and Industrial Organization in Communist and Capitalist Nations*, Indiana University Press, Bloomington, 1973, esp. chaps. 1, 4, and 9.

Holesovsky, Vaclav: "Revision of the Taxonomy of 'Socialism': A Radical Proposal," *The ACES Bulletin* (Association for Comparative Economic Studies), vol. 16, no. 3, Winter 1974, pp. 19–40.

Bettelheim, Charles: "State Property and Socialism," *Economy and Society*, vol. 2, no. 4, November 1973, pp. 395–420.

Schweitzer, Arthur: "Comparative Enterprise and Economic Systems," *Explorations in Economic History*, vol. 7, no. 4, Summer 1970, pp. 413–432.

Boissonade, P.: *Life and Work in Medieval Europe*, Harper Torchbooks, New York, 1964.

Coulborn, R., and J. R. Strayer: *Feudalism in History*, Princeton University Press, Princeton, N.J., 1956.

Strayer, Joseph R.: *Feudalism*, Van Nostrand, Princeton, N.J., 1965.

Goody, Jack: "Feudalism in Africa?" *Journal of African History*, vol. 4, no. 1, 1963, reprinted in George Dalton (ed.): *Economic Development and Social Change*, The Natural History Press, Garden City, N.Y., 1971, pp. 148–168.

Blum, Jerome: *Lord and Peasant in Russia*, Atheneum, New York, 1964.

Hall, John W.: "Feudalism in Japan: A Reassessment," *Comparative Studies in Society and History*, vol. 5, no. 1, October 1962, pp. 15–51.

Asakawa, K.: "Some Aspects of Japanese Feudal Institutions," *Transactions of the Asiatic Society of Japan*, vol. 45, part I, 1917, pp. 77–102.

Kamenka, Eugene, and R. S. Neale (eds.): *Feudalism, Capitalism and Beyond*, E. Arnold, London, 1975.

Preston, Lee E.: "Corporation and Society: The Search for a Paradigm," *Journal of Economic Literature*, vol. 13, no. 2, June 1975, pp. 434–453 (bibliography).

De Vroey, Michael: "The Separation of Ownership and Control in Large Corporations," *The Review of Radical Political Economics*, vol. 7, no. 2, Summer 1975, pp. 1–10 (bibliography).

Chapter 4

Classification
of Economic Systems
by Mode of Allocation

Unhappy is a society that has run out of words to describe what is going on.

Daniel Bell

What is it we were doing when ordering economic systems by type of ownership? We looked at the systems' participants and asked who had which kind of decision-making authority; how it was distributed within a production unit or within the economy as a whole; into what social-group or class patterns the distribution of ownership rights fell. We knew these patterns to have developed historically, to be subject to change and replacement by new ones, but basically the point of view was static. Now for the dynamic one. Classification by mode of allocation takes economic systems in their process of functioning. It searches for differences in the way participants are related to each other, via the process elements (see Chapter 2), in their two basic roles: as users and consumers of products, and as producers. The classification is after patterns of interaction between participants, individual and grouped, and of their integration into a coherent economic process.

THE ISSUES IN GENERAL

What Is Allocation?

We say in economics that we allocate productive resources to useful ends, but what we really mean is allocation of activities: Who is to do what with which part of material assets? Or who is being prevented from doing what he might do? In money-using economic systems of some complexity, there are many transactions involving purely financial assets, or rights, and they considerably complicate the allocation process, but in the end everything converges upon what happens at the level of real activities involving real assets and products.

This part of allocation concerns the production process. It is nothing else but regulation of the social division of labor, not just by occupational categories but by minute detail of individual operations. That is the content of custodial rights when they are being exercised: utilization of material assets, which implies directing human resources as to how they are to be utilized.

The other part of allocation concerns the distribution of the usufruct: Who is to receive what portion of the products which are the outcome of the utilization of productive assets? This is what is understood by "income distribution," but behind "income" are always claims to products. The claims may be exercised by the income receiver, or kept in abeyance, or passed on to someone else. In moneyless economies "income" is directly synonymous with "products."

What Are "Modes of Allocation"?

The integration of the participants' behavior, the coordination of decisions governing that behavior into a coherent, interlocking process, can be accomplished in a number of different ways. The differences hinge on the *manner in which information reaches the decision makers, and on how this information becomes processed into allocation decisions, under the admixture, at various phases, of motives and incentives influencing the decision-making participants.* Just as a living organism is biologically programmed to respond to inner urges by definite operations upon its environment, for the sake of its self-preservation and reproduction, so are human societies programmed socially through the structure of the allocation process. The basic problem is the same.

Direct Allocation   How does information reach decision makers? How is it processed into allocation decisions? The formulation may seem unnecessarily ponderous if one considers the simplest economic "system," a one-person economy of the Robinson Crusoe variety. Information on goals and possibilities, motivation, allocation decisions, and their implementation are all handled directly by a single human organism, its brain and its muscles.

One merely needs to elaborate this model, which one intuitively understands, to see that it applies, in all essentials, to all self-contained human societies that are small enough to organize their economic life via direct personal communication between their members. Competence and authority to make different decisions may well be socially structured, and so may the implementation. In other words, division of labor and functions is there, and even hierarchy, but the coordination task itself does not yet require a specialized set of acts for wishes to be communicated from the consumption "pole" to the production "pole," and for possibilities to be communicated in the opposite direction. Everything is clear, either because decision rules have been routinized and internalized by tradition, or because of direct orders coming from the person or persons in authority, who may themselves be merely performing according to tradition. Adherence to custom or obedience to authority takes the place of individualistic motivation.

The Medium of the Market   The person-to-person immediacy in communicating about economic goals and means needs to be contrasted with all those modes of allocation where such communication occurs through the intermediary of a special class of acts and type of behavior covered by the term "market." Social acts which constitute a market are acts of exchanging products, whether material products or personal services does not matter. What does matter is that the exchanges be not incidental isolated happenings but form a general, accepted pattern of behavior, stabilized by rules of conduct and even (though not necessarily) backed up by legal norms. This is what makes the market into a social economic institution.

In what way are markets means of communication? Exchange is a method of finding out whether the outcome of a production decision is acceptable to the users. An exchange consists of a bid which specifies the ratio between the quantity of product being offered and the quantity of product expected in return. If the bid is accepted, the transaction is ready to be made. If not, the bid may be answered by a counterbid, evolving into a Ping-Pong series of bids and counterbids, until an agreement is reached. Depending on whether the outcome satisfies producers, or disappoints them, they will adjust their subsequent production decisions. They got the message.

This elementary form of market behavior describes *barter* where products are exchanged against products. With the development of money, products are exchanged against symbolic product equivalents, i.e., monetary signs convertible into specific quantities of products. In the process, barter exchange ratios (which are the same thing as "commodity terms of trade," an expression used in economics of international trade) become expressed as prices. First traders think in terms of a physical quantity of product A as equivalent to some physical quantity of product B; then in terms of the same physical quantity of product A being equivalent to a given number of monetary units, these being in turn equivalent to the same quantity of B as before; finally, from the preceding equalities one calculates how many monetary units are equivalent to *one* physical unit of product A, or B, etc. These are then unit prices corresponding to the underlying exchange ratios of commodities. Barter exchanges become sales and purchases of products for money.

Instead of bargaining about the terms of trade, i.e., about relative prices, the market can convey information in a modified manner, one which is anonymous and more suitable to transactions involving plurality of buyers. The seller (producer) makes a firm bid and decides on a tentative flow of output to be offered.

If buyers want less, at the set price, the seller will be left with unsold inventories. If they want more, the seller will find out from inventories falling quickly down to zero, and from inquiries about "when do you expect the next shipment?" Again, the seller gets the message.

We have thus established the distinction between two basic modes of allocation, using as distinguishing characteristic the method by which information on goals is transmitted to participants in their role as providers of means. One amounts to direct allocation, the other uses the medium of the market. In the market mode of allocation, information on goals and purposes is generated through economic transactions—market exchanges—which allocate finished products among users, and the information feedback then influences allocation of resource-using activities. In the direct mode of allocation, economic transactions allocating products do not carry in themselves any such information. They constitute the category of *transfers*.

A Word about Transfers   Now that we have spelled out the fundamental nature of exchange transactions making up markets, it will be easy to be precise by adding a few remarks about transfer transactions (see Figure 4-1). We speak properly of transfers when products (or money) change hands without the recipient's giving in return any equivalent as a condition. In its pure and simple form, a transfer is a unilateral act. Its prototype is a gift (or its involuntary counterpart—theft). Such transfers consist in the direct transmission of a product or service by the supplier to the user. Examples abound: volunteer work, household chores, rearing children in a family, sick care, military draft, blood donations, free advice, etc. Other transfers are less direct and specific, and amount to a redistribution of income, through the government or other agencies, e.g., charity; scholarships; taxes that end up as welfare payments, grants, subsidies, or goods enjoyed by others than the taxpayer. There are voluntary and involuntary transfers; transfers in kind and money transfers. There are sinister transfers causing cost to the recipient, such as bullets and bombs.

We think of transfers mainly in the sphere of income and product distribution. However, the production sphere within a given plant or enterprise is ordinarily chock-full of transfers: an item of goods-in-process is passed on from one partial operation to the next, from one machine, or workshop, or division of a firm to another.

In principle, we said, transfers are *unilateral acts*. Therefore, if the recipient of a transferred product or service is expected to reciprocate, we are crossing the boundary of the transfer concept.

Bilateral transfers amount to a transitional form of allocation, halfway between transfer and exchange. There is reciprocity, as in exchange, but not yet any systematic tendency toward value equivalence of items or services changing hands.

The most striking instance of a bilateral transfer is the institution of *potlatch*, observed by anthropologists in its classic form among North Pacific Coast Indi-

Figure 4-1 Elementary forms of economic transactions (modes of allocation).

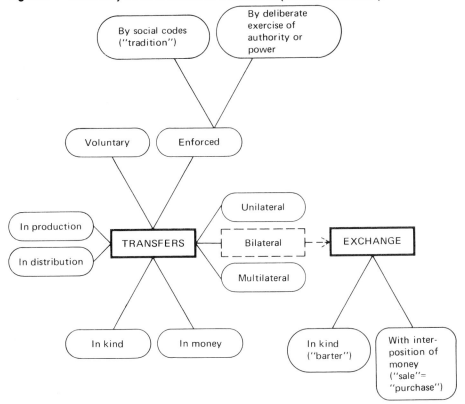

ans. It amounts to tribal groups taking turns in ceremonial gift giving, trying to outdo each other in conspicuous generosity. However, the phenomenon is much more general. Features of reciprocity may be observed in the economics of certain social functions in our type systems, such as invitations to dinner or party giving. They often seem to be offered in that certain (unspoken) spirit which ancient Romans expressed by the phrase *do ut des, facio ut facias*—"I give so that you would give, I do so that you would do."

War is another example of a collective set of bilateral transfers, involving products and "services" whose utility consists in causing disutility.

Some of the preceding remarks point to the fact of coexistence of the two basic modes of allocation within a given concrete economic system of reality, the same as with ownership models. Modern market economies are shot through with very important instances of direct, transferlike allocation. The entire household sector operates, as far as its productive and redistributive functions are concerned, on the transfer principle. However whereas markets rarely exist without being supplemented by transfers, there do exist primitive economic systems without any market exchange, except perhaps in the peripheral contacts with other economic systems, i.e., in their "foreign trade." In those cases, the universality of the mode of direct allocation leads necessarily to the concept of *multilateral transfer systems.*

When people try to imagine what mode of allocation might characterize a possible system of socialism vaguely discernible in the mist of postcapitalist future, they often think of a return to some such multilateral exchange system, at a much higher level of complexity, of course. This is what Marx seemed to be suggesting. It is not necessary to examine here the merit of the issue, but this is the place to mention it.

The Classification Scheme

Much of the preceding has already been part of the explanation of the proposed classification scheme (see Table 4-1). The fact that, in most empirical cases, different modes of allocation are interlaced with each other presents the same slight problem we met with ownership models, and we should be aware of it. A distinct mode of allocation *constitutes* a distinct economic system. The classification boxes are set up for such pure models which have unadulterated real counterparts only in exceptional cases. Most models entered at the lowest level of generality are therefore to be understood as representing just a segment of allocation processes going on in real systems designated by the same name.

The two broadest classification categories correspond to the two modes of allocation we set forth above: direct-allocation systems based on transfers and market systems based on exchange transactions. Transfer systems are further subdivided into unilateral, bilateral, and multilateral, and the unilateral ones into those based on transfers in kind and in money. (Bilateral transfers in money do not seem to play any great role; making change and mutual borrowing or sponging is all one can think of.) Further reflections on these systems will appear below in connection with some cases selected for illustration.

It is in the category of market-exchange systems that a clear understanding of the subdivision counts most for correct analysis of contemporary systems. The first two subdivisions of market-exchange systems parallel the subdivisions of ownership models labeled respectively "owner-operated units of independent producers" and "capitalism." In the first one, we encounter *only product markets.* In the second, product markets are *integrated with markets for hiring human resources, i.e., with labor markets.*

The parallelism between the two ownership models and the two allocation models is a natural consequence of the fact that independent producers combine in their person the ownership of all basic factors of production. In particular, they supply their own labor, which means that there is no explicit market for labor as such. What can be marketed is only the outcome of productive activities, i.e., commodities: farmers sell their grain and other produce, shoemakers their shoes, bookmakers their books, merchants their wares. In contrast, under capitalist ownership conditions, before any production can take place, the owner as custodian of material production assets has to hire labor as a complementary production factor. Or, the other way around, before workers can do anything, they have to lease their labor power. They have to become employees in order to

TRANSFER SYSTEMS

EXCHANGE SYSTEMS

Unilateral transfers

Bilateral transfers

Multilateral transfers

MARKETS FOR COMMODITIES AS WELL AS FOR LABOR (CAPITALISM)

MARKETS ONLY FOR COMMODITIES

Gift

Potlatch

Tribal economies

Taxes

War

Manorial economy

Subsidies

Grants

Theft

Free advice

Full "visible-hand" domination

Some "visible-hand" participation

"Laissez faire"

Compulsory cartelization

Microregulation

Macrocontrols

Voluntary self-organization

Atomistic

Organized

Atomistic

Centrally administered systems

Nazi system

Wartime market economies

Antitrust

Indicative planning

Full employment and price stabilization

Cartels

Oligopolies

Competitive

Competitive with monopoly elements

Guilds of owner-operated enterprises

Independent owner-operated enterprises

get hold of the complementary means of production they do not own, but which they need in order to produce things covering their needs. Then they buy them, for their wages, in the markets for products. Thus, capitalism may be defined, in terms of basic allocation processes, as a combination of product *and* labor markets.

The elementary difference between the two systems can be driven home by means of a few historical glimpses showing the emergence of capitalism as a consequence of disturbances upsetting the balanced ownership pattern in the system of independent producers. Each independent producer controls what we might call a "viable bundle of production factors," i.e., a combination of material assets and labor, as well as entrepreneurial skills, in quantities which make it possible—under prevailing conditions of technology—to put out marketable commodities.

What happens if the combination of production factors under the producer's control ceases to be "viable"? This may happen, e.g., through splitting up of farms among many heirs, which reduces the land/labor ratio below workable levels; or through the effect of the rule of primogeniture, under which the eldest son inherits his father's estate and the younger siblings are left without any land; or through the eviction of farmers and tenants from their fields by landlords, eager to make better money raising sheep, as happened during certain periods between the fifteenth and eighteenth centuries in England; or through the effects of competition, as in the case of the shoemaker who, overwhelmed by the on-slaught of new technology, sang:

> In the days of eighteen and four
> I said I'd peg those shoes no more,
> Throw away my pegs, my pegs, my pegs, my awl.
> They've invented a new machine . . .
> Prettiest little thing you've ever seen,
> Makes hundred pairs to my one—
> Pegs and shoes, it aint no fun. . . .

The by-product of all such historical processes was the emergence of individuals without land and tools—the birth of the proletariat, the wage earners—and with them the core of capitalist social relationships: polarization of labor and capitalist employers as separate groups, each owning one subset of complementary production factors.

"Market System" and "Market Forces" Are Two Different Things

The intricate task before us is to settle on a characteristic which, by its variability, could serve as basis for distinguishing subtypes of the capitalist allocation model.

To do that, we have to ask ourselves what is essential in a market system of exchanges, and what is not. What is it that *defines* market exchange, and what makes for *subsidiary* modifications producing its variants? Market exchange is definitionally present when a product changes hands against money (or against another product in the case of a barter market). *Being a sale-purchase transaction is the essence of market exchange.* It turns the "product" into a "marketed product," i.e., a "commodity."[1] What is secondary and nonessential is the exchange ratio, the commodity terms of trade or price, its exact value, and the manner in which it is determined. Equally secondary are the exact physical quantities being traded at those prices. Prices and quantities may emerge from an unfettered bargaining process between the transactors, but they need not. The process may be "fettered" without the transaction losing its essential property as sale-purchase.

The difference between the essential and the secondary may be explained most easily in reference to the system of independent producers. Imagine their sales taking place in markets with a sufficiently large number of producers of any given article selling to a sufficiently large number of customers for nobody to be able to dictate prices. A customer will always have the option to buy from a cheaper source and those charging higher prices will be stuck with their articles. On the other hand, should sales be so brisk that the low-price sellers can be expected to run out of merchandise before customers buy all they want, at that price, then sellers will be able to raise the price up to the level at which the whole market will be cleared. They would find out from the number of queries of frustrated customers facing empty shelves, whether such a clearing price was actually attained; they would find from the volume of unsold end-of-the-day inventory if the market price had been too high.

The main point is that individual pricing will have to conform to the general market situation, i.e., to demand-and-supply conditions. Furthermore, if the producers produce at differing cost levels—some are more efficient than others—those for whom the established market price is too low to cover their production costs will not be able to continue and will be squeezed out of the market. Now, this picture of how terms of exchange are determined by the "forces" of supply and demand leaves out many finer points and assumptions. These can be found in any book on price theory. Thus, no market day starts in reality from scratch. Prices are not determined every day anew through tentative offers and bids, but on the background of accumulated experience. There will usually be a continuity of today with yesterday; prices and quantities will be adjusted, from last night's starting point, within a relatively narrow range. Nevertheless, this pocket summary brings out the essentials of a market model where terms of exchange, prices, and quantities are determined through the unsupervised play of market forces.

However, this is only one possibility, and perhaps a rather unrealistic one at that, at least as far as some of the best-known historical systems of independent producers are concerned. The conditions of exchange may be heavily determined by interventions of collective organs of associated producers. Such, for example, were the medieval guilds which regulated the permissible volume of output of individual trades, fixed their prices, limited the number of production units, and controlled entry into the profession by limiting the number of apprentices and

---

[1] Transfer systems deal with products as products, not as commodities.

journeymen per master. We shall return to this model further below, among the "Selected Cases."

We would look at these arrangements as instances of monopoly and discretionary behavior. Still, we cannot deny that transactions take place in such markets through sales and purchases, i.e., in the form of market-type exchanges, even though the conditions of exchange are not determined by a free play of market supply and demand. In other words, *there may be market systems without "market forces,"* or with limited room for their operation.

This manner of putting the issue implies that, when we say "market-exchange systems," we are not saying anything yet about the ways in which prices and traded quantities are being determined. They may be determined by supply and demand in a competitive environment, but they need not. If they are not, this is an interesting subsidiary characteristic of the given market-exchange system but does not keep it from being a market-exchange system.

Variations of Capitalist Allocation Systems

The natural principle according to which one can distinguish subtypes within the general capitalist allocation model is the degree to which it is market forces that do or do not determine prices and quantities traded. The degree to which they do or do not depends on how much spontaneous decision making of direct transactors is modified by intervention or participation of agencies other than the transactors. Mixed up with the question of degree is also the question of the character of the intervention, as will soon become apparent.

Ranged according to that principle, subtypes of capitalist allocation form a spectrum going from one extreme, total reign of market forces, to another extreme, complete suppression of market forces. In the latter extreme, suppression of market forces means they have been superseded by outside instructions or orders, and that all autonomy of direct transactors was wiped out and replaced by the authority of some agency standing above all the transactors. We call the first extreme the "laissez faire" model, and the other extreme the "centrally administered" model of allocation.

An Argumentative Digression   It is probably wise to face up right away to possible objections to this treatment, before we go any further. In the conventional view, the centrally administered allocation system (what often goes by the alternative names "central-command planning" or "centrally planned economy") is so unlike the other variants of the capitalist mode of allocation that it must be treated as an allocation model of its own kind, and placed far outside the capitalist market mode of allocation. Now, there is no question about the centrally administered system being unlike any other system. It is on account of its very specificity we would never place it in the box labeled the "laissez faire" model, or in any of the other in-between types we shall come to shortly. It surely needs a special box. However, because of the one common and essential feature which it shares with the other subtypes, it belongs with them in a common larger box. The feature in question is *the formal presence of sales and purchases of products, and* *hiring of labor for wages, the twin characteristics that define the basic mode of capitalist allocation.*

It is generally accepted that the free play of market forces of demand and supply is not a necessary feature of the capitalist mode of allocation. They can be modified, constrained, limited, manipulated, distorted, and even suspended (as in wartime rationing systems)—and one does not conclude that capitalism has been therefore done away with. One understands that only the methods of determining prices and quantities traded have been varied. The price-quantity patterns are different, but not the formal mode of allocation via exchange. Thus, one acknowledges in practice the difference between what is essential and what is secondary. Our proposed classification does nothing else but continue in the same direction, all the way to the logical end.

One could, of course, quite legitimately counter by saying that, at a certain point, the change in the quantitative degree of suppression of market forces may lead to a qualitative jump—a transformation of the capitalistic market mode of allocation into a system of centrally directed multilateral transfers. This is an acceptable formulation, provided it is understood that these dictated transfers retain the form of sales-purchases and hiring of labor for wages, as under capitalist market-exchange transactions. From that point of view, the centrally administered system can be looked upon as a hybrid. (This is expressed by the peculiar location of this system in Table 4-1.)

The Spectrum of Variants   The laissez faire model of unfettered market forces has two further subdivisions. *Atomistic markets* is one, *self-organized markets* is the other. This reflects an important observation. Left to its own devices, the capitalist market mode of allocation does not necessarily produce an atomistic competitive system—the "invisible-hand" system of Adam Smith—made up of firms acting independently of each other, either as perfect competitors or as individual monopolists. Indeed, the allocation model of atomistic competition may not have any counterpart in reality at all. It may be a purely theoretical construction. It may be useful as an abstract reference model, but not as a model representing reality. One may expect individual firms to seek mutual agreements to coordinate their behavior in determining price-and-quantity terms, and thus to modify market forces of supply and demand through the force of deliberate voluntary organization. Tendency toward the formation of cartels and oligopolies is part of the laissez faire picture. It is so natural and spontaneous, so strong, that competitive behavior, corresponding to an atomistic allocation pattern, requires governmental intervention and enforcement to exist.

Next comes the *macrocontrolled* allocation model. Here, the visible hand of the government intervenes in the operation of market forces (however limited by actions of market transactors themselves) for the sake of influencing the outcomes *in the aggregate*, which is what the expression "macro" refers to. The underlying set of notions is this: Aggregate outcomes of activities, as determined by the operation of unattended market forces, may be found undesirable from the point of view of preferences of society. In that case, the government may be charged with the task of manipulating behavior through macrocontrols, so as to make aggregate output, its volume and growth, and the average price level conform to the desirable standard. In plain language, we are referring to capitalist systems subject to stabilization policies in the sense of full employment, growth rates, and price stability. (This model will occupy us at some length in Chapter 10 and parts of Chapters 11 and 12.)

In the allocation model labeled "microregulation," the visible hand of the government is concerned with the determination of specific price-quantity decisions. It interferes in the structure of relative prices and the product composition of output. The purpose is not to influence economic outcomes in the aggregate, even though that may also be a by-product. There is no dearth of concrete examples of microregulation: regulation of public utilities; price controls; rationing of commodities, credit, and foreign exchange; subsidization; direct controls of imports and exports. Antitrust policies are supposed to strengthen the role of market forces and independence of participating transactors in making their decisions. It amounts to an artificial enforcement of behavior corresponding to atomistic markets. (A section in Chapter 13 is devoted to an examination of this model in real national economies.)

The macrocontrolled and microregulated systems are thus contrasted by the purpose of governmental intervention: to influence aggregates in the first case, and price-quantity structure in the second. However, the fact that the purposes differ should not obscure the fact that the practical exercise of macrocontrols usually does something to the price-quantity structure, too. Conversely, the structure of prices and quantities may be manipulated in view of achieving certain aggregate outcomes. This last case refers to the model of so-called indicative planning (illustrated by the French example), as well as to techniques assisting the market in performing structural shifts of production factors, especially labor, as smoothly as possible, to prevent unemployment (illustrated by the Swedish system). Our classification permits us to identify such cases as hybrids straddling the models of macrocontrol and microregulation.

At one remove from the centrally administered model we have placed the system of *state compulsory cartelization*. Here, the government's visible hand does the opposite of antitrust regulation: instead of strengthening atomistic-type behavior, it enforces and imposes the system of organized market supply—cartelization, etc.—which otherwise would be neither universal nor durable. Historical systems which came closest to this model were those organized in Nazi Germany and countries under Nazi occupation during World War II. With wartime price and wage fixing, as well as priority rationing, these systems represented microregulation raised to the position of dominant principle. They were the closest relative of centrally administered systems outside the areas influenced by the Soviet example.

Did We Forget "Planning"? If it were not for a passing reference to "indicative planning" of the French type, there would not be a single trace of the concept of "planning" in the entire classification. The contrast between "market" and "plan" is, though, the favorite principle on which to base distinctions between allocation models. Why not use it?

At first sight, the distinction between "market" and "plan" seems to mean exactly the same thing as our distinction between "market forces" and intervention of some kind by the visible hand. If the meanings were indeed the same, nothing would be more reasonable than to say "market" and "plan." It certainly would be shorter. Unfortunately, the market/plan distinction is not parallel to the one we are trying to establish, and the words "plan" and "planning" are not at all as precise as they sound. There is no parallel, since normally the notion of "plan" does not cover, for example, our microregulation and macrocontrols. There is also lack of precision. "Planning" may mean formulating in a document a projected future comprehensive state of the economy and trying to make the economy behave accordingly. It may also mean adopting consciously, as an objective, *any* aspect of the future states of the economy, partial or comprehensive, and deliberately applying appropriate instruments to attain the objective.

It is the latter, broader meaning of "planning" that appeals to us. In that sense, planning (or its absence) gives *all* the different modes of allocation an extra new dimension. We then view allocation systems with the following question in mind: "How much effort do the participants make to act with a clear future purpose in mind?" Since participants always have some purposes on their minds, one can speak only of *degrees of* "*planningness*," according to the length of the planning horizon, clarity and consistency of goals, and adequacy of instruments used for the attainment of goals. From that point of view it may easily happen that economic systems traditionally considered as the paragon of planning, such as the centrally administered systems, possess a modest degree of "planningness," while systems combining the market-forces mode of allocation with macrocontrols, selective microregulation, and transfers, possess more "planningness" than, according to convention, one is inclined to grant them.

Ownership Models and Mode-of-Allocation Models   How are the two types of classification related? Is one of them more basic than the other? Do both have equal standing, each merely giving an X-ray picture of systems from a different angle? We find it difficult to decide these questions in any clear-cut way.[2] It makes for a certain feeling of uneasiness, but that need not be fatal. Perhaps the questions simply do not have much point, and the only useful thing to do is to collate the two sets of classification categories and see whether they are in some way correlated.

---

[2] Nicholas Spulber did not hesitate to answer the issue as follows: "Differences among systems arise from the predominant form of ownership prevailing in them . . . while differences within each system arise under a variety of impacts from the ways in which the instrumentalities—market mechanism or planning and administration devices—are combined with each other." (*American Economic Review*, December 1964, p. 1137.)

It is clear that products-only markets represent a mode of allocation reserved to ownership systems where labor and material production factors are under the united control of participants who function simultaneously as owners, entrepreneurs, managers, and workers. This covers individual independent owner-operators, and also producer cooperatives and communes, as far as allocation via transactions *between* such units is concerned.

It is also clear that product-and-labor markets are a mode of allocation corresponding to the large genus of capitalism, whatever its ownership variant. This correlation follows logically from our definition of these two sets of ownership categories.

Finally, it is clear that participants *within* closed economic systems where labor and material assets are controlled jointly by workers-entrepreneurs-managers-owners will, as a rule, allocate resources via direct transfer methods, not via market transactions. Thus, a commune, a simple tribal economy, a self-contained manorial economy will not know internal markets but only transfer systems.

Thus, it would appear that the trichotomy of modes of allocation (transfers, product markets, and product-and-labor markets) expresses only behavioral characteristics of definite ownership models grouped by three major subdivisions. (The neatness of this ownership/behavior correlation is spoiled by the fact that transfers also predominate *within* units of capitalist ownership models or slavery systems.)

However, the criterion used for subdividing the capitalist product-and-labor markets mode of allocation into subtypes—the criterion of mixture of market forces and the visible hand—may be appropriate to subdividing the two other major modes of allocation (products-only markets and transfer systems) as well, if it is suitably reformulated. We see that, within the category of products-only markets, the analogy is straightforward. The two-fold subdivision into atomistic and organized systems of owner-operated units follows the difference in the dosage of market forces and the visible hand of other agencies than the transactors themselves. We could easily add other subtypes where the intervening agency would be the governmental power; if we think of medieval kings checking the honesty of weights and dunking dishonest bakers into the river, we have an analogy to microregulation of terms of trade (on the side of early "consumerism").

The need for reformulation applies to transfer systems. Since, by definition, there are no markets, we have to substitute for market forces their underlying behavioral characteristic, i.e., autonomy of direct transactors in making decisions. Visible hand is then to be understood as the power of authorities standing above direct transactors and imposing a pattern of transfers different from the one which would prevail without the intervention of the visible hand.

What we are encountering here under a different nomenclature is the concepts of, on the one hand, *decentralization* and, on the other, *centralization* or *articulation of decision making* discussed in Chapter 2. We also conclude that, at this level of subclassification of economic systems, the view of Nicholas Spulber given in footnote 2 is valid.

SELECTED CASES

Primitive (Tribal) Economies   "Primitive" is not to be understood as inferior but simply as coming at some earlier stage in the historical genealogy of economic systems. A primitive economy naturally has to perform all the basic functions in the allocation of economic resources and distribution of output: production, replacement of discarded items of fixed capital goods, their maintenance, and possibly their accumulation, inventory management (food and material reserves), allocation of output among the members of society. What distinguishes this economic system from the more complex types is the *low degree of institutional differentiation of these functions*. In particular, "households" as the primary consumption units are not differentiated from "firms" as production units. Similarly, "work" is probably not perceived as an activity distinct from, and opposed to, other social activities, such as religious rituals, cooperative behavior through which kinship ties are expressed, etc. Income distribution is not distinct from other behavior denoting the status position of individuals in society and other types of social functions (such as festivities, weddings, etc.). This is what anthropologists mean when they say that economic processes are "embedded" in wider social needs and are inextricably mixed with politics, ceremonial, ritual, and general festivities.

(In contemporary systems we may observe small residuals of this interpenetration of functions, e.g., in office Christmas parties, coffee breaks, the tree-topping ceremony of construction workers having completed a rooftop, launching of ships with champagne bottles, dowries, etc.)

It may be presumptuous to construct a general model of a primitive economic system from the wide and colorful variety of documented cases in Africa, Asia, Oceania, and South America. However, they do exhibit certain basic similarities in economic organization which can be summed up as *systems of multilateral transfers in kind*, with strong elements of *bilateral transfers* (such as gift giving). Raymond Firth rendered the essence of the labor-allocation and output-distribution system in a memorable phrase: "From each according to his status obligations in the social system, to each according to his rights in that system."[3]

In a number of primitive systems we encounter certain embryonic forms of money, full of symbolic connotations, and minor market-type exchanges, especially between tribal societies, or tribal societies and the outer, more developed world (e.g., trade posts in contacts with North American Indians). These are either incidental features, or intrusions of another allocation model into the basic one. The obvious concomitant of the pure model is economic self-sufficiency.

The enforcement of behavior appropriate to the primitive allocation systems (i.e., motivation) is secured through social sanctions, mostly internalized by the individual's psyche: "Order is kept by direct force of everybody's adhesion to custom, rules and laws, by the same psychological influences which in our society prevent a man of the world doing something which is not 'the right thing.' "[4]

---

[3] Raymond Firth, *The Elements of Social Organization*, Watts, London, 1951, p. 142.
[4] Bronislaw Malinowski, *The Argonauts of the Western Pacific*, Routledge, London, 1922.

"Tradition" is just another word for this set of social codes. This system of motivation and behavior signals is, of course, dependent on the relatively small size of these economies and on technological processes of limited complexity. Small scale and relative simplicity—these are the prerequisites of what we call the *transparency* of economic relations. It means that supply of information is practically costless and may be treated as a free good available to all. Another way of describing transparency is to say that economic functions are implemented through direct relationships between members of society, i.e., relationships not mediated through the interposition of impersonal institutions such as markets.

Primitive economic systems have been frequently endowed with the aura of a golden age. Their romantic glorification may be a reaction to the experience with capitalism and its burden of social and psychological costs. Such positive evaluation of primitive systems often goes hand in hand with utopian mentality. A little bit of it seems to have rubbed off even on such a professed antiutopian as Karl Marx—see his occasional references to primitive economic systems as "primitive communism." However, whether economic systems of this type are particularly well suited to human needs is a wide-open question. Certain empirical observations suggest that these systems, too, contain a hidden (latent) dynamic of discontent. Often, when contact with alternative systems is established and the loyalty to tradition becomes corroded, individuals attempt to escape it. The weakening of internalized motivation is then made up for by sanctions and retributions in the form of explicit force (e.g., witchcraft) on the part of the conservative forces of tradition.

The *Jajmani* System   The *jajmani* system of Indian villages is a particularly well-developed—rigid and elaborate—case of economic organization based on multilateral transfers of services and products between members of a multilayered society. The stratification consists in a hierarchy of *castes*. These are social groups differentiated by their status position, as well as their economic functions with respect to each other. The village society is made up of high-caste landowning families called *jajmani* and a host of subordinate castes of *kamins* who specialize in different occupations. They are the Potters, Water Carriers, Carpenters, Sweepers, Laundrymen, Agriculturalists, etc. The artisan and serving castes have the traditional obligation to supply goods and services to each other and to the *jajmani*. They also work on the *jajmani* land. In return, they receive payments in grain, in the total supply of which they have stated shares. They also receive other benefits like free residence sites, food for animals, dung for fuel.

What comes immediately to mind is the analogy with the allocation arrangements in the manorial economy of European feudalism. The pivotal role of the *jajman* is parallel to that of the feudal landlord. In the closed circle of interdependence, mutuality, and reciprocity, the *jajman* has an important function—that of a central redistributive agency, responsible for social security benefits and grants in kind (in times of illness, family events, and festive ceremonies). In tribal economic systems, too, the redistribution of output is typically taken care of by some socially recognized central figure—king, chief, or priest—who collects tributes and then doles them out in ways consecrated by custom. The function of the feudal master was to some extent redistribution, but the analogy is mainly with his primary contribution, i.e., the supply of defense and security in times of lawlessness and weak central power. The interesting question is: How stable and self-enforcing are such systems?

The rigidity of the *jajmani* system rests on the self-perpetuation of the castes through birth ascription, the whole being supported by the accepted and internalized value system of Hindu social and religious doctrines. However, on the basis of Western experiences, one wonders about the relationships between social function and the corresponding position of power and privilege. To what extent does the *jajman* (or chieftain, or prince) conform to impersonal rules of tradition? Or might he perhaps be using his function and authority for the pursuit of subjective, hence potentially arbitrary, goals? To what extent is his social function really vital so as to justify his preeminence which, without that function, would amount to parasitism and exploitation?

The case of feudalism is a classic illustration of social function withering away under the luxuriance of privilege sustained by power alone. This process is made dramatically visible in the transformation of feudal architecture from a castle-fortress into the pleasure palaces of the later nobility. In the *jajmani* system, the latent tensions seem to come to the fore, not through open rebellion, but through individuals easily succumbing to the lure of opportunities offered by alternative systems, if and when they appear, e.g., production for outside markets or employment in manufacturing.

Ancient Incas of Peru   The problem of political power relations, economic function, and their link with the mode of allocation decisions is starkly illustrated by economic systems of certain ancient civilizations that existed mainly in the Orient and some parts of South or Middle America, but also in Hawaii and elsewhere.

In the ideal model of small-scale tribal transfer economies, the structure of authority and economic transactions seem to follow impersonal codes of tradition. Under such conditions the notion of a subjective, i.e., deliberate, exercise of power of persons over other persons would seem to have little application. Now we are examining cases where allocation still takes place via direct transfers, just as in the tribal, manorial, and *jajmani* systems, but with important differences. We are now dealing with large-scale societies, often heterogeneous in ethnic composition. Production techniques in agriculture are such that they need large-scale investment in "social overhead" as a prerequisite, e.g., irrigation systems, flood-control dams, or terracing of steep slopes. Those works in turn presume a rather complex organizing activity, mass mobilization of labor, coordination, preliminary statistical surveys of the population, geodesic measurements, and sometimes astronomic and meteorological observation. Furthermore, persons specializing in these tasks have to be supported by contributions from the rest of the population: a problem of taxation arises. The central, pivotal agents of the system thus assume essential economic functions. However, with the scale and complexity of tasks the transparency of economic relationships is considerably reduced. Sanctions and motivation provided by tradition and custom cease to be workable, and the explicit use of organized power comes to the fore.

Basically, the situation is not unlike that in feudal economic relations, except for two facts: the state power structure, incomparably more centralized, is articulated over the entire territory of the system; and the technocratic, managerial, and bureaucratic element is overwhelming.

The case of Inca Peru is noteworthy for the exceptionally methodical elaboration of the model's characteristics. Also, it displays some strikingly "modern" features.

It anticipates, at an early age and in an unexpected corner of the world, certain elements of totalitarian practices in our century. The Incas were military conquerors of an indigenous agricultural society which they forcefully reorganized according to a preconceived rational pattern. They built their system on the foundations of communal land tenure practiced by the original population. They brought the operation of the communal system under strict central supervision, but set aside two other types of landholdings: the "Inca lands"—a *demesne*—for the support of the Emperor and his nobility (the Incas); and the "sun lands" for the "Church officials." The exploitation of these lands took place under a system of compulsory labor (*corvée*, called *mita*) supplied by the peasants, in addition to some permanent governmental workers. Output of agriculture had to support, in addition, the staffs of appointed officials—administrators, organizers, statisticians, engineers—as well as those employed as governmental artisans and soldiers. Terracing and irrigation systems were the Incas' technical contribution to agriculture, and so was a systematic management of agricultural reserves in state warehouses. The political-economic conception seems to have been a combination of a benevolent integration of preexisting local units and cultures into the imperial state, with strict regimentation of society, held together, in that form, by external power constraints of the state.

Karl A. Wittvogel, who devoted a monumental study to systems of this type, was so impressed by the central role of water-management tasks as to call them "hydraulic systems."[5] He stressed particularly the correlation between the presence of such economic functions and the political superstructure of bureaucratic-managerial despotism. He also drew parallels between historical cases of the remote past, e.g., Chinese and Egyptian antiquity, and more recent cases, where despotic systems and centrally managed tasks of industrialization went hand in hand.[6]

The Russian *Mir* The word *mir* or *obshchina* refers to the Russian village commune, an agricultural organization which took shape, apparently, in the late

[5] Karl A. Wittvogel, *Oriental Despotism (A Comparative Study of Total Power)*, Yale, New Haven, Conn., 1957.

[6] An intriguing question is raised by these cases of despotism accompanying general social economic tasks: Does the economic function bring forth despotic political systems as necessary instruments, or is such political organization a prior and independent fact, which—sometimes—enables despotic governments to discharge broad economic functions? The issue was discussed, in the Soviet context, by Alec Nove ("Was Stalin Really Necessary?" in his *Economic Rationality and Soviet Politics*, Praeger, New York, 1964, pp. 17–39), but a definitive treatment is still lacking.

fifteenth century and survived in some form until Soviet collectivization of the 1930s. Analogous systems of collective landownership combined with actual cultivation done by individual households had existed in prefeudal Germanic Europe, among South Slavs (*zadruga*), and elsewhere. In the context of allocation models, it illustrates the case of direct allocation of resources through custom rather than through technical-economic calculation. The essence of the institution is in the communal ownership title to land, and its distribution among the commune households for temporary custody. The cultivated area was allotted to each household not in one contiguous piece but in the form of narrow scattered strips. Every few years, the commune authorities proceeded to a new redistribution of land which gave each household a new collection of strips to farm. The system had disastrous consequences for agricultural efficiency: strip farming limited the possibilities of technological exploitation of economies of scale, temporary occupancy foreshortened the individual peasant's planning horizon and led to neglect of the land. The ownership and allocation system compounded the effects of primitive technology which relied, for the restoration of nutrients to the soil, on letting the fields lie fallow in turn.

However, it was the ownership and allocation model for which the *mir* was undeservedly idealized by Russian romantics, who saw in it one of the expressions of the innate Russian spirit of collectivism. Russian agrosocialists ("populists" or *narodniki*) of the latter part of the nineteenth century saw in the village commune a predestined nucleus of coming socialism. Even some Russian Marxists wondered about such a possibility and confronted Marx with the idea. (Marx, aware of his insufficient acquaintance with the realities of *mir* and perhaps not wanting to hurt the feelings of Russian revolutionaries, hedged his opinion with provisos and, on the whole, remained noncommittal.)

Craft Guilds   The world peopled by independent producers is often connected in people's minds with an image of unfettered free enterprise. In historical periods when independent-producer systems flourished, this might have been true at the early stages, i.e., during the formation of urban handicrafts and trades economies, and then again toward the end, i.e., during the germination of capitalism, when free enterprise was legislated from above and independent trades were joined by independent peasantry, progressively liberated from feudal dependency. (We are obviously referring to the Western European experience from the Middle Ages on to the first half of the nineteenth century.) At the height of independent crafts and trades, between the twelfth and seventeenth centuries, the allocation model was that of a highly organized, autonomous regulation of the economic conduct of individual artisans (who were their own retailers), by their *guilds*. Guilds were exclusive associations of masters, journeymen, and apprentices active in a given specialty, usually very narrowly defined. They were dominated, as a rule, by an inner circle of prominent masters, participated in important ways in local administration, and served as framework for many social functions other than production (remember Richard Wagner's "Master Singers of Nuremberg" and Hans Sachs, who was "shoemaker and poet, too!").

The major economic function of guilds was to prevent factor allocation and price/quantity variables from being freely determined by demand-and-supply conditions. The guiding principle was to secure sufficient and dependable income for the master members. The ideological underpinnings were found in the doctrines of Scholastic church philosophers (Albertus Magnus and Thomas Aquinas) concerning the "just price." This was an early instance of the modern notion of "administered prices," where revenue is not the outcome of objectively ("parametrically") given price relations, but where desired ("targeted") revenue serves as the starting point from which prices are derived. What were the instrumentalities for achieving the guild objectives? We encounter regulations, many of which were to reappear in the capitalist setting of collusive agreements (see next section): prices were fixed by the guild; volume of output was controlled by fixing the permissible number of journeymen and apprentices, as well as working hours; wage rates were set uniformly; production methods (tools and technical innovations) were regulated; the number of production units was limited by restricting access to mastership and establishing territorial monopoly (e.g., by prohibition of conducting a trade freely within a 1-mile radius of the city). As secondary economic functions of guilds we may mention quality control of output, a task assumed by governments as consumer protection, and cooperative undertakings, such as acquisition of large-scale capital equipment by guild members. Despite the apparent intent of guilds to equalize the condition of member's standardization of allocation rules, differentiation of income and wealth could not be prevented. However, the rules prevented the rich from reinvesting their surplus revenue to expand productive capacity. For centuries, the potentialities of a capitalist development were thus kept under the lid.

Cartelization   Guilds are to independent-producer systems what cartels are to capitalism. The key words are "agreement," "collusion," "practices restricting competition." The purpose is to regulate the allocation and pricing behavior of firms so as to reduce uncertainty and wasteful errors (such as over- or underproducing, over- or underinvesting) with which competition is fraught, and in so doing, to realize monopoly profits for the industry as a whole. Cartel-type agreements make this possible by enabling a *multifirm industry* to act as a single monopolistic *multiplant firm*.

. In microtheory, cartelization is usually discussed and analyzed under the title of oligopoly. We come back to it in Chapter 8. In this survey we content ourselves with a summary description.

The *instruments* of cartelization parallel those of the guilds: price fixing, total output limitations and output quotas assigned to member firms, market sharing, joint selling, control of technology by patent sharing, coordination of financing, etc. These may be used singly—we then talk of price cartels, quota cartels, territorial cartels, etc.—or in combination. There are many degrees in the scope of cartelization.

The *forms* of cartel-type agreements are differentiated according to the stringency of enforcement. There are *formalized cartels* with written statutes, using internal sanctions and policing. The extreme case is the merger of individual firms into a single company. At the other end are *informal agreements*, or just effective behavior of firms indicating that some cartel-type considerations are at work, without there being any overt (or secret) communication between firms. Such is the case of so-called price leadership, where a given firm is tacitly recognized as the pacesetter and others follow.

The need for enforcement (sanctions and policing) indicates that cartels are not self-enforcing. The reason is that a cartel member is torn between two conflicting interests: to adhere to the agreement for the sake of *joint maximization* of profits, based on agreed rules of sharing the total loot; and to increase individual share at the expense of others, e.g., by letting others charge the agreed cartel price and secretly expanding sales by charging less. This makes for an inherent instability of *voluntary (autonomous) cartelization*. One may sometimes even observe a cyclical sequence of formation and collapse of cartels. The dissolution of cartels drives the lessons of "wasteful competition" home again, whereupon a new attempt at reestablishing the cartel may follow.

To help with the enforcement problem, the organized power of the state may be brought into the picture. The precondition is that the state must treat cartel agreements as legal acts. The way is then open to prevent noncompliance by resort to court action, as in the case of other civil contracts. In the extreme case, the state may consider a noncompetitive organization of economic branches so desirable as to legislate *compulsory cartelization*, and assume the task of enforcement as part of its administrative functions and application of the statutory law.

Fascist Regimentation   "Regimentation" is hardly a standard economic term, but it happens to be much more descriptive of the allocation model introduced under fascist dictatorships before World War II than if we called it "universal compulsory cartelization," although that is what it resembled most. Compulsory cartelization was only one aspect of the Nazi economic system, and its purpose was not quite the same as that of traditional cartels. Cartels in days of old, i.e., throughout the Weimar Republic, were motivated by the profit-maximizing instincts of business. However, business executives were told by Nazi representatives as early as 1934 that "any organization that represents the interests of employers will be regarded as illegal and disbanded, and the guilty parties will be prosecuted." According to Nazi conceptions, partial interests of social groups had no legitimacy. They were supposed to dissolve in the organic unity of the nation and be subordinated to the organizing will of the state.

The state followed through by taking crucial managerial decisions out of the hands of entrepreneurs and managers, such as price, wage, and capacity determination, as well as by severely curtailing their freedom of action in the distribution of dividends and raising corporate finance in capital markets. Outwardly, the organization of the economy gave the impression of a uniform monolithic structure. Every enterprise was made member of a "branch group," "branch groups" were tied into "economic groups" (industry had thirty-one of them), and "economic groups" were headed by seven "national groups" (for industry, trade, banking, insurance, power, tourist industry, and handicrafts). The pyramid was topped by the Ministry of the Economy. This organization by economic sectors and branches was supplemented by a coextensive cross-organization according to the territorial principle, binding the same organs into local, provincial, and national "chambers." It all seemed a marvelous arrangement for supervising and manipulating the economy from a single point.

In reality, the microregulation of the economy issued from a number of unconnected "ruling organizations," some of them created in an ad hoc fashion to implement specific policies and tasks, as economic or political needs arose. There were "supervisory agencies" (*Überwachungsstellen*, later renamed *Reichsstellen*) for control of foreign trade in specific raw materials and other bottleneck articles. They ended up regulating domestic production and rationing of these products as well. From 1936 on, the Four-Year Plan, a composite of agencies and their staffs, began to reorder economic priorities in the direction of armaments and import substitution through domestic sources of supply. (It was absorbed into the Ministry of the Economy in 1938.)

Before 1936, some preparatory steps were made to put into place an administrative machine for a central comprehensive direction of the economy, under the authority of the "Plenipotentiary for the War Economy." This was frustrated by the influence of powerful economic procurement offices of the Army, Navy, and Air Force, each of which dominated its own industrial empire. Another fulcrum by which allocation decisions were manipulated by administrative orders was the *Hermann-Goering Werke*, a state enterprise created in 1937, for the purpose of steel manufacture from the low-grade domestic ores. (Private steel industry, having refused to assume this task, moved to the back of the line in the allocation of labor and other resources.) This administrative pluralism in economic allocation corroborates the description of the Nazi system, given by H. R. Trevor-Roper, as a "confusion of private empires, private armies, and private intelligence services." We do not know, of course, how the system would have evolved further. Conceivably, it might have developed in the direction of Soviet-type centralism.

How does the system, as it actually evolved, compare with the early fascist model of a "corporatist organization"? Originally, starting with Mussolini's ideological notions, society and its economy were to be organized by "estates," welded on the basis of noncompetitive solidarity into a nation. This ideology had appealed mainly to the so-called old middle classes, small independent trades, artisans, and shopkeepers, threatened in their livelihood by big business and overshadowed by the claims and aspirations of the labor movement. The corporatist idea, refurbishing the ancient pattern of economic organization by guilds, seemed to offer a shelter from competition and class struggle.

However, having conquered political power in the state, the fascist movement scuttled all concern with the interests of its erstwhile supporters and turned to big business, the only economic power capable of supplying material means for the pursuit of political goals of the fascist state.[7] Thus, compulsory carteliza-

[7] Hitler confided privately: "I had to let the Party experiment with the corporate idea. . . . You can understand that I had to give the people something to do. They all wanted to help. They were full

tion with the accompanying measures led to a subordination of small business and "petty bourgeoisie" to "big capital," and their partial ruin. This, and the following armaments boom, gave credibility to the popular idea of fascism having been a political creature of the capitalist system. In the light of evidence, serious scholarship has discredited this all too simple formula. Notwithstanding the material benefits going to representatives of industry, regimented capitalism played the part of an instrument used by the fascist state, rather than the other way around. This interpretation corresponds to the modern understanding of totalitarian systems. They represent an inversion of traditional relationships: the state, instead of being an outgrowth of society and its functional organ, uses its coercive powers to mold and manipulate society to suit its own arbitrary ideological purposes.

Centrally Administered Systems   Although Trevor-Roper's characterization of the Nazi system applies, to some extent, to Soviet-type systems as well, we take them generally to be real-life representatives of economic centralization. An underground warfare between various interests may be going on—between the party apparatus, governmental bureaucracy of ministries, army, regional interests, managers, personal cliques—but the formal framework is one of complete centralization of decision making. Pluralism of interests has to move within that framework, which is an extreme expression of the totalitarian inversion of roles between state and society.

Soviet-type systems of centrally administered allocation are important not only because of their weight today in terms of geography, population, and share in world production but also because of their pedagogic value. Their analysis has helped deepen our understanding of other models, those we live under, as well as of issues involved in prognosticating a postcapitalist future. This is why a full chapter is devoted to the description of the mechanics of central allocation (Chapter 9), and substantial sections to their partial aspects: income distribution and inflation (in Chapter 11); growth performance (in Chapter 12); industrial organization (in Chapter 13); agricultural system (in Chapter 14); foreign-trade operations (in Chapter 15); treatment of the consumer (in Chapter 16) and the worker (in Chapter 17). All that is called for here is a gist of the allocation model, uncluttered and uncomplicated by any real-life features.

Universal cartelization, we said, is but a step removed from systems administered centrally by the state and its organs. The step is an important one: decision makers in the production sector proper, the direct transactors, lose all autonomy. Executives are demoted to a position of executants. They are merely to implement decisions made at the governmental tier of the command hierarchy. (This aspect is captured by the frequently used term "command economies.")

In such a model, we have to postulate an administrative center which is in

---

of fire. I had to offer them something. Well, let them have a crack at it. After all, the corporatist organization is not so important that it could do much damage." (Cited in David Schoenbaum, *Hitler's Social Revolution*, Doubleday, Garden City, N.Y., 1966, p. 130.)

the possession of all economic information (on available resources, technology, objectives, etc.) and is able to formulate detailed decisions, as well as issue corresponding instructions (directives, commands) to all participants in the production sector. The messages refer to physical quantities of inputs, to labor (which gets assigned to its place of employment), as well as to outputs. Thus, production units receive mandatory production targets, and their output is allocated by quotas to users. The principle of allocation is *direct rationing* (nobody can obtain more than he is given, nobody can produce more than he gets inputs for). Messages are issued periodically (annually) as comprehensive sets of instructions, in the form of "plans" covering the activities of the whole period. (This aspect is captured by another frequent term—"centrally planned economies.")

Physical flows of goods and services are accompanied by corresponding money flows going in the opposite direction. Goods and services have prices. Transactions have the formal attributes of sales and purchases, and labor is paid for its services in the form of wages. To repeat once more: It is this aspect which makes us treat this model as *a subspecies of the capitalist market-exchange system*, understood in this broad sense. It is the mode of determination of terms of exchange which distinguishes this particular subspecies from all the others, namely, the *elimination of market forces* of supply and demand, and their replacement by direct central administrative instructions. In this sense, it is a polar case lying at the opposite of the pole of atomistic allocation models.

BIBLIOGRAPHY

Dalton, George (ed.): *Tribal and Peasant Economies*, The Natural History Press, Garden City, N.Y., 1967.
———: *Economic Development and Social Change*, The Natural History Press, Garden City, N.Y., 1971.
Firth, Raymond, and B. S. Yamey (eds.): *Capital, Saving, and Credit in Peasant Societies*, Aldine, Chicago, 1964.
Mauss, M.: *The Gift*, Free Press, Glencoe, Ill., 1954.
Piddocke, Stuart: "The Potlatch System of the Southern Kwakiutl: A New Perspective," *Southwestern Journal of Anthropology*, vol. 21, 1965, pp. 244–264 (bibliography).
Dahl, Robert A., and Charles E. Lindblom: *Politics, Economics, and Welfare*, Harper, New York, 1953.
Boulding, Kenneth E.: *The Economy of Love and Fear*, Wadsworth, Belmont, Calif., 1973.
Robinson, G. T.: *Rural Russia under the Old Regime*, University of California Press, Berkeley, 1967 (on the village commune, passim).
Baudin, Louis: *A Socialist Empire: The Incas of Peru*, Van Nostrand, Princeton, N.J., 1961.
Metraux, Alfred: *The History of the Incas*, Pantheon, New York, 1969.
Murra, John V.: "The Economic Organization of the Inca State," unpublished Ph.D. dissertation, University of Chicago, 1956.
Moore, Sally I.: *Power and Property in Inca Peru*, Columbia, New York, 1958.
Wittvogel, Karl A.: *Oriental Despotism*, Yale, New Haven, Conn., 1957.
Encyclopedia of the Social Sciences (1932), entries "Guilds," "Just Price."
International Encyclopedia of the Social Sciences (1968), "Gilds," "Cartels and Trade Associations" (bibliographies).

Schweitzer, Arthur: *Big Business in the Third Reich*, Indiana University Press, Blooming-
    ton, 1964.
Neumann, Franz: *Behemoth*, Harper & Row, New York, 1966.
Schoenbaum, David: *Hitler's Social Revolution*, Doubleday, Garden City, N.Y., 1966.
Milward, Alan S.: *The German Economy at War*, The Athlone Press, London, 1965.
Eucken, Walter: "On the Theory of the Centrally Administered Economy: An Analysis of
    the German Experiment," *Economica*, New Series, vol. 15, no. 58, May 1948, pp. 79–
    100, and no. 59, August 1948, pp. 173–193; reprinted in Morris Bornstein (ed.):
    Comparative Economic Systems: Models and Cases, Irwin, Homewood, Ill., 1965, pp.
    157–197.

Evaluation Criteria

Only by making comparisons does one become aware of differences and learn who one is so as to grow fully into what one ought to be.

Thomas Mann

There is a class of economic systems which are out of this world: the ideal mental constructs, the utopias. For those we should make a classification, too, as long as we are at it. This ought to be the chapter on normative systems. However, practicality demands that we wedge in an examination of criteria by which economic systems can be appraised. Some of the normative systems, especially the academic theoretical models, cannot be understood without first explaining the criterion of optimality in resource allocation.

There is also a logical reason for considering the problem of evaluation before surveying normative systems. Normative systems are responses to the critique of the existing ones. Therefore, evaluation comes first, and designing something better, or ideal, comes after. However, the plan of this chapter is not yet to tell the reader how good or bad the various real-world cases are, but merely to suggest how one goes about judging them methodically.

GENERAL CONSIDERATIONS

What do we ask from an economic system? Performance. Or, more precisely, considering that the economic system is not the only factor influencing the performance of a given country's economy, we expect the economic system to contribute its best to that performance.

Can One Isolate the System's Part?

At this point, we stumble upon a serious difficulty. If there are several factors contributing to an economy's performance, how can one tell what their separate contributions are? What part is due to the country's endowment in natural resources? Some economies benefit by their geographical position. Insular economies (England, Japan) have the advantage of cheap ocean transportation. Large or mountainous countries (e.g., Russia or Norway) require unusually large resources to overcome distance. Some economies are lucky in having complementary resources in close proximity of each other (e.g., iron-ore and coal deposits in England or in the United States); others are disadvantaged, Mother Nature having placed such resources thousands of miles from each other (e.g., in the Soviet Union).

What part of observed differences in performance is to be credited (or debited) to cultural factors, such as psychological attitudes of the population? The Japanese national character is always mentioned in connection with the astonishing performance of Japan's economy after World War II. So is German *Tüchtigkeit* in connection with the West German postwar "economic miracle," as well as with East Germany's apparent ability to let hard work make up for the disadvantages of the Soviet-type system. On the other hand, a *mañana* mentality, contrasting with the restless spirit of striving and entrepreneurship, is often blamed for economic stagnation. Political and legal arrangements constitute an impediment in one place and a stimulant in another.

One must also never forget to ask whether observed performance of a given economy is due to the properties of its economic *system* or to economic *policies* adopted by its policy makers. One may get a bad ride because the car is bad or because the driver is bad. An economic system is not only an impersonal social and economic "mechanism." It is also subject to the influence of human decisions to which the "mechanism" responds. A workable economic system may not work so well under one set of policies, but it may perform quite acceptably under another. Since real functioning of modern advanced systems always takes place under the impact of *some* policies—absence of policy is also a policy—one must be careful not to ascribe to the system's characteristics what particular policies have wrought.

Total performance of an economy is therefore the outcome of many nonsystemic factors, operating in conjunction with the economic system. To evaluate a system's contribution, we would have to isolate its influence and link it with an identifiable portion of the total performance. This is practically impossible. First, the number of observed cases is ordinarily too small for the application of statistical multiple-correlation methods. Second, because many of the factors at play are difficult to quantify, they are unsuitable for econometric manipulation. Third, performance itself is not a clear-cut quantifiable notion, as we shall demonstrate shortly.

Thus, we have to grapple with the fact that evaluation must deal with motley evidence on loosely defined economic performance country by country, attributable to a set of factors, some of them institutional, some strictly qualitative, which all act simultaneously and are interdependent. How to evaluate the role and the merit of economic systems under these conditions is a perplexing question. However, the task is too important to be given up. What we should keep in mind is that the problem is essentially analogous to the econometric problem of isolating factors and finding their correlation with economic outcomes, even though the "data" are in many instances nonquantifiable. As usual in such cases, careful observation, knowledgeable interpretation, and judicious reasoning in making inferences have to make up for the missing precision of an econometric exercise. Sometimes, we may find the task easier if the systemic component is very pronounced (see, for example, differences in growth performance of Eastern European countries as a group, and Western Europe, in Chapter 12), or if a country undergoes a swift change in the economic system, and the performance afterward turns out to be dramatically different.

Dimensions of Economic Performance

Now to the notion of economic performance itself. As in the case of an automobile, performance of a country's economy has many "dimensions." A car is judged by mileage per gallon, speed, comfort, looks, trunk space, noise, pollution, and other aspects. An economy may be judged by its productive efficiency, i.e., output per unit of factor inputs; rate at which output grows; level and growth rate of consumption per head; degree to which the composition of output corresponds to preferences of the population; degree of income inequality, and so on. Economists have a general concept which covers all these partial aspects, namely, *welfare*.

Welfare of the population is the comprehensive objective which it is desirable to see maximized. This principle we treat, like all economists, as axiomatic, i.e., not requiring any further proof or justification. Welfare is a flexible notion, in that it has room for all the "dimensions" of economic outcomes one can think of. There was a time when economists, following the lead of A. C. Pigou, made a distinction between *economic* welfare (conceived as output "falling under the measuring stick of money"), and *noneconomic* welfare, such as political welfare, psychic income, etc. The distinction is artificial and arbitrary. With growing awareness of the interdependence of various aspects of welfare, and concern with social costs and benefits, it is being quietly abandoned, despite some residual lip service.

Thus, it has become customary to probe beneath published figures on gross national product, as conventionally defined, and seek answers about the social-cost aspects of the economy: which items in the GNP do not indicate a positive contribution to welfare; which economic outcomes are not even registered in the

GNP figures; etc. Even more important is the realization that economic systems are not innocent of changes in social and cultural values, psychic well-being, human personality traits, family patterns and family problems—in short, of what is suggested by the term "quality of life."

The extension of the relevant notion of welfare creates some further difficulties for the evaluation of systems. It is bad enough that one cannot follow through on all quantifiable dimensions of welfare with statistical comparisons because one does not have the proper data. It borders on the hopeless to try and make comparative evaluations of systems from the point of view of their non-quantifiable effects upon welfare. However, the stance adopted in this book is always to wait with agnostic shoulder shrugging and to utilize any evidence that is available. As the Czech saying goes, "If poor, use water when you cook."

QUANTIFIABLE DIMENSIONS

Performance aspects which lend themselves to definition in quantitative terms are the static efficiency aspects, rate of growth, efficiency in attaining growth, and the pattern of income distribution. From among the qualitative performance aspects we have singled out consumers' sovereignty and workers' sovereignty as being most amenable to systematic formulation. As we shall see, defining a performance dimension in quantitative terms does not automatically mean that it also is measurable statistically. For comparative evaluation, one may still have to fall back on nonstatistical observation.

In the following review, a disproportionately large space is devoted to static efficiency in allocation. The reason is, as indicated in the opening paragraph, that it is a prerequisite for understanding the rationale of theoretical normative models, such as those of Hayek, Lange, Lerner, and Vanek, to be surveyed in the next chapter. It underlies also much of the critical analysis of empirical systems, especially in Chapters 8, 9, 13, and 15. The other performance dimensions, for being shortchanged here, will be given a more extensive treatment in the chapters dealing with the corresponding topics: income distribution in Chapter 11, growth in Chapter 12, consumers' and workers' sovereignty in Chapters 16 and 17.

Static (Single-Period) Efficiency

The key words defining this criterion are "optimal allocation of resources" or simply "static optimality." Since no economic system is perfect, it makes sense to apply this criterion only by asking: "How close does this or that economic system come to achieving static optimality? Are some systems better at it than others? Which ones, and how can we tell?"

Allocation of resources which deserves to be called optimal must result in a volume and composition of output that cannot be improved upon. What that means will become clear as we proceed. Note that output has to be considered under two aspects: volume (or level) and composition (proportions of products). By volume we mean "physical" volume measured in "physical" units.[1] According

---

[1] "Physical" is in quotation marks to indicate that it covers also such items as kilowatt-hours of electricity or services like numbers of theater performances.

to convention, one adds up physically heterogeneous products by converting them into money equivalents, i.e., by giving each physical unit a money value, usually its market price.

Technological Efficiency: Volume of Production   The first condition of optimality is that the volume of output be as large as possible, given the system's available resources, and their full utilization at a normal rate. "Full utilization" is defined with respect to total work time obtainable from the available labor force.

Inefficiency on the production side may mean two different things. Resources may be fully employed but not used in the best possible proportions. For instance, labor may be redundant in one sector and there may be understaffing in another. A mere shift would then improve proportions in both places, and larger output would result.

The other type of inefficiency consists in less than full employment of resources. Resources are wasted if they are kept idle against people's wishes. This is a matter of wrong proportions, too, but in this case, they refer to the utilization of people's time. If output which does not get produced because of idleness of resources is valued more highly than the leisure time spent in idleness, there is clearly waste. We then speak of involuntary unemployment.

"Maximum output from available resources" does not say anything yet about its composition. It presents itself at first as a wide range of alternative output volumes, each of them maximal and each of a different composition. This range is usually called the production-possibilities frontier, or the product transformation function.

It is helpful to express this last concept geometrically by means of the production-possibilities (or transformation) curve. To make such a representation possible, one has to reduce the variegated world of goods to one pair only (as is usual with two-dimensional diagrams), for instance, to books and beer, guns and butter, etc. The curve plots all the maximal combinations of the two goods the economy could deliver. It encloses an infinity of other combinations it also could deliver, but which would represent less of one good, or less of both. Combinations that lie beyond the boundary are not obtainable at the normal rate of resource utilization.

In the usual presentation, the production-possibilities curve is negatively sloped and bulges outward (see Figure 5-1). It has a negative slope because if it were positive, it would mean we could increase the output of both goods simultaneously. Such a line would have to be within the area of production possibilities, either because some resources were idle or because they were not used in the best proportions. The negative slope means that the economy can produce more of one good only by using resources taken away from the production of another good. The economy "pays" for an extra amount of A by having less of B.

The outward bulge indicates a situation where the economy has to "pay" for every additional unit of A by increasingly larger loss of B as the B's scale of production shrinks.

Figure 5-1 Standard example of a production-possibilities curve: increasing costs case.

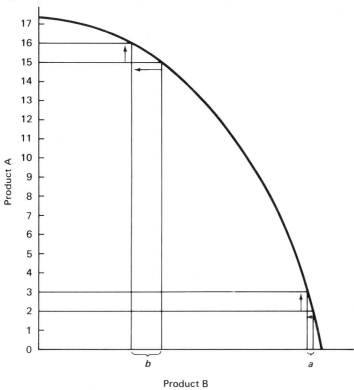

Product B

Raising output level of A from 2 to 3 units involves an opportunity cost in the form of a loss of an *a* amount of B. When the increase occurs at a higher level, e.g., from 15 to 16 units, the opportunity cost increases because the amount of B lost is now *b*, and *b* > *a*.

One can also imagine a situation where additional units of A would cost an increasingly smaller loss of output of B. In that case one would have to draw the production-possibilities curve bending inward. This would indicate that either A or B, or both, are being produced under conditions of increasing returns to scale, or, which is saying the same, under conditions of declining costs. There is an important class of economic activities which falls in the category of "declining-cost industries," such as transportation, public utilities, printing, pipelines, education.

A declining-cost situation exists whenever an extra unit of output—an extra passenger, student, or printed sheet—requires a less-than-proportionate addition to costs. Hence, the marginal cost falls, and so does the average cost.

Efficiency in Choosing the Best Product Proportions   The second condition for optimality is that the system be able to select, from among all the maximum feasible combinations of products, that combination which is more useful than any other. Which one is it? In abstract terms, it has been defined innumerable times. For instance, read this compact and elegant formulation of the "ideal output" given by A. P. Lerner: "If we so order the economic activity of the society that no commodity is produced unless its importance is greater than that of the alternative that is sacrificed . . ."[2] This principle, so simply stated, has a great many ramifications and implications which can hardly be given an adequate treatment here. We shall confine ourselves to touching a few bases which seem essential, without going through the step-by-step reasoning which underlies the results. We shall be compelled to assert where we would have preferred to demonstrate and prove.

Consumers' Perspective   Intuitively, we recognize in Lerner's formulation our everyday experience. We would surely not wish to buy a tenth winter parka before we bought at least a pair of skis (parka fetishists and ski haters excluded). We would not care for still another pack of beer if, having quenched our bodily thirst, we were thirsty for the printed word, though that would also depend a little on whether our tastes were closer to those of a Falstaff or a Faust.

Lerner's formulation of the optimality idea implies that, once we hit upon the optimal combination, we would stay with it. This would happen when switching a dollar's worth of expenditure from one particular commodity to any other would involve a utility gain exactly equal to the utility loss due to the switch. Whenever no feasible change could improve things, we can be sure that our situation is the best one attainable. Under those conditions, changing the proportions of our purchases would be pointless.

This is the perspective of the consumer for whom the personal valuation of the usefulness of products represents benefit, and money expenditure represents cost. And that means not just cost in the sense of money as such, but in the sense of what that money stands for. It stands for two things at once: the effort it cost to earn the money (most of us "pay" with hours and minutes of our work time when we pay with money earned as wages); and the utility of things one could conceivably buy for a given amount of money but has to forget about as soon as one decides to spend it on a particular commodity for the sake of *its* utility. This latter idea corresponds to the concept of "opportunity cost." It is the utility of alternative choices one has to forgo each time one makes a particular affirmative choice. This is Lerner's "importance of the alternative that is sacrificed."

The clever part of marginalist analysis in economics is the insight that it is not necessary to scan the benefit value and cost of every single unit of every commodity in order to make optimal choices. It is sufficient to deal with small adjustments of proportions, proceeding by small steps: a little more of this and less of that—would the change be worthwhile? This is what is meant by decisions made "at the margin."

Let us, then, restate the principle of optimal choice in marginalist language. A one-dollar shift in spending refers to the marginal dollar of expenditure. A

[2] A. P. Lerner, "Statics and Dynamics in Socialist Economics," *Economic Journal*, vol. 47, 1937, pp. 253–270.

switch of that dollar from commodity A would represent a marginal opportunity cost in terms of lost utility, represented by one dollar's worth of A forgone, and a marginal benefit in terms of utility gain obtained from one dollar's worth of whichever commodity one decided to buy instead. When proportions of products bought are optimal, the loss and the gain between any pair of commodities are equal. In other words, the *marginal cost equals the marginal benefit* involved in that marginal option concerning the marginal adjustment of proportions. This is the universal rule of conduct aiming at optimality.

The rule may be expressed alternatively in terms of relative prices of commodities, and utilities associated with marginal units of these commodities. A money amount of one dollar divided by the number of units of A one can buy for that dollar gives us the unit price of A, and the same for any other commodity. Under optimal proportions, a marginal dollar expenditure corresponds to the same marginal utility of any commodity. It follows that the ratio of the unit price of commodity A to the unit price of commodity B, C, . . ., N, must be the same as the ratio of utility of the marginal unit of A to the utility of marginal units of B, C, . . ., N. The *ratio of unit prices (i.e., relative prices) must be equal to the ratio of marginal utilities.*

Perspective of the Production Sector   We shall ignore at first how the production sector is organized, e.g., whether it is divided into independent firms, each producing a single commodity. That is not essential to the optimality argument. For the production sector, the benefit aspect is the revenue from sales of commodities. The marginal opportunity cost of supplying output in given proportions is the revenue obtainable under alternative proportions, e.g., by letting a certain portion of productive resources produce less of a given commodity and more of another one. Thus, a dollar's worth of revenue, earned thanks to a bundle of resources producing A, needs to be compared to the revenue which the same bundle of resources would bring if it were devoted to the production of B, C, . . ., or N. That is the opportunity cost of these resources producing A.

Exactly parallel to the consumers' perspective, producers supply an optimum assortment of products when the opportunity cost of producing a dollar's worth of any commodity is the same. It would then be pointless to change the assortment, since the marginal revenue of the marginal switchable bundle of resources would everywhere be the same.

Likewise parallel to the consumers' case, we may express the optimal situation in terms of unit prices and unit costs associated with the commodity units teetering at the margin of being dropped or added. One marginal dollar of revenue, divided by the number of commodity units yielding that revenue, gives us the unit price at the margin. This goes for all commodities. Under conditions of the optimum, the opportunity cost of earning an extra dollar of revenue is the same for any commodity. Opportunity cost per marginal unit of a commodity therefore is the same as its unit price. *The ratio of prices of any pair of commodities must be the same as the ratio of their marginal opportunity costs.*

The cost of a commodity has, of course, still another, and surely more basic, meaning: that of real resource inputs required to produce it. This is in the back of its opportunity cost. Marginal alternatives in production—less of this for the sake of more of that—always refer to a shift of a certain specific bundle of inputs from one production line to another.

Let us think of it in terms of the production-possibilities curve: Every point on that curve represents a different combination of products produced when all resources are fully and efficiently utilized. Therefore, any move along that curve, from one point to a neighboring one, means a release of a specific bundle of resources, and its transfer from the production of one commodity to another.

Under the optimum product composition of output, such a marginal shift of resources would generate the same revenue, whichever way it was shifted (which is why it would *not* be shifted). If the bundle of resources had a money value, one could calculate the money cost per unit of any commodity: one would divide the money value of the bundle of resources by the number of units of a given commodity such a bundle could produce. Since we are considering shifts and changes at the margin, starting from an optimal assortment of products, such money unit costs would amount to the marginal costs of commodities.

Note that, while *revenues* per marginal bundle of resources are everywhere equal, *marginal unit costs* are not, because the number of commodity units a marginal bundle of resources can produce will be different depending on which particular commodity we are talking about. However, *marginal costs of different commodities will stand in the same proportions to each other as their prices.* (In both cases, a given money value—revenue or cost—is divided by the same pair of numbers of commodity units. This is why.) Indeed, if the price received from selling a commodity is fully used in payment for resources, *marginal costs are exactly equal to prices of the respective commodities.* With this, we have arrived at the definition of optimality from the perspective of the production sector.

Communicating through the Supply-and-Demand Mechanism   To attain a fully optimal product combination, the economic system must be able to reconcile the perspective of the consumer with that of the production sector. This reconciliation brings the utility aspect in touch with the cost aspect.

In a Robinson Crusoe system, or taking you and me as we think how to spend our leisure time, the reconciliation of the two points of view takes place via an internal psychic process. We keep weighing and considering the benefit and the bother involved in different courses of action. One and the same question keeps popping up: "Do I find the result of an extra hour, or minute, of such and such activity important enough to justify the effort? Isn't there something more important I could do with the same effort?" The process of adjusting productive activities through the mechanism of supply and demand is supposed to solve such questions for the members of society when their roles as consumers and as producers are separated through the division of labor.

Let us recapitulate the basic principles. In any kind of economic optimum, marginal benefits should be proportionate, or equal, to marginal costs. To the consumer trying to choose the best product assortment, utility is the benefit, and price is the cost. To the organizer of production trying to maximize revenue, price is the benefit, and resources used are the cost. Applying the optimizing rule to consumers, proportions of marginal utilities of different products they acquire should be the same as those of prices. On the production side, proportions of prices of different products supplied should be the same as proportions of their marginal costs. If all these conditions are fulfilled, the two points of view are reconciled: *proportions of marginal utilities are equal to proportions of marginal costs, and both of them are the same as proportions of product prices.* In economists' shorthand, such a state is called the *Pareto optimum.*

Under the stated conditions, the system of relative prices makes economic sense. It expresses the hidden relations of utilities, i.e., "importance" of products, as well as their costs. This is what really matters, and this is what is meant by a *system of relative prices* being *rational*, in contrast to price systems which are arbitrary, i.e., lacking any systematic relationship between prices, benefits, and costs. (Keep this distinction in mind for the discussion of centrally administered systems in Chapter 9.)

The reason why the supply-and-demand mechanism is called upon to resolve allocation problems in complex systems is a practical one. Instead of saying "practical," we could put it in terms of "cost of information." It is just too difficult, i.e., costly, to gather information on people's subjective valuation of products and producers' objective production costs by using direct methods. It is cheaper to let this information emerge through the behavior of the two sets of partners in money-using, price-generating markets.

To see how the supply-and-demand mechanism operates in prodding allocation of resources toward the optimum, one starts best by considering consumers' and producers' reactions when product proportions and prices are not optimal for both sides simultaneously. Imagine that products were offered in a certain assortment, at prices proportionate to their respective marginal costs, and consumers felt marginal utilities to be of entirely different proportions. Some products would then appear as "tremendous buys," i.e., cheap considering their marginal utility. Other products would appear as "outrageously expensive" and "rip-offs," considering their "value" (read: marginal utility).

The response would be, on the part of consumers, to try to expand purchases of "good buys" beyond the amounts offered, in order to bring the marginal utility *down* into line with the marginal-cost price. (Marginal utility is assumed to *decline* with the expansion of purchases by successive units.) There would be a series of selling-like-hot-cakes situations and rapidly emptied shelves. On the other hand, in lines appearing as full of "overpriced items," merchandise would be moving slowly, creating a dead weight of unsalable inventories.

This experience would be enough for the organizers of production to realize the high opportunity cost of using that much of resources in the production of unsuccessful items. They would tend to shift some resources into the hot-cakes lines promising larger revenue. The signaling power of the movement of inventories might be reinforced by a transitional increase in prices above the marginal cost in the high-demand, insufficient-supply areas, up to the price level consumers would be willing to pay. A reverse movement of prices, a temporary fall, might obtain in the low-demand, excess-supply areas. These price signals, appearing on top of the inventory signals, would speed up the shift of resources. If the economic system were represented by means of a multitude of standard demand-and-supply diagrams, one for every commodity, these are the phenomena which the diagrams would describe (see Figure 5-2). Prices and quantities corresponding to the points of intersection of demand-and-supply schedules would then be those of an equilibrium having the properties of an optimum: price ratios equal to ratios of marginal costs and marginal utilities.

An Institutional Prop: Perfect Competition In the previous section we went beyond the abstract formulation of optimal allocation and its characteristics. The demand-and-supply mechanism tacitly assumed a specific institutional framework, i.e., a certain type of the market mode of allocation. It assumed incentives leading to a certain kind of response. Incentives consisted in the desire to attain the highest possible revenue per bundle of resources. As long as there were differences between the revenue payoff per bundle of resources, the response of organizers of production was expected to be a shifting of resources from the low-reward areas to the high-reward areas. On this response depended the sensitivity of the production sector to the point of view of the consumers. The discussion turns, as the reader has rightly guessed, around Adam Smith's idea of the invisible hand, which works through the incentive of private gain toward the achievement of a social good.

However, the nature of the response has to be specified more precisely if the social *good* is supposed to be also the social *best*. The response to a less-than-optimal disequilibrium must be of the following special kind: Organizers of production must have the will to direct, or attract, resources toward the areas of relatively high revenues per unit of resources; those who are already active in those areas must allow resources emigrating from the low-revenue areas to enter freely, i.e., to add their capacity and output; this additional output must be allowed to find room in the market for the given commodity by having its price lowered below the temporarily elevated disequilibrium level, and thus forcing the price of all output down; additions to output and lowering of the price must go on, together with the reduction of output in the low-reward areas, until the level of revenue per marginal unit of resources is equalized with that prevailing everywhere else. Mobility of resources, free entry, price competition—these are the major requirements of responses leading toward optimality.

Search for the highest revenue per unit of resources has been traditionally treated under the title of the *profit-maximization incentive*. This implies a further narrowing of the specifications of the allocational mode's institutional side. Profit maximization refers to net revenue, i.e., to revenue which remains after subtraction of payments for the use of resources, supplied to a given production unit (firm) from the outside, which includes payments of wages for the use of labor. Thus, profit maximization, maximization of net revenue, presupposes the institutional setup of the capitalist system.

However, it is also conceivable for the mechanisms of demand and supply and competition to operate when all revenue is distributed to labor, so that the distinction between profits and wages disappears. (We shall meet a form of this

Figure 5-2   The supply-and-demand mechanism.

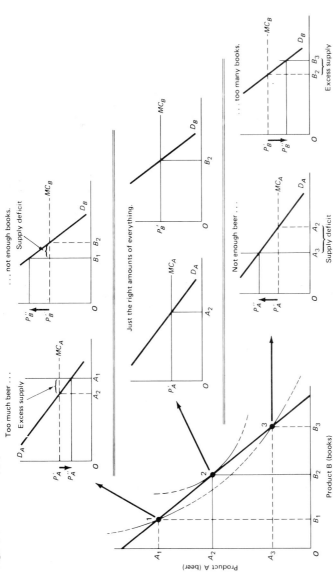

The production-possibilities curve on the left is a straight line: both products are produced under conditions of constant costs. This is why marginal-cost schedules in the demand-and-supply diagrams on the right (MC_A and MC_B) are horizontal throughout. D_A and D_B are demand schedules for beer and books respectively. P'_A and P'_B are tentative prices of beer and books at which they are initially offered by the producers. They are set at the level of marginal costs, here identical to average costs. P'_A and P'_B are the temporarily increased or lowered disequilibrium prices.

Lines crossing the production-possibilities curve at points 1 and 3 indicate the relative valuation of beer and books, at the margin, on the part of consumers. At point 1, an extra book has more utility than an extra book at point 3. At point 1, an extra beer can has less utility than an extra beer can at point 3. Therefore, at point 1, a book is worth more beer, in terms of relative degrees of utility the two goods represent, than is the case at point 3. This is expressed by the slope of the line crossing the production-possibilities curve at points 1 and 3. The solid line is a segment of an indifference curve indicated by the broken line.

arrangement, which subtly modifies the responses of production organizers, in the Vanek model, Chapter 6, and the Yugoslav model of the firm, Chapter 17.)

When the desirable optimizing responses are projected into the internal decision-making process of the individual firm or industry, they must take the following form: profit is allowed to be maximized only by means of adjusting output levels to the prevailing price, and never by manipulating the price. Output will then be expanded as long as the prevailing market price is higher than the marginal cost because as long as this difference exists, there is some extra net revenue to be gained through extra output. Output will stabilize at that level where price equals marginal cost, because losses lurk beyond that point.

In this conceptual framework, average unit cost hides an element which business executives, laypersons, and a number of economists outside the mainstream of the profession ordinarily do not count as cost. This is sometimes confusing.[3] It is the element called "normal profit." Its conventional definition is usually not very exact. For our purposes it is suitable to regard it as the equilibrium rate of profit. It is that rate which, if it prevailed universally at the margin of production of all commodities, would not make any organizer of production feel like switching.

In a state of disequilibrium, firms in a given industry may be earning a higher rate of profit than the "normal" one. They would attract enough factors of production entering variable cost to be able to expand output up to where the temporarily elevated price equals marginal cost. However, the abnormally high rate of profit would further attract investments into what constitutes fixed costs of a plant: additional capacities would be built. It is their output which, by being offered cheaper, would force the price, as well as the output of each individual firm, down to the normal profit level. That price would be just high enough to cover average cost with its hidden normal-profit element. Equilibrium further demands that output be carried up to the level where price is equal to marginal cost. Therefore, all these conditions are fulfilled when output is at a level where its marginal cost is equal to the price as well as to average cost. This is where average cost is at its lowest.

This concludes the basic outline of the theoretical model of perfect competition famous for its optimizing properties. This is the part which needs to be retained as background to the discussion of academic normative models (Hayek, von Mises, Lange, Lerner, and Vanek) in Chapter 6.

The Ugly Head of Monopoly   The model of perfect competition gives the exact rules of behavior under which the profit-maximization incentive leads to optimal product proportions of output. The major condition is that firms submit to the play of supply and demand, that they do not try to set prices on their own, and that they desist from blocking the free movement of resources. There are still other conditions, such as increasing cost curves, to which we shall give some attention later.

---

[3] One sometimes reads that, in competitive equilibrium, all profits are competed away and down to zero. It should read "all above-normal disequilibrium profits."

Optimizing rules and the rules of perfect competition stand and fall with the rule that higher prices should invite an expansion of output. However, this is a highly unnatural response if we think of the profit-maximization incentive. One of the elementary lessons of the supply-and-demand mechanism is that higher prices are associated with the supply of smaller quantities of products. Managers of firms in an industry, be they few or numerous, would have to be particularly dense not to get the idea that, by coordinating production decisions, they might keep output permanently at low disequilibrium levels. Prices and profits could then be kept at high levels above normal. Besides agreeing among themselves on restricting output, firms would just have to block access to resources tempted to join in the feast. The possibility of circumventing competition via monopolistic behavior thus follows from the downward-sloping shape of the ordinary demand schedule.

Large number of firms in an industry is no guarantee against such collusive behavior. It just makes agreements more difficult but by no means impossible. The section on cartels in Chapter 4 referred precisely to this phenomenon. Nonetheless, it helps if there are only a few firms producing a given commodity, or just one. Of particular interest is the case of *declining-cost industries* which give rise to the one-firm-per-industry situations.

In most firms, average and marginal costs decline over a certain range of output. Usually the demand schedule intersects the cost curves when they are horizontal (constant-cost) or rising. If the demand schedule meets cost curves in their declining portion, we speak of declining-cost industries. This constellation of circumstances has three serious consequences. First, it would be inefficient to have more than one firm in operation because any greater number would have to divide up the output demanded among themselves, which means that each would operate at a higher cost level than a single firm supplying all. Second, the optimizing rule (price equal to marginal cost) cannot be reconciled with earning normal profits. As long as average cost is falling with increasing output, marginal cost is less than average cost. Hence, if price were equal to marginal cost, sales revenues could not cover all costs and the firm would be incurring losses. On the other hand, if such a firm sells at a price which does cover cost, it cannot be equal to the marginal cost (see Figure 5-3). For this technical reason alone the competitive model loses all relevance in this case. Third, price competition allows for only one firm to survive. Once there is only one firm in the industry, the temptation is irresistible to exploit the monopoly position by keeping output at a level sufficiently low to allow charging a price not only above the marginal cost but above average cost, covering normal profit, as well.[4]

The Income-Distribution Proviso As we discussed the problem of optimum product proportions from the perspective of consumers, we kept silent about how

---

[4] The cost curves in question refer to total cost. Declining-cost industries appear in production lines where the fixed-cost component is very large compared to variable cost. As the fixed cost becomes distributed over an increasingly large number of product units, average fixed cost falls. Since variable cost is a minor matter, the average total cost falls also. Typical examples of such industries are transportation, electricity, pipelines, printing, etc.

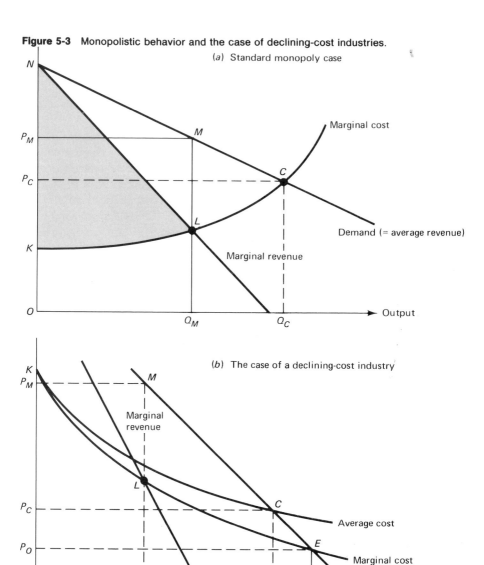

Figure 5-3 Monopolistic behavior and the case of declining-cost industries.

(a) Standard monopoly case

(b) The case of a declining-cost industry

Panel *a*: A firm aware of facing a downward-sloping demand curve for its output is in a position to choose an output level and to set a price such as will maximize its private net revenue. Following the maximization rule, it will compare the level of gross revenue with the cost level associated with each additional unit of output, i.e., the marginal revenue with marginal cost. As long as *MR* is higher than *MC*, there is gain in net revenue from expanding output further. The gain disappears at point *L* when *MR* = *MC*. This is when net revenue is maximized (= *KLN*).

Panel *b*: The same rules of profit-maximizing monopolistic behavior apply when the demand curve intersects the marginal-cost curve in its declining portion (output *OQ_m*, price *P_m*). However, the socially optimal alternative (output *OQ_o* at price *P_o*) is not attainable under conditions where the firm is supposed to cover its average cost from average sales revenue (i.e., price). At output *OQ_o* and price *P_o* the operation would not be "self-liquidating." It would require subsidization, which raises a new set of problems for the attainment of the social optimum.

consumers come into possession of the necessary purchasing power, although it was of considerable relevance. Proportions according to which total purchasing power is distributed among households influence what the optimal product proportions are going to be.

At this stage we are not concerned with the question of what an optimal income distribution might be. This will be taken up below, in the short section on income-distribution patterns, and then again in Chapter 11. All that needs to be said here is that the pattern of demand for different products depends, among other things, on how much money different types of consumers have to spend. This is because tastes and needs of consumers vary. If total purchasing power goes in larger chunks to the Falstaffs among us than to the Faust characters, "optimal" composition of output will be slanted more toward alcohol than toward books. If the proportion of distributed profits to wages rises, chances are there will be greater demand for luxuries than before. If young couples start receiving family allowances, there will be greater demand for diapers and toys. In each case, there will be a different optimum proportion of products. Therefore, speaking of optimal allocation, we always have to add the proviso: optimal— *relative to the given distribution of purchasing power.*

Observable Symptoms of Static Optimality   We are now back to the question: In what way are all these theoretical thoughts applicable to the practical evaluation of economic systems from the point of view of efficiency in allocation? The answer is that none are easy to apply, but some are easier to apply than others.

It would seem relatively easy to judge whether an economic system operates on its production-possibilities frontier. All one needs to check is the *rate of unemployment.* If there are any persons who would like to work but cannot find jobs, their percentage in the total available labor force reflects the distance from the production-possibilities frontier. Alternatively, one can calculate the potential-output path, i.e., hypothetical output volumes obtainable with a fully employed labor force and a certain trend of labor productivity, and compare it with output figures actually achieved. Negative differences will appear as the so-called production gap, i.e., a shortfall in output which reflects given rates of unemployment. (See Figure 5-4.)

However, it is also possible to have full employment and *not* be on the efficiency frontier. Labor and specific material inputs may be distributed throughout the system in local patterns which are technically inappropriate, so that deficits and excesses, or unused physical capacities, exist while everyone is employed. On the other hand, there may be temporary deficits of material inputs, which keep labor idle without registering as unemployment. This has been known to happen everywhere, but phenomena of this type have been plaguing Soviet-type centrally administered systems in particular (see Chapter 9). The rate of labor employment is therefore not fully conclusive evidence. It does not register the degree of optimality in input proportions.

One has to be equally careful using data on comparative *labor productivity,*

Figure 5-4   Measuring the performance of a system with respect to full utilization of resources.

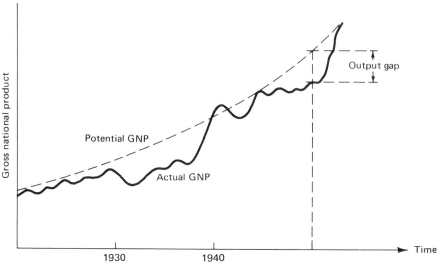

or output (consumption) per head of population. All other things being equal, these statistics are significant indicators of efficiency in allocation. However, "all other things"includes the level of technology and overall degree of economic development. These are precisely the aspects which vary from one country's economy to another even though their economic systems may be the same. It is extremely difficult to say whether a given economy displays lower values of these indicators because it is less efficient in allocating resources, or because it started on the path of modern economic development at a later date than others, and therefore could not accumulate as much real capital per worker or absorb advanced skills and technology.

As for indications of efficiency with respect to the composition of output, it is necessary to make do with *inferences from circumstantial evidence*. This evidence consists in signs indicating competitive behavior at work, or actions of the visible hand engaged in stemming noncompetitive behavior, in controlling it, or correcting its results. On the other hand, interference of the visible hand such as arbitrary price fixing, rationing, direct allocation in physical terms unaided by rational prices, chronic queues and shortages, all these are prima facie signs indicating probable distance from optimality, the wider the more pervasive they are. Abnormally high profit rates could be simply temporary signs of changing demand or cost conditions. The firms may be on the forefront of technical innovation or may be leaders in introducing new growth articles. However, if profit rates in certain sectors are permanently abnormally high, it may be taken as a sign of monopoly, hence suboptimality.

Not to skip any relevant evidence, let us be conscientious enough to ask whether a given economic system might be achieving optimality without any use of market forces. It may be allocating resources through visible-hand orders based on paper calculation of optimal input and output proportions. In that case, *perfect computation* would take the place of perfect competition.

If such attempts take place in a restricted area, e.g., by governmental agencies, it may be taken as a sign of conscious search for optimality. This would seem better in comparison with cases where no such effort is made. Still, it would be necessary to go over such calculations critically before one could say whether or how well optimality was being served. However, if claims are made for perfect computation on a scale of nationwide economies, in the present state of the art we are well advised to take them with a huge grain of salt. Egon Neuberger coined the term "computopia" for such allocation methods, which tells clearly what to think of them.[5]

An extremely important aspect of optimality in the composition of output is the choice of proportions between current-consumption goods and the class of producer durables. In complex economic systems, the choice is made in very roundabout ways. Members of society in their role as consumers indicate their preference for producer durables indirectly, and most of them unknowingly, by not spending, i.e., saving a portion of their purchasing power. However, from the point of view of society as a whole, saving is possible only through the supply of new producer goods, i.e., through investment. Saving decisions have to be indirectly "validated" through the system's investment decisions. This real counterpart of saving can be looked at as a reserve to be drawn upon later, i.e., as deferred consumption.

Additions of new producer goods to the stock of producer goods inherited from the past play a crucial role in the expansion of a system's production potential. Therefore, composition of output as between current-consumption goods and producer goods is a matter of choosing a certain rate of increase of the system's total output in the future. Thus, the issue of optimal allocation shades over into the second quantifiable performance criterion, that of growth efficiency.

Dynamic Efficiency

Discussion of this criterion can be made fully symmetrical with that of static optimality. The notion of static optimum starts with the "menu" of production possibilities. The notion of an optimum rate of growth, which refers to a system's aggregate output, might start with the range of feasible growth rates. This range can be also seen as a "menu": a set of alternative growth rates, from zero (or below) up, from which to pick the best one. Each higher rate would be related to an increasingly higher proportion of new producer goods in total output, i.e., to a higher investment (= saving) ratio. Thus, the opportunity cost of raising the growth rate of output would be consumption given up in favor of extra producer goods.

We could then try to formulate the optimal growth rate from the point of

[5] See Egon Neuberger and William Duffy, *Comparative Economic Systems: A Decision-making Approach*, Allyn and Bacon, Boston, 1976, pp. 84–88.

view of society's preferences. Extremely high growth rates, though desirable in themselves, might be considered too costly in the light of reduced consumption shares. On the other hand, overcoming stagnation may be worth paying the cost of a lowered consumption share—up to a point. It would be that point beyond which *today's valuation of the extra flow of output in the future*, made possible by an extra parcel of producer goods in current output, *would be less than today's valuation of current consumer goods which would have to be forgone for that purpose.*

This type of reasoning underlies the notion of the "golden rule of accumulation" which, in the area of growth economics, is the equivalent of the notion of Pareto optimum of static allocation.[6] Unfortunately, it is even less directly applicable to the practical evaluation of economic systems than Pareto optimum. Usable circumstantial evidence is hard to come by, but there is some. There is, for instance, circumstantial evidence on "forced saving." This is an invisible method of the visible hand to make the population save and finance investments involuntarily. It may indicate that growth rates are above the optimum that would be chosen if people had the opportunity to express their own ideas about the rate of saving. On the other hand, low growth rates need not mean bad performance if one can find convincing signs that society really does not care for higher ones. However, in practice, most comparisons assume without question that, as far as growth rates are concerned, the higher the better.

We shall defer the rest of this discussion to Chapter 12. There we go more deeply into the question of appropriate indicators of growth efficiency. Let us merely note that the observed growth rates of national product country by country are a very unsophisticated measure. We call this readily available statistic the "crude growth rate." If we are interested in comparing the efficiency with which different systems achieve their growth rates, we have to go beyond "crude growth rates" and take into account the costs of growth achievements. This will be the purpose of our emphasis, in Chapter 12, on performance with respect to the rate of growth of labor and capital productivity.

Income-Distribution Patterns

This performance criterion refers to the size distribution of incomes. Its observable and measurable aspect is the degree of equality (or inequality). Different degrees of inequality are imaginable in any economic system. They correspond to the range of feasible alternatives, analogous to the range of production possibilities or feasible growth rates. The difficult question here is to define an optimal standard of income distribution against which we could evaluate observed data for different systems, or rank them.

We have come across this issue in our examination of static optimality which, we said, is relative to a given income distribution pattern. The pattern

---

[6] Incidentally, as far as the item-by-item composition of the class of producer goods is concerned, similar principles of optimal choice apply as in static allocation. After all, demand for specific items of producer goods is derived from the demand for final consumer goods which they are meant to bring forth, directly or indirectly. Hence, consumers' choices must be reflected in producers' choices of producer goods.

itself needs to be evaluated on its own ground. The ordinary way of handling the issue is to say it is the subjective business of the evaluator, whose own values determine whether the standard is to be complete equality, or the status quo, or some qualified degree of inequality. In Chapter 11, we shall mention the attempts of various economists to find theoretical arguments for one or another distribution standard, mostly for equality.

The trouble with this performance criterion is that most economists suspect it cannot be treated in isolation. Concretely, it interacts with technological efficiency in allocation. It influences the position of the production-possibilities frontier. Equality, it is believed, tends to suck it in, inequality tends to push it out. This aspect of technological efficiency is not a matter of engineering and organization. It has to do with human incentives which lie behind engineering and organization, as well as plain work, i.e., with motivation to take care of all these functions with greater or less zeal, in accordance with higher or lower income. If the connection is what it is believed to be, then systems have to pay for greater equality by having less output. The cost of greater output would be more inequality. There may be some theoretical happy medium which could serve as standard. As we shall see in Chapter 11, to define it verbally is not hard, but to make it operational is an elusive task.

NONQUANTIFIABLE (QUALITATIVE) DIMENSIONS

In a sense, we have worked with nonquantifiable aspects of economic performance all along. Utility, which is another way of saying economic welfare, is not quantifiable—at least not in a cardinal sense: one cannot measure it in units which can be added up. However, utility does have a quantitative side in an ordinal sense. It exists in degrees of intensity. In that sense, there can be more of it or less. Degrees of intensity can be ranked, as well as compared, but not added up. In a pinch, they can be expressed in terms of measurable amounts of goods (or purchasing power) which serve as equivalent expressions of the degree of utility they yield. This makes it possible to work with *ratios* of degrees of utility, as we did in the formulation of the static optimum, but never with any absolute quantity of utility.

As we turn to the nonquantifiable aspects of economic performance, we continue to have in mind degrees of utility, or welfare, with which they are associated. In that ordinal sense, in the sense of intensity of satisfaction, they are quantifiable. They are amenable to being ranked, both in theory and in people's lived experience.

Consumers' Sovereignty

The entire discussion of optimality in the composition of output, as well as in growth rates, was based on the image of consumers who made choices, knowing perfectly well what they wanted. What their preferences were, and how they came to be formed, was none of our concern. In this, we followed the usual practice of economic analysis, which takes consumer preferences as an exogenous datum. It is treated as fully formed outside the economic sphere. However, in studying economic systems, exogenously given consumer preferences are an artifice. They have to be regarded as one of the endogenous elements of the system, interacting with other elements in a process of mutual determination.

The assumption of exogenous preferences goes hand in hand with the related notion of the "sovereign consumer." He or she is the master catered to by the production subsystem, the arbiter of the correctness of decisions made by the organizers of production. If there ever was a value-laden theoretical construct, this would be it. More than once the observation has been made that this part of economic analysis was intimately tied up with the democratic world view. "Sovereign consumer" is not just an analytic assumption. In it there vibrates the value judgment that this is how it should be.

But is it so actually? Or to what extent? These are the questions one asks when one tries to evaluate economic systems by this criterion. The reason why consumer sovereignty cannot be taken for granted is that it may suffer various restrictions imposed by the power and influence of competing interests aspiring to dominate the field of preferences: government, planners, ideological power groups, or the point of view and the needs of the production sector itself. One can argue that whenever optimality in allocation, or growth rates, is being violated— via rationing, arbitrary production dictates, etc.—consumer sovereignty is violated. True enough. If that were all, we would not need to treat it as a separate criterion. But there is more to it.

Consumer preferences do not sprout spontaneously from within the consumer's self. They also are one of the outcomes of economic processes. They, too, are being produced, though not exactly like dishwashers in a factory. The essential input ingredient, in this case, is information. Whoever controls the supply of relevant information controls consumer sovereignty. It is from this vantage point that the issue is further explored, and economic systems are compared, in Chapter 16.

Workers' Sovereignty

The concept of workers' sovereignty received the stamp of academic respectability, though not universal acceptance, when it was intimated, at the 1961 meeting of the American Economic Association, by William J. Baumol. Discussing two papers on consumer sovereignty, he remarked: "I am somewhat surprised that none of the papers has pointed out that the term 'consumer' in 'consumers' sovereignty' narrows the reference group excessively. . . . Considering the proportions of an individual's time which is typically spent at work, working conditions may be as important for his welfare as the flow of consumables which he receives."[7] Three years later, Benjamin Ward worked on the same theme further by relating the distribution of power and influence in decision making within production units to the state of welfare of the participants.[8] Workers' sovereignty has been a natural component of Jaroslav Vanek's conception of a "participatory economy" (see Chapter 6). For socialists and other leftists, it has been a traditional part and parcel of their ideological equipment.

---

[7] William J. Baumol in *American Economic Review*, vol. 52, no. 2, May 1962, pp. 289ff.
[8] Benjamin Ward in *American Economic Review*, vol. 55, no. 2, May 1965, pp. 71–72.

The probable reason why the notion of workers' sovereignty has not yet received official citizenship papers in the economics profession is that it smacks of a political line. It is therefore necessary to face up honestly to this source of suspicion. The suspicion would be entirely justified if workers' sovereignty was made to mean a pure and simple takeover of the positions of command, within firms and in the economy, by blue-collar workers or their representatives. However, this is not what William Baumol had in mind when he spoke of "the public's desires in its role as producers." Neither do we wish to have it understood in that sense in our context, as a performance aspect of economic systems.

It has been acknowledged by economic analysis that labor services have a dual character: that of cost ("disutility") and that of source of satisfaction ("psychic rewards," i.e., utility). The dosage of the two aspects differs from one job to another; it differs between technologies (e.g., manual handicrafts versus the assembly line) and between economic systems (e.g., slavery versus commune). The relative dosage between disutility and satisfaction associated with work is therefore a significant economic variable.

Workers' sovereignty, as understood here, refers to the power of people, in their role of suppliers of labor services, to influence their working conditions so as to maximize the satisfaction part and to minimize the disutility or cost part. This, too, is an aspect of economic efficiency, like any other cost-benefit calculation.

How one can compare economic systems under this performance aspect is, of course, a challenging question. One might wish to distinguish, as in the case of resource allocation, between the *state* of workers' sovereignty at a point of time, and its *rate of change*.. In either case, one has to make do with circumstantial evidence, although certain statistical measures may be helpful (such as the rate of industrial accidents and occupational diseases), but not always conclusive (such as the number and scope of strikes). Circumstantial evidence which has an indicative value is the presence of certain social institutional machinery, one that makes it loud and explicit how labor perceives the cost side of its productive activities, and allows for negotiated improvements. Discussion of these arrangements—trade unions, schemes of workers' participation in management, etc.—in different systems will be the subject of Chapter 17.

Other types of circumstantial evidence are of a still more indirect, though telling, kind. The geographic direction of actual, or desired, migration of labor between different systems; governmental measures preventing such migration; measures blocking sources of information about the conditions of labor in different countries, or even within the same country—these are some of the pieces of symptomatic evidence whose significance for the state of workers' sovereignty should be obvious.

IS A COMPREHENSIVE EVALUATION POSSIBLE?

We have gone over five separate aspects of the performance of economic systems. Now we have to ask ourselves how one can combine them in order to arrive at a balanced overall evaluation of systems, taking into account pluses and minuses, and perhaps some additional performance aspects as well.

There is no problem if one economic system performs in every respect better than another. In that case the ranking is clear. But what if one system excels in growth rates and does poorly allocating resources in optimal proportions and safeguarding consumer sovereignty? What about Joseph Schumpeter's classic defense of monopoly profits? Bad for optimality in static allocation, they may benefit growth efficiency by providing massive financing for innovations through research and development. "A system—any system, economic or other—that at *every* point of time fully utilizes its possibilities to the best advantage may yet in the long run be inferior to a system that does so at *no* given point of time, because the latter's failure to do so may be a condition for the level or speed of long-run performance."[9] Or how do we balance income equality against possible losses in production possibilities?

One could proceed using a similar method by which college teachers arrive at the final grade for their students. In examining a system, one would "grade" each partial performance aspect on some scale, give each partial grade some "weight" (percent in the total, number of points), add up the weighted figures, and then compute the weighted average for every system under comparison.

Evaluators could also establish *in their minds* a system of "indifference curves," mapping various combinations of partial performance indicators. A better performance in one respect (growth efficiency) would make up for a certain degree of slipping in another respect (allocation efficiency, income equality). A set of equally satisfactory combinations of partial performance indicators, i.e., of their specific values, would form an "indifference curve," exactly as in analysis of consumers' utility valuation of different product combinations. There would be a series of such sets of equally satisfactory combinations, each set being better or worse, in an overall sense, than other sets. One could then take the *observed combinations* of performance indicators for individual systems and see where they fit on such an "indifference map," and whether combined indicators of a pair of country systems fall on the same indifference curve or not.

The indifference-curve approach is obviously more sophisticated than the grading-by-weighted-average approach, but both of them probably strike the reader as utterly impractical. It would surely be foolish to pretend that one could assemble adequate statistical performance indicators, quantitative proxy measures of various types of circumstantial evidence, and set up a precise indifference map expressing the valuation of such indicators. This is not the point, though. Of course the evidence will mostly be inadequate and our valuation standards fuzzy, uncertain, and intuitive. However, no matter how fuzzy and intuitive, the indifference-curve approach does give us a formal model of the mental processes we go through when we try to evaluate economic systems comprehensively.

Nonetheless, the method of evaluation suggested by this formal model may

[9] J. A. Schumpeter, *Capitalism, Socialism, and Democracy*, Harper, New York, 1942, p. 83. The same idea was propounded by Peter Wiles with respect to optimality of allocation and growth in the Soviet economy. See his "Growth versus Choice," *Economic Journal*, vol. 66, no. 262, June 1956, pp. 244–255.

still not fully come to grips with all that is involved. Mentioning intuition as part of the evaluation process leads up to still another problem, to that of *interpretation* of certain observed systemic characteristics which we have left for the end.

Evaluation and Interpretation   As soon as we admit that consumers' preferences are partly the outcome of how the economic system works, we are broaching problems having to do with the impact of economic systems upon cultural values in general. A few remarks on that subject were made above (in the section on "Dimensions of Economic Performance"), in connection with various aspects of "quality of life." This takes the evaluation task beyond the issue of how responsive the supply side of the economic system is to given preferences. The question now takes the form: "How do we feel about the various social, aesthetic, moral, spiritual aspects of society, insofar as they can be traced to the character of the economic system? How do we go about evaluating that part of its performance?"

Let us list a few of the more conspicuous outcomes in this category. Humanity has been made aware of them mostly through observation of modern Western capitalism, but they have to be assumed to exist, in one form or another, in other systems as well.

Speaking of the transition from medieval slavery to feudalism (in Chapter 3), we mentioned in passing its beneficial effect upon family structure and private life of the common people. The split capitalism caused between the household and the workplace; the premium it places upon labor mobility; all this contributed in turn to the transformation of the family structure from the earlier "extended family" to the contemporary "nuclear" type. The effects of this change upon psychic well-being have not necessarily been beneficial. True, it weakened the oppressive character of patriarchal authority; but it also created new uncertainties in the structure of authority in general. It created new problems in the loneliness of the housewife and of old people, in the mental stress connected with occupational choice when clear and closely witnessed models of professional roles are absent.

We know from other sciences that organisms require a certain equilibrium of environmental factors for their successful existence. Similarly, psychic structures need a balance between stability and change. If the stimuli of change are too powerful, or follow too quickly one upon another, adjustment becomes difficult. This is one reason why transitions from one economic system to another are often so painful. Some systems, certainly Western-type capitalism in its advanced stages, thrive on change and promote change actively, perhaps to the point of discomfort. On the other hand, there also may be not enough change, as witnessed by underdeveloped countries or by consumer complaints under Soviet-type systems. This, too, ought to be taken into account.

Allied to the problem of excessive rate of change under Western-type capitalism has been the tendency of playing up values of materialist hedonism and playing down the word "enough." This sensuous stimulation of greed has been the tenor of advertising messages originating with the economic system. Side by side with tendencies of excessive rate of change, established patterns of production may subtly resist the articulation of human wants which would need a profound reorientation on the supply side (e.g., from material output to education and to services catering to the need for personal creativity, which seems to be an obvious necessary complement to increased leisure).

There is a welter of adverse psychic and moral phenomena that go under the name of *alienation*, which has been regularly associated with the character of the economic system. The multilayered concept of alienation has been rather overworked in recent years, and its meaning devalued close to cant. Nonetheless, it does correspond to some highly significant realities, attributable to economic systems.

Of the several layers of meaning of alienation, the simplest are the psychological effects of certain technologies upon labor (blue-collar as well as clerical white-collar): monotony; personal isolation; low demand on skills; high demand on attention to repetitive tasks; performing machinelike operations and being paced by machines; insufficient insight into how one's part in the production process fits in with other parts leading to the finished outcome (lack of meaning); absence of a completed job one could take pride in, etc. Another aspect of alienation stems from the individual's being inserted into an organizational system of social hierarchies: lack of autonomy; passive submission to the authority of others; being manipulated like a thing within a social structure which itself resembles a machinelike mechanism. Finally, participants in the economic system may feel a lack of control over their own life owing to the effects of the way its impersonal "economic laws" work: uncertainties of technological and structural unemployment, as well as unemployment of the cyclical variety; pressures of competition; pressures due to the growth propensities of the system.

Much of the current usage goes back to Marx's application of the recondite philosophical concept of alienation to the analysis of human existence in a concrete economic and social setting. It can be boiled down to the following two propositions. On the one hand, alienation arises from the inversion of the natural relationship between humans and objects of their creation: instead of being masters of their instruments, people become subject to the often strange logic of their shape and use, dictated by the working of the economic system and its mechanics. On the other hand, humans become estranged from each other as members of the same species by virtue of the divisive social roles into which they are pressed, and whose character corresponds to the nature of the given economic system.

After this illustrative survey, it is unavoidable to raise the delicate question of *evidence, verification, and comparability*. It is surely apparent that methods relying on quantification, and even on simply definable circumstantial evidence, are not of much use here. We are dealing with aspects of economic systems which cannot be converted into objective brute facts that could be counted, fed into a computer, and correlated with each other. This is where the study of economic systems links up with humanities, whose business is *interpretation of meaning*. This task is of a different order from systematic reconstruction of regularities in the behavior of facts, which is the method of natural sciences.

What makes the task so different? It can be put simply as follows. In natural sciences, as well as in behaviorist social science, the observer and the facts are strangers to each other. The observer has the eye to the microscope, the fact is the microbe at the other end. In the reconstruction of meaning, the observer and the facts are in communication: they are part of the same human world of values and purposes, of strivings and frustrations. There is a shared human frame of reference, even though neither the specific values nor the means of expressing them need be shared by the observer and the observed. In this case, the facts are not mute. They "speak" to the observer who "reads" their meaning through empathy and identification with the objects of observation.

This is how one has to approach the evaluation of the impact economic systems have upon those aspects of social life which have to do, broadly speaking, with cultural values. It is clear that the evaluation is possible only from the point of view of other cultural values which the observer chooses as a standard. That is not a special problem. Subjectivism is part of all evaluation. One cannot gauge a system's performance except against some chosen preference standards, be they one's own or someone else's. The difficulty lies with the possibility of different observers communicating with one another.

Whenever values are involved, a given ensemble of social facts will have an entirely different meaning for different observers. Their perception of reality will depend on the makeup of their minds and hearts. Some will be colorblind to the alienation issue or to the value-forming powers of economic systems (e.g., Milton Friedman, presumably). Others will see oppression and alienation everywhere, even in the growth of living standards (e.g., Herbert Marcuse). Still others may be subtly aware of the ambiguity of a system's cultural effects as, for instance, Marx was.[10] The validity of this part of the evaluation enterprise, including its premises in observation, are not accessible to impartial testing. However, it may be of the greatest moment.

TWO FOOTNOTES ON THE EVALUATION METHOD

As an afterthought—and afterthoughts need not be unimportant—one minor remark and one major methodological remark are offered for consideration.

Intrinsic versus Relative Standards

Evaluation of economic systems need not always be conducted by comparing the performance of one system with that of another. It is also possible to evaluate a given system in isolation and use the estimate of its own potential as evaluation

---

[10] Thus, he wrote: "Accumulation of wealth at one pole is . . . at the same time accumulation of misery, agony of toil, slavery, ignorance, brutality, mental degradation, at the opposite pole." (K. Marx, *Capital*, vol. I, p. 645.) But at the same time he stated: "It is one of the civilizing aspects of capital that it enforces this surplus-labor in a manner and under conditions which are more advantageous to the development of the productive forces, social relations, and the creation of the elements for a new and higher form than under the preceding forms of slavery, serfdom, etc." (Ibid., vol. III, p. 819.) One could make a collection of such contrasting statements which, to Marx's way of thinking, did not exclude each other but reflected the two-faced character of reality.

standard. An economic system may be an "underachiever" in terms of its own unutilized capabilities. To the extent humans are innate improvers, observed performance will always be found wanting. We shall call this approach the *intrinsic-standard evaluation*.

The other approach is the obvious one—to take the performance of other economic systems as standard of reference. In that case, an intrinsically poor performance may appear good by comparison—among the blind the one-eyed is king. This procedure constitutes the *comparative*, or *relative, evaluation*.

Gestalt Perception in Evaluating Performance

To be systematic in going about any complex task usually means breaking it up into manageable parts and tackling these, one by one, in some convenient sequence. There is nothing wrong about understanding systematic procedures in this manner. We prepared the ground precisely for such methodical appraising of economic systems by singling out several partial aspects of performance. However, as we examined the possibilities of comprehensive evaluation, it became clear that systematic comparison, one aspect at a time, was only part of the job. Systematic procedures, which see total performance as a mechanical collection of scores on partial counts, fail utterly as soon as we include nonquantifiable aspects, and especially the impact of economic systems upon the "quality of life," and cultural values. What other way is there? Is there another way?

The insights gained by the psychology of perception may be of some help. It has been established that we do not recognize objects, or grasp their meaning, by going methodically down some checklist of partial characteristics. We proceed through a simultaneous global perception of the "pattern" formed by the innumerable characteristics of any particular object. We recognize objects for what they are because we see each characteristic *in the context* of all other characteristics. We go by the particular way in which they are combined. When people talk of an "intuitive grasp," this is probably what they mean. Psychologists call it the gestalt form of perception, *Gestalt* being the German word for "form," shape, or pattern.

Comprehensive evaluation must rely, at some point, on this kind of global perception of the systemic performance. There is no need to be apologetic about it. On the contrary, stopping short of it (because it presumably is not exact in the natural-science sense) leaves the evaluation truncated. This is of immense importance, for instance, to observers who wish the concept of consumer sovereignty to refer also to the supply of governmental services of a political nature. (Some call it "citizens' sovereignty.") In the context of these services, depending on their character, the other performance criteria may acquire a profoundly different meaning.

Let us illustrate by contrasting an instance of the piecemeal approach with a comprehensive gestalt approach. Thus, in an evaluation of a segment of the Soviet economy, we read:

As for the fate of the Estonian, Latvian and Lithuanian peoples, it is difficult for this recent observer of the Baltic area to muster up any great sympathy for their "plight." As a generalization, these republics today enjoy the highest living standards in the Soviet Union. . . . [11]

An alternative evaluation of the same performance aspect, this time of the Czechoslovak economic system and the increase in consumption levels after 1969, comes out as follows:

By nailing a man's whole attention to the floor of his mere consumer interests, it is hoped to render him incapable of appreciating the ever-increasing degree of his spiritual, political and moral degradation. Reducing him to a simple vessel for the ideals of a primitive consumer society is supposed to turn him into pliable material for complex manipulation.[12]

It is obvious that the two observers would have a hard time communicating, reconciling the results of their individual evaluations. We spoke earlier of the problem of proving the validity of a given evaluation. The upshot is that evaluators have to get used to the impossibility of proving the validity of their results, except to those who are on the same wavelength.[13]

As we now prepare to review a number of normative models, let us be alert to which performance aspect, or aspects, these products of economic imagination respond to. Some represent a response to deficiencies in static allocation, some are concerned with economic expansion and growth, some with income distribution, and still others with the qualitative impacts. They have one thing in common: they are responses to the experience of humanity with modern capitalism.

BIBLIOGRAPHY

Koopmans, Tjalling C., and John M. Montias: "On the Description and Comparison of Economic Systems," in A. Eckstein (ed.): *Comparison of Economic Systems*, University of California Press, Berkeley, 1971, pp. 34–35 and 41–48.

Boulding, K. E.: "Welfare Economics," in B. F. Haley (ed.): *Survey of Contemporary Economics*, Irwin, Homewood, Ill., 1952, vol. 2, pp. 14–23.

Balassa, Bela: *The Hungarian Experience in Economic Planning*, Yale, New Haven, 1959, pp. 5–24 (on criteria of comparison), reprinted in Morris Bornstein (ed.): *Comparative Economic Systems: Models and Cases*, Irwin, Homewood, Ill., 1965, pp. 3–18.

Dorfman, Robert: *The Price System*, Prentice-Hall, Englewood Cliffs, N.J., 1964.

Bator, Francis M.: "The Simple Analytics of Welfare Maximization," *The American Economic Review*, vol. 47, March 1957, pp. 22–59.

Mansfield, Edwin: *Microeconomics*, Norton, New York, 1970.

[11] Lynn Turgeon in *Society*, vol. 13, no. 1, November–December 1975, p. 38.

[12] Vaclav Havel, "An Open Letter from Prague," *Encounter*, vol. 45, no. 3, September 1975, p. 18.

[13] For a helpful elucidation of these issues, the philosophically inclined reader is referred to the article by Charles Taylor, "Interpretation and the Sciences of Man," *The Review of Metaphysics*, vol. 25, no. 1, September 1971, pp. 1–51.

Chapter 6

Normative Models
of Economic Systems

Let us admit the case of the conservative: if we once start thinking no one can guarantee where we shall come out, except that many objects, ends and institutions are doomed. Every thinker puts some portion of an apparently stable world in peril and no one can wholly predict what will emerge in its place.

John Dewey

"Normative" means that which ought to be but isn't. It is the realm of standards, of ideal objectives to be striven for. "Normative" is the opposite of "existing" or "descriptive." When we think or dream about the Good Society, we deal with a normative idea. At the same time, a norm is, as a rule, an implied critique and negation of the existing state of affairs.

Normative thinking is a steady companion of human existence. Even those who are well satisfied with the way things are think normatively: they treat their empirical reality as a cherished norm that other societies might do well to emulate. They also wish all other members of their society would accept it as their norm, and stop grumbling. In that sense, each of the descriptive models of real economic systems of Chapters 3 and 4 can be used normatively. This is what happens when, for instance, developing countries are told by some to adopt the market-capitalist system of free enterprise, and by others to follow the Soviet, Yugoslav, or Japanese example. Having noted this normative use of models which describe reality, we shall devote the rest of the chapter to normative models which arise from opposition to reality.

Why is construction of ideal systems such a widespread, not to say universal, phenomenon? Why do such ideas strike a responsive chord in so many people's hearts? They range from Plato's ideal utopia, from infantile rock-candy-mountain type of dreams—the *Schlaraffenland* of the Germans, *pays de cocagne* of the French, the cargo cults of New Guinea aborigines[1] —all the way to elaborate schemes of socialist utopians and social reformers.

We have to conclude that the adjustment of humans to social organization, or of social organization to humans, has been imperfect most of the time. From the point of view of the defender of the status quo, the fault is with people. One can point to the findings of anthropologists concerning the amazing variability of personality structures in different societies, and draw the quick conclusion that it is up to individuals to make a flexible adjustment. After all, there is no such thing as "human nature" in general! From the point of view of a critic of society, on the other hand, the widespread occurrence of discontent and of normative thinking is itself a proof that there is some basic core of universally valid human needs which are frustrated by existing types of social organization and yearn to be satisfied. Of course, the existence and intensity of such yearnings are also a question of where one is situated in a given socioeconomic space or with whom one identifies. The "view from the top" is usually not the same as that from under the proverbial bridge sheltering the outcasts of society.

TYPES OF NORMATIVE SYSTEMS

We shall not produce any systematic classification in this instance, but merely indicate in what respects normative models differ from one another.

Every systems designer lays emphasis on a particular favorite element, or set of elements, in the proposed model. The rest is underplayed, ignored, or left in a state of hidden assumptions which are not properly spelled out. Some stress the element of ownership rights and structure of decision making; others, the outer organizational arrangements and rules of conduct. Some put at the center incentives, often in the form of idealistic personal motivation; others, the manipulation of the mode of allocation. Some utopian extremists construct their models almost from scratch, giving free rein to their sociological imagination; others are content to modify models of existing systems ever so slightly.

Leaving aside which particular element receives emphasis, normative models

[1] "Cargo cults" refers to myths that emerged among aborigines of the Pacific after their World War II experience with American airlifts of material. When these stopped, there arose beliefs in their "second coming," to be accompanied by new affluence. (See Peter Worsley, *The Trumpet Shall Sound: A Study of "Cargo Cults" in Melanesia*, MacGibbon & Kee, London, 1957; Guenter Lewy, *Religion and Revolution*, Oxford University Press, New York, 1974, pp. 221–236 and bibliography on pp. 622–624.)

can be arranged according to their degree of elaboration. At one end are systems designers who pay loving attention to every specific detail. In some early utopian models it was specified, for instance, that clothing should have buttons in the back, so as to promote the spirit of mutual help among people. This is the *formalistic blueprint approach*. Fourier was its prime representative (see below). At the other end are systems which are barely described at all, merely defined in terms of some very *general operating principles*, such as optimality in allocation (A. Lerner) or "free association of producers" (Marx).

From still another point of view, a very important one, normative models can be examined as to the process which they assume to be required for their practical realization. The basic division here is between those normative models which are conceived as *immediate substitutes or alternatives* to existing systems and those which are conceived as objectives, or as images of the future, *to emerge through the development of existing systems*. Behind each of these conceptions of normative modeling there is an entirely different idea of the internal structural makeup of society and of what it takes to achieve a true structural change. There are also different political philosophies underlying each of them.

The *immediate-alternative conception* assumes it is possible to "introduce" the normative model by making a clean break with an existing one. The existing one is "overthrown," "abolished," or "collapses" in one way or another. The normative model is realized by means of a series of deliberate measures over a relatively short period of time. Through these measures, the new system is "constructed," or "built," on the vacant lot left by the old one.

In other words, the method of realization relies on *exogenous means of action*, exogenous to the economic sphere—physical force of social groups, political power, legislation—which operate changes in the socioeconomic structure. It is the method of social engineering. Alternatively, realization may be expected through an *inner psychological change* among the system's participants. Change of mind and motivation, release of people's assumed basic goodness, are the result of proselytizing or propaganda. They are seen as the moving force changing the economic system. The inner-rebirth method has usually been tried in the realization of normative models on a small scale, say on the scale of one production unit, such as a commune. However, it can also become part of social engineering on a nationwide scale, if the attempt is made to change people's subjective attitudes through propaganda emanating from some power center.

The other conception—let us call it *the pragmatic evolving-system conception*—accepts the existing system as a starting point. It formulates the normative model as a modification of the existing one, not as an a priori construction. The normative model is developed *from* the existing one. It is its extrapolation. It is a *phase of its development*. However, it is not a phase as it would automatically emerge through the system's own working. Therefore, it is not a simple forecast. It is perceived as a possibility among the many possibilities which are practically feasible, but one that is at the same time adopted as a desirable goal requiring deliberate intervention, or action, in order to become reality.

Examples of such pragmatic normative models abound. Every economic policy works with some normative model as a goal. In a capitalist system subject to economic fluctuations, full employment and steady growth without fluctuations represent a normative model of this type. In the gallery of famous historical examples, the model of technocratic productivism advocated by Saint-Simon belongs here, too (see below). Interestingly enough, as we shall try to show, Marx's model of socialism-communism was also conceived as a developmental phase emerging from the capitalist system, partly owing to its own working, partly carried forward by conscious activities and actions.

As to the methods of implementation associated with the pragmatic normative modeling, they do not shy away from social action, power of persuasion, political power, and legislative measures. However, there is a fundamental difference in the use of these instruments on the part of pragmatic model makers, in contrast to proponents of models of the immediate-substitute kind. The immediate-substitute school would *force* existing structures into a preconceived mold of the normative model. The pragmatic school takes into account the natural resistance of established structural patterns to change and weighs the practical adequacy of chosen means to normative ends. It swims along with the current, while steering the course.

NINETEENTH-CENTURY UTOPIANS
AND OTHER PRE-MARXIANS

It would be a mistake to approach the group of authors chosen for review as a set of old-fashioned museum portraits preserved from a dusty past. There can be no question about their relevance to modern times. Radicals and revolutionaries far and wide have been treading and retreading utopian paths opened some hundred and fifty years ago. Curiously, even many "Marxists" remained confined to pre-Marxian modes of thinking about social change, regardless of their vocabulary. On the other hand, important insights of the early socialist and parasocialist thinkers often did not receive their due, even when these insights were quietly integrated by Marx into his own system.

Fourierism

Charles Fourier (1772–1837) was one of the most original designers of social systems. He can be treated either as an eccentric fool or as a genius—there is enough material in his work for both. For condescending ridicule, there are his bizarre notions about the laws of the universe animated by emotional categories; his private terminology, often as grotesque as it was inventive; his pedantic elaboration of inconsequential details; and other features that made him sound like many another crackpot. It seems more fruitful for our purposes not to dwell on the idiosyncratic side, but instead to extract from his writings what is sound and lasting.

Fourier's great general achievement was to claim for social science the right to view the social system as a deviation from an ideal norm and to explore the problem of its "destinies" and the possibility of "universal harmony." Bourgeois revolutions, after having destroyed the absolutism of kings and religion, came to view their own world of bourgeois social and economic institutions as untouchable creations of absolute validity. It was up to the socialist thinkers to reduce, in turn, these new absolutes to mere historical phases, subject to fundamental critique and open to change by human acts.

Fourier gave relatively little space in his writings to explicit criticism of his contemporary bourgeois world. He also neglected the problem of the passage from the existing to the desirable. His major contribution lay in a formalist proposal of the ideal social system: a detailed description of the internal basic social unit (the *phalanx*), and of the physical layout of structures provided to house it (the *phalanstery*). According to ownership arrangements, it was to be a shareholding production cooperative, which is saying too little: the phalanx commune was to serve as framework for a harmonious integration of all social functions, not only of production.

In formal terms, the phalanx had all the standard features to be expected in a cooperative: subscription of shares, allocation of revenues between interest on subscribed capital, compensation for work, and a bonus fund for rewarding extra contributions to the work process. As for substance, the originality of Fourier's scheme was in the consequent implementation of the following guideline: Make all formal arrangements fit natural propensities and psychological needs of people. In other words, the human "operating unit" was not to be adapted to the system's objectives. The satisfaction of human needs was itself treated as an objective, and not only at the consumption end, but in the very process of production. The principle was, and still is, revolutionary: Instead of viewing individuals at work as technical components of a technical process, to view them as social beings who obtain their identity as humans only through interaction with other humans. Thus, humanism is placed at the center of solving technical problems.

Consequently, Fourier pays great attention to the microsociology and psychology of work teams: balance between variety and specialization; elimination of boredom and fatigue; balance of age and sex composition of work teams; balance between spirit of cooperation and competitiveness; and the combination of material and social-psychological incentives. Fourier's solutions reveal amazing powers of psychological intuition, especially for a man living the life of a recluse. The limited size of a phalanx (up to 1,800) was to facilitate direct social intercourse, in contrast to the lostness of the individual in mass society. On the other hand, the tyranny of the collective was to be prevented by a balance of options between privacy and communal living.

Because of its detailed specifications, Fourier's model undoubtedly belongs to the class of *formalist blueprint designs*. However, the formalist label fails to do justice to the presence of profoundly humanistic operating principles around which the model is constructed. Fourier's ideas about human nature and his theory of motivation were sufficiently lifelike to create a distinctive tension between the a priori character of the model as a whole and the realism of individual ingredients.

Fourier's recipe was tested on American soil in the eighteen-forties and found, at least for a while, viable.[2] It was also a source of inspiration for the early kibbutz movement in Israel. In all cases, however, it was a matter of isolated ventures in the margin of society.

Saint-Simonism

Fourierist conceptions, if universally implemented, would require a clear break with established social and economic trends. New social patterns would have to be poured as from a mold, using existing social material. This unconcern with the question of transition is typical for all utopians proper. With some authors, it is due to the fact that they do not even seriously contemplate realization; for them, positive utopia is a roundabout way of expressing negative social criticism, and nothing more. With others, cavalier treatment of real circumstances is due to their illusions about the ease of implementation. They seem to feel: "Once the virtues of my model are demonstrated, who would not want to follow?"

Thus, utopias are by definition not properly inserted into the realities of the actual development of society. This has grave consequences, should implementation after all be tried. Since realization is treated as if it were a matter of free choice and will to act, the main burden must be placed on persuasion and propaganda. If reality turns out to be too recalcitrant, there are two possible outcomes. Either the attempt ends in a few individual pilot projects and fizzles out as harmless escapism; or else the utopians gather sufficient political power to force events. In that case, the hidden totalitarian implications of utopianism become manifest. Society is then coerced to conform to the preconceived utopian model. (It may be instructive to try this approach in interpreting certain aspects of Chinese or Cuban developments under Communist rule.) Whether the results obtained under duress can correspond to the original utopian intentions is, of course, another question.

In contrast to utopians, the Saint-Simonian school of "normative modeling" applies its efforts to real tendencies in the existing social and economic system. We shall gloss over the blow-by-blow development of the doctrine from the remarkable writings of Count Saint-Simon (1760–1825) through the amplifications undertaken by his disciples. We shall also ignore, as with Fourier, the cranky and cultist side of their activities. At the cost of many interesting details, we shall reduce Saint-Simonian ideas to what seems essential from the point of view of current relevance.

As hinted above, Saint-Simonians said yes to the upsurge of capitalism. They embraced the idea of industrialization and singled out *production* as their leading objective. Thus, their normative model amounted to perfected capitalism. Their improved version would have been pruned of all parasitic elements without productive functions. They advocated what today would be called the principle of

---

[2] The foremost American followers of Fourier were Albert Brisbane and Horace Greeley. From among more than thirty projects, the Wisconsin Phalanx and the North American in New Jersey lasted for six and thirteen years respectively. The Brook Farm commune (1841–1846) was also of Fourierist inspiration.

meritocracy: social elite based on achievement, not on inherited or ascribed status. Their hero figures were the bankers, industrialists, and scientists. Their sociology of capitalism ignored the categories of wage earner, proletarian, or labor, as
opposed to capitalist employer. In their view, the significant category was "producers," a concept which lumped together all participants linked functionally by
the technical process, no matter what their position in the hierarchy.

At the same time, private ownership was expendable if it did not serve the
goal of production adequately. Private owners held capital and land in trust on
behalf of society, and if they failed to keep up production and employment, they
could be dispossessed. In its later version, Saint-Simonism incorporated the idea
of *public* (i.e., *state*) *ownership and a system of central regulation by a supreme
planning body*:

> The social institution of the future will direct all industries in the interest of the whole
> society. . . . The system will include in the first instance a central bank which consti-
> tutes the government in the material sphere; this bank will become the depository of
> all wealth, of the entire productive fund, of all the instruments of production. . . . [3]

The movers of the system were still to be the "captains of industry," and the mass
of working people its beneficiaries.

The relevance of Saint-Simonism for subsequent system designs cannot be
overestimated. It provides the first rudimentary model for all modern conceptions that share its principal features: (1) production and industrialization as
primary goals; (2) betting on the crucial role of managerial elites; and (3) rejection of class conflict between the guardians of the means of production and the
workers. Two notable examples from twentieth-century history are *Mussolini's
productivism* and *Stalinism* in the Soviet Union.

Priority of production goals, glorification of "captains of industry," and
condemnation of class struggle marked "Mussolini's transition [after 1917] from
his original revolutionary radicalism to his subsequent stand as the man of law
and order."[4] Only the elements of planning and the state's visible hand were
underdeveloped. These were present with a vengeance in the ideology of Stalinism, which contained all the principal elements of the Saint-Simonian creed (with
the exception of egalitarianism, and with the role of the Communist party added). That they were expressed in Marxist vocabulary is irrelevant. Besides, Stalinism modified that vocabulary in significant ways. Thus, for instance, the term
"working class" was phased out and replaced by the concept of "toilers" or
"working people," analogous to the Saint-Simonian all-inclusive concepts of
"producers," or "industrials," covering workers and entrepreneurs alike. To trace
the ideological progeny of Saint-Simon further, we may identify his ideas with

---

[3] Celestin Bougle and Elie Halévy (eds.), *Exposition de la doctrine de Saint-Simon*, Paris, 1924,
pp. 272–273, cited in G. Lichtheim, *The Origins of Socialism*, Praeger, New York, 1969, p. 53.

[4] Roland Sarti, *Fascism and the Industrial Leadership in Italy, 1919–1940*, University of California Press, Berkeley, 1971, p. 22. See also A. James Gregor, *The Ideology of Fascism: The Rationale of
Totalitarianism*, Free Press, New York, 1969, pp. 147–149, 161–163, 180.

members of certain new elites in underdeveloped countries. In Lichtheim's words, he was "the ancestor of the 'technocratic' faith which in our days has become the doctrine of self-styled socialists in charge of newly independent countries in Asia, Africa, and Latin America."[5]

Louis Blanc

The name of Louis Blanc (1811–1882) has been traditionally associated with the ideas of *reformist, democratic socialism*. What made him dear to social democrats and some other socialists of non-Marxian persuasion was the role assigned in his scheme to a democratic state and government, elected by universal suffrage. The major economic goal was to be full employment. Modern readers will recognize in Blanc's model the essentials of what is now called the "welfare state" with its Keynesian policies.

However, Blanc is at the same time the precursor of present-day models of labor-managed economic systems. In contrast to many latter-day democratic socialists, Louis Blanc did not advocate nationalizatons and state control of industry. Management of economic enterprises was to be discharged autonomously through executives elected by workers. In contrast to the cooperative form in the narrow sense, capital was to be supplied by the state via an initial capital grant, and accumulated later from allocations of undistributed revenue. Once launched by the state, the system would spread by its force of appeal to workers in private enterprises, until they, too, would be forced to convert to the labor-managed form. Insofar as there was to be planning, it was not to become synonymous with "running the economy."

Although Louis Blanc's name has not become a household word, not even in socialist households, his ideas are still very much alive. Thus, if contemporary Yugoslavia were governed along democratic lines and carried forward the development of its model of labor-managed enterprises, the system would probably answer the description of Blanc's design surprisingly well. At any rate, models of this kind have been enjoying a secret popularity among many Eastern European economists. When, at certain periods, alternatives to existing systems could be discussed publicly, as in Czechoslovakia in 1968–1969, the Blanc-type models surfaced immediately. They were advocated under the title of "socialist group ownership," as opposed to state ownership. An interesting reincarnation of Blanc's ideas may also be found in Jaroslav Vanek's model of "participatory economy" (see below).

Proudhon, Syndicalism, Guild Socialism

The inclusion of Proudhon in this survey is justified by the influence rather than by the intrinsic quality of his thought. Pierre Joseph Proudhon (1809–1865) is considered to be the spiritual father of *syndicalism*, or *anarcho-syndicalism*. His ideas also bear a family resemblance to the doctrines of *guild socialism* in England. With Louis Blanc, Proudhon has in common the emphasis on workers'

[5] Lichtheim, op. cit., p. 40.

self-management, but he differs from him in totally rejecting any role of government, not only in the economy but in society altogether.

Proudhon's design could be described as a horizontal configuration of component units, with no hierarchies, no centrally articulated functions, and no complex structure. Insofar as individual units had to be grouped into larger sets, e.g., individual workshops or enterprises into industries, it would be done on principles of federation. (Local administrative units would be similarly federated, and there might be federations of federations, but never a centralized state or government acting upon society "from the outside.") Interaction between participants would be based on the universal application of free contract, as guarantee of fairness and justice.

Thus, at the bottom of Proudhon's system are the values of individualism. This sets it apart from, as well as against, self-governing schemes of collectivist inspiration, which he called "associationist." It is also in opposition to the elitism of Saint-Simonians, or etatism, be it ever so mild and democratic as that of Louis Blanc. Only one central institution found room in Proudhon's scheme, and that had the task of supporting individualism: a central bank dispensing free credit to producers.

It is sometimes difficult to distill the precise meaning of Proudhon's proposals from his writings. As a writer, he was stronger on rhetoric than on clarity of expression. In particular, there is ambiguity in Proudhon as to whether his scheme was to answer the needs of small independent producers or to solve the problems of the industrial proletariat. However, one may also take these very ambiguities and moral rhetorics as archetypical for a certain strain of "populism" in modern socialist movements.

Proudhon's vague scheme of federated producers was carefully elaborated by authors belonging to the movement of *guild socialism* in Britain, which attained its greatest popularity in the years before and after World War I. Inspired originally by the idealized image of the medieval craftsman and his work, guild socialists adapted the idea of federated self-governing associations of "workers by hand and brain" to modern industrial conditions.[6]

In the French syndicalist offshoot of Proudhonism, the main accent is placed on the spontaneous action of the working class in making the transition to a system of economic self-determination at the production-sector level. In the new system, all management functions and entrepreneurial decision making would be absorbed by workers grouped in production syndicates. This is in contrast to trade unions conceived as wage-earners' interest organizations. The reason for associating this conception with anarchism is in the elimination from the model of all government functions and a complete reliance on society's capacity of voluntary self-regulation.[7]

---

[6] See. G. D. H. Cole, *Guild Socialism Re-stated*, Leonard Parsons, London, 1921; for excerpts, see Marshall I. Goldman, *Comparative Economic Systems: A Reader*, Random House, New York, 1964, pp. 13–30.

[7] Anarchism as a political tendency does not advocate anarchy in the sense of lawlessness, but an absence of centralized political power governing society by force, no matter how legitimized.

ACADEMIC UTOPIAS

Today, normative models of the type discussed in the preceding section would be branded as "institutionalist." They are, indeed, long on description of institutional arrangements, and short on the nature of the economic allocative mechanism. Objectives are not clearly specified, and superior performance is taken for granted, without much concern for proof or convincing demonstration. In contrast, proponents of normative systems among modern academic economists concentrate on the properties of the allocative mechanism and its ability to attain economic optimum.

This is true for each of the two broad types of academic normative models: the "capitalist" and the "socialist" ones. The main contending arguments are about the virtues of the respective allocation mechanisms, ownership arrangements, and incentives associated with them. They do not differ on objectives. For both, attainment of economic efficiency, i.e., optimality, is the goal.

Theory of Choice and Theory of Institutions

Thus, academic authors try hard to make their models professionally competent where institutionalist models look amateurish. Their lodestar is economic theory of allocation, which was reviewed in Chapter 5, as a prerequisite to the following survey of academic models. This tells something very important about the theory itself. The use of economic theory in the construction of normative models reveals its essentially normative character. Insofar as modern economics is grounded in the theory of choice and optimal allocation of resources, *it is not meant to describe or explain historical events but to formulate general rules of rational choice.* To account for that aspect, economic theory is sometimes interpreted as praxeology.[8]

Authors on the socialist side were particularly careful to stress this point. They wished to avoid having their use of bourgeois economic categories mistaken for advocacy of capitalism. William S. Vickrey, an exponent of applied welfare economics, expressed the issue in a paradox: "As a prescriptive theory, classical economics may be said to be the economics of socialism, in that it has a great deal to say, rightly or wrongly, about how a socialist regime ought to be run."[9] The same idea echoes in a statement by Abba P. Lerner, a prominent author of a normative model of mixed type: "The results of bourgeois economics are useful, not so much for describing the capitalist economy as for providing principles on which to run an economy organized in the general social interest (whether we call it socialist or not). The remoteness of a great part of economic theory from reality is nothing but a reflection of the remoteness of our existing economy from such an ideal state of affairs."[10]

The enunciation of abstract "principles on which to run an economy" leaves

---

[8] Oskar Lange, *Political Economy*, Pergamon, Oxford, 1963, vol. 1, pp. 148–207; Ludwig von Mises, *Human Action*, 3d rev. ed., Regnery, Chicago, 1963, pp. 30–71.

[9] William S. Vickrey, *Microstatics*, Harcourt, Brace & World, New York, 1964, p. 11.

[10] Abba P. Lerner, "Marxism and Economics: Sweezy and Robinson," *Journal of Political Economy*, vol. 53, no. 1, March 1965, p. 87.

the problem of rational choice suspended halfway. There remains the task of specifying what kinds of organizational arrangements—ownership, allocation mechanism, incentives—are optimal for the attainment of the optimum. Economic praxeology leaves off having formulated *operating principles* which are valid in the abstract. Theory of economic systems has to take over and complete the job: it has to investigate the relationship between the stated operating principles and alternative *institutional instrumentalities*. This part of theory proceeds on the assumption that different kinds of economic organization will not do equally well in making those principles work, and hence feels obliged to make normative recommendations as to appropriate institutions.

The contending recommendations of the "capitalist" and "socialist" system theorists revolve around the following question: *Is market the necessary institutional requirement for making rational economic calculations and optimal decisions?* What is known as the "socialism controversy" belongs to those famous great economic debates which punctuate the development of economic thought. Major contributions to the debate were made in the interwar period. In retrospect, it is clear that the debate, seemingly academic, dealt with issues of immense practical importance. This was brought home in particular in the sixties, when the debate was rekindled by the problems surrounding economic reforms of centralized systems in Eastern Europe and the Soviet Union.

The field of battle was predetermined by the formal definition of socialism given by most socialists of the time, or imputed to them. The distinguishing features of socialism, according to convention, were taken to be two: *public ownership of the means of production* (understood, most often, as plain state ownership) and *economic planning* (understood as the socialist alternative to capitalist markets). To look at the market as primarily a tool of coordination was dismissed out of hand because of its evident malfunctions. "Anarchy of the market" became the battle cry which, on the verbal plane, made planning appear superior by definition. The critique of the market seemed to absolve socialists from the obligation to demonstrate exactly how they imagined planned allocation without markets would work.

It is on this point that socialists were pressed for an answer by the advocates of capitalist models. *Ludwig von Mises* of the Austrian school, *Friedrich A. Hayek* of the Freiburg school, and *Lionell C. Robbins*, to name some of the best-known challengers, claimed that rational economic calculation was not feasible without actual markets. They did not deny that it was theoretically conceivable for rational calculation to take place in some central planning headquarters. Of course it was conceivable, provided one made the necessary assumptions about the planners' ability (1) to collect all the necessary information on consumer preferences and production functions, (2) to set up and solve fast enough all the corresponding simultaneous demand-and-supply equations for their equilibrium values, and (3) to assure implementation of these targets by the production sector. To "demonstrate" or, rather, to define such an abstract possibility was what Enrico Barone, the Italian disciple of Pareto, attempted in his article of 1908 "The Ministry of Production in the Collectivist State."[11] However, the quarrel was not about abstract possibilities based on assumptions concocted by freewheeling fantasy. It was about practical feasibility. In that respect, the challengers did not see any workable substitute for the market mechanism. They insisted further that, for a market to work optimally, there is no substitute for private property and the profit incentive.

The Lange Model

In the interwar period, most theorists of socialism still thought that the socialist economic system must be conceived as an antithesis of the market system. This is why academic critics of socialism could organize their attack around the thesis that socialism could not allocate resources rationally because it would be deprived of the necessary information which only market prices, as determined by market supply and demand, could provide. This is also why academic advocates of socialism felt they could answer the critics only by demonstrating the possibility of economic models capable of rational economic calculation without the instrumentality of markets and without private property. The most reputed version of such a model was devised by Oskar Lange in 1935–1937 in his article "On the Economic Theory of Socialism."[12] The article attained the status of a classic. This does not necessarily signify merit as to the quality of thought. A classic may be simply a piece of writing which was found convenient for use as a point of reference, or as training apparatus on which to exercise critical thinking of students.

Did Lange's essay really finish off the arguments of von Mises, Hayek, and their followers? Lange sincerely believed so. His triumphant conclusion reads as follows: "The Central Planning Board performs the functions of the market. . . . It follows that a substitution of planning for the functions of the market is quite possible and workable."[13]

In making this claim Lange must have momentarily forgotten that, a few pages earlier, he had explicitly mentioned a number of markets as elements of his model of socialism. Lange did not do away with the market. As we shall see, his central idea was merely to take out of the hands of "socialist managers" the authority to set prices and determine output levels according to the principles of profit maximization. The irony has been that most interpreters of Lange's essay have chosen to ignore the author's claim. His model has entered the history of economic thought as the first theoretical model of "market socialism," an intellectual Pyrrhic victory which left the fundaments of von Mises' arguments unshaken.

[11] Reprinted in Alec Nove and D. M. Nuti (eds.), *Socialist Economics*, Penguin, Hardmondsworth, England, 1972, pp. 52–74.

[12] Oskar Lange, "On the Economic Theory of Socialism," *Review of Economic Studies*, vol. 4, no. 1, October 1936, pp. 53–71, and no. 2, February 1937, pp. 123–142, reprinted in Oskar Lange and Fred M. Taylor, *On the Economic Theory of Socialism*, McGraw-Hill, New York, 1964, pp. 57–142, and excerpts in Nove and Nuti (eds.), op cit., pp. 92–110.

[13] Lange and Taylor, op. cit., pp. 82–83.

Let us summarize the main features of Lange's model. The model contains households supplying labor on the labor market and buying consumer goods on the consumer-goods market. Further, it contains publicly owned firms run by appointed socialist managers according to specific rules. The network of dealings in intermediate (capital) goods among firms is not considered a market, "in consequence of public ownership of the means of production."[14]

Production decisions are made by managers on the basis of *accounting prices of inputs* supplied by the Central Planning Board (CPB), and prices of final output sold to consumers.[15] Thus, the socialist manager is placed in the position of a textbook entrepreneur under textbook competitive conditions: He has no influence upon prices. He is a "price taker" or, as Lange puts it, he "is forced to regard prices as constant parameters independent of his behavior."[16] However, to make sure that all possibility of monopolistic maneuvering is excluded, Lange strikes out profit maximization as objective and incentive for his model. Profit maximization, as we know, might induce managers to manipulate output. By creating relative scarcity, managers might fool the Central Planning Board into raising the price and letting abnormal profits arise. In place of profit maximization, the manager is *instructed* directly to pursue the objective of optimal allocation. He receives *two categorical imperatives* to act by: (1) operate on the lowest attainable average cost schedule and (2) set the output flow at a level at which the parametrically given price is equal to marginal cost. The two rules trace out the path toward efficient, i.e., rational, allocation, provided prices reflect objective social valuation of inputs and products in terms of costs and benefits.

Thus, we are led back to the question of how the CPB goes about determining prices. In principle, the method is extremely simple. At the start, prices may be set arbitrarily, even though, in practice, the socialist regime would begin with prices inherited from capitalism. After that, prices would be adjusted by trial and error. All that was necessary would be to watch the movement of inventories: surpluses would indicate that lowering of prices was in order, shortages would call for raising prices, until equilibrium between demand and supply was reached.

Thus, on the basis of inventory movements, prices and wages are *set* by the CPB and then communicated, via detour through the CPB, to the participants in the system. Lange's managers are forbidden even to look at inventories, let alone to respond to their movements. They are screened off by the CPB agents, who take the reading of inventories themselves, adjust prices, and then show them to managers. Managers are to keep their eyes only on the price and marginal-cost gauge. Can one say in any meaningful sense that the CPB engages in "planning"? That it dispenses with the market? Doesn't the CPB in reality passively register what is happening as a result of quantities offered for sale and quantities actually bought? Isn't therefore the equilibrating price ultimately determined by what amounts to an interplay of supply and demand, i.e., of market forces?

---

[14] Ibid., p. 61.

[15] To distinguish accounting prices from market-determined prices, Lange also refers to them, following Wicksteed, as indexes of the "terms on which alternatives are offered." (Ibid., pp. 60–61.)

[16] Ibid., p. 65.

The answer to these questions decides the issue. What does take place in Lange's model is that pricing decisions are split off other managerial functions and made the exclusive preserve of a specialized agency—the CPB. True, this arrangement leads to a price structure different from what would emerge in a capitalist market under the impetus of profit maximization. (In particular, as we have noted, monopolistic price distortions could not arise in Lange's world.) However, the central point is that the primary source of data for price setting is the buying and selling behavior in the market. To refer to it as nonmarket planning is nothing but verbal legerdemain. The CPB activity is meant to simulate perfect competition and the attainment of the Pareto optimum. It does not replace the market itself.

There is one area of decision making where the market is fully superseded, however, and that is the aggregate rate of investment. The Central Planning Board takes upon itself this decision and sets the rate "arbitrarily," a method Lange considers more appropriate to socialism and superior to individual savings decisions. The global quota of investment funds is to be allocated among alternative uses by means of an interest rate charged to investors and set at a level such as to let the available investment fund be fully used up.

The distributed portion of nonwage incomes, the "social dividend," would be allocated among the population according to a rule of equality.[17]

There are many loose ends, unfilled gaps, and some inconsistencies in Lange's original account of his model. The trial-and-error method was to be used in determining prices of production resources and intermediate goods, as well as of consumer goods and wages of labor.[18] However, at an earlier place, Lange writes that "in the case of consumers' goods and services of labor [prices] are determined on a market; in all other cases they are fixed by the Central Planning Board."[19] If the second statement were allowed to stand, then prices could not be given parametrically to firms selling consumer goods, nor wages in their hiring of labor.

One of the unresolved and untouched questions of the model is the determination of prices in declining-cost industries. If prices were adjusted as a function of inventory movements following the ordinary trial-and-error rules of the model, the results in a declining-cost industry could be perverse. Setting the price tentatively higher than the marginal cost at its point of intersection with the demand schedule would lead to a supply deficit, decline in inventories, and queuing. The CPB would raise the price to encourage larger output. However, the rule ordering firms to produce up to where price equals marginal cost would lead to a still lower output (see Figure 6-1)!

However, these are minor points which Lange could have taken care of in a more definitive treatment. The element which could not be easily corrected is the unsatisfactory treatment of the problem of *managerial incentives*. The place of the

[17] Ibid., pp. 99–103.
[18] Ibid., p. 86.
[19] Ibid., p. 78.

Figure 6-1 Lange's model: where the pricing rule fails.

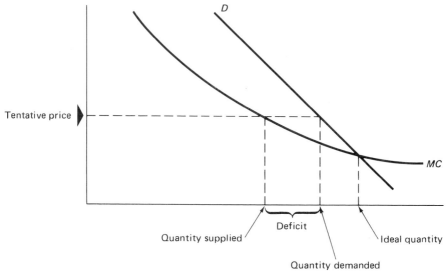

Changing prices according to the movement of inventories would lead to perverse results in declining-cost industries. If the price is set tentatively above the level of intersection between the demand schedule and marginal cost, and managers follow the rule of producing at the point where the price equals marginal cost, demand will exceed the quantity supplied. Depletion of inventories would lead the price administrators to raise the price, which would only make the situation worse.

profit motive is presumably taken by the *internalized professional ethic* of a manager trained in the skill of following the system's rules. It would be rash to dismiss this type of motivation as inconceivable. To some extent it operates even under capitalism, and a large stretch of the human race's journey toward higher and higher productivity was traversed, after all, without capitalist profit incentives! Nevertheless, Lange himself was not quite sure about the dependability of moral and professional incentives under advanced industrial conditions, and he voiced concern that "*the real danger of socialism, is that of a bureaucratization of economic life.*"[20] Therefore, F. A. Hayek's emphasis on the compelling force of competition should not be taken lightly: "The force which in a competitive society brings about the reduction of price to the lowest cost at which the quantity saleable at that cost can be produced is the opportunity for anybody who knows a cheaper method to come in at his own risk and to attract customers by underbidding the other producers. But if prices are fixed by the authority this method is excluded."[21]

Lange's ideas bear a mark of the times in which they were formulated. The Great Depression, which engulfed most advanced capitalist economies in the

[20] Ibid., p. 109 (italics in the original).

[21] Friedrich A. Hayek, "Socialist Calculation: The Competitive 'Solution,'" *Economica*, New Series, vol. 7, no. 26, May 1940, p. 139. Reprinted in M. Bornstein (ed.), *Comparative Economic Systems*, Irwin, Homewood, Ill., 1965, p. 88.

nineteen-thirties, made argumentation about the superiority of market allocation sound hollow. Capitalist response to the Depression was often in a retreat from competition to cartelization, retrenchment of investment activities, and reluctance to innovate. If critics discovered flaws in Lange's reasoning, he could always counter by pointing to the real flaws of capitalism at the time of his writing.[22]

However, on the principal theoretical issue, the academic designers of socialist alternatives to the capitalist market model have effectively lost the argument: market forces had to be acknowledged as a necessary socioeconomic mechanism for revealing, through prices, the cost and benefit relations on which rational economic calculation must be based.

Lerner's Model

With Oskar Lange, as we have seen, the point was conceded implicitly since overtly Lange apparently remained confused about the meaning of his demonstration. The pretense was entirely dropped in the next generation of models after Lange. In the economic system constructed by Abba P. Lerner,[23] we find the author reintroducing, with no apologies, market competition and private profit incentives. The operating principle of Lerner's model is the same as that of Lange's, namely, running the economy in the general social interest, technically defined by marginal-cost pricing and all the other conditions of optimality in allocation. In economic literature one often comes across references to a "Lange-Lerner model," presumably because the basic operating principle is the same for both. This is rather misleading since, with respect to institutional instrumentalities, Lerner's model is profoundly different. Lerner is undogmatic about ownership relations. His model "denies both collectivism and private enterprise as *principles* for the organization of society, but recognizes both of them as perfectly legitimate means."[24] Whatever works in the direction of the objective is acceptable:

> Where private enterprise would lead to an optimum division of a factor among its products *and is not in conflict with any of the other aims of society* it is preferable to its alternative of state enterprise with the managers subject to the Rule. . . . Private enterprise is preferable because there is a closer identity of the interest of the manager with the social interest.[25]

However, Lerner is concerned, just as Lange was, about the danger of monopolistic tendencies, where the interest of the private-enterprise manager departs from the social interest in optimal output proportions. Lerner's safeguard is

---

[22] See Lange and Taylor, op. cit., pp. 110–115. For example, "The real issue is *whether the further maintenance of the capitalist system is compatible with economic progress*" (p. 110; italics in the original). Or "In present capitalism the maintenance of the value of the particular investment has become the high concern. Accordingly, interventionism and restrictionism are the dominant economic policies" (p. 114).

[23] Abba P. Lerner, *The Economics of Control*, Macmillan, New York, 1944.

[24] Ibid., p. 5 (italics in the original).

[25] Ibid., pp. 83–84 (italics in the original).

the device to which he gave the puzzling name of "counterspeculation." It amounts to the government's estimating "what would be the price of the good that would make demand equal to supply if there were no restrictions of the kind we wish to abolish."[26] The actual market price is allowed to emerge from real transactions in the market. The previously estimated price is, however, the one that is made legitimate for firms to earn and keep. If the actual market price turns out higher, the firm is expected to turn the difference over to the government. If it is lower (because, for instance, firms produced too much), the government reimburses firms for the difference. In that sense, the price is "guaranteed," as Lerner puts it.

The device would seem to be effective in allaying the fear of excessively low prices, a fear counseling firms to hold output down out of caution.[27] However Lerner had difficulties explaining how firms would be prevented from playing monopolistic games through output restrictions which were not motivated by caution but by a desire of monopolistic prices and profits. It is clear that "counterspeculation" contains no automatic mechanism to prevent that, and some administrative intervention would be necessary.[28]

In the determination of the investment rate and the allocation of investment funds, Lerner follows Lange quite closely. The real forte of Lerner's model is the treatment of *macroeconomic problems of stabilization*, which overshadow by far the prescriptions touching on microallocation. Thus, in the distribution of the "social dividend," concern with stabilizing aggregate demand is paramount. Social dividend is the equivalent of profits available for distribution, presumably collected centrally and distributed in equal shares to the population. However, the volume of such payments would be varied according to the needs of stabilizing aggregate demand. This and similar principles in government taxation and expenditure made up Lerner's concept of "functional finance." Obviously of Keynesian inspiration, the concept became part and parcel of pragmatic normative models, used in modern policies of stabilization through demand management (see Chapter 10).

In contrast to Lange, Lerner eschews the designation of his model as socialist. Interested as he is in expounding the real content of his system, he fears the danger of labels. Even though he refers occasionally to "collectivist society," he favors the term *"service economy*, since it is the question of which method *serves best* that determines which is to be used."[29]

Vanek's "Participatory Economy"

Among academic normative models, the most recent one, worked out by Jaroslav Vanek in the sixties (the published version appeared in 1970), is probably also the

---

[26] Ibid., p. 55.

[27] This reflects the experience of the Great Depression with relative overproduction, ruinous declines of prices, and attempts of firms at coordinating production, keeping it at lower levels, through the formation of cartels. Thus, Lerner's model also bears the mark of the times, as Lange's does (see footnote 22 above).

[28] See Abba P. Lerner, "An Integrated Full Employment Policy," in A. P. Lerner and F. D. Graham (eds.), *Planning and Paying for Full Employment*, Princeton University Press, Princeton, N.J., 1946, pp. 174–176. For an evaluative interpretation, see William J. Baumol, *Welfare Economics and the Theory of the State*, 2d ed., Harvard, Cambridge, Mass., 1969, pp. 105–108.

[29] Lerner, *The Economics of Control*, p. 5 (italics in the original).

one which is most elaborate and thought through. Its full "official" title is the *labor-managed market economy*, whereas "participatory economy" is its popular brand name. The emphasis is on the democratic process of decision making within the firm and on the nature of incentives. The highest source of decision-making authority is the full working staff of a firm—one cannot call them "employees" because they are essentially self-employed—even though specialized elective management may be charged with executive tasks. The central target variable of the firm is income per worker, or disposable value added per worker, which the working staff has an incentive to maximize.

Striving for optimality (on the system's terms) follows automatically from that objective, and from the fact that firms operate in a competitive market environment, which may be upheld against monopolistic temptations, if need be, by external price fixing on the part of central authorities. There are no special formal rules for the managers to follow, as in Lange's model. There are no profits to maximize, as in the model of perfect competition, or in Lerner. As a separate category, profits are gone. They fuse, so to speak, with wages into a single category of labor income.

It would be wrong to interpret Vanek's model as a simple formalization of a system of producer cooperatives. With these it does have one feature in common: democratic structure of authority within the firm. However, the ownership of material assets has an entirely different form. The working staff of the firm does not have any collective ownership title to the managed assets. There are no personal ownership shares either. If anything, the staff *owes* the value of its capital, though not to any titular owners, such as stockholders in a capitalist corporation, nor to any nebulous titular owner, such as the nation or the state under state capitalism. Indeed, there may not exist any *titular* owners at all, but only creditors. This has to do with one of the truly original features of the model, which is the method firms are obliged to use to finance their investments, namely, by long-term renewable credit.

This arrangement has a number of important prerequisites, as well as consequences. The essential prerequisite is a well-developed market for investible funds, i.e., "capital market," in the usual terminology. Investible funds are raised exclusively through the sale of securities having the character of bonds bearing fixed interest. On the point of who sells these securities, and how the funds reach the labor-managed firm, there seem to be some variations in Vanek's writings. It may be a bank, the government, or some other financial intermediaries, which then lend the money to the firm for projects deemed worthy of undertaking, or it may be the labor-managed firm itself, offering bonds directly to the public. Whatever the case may be, in principle, all such funds must be repaid, with interest, to the bondholders, and resold again for a new run of maturity.

The major consequence of this arrangement is that labor-managed firms are prevented from using their own earnings for reinvestment. Autofinancing from internally generated funds (equivalent of "retained profits") is excluded. Such funds (e.g., depreciation allowances used for repayment of borrowed principal, together with interest) always return to the social "pool" of investible funds and are always reallocated afresh among the firms under nondiscriminatory conditions. This makes it difficult for particular firms to perpetuate an initial advantage they may have, to consolidate their financial position, and to create private investment empires of the capitalist type.

It is understood that the interest rate must not be set at an arbitrarily low level but be as high as warranted by the scarcity of savings and productivity of real capital accumulated thanks to the savings. Since the collected interest payments are to be the major source of net investment financing, it is clear that the level of the interest rate strongly determines what the proportion of saving in national income would be. Vanek seems to favor this proportion to be decided centrally, though democratically. This implies setting the interest rate on loans at a corresponding level, and possibly overriding the lower rate which would probably be established through individual saving decisions in a free and atomistic capital market.

In this manner, Vanek's scheme solves a dilemma which has bothered many analysts of labor-managed systems. In his model, the question of how much to save is taken out of the hands of firms and their collectives. They do not have to struggle with their consciences about how to divide the firms' revenues between the immediately distributed portion and the portion to be saved and reinvested. They do not have to worry about people contributing to savings in one firm, and then not being entitled to any of the earnings when they move out or retire (which is why there may be widespread reluctance to reinvest the firm's revenues). These are the typical concerns in a Yugoslav firm (see Chapter 17), but not in Vanek's model, although it has been sometimes identified, wrongly, with the Yugoslav system.

However, aside from the formal arrangements which are meticulously specified, the author sees the greatest source of efficiency in the unshackling of incentives to work longer, better, more intensively, and with enthusiasm. With the opposition between the interests of labor and employers gone, the motivation to hold back on performance evaporates. Harvey Leibenstein incorporated these aspects of productivity in his concept of X-Efficiency, i.e., efficiency traceable to factors other than the formal rules of optimizing discussed in Chapter 5.[30] Vanek's estimate of the potential gains due to the transition to his model may strike some readers as extravagant—"effort" may be reasonably expected to increase up to eight-fold[31]—but he undoubtedly touches upon an important aspect of economic systems performance which had not been getting due attention before Leibenstein and Vanek.

Eastern European "Revisionists"

The final vindication of the market came from economists in countries which underwent the practical experience with systems which had suppressed market

---

[30] See H. Leibenstein, "Allocative Efficiency vs. X-Efficiency," *American Economic Review*, vol. 56, June 1966, pp. 392–415; also "Aspects of the X-Efficiency Theory of the Firm," *The Bell Journal of Economics*, vol. 6, no. 2, Autumn 1975, pp. 580–606, and his book *Beyond Economic Man*, Harvard, Cambridge, Mass., 1976.

[31] J. Vanek, *The General Theory of Labor Managed Market Economies*, Cornell, Ithaca, N.Y., 1970, p. 237.

forces almost completely. In the Soviet Union and Eastern Europe, centrally administered systems operated for decades on the basis of planners' subjective judgments. In this, planners acted unassisted by objective valuation of costs and benefits, neither of their own nor of the consumers. As far as choices in allocation were concerned, decisions were made either by ignoring the optimality problem, or by following routine, or various rules of thumb, i.e., by groping in the dark. The economies "worked," but efficiency manifestly suffered.

We shall have occasion to examine the matter more thoroughly in Chapter 9. Here we only wish to note that, from criticism of centralized allocation, numerous Eastern European economists moved in the sixties toward proposals of various "new economic models" which reserved a prominent role for the market mechanism. However, unlike A. P. Lerner, they had to reaffirm at every step their allegiance to socialism as the official ideology. For political reasons they were not free to explain the merits of their market models on pragmatic grounds and leave it at that. Hence, the old idea of socialism replacing the market by planning had to be revised. As for "public ownership," "revisionists" held on to it as of old. As for planning, it also was kept but it was not presented any more as an *alternative* to market allocation but as an activity complementary to the market, and conducted on the foundation of a market economy.[32] The best-known representatives of this new doctrine of "market socialism," which owes very little to Lange, are the Polish economist W. Brus and the Czech economist Ota Šik.[33] However, it would be misleading to connect these normative models with any particular personality. They emerged as truly collective work of a host of capable economists in Poland, Czechoslovakia, and Hungary, following independently in the direction started in Yugoslavia around 1951.[34] Even the Soviet Union has a few representatives who were able to publish their views during a transitory period of relaxation after 1965.[35]

While conceding the importance of the market for rational economic calculation and allocation, the new doctrine seems to be successfully disputing the other fundamental tenet of the von Mises–Hayek market-capitalist school, namely, the necessity of private ownership for the functioning of the market. Eastern European "revisionists" present market allocation as being just as compatible with public ownership of means of production. All that needs to be done is to grant *operational autonomy to individual production units.* Prices and profits can serve as signals for allocation, without the pursuit of profit supplying motivation and incentives.

However, at closer inspection it turns out that, even in that respect, Eastern

[32] As a postscript to Vanek's model, it also has room for planning activities of the "indicative" sort (see Chap. 10, section on France), supplementing, assisting, and guiding the market.

[33] See Wlodzimierz Brus, *The Market in a Socialist Economy*, Routledge, London, 1972 (Polish original appeared in 1964); Ota Šik, *Plan and Market under Socialism*, International Arts and Sciences Press, Inc., White Plains, N.Y., 1967.

[34] Deborah D. Milenkovitch, *Plan and Market in Yugoslav Economic Thought*, Yale, New Haven, Conn., 1971.

[35] For example, G. S. Lisichkin, *Plan i rynok* (Plan and the Market), Izdatelstvo "Ekonomika," Moscow, 1966.

European models contain significant concessions. Managerial incentives are, as a rule, tied to managerial performance in terms of realized profits. Thus, models of market socialism simulate an important element of private ownership as well: Managers exercise not only the function of custody, but combine it also with an incentive system based on certain rights of usufruct.

*   *   *

Be it said in conclusion that the victory of promarket arguments does not signify that market allocation is thereby vindicated in all respects. F. Hayek and von Mises never spent much time on questions of declining-cost industries, external effects, public goods, and tendencies of market economies to fluctuate. This happens to be the class of economic phenomena where competitive markets fail, for one reason or another, to lead to optimal solutions. These "market failures" will occupy us in Chapters 7, 8, and 10, which examine the working and performance of market-capitalist systems at a more concrete level. There exist no general normative models offering a design of an institutional setting capable of optimally taking care of these problematic areas of "market failures." There are some piecemeal suggestions, such as that of Kenneth Arrow's "courts of externalities" (see Chapter 8), but otherwise we have only the abstract normative prescriptions of welfare economics devoid of any institutional grounding which, however, is what economic systems are about. Models that would incorporate markets' virtues, while also dealing optimally with areas where markets fail—such models are still in search of their authors.

MARXIAN MODEL OF THE POSTCAPITALIST SYSTEM

Marx's approach to setting up a normative model belongs definitely to the "evolving-system" school. Among the socialist systems designs, his is the most consequent elaboration of the idea that normative systems cannot be imposed upon society at will, and by will alone. In fact, Marx developed his conception through the critique of utopian blueprints and in opposition to socialist currents whose representatives, such as Auguste Blanqui, advocated introduction of some a priori "socialist alternative" from above, after a successful takeover of political power by a group of determined revolutionaries. Marx's as well as Friedrich Engels's disdain for such notions cannot be emphasized strongly enough because, by curious twists and turns of history, those very notions came to be tagged Marxist, in the public mind as well as in the mind of many latter-day Marxists.

Process of Realization   "Setting up a normative model," therefore, does not quite correspond to Marx's understanding of the relationship between, on the one hand, the socialist system as a goal and, on the other, existing capitalist reality. Socialism for him is not an *alternative* to capitalism. It is not some kind of an ideal system, ready to be introduced after an "overthrow" of capitalism, or *instead* of capitalism (in countries set for industrialization), any time its adherents feel they have the political power to do so.

Socialism for Marx was a developmental stage to emerge through the working of certain key tendencies inherent in capitalism itself. In his view, the "elements" needed "for a new and higher form" are prepared "within the womb" of capitalism, the central one being the *secular increase in labor productivity*. These elements are "set free" when the hierarchic organization of production relations on the basis of classes becomes "incompatible" with labor productivity, once that variable attains a certain critical level.

One can grasp this conception fully only by referring to Marx's structuralist model of society and its dynamics, in its sophisticated version presented in Chapter 2. We shall take it up once more in Chapter 18, dealing with the change and succession of economic systems, where it belongs. Here we jot down a rough outline, just enough to frame the discussion of the features of Marx's image of socialism.

In what sense is the key tendency, growth of labor productivity, supposed to become incompatible with the systemic features of capitalism? The point is that growth of labor productivity is itself just an aspect of the structural development of capitalism which involves constant changes in its systemic features. It is their effect, but it also provokes them. It is at the crossroads of a host of interdependent and interacting phenomena. Labor productivity plus the wage-labor system generates profits; profits lead to accumulation of real capital; expanded scale of enterprises leads to the discovery of new technologies, new division of labor; workers become at first stunted live appendages of machinery; their protest movement leads to shortening of the working time; this leads to further development of laborsaving technology; constant change requires a broader training of workers to secure flexible, all-purpose operatives; growth of enterprises in scale is facilitated by the development of the capital market, securities (bonds and stocks), and the corporate form; this is part of the process of concentration of output in a smaller number of firms; mergers and bankruptcies mean expropriation of some capitalists by others, and the corporate form downgrades capitalist owners to mere investors; shorter work hours, higher real wages, improvements in working conditions, and organized struggle through which they are obtained are all part of the process of emancipation of the working class from a state of poverty, uncertainty, and passivity of manipulated objects. It is by going through this complex historical experience that the system, as well as its human participants, "matures" for an eventual transition to a system which is not capitalism anymore.

That transition raises the issue of the socialist revolution. While the above reconstruction of the process of change is easy to document, statement by statement, from Marx's writings, his idea of the socialist revolution requires careful interpretation of all the relevant passages. What is certain is that Marx's structuralist conception of the dynamics of social change precludes a simple reduction of the concept of socialist revolution to a dramatic one-time event of a political nature. However, more will be said about that in Chapter 18. Now we shall try to assemble a few of the specific features of Marx's model of the postcapitalist system, insofar as they can be gleaned from his not too numerous and mostly incidental remarks.

"What Would Marx's Socialism Be Like?"   It has been repeatedly stated that Marx did not leave any blueprint for the socialist system of the future. He seems to have adopted the attitude that humanity would cross those bridges when it got to them. It was not up to him to indulge in painting programmatic pictures of the future. He was saying, in effect, he would then be regressing to utopian daydreaming. Building socialist air castles might have been an understandable occupation as long as there was not yet any real workers' movement. Once that was established, the task of a "scientific socialist" was to participate in its concrete struggles, to try and clarify its perspectives, and thus to advance practically both the self-dissolving tendency of capitalism to increase labor productivity and the process of self-emancipation of workers.

Now, it is quite correct that Marx, in talking about the socialist future, kept away as much as he could from descriptive detail. He preferred to remain at the level of general definitions such as "community of free individuals, carrying on their work with the means of production in common,"[36] or "associated producers rationally regulating their interchange with Nature, . . . and achieving this with the least expenditure of energy and under conditions most favourable to, and worthy of, their human nature,"[37] or, in the words of the *Communist Manifesto*, "an association in which the free development of each is the condition for the free development of all." However, he could not avoid specifics entirely. It is, therefore, possible to speak of Marx's model of socialism at least in terms of a few major operating principles.

One set of specific features of the postcapitalist system one sees regularly mentioned are the rules governing the distribution of output. Commenting on a program draft of the German socialist party, Marx argued against the illusion that a postcapitalist system could leap directly into a state ruled by the principle: *From each according to his ability, to each according to his needs.* True to his evolving-system conception, he foresaw a transitional phase "which is . . . in every respect, economically, morally and intellectually, still stamped with the birthmarks of the old society from whose womb it emerges."[38] During this "first phase of communist society," claims to the consumable portion of output would be distributed in proportion to individual contributions of labor time.

As for the mode of resource allocation, Marx's writings contain a few vague utterances concerning a "definite social plan" which would allocate labor time so as to maintain "the proper proportion between the different kinds of work to be done and the various wants of the community."[39] Marx contrasts this kind of conscious attempt "to socially control and regulate the process of production" with capitalist market processes which tend toward equilibrium only through the anarchy of trial and error, "chance and caprice," and a constant upsetting of equilibrium.[40] It is understandable that most Marx interpreters should have con-

---

[36] K. Marx, *Capital*, vol. III, p. 78.

[37] Ibid., vol. III, p. 820.

[38] K. Marx, *Critique of the Gotha Program*, in Robert C. Tucker (ed.), *The Marx-Engels Reader*, Norton, New York, 1972, p. 286.

[39] K. Marx, *Capital*, vol. I, p. 79.

[40] Ibid., pp. 355–356, passim.

cluded that the mechanism of supply and demand had no place in his socialist scheme of things. Some have even read into his words a prescription of central-command planning of the Soviet type. However, the issue is much more complex.

First of all, it is necessary to realize that the allocation problem under socialism was very much on Marx's mind, even though he was unable to give it an exact formulation which he might have chosen had he worked out his theories after Marshall, Edgeworth, Walras, and Pareto. Marx thought of allocation primarily as a matter of economy of time. Thus, he wrote:

> Assuming communal production, the time aspect remains, of course, essential. . . . As with the single individual, the integrality of [society's] development, of its gratifications and its activity depend on saving time. All economy boils down to economy of time, after all. Likewise, society must allocate its time purposefully in order to secure a correspondence between production and the totality of its needs.[41]

Such allocation would draw upon information supplied by bookkeeping which "becomes the more necessary the more the process assumes a social scale and loses its purely individual character. It is therefore . . . more necessary in collective production than in capitalist production."[42] However, Marx did not provide a satisfactory answer to the question of socialist pricing, nor did he elaborate on the mechanics of communication between individual wants and the production sector.

In a few spots, Marx seems to have taken it for granted that products would be priced in proportion with the amount of labor time needed in their production.[43] However, in another set of passages, Marx and even more his close friend and collaborator, Engels, have criticized those doctrines of socialism which would introduce direct calculation of product "prices" in terms of labor time and thereby abolish the capitalist system of commodity production and exchange.[44] The clearest (though not absolutely clear) statement as to the indispensable role of demand under socialism is contained in Engels's critique of the socialist allocation system devised by the German economist J. K. Rodbertus:

> Only through the undervaluation or overvaluation of products is it forcibly brought home to the individual commodity producers what things and what quantity of them society requires or does not require. But it is just this sole regulator that the utopia in which Rodbertus also shares would abolish. And if we then ask what guarantee we have that necessary quantity and not more of each product will be produced, that we shall not go hungry in regard to corn and meat while we are choked in beet sugar and drowned in potato spirit, that we shall not lack trousers to cover our nakedness while trouser buttons flood us in millions—Rodbertus triumphantly shows us his famous calculation, according to which the correct certificate has been handed out for every

---

[41] K. Marx, *Grundrisse der politischen Ökonomie*, Dietz Verlag, Berlin, 1953, p. 89 (our translation). See K. Marx, *Grundrisse* (English translation by Martin Nicolaus), Random House, New York, 1973, pp. 172–173.
[42] K. Marx, *Capital*, vol. II, p. 135.
[43] See Joan Robinson, *An Essay on Marxian Economics*, Macmillan, London, 1949, pp. 23–28.
[44] See F. Engels's introduction to K. Marx, *The Poverty of Philosophy*, International Publishers, New York, 1963, and Marx's appendix, pp. 203–206.

superfluous pound of sugar, for every unsold barrel of spirit, for every unusable trouser button. . . . [45]

If this passage means what it seems to mean, then it badly needs to be reconciled in an outspoken way with Marx's assumption that, under socialism, products would not be exchanged in markets as commodities anymore but would be handled through some kind of transfers, as results of "directly socialized labor." However, this is not a place for critical exegesis of texts. What mostly comes across from Marx's and Engels's treatment of allocation under socialism is that they kept coming to the edge of the problem, could not get a solid grip on it, and so left it at generalities.

In dealing with the question, one should probably distinguish between the postcapitalist medium-term and the very, very long-term development. Marx took it for granted that numerous institutional elements would be initially carried over, as a legacy of capitalism, into the postcapitalist era. There is no reason to assume he thought the mode of allocation would be an exception. In the long run, however, technological developments would pull the rug from underneath item-by-item cost calculations based on the input of labor time.

This is what Marx is effectively suggesting in a most remarkable passage, bordering on science fiction socialist style, in the *Grundrisse*.[46] There, Marx paints a state of technology amounting to full automation and analyzes its consequences. Work as we know it will have ceased to be part of the production process. Wielding of instruments will be superseded by mere external supervision of natural forces adapted to industrial ends. Current labor input will be minimal. The true source of productivity will be mankind's "understanding of nature and mastery thereof via its existence as a social collective—in one word, the development of the socialized individual, which appears as the great center post of production and wealth."

Speaking in narrow economic terms, we might say that, under these conditions, productive activities become all fixed general overhead. Not being part of variable cost, and being in any case of negligible duration, "labor time stops, as it must stop, being the measure [of wealth], and hence exchange value [the measure] of use value." Nowhere else did Marx provide a better glimpse of what he meant by level of labor productivity becoming incompatible with the transitory economic and institutional categories of capitalism.

In Marx's model, or rather image, of the postcapitalist future, it is the cultural impact of changes in the economic system which matters most. In its ultimate form, the postcapitalist system is a single worldwide system—an extrapolation of the expansionist tendency of capitalism. Art, literature, science, the world view have leveled nationalist boundaries with the help of economic relations. Division of labor has ceased branding individuals as members of narrow occupational and class categories; humans have become "species-beings" who happen to be active in this or that specialty, without being defined by it. Mutuality in human rela-

---

[45] Ibid., p. 19. The "correct certificate" refers to the count of labor time used up in producing different articles.

[46] K. Marx, *Grundrisse der politischen Ökonomie*, German original, pp. 592–594 (our translation); English translation by Nicolaus, op. cit., pp. 704–706.

tions has replaced antagonism. Individualism has ceased to be an assertion of oneself against others. Humanity has become free to create its own identity instead of being shaped by uncontrolled forces of history. From that point of view, changes in the economic system are seen by Marx as mere preconditions enabling mankind to get down to its real business. This is presumably what young Marx tried to convey when he wrote that "communism is not as such the goal of human development."[47]

* * *

Our survey is completed. It has covered only a selection of cases illustrating major approaches to the art, or sport, of designing normative economic systems. There would be no end to the list of utopian models. Neither could we go into popular versions of the model of "ideal capitalism," such as many readers might have come across in the writings of Ayn Rand[48] or L. O. Kelso.[49] We also have had to be satisfied with only an occasional hint at the various simplified or distorted versions of the Marxian model, without taking them apart. However, enough was said to provide the normative territory with markers enabling the students to cruise on their own.

We now turn to examining, in Chapters 7 and 8, the working of the real, not normative, model of market capitalism. However, the exposition of input-output accounting, which follows, provides also a theoretical framework for better understanding of centrally administered systems, to be discussed in Chapter 9, as well as of the French-type indicative planning we come to in Chapter 10.

BIBLIOGRAPHY

Boguslaw, Robert: *The New Utopians*, Prentice-Hall, Englewood Cliffs, N.J., 1965.

Lichtheim, George: *The Origins of Socialism*, Praeger, New York, 1969.

International Encyclopedia of the Social Sciences (1968), entries "Utopianism," "Fourier, Charles," "Saint-Simon," "Proudhon, Pierre Joseph" (bibliographies).

Encyclopedia of the Social Sciences (1932), entries "Communistic Settlements," "Communism," "Socialism," "Anarchism," "Utopias," "Owen and Owenism," "Fourier and Fourierism," "Brook Farm" (bibliographies).

von Mises, Ludwig: "Economic Calculation in Socialism," *Socialism: An Economic and Sociological Analysis*, Yale, New Haven, Conn., 1951, reprinted in Morris Bornstein (ed.), *Comparative Economic Systems: Models and Cases*, Irwin, Homewood, Ill., 1965, pp. 61–67.

Hayek, Friedrich A.: "Socialist Calculation: The Competitive 'Solution,'" *Economica*, New Series, vol. 7, no. 26, May 1940, pp. 125–149, reprinted in Morris Bornstein (ed.), *Comparative Economic Systems: Models and Cases*, Irwin, Homewood, Ill., 1965, pp. 77–97.

Lange, Oskar, and Fred M. Taylor: *On the Economic Theory of Socialism*, McGraw-Hill,

---

[47] Economic and Philosophical Manuscripts (1844), in David McLellan, *Karl Marx: Early Texts*, Basil Blackwell, Oxford, 1971, p. 157.

[48] For example, Ayn Rand, *For the New Intellectual: The Philosophy of Ayn Rand*, Random House, New York, 1961; A. Rand et al., *Capitalism: The Unknown Ideal*, New American Library, New York, 1966.

[49] Louis O. Kelso and Mortimer J. Adler, *The Capitalist Manifesto*, Random House, New York, 1958.

New York, 1964.

Nove, Alec, and D. M. Nuti (eds.): *Socialist Economics*, Penguin, Hardmondsworth, England, 1972.

Ward, Benjamin N.: *The Socialist Economy: A Study of Organizational Alternatives*, Random House, New York, 1967.

Lerner, Abba P.: *The Economics of Control*, Macmillan, New York, 1946.

Roberts, Paul Craig: "Oskar Lange's Theory of Socialist Planning," *Journal of Political Economy*, vol. 79, no. 3, May–June 1971, pp. 562–577.

Rosefielde, Steven: "Some Observations on the Concept of 'Socialism' in Contemporary Economic Theory," *Soviet Studies*, vol. 25, no. 2, October 1973, pp. 229–243.

Vanek, Jaroslav: *The General Theory of Labor Managed Market Economies*, Cornell, Ithaca, N.Y., 1970.

————: *The Participatory Economy*, Cornell, Ithaca, N.Y., 1971.

————: "The Yugoslav Economy Viewed through the Theory of Labor Management," *World Development*, vol. 1, no. 9, September 1973, pp. 39–56.

———— (ed.): *Self-Management: Economic Liberation of Man*, Penguin, Harmondsworth, England, 1975.

Brus, Wlodzimierz: *The Market in a Socialist Economy*, Routledge, London, 1972.

Šik, Ota: *Plan and Market under Socialism*, International Arts and Sciences Press, Inc., White Plains, N.Y., 1967.

Milenkovitch, Deborah D.: *Plan and Market in Yugoslav Economic Thought*, Yale, New Haven, Conn., 1971.

Sherman, Howard J.: "The Economics of Pure Communism," *Soviet Studies*, vol. 22, no. 1, July 1970, pp. 24–36.

Tucker, Robert C.: *The Marxian Revolutionary Idea*, Norton, New York, 1969.

Banks, J. A.: *Marxist Sociology in Action*, Faber, London, 1970.

Chapter 7

Coordination
of Economic
Activities

A lack of coordination of the parts resulting in a poor overall performance can create a tyranny of circumstance over individuals, an absence of effective choice. . . . A failure of the government to intervene can be destructive of private discretion no less than its intervention.

Neil W. Chamberlain

To provide the wherewithal for the satisfaction of human wants, society must have a way of apportioning the global production task among its members. We know the distribution-of-tasks phenomenon under the name division of labor. We have surveyed the ways in which society may go about apportioning the global task when we discussed classification of systems by mode of allocation in Chapter 4. In Chapter 5, we have examined what conditions must be fulfilled if a system using a given mode of allocation cares about having the reputation of a system tending toward optimality. However, we have not yet talked much about the hurdles which real economic systems must negotiate if they are to come anywhere near their full production potential, to say nothing of their ability to attain optimal product proportions.

To prepare the ground, we have to stop treating the production sector as if one firm had nothing to do with other firms. We cannot concentrate exclusively on their contacts with customers. Most firms do not produce their articles from scratch. They use inputs of material and producer durables produced and supplied by other firms. Therefore, consumers' demand for final goods requires coordination between firms catering to final demand, their suppliers, and suppliers of their suppliers.

Clearly, we are talking of coordination in economic systems of some complexity. We do not want to lose time on small-scale systems, such as tribal economies, where relevant information is easily available by direct observation. There the system is "transparent." Coordination can be taken care of by means of direct communication between members interacting in direct social contact with each other, and adjustments are easily arranged. It is in situations where the system is not so easily surveyable, where participants are too numerous and their relationships too complex to be grasped and controlled directly, that the problem of coordination begins.

Intellectually, the problem of coordination can be grasped, despite its complexity. The structure of transactions between firms, as well as between firms and final demand, can be presented compactly with the help of the ingenious device of *input-output accounting*. To explain its principles is the object of the first section.

We further need to gain insight into the process of adjustment to various changes in demand, be it final demand or intermediate demand for inputs. The question of speed of adjustments is of special importance. If they drag, the system as a whole may slack off and slide away from its full employment potential. We shall examine this mechanism under its usual name of the *multiplier effect*.

There are other hidden responses of firms to decisions made by other participants in the system. Especially reactions in the area of investments with respect to demand changes and multiplier effects may be of the sort that aggravates these effects further. We are alluding to the *accelerator effect*, also to be taken up later.

A streak of the tragic attaches to these economic mechanisms: Normally, there is nobody who wants these chains of repercussions to be activated. They just happen, but when they do, they force participants in the system to do things they do not want to do. There seem to be built-in obstacles to a smooth adjustment between the wishes of participants and the actual working of the system.

As we discuss these obstacles, we shall be circling around such perennial questions as: Can decentralized markets do a dependable coordinating job? Or do they need assistance on the part of the government? Is central administrative planning able to improve upon the performance of decentralized markets? Is it in control of economic mechanisms, or is it just suppressing their overt manifestations? Or is it beset by other flaws which make the abandonment of the market system a costly affair?

THE INPUT-OUTPUT FRAMEWORK

The purpose of input-output accounting is to make transparent the structure of transactions linking up the system's participants (firms and final users) into an interconnected network. We shall first show how this network presented itself before one hit upon the input-output method.

Let us take, as a starting point, an imaginary economy that lives by bread, furniture, and cars alone. Let us follow, first, some of the most obvious transactions between the production units and the final users.

The opening set of "transactions" consists of "extractions." Iron-ore- and coal-mining firms, logging outfits, and farms extract, or otherwise obtain, raw materials from the natural environment. Raw material is passed on for further processing into semifinished products by flour mills, sawmills, and steelworks. Semifinished products are shipped to be transformed into finished products by bakeries and furniture, machinery, and car manufacturing companies. Actually, the "production" process is truly completed only at the point where these finished products are sold to final users, either directly, or by being forwarded to retail trade outlets. All these obvious transactions, moving in the direction from nature through the production sector down to final users, are represented in Figure 7-1 by solid arrows.

There is another set of transactions, a shade less obvious, which complicates the picture. Some producing units sell to other producing units either in the opposite direction, or in the main direction by way of all sorts of detours. Steel mills sell some steel products to iron-ore mines and coal mines, sawmills sell boards and plywood to the logging companies; furniture manufacturing sells to practically everyone else, and so does machine-tool and car manufacturing. These transactions are represented by broken-line arrows. Finally, households sell labor services to all production units, as well as to the government (in a sense, a production unit, too). Sales of labor services are indicated by the lighter solid arrows.

The diagram is a maze of links between the various participating units. It conveys the impression of the complexity of economic relationships rather well, but otherwise it is rather confusing. Is it possible somehow to make it more orderly? Fortunately, there is a standard method of presenting the same complex relationships in an amazingly simple way. This is the so-called *input-output method*.

The method is based on the same principle which is used when a score table is set up in a round robin tournament, where each contestant is matched against every other contestant. Here it is every firm, or industry, that plays a cooperative game of supply and demand with every other firm, or industry, at least in principle. (In practice, there will be many firms, or industries, which will hardly ever be paired in a supplier-customer relationship, e.g., chicken feed and textile manufacturing.)

The input-output method can be explained best by taking first a single production unit, say, the coal mine, and considering what happens to its output of coal. Obviously, it is sold to the various customers. We may, therefore, break down these sales according to their destination. We list the buyers on top of the line (as in Table 7-1) and enter in each cell the dollar value of sales going to the buyer marked in the heading of the cell. Instead of filling in invented figures, we

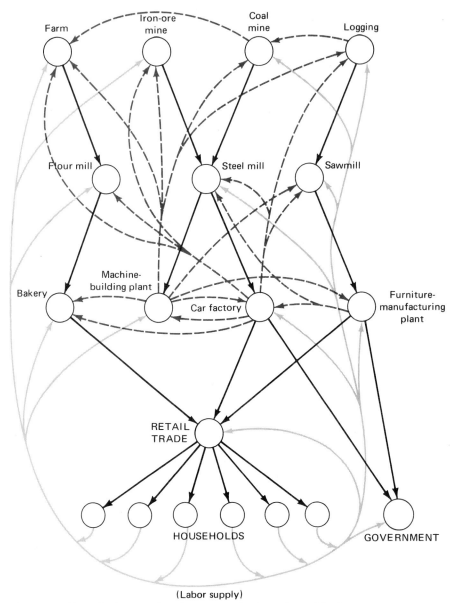

Figure 7-1 Network of transactions between production units and final users.

use simply checkoff marks, reserving a large mark for the cells of what would presumably be the largest customers.

Some entries call for an extra word of explanation. Cell number 7 contains the value of coal retained by the coal mine for its own use ("sold" back to itself).

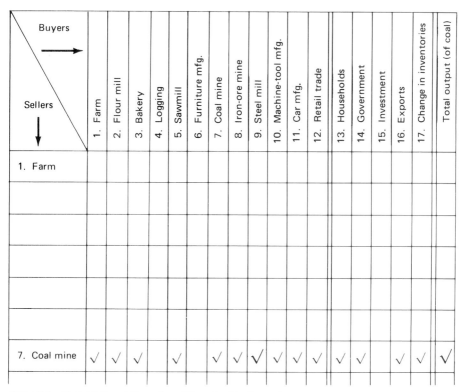

Table 7-1 Coal mine and the sales of its output to its customers.

If we dealt with sales of the farm (or agriculture), the corresponding cell (in that case cell number 1) would contain the value of the grain kept for seed, hay for feeding cattle, eggs for hatching chickens, etc.

The other cells in the row up to cell number 12 contain sales of *coal used as input* for producing other firms' outputs. We call these the *intermediate sales* because the value of that coal will become part of the value of other output intended to be resold. Cells 13 through 16 contain sales to customers who are *not planning to resell* the coal any further, at least not within the given year. This is how the category of *final sales* is defined. In light of this definition it should be clear why final sales contain such obvious *final users* as Households or Government, and also Exports, and output not yet sold to anybody but piled up, for the time being, as net addition to the inventory (stock) of coal at the coal mine or at other industrial coal users (cell number 17).

In the case of coal, we left the cell for Investment (cell number 15) empty. The reason is that coal is not a producer durable. Investments refer to sales of producer durables having a lifetime of more than one year. Thus, in the case of sales by machine-tool manufacturers (or cars, or furniture), we would enter under

Investment sales to those customers (i.e., other firms) who will use the machine tools or cars, or furniture, as part of their stock of producer durables.[1]

The final cell contains the *total value* of coal produced during the given period. In other words, it amounts to the summation of all entries in cells 1 through 17, or, the other way around, entries in cells 1 through 17 represent a detailed breakdown of the total value of output at the end.

If we now proceed with every production unit as we did with the coal mine, and write out its sales in a row form according to their destination, we obtain a table like Table 7-2. It is customary to treat the double lines as vertical and horizontal axes dividing the table into four quadrants. We number them counterclockwise, starting with the northeast corner: quadrant I contains final uses; quadrant II—the most extensive one—contains sales for intermediate use, i.e., sales of outputs to be used by other production units as inputs; quadrants III and IV list sales of labor services by households to production units (as labor input) and to final users (mainly government). (Entries beyond the *broken* double lines are mere summations of individual entries by rows or columns.)

The table as set up does not represent a full-fledged input-output table. A standard input-output table would contain additional rows in quadrants III and IV, besides sales of labor services (expressed in terms of wages earned), namely, rows that correspond to categories of value added other than wages (such as profits) and depreciation. A note is necessary to explain the place of transactions with foreign firms. The sales by foreign firms to domestic buyers (i.e., imports) are lumped together with the sales of those domestic firms which sell the same products, for reasons that will become apparent later.[2]

The table can be read horizontally (by rows) or vertically (by columns). Read horizontally—which is what we have been doing until now—it answers the question: "Where does output go?" This is the sellers' perspective. Now, we are well aware that a given sale is the same thing as purchase: it is but one single transaction looked at from two different ends, the seller's end and the buyer's end. Recall that the top headings of the table list the various buyers, i.e., other firms (quadrant I) and final users (quadrant I). Therefore, if we take a single column in quadrant II, it will contain all the purchases, made by the production

---

[1] It is true that, in a deep sense, such producer durables are actually intermediate products, and it is equally true that they eventually will be "resold" to other users, although not bodily. Their value will enter the value of other commodities over the years in the form of depreciation charges, as one of the cost elements constituting price. However, here they qualify as part of final sales by virtue of the conventional definition of final sales given above: sales of commodities not meant for resale either at all or in the current period.

[2] In a full-fledged input-output table, imports of articles not produced domestically (e.g., banana imports to the United States economy) would receive a special row, as if they were another production unit, or industry. In the final-use quadrant (I), there would be a special column labeled Imports. Cells in this column would contain the value of all the imported items—those lumped with sales of domestic industries as well as those having a special row to themselves—except that they would have a minus sign. The (negative) Imports column, taken together with the (positive) Exports column, would then represent *net exports* (or imports); this corresponds to the category "net foreign investment" in the gross national product. The bottom summary of the columns in quadrant I would then be the gross national product.

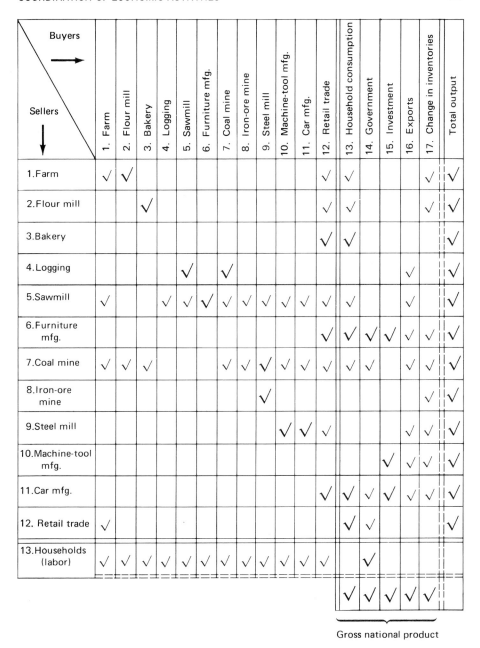

Sellers \ Buyers	1. Farm	2. Flour mill	3. Bakery	4. Logging	5. Sawmill	6. Furniture mfg.	7. Coal mine	8. Iron-ore mine	9. Steel mill	10. Machine-tool mfg.	11. Car mfg.	12. Retail trade	13. Household consumption	14. Government	15. Investment	16. Exports	17. Change in inventories	Total output
1. Farm	√	√										√	√			√		√
2. Flour mill			√									√	√			√		√
3. Bakery												√	√					√
4. Logging					√	√									√			√
5. Sawmill	√			√	√	√	√	√	√	√	√	√	√			√		√
6. Furniture mfg.												√	√	√	√	√	√	√
7. Coal mine	√	√	√				√	√	√	√	√	√	√	√		√	√	√
8. Iron-ore mine									√							√		√
9. Steel mill										√	√	√				√	√	√
10. Machine-tool mfg.														√	√	√		√
11. Car mfg.												√	√	√	√	√	√	√
12. Retail trade	√											√	√					√
13. Households (labor)	√	√	√	√	√	√	√	√	√	√	√	√	√					
													√	√	√	√	√	

Gross national product

Table 7-2 A simplified version of an input-output table.

unit listed on top, from all its various suppliers listed at the left of the table. Thus, *the column of an industry will contain the values of products bought as inputs necessary for the production of the given industry's output*, the value of which we shall

Table 7-3 Matrix of Transactions Involving Real Resource Flows between Participants

	1	2	3	$\cdots$	n
1	a_{11}	a_{12}	a_{13}	$\cdots$	a_{1n}
2	a_{21}	a_{22}	a_{23}		a_{2n}
3	a_{31}	a_{32}	a_{33}		a_{3n}
⋮	⋮	⋮	⋮		⋮
n	a_{n1}	a_{n2}	a_{n3}	$\cdots$	a_{nn}

find in the *last cell* of that industry's *row*. The vertical reading of columns answers the question: "Where did the inputs come from?" The horizontal and vertical readings combined explain the name of the input-output table.

These are the elementary aspects of input-output accounting. Before we return to the main subject, which is to elucidate the coordination problem, let us present the input-output relations once more, this time in a symbolic form and from the point of view of communication between participants required for the transactions to take place.

THE INFORMATION NETWORK

In passing to the symbolic language, we shall drastically simplify and generalize. We wipe out all specific distinctions between production units, final users, households as suppliers of labor, etc. We call them all "participants" engaged in transferring "resources" from one to another. The term "resources" as used here covers commodities at all possible stages of transformation, including final products. The participants are not designated by name but simply by number. The value of a sale-purchase transaction is designated by an *a*. A subscript made up of two numbers will indicate which industry is on the selling and which on the buying side of the transaction. Thus, a_{35} means a flow of resources from participant number 3 (listed on the left) to participant number 5 (listed on top).

When we arrange the symbols in a manner analogous to an input-output table, we obtain an arrangement such as in Table 7-3. Such a rectangular array of numbers is called a *matrix*. If the number of rows and columns is the same, as it is here (namely, n of each), we have an $n \times n$ *square matrix*. Since the symbols represent values of resources transferred from one participant to another, we may call it a resource-flow matrix.[3] It is clear that many entries will have zero values, i.e., usually not all participants will be in touch with all the others. If we wish to

---

[3] Leonid Hurwicz, "Optimality and Informational Efficiency in Resource Allocation Processes," in K. J. Arrow, S. Karlin, and P. Suppes (eds.), *Mathematical Methods in Social Sciences*,

refer to a transaction in general, without specifying the partners, we use the standard notation a_{ij} (transfer from the ith row unit to the jth column unit). The full set of all such unspecified transactions—i.e., of *all* transactions in the matrix—can be written compactly as A.

The Information Matrix A is the summary expression of all the interlocking relationships in the production and distribution processes of a given economy. They represent the material outcomes of economic activities. Now, it is obvious that these outcomes must be accompanied and/or preceded by some *information flows*. For any transfer to take place, there must be some terminal communication that "clinches the deal." We may think of such *messages* as *contracts* just preceding the transactions. These terminal messages are bilateral in nature, exactly as the material transactions are. Therefore, they can be represented by a matrix exactly duplicating the resource-flow matrix in Table 7-3, except that we use a different symbol for the information exchanged, not a but, say, m. These communications are "addressed" from one participant to another, i.e., they are not "anonymous." Therefore, the message symbols have the same subscripts as the related transaction symbols. An unspecified element of these terminal messages can then be written as m_{ij} and the full matrix as M.

The matrix of terminal messages M covers, of course, only a small set of information flows, most of them having taken place beforehand. The big question is: *How does the economic system get to this terminal stage?* The second even bigger question is: *How does the economic-communication system assure that these terminal messages (and related transactions) correspond to the expectations of all participants?* The last one is the coordination question.

How does the economic system arrive at the terminal stage of messages and actual transactions between units? In the background, there is obviously an enormous amount of detailed information which is generated and processed *inside* each participating unit. Production units will normally know, more or less imperfectly, the facts about their current state of capital equipment, employed labor force, production methods, input needs for various levels of operation, alternative cost schedules, and the level of *minimum* acceptable financial net returns, as well as their *desirable* level. Final users, especially consumers and the government, will know about their current needs (preferences) and disposable revenues. The information, which is *internal* to the participating units, is the basis of information messages exchanged *between units*. It does not show up in our information-flow matrix (or matrices) and will be taken for granted.

Production by Prearrangement   Before we delve into the real-world information processes, let us go through an abstract exercise, using the power of economic imagination. The exercise consists in imagining one possible way

Stanford University Press, Stanford, Calif., 1960, pp. 27–46, reprinted in K. J. Arrow and T. Scitovsky, *Readings in Welfare Economics*, American Economic Association, Irwin, Homewood, Ill., 1969, pp. 61–80. Our exposition draws its inspiration from this article, as well as from Hurwicz's contribution on "Centralization and Decentralization in Economic Processes," in A. Eckstein (ed.), *Comparison of Economic Systems*, University of California Press, Berkeley, 1971, pp. 79–102.

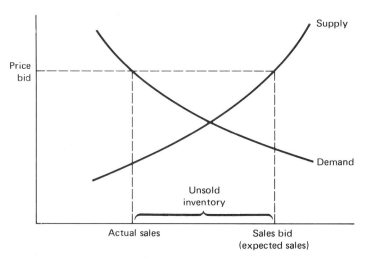

Figure 7-2 Communication between suppliers and market demand: learning process based on the movement of inventories.

whereby the participating units arrive from what they know internally to the terminal stage expressed by M and A. One can conceive a system where participants first "talk over" what is to be done before actually doing it. Producing units start out by issuing initial messages (which may consist of *bids*, or *offers*, in terms of prices related to their ware). These initial messages are not addressed to anyone in particular; they are emitted into the economic "space" anonymously, in expectation of some return signals. Then the return signals come in. Interested units answer with counterbids consisting of buying proposals. Production units examine these counterbids, and if they are not compatible with the requirements of their internal situation, they issue a new round of revised bids. Then they receive a second round of counterbids, and repeat the procedure as many times as necessary to arrive at a mutually consistent set of bids and counterbids. Only after this preliminary dialogue is over will production activities be undertaken. The last consistent set will serve as basis for the terminal contract messages M and physical transactions A. The procedure guarantees that outcomes will correspond to everybody's expectations or plans.[4] It is a world of complete *certainty*.

What we have described is nothing else but a process of arriving at a demand-and-supply equilibrium for every commodity and service as we know it from elementary price theory. The difference is that this imaginary process takes place "on paper," before the equilibrium solution is implemented in fact.[5] The back-and-forth process of preliminary messages, and their mutual adjustments, is

[4] The initial set of messages could also be started by final users, with production units responding. In that case, we would have an economic *system of active consumer (or user) demand*, something of the order of a generalized custom-made production, which is the proper realm of *consumers' sovereignty*.

[5] Such a process was expounded by Leon Walras in his theory of general equilibrium; it is frequently mentioned in literature as *tâtonnement*, "groping."

an instance of what is often called *iteration*, i.e., a repeat process, from the Latin *iterum*, "again." Such a process, if fully executed, would save the cost of mistakes due to discrepancies between bids and counterbids which, in the hard school of reality, would take the form of unexpected and unwanted changes in inventories (see Figure 7-2). On the other hand, this process assumes that the economy can afford it, i.e., that the exchange of messages is cheap—does not cost any resources—and quick; or else that the world stands still while it goes on.

Cutting Down on Information Flows   The real world does not, of course, stand still, and transmitting information *is* costly. Therefore, real economies try to find shortcuts to the iterative chain of messages, and at the same time avoid the cost of discrepancies between selling and buying plans. On the one hand, they use the lessons of accumulated experience. After all, the coordination process does not have to start at every step from a state of complete ignorance. Participants have already learned a lot by doing. They may have to make only relatively small corrections in a largely coherent network of relationships, established through the continuity of actual past development of the economy. Routine based on past experience is a great saver of information effort.

On the other hand, insofar as decisions concern an uncertain future, participating units try to guess the outcomes ahead of time. They use market-research techniques of varying sophistication. This is a way of circumventing the need for costly direct individual exchange of messages with other units. They take the consequences of eventual errors in stride as best they can. In all this, messages are rarely completely anonymous (i.e., undirected), as we assumed in the abstract account. The field of communications is restricted, in practice, only to relevant partners in relevant markets. In the extreme, it may end up, and often does, in stabilized pairs of customer-supplier relationships. These then provide basis for a stable core of coordinated economic activities. Once the effective field of a unit's concerns is thus reduced, the amount of preliminary information flows is correspondingly reduced and the degree of certainty enhanced.

The foregoing gives a simplified idea of the realistic structure of basic information flows in a *market economy*, where decision making and communication are *completely decentralized*, i.e., left up to the participating units, acting autonomously, without interference or assistance from any third party.

At the other extreme lies the *completely centralized model*. In abstract terms, parallel to the abstract imaginary decentralized process described earlier, it could be defined as follows: One unit (a "center" or a Central Planning Board) would stand outside and above all the other participating units. These would not be allowed any direct communication with each other. The "center" would collect all the internal information of the participating units, process it into production decisions with the resulting matrix A in mind, and issue appropriate terminal messages M, this time not contracts but instructions or commands, back to the production units. Having executed them, production units would transfer the resources routinely to other units, according to the centrally predetermined matrix A. We shall come back to this model, and its real-life modifications, in the section on Soviet-type central planning.

Decentralized Information: Cheaper and Better   It is the great merit of F. A. Hayek to have examined the decentralized market model from the point of view of efficiency in handling information and ability to coordinate economic activities.[6] His classic statement, which the reader should by all means get acquainted with, emphasizes the fact that knowledge (information) in society exists necessarily in a state of *dispersion* among participants. Dispersed knowledge has the advantage of being rich knowledge: rich in detail, rich by the intimate acquaintance with particular circumstances of time and place. He writes: "It is with respect to this that practically every individual has some advantage over all others in that he possesses unique information of which beneficial use might be made, but of which use can be made only if the decisions depending on it are left to him or are made with his active cooperation."[7]

Continuing the argument, Hayek interprets the price system as a method of communication (today we would say "language") which coordinates activities between units without anybody needing access to the internal information of these units:

> The most significant fact about this system is the economy of knowledge with which it operates, or how little the individual participants need to know in order to be able to take the right action. In abbreviated form, by a kind of symbol, only the most essential information is passed on, and passed on only to those concerned. It is more than a metaphor to describe the price system as . . . a system of telecommunications which enables individual producers to watch merely the movement of a few pointers . . . in order to adjust their activities to changes of which they may never know more than is reflected in the price movement.[8]

A special place should be reserved for these passages in the reader's memory. Not only do they express eloquently the assumptions underlying models of market capitalism, from Adam Smith's invisible hand to von Mises and Milton Friedman. Their spirit has also been revived and gloriously rehabilitated in Eastern Europe, in the course of the revisionist revulsion against centralized planning (see Chapters 6 and 9).

DISTURBANCES AND TREACHEROUS RESPONSES

However, a number of serious doubts throw a shadow on the alleged ability of decentralized market systems to assure a flexible coordination of economic activities under all circumstances. We mentioned earlier an important shortcut on the informational iteration process that would lead to an ex ante matching of production and selling plans with buying plans: guessing, or estimating, future demand on the part of production units. This shortcut means that the iteration process is not carried through before actual decisions about production (supply)

---

[6] Friedrich A. Hayek, "The Use of Knowledge in Society," *American Economic Review*, vol. 35, no. 4, September 1945, pp. 519–530, reprinted in M. Bornstein (ed.), *Comparative Economic Systems*, Irwin, Homewood, Ill., 1965, pp. 39–50.

[7] Ibid., p. 42.

[8] Ibid., pp. 46–47.

are made. Things are not "talked over" beforehand. *Plans of sellers and buyers are made independently of each other.* The shortcut, which saves on information costs, is heavy with consequences. A guess is still a guess.

We remarked earlier in passing that participants "take the consequences of eventual errors in stride as best they can." The time has come to examine their ability to cope more closely. If selling and buying plans are made independently of each other, this very fact creates the possibility that they will not match up, and someone is going to be disappointed. *Uncertainty* enters the stage. Firms make their production decisions on the basis of their expectations. Then they wait for customers. They submit their decisions to the "test of the market." What happens if the decisions fail the test? Failure here means inability to sell expected quantities at expected prices: unexpected accumulation of unplanned inventory.

The first natural reaction is to correct the course, to lower the price in order to get the inventory moving, or to reduce the flow of output, or both. Let us assume that the error in expectations—due, for example, to a fall in demand for the particular article—was serious enough to require a cutback in output for correction. In that case, part of the labor force will be discharged, and orders of material inputs cut. Consequently, incomes and sales revenues will fall, unless substitute jobs are quickly found for discharged labor, and substitute customers for suppliers experiencing a drop in sales. What is the chance of this initial disturbance being contained?

The Multiplier   The disturbance could be contained if there appeared a compensatory disturbance pulling in the opposite direction, and the factors of production released in one place moved instantaneously, or were adapted, to fill the requirements of the compensatory demand. However, there is no guarantee that such a compensatory increase in demand will be kind enough to make its appearance when needed. And even if it did, would information reach the holders of idle resources fast enough? And even if the news did travel fast, could labor? Could idle producer goods be quickly remolded and reassigned?

If not, the reduction of incomes earned through sales revenues would become an uncompensated accomplished fact. However, the matter would not rest there. Income from sales revenues are, in turn, the major source of consumer demand. If they fall, demand for other articles, beyond the spot of the initial disturbance, is bound to fall, too. The disturbance spreads. New rounds of lay-offs, and reductions in incomes and consumption spending, follow. We are in the presence of the familiar *multiplier mechanism*, operating on the downgrade and producing a general contraction.

The multiplier effect works also in the opposite direction. When there is unemployment and idle capacity, and demand increases for one reason or another, the multiplier magnifies the expansionary effect. If there is full employment, it magnifies the expansion of aggregate excess demand which feeds inflation. However, it is its negative manifestation, the cumulative contraction of incomes and demand, which makes the multiplier appear as one of the most serious flaws of the capitalist market mode of allocation.

The multiplier effect is not triggered by any failure of the system to signal, through inventory movements and prices, the need to adjust production decisions. It is due to changes in demand, where downs are not compensated by any ups. More basically, it is due to the slow speed in the movement of production factors. Even when there is an up in demand compensating for a down, before production factors have had time to relocate, they are overtaken by the falling-dominoes effect which works through the reduction of incomes and spending. The principal conclusion is that discrepancies between expectations (plans) of sellers and buyers create partial disturbances which have a tendency to spread and hit innocent bystanders. Decentralized market systems lack an automatic adjustment mechanism that is capable of quickly restoring coordination before economic activity in general is substantially reduced.

The Accelerator The multiplier effect is a chain response to demand disturbances; it operates via changes in spending on consumption, financed from incomes earned in production. Alongside there exists another effect which represents a chain response to those changes in consumption spending. It operates through spending on the acquisition of inventories and items of fixed producer goods. It is called the *accelerator*. As the multiplier effect tends to magnify the initial effect of a disturbance, the accelerator in turn tends to magnify the multiplier effect. Furthermore, it becomes the source of new multiplier chains of its own, to which in turn it responds. The two effects together can be quite a combination.

The essence of the accelerator effect is best explained when we put ourselves in the shoes of merchants managing their inventory of goods. Whenever there occurs a disturbance in demand, good or bad, the immediate impact is upon inventories: their stock piles up annoyingly above the expected level, or it is depleted, to the merchants' delight, below the expected level.

Now, firms like to keep a steady proportion between their sales volume and their stock of inventory. This is why unexpected pileups make them cut down on reorders. Unexpected depletions make them raise reorders. Normally, as long as demand is steady, reorders also follow a steady course. Just enough is reordered to replace the items sold. Similarly, as long as demand increases smoothly at a steady pace, reorders also increase at the same steady pace, so that the proportion between inventory on hand to volume of sales would remain the same.[9] Such changes in reorders are no problem because they are deliberate. They are planned. They are expected.

Any increase in reorders results in an addition to the stock of inventory, which is called "net inventory investment." Any decrease amounts to "inventory disinvestment." Now to the crucial point: It is when demand speeds up or slows down (it does not have to fall absolutely) that unexpected depletions or pileups show up. It is exactly analogous to what happens to water level in a sink when the faucet is open and the drainpipe either gets partly clogged or suddenly expands.

---

[9] Merchants often measure this proportion as a multiple of monthly sales: for instance, they keep a stock of inventory equal to three months' sales. This is their inventory/sales ratio.

To adjust the water level, one has to turn the faucet either down or up. When merchants adjust the inventory level, they do it by turning the faucet of reorders down or up. This is when reorders take a plunge or jump.

The change in reorders is a secondary disturbance. It is the more serious as merchants may decide to stop reorders for a while completely, until the inventory which had piled up against their will is worked off. Only when it is down to the desired level will they start ordering again. However, they may have trouble bringing the level down because demand may continue sluggish. And it may be their very own decision to cut down on reorders which is at fault. The reason is that reducing spending on inventory investment means reduction in incomes earned in the firms of their suppliers and in their consumption spending. This is the beginning of a multiplier chain of responses. And the merchant may easily be one of its victims.

What stands to reason in the case of inventories of merchandise applies also to inventories of industrial materials and to inventories of fixed producer durables which constitute the base of productive capacity. (The latter are usually called the "stock of capital," but stock is just another word for inventory.) Just as there is a desired inventory/sales ratio, there also is a desired ratio between the stock of fixed producer durables ("capacity") and the volume of production for which there is demand. It is called the capital/output ratio, and it is also usually expressed as a multiple of the annual output.[10] Ordinarily, reductions or additions to the stock of fixed producer durables (i.e., "net fixed-capital investment") are not as sensitive to changes in demand as reductions and additions to inventories of material and merchandise. The timing is slower; adjustments are more spread out, and the accelerator effect is overlaid by a class of forward-looking investment decisions which are completely oblivious of short-term wiggles in current demand. This is the so-called autonomous investment. Nonetheless, in a modified fashion, the accelerator operates in the area of fixed-capital capacity adjustments, too. (For a diagrammatic presentation, see Figure 7-3.)

Trigger Factors   So far, we have kept rather vague what makes for the initial disturbances in demand. This was intentional. We wanted to concentrate on the treacherous response mechanisms which tend to make bad things worse. Now we can survey the major sources which are likely to start trouble.

Closest to one's experience are changes in the structure and/or volume of *consumer demand*. Hoola hoops came and went, long hair ruined the barbers, cooling off toward denim fashions hurt Levi's, advent of television emptied movie theaters. As for the volume, there have always been seasonal, or irregular, consumer buying sprees as well as consumer "strikes." There also seems to be a certain regular tendency for consumer spending to slow down as production activity grows during economic expansions. This also may act as a disturbance, as we have seen in the course of explaining how the acceleration principle oper-

---

[10] Capital/output ratio varies among different industries and among national economies. It may be of the order of 7.0 in housing, high in transportation. For national economics as a whole, the ratio may fall anywhere between 1.5 and 4.0.

Figure 7-3 Steady growth and accelerator-multiplier interaction.

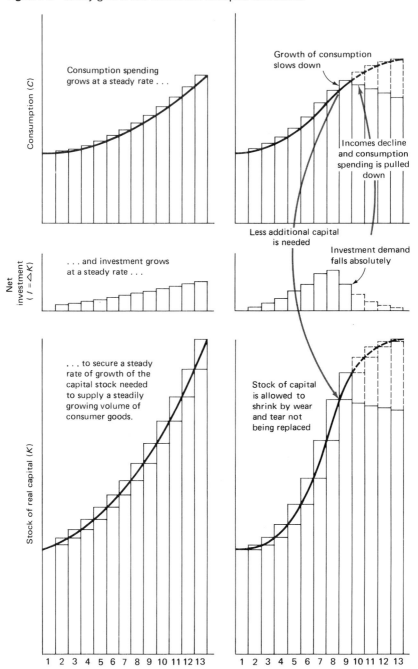

The broken portions of the diagrams on the right-hand side represent a development that will not be realized. In the ninth period, the rate of growth of consumption diminishes. Therefore, lesser additions to the stock of capital are needed. Net investment demand falls absolutely. Incomes earned in investment-goods industries decline, consumption spending declines, demand for investments completely disappears, and incomes and consumption decline still further.

ates in the area of inventory investment. The initial disturbance may also come from *intermediate demand for inputs.* A technological innovation appears and knocks out the ground from under certain manufacturing branches, as pocket calculators did with respect to slide-rule manufacturers, transistor technology to producers of coil transformers, artificial fibers to silk, wool, and cotton. Some changes of this type are extended over a longer period, such as substitution of oil for coal or spatial relocation of the textile industry from New England to the South of the United States. The mobility and adaptability of production factors, especially labor, may be so low that part of them may never move, but may stay in the original location as chronic pockets of poverty. One usually does not consider chronic regional or technological unemployment as part of short-run market-adjustment phenomena. However, it is not at all far-fetched to interpret such cases as petrified remnants of earlier multiplier-accelerator effects.

   We shall continue the list of major culprits that disturb economic equilibria, after a brief digression on the patterns in which multiplier-accelerator mechanisms tend to spread their effects.

   Tremors, Epidemics, Prairie Fires   These metaphors are meant to convey once more the idea of propagation of economic effects from their original source. If we wish to gain a more technical and less poetic insight into this process of propagation, nothing can help us more than a closer look at the input-output scheme of Table 7-2.

   Let us start with the assumption of an uncompensated decline in car buying by consumers (cell at the intersection of row 11 and column 13) and patiently trace the consequences. The first consequence will be a temporary increase in car inventories (row 11, column 17), then a reduction of total car output (last cell in row 11).

   This will involve a second-round reduction in the demand for inputs into car manufacturing. These are listed in *column* 11. Car inputs happen to be purchased from industries in rows 5, 7, and 9, and labor from households in row 13. The material inputs into cars represent parts of the output of industries in rows 5, 7, and 9, shown in the last cells of these rows.

   Since demand for these outputs declined, demand for inputs needed in the production of *these* outputs declines, too. This is a third-round series of reductions. This last set of inputs is listed in columns 5, 7, and 9. That involves, for inputs in column 5, supplier industries in rows 4 and 5; for inputs listed in column 7, supplier industries in rows 4, 5, and 7; and for inputs in column 9, supplier industries in rows 5, 7, and 8. In sum, the third-round decline in demand will affect output of input-supplying industries in rows 4, 5, 7, and 8. In the fourth round, supplier industries of this last set of input-supplying industries will suffer a decline in demand, and so forth.

   In the meantime, with every round of decline in demand for inputs into a given output, and inputs into inputs, demand for labor services in row 13 declines, too. Thus, wages decline. With sales declining, profits decline. And with the decline of these incomes, consumption spending is bound to suffer, too. This will affect a great many cells in column 13, though not across the board. Demand for expendable luxuries and consumer durables will shrink first, for necessities last. However, decline of demand in any cell of column 13 will start its own series of repercussions, analogous to that started by the original decline in the demand for cars with which we began. Finally, any industry suffering a decline in demand for its output may also have to reduce its purchases of durable equipment. This will put a squeeze on figures in a number of cells in column 15. The accelerator effect is beginning to take hold. Decline in any cell of column 15 will, in turn, start its own chains of repercussions as the original decline in the demand for cars did, followed by the secondary declines in demand for other consumer goods. Eventually, the accelerator-induced decline in investment demand will be reinforced by further waves of declines in investment demand of the same accelerator kind.

Once we have gone through these successive chains of repercussions, behind the pedestrian recital we shall begin to feel the nature of economic tremors and vibrations to which capitalist market systems are subject. *If unchecked*, disturbances have a tendency to reverberate throughout the system as multiple echoes. They testify to the interdependence of the system's elements. The lesson they teach is that, *in a closely interdependent system, no element can act without affecting the situation of other elements, and being affected, in return, by the situation it had created.*

Further Trigger Factors   The account of cumulative mechanisms, a trifle dramatic so far, will be toned down considerably if we drop the assumption of *uncompensated* disturbances in demand. Changes in demand for consumer goods and technical inputs are largely changes in the *structure* of demand. This means that declines in one kind of demand are mostly compensated by increases in another kind.

It is true that increases in demand will not be able to draw immediately on factors of production which are being simultaneously released in spots of declining demand. However, they will be able to draw on factors which were released in areas of declining demand somewhat earlier, had time to arrange for the move, and are ready to be reemployed. Market economies, subject as they are to constant changes in the structure of demand and production, develop a relatively stable pool of factors of production, especially labor, which are in the process of transition from one corner of the economy to another. This pool cushions the impact of changes in demand. It prevents their spread via the multiplier effect and assures the needed flexibility in factor allocation. As far as labor is concerned, this reserve pool is called "frictional unemployment."

If such is the case, are there any typical instances of uncompensated demand disturbances at all that do send the economy into the multiplier-accelerator tailspin? Historical experience points to four major sources of destabilizing effects. They are not of the random variety where declines tend to be checked by expansions, and they can be so large as to cause very serious dislocations. We count here *government spending* and raising revenue; *investment spending* of business firms; changes in the *quantity of money* regulated by monetary authorities; and *foreign demand* for exports of a given national system. We shall devote to each of them a few words of comment, although a chapter each is what they deserve.

Government spending and raising revenue, or *fiscal operations*, as it is summarily called, can be disconcertingly fickle. What in an individual would appear as unpredictable moodiness becomes a source of economic woes in the case of fiscal operations because they weigh so heavily in the aggregate demand of modern market-capitalist societies. (Around 1960 government spending ranged roughly from 25 to 33 percent of national output; ten years later, the upper end reached beyond 45 percent; see Figure 7-4.) For instance, in the United States, during the postwar period, federal spending outranked all other spending categories in degree of instability.[11] Thus, despite its reputation as handmaiden of the "industrial-military complex," the government can be ruthless in either raising or slashing military expenditures. Hence the economic recessions after the close of every war episode.

Investment spending is another component of aggregate demand which is known for its volatility. Partly this is due to the accelerator effect: Investment responds by an absolute fall to a mere slowing down of final demand. Partly it is autonomous investment which moves by erratic jerks depending on the business judgment of investment opportunities.

Supply of money, to serve the stability objective, has to keep pace with the payment needs of the economic system in a state of full employment. If the supply of money lags behind the needs of the economy, or moves in the opposite direction, participants in the economy experience it as shortage of money and credit. This reduces their ability to spend and produces disturbances in demand. An important subsidiary effect upon demand operates through the increase in interest rates. These throttle in particular those components of demand which are regularly financed on credit, such as housing construction, consumer durables, investment spending by local government of municipalities, and the like.

Foreign *demand for exports* operates upon an economic system from the outside, and there is very little the system can do about it. A fall in the demand for exports is usually the consequence of a contraction of economic activity abroad. Thus, demand for exports is the vehicle through which disturbances and multiplier-accelerator contractions are propagated from one country to another. This is the phenomenon of the *international transmission of business recessions* and depressions. If a country suffers a decline in domestic demand and economic activity, demand for goods from abroad is automatically drawn into that decline. From the point of view of foreign suppliers, this appears as drying up of demand for articles produced for exports. Such disturbance is likely to cause a contraction in their economies. Hence, they will also have to slash their demand for goods from abroad. But now, "abroad" means the country where the original trouble came from. It will now experience, in its own turn, a fall in demand for its

[11] See Bert G. Hickman, *Growth and Stability of the Postwar Economy*, Brookings, Washington, 1960, pp. 208–215.

Figure 7-4 Public-expenditure ratios (percent of gross domestic product).

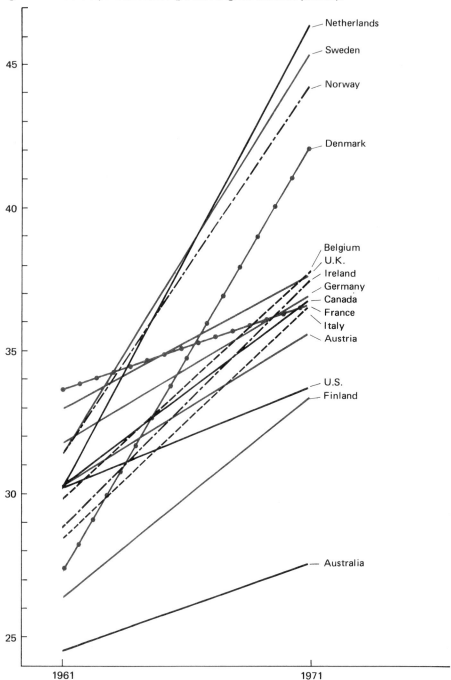

Note: Figures include all current expenditure and gross fixed investment at all levels of government and social security.

Source: Organization for Economic Cooperation and Development, *Economic Surveys: Netherlands,* June 1974, p. 22; based on national account statistics of OECD countries, OECD.

exports, which will make domestic matters still worse. Call it feedback, or ricocheting, we are here observing the operation of the multiplier effect across national boundaries.

*   *   *

We have been discussing the coordination problem as it appears when the market-capitalist system is left to the mercy of its built-in mechanisms consisting in cumulative responses to the shocks of partial disturbances. Many economists have tried their hand at linking up the behavior of all the relevant elements. They have constructed complete models of their interaction, tracing out the direction of causality and of feedback effects. This is how theories of "business cycles" or "economic fluctuations" came into being. Whatever their favorite explanatory hobbyhorses, the upshot of all these theories has been the finding that the capitalist market system is inherently unstable. It has no self-correcting inner stabilizer, no gyroscope to keep the system's course close to the full-employment production-possibilities frontier. If it is to be kept on such course, it needs some outward steering. It needs the assistance of conscious deliberate intervention, i.e., the application of proper economic policies.

Thus, we have touched once more upon the important distinction between, on the one hand, the characteristics of an economic system as such and, on the other hand, policies which determine its actual behavior and performance. In the latter part of this chapter, we were concerned with those intrinsic characteristics of the capitalist market system which constantly threaten to trip up the coordination between the wishes of its participants and productive activities. In Chapter 10 we shall examine the actual behavior and performance of capitalist market systems when they are regulated by various full-employment stabilization policies. In Chapters 8 and 9, however, this point of view is temporarily put aside. Attention is shifted mainly to questions of coordination from the microeconomic point of view of product composition of output: in Chapter 8, under the capitalist market system, and in Chapter 9, under the system of central administration of the Soviet type.

BIBLIOGRAPHY

Miernyk, William H.: *The Elements of Input-Output Analysis*, Random House, New York, 1965.

Yan, Chiou-shuang: *Introduction to Input-Output Economics*, Holt, New York, 1969.

Leontief, Wassily W.: "Input-Output Economics," *Scientific American*, vol. 185, no. 4, October 1951, pp. 15–21 (reprint: Freeman, San Francisco).

(For latter portions of the chapter, consult any standard text in elementary economics or intermediate macroeconomics.)

Chapter 8

Market Capitalism and the Government Sector

I have great admiration, even fondness for the logic and the calculus of the classical market—as a benchmark. But it is neither an infallible nor a universal guide for the economizing conduct of great societies of men living together.

Ben W. Lewis

In the preceding chapter we outlined the process by which economic transactions between sellers and buyers get integrated into an economywide network. In a somewhat offbeat language we talked about the interaction of market supply and demand. After a bow in the direction of F. A. Hayek, we proceeded to debunk the notion that the integration can always be smoothly accomplished. We put emphasis on uncompensated disturbances which tend to drag the system down and away from its full-employment equilibrium, i.e., from its production-possibilities frontier. We have reserved for Chapter 10 a survey of methods used by market-capitalist systems to counteract this tendency, but for the time being we shall put that aspect aside. Here we assume that full employment is being safely maintained, and we examine the ability of the market-capitalist systems to secure optimal allocation with respect to product composition of output.

The examination will lead up to another debunking, although showing up market economies for their shortcomings in allocation is like beating a dead horse. It has become almost a theoretical commonplace that real capitalist markets are unlikely to achieve optimality unaided. On the other hand, market systems have some valuable properties, which proponents of alternative systems would do well to learn to appreciate. Alternative systems had better be able to develop allocation methods which possess these valuable properties in the same, or greater, degree. As long as they cannot, it is hard to see a better alternative to some form of the market mechanism. Obviously, "some form" does not mean an unaided capitalist market, or necessarily the capitalist market of contemporary experience, modified as it is, for better or for worse, by government's visible hand.

The "valuable properties of the market" will be spelled out in the closing section, but we have had to announce them at the outset for the sake of balance. The account might otherwise appear excessively dark, because much of what follows will deal with the failings of market allocation in its capitalist variant. From the perspective of comparative analysis, there is little one can say about the relative merits of one or another market-capitalist specimen. The United States, West Germany, Japan, France, etc.—each has its own peculiarities in coping (or not coping) with failures of the market to optimize. These failures are due to a multiplicity of reasons and are difficult to measure with any precision. It is out of the question to rank systems of individual market-capitalist countries with respect to efficiency in allocation. The evaluation implicit in the following discussion is very general and belongs to the "intrinsic-comparison" type (see end of Chapter 5): the standard of comparison is the system's own potential. Its failures are those of underachievement, whereby conditions of optimality serve as a theoretical point of reference.[1]

There is one category usually counted among market failures which does not refer to the market allocation doing a poor job, but to its natural inability to do that particular job at all. We are thinking of the supply of so-called public goods. The market mode of allocation is simply unsuitable to operate in this area, as we shall explain in a later section. (It is, therefore, questionable whether economists should classify it as market failure. After all, we do not call it a swimming failure when fish are unable to walk. Just as the market is suited to handle the supply of so-called private goods, so are the government and similar collective agencies suited to provide for the supply of public goods.)

We have managed so far to keep public goods out of the discussion of allocation criteria (in Chapter 5), and of normative models as well (Chapter 6).[2] The notion of public goods was implied in our discussion of the visible hand of the government modifying the market mode of allocation (in Chapter 4, especial-

---

[1] One could also say, of course, that if the system did achieve this potential, it would not be market capitalism any more. From that point of view, the optimality potential lies outside and beyond capitalism, in the far distance of some future system that may develop with time out of capitalism.

[2] It is symptomatic for the difficulty of this subject that most normative-model designers— F. Hayek, von Mises, Lange, Lerner, Vanek—have very little to say about it and rather leave their models incomplete in that respect.

ly the explanation of Table 4-1). Government activities intervening in the market process are one type of public goods, which includes governmental services. Now that we are about to deal with the specifics of real economic systems, the government has to be brought in explicitly. Its performance must be included in the account of the real systems and their evaluation.

The visible-hand services of the government are intertwined with the operations of the enterprise sector. This part of the supply of public goods cannot be treated as if it existed in an insulated cubicle called government, alongside another insulated cubicle called the market sector. Hence, in the following, we have to deal realistically with a "mixed economy," mixed in the sense of government participation in market processes. Besides that, there exists a category of public goods which do exist alongside, or as a supplement to, the market sector. We shall deal with these under the section titled "Government Doing Its Own Thing."

MARKET FAILURES

The true market failures are those where failure to achieve optimality in allocation concerns the supply of private goods. They are due to the existence of conditions leading to *monopolistic behavior*; to *external effects* whereby prices paid by users of products fail to reflect fully the costs and benefits associated with these products; and a *number of other circumstances*, practices, customs, etc., which distort economic outcomes each in its own peculiar way. We shall discuss each of these three groups of market failures in its turn.

Monopolistic Behavior

We shall combine the survey of conditions which lead to monopolistic behavior with a brief comparison of how various countries use the visible-hand intervention in trying to counteract monopolistic tendencies and thus to improve allocation.

Through Competition to Concentration   The counteroptimal nature of monopolistic behavior was explained in the ugly-head-of-monopoly section in Chapter 5. There, it was treated mainly from the point of view of logic of decision making: how the profit-maximization incentive becomes a motive for firms to agree among themselves not to engage naïvely in price competition, to smartly limit output instead, to let the price climb, and to make above-normal profits a permanent condition. The section on cartelization in Chapter 4 provided an illustration by citing some of the techniques used in such collusive agreements. Here, we shall explain how conditions enabling firms to behave monopolistically arise through a preliminary stage during which firms do engage in classic competition, whereby their number is reduced and collusive behavior is facilitated.

It is more precise to speak of an increase in the *degree of concentration* of firms in a given industry. It has to do with a progressive change in the size distribution of firms: a few large firms end up being responsible for most of the industry's output, and the remaining fraction of output is split among a mass of small firms.

The most common measure of concentration is the share of the largest firms (usually four) in total sales of the pertinent industry. Offhand one would assume concentration to be less pronounced in large national economies than in small ones: in a small country fewer firms of technically optimal scale are needed to fill out the economic space, than in a large country. However, if one takes into account concrete circumstances, the degree of concentration in most Western countries is almost uniform.

In the United States, the degree of concentration is expressed by the fact that in about one-half of manufacturing industries the four largest firms supply more than 40 percent of the given industry's output.[3] For manufacturing as a whole, the four largest firms in an average industry supply just about 40 percent of its output.[4] The following countries have an average degree of concentration very similar to that of the United States: France, West Germany, Italy, Japan, and the United Kingdom. The group with a higher degree of concentration (by a factor of 1.2 to 1.6) consists of Belgium, Canada, Sweden, Switzerland, and the Netherlands.[5] In this last group the rule "small economy—higher concentration" apparently applies.

Much more than the average degree of concentration between countries, the degree of concentration varies from one branch of industry to another within a given economy. Frederic Pryor found that, in manufacturing of twelve Western economies (including Yugoslavia), concentration is invariably lowest in furniture, lumber products, and clothing branches, and frequently in food processing, paper products, beverages, and textiles. It is highest in the tobacco, transport equipment, machinery, and petroleum plus coal products.[6] This listing does not include construction, retailing, eating places, and other branches outside manufacturing which all have a low concentration ratio. As an illustration, Figure 8-1 presents a graph showing a sample of economic branches in France according to their degree of concentration.

However, what interests us here is the process by which capitalist market economies arrive at this degree of concentration. We generally presume that concentration is the result of a process which starts from a state where economic activity is dispersed among many firms of not too unequal sizes. We may be too much under the influence of the textbook model of perfect competition. In real economies, there always was *some* degree of concentration. There always were smaller and bigger firms from the beginning, some even exceptionally large.

It is to be expected that some firms start out better endowed than others. Entrepreneurship is not a homogeneous factor—there are geniuses and duds in

---

[3] F. Scherer, *Industrial Market Structure and Economic Performance*, Rand McNally, Chicago, 1970, p. 60.

[4] F. Pryor, *Property and Industrial Organization in Communist and Capitalist Nations*, Indiana University Press, Bloomington, 1973, p. 203.

[5] Ibid.

[6] Ibid., p. 206.

Figure 8-1 Curves of concentration of enterprises in selected branches of French industry.

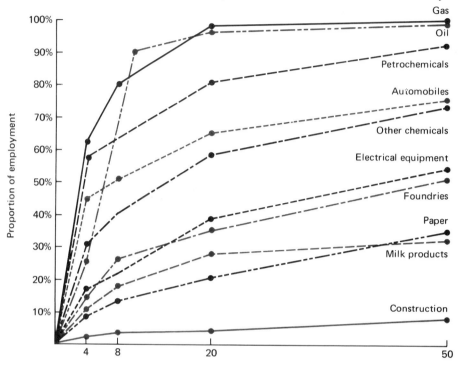

The number of largest enterprises arranged in descending order by size

The vertical scale indicates the percentage of persons employed by the four, eight, twenty, and fifty largest enterprises of a branch in total employment of that branch.

Source: Yves Morvan, *La concentration de l'industrie en France*, Librairie Armand Colin, Paris, 1972, p. 22.

capitalist management as in any other occupation. Some start with larger nest-egg capital. But once a firm gets ahead of its competitors in one or another respect, its advantage tends to be self-perpetuating and cumulative. Success begets success. Higher profits generate higher internal funds. They improve credit standing and attract new investors. Enlarged scale of financing leads to enlarged technical scale and scale of economic operations, to innovation, and to increased freedom of competitive maneuvering. The flow of higher returns keeps the process going. It is significant that the position of firms among the top 200 or 500 companies tends to be permanent, while bankruptcies and high turnover are the order of the day among the small ones.

To fix the process in our mind, let us consult Figure 8-2, where an industry is represented in the upper portion by three firms of unequal efficiency (as shown by the level of their marginal-cost curves) and capacity. In the right-hand figure, the marginal-cost curves have been summed up horizontally—the result is a scalloped upward-sloping industry supply curve. This is the picture of a situation

Figure 8-2 Process of industrial concentration by elimination of high-cost firms.

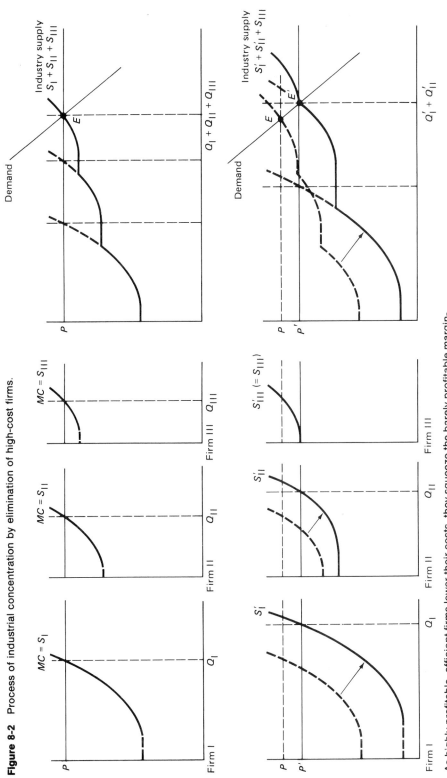

As highly profitable, efficient firms lower their costs, they squeeze the barely profitable marginal firm out of the market, while the equilibrium price declines from P to P'.

which can hardly be expected to be permanent. The profits of the most efficient firm are there to finance expansion and technological innovation. The firm lowers its cost curves and increases the scale of its capacity. This is shown in the lower portion of the diagram. As a result, the industry supply curve shifts to the right. If demand remains the same, there is no room for the high-cost inefficient marginal firm. If demand increases, the most efficient firm has lots of room to lower its price temporarily to force the marginal laggard into bankruptcy, and then raise the price again.

We are analyzing the process of competition under conditions of economic growth which implies the growth of individual firms. It is not immediately obvious that, competition apart, a mere incidence of chance in a growth economy would make, after a while, for a substantial size inequality. Even if all firms had been created equal on day zero, chance alone would produce variability in growth rates. It would smile on some firms more than on others, and even favor some of the lucky ones repeatedly. The initial advantage would be consolidated and cumulated. Mathematical simulations of such chance processes result in size distributions remarkably similar to those observed in market-capitalist economies.[7]

Through Concentration to Collusion   Once the size distribution of firms becomes so drastically slanted toward bigness and fewness, competition may turn into a ferocious contest among the few for the first place, or it may be replaced by a combination of collective domination of the market by the few, and new forms of rivalry between them. The latter outcome, the so-called oligopolistic competition, is a manifestation of monopolistic behavior, even though there is more than one seller on the scene. The point is that, whatever the number of sellers may be, in some respects they try to act as if they were a single firm which happens to operate several production units.

To show the essence of this collusive behavior, we have adapted the diagrams of Figure 8-2, so as to bring out the issue clearly. The issue is the same as encountered in our thumbnail sketch of cartelization in Chapter 4. Figure 8-3 should, therefore, also be useful as a supplement to that earlier section. In the right-hand diagram, the industry demand curve is the starting point from which one can derive the marginal revenue schedule of the industry. Following the usual profit-maximization principles, maximum-profit output of the industry corresponds to the point where the marginal revenue schedule intersects with the composite marginal-cost curve of the industry. The practical problem is how the firms composing the industry will divide up the production task among themselves. We have shown one possible solution in the diagrams on the left, though there could be other, more advantageous solutions. All we want to show is that the profits in the aggregate, and for each firm, are higher than they would be in the absence of the gentlemen-oligopolists' agreement.

The rivalry then consists in each firm's trying to capture a larger share of the

---

[7] This phenomenon, often referred to as "Gibrat's law," is discussed in Scherer, op. cit., pp. 125–130.

Figure 8-3 Cartelization or merger of two independent firms.

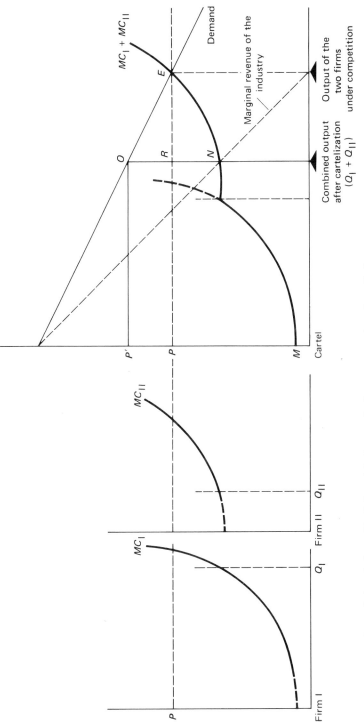

The two firms will maximize their profits if they join in a collusive agreement, reduce their combined output, and raise the price from P to P'. Their combined profits after collusion (*MNOP'*) will be larger than the sum of their profits before collusion (*MEP*), because *PROP'* > *NER*. How they shall divide up the combined profits among themselves is indeterminate; that problem disappears in an outright merger.

market demand without, however, charging a lower price. This would invite retaliation. The term "throat-cutting competition" is a trifle exaggerated, but profits surely would be cut down from the privileged high levels. The rivals know why they submit to the code of behavior which forbids price competition, and they are satisfied with a form of rivalry which is only about shares in industry monopoly profits but does not endanger their total.

Having explained the essence, we should survey the techniques of implementing the necessary agreement between firms in practice. We have described one technique—that of *overt cartelization*, which does not require, in principle, that the industry be highly concentrated, though it does make the arrangements and their policing easier. Another technique consists in the *horizontal merger* (takeover) of independent firms into one large superfirm. The problem of agreement and supervision disappears by being internalized and taking the form of a dictate by central management. A more subtle technique is deliberate *parallelism* of behavior. A group of oligopolists may let one firm act as the price leader while the rest tacitly imitate its actions (*tacit collusion*). For further detail, of which there is plenty, the reader is advised to consult specialized treatises, such as the book by Scherer (see footnote 3).

Any Socially Redeeming Value?   The usual graphic devices economists use to demonstrate the antioptimum nature of monopolistic behavior refer to a static situation. They seem to be out of place in the world of real oligopolies, which is a world of growing firms, product innovation, research and development, and everything dynamic. Responsibility for pointing out these aspects of monopoly as its redeeming feature goes back to Schumpeter, whose eloquent statement to this effect we quoted in Chapter 5 (in the section "Is a Comprehensive Evaluation Possible?"). Monopoly profits are there—so runs the argument—not just to make some people richer than others but also to finance research and technical innovation, introduction of new growth items, improvement of old ones, and stimulation of demand. We are about to discuss policies of the visible hand aiming at control and limitation of monopolistic behavior. It is, therefore, time to examine this redeeming-features argument because, if it were valid, it would considerably weaken the rationale of antimonopoly critique and policy.

We know from Chapter 5 why monopoly gets bad marks: it amounts to a betrayal of the allocative function of profits. Where monopoly profits appear, spontaneous entry to factors of production from low-profit areas is barred so as to keep output limited, prices high, and profits above normal. The rigged price structure results in a misallocation of spending and production. Considering demand and cost conditions, there is too little output forthcoming from sectors operating under monopoly conditions. Too much output is supplied by the competitive sectors. Society suffers a loss of welfare. This loss is not directly visible, except in diagrammatic presentations such as in the top panel of Figure 8-4.

From the preceding it is clear why monopolistic behavior should often be summed up in the expression "restrictive practices." However, when monopolistic profits are plowed back, the firms expand, and output grows—and grows faster than in the competitive sector—it seems absurd to raise the accusation of restrictive practices. Nonetheless, it is not absurd.

The analytic insight gained from the static diagram is not invalidated, but it helps us understand the disconcerting paradox of the ways in which monopolistic behavior manifests itself. In the bottom panel of Figure 8-4, we depict a dynamic

Figure 8-4 Monopoly output under static and dynamic conditions.

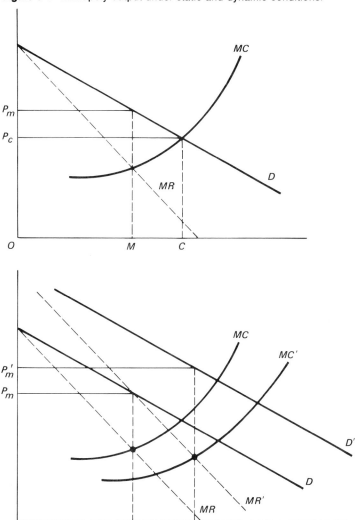

In the top panel, under static assumptions, we are comparing the hypothetical output of the firm which would be socially optimal (i.e., *OC*, determined by the intersection of the demand schedule, tracing marginal social benefits, and the marginal-cost schedule) with the *smaller* monopoly output *OM*, determined by the intersection of the marginal revenue curve and the marginal cost curve.

Under dynamic conditions (bottom panel), the demand schedule shifts to the right (*D* → *D'*), and so does the marginal-cost schedule (*MC* → *MC'*). We observe monopoly output *increase* over time from *OM* to *OM'*.

situation where all schedules shift to the right, as time passes, and output of the monopoly sector increases from *OM* to *OM'*. At any point of time, the portion of output coming from the monopolistic sector is smaller and more expensive than would be optimal. Over time, the output of the monopolistic sector may grow faster than in the less profitable sectors, it may be able to lower its price relatively, and its share may turn out *larger* than might be optimal! And the output of the competitive sector may be chronically more costly than it could be if it had access to some of the profits of the monopolists.

Instead of jubilating at the growth rates of the monopolistic sector, Schumpeter might, therefore, have reasoned as follows: There is no reason in the world why, given a certain global investment quota, the various sectors ought to share in it according to their ability to hold prices and profits above competitive levels, thanks to their degree of monopoly power. Neither is it clear why monopoly power should be necessary for society to obtain high global investment and overall rate of growth. What looks superficially like a redeeming feature is just another incriminating point.

What Can the Visible Hand Do?   How can society get producing firms to behave as if they were under competitive pressures when they are not? And how can it make sure the payoff is large enough to make the effort worthwhile?

We should realize that, in this case, the law is expected to suppress a strong spontaneous tendency of an enterprise sector where profit maximizing is the accepted objective, no matter by what means. Anticompetitive behavior is usually a consequence of growth, technological progress, economies of scale, and concentration of production into a smaller number of production units. Therefore, to suppress it by means of legislation may be a labor of Sisyphus, as monopoly will try again and again to reassert itself.

There are two basic approaches to monopoly control, each of them problematic in its own way. One approach tries to *prevent concentrated market structures from emerging*, especially by obstructing tendencies toward mergers or by splitting up giants. However, a mechanical application of this approach may work against the economizing effects associated with concentration, i.e., against its beneficial side. Besides, anticompetitive collusion, price cartels, and restrictionism of all kinds can also occur when the number of firms is large (as in retail trade). Indeed, to focus blindly on the maintenance of a large number of firms may effectively assist cartel-type structures: if the law shields inefficient firms from the price-cutting power of the efficient ones, it ends up, as the saying goes, by protecting *competitors* instead of promoting *competition.*

The other approach tries to *prohibit practices through which monopoly power is exercised.* It outlaws collusive agreements about prices, terms of sales (such as discounts), creation of captive markets through carving up a given territory among member firms, setting up production and sales quotas, etc. The problematic aspect consists in the fact that the law has no grip on anticompetitive practices if they are due to some tacit understanding or unwritten code of behavior, rather than to formalized agreements, such as "price leadership." With some effort and imagination, business is able to find ways of circumventing the intent of the law.

There is a third option. Instead of battling perennial monopolistic tendencies of the private-enterprise sector, the state may attack the problem from within. It may entrust the management of certain firms to its own appointees, or subject them to *state controls* as far as pricing, investments, volume of output, and its distribution are concerned. This kind of conversion from private to state-run status comes in many shades. Public enterprises may be entirely assimilated to other administrative segments of the government and thus be exempt from the rules of the marketplace. They may be given operational autonomy and told to fend for themselves as if they were private. They may be subject to managerial controls split between executives at the enterprise level and government administrators. Finally, "publicness" may take the form of subjecting certain aspects of the firms' decisions to governmental regulation but otherwise letting them have their private status and autonomy. This is frequently the case of public utilities or other regulated industries.

What Does the Visible Hand Do? The issue of public enterprise, which is part of the third option, will be examined comparatively in Chapter 13. As for the case of regulated industries, the reader is again referred to specialized literature. In this section, we confine ourselves to surveying some of the policies in the first and second category of options, popularly known as *antitrust*. Trusts were a special form of cartel-type organization in the United States in the 1880s. "Antitrust" means generally antimonopoly laws and policies: distrust of trusts, trust in competition.

Traditionally the United States has been presented as the pacesetter of fierce antimonopoly legislation, in sharp contrast to other countries where governments were believed to live in cozy coexistence with private industrial cartels. This impression is a carry-over from a rather distant past. Present-day contrasts, that do exist, are much more subtly modulated.

In the past, around the time the United States was putting its first piece of antitrust legislation on the books (Sherman Act, 1890), Europe adhered to the principle that freedom of contract also meant freedom to conclude restrictive agreements; in other words, business was not duty-bound to compete. Indeed, it was sometimes assumed that, once private business firms had voluntarily entered a cartel-type agreement, it was up to the state to enforce it. Until World War I, cartels flourished unimpeded, though clamor that "something ought to be done" grew louder.

Between World War I and the Great Depression, in a number of European countries (e.g., Germany, Norway, Denmark, the Netherlands)[8] a beginning was made to subject cartels to legislative controls, at least by ordering them to register publicly. The doctrine was gaining ground that, while there was no need to make cartels illegal or to regard absence of competition automatically as harmful, society ought to be on guard against "abuse" of cartelization.

This start, modest and ill-defined as it was, suffered a reversal in the period of the Great Depression and World War II. Cartels were then more than tolerat-

---

[8] See John Perry Miller (ed.), *Competition, Cartels, and Their Regulation*, North-Holland Publishing Company, Amsterdam, 1962, chaps. 3 and 5.

ed. In Italy, Germany, and Japan cartelization was even made compulsory. Only after the end of hostilities was the earlier antitrust tendency resumed.

At first, the United States appeared as the leading postwar trustbuster, breaking up the industrial empires of German giants, such as Krupp and I. G. Farben, and of the Japanese *zaibatsu* (see Chapter 13). As soon as the United States turned its back on the role of occupying power and governments progressively shed wartime controls, it looked as if prewar anticompetitive tendencies were to be resurrected. To some extent, this is what began to happen, but the main trend was for European governments to take a stronger hand in combating attempts at collusion against competition.

In one country after another, national antitrust legislation appeared throughout the fifties and early sixties, usually after preliminary study of the problem by appointed investigative commissions.[9] However, the strongest push came from the efforts of governments to reduce international trade barriers. It was realized that it would not make much sense to abolish import restrictions, which are supposed to encourage mutual penetration of national markets, and at the same time to allow agreements *limiting* such competitive penetration of markets.

Strictures against collusive agreements were inserted in the texts of the early charter establishing the European Coal and Steel Community (Paris Treaty, 1952).[10] The culmination of legal enactments came in the document establishing the six-nation customs union known as the European Economic Community (Treaty of Rome, 1957). Its famous Articles 85 and 86 are directed, essentially, against the same restrictive business practices as the United States Sherman Act (1890), the Clayton Act (1914), and the Robinson-Patman Act (1936).[11]

What generally distinguishes European legislation from that of the United States is the existence of escape clauses which provide for the possibility of allowing some cartel structures, after all. A distinction is made between "bad cartels" and "good cartels." Thus, Article 85(3) of the Rome Treaty exempts business restrictions "which contribute to the improvement of the production or distribution of commodities or to the promotion of technological or economic progress." The idea behind such exemptions is that certain kinds of scale economies (say reducing transport costs by eliminating crosshauls which occur under competition, or pooling research) may require explicit arrangements between firms. Such agreements should then be condoned, if not encouraged.

In terms used by American analysts, the European conception of antitrust leans toward the application of the *rule of reason*. This principle forces each case

---

[9] For a chronological survey, see Corwin D. Edwards, *Control of Cartels and Monopolies: An International Comparison*, Oceana Publications, Inc., Dobbs Ferry, N.Y., 1967, pp. 337–341.

[10] See D. L. McLachlan and D. Swann, *Competition Policy in the European Community*, Oxford University Press, London, 1967, pp. 117–129; Miller (ed.), op. cit., chap. 9, pp. 347–377; Edwards, op. cit., pp. 243–280.

[11] See McLachlan and Swann, op. cit., pp. 129–194; Edwards, op. cit., pp. 281–320; and Sigmund Timberg, "Antitrust in the Common Market: Innovation and Surprise," *Law and Contemporary Problems*, Spring 1972, pp. 329–340. For a survey of the United States legislation and its application, with side glances upon conditions abroad, see Scherer, op. cit., pp. 422–517.

to be examined on its own merit by courts and authorities. However, this is just what some critics find objectionable. Even if lawyers possessed the necessary expertise in social cost-benefit estimation, which may be doubted, it is questionable whether they should be called upon to arbitrate between conflicting interests. These are political decisions which do not belong within the province of the judiciary.[12]

The American approach, though far from consistent, leans more toward the principle of treating all collusive agreements "in themselves" as illegal (the *per se doctrine*). This relieves courts of the necessity to evaluate economic and social merits of individual cases. On the other hand, it is not satisfactory insofar as emphasis on judicial formalities (such as the definition of the punishable act, rules of evidence, etc.) may miss the economic purpose which is the rationale of antitrust legislation.[13]

It is not clear which of the two approaches is better, or whether a choice should be made. Each may be best suited to its own local historical background, as Corwin M. Edwards suggests in a most subtly illuminating chapter on the connection between style in antitrust matters and the cultural and political inheritance.[14] The same author stresses that laws outside the United States are not uniformly more permissive, and he points out one particular area where European legislation is stringent and the United States neglectful: European business is legally obliged to sell to any comer, whereas in the United States the law generally permits sellers to choose their own customers.[15] This liberty can become a mighty weapon against those who would try to engage in competition instead of observing an oligopolistic code of behavior. How uncertain observers can be when weighing the relative merits of European and United States antitrust legislation is nicely illustrated by an otherwise informative article, where we read that "the enforcement bite of the American antitrust laws is much deeper than that of Common Market antitrust policy," and a few pages later, that nobody who knows conditions in the United States "can arrive at an optimistic evaluation of the effectiveness of its antitrust enforcement."[16]

Are capitalist market economies more efficient *with* antitrust legislation than they would be without it? Or with vigorous enforcement in contrast to a lenient one? Everybody seems to be unhappy about the difficulties encountered in trying too hard to prevent economic systems from swerving too far away from competitive behavior. However, there is a widespread feeling among economists that the effort does act as a deterrent and is well worth pursuing. The value of the welfare loss due to monopolistic distortions in the structure of output has been estimated

[12] See Robert H. Bork, "The Goals of Antitrust Policy," *American Economic Review*, May 1967, pp. 242–253.

[13] This is why United States enforcement agencies have been searching for techniques allowing prosecution "even in the absence of direct evidence of agreement," e.g., by inference. See *Business Week*, June 2, 1975, p. 75.

[14] See Edwards, op. cit., pp. 15–23. The importance of the cultural background for attitudes toward noncompetitive behavior is even more strikingly illustrated by the case of Japan; see below.

[15] Ibid., chap. 13, pp. 208–220.

[16] Timberg, op. cit., pp. 333 and 340.

to fall, in the case of the United States, anywhere between 3 and 12 percent of the GNP, depending on how many plausible effects are included and how cautious, or wild, is the estimating procedure applied; one conservative estimate sets the loss at 6.2 percent of GNP.[17]

On the other hand, no amount of antitrust legislation will breathe a dynamic spirit into an economy if it is lethargic, and the other way around: if an economy is bursting with dynamic energy, it is not because it has excellent antitrust laws. However, it surely is safe to state that, other things being equal, antitrust legislation and its enforcement cannot do any harm and may significantly improve performance.

External Effects

This class of phenomena has an alternative name which the reader may like better, as we do, because of its suggestive power: the "spillover effects." Their common feature is that the amount of costs or benefits exceeds the price paid by the direct buyer. The cost that spills over above the market price is paid by someone else, if not in money, then in the form of suffering of some sort. If benefits spill over, it means that someone buys and pays and, beside him, someone else enjoys the benefits, getting a "free ride."

If a smoke-spewing chimney of a widget-manufacturing plant raises the dry-cleaning bills of the local population, the widget price does not include this nuisance although it is part of the production costs: it would not arise if no widgets were produced. The relative widget price being too low, the proportion of resources devoted to their production is too high. How one can best remedy this distortion is offhand not clear. Make the firm pay a penalty? It may raise the price and reduce the demand for widgets, but not abate the smoke, chimneys being a fixed overhead. Charge a penalty and compensate local people for the cost of extra soot? It may be cheaper to prohibit the emission of smoke and force the firm to install smoke-filtering equipment.

Issues of air, water, and noise pollution and environmental concerns have penetrated public consciousness within the last decade, so that further elaboration is hardly necessary. The problem is: What is it the market mechanism lacks to be able to respond effectively to demand for cleaner and quieter environment? One usually answers by explaining difficulties to establish a "right" not to be victimized by noxious spillover effects, to have it protected as a private asset, or to "sell it," in the sense of charging for its violation. The market can handle articles or services whose cost-benefit effects are concentrated enough to be appropriated privately. As soon as costs or benefits are widely diffused over many individuals beyond the actual buyers, two problems arise: that of collective organization needed to formulate the nature of the diffuse costs or benefits, and second, the problem of expressing these costs and benefits as a quantified value, i.e., giving them a "price tag" and thus making them tractable objects of economic transactions (through negotiations, bargaining, government action, etc.).

---

[17] Scherer, op. cit., pp. 400–409. For a view underplaying the relative importance of monopolistic distortions see Mancur Olson, "On the Priority of Public Problems," in Robin Marris (ed.), *The Corporate Society*, Macmillan, London, 1974, pp. 294–336.

To illuminate what the market mode of allocation lacks, and to avoid throwing the solution automatically into the lap of the government, let us give a thought to an institutional innovation proposed by Kenneth J. Arrow. Arrow takes his point of departure in the two-pole structure of markets. The supply and the demand poles are "informationally specialized," one in providing information about production, the other about needs. The two sets of information are reconciled through market transactions and prices. Arrow then draws a parallel with the judicial system. There also two "informational structures" confront each other, the plaintiff and defendant, and are reconciled through the verdict of the court. He then comes to the point:

> I suggest that an analogue is appropriate for the handling of externalities. Once an externality is recognized, there is need for two public organizations, as distinct from each other as prosecuting attorney and a court. One is in charge with an adversary role—to establish the social costs of the externality and suggest remedies, whether of the tax-price variety or regulation. Having a well-defined goal, it should be possible for it to structure its informational channels appropriately. There is no reason to give such an agency a monopoly in its role of expressing the cost side of the externality pseudo-market. Citizens' groups, private foundations, other government agencies and the like should all be highly eligible to enter briefs for the existence, costs and mode of regulation of an externality.
>
> The final decisions will be made by a quasi-judicial agency. It will receive the cases as presented by the complainants, whether the officially-designated agency or a volunteer organization, and by the firms affected by the order. Over a period of time, rules should emerge for the form in which evidence is accepted, in part a codification of present practices in cost-benefit analysis. Like the ideal market or the judiciary, there will be an appropriate specialization of informational functions.[18]

Thus, the fundamental precondition of optimality covering spillover effects is to find ways of making all hidden and diffuse costs and benefits explicit: lend them voice, make them tractable, deal with them.

An adversary relationship exists also in spillover effects associated with consumption: use of stereo sets in dormitories offending demand for quiet; smoking; motorcycles under one's windows; weapons in the hands of criminals. All spillover effects belong under the mode of allocation we defined as unilateral transfers, a kind of transfer which is an offshoot of market transactions. When these transfers consist in the spread of nuisances, in order to eliminate, or limit and regulate them, the market mode of allocation needs to be supplemented by the operation of informal moral codes (self-restraint); political processes on a microscale (request to desist, quarrel, threat) or on a macroscale; formal rules and prohibitions; punitive fines; and the juridical system of sanctions and enforcement. There are no other ways of solving allocation conflicts when benefits enjoyed by some participants inflict costs upon others, and an area of incompatibility is created.

To complete the roundup, a few words are in order about *positive spillover effects*, where benefits extend beyond the sphere of direct buyers. If this situation

---

[18] Kenneth Arrow, "On the Agenda of Organizations," in Robin Marris (ed.), *The Corporate Society*, Macmillan, London, 1974, p. 233.

is left to the market alone, direct buyers pay the cost, and additional nonpaying participants share in the enjoyment of benefits. Thus, cultural events or education may be of great benefit to those who rarely go to concerts and operas, never set foot in a lecture hall, or never open the pages of a high-class journal. There is such a thing as "trickling-down" effects, whereby quality of life in general is enhanced in imperceptible ways by activities in which we are not participating in person. It is then fair for the indirect beneficiaries to be asked to share in defraying the costs. As a result, the market price of the activities in question may fall and lead easily to an increase in the quantity demanded. This reasoning provides the rationale for paying private and government subsidies to culture and education, and treating them, partly at least, as public goods.

Miscellaneous Failings of the Market

In contrast to monopolistic behavior and spillover effects, market failures to be reviewed in this section do not fall under any precise definition. Some contain an element of monopolistic behavior, some bear the stamp of spillover effects or public goods, and some may actually be a matter of general human imperfection showing up in the market phenomena. The listing is definitely incomplete; and Chapter 16, which deals with consumer sovereignty, is an overgrown item that would properly belong here.

Improvidence   The capitalist market mechanism is not very good at taking into account some important consequences of decisions taken within its institutional framework. It tends to operate within a relatively *short time horizon* and to proceed by *piecemeal decisions* which bar from view their global outcomes.

Limited Time Horizon   The shortsightedness of the capitalist market and its competitive profit maximization is best seen in the use of exhaustible natural resources. The unsupervised behavior of firms often recalls, in this respect, a nomadic mentality. Popularly denounced as plunder, it is being described by economists tactfully as "treating natural resources as a free good."

For the production sector, unextracted and unprocessed natural resources are indeed a free good. They are gifts of nature. No costs are involved in placing salt, ores, or fish in their sites—production costs begin only with the process of changing their natural state or location. However, this also has its opportunity costs, and in that sense natural resources are not free. One of the opportunity costs concerns future availability. The opportunity cost of using up a quantity of ore or whales today is not having it ten or fifty years later. Where the supply is, for all practical purposes, infinite, as in the case of wind or sunshine, this opportunity cost is zero. The resource is inexhaustible, and there is no economic problem. If the resource is exhaustible, optimality requires that the opportunity cost of going without it in the future be taken into consideration.

What is the economic system supposed to do today to take into account adequately future market-created shortages of natural resources? "Taking into account" means here preventing them or compensating for them. However, the problem is different depending on whether we think of natural resources which are exhaustible but replaceable, or exhaustible but not replaceable. In the first case, shortages can be prevented. In the second, they can only be compensated for.

In the case of replaceable natural resources, the above-mentioned nomadic mentality needs to give way to economic mentality that started with sedentary agriculture. Nomadic mentality is dominated by the idea of ever present fresh substitutes: from one green pasture, or hunting ground, people move to another. Sedentary agriculture develops the practice and notion of maintenance and replacement. Capitalist market systems inherit this mentality; they carry it further in their bookkeeping, which keeps track of fixed capital depreciation and replacement needs. However, in using nondomesticated plant and animal resources, the first impulse of capitalist firms is to ignore future shortages, concentrate on lowering costs in the short run, and count as part of profits what should actually be a depreciation charge financing replacements. Left to their own tendencies, they leave in their wake overcut forests, overexploited fishing grounds, gaps after extinct species, dust bowls. It takes usually the visible hand to unteach individual firms their habits of reaping without sowing and hold them to the rules of proper husbanding of resources.

As for nonreplaceable resources, the husbanding rules apply in the form of recycling material from discarded articles, but in growth economies, the eventual exhaustion of limited resources currently used must be faced. The problem is to make sure that substitute resources be secured in time, so that material welfare of present generations is not paid for by a decline in welfare of future generations. To a large extent, the competitive market mechanism does provide incentives to search continuously for substitutes. It is part and parcel of technological progress which receives an impetus from the rise in cost of resources that accompanies their progressive exhaustion. On grounds of historical experience, it seems unrealistic to think in terms of an abrupt ending to the supply of a given natural resource and facing the future empty-handed. Panic-inspiring projections of the future suffer greatly because they do not take into account the *possibilities of substitution* through time.[19] Nonetheless, belief in *certainty* of substitution may again err on the side of overconfidence in the market mechanism and human capabilities. We just do not know for sure.

"Tyranny of Small Decisions" The phrase is taken from the title of an article by Alfred E. Kahn dealing with this particular "market failure."[20] At its core is the fact that the market price system is limited in its guidance function to marginal adjustments of proportions. Market choices scan only a narrow range of marginal alternatives. They focus on small shifts around established positions of the moment. And they handle ordinarily one isolated article at a time. What tends to escape attention is the interdependence of isolated choices. One small choice leads to another, and their cumulation may result in surprising outcomes which the step-by-step choosers really did not want.

---

[19] See the papers by S. Gordon, N. Rosenberg, and P. G. Bradley in *American Economic Review*, vol. 63, no. 2, May 1973, pp. 106–128.

[20] A. E. Kahn, "The Tyranny of Small Decisions, Market Failures, Imperfections, and the Limits of Economics," *Kyklos*, vol. 19, no. 1, 1966, pp. 23–47.

This can be seen most dramatically in the example of major innovations which are initially accepted by the public on grounds of their merits perceived in isolation, but then induce further changes which, had they been foreseen, would have made people think twice about the innovation which had started it all. The automobile seems to be a case in point. Its introduction was not just a substitution of one mode of transportation by another. Footloose, because freed from tracks, the new vehicle opened the possibilities of new patterns of habitation: dispersed, individualistic, and pushing the zone of recreational nature areas farther and farther away from the center of cities. Such cumulative chains of consequences could be traced in other directions (effects on health, atmosphere, etc.). William Baumol identified another phase in the cumulative process

> whereby the movement of high income groups out of the cities and into the suburbs has reduced the economic resources at the disposal of the municipal government and at the same time decreased the average per capita income of those who remain. The result has been a deterioration in living conditions within the cities—poorer schools, neglected streets, etc.—which have made it even less desirable to remain in the city. This has led to a further exodus which, in its turn, caused another reduction in the per capita wealth of those who continue to inhabit the city, and so on ad infinitum.[21]

For every individual it might have seemed rational to make his or her small decision the way he or she did, but in the end few are enchanted by the global outcome. Step by step, marginal adjustments through market choices produce unforeseen, and perhaps unwanted, new global patterns. At no point does the market offer society the option of refusing the entire evolving package deal of consequences and their ramifications. It would take a different mode of allocation to break, as Kahn says, "the market-determined spiral of history."

Option Demand   There is no bargain counter in the pure market system where one could shop for the sheer availability of a commodity, or service, without right away buying it, although people may enjoy merely having the option of using a good, and be willing to pay a contribution. However, the paying demand on the part of actual users may be too weak to cover the cost of such goods; hence, the market does not provide it. For instance, on market principles, we may not have any national parks, or special transportation service for the elderly. But the point is, as Kahn puts it, that there are "people who may never travel to the parks yet for whatever reason derive satisfaction from their availability, and who would feel a loss if they were to disappear."[22]

There is a basic similarity between option demand and demand for insurance against various risks. It is true that capitalist market systems do supply insurance services against a number of risks, on a voluntary basis, to paying customers. Whether they do so with all the attainable efficiency and respond to all existing demand is a different question. Insurance services have the property of becoming cheaper with increasing numbers of customers. However, a private

---

[21] William J. Baumol, *Welfare Economics and the Theory of the State*, 2d ed., Harvard, Cambridge, Mass., 1965, p. 37.
[22] Kahn, op. cit., p. 29.

insurance company has limited ways of addressing such offers to the public collectively, although many (or all) might join if they were told how much lower the price would fall as a result of their joining. Besides, reaching customers individually involves costly arrangements (selling costs) which nonmarket allocation can do without.[23]

Pricing Practices In the economic theory of competition, pricing is treated as an automatic outcome of market forces. In business literature it is approached as an art or a game. Theoretical treatment of monopoly or oligopoly pricing and output determination represents a bridge between economics and business because it allows for the element of willfulness. Willfulness, strategy, game playing, image creation through manipulation of prices—these are the ingredients of which real business behavior is made. How does optimality come off?

It does not come off unscathed, that much is certain. Without any wish to engage in moralizing, it is worth pointing out that an ideal price structure would require total candor and truthfulness in order for the relative cost structure of products to be revealed to buyers with precision. The value of competition lies in its ability to unmask instances of willful attempts at divorcing prices from relative costs. Collusive behavior has the flavor of a rigged contest with prearranged results. Pricing practices that consist in making relative prices deviate from relative costs are by definition antioptimal.

Analytically speaking, much of the art of setting prices at the most profitable level is the "small change" of monopolistic behavior and discrimination. It tries to create or exploit temporary monopoly situations. There are strategies of "skimming the market" at high season, and later offering "sales prices" to less pressed customers, satisfied with a shrunken choice. Prices are set high during the initial monopoly position of a new product, before competition invades the field (see electronic pocket calculators of recent memory). Prices are initially set low in order to bait buyers, and when they are hooked (i.e., when demand becomes inelastic), prices are raised. Psychology enters—a price may be set high because a low price may connote shabbiness and keep customers away. There is no end to factors to be weighed.[24]

A special case of arbitrariness in price setting is the so-called *cross-subsidization*. If a firm produces a number of different articles, some may be priced below actual cost. The resulting losses will then be covered ("subsidized") by profits realized on other items. Such so-called cross-subsidization could be unintentional, but it may also be a matter of conscious policy. For instance, publishing houses, before they were taken over by unsentimental conglomerates, are said to have produced low-circulation scientific monographs at a loss, and recouped the

---

[23] One-half of health insurance premiums for individual policies goes to cover expenses of the companies; for group insurance policies the proportion is one-tenth. (Under socialized insurance it would presumably fall even further.) See H. M. Somers and A. R. Somers, *Doctors, Patients, and Health Insurance*, Brookings, Washington, 1961, p. 272, cited in K. J. Arrow, "Uncertainty and the Welfare Economics of Medical Care," *American Economic Review*, vol. 53, no. 5, December 1963, p. 963.

[24] See, for example, Alfred A. Oxenfeldt, *Pricing Strategies*, AMACOM, New York, 1975.

loss on best sellers. By privately assuming such public-service tasks, the firm plays God, or at least angel, essentially redistributing income in social-welfare interests. Similar are the Robin Hood–spirited physicians who allegedly overcharge the rich and treat the poor for free.

Weird patterns of pricing sometimes emerge in cases where consumers are sold an article whose price serves to finance the supply of still other products distributed free of charge or at an unrealistically cheap rate. Thus, the public may buy its papers and magazines at a price far below cost, and get its television programs free, having paid for them unwittingly when buying cereal or aspirin. There the price covers not only the cost of cereal and aspirin but also the cost of commercials and advertising which, in turn, "subsidize" papers, magazines, and television. This is possible only because the capitalist market treats merchandise plus advertising information plus part of the media production as a single package, at least from the point of the consumer who pays for them in one lump sum at the supermarket. From where he stands, he is faced with a disguised case of a *tie-in sale*: buy the whole package or leave it. Putting it differently, he is effectively paying a *hidden private sales tax*, collected by Nabisco or Bayer; the firms then use this revenue to finance commercials and media production which is distributed as a public good. From the vantage point of the manufacturing firm, the transaction appears as *selling cost* and is usually treated as such in economic theory. However, what is relevant, from the point of view of optimal allocation, is the fact that several independent products, each of which could be priced separately, are produced and distributed in a manner which makes it impossible for the consumers to choose knowingly how much they want of each.[25]

Information Data Base   The capitalist market system can rightly boast of having developed a highly effective system of keeping economic records. Accounting, allied to computerization, is part of the forever-improving technology of organization. Techniques of market research and product testing have enormously *reduced the degree of uncertainty* of earlier hit-or-miss methods which made the phrase "anarchy of the market" sound self-evident. However, other aspects of the system, such as prolongation of the development and investment cycle of new products, have again tended to *increase uncertainty*, and some, such as inflation, have been undermining the validity of data supplied by improved accounting methods.

The capitalist market system has traditionally been future-oriented. Stretching imagination and building ahead of demand have been its features, side by side with shortsightedness noted in the exploitation of natural resources. The longer the time horizon of innovators, the less the reliability of estimated data on which decisions are based, and the higher the risks. Thus, technology and innovative drive generated by the system have created an uncertainty problem with which it has to cope. J. K. Galbraith suggested that the system's way of coping is

---

[25] See Nicholas Kaldor, "Economic Aspects of Advertising," *Review of Economic Studies*, vol. 18, 1950–1951, pp. 1–27, reprinted in his *Essays on Value and Distribution*, Free Press, Glencoe, Ill., 1960, pp. 96–140.

to manipulate demand and adapt it to the investment and innovation plans of business: hence his claim that the system is informally planned rather than subject to market forces.[26] At first sight, this is plausible and appears inferior to production by prearrangement, catering to consumers' orders, a system which was theoretically explored in Chapter 7. For that reason, it is mentioned among the failings of market capitalism. However, this is a provisional appraisal. We return to it in Chapter 16, where the attempt is made to deal more fully with the complexity of the issue.

Accounting data serve as one of the information inputs into firms' decision making. This is not the place to analyze critically the detail of accounting procedures in use. What must be noted in the analysis of economic systems is the general character of accounting data which creates uncertainties in pricing of a special sort and impairs the possibilities of optimality to an unknown degree. One problem is the apportioning of fixed overhead costs (such as administration, accounting itself, research, etc.) and fixed capital depreciation among prices of individual products. The rules in use bring an element of arbitrariness into price determination. Another problem worth mentioning is the erosion of the validity of accounting data through time. Accounting starts from "historical" prices of inputs, i.e., from original acquisition costs. However, in the course of their use in the production process, current values of inputs, especially of the more durable ones, change. On the one hand, their relative price may decline over time (because of increases of productivity or appearance of substitutes). On the other hand, their absolute level may increase over time, if there is inflation. Thus, the current replacement value of inputs, especially of fixed capital, but of material inventories as well, ordinarily deviates from data furnished by accounting. However, it is the current replacement value, which can be only vaguely known, which is relevant for many decisions.

GOVERNMENT IN FAILURE-RIDDEN MARKET SYSTEMS

After such a survey of market failures one is bound to ask whether and how they can be corrected. A likely response is to issue a call for the government to come to the rescue with its visible hand. This is legitimate because the government is supposed to be, among other things, the guardian of the interests of society and its agent with respect to that segment of the economic system which is not government. However, one should be forewarned against the optical illusion which makes it appear that, where the government takes over, failure stops. This is just the obverse of another optical illusion which starts with nausea over "inefficiency in government" and ends in declaration of faith in the shining virtues of the market. Ronald H. Coase struck the right balance when he said: "Until we realize that we are choosing between social arrangements which are more or less failures, we are not likely to make much headway."[27]

---

[26] J. K. Galbraith, *The New Industrial State*, Houghton Mifflin, Boston, 1967, pp. 16–17, 198–218.

[27] Ronald H. Coase, *American Economic Review*, May 1964, p. 195.

Components of Government Output

Let us revive in our mind the notion that government with its activities belongs to a country's economic system. Their outcome is the output of governmental services and government-supplied goods which are part of the system's total output. Therefore, *activities of the government's visible hand,* which spell intervention in the operation of the nongovernmental sector, *are also part of governmental output.* They are a special category of public goods, namely, services of economic intervention, regulation, prohibition, etc., which nobody buys by the piece or by the pound, but which society, nevertheless, uses, i.e., "consumes," even though the "enjoyment" is indirect and diffuse. Besides these services of the visible-hand category, the government supplies goods and services which are *supplementary* to the output of the nongovernmental sector. Some of these are public goods, and some are not—a difference we shall explain shortly. This is the area of activities we nicknamed "government-doing-its-own-thing."

This distinction provides a clear image of the composition of governmental output in a breakdown suitable for analysis of economic systems. This elementary outline is presented in Table 8-1, where the two basic components are further divided into major subcategories. Further explanations follow.

First, it is necessary to clarify the concept of public goods, which has a precise meaning in economics. Pure *public goods* differ from *private goods* in two respects. First, there are no feasible ways of excluding any users from enjoying the good (even if they do not enjoy it). It cannot be sold for exclusive possession and use. Second, the use of the good by one person does not diminish the amount available to others. Conversely, adding extra users does not require additional supply. These characteristics, especially the technical impossibility of barring access to such goods unless a price is paid, make them totally uninteresting to private firms.

Public goods appear both under the category of government output supplementing that of the rest of the system and under the category of visible-hand services. The latter have, all to the last one, the character of public goods. The collective nature of public-goods "consumption" creates a special problem in cases where there is no unanimity among participants as to the given need or its degree of intensity and urgency. Especially when opposite views clash and fulfillment of wishes is mutually exclusive, the notion of optimality loses its normal significance. The content of public goods and services is then determined by rules of political decision making, i.e., by power relations. This is a process of a different sort from market "voting by the dollar" for juxtaposed and compatible components of output.[28] If you wish, you might interpret the frustrations of the defeated party as an "externality" of decisions made by the victors. However, it is an external diseconomy which cannot be remedied without creating an external diseconomy in the opposite direction, i.e., by frustrating the other side. In other words, it cannot be remedied.

Examples of more or less neutral and compatible public goods are orienta-

---

[28] As a half-serious teaser, one could claim that political science is in effect a branch of economics because it deals with processes of choice determining the supply of public goods.

Table 8-1 Components of government output.

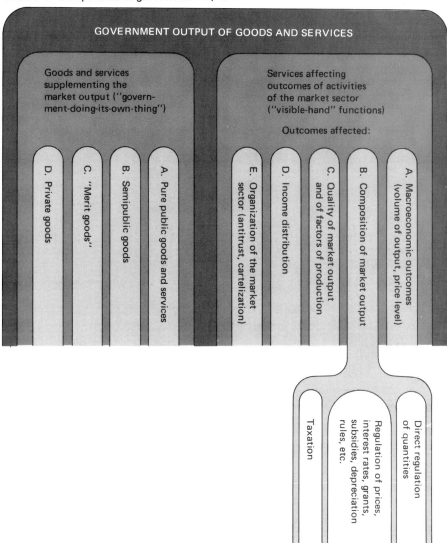

GOVERNMENT OUTPUT OF GOODS AND SERVICES

Goods and services supplementing the market output ("government-doing-its-own-thing")

Services affecting outcomes of activities of the market sector ("visible-hand" functions)

Outcomes affected:

D. Private goods

C. "Merit goods"

B. Semipublic goods

A. Pure public goods and services

E. Organization of the market sector (antitrust, cartelization)

D. Income distribution

C. Quality of market output and of factors of production

B. Composition of market output

A. Macroeconomic outcomes (volume of output, price level)

Taxation

Regulation of prices, interest rates, grants, subsidies, depreciation rules, etc.

Direct regulation of quantities

tion signals on the high seas, traffic regulation, and very little else. Among politically tinged public goods are political leadership and representation itself; national defense; provision of the legal framework for economic and other social transactions; etc. The distinction between neutral and politically tinged activities applies to all other subcategories of government output.

Government-Doing-Its-Own-Thing

We have dealt with the pure-public-goods component. *Semipublic goods* are those where exclusion of customers is feasible and scarcity does set in when capacity is filled (as in the case of public roads, bridges, etc.). However, optimality requires a zero price as long as the marginal cost of admitting an extra user is zero, whereas a private firm could operate only by charging admission. Hence, supply of such goods through the government is indicated.

Merit goods is a somewhat fuzzy concept. It applies to goods and services which could be supplied as private goods through the market but yield such important external benefits that the undersupply would be perceived as serious. Examples are: immunization against communicable diseases, preventive health care, cultural goods (such as museums, monuments, scientific research), collection of statistical information. An added element is, in certain cases, the interest of society in keeping direct control, through its collective organs, over the product (quality and content of education, reliability of postal service).

There is no economic justification for the government to go into the business of supplying *strictly private goods* (as sometimes happens with so-called fiscal monopolies—tobacco products, alcohol, matches, etc.). From the point of view of efficient allocation, and all other things being equal, the decision to let the government take over is arbitrary and unjustified.

The above distinctions are not absolute and no claim is made concerning their precision, especially since concrete instances often do not fit neatly into one or another category.

The Visible-Hand Services

The visible-hand activities of the government—the extent of governmental intervention—were used as a criterion for establishing classification categories of the capitalist market mode of allocation in Chapter 4 (see Table 4-1). Here we are meeting them again in a finer breakdown. Under A we have put activities affecting *macroeconomic outcomes*, mainly the state of employment of economic resources and general price stability. Interventions affecting *microeconomic relationships* (mainly relative prices and product composition of output) are listed under B through E.

As we have pointed out on earlier occasions, and will repeat again in Chapter 10, this subdivision follows the conscious purposes of the different activities, not the instruments used. The reason is that interventions affecting macroeconomic outcomes operate through instruments which are of the microeconomic variety and affect microeconomic outcomes as a by-product, as well as the other way around. As for the specific types of microintervention under B through E, they are self-explanatory. Those under E have already been treated in the earlier section on antitrust policies; interventions affecting income distribution (D) will come under discussion in Chapter 11. Here, let us still comment briefly on category C, dealing with quality control and licensing of professions.

Surveillance in the area of product quality and people's professional qualifications is plain common sense. Although economic justification seems superfluous, let us provide it just the same as a matter of analytic exercise. Market forces are undoubtedly capable by themselves of identifying and eliminating goods of less-than-minimal quality, as well as quacks, impostors, or habitual contract breakers. However, the cost of finding out may be too high: deaths from poisoned food cans and false doctors are an unacceptably costly and slow search process. If government agencies insinuate themselves preventively into quality control, it simply amounts to cutting the cost of market information and search.

Government Failures

On a priori grounds or from experience, many people doubt whether the government in its area uses resources as efficiently as private firms do in theirs. The a priori grounds usually turn on the absence of the profit incentive and competition. There may be quarrels about the comparative degree of inefficiency. But as long as the market is constitutionally incapable of delivering the particular category of goods, the inefficiency in execution is no reason for stopping the government activity altogether. That would be even more inefficient. As Francis Bator puts it, if a public program is needed, "then to eliminate it because it is wastefully administered and because consumers would spend the money on efficiently produced consumer goods is to follow the example of the man in Atlanta who wanted to go to New Orleans but decided to take the train to New York because it was faster."[29]

However, government failures do have to be faced as much as market failures. Collective economic choices through nonmarket decisions suffer from several serious disabilities. For one, there are no visible, objectively generated prices of government-supplied goods and services. The difficulty of valuation does not come so much from the cost side—inputs purchased from the market sector have their prices, and labor services of state employees have their wage and salary rates which must more or less match the market rates. It is the information on the demand side which is highly imperfect. Hence, the determination of both the global volume of governmental output, and its composition, takes place in a mist of ignorance, uncertainty, and economically arbitrary rules.

In the background, there is the supposition of some structure of demand for governmental output on the part of the citizenry. It has the same character as any other demand: schedules of quantities demanded at various levels of hypothetical prices.[30] However, the clarity of such schedules is very poor, and the point of actual allocation of resources is reached through a circuitous route. Citizens delegate the decisions to their elected agents, either trusting they will give their demands faithful expression or charging them with articulating such demands on behalf of the voters. These tasks are then divided between the executive and legislative branches, and execution is delegated further to the bureaucracy. In the process, the tasks are fragmented among committees, subcommittees, depart-

---

[29] Francis M. Bator, *The Question of Government Spending*, Collier Books, New York, 1962, p. 107.

[30] There is, however, one difference. For market demand schedules, the question is phrased: "Given price P, how much Q of commodity X would you buy?" In demand schedules concerning public goods, it has to be phrased: "If offered a quantity Z of public good Y, how high a price would you be ready to contribute, no matter what anyone else is doing?" In the market for private goods, individual demand schedules are added horizontally because every user needs his own extra private batch of the good to derive any utility from it. In the nonmarket for pure public goods, individual demand schedules are added vertically: added-up utilities derived by individual citizens refer, at each point, to a given quantity of the good enjoyed in common, without requiring additional amounts to satisfy additional users.

ments (or ministries), and administrative offices. Initiatives originate in one or another branch; they are subjects of backroom negotiations; submitted to partial review, approval, or veto by others; influenced by secret or disguised bribery. How adequate this process of communicating citizens' demands to the implementing stage is, or how it could be improved, is anyone's guess.

Several major circumstances make for its inadequacy. One is the standard majority voting rule. If the demands of the majority and minority are absolutely incompatible and mutually exclusive (e.g., hawks versus pacifists), there is no way of arriving at decisions except by overriding the minority. This is a pure reflection of Arrow's theorem of the impossibility of having a consistent social-welfare function; it has already been mentioned in connection with the concept of public goods. However, majority voting is also likely to stand in the way of optimality when citizens' demands *are* compatible. In that case, if every minority demand were backed up only by the interested minority votes, none of them could be satisfied. Hence, optimality calls for accommodation between minority demands. Logrolling and trading votes are methods believed to accomplish that to some extent, but their use is very unsystematic and coarse.

Furthermore, the budgetary process splits total fiscal outlays into annual or long-term appropriations by compartments. Once earmarked, funds are well-nigh impossible to transfer from one purpose to another even if, on balance, the shift would increase social benefits.[31] Within these compartments, politicians or administrators sometimes ask economic experts to help visualize public demand through a cost-benefit analysis on paper. If competently done, this improves allocation, but only within the compass of broader allocation decisions which may be entirely wrong.

Towering above all these considerations is the problem of choice in the supply of that most critical of public goods—services of political decision making, representation in international affairs. Economists shy away from this part of resource allocation. They leave it gladly to the political scientist and, though not very gladly, we shall follow their lead. The "product" is unique and unpredictable. The process of "choosing the choosers" is unlike any other economic choice. It is heavy with risk and uncertainty. It offers very limited possibilities of learning from past experiences.

Comparing the performance of economic systems in this respect would mean comparing their political systems. While comparative evaluation is fairly easy between despotic and democratic systems as a group, it would take an extremely well-informed, rather subtle, and daring analyst to pass judgment on the relative allocational merits of national variants of the democratic system existing in various market-capitalist systems. This is unfortunate because this crucial class of most risky choices happens to have the gravest consequences for the rest of allocation in the government and nongovernmental sector, and for the "quality of life" in general.

Optimality failures in the process of choosing the choosers will, of course,

---

[31] See Murray L. Weidenbaum, "Budget 'Uncontrollability' as an Obstacle to Improving the Association of Government Resources," in U.S. Congress, Joint Economic Committee, *The Analysis and Evaluation of Public Expenditures: The PPB System*, 1969. (Browsing through this compendium of scientific papers is most illuminating for the issues at hand.)

show up in the quality of the visible-hand activities of the government. The two are interdependent, because chosen agents in turn choose their economic advisers and appointees. However, we have to think carefully before we start blaming (or praising) the system as such, or the particular choices that were made. In choosing their political agents, citizens may make mistakes of judgment of the same kind that occur when one buys a "lemon" in the sphere of private goods. Furthermore, choosing political leaders and representatives is *the* area of incompatible preferences. In either case, whether it is a question of mistaken choice or of frustrated preferences, the damages are naturally more widespread in the case of public goods than private ones. That does not necessarily inculpate the political system as such. At least those inconveniences which are created by the incompatibility of preferences are due to the interest structure of society, not to the form of making political choices.

Let us now narrow our focus on the more technical side of government failures in the visible-hand sphere. Notice that "altering" hypothetical outcomes in the market sector may mean either improvement or departure from optimality. As for the sphere of macroeconomic intervention, we shall venture the guess that, if the government succeeds in maintaining full employment, it will have richly made up for any distortions in allocation it may cause otherwise. As for decisions altering microeconomic allocation, the net balance of harm and improvement actually caused is probably of a smaller order of magnitude than losses in the form of the output gap due to unemployment, once it rises beyond, say, 4 or 5 percent of GNP. However, it is a guess, not an estimate based on calculation.

Calculating the gross value of harm and improvement caused by microeconomic interventions of the visible hand is in any case an impossible task. The market terrain is mined with opportunities for the government to distort further an already-distorted allocation. Chances for improvements are rare and far between. Indeed, if government agents were economic theoreticians, they might despair of any possibility of knowing for sure which way improvement lies. They would be especially inhibited if they were familiar with "the general theory of the second best," formulated in 1956 by R. Lipsey and K. Lancaster.[32] The two authors argued convincingly that, in an economy beset with deviations from the optimum, it is futile to make piecemeal corrections. Thus, to enforce competitive prices in a single industry could make allocation worse. It might thus be better to tolerate various degrees of monopoly as they happen to pervade the economy.[33]

This dousing of beliefs in the possibility of piecemeal improvements of market misallocations did not stop governments from trying, and economists from making recommendations. This is particularly true in the area of antitrust policies and pricing rules of public enterprises and regulated industries. In many instances, government intervention changes market prices and quantities, but

[32] See Richard Lipsey and Kevin Lancaster, "The General Theory of the Second Best," *Review of Economic Studies*, vol. 24, December 1956, pp. 11–31.

[33] A simpler version of the Lipsey-Lancaster thesis would argue that unequal pressure of the government to conform to competitive pricing achieves only an unequal distribution of aggregate profits among industries. Thus, Gunnar Myrdal writes: ". . . Pricing policies pursued by public enterprises are usually such that, by holding down prices, they swell the profits of the private sector." See his *Asian Drama: An Inquiry into the Poverty of Nations*, Pantheon Books, New York, 1968, vol. 11, p. 819.

actually wants to change income distribution—free Shakespeare in New York's Central Park, United States food stamps, etc. This is where the Lipsey-Lancaster strictures do not apply.

Otherwise, economists make it a favorite sport of theirs to point out cases and cases of distortions caused by government intervention: rent controls contribute to the creation of slums; guaranteed prices and subsidies to agriculture lead to surpluses of butter or tomatoes; building and operating airports on government expense makes air travel appear cheaper than it is; same for financing roads and traffic regulation in the case of automobile transportation. In the United States, keeping natural-gas prices artificially low and thus creating shortages became another textbook example.[34] Distributing semipublic or private goods free of charge leads to excessive use and creates situations of congestion; and so on.

Frequently, government intervention is a response to demands of social groups wishing to be protected against free market outcomes. The economist always argues against such protection of partial interests from the vantage point of general social welfare. The government could counter by another cost-benefit rationale. It could claim that the loss in aggregate welfare is a price well worth paying to avoid the cost of social disruption through freely operating market forces. This, at least, is implicit in many cases of piecemeal intervention. Now, it might turn out that it would be more economical to let market forces do their work and to finance the cost of social adjustment by direct assistance to those adversely affected (as Sweden does by its active labor market policy—see Chapter 10). The point is that protection against social disruption is something that ought to be taken into account by economists on the prowl after government failures. Glancing back over the many possible sources of government failure can be discouraging. Therefore, it is good to remember once in a while Francis Bator's man from Atlanta. Skepticism about governmental efficiency and fulminations against big government are useful only if they promote public demand for better ways of articulating public demand, applying cost-benefit analysis, and following through in the implementation stage.

SUSPENDING THE MARKET MECHANISM

Are there situations in which the government is forced by the nature of the case to exempt a segment of the enterprise sector from market rules altogether? Are there times when a capitalist market economy must temporarily suspend the operation of the market mechanism so as to speed up reallocation of resources when preferences suddenly change? The two instances, analytically different, are too important to be dismissed in a footnote. At least a few paragraphs are in order for each.

The Military-Industrial Complex

Demand for the public good called "national security" takes a long and winding path before it reaches the resource-allocation stages. Vague at the point of origin,

---

[34] See "The FPC Is Backing Away from the Wellhead," *Fortune*, November 1972.

it is articulated at various levels by public-opinion makers and finally by governmental agents. Its concretization is entrusted to the appropriate department or
ministry. The military buy material inputs from the enterprise sector, secure human resources by conscription, enlistment, or hiring, and proceed to transform
them into the particular utility: capacity to prevent an enemy from inflicting
war-type costs upon the country (defense) or to inflict such costs upon the enemy
(deterrence or ability to attack). Here we are interested mainly in the special
aspects of buying material inputs.

To start with the conclusion, military procurement is intrinsically unsuited
for the ordinary market mechanism. Usage itself reflects this fact: one does not
say "buying weapons"; one says "weapons acquisition process"—in the United
States, anyway. Modern weaponry can hardly be privately developed by different
independent companies and then advertised for sale across the counter. While
the absurdity may be obvious, it is interesting to spell out the major reasons.

There is much more to it than need for secrecy. M. J. Peck and F. M.
Scherer cite four groups of basic reasons why weapons markets cannot exist: (1)
the cost of development of most weapons systems is so high as to make private
financing virtually impossible; (2) there exist unique uncertainties due to changes
of mind of the customer, as well as unforeseeable technical difficulties; (3) the
customer has to keep constantly in touch to determine the desired characteristics
of the product—it is truly a case of "bespoken" purchases, i.e., custom-made
production to exact specifications, with few parallels in the civilian sector; (4) the
product being unique, the customer being a monopsonist (with no alternative
buyers around), and the supplier having something of a monopoly position, cost
and price cannot arise through the interaction of market forces but only through
individualized bargaining.[35]

All these circumstances together, but especially the last set, conspire to let
inefficiencies in by droves. Because the government does not like the risk of
changing horses in midstream, the chosen contractors do not feel the same pressure to perform as they would if they were replaceable. Because the government
acknowledges the riskiness of military contracting for private companies, it is
agreeable to paying for part of the necessary capital out of its own pocket. An
extra invitation to be inefficient is provided by the method of payment. Prices are
negotiated on the basis of costs incurred plus a profit margin as a percentage of
cost. Whatever this percentage may be, it will always be true that the higher the
cost, the more dollars of profit.[36] This is just the reverse of the economizing
pressures of the market. It is true that government agencies try to watch costs
through administrative methods (rules on admissible costs, auditors, etc.). How

[35] Merton J. Peck and Frederick M. Scherer, *The Weapons Acquisition Process: An Economic Analysis*, Division of Research, Graduate School of Business Administration, Harvard University, Boston, 1962, pp. 57–60.
[36] See Arthur E. Burns, "Profit Limitation: Regulated Industries and the Defense Space Indus-tries," *The Bell Journal of Economics and Management Science*, vol. 3, no. 1, Spring 1972, pp. 3–25. Also Walter Adams and William James Adams, "The Military-Industrial Complex: A Market Struc-ture Analysis," *American Economic Review*, vol. 62, no. 2, May 1972, pp. 279–287, and the papers by Richard F. Kaufman and James R. Kurth, *American Economic Review*, vol. 62, no. 2, May 1972, pp. 288–295 and 304–311.

successfully is uncertain. When government-oriented corporations try to diversify into the commercial sector, they find the going very rough, and comparative inefficiency seems to bear part of the blame.[37] It acts as one of the exit barriers which keep companies locked in to the government business.

A much more fundamental set of questions has been repeatedly raised concerning waste in this area. The suspicion, or assertion, is that demand for "defense" is an artificially fabricated demand, that it is fictitious. It is said to cover up for an underlying *true* demand which is of a very peculiar sort. It does not originate in any specific need, but in a general search of the capitalist system as such for production and profit opportunities. It is asserted that civilian demand (private and public) is not suited to keep pace with the built-in drive to expand the overall supply capacity of the system, mainly because that would upset the social structure implied by the capitalist system. Need is for a demand outlet which is neutral in that respect, has a high degree of built-in obsolescence, and does not compete with the civilian-goods sector. Military spending, though not absolutely necessary in abstract terms, is ideal under the concrete circumstances of the capitalist system. The system does not quite dare to ask the government to finance digging of holes and filling them up, as Keynes had suggested for a possibility, so military spending provides a plausible pretext, i.e., demand for defense, masking the authentic demand of the capitalist system for its self-perpetuation.[38]

Radical economists, who hold to this interpretation, have not explained satisfactorily why capitalist systems in many countries other than the United States have thrived without recourse to armaments (Japan, for instance). Nor have they explained why defense spending fluctuates, and is often raised or slashed in response to exogenous events, or to their perception, without regard to the need of capitalism for self-perpetuation, which is presumably steady and permanent. Nor does the theory explain why increase in armaments should have started in some countries (e.g., Nazi Germany) and have been answered very reluctantly by other capitalist countries, though the self-perpetuation need is being attributed to capitalism in general.

There are some valid points in this interpretation of defense expenditure. Once established, the structures of the production sector, society, and political ideas surely contain forces of inertia interested in protecting the existing state against change. Imagination always had to battle lack of imagination, and general interest, vested interests. This conflict, which is not unique to the capitalist system, happens to be constantly enacted around the issue of the composition of government output. However, not to even consider the possibility that vested interests promoting a defense-oriented supply structure might be intertwined with

[37] See Murray L. Weidenbaum, *The Modern Public Sector*, Basic Books, New York, 1969, pp. 67–92.
   [38] See Michael Reich, "Does the U.S. Economy Require Military Spending?" *American Economic Review*, vol. 62, no. 2, May 1972, pp. 296–303. See also an informative collection of papers in Steven Rosen (ed.), *Testing the Theory of the Military-Industrial Complex*, Lexington Books, D. C. Heath and Company, Lexington, Mass., 1973.

a well-founded authentic demand for defense (which need not be universally shared) seems to result in a seriously incomplete analysis.

Wartime Mobilization Controls

At first sight, increases in defense spending during wartime only mean more of the same features discussed above. However, this quantitative jump changes the quality of the problem. It becomes a problem of sudden adjustment to a new structure of demand, of sudden revision of plans and reallocation of resources, all this under extreme pressure. Gone overnight is all patience with price signals and market responses. These may have worked reasonably well as long as change was marginal and continuous. They are not up to emergencies.

The change in the structure of demand is simple enough: a vast increase of demand for military supplies, i.e., of output not available to civilian consumption. The problem of adjustment has four distinct aspects: (1) need to raise the capacity of the armaments sector by expanding its labor force and constructing additional productive facilities; (2) need to shift resources by reducing the volume of civilian consumption absolutely when redeployment of unused resources or net new additions fall short of the task under (1); (3) need to change the composition of civilian consumption so as to cut down on the use of inputs needed in the defense sector (e.g., gasoline); and (4) need to arrange appropriate financing for the increase in government demand. This four-fold breakdown of the issues should help us make sense of the many practical measures employed by mobilization economies. The first three aspects, though technically quite complex, are relatively straightforward in principle. It is the fourth aspect that will require special attention because it is economically more intricate, and in some ways more interesting.

To implement the first three tasks, direct controls supersede market processes. Consumer-goods industries are told to reduce production down to an essential level, determined as some proportion of an earlier bench-mark year or other limit. Production of nonessential items may be outright prohibited, and the same for hiring of labor. Key material inputs are subject to centralized tallying and allocated according to some rules defining priorities. Labor is usually channeled to high-priority branches through a central employment agency. Limitations are placed on the normal process of bargaining about working conditions, and turnover is discouraged by various administrative stipulations inhibiting labor mobility.

No matter how drastically demand changes and direct controls supersede the market mechanism, the general rules of optimization still hold, with respect to the new wartime cost and demand data. However, direct controls do not have it in them to generate an automatic system of allocation signals. One poor substitute has traditionally been the priority system. It works by giving specific orders of specific customers a preference rating, corresponding to the order of urgency with which they have to be filled. When total demand for a priority material exceeds available supply, the priority system breaks down. The various claimants push and shove to get satisfaction. Higher administrative authorities spend their time arbitrating between competing demands, without being able to tell which is more meritorious at the margin.[39]

A considerable improvement over this crude method was introduced in the United States in 1942. It consisted in obtaining independent estimates of availabilities and claims, and on that basis deciding on a fair and comprehensive allocation among the various claimants.

Let us now turn to allocation problems associated with the method of financing the increased defense expenditures. From a purely formal point of view it would seem logical to keep disposable income down to the value of output available for consumption. In order to match these two aggregates, one would deduct from incomes earned in production, through taxes, an amount equal to the value of the nonconsumable part of output, which includes the war material. This method has been called *pay-as-you-go*. It is completely honest, and it is capable of minimizing inflationary pressure on prices of consumption items. Nonetheless, it is not the preferred method.

Such honest transparency impairs incentives whereas the alternative method, under which people get more money than they can spend, is believed to safeguard incentives. The alternative method, called the *disequilibrium system* of financing, amounts to a game based on the money illusion. The gist of it is as follows: Do not tax people's income to the full amount of the value of nonconsumption output. Let their disposable income be larger than the available volume of consumer goods at given prices. They will save the difference, which they cannot spend because its counterpart is the guns and bombs in the battlefield. They will have the feeling of getting something they will be able to spend later, after the war is over.

However, for this psychological effect to work, prices of consumer goods must not be allowed to rise. Otherwise, price rises would swallow up what people are expected to save, whereas if prices are fixed and the volume of goods lags behind incomes, people are automatically left with unspendable money savings on their hands. This is why mobilization systems put such great emphasis on price controls and rationing of consumer goods. Price freeze prevents disposable income from being dissipated on inflation-hoisted price tags. As for rationing, by restricting everyone to a fixed amount, it is meant to prevent savings from being used in attempts to increase one's share at the expense of others.

In practice, the disequilibrium system of financing usually is not leakproof but, within limits, it does work. Let us add that, when market rules are back in force, savings accumulated during the war have a tendency to be quickly spent, while production is only slowly converted to civilian demand. Hence the phenomenon of postwar inflations. Repressed by the mobilization system, inflation is said to be deferred until its aftermath.

---

[39] See Walter Eucken's analysis of the parallel German experience in *Economica*, New Series, vol. 15, no. 58, May 1948, pp. 79–100, and no. 59, August 1948, pp. 173–193, reprinted in Morris Bornstein, *Comparative Economic Systems*, Irwin, Homewood, Ill., 1965 (2d ed., 1969).

ALL THINGS CONSIDERED—

The multitude of topics covered in this chapter may leave the reader with a feeling of overeating, and the author with a feeling of not having done justice to any single one of them. We have surveyed a number of important *market failures* which militate against the ability of the capitalist market system to lead toward optimal allocation with dependable automaticity. We have surveyed the possibilities of *government failures*, both with respect to correcting market failures through the intervention of visible-hand activities and with respect to allocating resources optimally in the sphere of the government output proper. Finally, we have examined important instances where the operation of market forces must be drastically curtailed and submitted to *direct governmental controls*. (Peacetime anti-inflationary wages and price controls, which also might belong here, will be touched upon in Chapter 11.)

Considering all the market failures, the system's participants keep turning to government for assistance in improving the performance of the market sector, and sometimes even wonder about the advantages of some kind of "planning." Then again, considering the crudity and clumsiness in allocating resources via nonmarket methods, where demand has only vague and indirect ways of communicating with the organizers of supply, where price and profit signals are missing, and competitive options are not available, one is bound to have second thoughts about the deficiencies of the capitalist market mechanism.

We cannot do without nonmarket modes of allocation, neither in normal circumstances nor in emergencies. We *could* do without the market mode of allocation, but we hesitate to make the step from critique to condemnation. Notice that the critique sets up as standard for the market the *theory* of optimization, not the behavior of governments in allocating resources. On the other hand, governments, although subject to the same theoretical standards as the market, are often able to lean on real market behavior as a practical second-best reference point. They borrow market prices as ingredients for their cost-benefit calculations; they prefer to shop in the market for material ingredients needed in the supply of public goods; they think of ways of transplanting market-type incentives into governmental offices. Abstracting from all the negative features of capitalism, there is something basically positive about the market system itself which makes it attractive.

That "something" is an elementary vitality of response between demand and supply, between people as users and people as producers. It is at its most palpable in an old-fashioned European small-town market in the square. It is familiar to anyone who, as a child, ventured to sell lemonade in front of the porch. The same good feeling of a pat on the shoulder is repeated, in more sophisticated forms, up to top corporate decisions that turn out well—the Xerox adventure, the ballpoint pen, the Polaroid camera, etc. The market process is a process of striving for social approval: social incentives and sanctions at work.

The incentive aspect which takes the form of financial rewards—the profit motive—will come up for discussion in Chapter 11. As for the sanction aspect, it operates through two channels: the necessity for products to gain acceptance on the part of buyers; and the necessity to adhere to social standards of efficiency— "cost must fit into the price." Competition in some form must be part of the process because it secures the availability of options, and these prevent individual participants from dictating their conditions. And options are the prerequisite of freedom.

Competition, though, evokes mixed feelings. The setting-people-against-each-other is the aspect which is found alienating. However, we have to ask ourselves whether this element of antagonism is not just one pole of a dialectical situation, its other pole being social complementarity and cooperation. Could it be the market system is only a special manifestation of a more general polarity proper to the human condition? Simultaneous competition and cooperation are present in many forms, informal or institutionalized, in widely different societies and social settings. Perhaps it is illusory to dream of preserving the cooperative pole and eliminating the competitive one. The tension between competition and cooperation may be a symptom of life rather than of pathology.

Shall we say then: All things considered—the market, after all? But competitive markets need the government's visible hand to be preserved and promoted, and some types of social output can be supplied only by collective agencies such as government. Indeed, newest forms of competition involve governments much more directly in the very competitive market process than mere protection of the legal framework used to.

In a growth economy, where expansion and continuous product innovation go hand in hand, competition acquires a new face. It becomes a high-powered game of betting on new growth items. It has nothing to do any more with petty questions such as "Shall we cut the price a little and gain on volume? Shall we raise the price a little to gain on the unit markup?" Competition becomes a matter of a long lead in developing a product or process, devising a strategy for testing, launching, and marketing it, and then throwing into the competitive game a large block of complex new production capacities, in the hope that the new product will survive the derby and generate sales far beyond the break-even point.

Modern technological innovations have characteristics which raise competition another few notches, as far as grandiosity of action is concerned. The requirements on research and development resources are such that nations have to choose among different strategies of technological development. Only a superpower can dare to push the competitive research and development effort on a broad front. Small and medium nations have to choose a strategy of concentrating resources in an area where they have a chance. Should a medium-size country, such as France, attempt to compete in atomic energy, computers, electronics, high-performance aircraft, space technology, color television, and so forth, resources will be spread so thin that failures and disappointments are a foregone conclusion.[40] Thus, market competition becomes competition between national

---

[40] A comparison of the French, American, Swedish, and Japanese strategies is contained in an illuminating article by Robert Gilpin, "Technological Strategies and National Purpose," *Science*, vol. 169, no. 3944, July 31, 1970, pp. 441–448.

strategies in the design of technological development, and puts governments in the role of top-level advisers, initiators, and coordinators.

Shall we say then: All things considered—the market *and* the government, a mutually corrective and complementary symbiosis of the invisible *and* visible hand, after all? The issues will appear in a sharper light after we have worked through the problems of allocation under centrally administered systems, in Chapter 9.

BIBLIOGRAPHY

Miller, John Perry (ed.): *Competition, Cartels and Their Regulation*, North-Holland Publishing Company, Amsterdam, 1962.

Edwards, Corwin D.: *Control of Cartels and Monopolies: An International Comparison*, Oceana Publications, Inc., Dobbs Ferry, N.Y., 1967.

McLachlan, D. L., and D. Swann, *Competition Policy in the European Community*, Oxford University Press, London, 1967.

Marris, Robin (ed.): *The Corporate Society*, Macmillan, London, 1974.

Galbraith, J. K.: *The New Industrial State*, Houghton Mifflin, Boston, 1967.

U.S. Congress, Joint Economic Committee: *The Analysis and Evaluation of Public Expenditures: The PPB System*, vol. 1, 1969 (compendium of papers).

Weidenbaum, Murray L.: *The Modern Public Sector*, Basic Books, New York, 1969.

Margolis, J., and H. Guitton, *Public Economics: An Analysis of Public Production and Consumption and Their Relation to the Private Sectors*, Macmillan, London, 1969.

Peck, Merton J., and Frederic M. Scherer: *The Weapons Acquisition Process: An Economic Analysis*, Harvard Graduate School of Business Administration, Division of Research, Boston, 1962.

Rosen, Steven (ed.): *Testing the Theory of the Military-Industrial Complex*, Lexington Books, D. C. Heath and Company, Lexington, Mass., 1973.

Pursell, Carroll W., Jr.: *The Military-Industrial Complex*, Harper & Row, New York, 1972.

Backman, Jules (ed.): *War and Defense Economics*, Rinehart, New York, 1952.

Hart, Albert G.: *Defense Without Inflation*, Twentieth Century Fund, New York, 1951.

Galbraith, J. K.: *A Theory of Price Control*, Harvard, Cambridge, Mass., 1952.

Scitovsky, Tibor, Edward Shaw, and Lorie Tarshis: *Mobilizing Resources for War*, McGraw-Hill, New York, 1951.

Pryor, Frederic L.: *Public Expenditures in Communist and Capitalist Nations*, Irwin, Homewood, Ill., 1968.

Chapter 9

Central
Administrative
Planning

If there existed the universal mind that projected itself into the scientific fancy of Laplace . . . such a mind could, of course, draw up a priori a faultless and an exhaustive economic plan, beginning with the number of hectares of wheat and down to the last button for a vest. In truth, the bureaucracy often conceives that just such a mind is at its disposal; that is why it so easily frees itself from the control of the market and of Soviet democracy.

L. D. Trotsky

The purpose of this chapter is *not* to tell in detail the story of how central administrative planning was invented, around 1930, in the Soviet Union; what type of industrialization policies were pursued in its framework; how the system was exported, after World War II, to the countries of Eastern and East Central Europe, China, and Cuba; what the economic outcomes have been, over the years, in the individual countries; what have been the nuances of form in the local adaptations of the system; and what nuances of reform have been planned, adopted, dropped, or modified, in the individual countries, since the midsixties.

The purpose of the chapter is something else, namely, to help the student grasp the problem of the decision makers at the top, the "central planners," who wish to run an entire national economy from the center, and who wish to run it in a special way: not just by holding the reins to steer the horses, but by instructing the horses where to step, how to lift their legs, and how to breathe. The intention is to go about the explanation in a rather technical, rigorous, and systematic way. At the core is the economics of a particular mode of allocation which attempts to substitute vertical flows of information (instructions down, reports on execution up), for lateral, horizontal flows of information between buyers and sellers, i.e., central command for market forces. Hence, the reader is advised to consult some of the sources listed at the end, to acquaint himself with the basic facts of economic history of the countries in question.

The image with the horses is really not very farfetched. Before we go into the technicalities of central planning, it is useful to point out that the system has its mainspring in a certain political philosophy, in a mentality characteristic of a certain attitude toward the human being and society. Its hallmark is distrust of spontaneity: in thought, in social relations, in economic processes. Without supervision, it says, there would be chaos. Order, action, and performance can be secured only through the authority of leadership and instructions from above, the more detailed the safer. The notion of an organic order which springs from natural propensities and motives of members of society, and is maintained through self-regulatory adjustment processes, is abhorred. It reeks of anarchy.

In the opening sentence we said the system *was invented.* Indeed, it is a preconceived economic system which *did not develop,* as did the capitalist market system, through spontaneous historical processes. The centrally administered variety of state capitalism can be imposed by decree upon whatever economic system precedes it. In the Soviet Union, it supplanted a market-type state capitalism of the 1921–1928 period known as the New Economic Policy (NEP). Elsewhere, it supplanted private capitalism directly, or served as the organizational mold for modern industrialization on a more or less precapitalist territory (China, Bulgaria, Albania). In a sense, it is a preconceived utopian model—somewhat along the lines of Barone's "Ministry of Production in the Collectivist State" (see Chapter 6, footnote 11)—which got a chance to be put to a test, thanks to the political power of its sponsors. The hidden totalitarian implications of one class of utopianism were thus demonstrated in historical practice.

The first and longest part of the exposition presents the system in its classic form, as it prevailed in the Soviet Union until 1965, the first year of an economic reform, and throughout the fifties in the Eastern European countries. It is essential to understand the classic version, in order to understand its reforms: their rationale, the modifications they introduced, and their difficulties. The reforms are outlined in the later sections, and the Chinese and Cuban variants are summarized. Further aspects of the system—its growth performance, income distribution and the inflation issue, industrial organization, the agricultural sector, foreign trade, position of the consumer, and labor relations—are taken up in the appropriate subsequent chapters of the book.

CENTRAL-COMMAND PLANNING:
THE CLASSIC VERSION

Under market capitalism, coordination calls for a combination of spontaneous market processes and deliberate regulation of global activity levels. Market processes take care of the detailed microadjustments of demand and supply. Macro-controls provide antibodies against cumulative mechanisms of decline, to assure operation at a level which leaves no labor unemployed. In a centrally planned economy—we shall be using from here on the abbreviation CPE favored by American scholars—this duality disappears. *Both microeconomic and macroeconomic results are secured via centralized assignment of microeconomic activities in the form of planned tasks to be fulfilled by the system's participants*: enterprises, government agencies, and their pertinent officials, managers, and employees.

An Input-Output Overview

What is involved in assigning production units their microeconomic activities from central-planning headquarters? To see that clearly, let us capitalize on our previous work with input-output relations in Chapter 7. In Table 9-1, we present once more the input-output schema, in a form suitable for a solidly grounded discussion of planning. Industry (or production unit) number 4 was chosen to recapitulate the meaning of a given row or column. The novelty, in comparison with Table 7-2, is the detailed breakdown of transactions involving fixed producer durables. In Table 7-2, purchases of fixed producer durables were given in column 15, in the final-use portion of the table. There, they were broken down by suppliers with whom they originated, but obviously not by the industries of destination, who bought them. To show this breakdown by customers, the investment column 15 would have to be split up into as many subcolumns as there are customer industries. This is exactly what we have done by placing a second input-output table, transactions in fixed producer durables, underneath the standard quadrant involving only transactions in current material inputs. It amounts to a blown-up investment column 15. The reason is that such itemized information on investment goods is of particular importance to CPEs, as we shall see.

In a market economy, the statistician constructing an input-output table collects the data on transactions between sellers and buyers *after the act*. The actual coordination of activities is achieved by the spontaneous operation of the market, and the input-output table represents its ex post record. Under perfect centralized planning, the planners would have to construct an input-output table for the coming planning period *beforehand*. It would serve as a blueprint according to which production units would then conduct their activities. Such an ex ante input-output table would constitute a *comprehensive central plan*.

How specific would the production units have to be in such a central plan? Ordinarily, input-output tables record aggregated transactions between entire "industries"; this is good enough for purposes of practical economic analysis in capitalist market economies. However, for operational purposes of centralized planning, the breakdown of transactions would have to be much finer. In the extreme, there would have to be an input-output table organized *by individual commodities*.

Table 9-1 Central planners' ex ante allocation of material inputs, labor, and fixed capital.

Enterprises buying outputs for intermediate uses (as material inputs)

Buyers of outputs for final uses

	1	2	3	4	5		n	C	G	I	X	Total gross output
1				enterprise #4				sumption	purchases	investment	Exports	Q_1
2												Q_2
3												Q_3
4	Shipments of output by enterprise #4 to other enterprises							Final uses of output supplied by enterp. #4				Q_4
5			Purchases of inputs by					Private civilian con-	Government	Fixed capital	Exports	Q_5
n												Q_n
								Total	Total	Total	Total	Gross total

Enterprises supplying outputs for intermediate uses by other enterprises and/or for final uses

LABOR ALLOCATION PLAN	Labor	L_4 assigned to individual enterprises	L_G	L

Total investment broken down by enterprises receiving fixed capital equipment

	1	2	3	4	5		n	
1								I_1
2	Deliveries of fixed capital equipment to investors							I_2
3								I_3
4								I_4
5								I_5
n								
INVESTMENT PLANS	IP_1	IP_2	IP_3	IP_4	IP_5		IP_n	I

Enterprises supplying fixed capital equipment to other enterprises

Column I, same as in upper part of table

C = civilian consumption (private)
G = government use of material goods
I = investment in fixed capital
X = exports
Q_1, Q_4, etc. = gross output of enterprise #1, #2, etc.
L = total labor force
L_4 = labor force allocated to enterprise #4
L_G = labor force employed in government
IP_1, IP_2 = investment plans (allocation of fixed capital items to enterprise #1, #2)

In addition to that, considering that a given commodity may be produced in a number of firms, and a given firm may produce a number of different commodities, transactions from the commodity table would have to be regrouped into rows and columns arranged *by individual firms*. The entry in the last cell (the total-output cell) of a given firm's horizontal row would be that firm's *output plan*; all the other row entries would together make up its *sales plan*; and entries in that firm's vertical column would be its *input-purchase plan*. Let us make a careful note of these distinctions because they will help us greatly in penetrating the mystery of the basic practical planning instruments of a CPE, the *material balances*, and the enterprise *operative plan* (*tekhpromfinplan*).

For purposes of a fully centralized planning it would also be necessary to determine the *time path* of all transactions of the planning period. Western input-output tables normally sum up transactions over a given year. This does not say anything about when all the small individual batches of output were delivered in the course of the year. However, such specification would be indispensable in a central plan. "Dating" transactions by smaller installments would be necessary to make sure that each batch of input arrives at the rendezvous with other inputs at the appropriate time. Otherwise, the planned activities could not proceed without hitches. In other words, production and related transactions would have to be coordinated not only in their annual summations; they would have to interlock smoothly at every point of time.

Basic Planning Instruments of a CPE

So much for the ideal picture of fully centralized planning. Actual planning procedures under Soviet-type central planning may be seen as a very partial implementation of the abstract planning scheme outlined above. Its full implementation in practice hurts itself against a number of real obstacles. They have to do mainly with limits to the amount of information that can be collected, processed, and communicated downward by the central planning agency. Central planners are able to handle the detailed planning for only a limited number of commodities. For the rest, they have to resort to shortcuts or leave decisions up to enterprises.

Material Balances   The first task of coordination through centralized planning is to make sure that the assigned production targets will be mutually consistent. It must be clear ahead of time *whether sufficient quantities of inputs are being planned to make the planned production targets of any given commodity possible*, and *what use will be made of the planned output of any given commodity*. This is the gist of all input-output relationships. It amounts to the requirement that the sum total of the various uses of a commodity must be in exact balance with the available quantities (sources) of that commodity: quantity demanded must equal quantity supplied. In a CPE, this relationship of equality is dealt with by placing the planned figures of output side by side with its uses, in the simple form of material balances.

A material balance is nothing else but one row of a fine-grain input-output table, i.e., one presented in a breakdown by single commodities, rather than by

Table 9-2 Material Balance for Commodity X

Sources	Uses
1 Total domestic output	1 Deliveries to be used as inputs in production
2 Imports	2 Distribution for domestic final uses (e.g., retail)
3 Inventories at the beginning of the planning year	3 Exports
	4 Inventories at the end of the planning year
	5 Reserves

broad industries. That row is usually rewritten in the form of a T account, as shown schematically in Table 9-2. Just as, in an input-output table, the figure in any last total-output cell of a row must naturally equal the sum of all the figures on specific uses in the preceding row cells, in a material balance the sum on the left (availabilities) must be equal to the sum on the right (uses).

In other words: The last entry in a row, i.e., total output of the given commodity, appears on the left-hand side of the material balance, under Sources. Domestic output is here augmented by imports and the available initial stock of inventories. All other entries of the row, i.e., sales to individual users, appear on the right-hand side of the material balance, among Uses (items 1 through 3). The fifth item, Reserves, represents a buffer: an amount to be allocated in the course of the year as the need arises. This reserve permits planners to plug up shortages that may appear in the course of the execution of the plan, owing to emergencies or mistakes. (Reserves may also contain strategic stockpiling for the case of war.) Item 4 represents end-of-the-year inventory which will appear on the Sources side in the material balance for the next year.

Planned allocation of commodities through material balances amounts basically to their *rationing*. First, figures on available quantities are assembled, on the basis of capacities foreseen for the coming period. Productive capacities are gauged on the basis of past performance and capacity expansion, expected from planned investments as well as from increases in productivity. Then, expected availabilities are earmarked for delivery to users.

The *Tekhpromfinplan* How do planners know how much to earmark for delivery to users, especially to those users who need the given commodity as input for their own production? To determine this side of the planned allocation process, figures on input uses in the row cells have to be considered with an eye on the production tasks of the various input users. In other words, how large a coal ration should go to a steel mill depends on how much steel the steel mill is expected to produce.

To set up these two related figures, the best place to start with is the steel mill itself. It has a concrete idea of its steel-production possibilities, as well as of its coal input requirements per ton of steel. The steel mill has also an idea of the other input requirements per ton of steel besides coal (iron ore, lime, electricity, nonferrous metals, etc.), so that, once it puts in the request for coal, it can put in requests also for other material inputs which concern a number of material balances for these other commodities.

Thus, it should be obvious that, as we go from one enterprise to another, we encounter all over again the same entries for planned data as in material balances. The operative plans of enterprises contain, too, output plans (availabilities) and input uses of output. But there is a difference: These input uses draw on portions of output listed in many different material balances, not on its own output. Thus, the operative plan of an industrial enterprise, a steel mill, is connected, via its output plan, to one material balance, that for steel (where its output is part of the figure on availabilities); and, via its planned input requirements, it is connected to a number of material balances in charge of the corresponding commodities (where these input requirements will be part of the figures on uses).

In speaking of *operative plans* of enterprises, we are coining an English equivalent of the clumsy term used in Soviet planning terminology, the *technical-industrial-financial plan*, usually abbreviated as *tekhpromfinplan*. Planned output and planned input requirements are at its core. We shall call this core the *enterprise production plan*.

To show the exact interdependence between enterprise production plans on the one hand and material balances on the other, we have drawn up a simplified schematic example in Figure 9-1. We urge the reader to trace the various connections with the help of the arrows. Having gone through the exercise, some will certainly ask: Why didn't we simply use the familiar input-output vocabulary? Why didn't we say straight that an enterprise production plan includes the vertical inputs column of the enterprise, as it is related to the last cell in the supply row of that enterprise, which is its total output? Quite so; it would have been a shortcut. However, something would have been lost. With the help of Figure 9-1, we can show better than any other way what the crucial requirement of consistency in production plans and material balances means.

The left half of the diagram can be interpreted, by itself, as a market economy consisting of three firms. (The picture is incomplete in that it leaves out the input of labor services and final uses of outputs delivered to consumers. It shows an economy that runs itself without people, which brings out clearly the strictly material input-output relations.) The firms sell to each other their outputs, and use them as inputs to produce those outputs. Consistency is assured because firms are in direct contact with each other. They produce as much as the others order, and each firm orders from the others what is needed to produce its output. Thus, demand for commodities (on the left side of their production-plan accounts), when summed up by individual products, is automatically equal to supply of these products (on the right-hand side of their production accounts). At the same time, each enterprise can be expected to order the amounts of inputs actually needed for its volume of output.

Figure 9-1 Enterprise production plans, material balances, and their relationship.

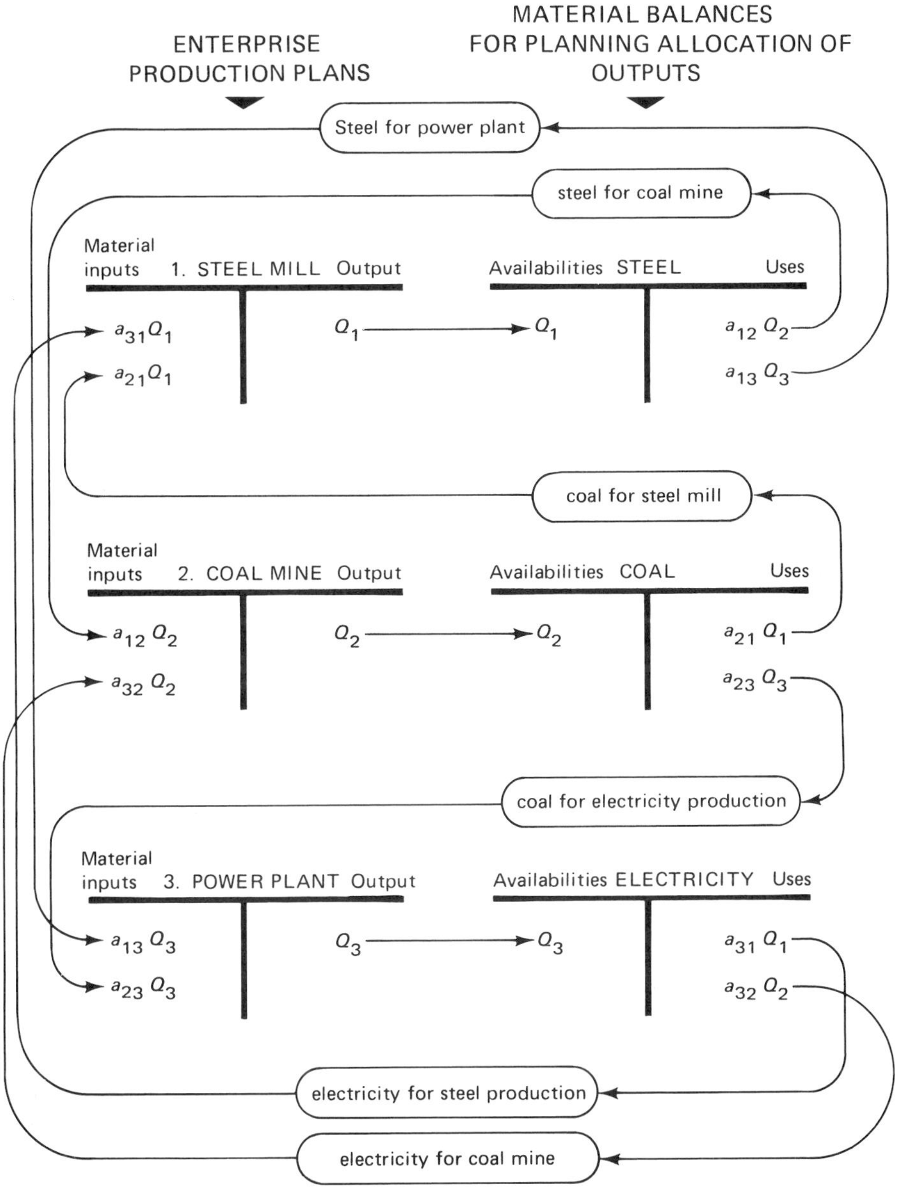

Material balances allocate output on materials "on paper." Actual shipments then follow the instructions indicated by the arrows. Outputs are shipped physically from the steel mill, coal mine, and power plant to the respective receiving enterprises, as they would in a market economy, except that there they would follow customers' orders directly, without the intermediary of material balances.

Symbols a_{31}, a_{21}, etc., are technical input coefficients per unit of a given output. Thus, a_{31} reads: amount of input 3 (electricity) per one unit of output 1 (ton of steel). Multiplication of a unitary technical input coefficient by the number of units of output that is to be produced (e.g., $Q_1 = 150,000$ tons of steel) yields the total quantity of electricity needed to produce that output of steel.

The CPE must secure the same kind of consistent results, but it complicates the task for itself by not letting enterprises deal with each other directly. It tries to figure out centrally what the outputs of individual enterprises shall be, and how these outputs shall be shared out when the enterprises in the set need them as inputs. Whether central planners can achieve such consistent output flows is a question that will have to be examined more closely.

Khozraschot   This is another of those Russian abbreviations, standing for "economic accounting." It is a very important additional instrument of planning, the more important as it represents a bridge to economic reforms of the system and, to tell it all, to a market mode of allocation. Material balances and the related enterprise production plans treat the allocation task, in principle, in terms of physical units. However, transactions between enterprises have the form of sales and purchases; compensation of employees has the form of wages which are spent on purchases of consumer goods; and government acquisitions of goods are also done via purchases financed from revenues raised as money taxes.

Hence, operations of enterprises in physical terms are replicated in corresponding financial flows. Sales of output bring enterprises revenue which is used to pay for material inputs, for wages of employees, for part of fixed producer durables, and for various contributions (including taxes), levied and collected by higher administrative units. These financial flows are what the expression *enterprise khozraschot* refers to. It is a key part of the financial portion of the enterprise *tekhpromfinplan*.

A highly simplified schema of an enterprise *khozraschot* is presented in Table 9-3. It looks very much like an income statement (a profit-and-loss account) of ordinary capitalist accounting. Value of output of goods for sale ("gross value of output") is on the right-hand side of the account; costs of inputs bought and of labor services are on the opposite side. If costs are smaller, the difference, profit, appears on the same side as the balancing item. A capitalist firm is likely to draw up periodically tentative statements of this kind, too, to see where it is going. In the CPE framework, the *khozraschot* statement amounts to a mandatory plan. It duplicates in financial terms what the production plan specifies in physical terms.

The last statement is fully true only if all output items, as well as inputs and labor, are physically planned. In principle, prices of outputs and inputs, as well as

Table 9-3   *Khozraschot* of a Soviet Enterprise

Outlays and profit (in rubles)		Value of output (revenues)	
1 Cost of material inputs	800,000	1 Gross value of output	1,000,000
2 Planned "wage fund"	150,000		
3 Planned profit	50,000		
	1,000,000		1,000,000

average wages, are given to the enterprise fixed. They are not allowed to vary with demand-and-supply conditions, or to be manipulated as part of some salesmanship. They are taken from centrally issued price lists. Therefore, prices being fixed, financial quantities really act as mere proxies of physical quantities. *Khozraschot* appears as a monetary veil draped over the planned physical magnitudes. Monetary corset might be a better word, since the financial plan is supposed to control the shape of real economic events.

However, the correspondence between the financial and physical aspects of production plans is not perfect, mainly because only a limited number of commodities is subject to planned allocation via material balances.[1] Besides, only some firms are so specialized as to handle only one or few products, and only some types of output are sufficiently homogeneous to be adequately recorded in physical units. Therefore, monetary values have to do the duty of physical quantities in all these instances. *Khozraschot* is an auxiliary instrument in the case of commodities allocated via material balances, but it has a primary role to play in many other respects. It is a softer instrument under which enterprises can, and often have to, make their own arrangements with each other.

Instruments—for What?

The basic instruments we have just described serve the implementation of the annual plans, the operational segments into which the much more general medium-term *five-year plans* are subdivided. The five-year plans give the broad aims and strategy: growth rates; development of new branches, regions, or technologies; major investment projects; relative emphasis to be placed on different sectors (agriculture, manufacturing) or fiscal uses (consumption, investment). The *annual plans* supply the tactics and take care of logistics. Now, is there any single pivot around which the annual-plan construction turns? Is there a so-called objective function to give the planning process direction?

According to ordinary economic logic, it should be the *bill of final goods*. One would expect planners to shoot for a maximum of commodities for final use, particularly for private and public consumption, given the range of feasible production levels. In terms of an input-output planning scheme, the starting point should be entries in the final-use columns. However, this is not the principle followed in a CPE of the Soviet type.

Soviet planners take their starting point from a set of preliminary targets concerning *gross output levels* of a number of important commodities and *aggregated gross output levels* of individual industries. They do take into account selected specific projects of high priority which fall into the final-use category (especially investments and military spending). Final consumption is treated more or less as a residual of less priority. However, the planning process centers around gross output data and intermediate input uses.

Preliminary figures serve as orientation points for subordinate organs (from

---

[1] The number of these so-called funded commodities has been limited but still quite large. Also, it has been changing over the years. For the Soviet economy, the upper range seems to be 40,000 products, though 20,000 is the most frequently cited number.

ministries down to individual enterprises) who are expected to draw up their own provisional pledges concerning output levels, and send in the corresponding preliminary requests for allocation of inputs. This activity coming "from below" is called *counterplanning*. Having compiled all this information, the planning center proceeds to test it for consistency. There is inconsistency if, for instance, the requests for a particular input add up to more than what its producers propose to supply. The planning center then tries to reconcile the figures by raising some (that goes for output proposals) and lowering others (that goes for input requests).

While the early sketchy plan drafts get progressively filled with more precise figures, the planning center pays attention also to global relationships between components of national income ("consumption fund," "accumulation fund," etc.) and to the balance of financial flows (revenues and outlays of the major economic sectors, volume of bank credit). The planning process culminates in the assignment of activity plans to the leading administrative organs (ministries and their economic-branch sections) and their concrete breakdown among individual enterprises. These final plans then provide the basis for the elaboration of an internal operative *tekhpromfinplan* within each enterprise. On that basis only can enterprises proceed to the conclusion of concrete *contracts* between one another concerning deliveries of output and the details and terms of their transactions.

This rudimentary account of the planning process is far from doing full justice to its actual complexity. It would lead us into dreary description of organization tables if we wanted to follow the planning process through all the various echelons of the administration, regional subdivisions of ministries and planning organs, organs of allocation and distribution (the *snabsbyt* system), etc. Besides, the administrative setup is subject to frequent reorganizations. What we need to know is how the system performs from the point of view of efficiency in allocation.

Malfunctions in Coordination

Just as we concentrated on market and government failures in the case of the capitalist market system, the following account also concentrates on failures. However, the procedure is not exactly parallel. In the market case, we took for granted a fundamental point in favor of the system: the final consumer and citizen having a say in the determination of output. In the case of a Soviet-type CPE, we shall take for granted a fundamental point in its disfavor: the final consumer and citizen being a very passive participant in the process of determination of output. What follows is an account of failures in the achievement of what the planners want to achieve, and think the consumer and citizen should want, too.

These failures are of a technical sort, owing to the system's characteristics. However, some of the malfunctions could be put at the door of *specific policies* of the planners, without which the *system itself* might work better. This is a most interesting issue. It is in line with our repeated warning not to confuse the characteristics of an economic system with the effect of policies adopted by the visible hand.

In this case, the policies that might be blamed for many malfunctions are summarized in words such as "taut planning," "overfull-employment planning," or simply "pressure planning." They seem to be strictly a reflection of the planners' lasting *policy preference for high growth rates*. But, on reflection, this separation of "policies" from "the system as such" may be too simple in this case. The policy of pressure planning is also supposed to substitute for market-type competitive pressures which are missing in a CPE. Would it, then, not be more appropriate to see such policy, at least to a degree, as part of the system's characteristics?

Inefficiencies of central planning do not mean that, in some basic and crude ways, the system cannot be extremely effective. The method of specific projects and material balances enables the system's directors to produce fast changes in the structure of an economy. This is what has to happen in the early stages of a country's industrialization. Central planning is not the only way, and perhaps not the optimal one, to achieve this developmental goal. Nevertheless, successes of forced industrialization in the Soviet Union of the 1930s, in Bulgaria, Romania, or Poland of the 1950s led to the widespread opinion that central planning is particularly suited to the accelerated creation of an industrial structure.

At those stages of development, plans typically consist of a collection of industrial investment projects ("leading links" in Soviet parlance) to which the rest of the economy is forced to adapt as best it can. Complex coordination is not the major order of the day. Once industrial capacities are installed and ready to operate, the problem of differentiated choices comes to the fore: what commodities to produce, and how to integrate their flows.

The ability of centralized procedures to coordinate is subject to increasingly severe testing as the number of products increases, or as sudden shifts are decreed in the already-established industrial structure (e.g., Soviet shift toward chemical industry in the early sixties). At that stage, deficiencies of central planning become universally apparent. Efficiency losses are too painful to be plastered over by dogmatic assertions about the superiority of the centralized system. The hour strikes for economic revisionism and reforms.

Criticism of central planning is not an exclusive preserve of Western observers. Indeed, material for all the negative points usually made has been gleaned mainly from Soviet and Eastern European publications. In a great number of cases, Eastern European economists turn out to be much the most severe critics, whereas in the West and in Japan, one often tends to lean over backward and to express judgments with extreme caution.

The system's malfunctions would make long and tiring reading if we were to make an exhaustive list. To give the account rhyme and reason, we have decided to include only features that find room under the following three headings: (1) "The Elusiveness of Consistency"; (2) "Means of Measuring Performance"; and (3) "The Question of Timing." We shall conclude the survey with an estimate of the net effect of the malfunctions.

The Elusiveness of Consistency   The requirement of plan consistency was already explained in connection with material balances. There are two main reasons why consistency is difficult to achieve. One has to do with the uncertain information basis for determining precise input-output targets. The other is the consequence of the bargaining tug-of-war between enterprises and planners.

Sources of Inconsistencies The *information basis* for target setting is weak because the plan for the coming year has to be prepared before statistical reports on the production performance for the current year are in. Hence, current-year data, the bench mark for the plan next year, have to be estimated. Furthermore, enterprises are expected to furnish their input requests before they know for sure what their output tasks will eventually be. Hence, they prefer to overstate their input requirements, just in case.

On the other hand, enterprises develop a habit of understating their production possibilities when they make their preliminary pledges of output next year. They know their planners. Year after year, without respite, planners set output targets by extrapolating past growth, taking as base figure the most recent performance. Only a foolish director would push output to the limit of the true enterprise capacity. Especially, extra high increases that could be achieved thanks to transitory circumstances are to be avoided. Planners would then expect the same high increases forever after. Always up, never down, is the "ratchet effect" at work. As a protective defense against excessive production tasks, enterprises, as well as their protectors at higher administrative echelons, have learned to hold back on output pledges during the stage of "counterplanning." They hope that, even if the final output plans are pushed above the preliminary pledges of the counterplanning stage, they will end up reasonably realistic. Overstating input requirements and understating output possibilities amount to a *search for slack*, for safety margins, or—as it is called in Soviet managerial folklore—*strakhovka*.

This behavior pattern leads to a serious impairment of "truth in planning." Basic information ingredients are thus inconsistent from the early stages of annual-plan construction. In terms of our Figure 9-1, it means the following: when firms specify their needs of output from other firms (left-hand side of their preliminary production plans), they exaggerate; when they propose their own output figures which are supposed to fill those needs (right-hand side of the production plans), they set them low. Thus, the two sides do not balance. When these preliminary needs and output proposals are rearranged into preliminary material balances, it turns out that, as a rule, the availabilities of a material its producers say they can deliver are less than the sum of amounts its users say they must have.

Planning authorities, of course, know, or suspect in any case what game is being played on the part of enterprises and their superior organs. The same pattern of behavior is repeated at every echelon: upward resistance to high production assignments, downward pressure for trying harder. A system of pervasive bureaucratic haggling and bargaining about input and production quotas thus becomes the unseen part of the planning process. It is officially known as search for "hidden reserves."

Eventually the central planning agencies have to proceed to reconcile the two sides of material balances, but their methods are crude. They boil down to raising output plans and paring down input appropriations. There is usually little time to make adjustments assuring full consistency and correspondence to the real conditions of production of individual plants. The upshot is that *input appropriations incorporated in the definitive plans tend to correspond poorly to the planned output targets*. This becomes manifest in the pervasive appearance of *shortages* in the course of the execution of plans.

   Correcting Inconsistencies in Practice   How do enterprises react to this state of affairs? They resort to a series of *corrective actions* on their own. This "informal behavior of the Soviet firm" is often very picturesque. It is the real-life hustle and bustle taking place in stark contrast with the niceties of formal planning schemes. It is frequently illegal; as such, constantly deplored and denounced. Nonetheless, it is indispensable and therefore tolerated.

   If the firm finds its plan inconsistent—not enough inputs in relation to its output plan—the simplest way out is to neglect production of items of lowest priority. In doing that, managers follow an unwritten, but universally known, *scale of priorities* which mirrors relative preferences of the planners. Thus, supplies for specific high-priority projects receive first attention; supplies for the consumer market are cut down to residual capacity that is available after priority deliveries have been taken care of. Simultaneously, through contracts and lobbying, the firm will try to have its output plan formally revised downward. It will then not have to report underfulfillment of the original plan and lose managerial bonuses.

   Another set of practices helps the firm obtain materials in short supply through unofficial channels. This amounts to a black or gray market that thrives in the interstices of planned allocation. It happens regularly that shortages in one place correspond to excess appropriations in another. The problem is to arrange informally for a suitable reallocation. To this end, firms employ services of special agents, the so-called pushers (*tolkachi*), whose talents lie in locating such supply sources and arranging deals, often in the form of barter.

   Inconsistency in allocation creates a pervasive *climate of uncertainty* concerning supplies. Ministerial organs try to protect themselves against breakdowns in deliveries from other ministries by constructing supply facilities for important inputs under their own jurisdiction. Thus, the chemical industry may build its own plants for transportation equipment, in order not to depend on the engineering industry. Tendency toward diversification of this type has been known as *empire building* or *subordinate autarky*. An analogous phenomenon exists within regional units: Regional organs tend to secure deliveries for local users in preference to those in other regions—a tendency denounced as *localism* (*mestnichestvo*). Exactly as in international trade, all such tendencies toward autarky (self-sufficiency)—whether within administrative or regional units—carry a cost. Autarky works against fuller specialization which normally yields benefits in the form of lower cost. However, the higher cost of autarky is gladly borne if it protects enterprises against uncertainty in deliveries.

   Means of Measuring Performance   Economic performance of a firm has many aspects which, under market capitalism, tend to be reflected in the rate of net financial returns, i.e., in the profit rate. The profit rate expresses *synthetically* all the relationships between the firm's decisions in the choice of articles produced and their success with the buyers, as well as its decisions in choosing and organizing the elements of the production process. The profit rate is the net outcome between sales and costs, the two basic dimensions of the firm's operations.

The *khozraschot* of a Soviet firm reflects them too, although in a clumsy and somewhat distorted way. Where is the fundamental difference? In a market-capitalist firm, accounting cost-and-profit data correspond to objective relationships—market demand, technology and internal organization of the firm, its comparative standing with respect to competitors, the quality of decisions made autonomously from within its management. Under state capitalism of the Soviet type, the performance of a firm is judged *against how outside authorities define it*.

The planners' a priori notions are expressed in the planned *khozraschot* and in a number of related *performance indicators* not mentioned so far. Thus labor costs are controlled through the planned ratio of gross value of output to the number of worker-hours (the labor-productivity indicator). Reduction of production costs is enforced and checked via the planned ratio of unit production costs in the given plan year and the preceding years. The average wage of workers is planned. Overall "financial discipline" is checked via the volume of planned profits. Efficiency in the utilization of various capital assets is followed by means of various partial capital-output ratios.

"Red executives" are constrained in their decisions by a battery of such piecemeal *performance indicators* they are expected to fulfill. However, since it is not easy to fulfill them all, they tend to pay greatest attention to that indicator they have learned from experience to count most, especially as basis for managerial rewards. That indicator was, in the classic form of Soviet central planning (up to 1965), the *gross value of output*. This indicator acquired central significance for the functioning of the Soviet firms, and many farcical curiosities have been traced to the almost exclusive reliance on its use. (After the denunciation of Stalin in 1956 under the code words "cult of personality," the status of this performance indicator was rendered through the expression "cult of the gross value of output.")

If a firm happens to produce a homogeneous type of product measurable in physical units, the system falls back on expressing performance in terms of *gross volume* (rather than *value*) of output. Unfortunately, the choice of the physical unit used for measurement of output can be very tricky. A given commodity may have a number of relevant physical "dimensions" according to which it can be measured: weight, surface area, volume, piece units, or other aspects that count for its usefulness. For instance, sheet metal is measurable in area units, but there are also thickness, various widths, and different finishes. In such cases, it has been observed, there will be a tendency on the part of managers to twist the assortment of products in favor of those types which will yield the largest quantity, with least work, in terms of the physical units in which performance is measured. Thus, if sheet-metal output is measured in square meters, there will tend to be lots of thin types, in large widths and rough finish, and not enough of other types. The assortment will not correspond to actual demand.

The use of gross *value* of output has similar defects leading to undesirable assortments of products. The game will then be played by taking advantage of (1) relative prices at which products are valued and (2) the fact that the gross-value indicator is "gross"; i.e., it covers not only the net productive contribution of the firm (its "value added") but also the value of material inputs purchased from other firms. Conservatism in product types can also be partly traced to the working of the gross-value indicator. Let us explain.

(1) The financial character of the gross-value-of-output indicator implies that the products are expressed in some prices. Here, the old customary principles which ruled Soviet price formation until 1967 (and still survive) come into play. Soviet prices were traditionally not meant as signals affecting or guiding managerial decisions. They were conceived as mere *accounting prices*, used for aggregating physical quantities in production plans and for controlling their execution. Therefore, the standard notion that prices should be systematically related to production costs and demand conditions was ignored. Prices were fixed centrally, through a periodic issue of voluminous price lists, and with a great deal of arbitrariness (see below). As a result, products were priced above money costs, with different profit markups, and frequently below cost. [This is why the *khozraschot* in certain firms or industries displayed, as balancing item, a *planned loss*, rather than planned profit (see Table 9-2), without being a sign of failure—as long as performance corresponded to the planned figure.]

Thus, in theory, prices were an entirely passive element with no effect upon managerial decisions. However, as they were used to express the gross value of output, prices did acquire an active role in influencing managerial strategy. Again, managers tended to twist their output mix toward a larger share of "advantageous" products, i.e., those whose money value happened to be highest in relation to the cost of production. Such manipulations made it easier for the firm to fulfill the planned gross value of output, as well as the planned-profit and labor-productivity indicators. The fact that this practice created shortages of the less advantageous items was another matter, of minor concern to the producing firm.

(2) The *gross* nature of the gross value of output was the source of another set of economic irrationalities. It is easy to see that a firm will have less trouble to show a high gross value of output if it chooses to produce by using as much material inputs purchased from other firms as possible, and minimizing labor input of its own workers. This amounts to a tendency to inflate item 1 and compress item 2 on the left-hand side of the *khozraschot* in Table 9-3.

In practice, it leads to a bias toward production of highly material-intensive products which require minimal processing, or simply to cutting corners in processing. Hence the chronic complaints about the excessively great weight of Soviet and Eastern European machinery products, poor finishing, use of high-priced materials, and the general shortage of spare parts in Soviet-type economies. (Spare parts are usually relatively labor-intensive both in production and in distribution.)

We also mentioned conservatism in product types as being partially due to the gross-value indicator. The reason is simple: It is easier to fulfill the gross-output target by concentrating on traditional products where operations are routinized than by innovating. As Khrushchev said, using steel as an example: "The production of steel is like a well-traveled road with deep ruts; here even blind horses will not run off because the wheels will break." Aversion to new products is at the source of the observed anti-innovation bias of Soviet-type central planning, and it has to do with the retardation of technological progress as a factor of economic growth. (Make a mental note for Chapter 12 on growth performance.)

The Question of Timing   To continue with the last type of malfunction, dislike of innovation has an additional reason in the chronology of checking on plan execution. Output plans of a firm are, as a rule, broken down into installments by regular time segments: quarters, months, and—in earlier days—even by ten-day periods. Periodic payments of managerial bonuses depend on the plan fulfillment in the successive periods. The breakdown of annual plans into short-term installments is done rather mechanically, with little allowance for possible fluctuations in the level of production. As one might expect under these conditions, anything that might disrupt the even flow of operations (such as retooling for a new product or a breaking-in period at the beginning of a new run) is disliked. Even if research-and-development institutes were spewing forth useful inventions, the production sector would be inventing reasons for not adopting them.

Another consequence of periodic checking on plan fulfillment is a peculiar "seasonal" pattern in the intensity of operations. Periodicity of controls brings out what is a rather general phenomenon: the propensity of humans to postpone effort. Soviet firms tend to start the month (or quarter) at an easy pace, then to accelerate, and to end up in furious tempos as the date of reckoning approaches. This aspect of central planning is known as "storming" (*shturmovshchina*) and has always been criticized as one of the major obstacles to efficiency.

The Net Effect   The question is sometimes asked: How seriously is one supposed to take all these stories on malfunctions and inefficiencies under central planning? Couldn't one compile a similar collection of anecdotal evidence, just as damaging, about market capitalism? Probably yes. Therefore, it is in order to point out a few general considerations and estimates for the benefit of the wary.

Speaking in comparative terms, the fact is that Soviet-area economists and officials are the ones who have been looking over the fence in the Western direction, to learn how to do things better, not the other way around. And Western companies doing construction work and other business in the Soviet Union have made very unfavorable comparisons on the spot, as repeatedly reported in the press. Besides, there exists a vast Polish, Czech, and Hungarian literature as witness to the profound disenchantment with the central-planning experience. (See Chapter 6, footnotes 33 and 35.)

In the Soviet Union itself, prominent economists of worldwide reputation have estimated the loss of potential output due to the system's malfunctions. L. V. Kantorovich, the winner of the Nobel prize in 1975, estimated in 1959 that the irrationalities of economic planning cost the Soviet system an extra potential industrial output equal in various branches up to one-half of their actual output, and V. V. Novozhilov put the loss of industrial output due to the malfunctioning of the supply system at 25 percent.[2] According to another more recent Soviet source, 25 percent of all working time is lost through difficulties with the supply system.[3] Whatever the basis of all these estimates, it is safe to conclude that losses attributable to the system's malfunctions add up to magnitudes far beyond allocation losses of capitalist market systems, even if we count in observable losses due to the unemployment output gap. (We shall return once more to a comparative evaluation of the two variants of capitalism in the last section.)

"But It Works"   This phrase, which can occasionally be heard, is absolutely true, saying, as it does, the obvious, but it does not take away an iota from the preceding observations. Rube Goldberg's intricate contraptions also work, which does not make them less absurd. The but-it-works idea sometimes takes the form of pointing to high growth rates achieved under the CPE systems, as a redeeming feature of inefficiencies in allocation. This would make sense if inefficiencies in allocation were the *cause* of high growth rates, i.e., if it were a question of "choice versus growth."[4] In reality, inefficiencies in allocation due to systemic malfunctions only mean that, without them, the growth rates might have been even higher, or less costly in terms of effort and consumption sacrificed (see Chapter 12).

Growth itself can never be divorced from the issue of choice. Growth implies construction of new capacities. What these capacities are going to be is a matter of economic choice. The choice predetermines what will be the future patterns of production possibilities. It fixes the precise *shape* of the production-possibilities curve, not only its *position*, as it moves outward.

The importance of efficient choice in the process of growth was admirably stated by P. Wiles:

> It is a mere fallacy, however often it is repeated by however high authority, that

---

[2] Cited by Leon Smolinski in *Foreign Affairs*, vol. 42, no. 4, July 1964, pp. 603 and 606; on Kantorovich see also P. J. D. Wiles, *The Political Economy of Communism*, Harvard, Cambridge, Mass., 1962, p. 94.

[3] *Khozyaistvennaya reforma i problemy realizatsii*, 1968, p. 36, cited in Michael Ellman, *Planning Problems in the U.S.S.R.*, Cambridge University Press, London, 1973, p. 32.

[4] This was the title of a celebrated article by Peter Wiles in *Economic Journal*, vol. 66, no. 262, June 1956, pp. 244–255; the theme is resumed in his *The Political Economy of Communism*, pp. 206–221. The same false dilemma, as propagated by Schumpeter, was analyzed in Chap. 8, section on antitrust.

poverty and underdevelopment give us more excuse for arbitrary choices, while rationality becomes important only when a certain prosperity has already been achieved. Obviously the exact opposite is the case. For arbitrary choices are wasteful choices, and a poor man can afford waste less than a rich.[5]

This brings us to an opposite misconception about the CPE of the Soviet type, namely, that the planning activities have been altogether a sham.

We owe the most extreme formulation of this judgment to Michael Polanyi, who, at one time, had disputed the ability of planners to subject the economy to central *direction;* he saw only "ubiquitous central pressure" which merely imposes "the continuous general expansion of an existing network of mutual adjustment," which is, in its nature, identical with a market network of relationships.[6] If this is understood in the sense that the planners lack any "objective function" and only blindly insist on forever expanding production as such, then it surely is wrong. It is, of course, true that the planning process, which starts with gross production targets (see above), supports the impression as if the system were geared to an "ideological consumption of semi-fabricates," to use P. Wiles's expression.[7] However, output targets contain a definite structure of final objectives. In particular, they cover specific projects which are not just a routine expansion of the existing structure of output. These are typically major undertakings of capital construction (new plants, power stations, pipelines, etc.), "prestige projects" (space exploration, international aircraft), and military equipment. These represent, so to speak, custom-made portions of the general plans. They are closely supervised by the appropriate agencies and enjoy a high-priority status in the allocation of inputs, labor, etc. By directing inputs into these preferential-treatment areas, the planners are molding the structure of the production sector in a very real sense by design.

The allocation methods may be as *inefficient* as they are, but they are extremely *effective* in determining the structure of the economy according to the planners' preferences. In considering the merits of a CPE, *effectiveness* in this latter sense is a notion to be kept carefully apart from the question of the system's *efficiency*. A sledgehammer may be very effective driving in a thumbtack, but it hardly is an efficient method.

REFORMS OF CENTRAL PLANNING

At one earlier point, the reader might have been struck meeting the term "contract," normally associated with market systems, in connection with the CPE model. Enterprises, having received the final version of their production plans from above, are supposed to give them concrete content by concluding contracts horizontally with one another, or with intermediary distribution organs, about

[5] P. Wiles, *The Political Economy of Communism*, p. 95.

[6] M. Polanyi, "Towards a Theory of Conspicuous Production," *Soviet Survey*, no. 34, October–December, 1960, pp. 90–100, and comments by G. Grossman, N. Jasny, A. Nove, and P. Wiles, pp. 101–110.

[7] P. Wiles, *The Political Economy of Communism*, p. 282. The passage continues: "Steel happens, in the minds of Communists, to be more beautiful and desirable than saucepans or even guns. . . . 'Steel was a final good to Stalin, and bread an intermediate one.' "

specific delivery of specific articles. Whatever the roundabout channels through which planning information shuttles between the government ministries, their various administrative echelons, the central-planning office, and their regional organs, it is a fact that for the economy to actually work, enterprises have to be somehow in touch with each other, independently of the planning superstructure.

We have also seen that the planning superstructure depends for much of its basic information input on upward communications from enterprises "in the field." Naturally, at some point someone begins to ask whether all that vertical information traffic is really necessary. Couldn't one perhaps leave it to enterprises themselves to establish their own links with suppliers and customers? They have to do it to a large extent in any case, even under central planning. So it may save much effort, and result in better coordination to boot.

What we have just said is the gist of all attempts at reforming central administrative planning. The designs of reforms may contain a swarm of other detailed arrangements, but underneath them all is the fundamental idea of activating the horizontal relationships between production units and their customers. It means bowing to the natural structure of economic relationships, to their spirit which is so vividly expressed in an input-output table and in every supply-demand diagram. It means mustering the confidence that people will work, managers manage, enterprises produce, sell, buy, and the sun rise even without a detailed central plan.

However, to acknowledge the objective logic of economic behavior and to follow through with practical measures is, first, a dizzying prospect, and then a politically and socially difficult enterprise which some have even perceived as dangerous and subversive. Not every country, in fact, *no* country was able to travel the full distance from the classic CPE model to the model of a market economy of autonomous state enterprises, and from "imperative" command planning to "indicative" steering. Theoretical *discussions* about reforms, practical *designs* of reformed systems, and actual *realization* of the approved designs come in various degrees of radicalism. In all three aspects, there are tame reforms tampering superficially with an arrangement here and there, and there are far-reaching reforms. There is limited experimenting, there are cases of arrested reforms, and there is backsliding. We are witnessing a confused and unfinished process.

We shall organize the explanation of basic principles of the most radical conceptions around two topics: *new incentives* and the *price reforms*. We shall then point out the reasons which make for caution, or outright opposition to reforms, resulting in the tame variants, or even in cases of "the reform that never was," as Alec Nove once characterized the Soviet reform of 1965.[8]

The New Incentive Design

The old system of incentives gravitated around the fulfillment of the planned gross value of output. We are speaking of managerial incentives because they are

---

[8] See L. A. D. Dellin and Hermann Gross (eds.), *Reforms in the Soviet and East European Economies*, D. C. Heath and Company, Lexington, Mass., 1972, p. 19.

the strategic element in the systemic behavior of the enterprise; they are what shapes decision making. In the classic CPE model, managerial bonuses—a substantial, though conditional, part of managerial rewards (up to 30 percent of basic salary)—were linked to those imperfectly and ambiguously specified production targets. Under the cult of the gross-output "success indicator" the central operating principle of a CPE became "production for the sake of production, not use," as Eastern European economists liked to say. The new system was to emphasize production for use.

In terms of success indicators, volume of *output* was replaced, first of all, by volume of *sales*. The idea was that usefulness of output is revealed only when customers actually buy it, not when it just exists, because it may also sit around in the form of useless accumulation of inventory that may eventually have to be recycled (as part of the fulfillment of planned scrap collection).

Since volume of sales in itself does not say anything about efficiency in production, the spotlight shifted further to an indicator capable of capturing that aspect of performance. Efficiency in production is revealed primarily in the level of cost outlays. Lower cost means higher profit margins, other things being equal. Hence, the indicator on which the spotlight rested was the profit volume. Now, *profit volume* increases not only when unit costs are lowered but also when the volume of sales increases. Therefore, profit volume reflects not only the quality of technological efficiency but also of decisions as to articles produced and marketed. It is a perfect "synthetic" indicator: it captures two basic aspects of operations in one figure. And if it is used as basis of incentives, it stimulates managers automatically to expand production of output that sells, an objective that planners sought vainly to achieve under the old system.

To distinguish the new system from the market-capitalist "profit motive," and to make it up as a descendent of the old model, Soviet sources have learned to discuss reforms using the code phrase "raising the significance of the *khozraschot*." If the reader relates the last two paragraphs to our Table 9-3, the point will be clear. The difference from the old *khozraschot* is that, in the most radical versions of the new model, none of the figures are planned from above. They emerge from the *self-motivated behavior of the enterprise, acting as an autonomous decision-making unit.*

The aspect of self-motivation has been expressed, in Eastern Europe, in the postulate that, under the new arrangements, "what is good for society should also be good for the enterprise." A corollary has been that "the enterprise must earn its own way," a phrase directed against the practice of subsidizing enterprise losses as long as the planned gross value of output was attained, or as long as high costs could be justified by "objective circumstances" beyond the control of enterprises.

We have to go back for a moment to the tug-of-war, under a CPE, between enterprises and the superior organs over their true production capabilities, input appropriations, and assigned output targets. There, pressure planning acted upon enterprises as an external force. The interest of participants on the enterprise end was to lie about production capacities in order to secure low output plans which would be easy to fulfill.

Outsiders have been impressed mainly by the sound and fury of planners' exhortations. There is no doubt that Soviet-area managers have been continuously under tension. They did supply their share of cases for the statistics on heart attacks. On the other hand, the account of the system's malfunctions revealed a number of practices that enabled participants to circumvent the harshness of planned tasks and to soften their impact. The daily run of the system allowed for accommodation between the managers of the production sector and the supervisory bureaucracies. Malfunctions served as a plausible pretext for grants of reprieve, exemptions, adjustments of plans, etc. The process was enervating, but it was also accommodating.

Thus, the paradox of exogenous pressure is that it provokes foot dragging and is less effective, in the end, than internalized pressures that characterize the system of capitalist market competition, as well as the radical Eastern European reform models.

Returning to the profit-volume indicator, there is a third efficiency aspect which it can be made to reflect synthetically, besides volume of sales and production cost level. Instead of dealing with it as an absolute sum, or as a percentage of the value of sales, one can relate the profit volume to the value of fixed capital equipment with which the enterprise works. The ratio of the two magnitudes is a type of *profit rate*. If it is used as a basis of incentive rewards, it provides a stimulus not only to minimize current productive costs but also to operate with as little fixed equipment as possible. Since that value appears in the denominator, the smaller it is the higher will be the profit rate.

This wrinkle is supposed to work against the old CPE tendency to "hoard" capital equipment, even if it had been allocated by error, or if the production program was changed and the equipment became superfluous. To put pressure on managers to get rid of such items, and in general to use capital sparingly, has been also the purpose of the *capital charge*. This instrument, or "economic lever," in the reformist lingo, has become an early standard feature of all reforms. It is imposed upon enterprises as a kind of property tax in the form of interest on the value of fixed equipment (usually set at 6 percent), to be paid to the treasury. In the CPE model, capital equipment was allocated free of charge as a nonreturnable grant. By putting a cost on its use, and in some cases treating its value as a repayable long-term credit, reform designers wished to put a stop to what looked like insatiable appetite of managers for capital equipment.

Reforming Prices

As in so many other things, Karl Marx has been also made responsible, by many Western writers, for Soviet-type price systems. In reality, he has been innocent. Their fault has not been to have followed any single principle, but so many different principles that the resulting structure of prices has been highly arbitrary. Still, it has not been so arbitrary as to defy description.

The major features of a classic Soviet-type price system can be summarized as follows:

(1) Enterprises sold their products to their intermediate distribution organs at *wholesale prices* constructed from a calculated *average* production cost for the

branch firms producing the article, plus a standard and very modest profit mark-up, practically a formality. Obviously, if actual production costs of an individual enterprise were considerably higher, they could not be covered from sales reve-nues. Such enterprise incurred losses which were covered by an injection of subsi-dies. Hence the normal and widespread phenomenon of "planned losses."

(2) Intermediate distribution organs transformed the enterprise wholesale price into an *industry wholesale price* by adding their own, not very significant, cost and profit markup. However, consumer goods received a massive dose of the so-called turnover tax—at certain periods one-third to one-half of the enterprise wholesale price on the average, though in individual cases it might have been several times its multiple. Thus burdened, industry wholesale prices of consumer goods were transformed into *retail prices*; retail organs merely had to add their own cost and profit markup. As a result, the price level of intermediate industrial goods, as long as traded between enterprises and government organs, was dispro-portionately low compared to the price level of consumer goods sold to the public. This is why a Soviet-type price structure is sometimes characterized as a "two-tier" price system.[9]

(3) If one considers also prices of *agricultural products*, it would be proper to speak of a three-tier price system. Just as consumer prices have been high, so prices of agricultural products paid to farm units have been traditionally low, relative to the wholesale price level of intermediate inputs of industry. Agricultur-al prices have also been low relative to realistic production costs, counting in assumed realistic wage rates farm labor should be getting. Why? Considering that direct taxes in agriculture have been light and the incidence of the turnover tax passes the rural population by (it has not been a great shopper in retail stores), low agricultural prices mean a method of taxing rural incomes: low prices keep incomes low enough so that they would not need to be taxed any more in a visible way.

Scattered around this low general level of agricultural prices have been spe-cific product prices, some priced more advantageously and some less, in view of their production costs; besides that, they were usually subject to graduated ad-justments according to agricultural regions, and were lower for obligatory deliv-ery quotas and higher for quantities delivered in excess of the quota.

The agricultural part of the price system does not concern us directly in connection with reforms of the CPE model. Revisions of agricultural prices have been part of another set of policies aiming, since the late fifties, at breathing new life into incentives in agriculture (see Chapter 14). As for the set of nonagricultur-al prices, it should be clear even from our summary account that they could not stay that way if profit and rate of profit were to become a major active regulator of managerial decisions. As a minimum, prices needed to be set high enough not

---

[9] Whether the turnover tax is a *disguised form of profit* or a form of sales tax paid by the consumer but collected at the point of sale between manufacturing and retail trade is a subject for endless theoretical discussions. It is probably best seen as a combination of the two. In any case, it has been a major source of fiscal revenue (in the Soviet Union at times almost 70 percent, now down to 30 percent).

to lead to planned losses, a category easily camouflaging losses due to misman-agement.

Price reforms undertaken since the midsixties in Eastern Europe and the Soviet Union have tried to do more than that. They were ambitious undertakings intended to yield a coherent set of industrial product prices, or at least a coherent scaffolding on which to construct such prices. They were to be rational to the extent of bringing relative prices closer in line with relative costs of production. To let them vary with supply and demand conditions would have been expecting too much, even though a small subset of prices was, as a rule, taken out of the category of "fixed" or "ceiling" prices and put into the free-price category. The key word has not been, as yet, "scarcity prices" or "optimal prices," but merely *prices constructed coherently and consistently according to one chosen price formula*, defined by the manner of calculating the profit markup.[10] The results have not been absolutely perfect, even on those terms; however, every step toward a great-er degree of coherence in the structure of prices can be considered progress under the circumstances.

Tame Reforms and Halfway Houses

If one abstracts from the ownership aspects, is the incentive structure of a re-formed CPE at all different from the market-capitalist profit-maximization objec-tive? Theoretically, the reform design could be pushed so far as to transform state capitalism of the classic Soviet type into a system of autonomous state corpora-tions, without stock and stockholders, operating in an authentic market environ-ment, under the only obligation of turning in some form of "dividend" (or profit tax) to the state budget and paying their loans back, with interest, to the state bank.

However, even the most daring reform designs of the late sixties (Czechoslo-vakia, 1967–1968, Hungary, 1968) did not dare project such images of the future (even though the Czechoslovak long-term "target solution," entertained before the Soviet invasion of 1968, came close to it). They do have a number of achieve-ments to their credit. They have convincingly demonstrated in practice that plan-ning with material balances can be dropped overnight, and the unwieldy system of distribution organs drastically curtailed, without any risk of chaos and with considerable benefits to efficiency. Financing of investments can be better han-dled through long-term bank credits than through central capital grants. But when it comes to profits, nowhere were managers allowed to dispose of net after-tax profits according to their own judgment.

Changing profit from a mere economic indicator into an active "economic lever," i.e., into an incentive, has taken the form of allocating a certain percent-

---

[10] If the profit markup is calculated in proportion to the value of fixed capital, the formula is called the *production price* (applied, for example, in East Germany). If it is calculated as a composite of two parts, one a percentage of fixed capital and the other of wages, we get the hybrid formula for the so-called *double-channel price* (used in Czechoslovakia and Hungary). If profit were calculated in proportion to wage cost, it would be the so-called *value price*, approximating the Marxian concept of labor values. (This last formula has not been used anywhere, except in theoretical discussions and dry-run computations.)

age of profit into an "incentive fund" from which bonuses and other extras are paid. It is the same principle as in selling on commission. Usually, an allocation is also made into a "social fund," meant to finance various amenities for use by employees, and into an "investment fund" available for smaller capital expenses at the discretion of managers. The large outlays are financed partly by bank credit, but mostly still through grants from the government, fiercely jealous of its controls over the crucial element of central planning, the investment plan.

This describes the essentials of the most advanced type, the halfway-house reforms, such as that of Hungary. The tame reforms have their best example in the Soviet reform, implemented gradually, and up to a point, in the years after 1964, when it was announced. The tameness consists in not letting enterprise managers have enough freedom of decision for profits to become a true test of their abilities, sink or swim. The *khozraschot* does have its significance raised, but the value of sales, profit, increments to profit, etc., continues to be handed down as *planned* financial magnitudes, and rewards to be based on their fulfillment. Thus, profits act as success indicators in the old CPE sense. Also, allocation with the help of material balances is not relinquished, which deprives the incentive, social, and investment funds of much practical significance: even if rates of achievement are high in money terms, the money cannot be easily spent on goods if no provision was made for them in material balances and production plans.

Two deep-seated reasons are often cited to explain why the progress of reforms has been so halting. First, there are the vested interests of the planning bureaucracy. Fearful of being robbed of jobs and function, they use ideological conservatism as cover for what amounts to a vast collective featherbedding enterprise, i.e., salvaging as much of the classic CPE as can be salvaged. Second, Communist leaders, especially those in the Soviet Union, seem to associate in their minds radical economic reforms with the movement for democratization. The democratic upheaval of the Prague Spring of 1968, which erupted a year after the enactment of the Czechoslovak economic reform, seems to be a case in point. However, this "clear lesson" could easily be a fallacy.

Economic reforms become a political issue only if Communist leadership makes them into one by opposing them. The idea is usually promoted by members of the establishment farsighted enough to see its advantages for the regime in power. It then becomes an issue in the factional strife within the power structure. Reforms can, of course, be further politicized if the issue is utilized by forces striving for democracy, provided these are strong enough.

However, if reforms are enacted by the regime on its own initiative, they become simply part of the official creed and are politically sterilized. The lesson of history which may be far more relevant is that of the Nazi regime in Germany: The profit motive was allowed to operate in a controlled way, and industrial management kept a wide decision-making autonomy, but in no way did that endanger the totalitarian power structure.

THE CHINESE VARIANT

For someone acquainted with the operation of the classic CPE in the Soviet Union and Eastern Europe, the case of mainland China does not seem to add much that is genuinely new. One expects the Chinese system to be profoundly different because it is Chinese and because the Soviets have been accused by the Chinese of "revisionism" and of "taking the capitalist road." As far as one can tell, differences do exist, but they have more to do with the less-advanced stage of industrialization in China, the peculiarities of the strategy of development, and especially the obscure peculiarities of the political system with its factionalism and ideological puzzles.

"As far as one can tell" is an important preamble because information about China is so much scarcer than about the European CPEs. Scholarly accounts must largely make do with formal descriptions based on official sources, and stretch meager factual material by dint of imagination and deductive reasoning. This is how one was forced to study the Soviet Union in prewar days, before it became possible to interview in depth masses of Soviet managers and workers who found asylum in the West;[11] before censorship of the printed word and statistical information was relaxed after Stalin died in 1953; and before Eastern European economists analyzed the CPE system to pieces. With this in mind, what can be pointed out as special to the Chinese CPE?

The classic form of Soviet-type planning was introduced into the virgin territory of postrevolutionary China in the early fifties by Soviet experts. While the Soviet mentors had since moved away from a strict allegiance to the classic version, their Chinese pupils made but a few minor adaptations. It seems that centralized allocation has been practiced in China in a much looser way. The number of commodities allocated centrally has always been much smaller, and a good deal of substantive planning activity was shifted to provincial organs. This amounted to decentralization of sorts, in the sense of delegating administrative command. (Coming in 1957–1958, still under Soviet influence, it may have been the Chinese analogy to Soviet post-1956 decentralization through the creation of "regional economic councils," the *sovnarkhozy*, abolished after 1964; see Chapter 13.)

Under this system, provincial enterprises were placed under the joint authority of local organs and organs of central ministries. The center has retained an iron grip on the geographic allocation of investments through financial quotas of investment funds, while giving local organs leeway in the choice of projects. One of the purposes has been fostering regional self-sufficiency and minimizing transportation requirements. Hence the greater variation in scale between manufacturing enterprises (down to midget plants associated with rural agricultural units) in China; the Soviet Union has traditionally preferred giant specialized plants, with railroads carrying a heavy burden of transportation.

The Chinese system has also been less strict on the precise numerical fulfillment of planned targets. Hence, managerial bonus incentives tied to success indicators never had the importance they have enjoyed in the Soviet-area coun-

---

[11] Material based on impressions of visitors to the countries in question has to be used extremely carefully. To sift truth from make-believe is a subtle art which has not been mastered by too many eyewitnesses from the West, be they movie actresses or academicians. It has also been known to happen that scholars, having been admitted to a Communist country, have afterward censured themselves in their work in order to keep the door open for future visits.

tries. Incentives in general have been less in the nature of differentials in financial remuneration and more of the direct personal-exhortation kind. There may be a secret link between this aspect and deeply ingrained cultural traits of the population. However, the frequent emphasis on traditional values of hard work and willing acceptance of authority, and on motivation based on "revolutionary idealism," seems to be overdrawn. There have been enough telltale signs indicating that many features attributed to Chinese mentality, or power of ideology, have been enforced by various pressure instruments of the political regime, whereas people's real propensities have been much closer to what Westerners consider normal than to the propaganda image of the "new man."[12]

No account of the Chinese CPE, be it ever so concise, can afford to skip two major episodes which marked its development. Interestingly, each episode had its historical counterpart in the Soviet Union during the thirties.

In 1929, the Soviet economy resumed the process of czarist industrialization, interrupted by World War I and the Civil War, with the first Five-Year Plan, which coincided with forced collectivization of agriculture. In 1931, its ambitious targets were revised dramatically upward. Industrial output as a whole was to increase annually by 45 percent, instead of 20 percent, as originally planned, and the slogan was issued to fulfill the Five-Year Plan in four years. This period of "bacchanalian planning," as it was characterized by Naum Jasny, resulted in a chaotic slowdown or decline of production in various industries between 1931 and 1934, and in a catastrophe in agriculture. The Chinese reenactment of this episode, known as the *Great Leap Forward*, falls in the years 1958–1960. It was an attempt at forcing the pace of industrialization, together with a reorganization of agriculture into "communes." It ended in complete disorganization and a disastrous decline in both industrial and agricultural output.

The second set of episodes was also one of slowdown and stagnation. In the Soviet Union, it occurred in the years 1937–1940, during Stalin's Great Purge, when police terror and mass arrests took their toll on economic performance. The Chinese counterpart was the period of the so-called *Cultural Revolution* lasting from 1966 to 1968. Although the motivation and particulars in the Chinese case were rather different, the similarity lies in the fact that in both cases the origin of economic troubles was an upheaval in the political sphere. The wild events of those years are difficult to summarize, and even more difficult to explain rationally, but as far as the impact on the economy is concerned, the shake-up meant an attack on the authority of industrial managers and technical experts, in the name of certain Maoist revolutionary conceptions.

As pointed out at the start of this chapter, the CPE is a preconceived model imposed upon an economy, and maintained by political power. It is to be expected, therefore, that its performance and reorganizations should be extremely sensi-

---

[12] Witness the short-lived campaign of officially enjoined freedom of expression, conducted in 1957 under the slogan "Let hundred flowers bloom." As soon as a wave of spontaneous criticism and social unrest began to gather force, the campaign was called off. Periodic reports on slowdowns, strikes, resistance to forced relocation of urban youth to rural areas, informal profiteering, etc., indicate a pattern of attitudes and tensions common to most societies living under the system of CPE.

tive to arbitrary fits of grandeur and to the kind of internal political conflicts which have been endemic to Communist regimes.

There is, of course, much more that could be said about the content of concrete policies pursued by different countries under the form of the CPE, in particular about evolving choices in the strategy of development: structure of industry, relative emphasis on agriculture, consumption, etc. We shall touch upon the treatment of agriculture in Chapter 14, but otherwise we have been intentionally trying to stay away from questions of content that belong in economics of development, and to focus on problems of systemic form. From that point of view, the story of China, as well as the other CPEs, must remain incomplete.

POSTSCRIPT ON CUBA

The same applies to Cuba, a relatively underdeveloped country with ambitions to industrialize, belonging, in its own maverick way, to countries of the CPE model. The vagaries of the Cuban search for a clear-cut systemic solution, lasting since 1959, would deserve a special study. The following remarks are merely for the purpose of a very general orientation.

The image of the Cuban economic system, which lingers in the minds of outsiders, has been dominated by the notion of moral incentives. Revolutionary enthusiasm, self-motivation, and responsibility toward the collective had presumably taken over the incentive role of financial rewards. This well-publicized myth, which caught the imagination of many young people in market-capitalist countries, dates from the years 1965–1970. This is when the idea was seriously tested, under the influence of Che Guevara, then still a man of power and influence. The test was negative, as could be expected in most attempts which start the transformation of society by decreeing a wholesale reform of consciousness. Since 1970, production norms and incentive wages have been brought back.

Another feature of the Guevarist model of planning, which is being phased out, has been the low status of financial calculation, cost accounting, and profit (which had served only as a source of taxation). Downgrading of the *khozraschot* concept was, however, not being compensated by upgrading precision in physical allocation. The instruments—Central Planning Board (JUCEPLAN), material balances and output targets—were all there, but central coordination was undermined by the custom of independent sectoral plans and Castro's brainstorm projects ("miniplans"). While the Chinese adaptation of the CPE model could be characterized as looser, compared to the rigorous classic version, sloppiness and improvisation seem to apply in the case of Cuba.

The state of affairs has been apparently changing since about 1972, when the Soviet Union began to assert its power and influence in the economic sphere. With respect to its Soviet mentors, Cuba may be entering the stage China was at in the early fifties. With many Cubans getting their training in the Soviet Union, and Soviet advisers operating in Cuba, the implementation of a Soviet-type model of the CPE may be under way. However, there could be a difference in the technology of planning. Whereas Chinese apprenticeship took place at a time when the abacus was still widely used in the Soviet Union, Cubans have been receiving computers, since 1970, for planning purposes. The first serious Cuban Five-Year Plan was promulgated to cover the years 1976–1980.

*   *   *

The capitalist market system has its market failures, central administrative planning has its malfunctions. Can one tell, under these circumstances, with some degree of assurance, how the two systems fare, comparatively speaking, with respect to efficiency in allocation? To answer that, we first have to realize that malfunctions of the CPE model are not the counterpart of market failures of the market system. They exist *in addition* to the latter, because much of what we call market failures is inefficiencies in allocation which exist just as much, if not more, under the CPEs. Monopoly is much more pervasive under the CPEs because there, buyers truly have no alternative options which usually do exist under competition or oligopolistic rivalry, and they can feel it at every step. External effects exist just as much under the CPEs—air and water pollution know no ideological barriers. Monopoly in a CPE is particularly obnoxious not because it erects "barriers to entry," as under market capitalism, but "barriers to exit" of those resources which may want to cater to existing demand on their own. This refers especially to small repair and maintenance services, or to housing. Insofar as resources do move, it has to happen on the sly, illegally, and that is not a merit of the CPE. The inability of a CPE system to adjust supply directly to demand, except when radically reformed, is the gravest general source of misallocations.

The fact is that reforms of the CPE model have been always in the direction of the market model, whereas nobody thinks seriously of improving market capitalism by borrowing from the CPE model. Thus, provided full employment is secured, market capitalism comes out definitely superior. How that proviso can be taken care of is the subject of Chapter 10.

BIBLIOGRAPHY

Bornstein, Morris, and Daniel R. Fusfeld (eds.): *The Soviet Economy: A Book of Readings*, 4th ed., Irwin, Homewood, Ill., 1974 (bibliography).

Gregory, Paul R., and Robert C. Stuart: *Soviet Economic Structure and Performance*, Harper & Row, New York, 1974, chaps. 5, 6, and 10 (bibliographies at the ends of chapters and in footnotes).

Ellman, Michael: *Planning Problems in the U.S.S.R.: The Contribution of Mathematical Economics to Their Solution*, Cambridge University Press, London, 1973.

Richman, Barry: *Soviet Management: With Significant American Comparisons*, Prentice-Hall, Englewood Cliffs, N.J., 1965.

Kaser, Michael, and Richard Portes (eds.): *Planning and Market Relations*, Macmillan, London, 1971.

Bornstein, Morris (ed.): *Plan and Market: Economic Reform in Eastern Europe*, Yale, New Haven, Conn., 1973.

Osteuropa-Institut München: *Jahrbuch der Wirtschaft Osteuropas*, Yearbook of East-European Economics, Gunter Olzog Verlag, Munich, vols. 1–6, 1970–1975 (annual compendium of studies, mostly in English).

Donnithorne, Audrey: *China's Economic System*, Praeger, New York, 1967.

Perkins, Dwight H.: "Industrial Planning and Management," in Alexander Eckstein, Walter Galenson, and Ta-Chung Liu (eds.): *Economic Trends in Communist China*, Aldine, Chicago, 1968, pp. 597–635.

Eckstein, Alexander: *China's Economic Development*, The University of Michigan Press, Ann Arbor, 1975.

U.S. Congress, Joint Economic Committee: *An Economic Profile of Mainland China*, vol. 1–3, 1967.

———: *China: A Reassessment of the Economy*, 1975.

Mesa-Lago, Carmelo (ed.): *Revolutionary Change in Cuba*, The University of Pittsburgh Press, Pittsburgh, 1971.

———: *Cuba in the 1970s*, The University of New Mexico Press, Albuquerque, 1974 (bibliographical references, pp. 153–174).

Chapter 10

Coordination
for Full Employment

As much competition as possible, as much planning as necessary.

Karl Schiller

One can get a bad ride in a perfectly good car, if the driver is bad; one can get a reasonably good ride in a bad car provided the driver is good; and a bad car can have also a bad driver. We resurrect this thought from Chapter 5 again because now the need becomes acute to distinguish between *the economic system as such* and *policies of the visible hand*. Market capitalism as such is not a perfect car. It has a tendency to shimmy and to swerve away from the rim of full production possibilities. It needs a driver who knows how to compensate for this fault, especially since it has otherwise a number of good points making it preferable to the CPE model which, on the face of it, holds the road of full employment so much better.[1]

---

[1] Actually, the Soviet-type CPE model only knows how to hide its unemployed better: supply shortages due to misallocation keep creating spots of periodic idleness but labor, instead of being laid off, is kept on the payrolls. Hence, ordinary wages partly assume the function of unemployment benefits, which the system boasts not to need. (The Russian term for this unemployment-on-the-job, *prostoy*, made its appearance in Eastern European countries in the fifties, together with the CPE system.) The difference is that, in a CPE, idleness of resources is caused not by demand deficiencies but by supply bottlenecks. For estimates which bear on the extent of such idleness, see Chap. 9, footnote 2.

We now abandon the automotive imagery which was meant to bring home the fact that observed performance of market-capitalist country systems is not a matter of just the market sector but also of the government, and very much so. The response mechanism of the market is characterized by cumulative multiplier-accelerator sequences (see end of Chapter 7). However, the disturbances ("shocks") to which the market responds may come either from within the market sector or from the government sector, or—most sadly—from faulty responses of the government to what happens in the market sector.

DEMAND MANAGEMENT

In terms of the classification of Table 4-1, we are embarking upon a closer examination of *macrocontrolled systems* of market capitalism. Putting the goal of the controls most broadly, it consists in making sure that the buyers of final products be continuously able and willing to buy the aggregate volume of output the economic system is capable of supplying when factors of production (i.e., primarily labor) are fully employed. It means minimizing the production gap (see Figure 5-4), by keeping an eye on the global amount of final expenditure made up of private consumption spending, business investments, government spending, and foreign demand for exports. This is the significance of terms such as *aggregate-demand management, anticyclical policies*, or *full-employment stabilization*. The policy comes down to a single general rule: *to prevent, or to compensate for, any change in spending that would make aggregate spending deviate from the figure required to take off the hands of suppliers the full-employment volume of output*. More specifically, the guardianship of aggregate spending means three things: (1) *protecting* the market sector from the effects of sudden arbitrary shifts in governmental spending and taxation decisions, and the volume of money created; (2) *compensating* for spontaneous disturbances or fluctuations in the major components of spending in the market sector (such as investments, private consumptions, exports and imports); (3) *influencing*, indirectly or by direct controls, the flow of spending in the major spending components of the market sector, so as to minimize the need for compensatory action by the government and the monetary system.

Instruments, Targets, Ultimate Objectives

In the terminology that has been developed for analyzing economic policies, aggregate spending represents the key *target variable*, which consists of a number of component target variables. The *policy objective* which is pursued determines what value the target variable should take. If the policy objective is full employment, this determines the size of aggregate spending, the target variable. (We can always look beyond the stated policy objective to discover some ultimate goal behind it, such as welfare, national power, prestige, or winning the next elections, but that does not add anything to the economic analysis.)

Then there are *instrumental variables*, i.e., economic magnitudes which are under the control of the policy makers. They can be deliberately varied, and because of the inner interdependence between *all* variables in the system, they can influence the values of the target variables. They are not push buttons, but they can be called realistically enough economic levers. Examples are government spending, tax rates, and supply of money through bank credit.

Besides these *general instruments*, policy makers have at their disposal *selective instruments*. These affect aggregate target variables by pinpointing the action upon some smaller component. Such are subsidies, particularly export subsidies; subsidies or taxes on specific consumer items, that can be imposed or removed; regulation of depreciation allowances and business taxes affecting investment decisions; etc. Still other instruments act upon the volume of target variables not via changes in the instrumental variables but directly. These are *direct controls*, such as import licenses, housing construction permits, etc.

Full employment is not the only objective that economic policies aim for. Indeed, as we have pointed out at other places, instrumental variables cannot act upon aggregate target variables without at the same time doing something to the microeconomic composition of output, incomes, and other magnitudes. Thus, instrumental variables serving a full-employment policy overlap in their effects with conscious or unconscious policies interested in target variables such as volume of investments, demand for housing and consumer durables, components of government spending, imports, exports, etc. Policy objectives which are affected by these target variables range from the economic growth rate (e.g., lowering interest rates stimulates investments and thus raises growth rates) through income distribution, product composition of output, and balance of payments, all the way to the level of economic activity in other countries.

Some of these other policy objectives are compatible and some conflict with the objective of full employment. Thus, in the illustrations which follow, but especially in the section on Great Britain, we shall encounter a conflict between the full-employment objective and a balance-of-payments equilibrium. A major and well-publicized conflict of policy objectives is believed to exist between full employment and price stability, forcing policy makers to choose between full employment with inflation and price stability with unemployment. (This question will come under closer scrutiny in Chapter 11.)

In Figure 10-1, we present systematically a selection of instrumental and target variables, so as to show the direction of the major first impact of the various instruments and their relation to the policy objectives. Among the subdivisions of the instrumental variables, the reader will discover the familiar categories of fiscal and monetary policy instruments. The schema should serve as a preview of the discussion of econometric policy models in the illustrative section on the Netherlands below.

What Do the Illustrations Illustrate?

The several case histories that fill the rest of the chapter have been selected with a certain purpose in mind. We wish to discuss a number of techniques and approaches to demand management, and a few problematic aspects encountered in their application. Each country case gives us an opportunity to highlight that aspect or technique which it happens to exemplify in a particularly striking fashion.

Figure 10-1 Macroeconomic regulation: policy instruments (left), target variables (center boxes), and policy objectives (right).

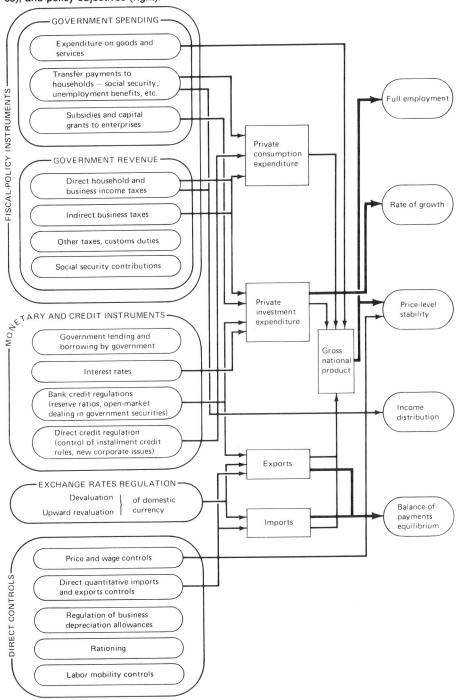

We start with the *Dutch planning system,* as an instance of the most systematic approach to global management of the economy which tries to work through adjustments of aggregate flows. The *Swedish case* allows us to study techniques which try to stabilize economic activity by stabilizing investments and facilitating microeconomic adaptation to structural changes (the "factor-mobility" approach). The special contribution of *French indicative planning* lies in the attempt to orchestrate and stimulate sectoral activities through comprehensive sectoral projections based on an input-output framework. The case histories of the *United States* and *West Germany* illustrate the problems of acceptance of deliberate market-management policies against a background of political opposition to public intervention in the economic process. The case of the *United Kingdom* is interesting because of the struggle of policy makers with the dilemmas posed by conflicting policy objectives, especially that of domestic full employment, price stability, and the balance-of-payments equilibrium.

We should keep constantly in mind that these are merely national variants of the macrocontrolled market-capitalist system and therefore share in different degrees and forms most of the features which individually receive special emphasis in every given illustration. One last preliminary remark: Being meant as illustrations, the histories are not followed up to the latest year on record, but refer mostly to the postwar period of the fifties and sixties, when the features discussed were taking shape.

THE NETHERLANDS: POLICY PLANNING AS ACCEPTED ROUTINE

The Dutch have gained the reputation of going about the task of macroeconomic management in the most systematic, calm, and matter-of-fact manner. The issues of macroeconomic policies have been largely removed from the arena of political and ideological controversy. They have become an almost purely technical matter, thanks to the broad consensus of opinion about the virtue of using the judgment and advice of economic professionals as basis of policy. This does not mean that the professional judgment is necessarily perfect, or policy decisions infallible. It is the climate in which they are made that makes the Dutch case appear as an example which other countries may wish to emulate.

The Home of the Econometrician

The Dutch are proud of having governmental policy decisions anchored to an elaborate quantitative model of their economy. They do not rely on rules of thumb, crude judgments, or educated guesses when they try to estimate the future development of their economy and the size effect of various contemplated policies. The Dutch Central Planning Bureau (CPB), established in 1945, provides governmental officials on a running basis with quantitative forecasts of future developments and probable effects of alternative policy actions. These forecasts and estimates are derived from an econometric model that simulates on paper the operation of the economy and is able to trace the effects of changes in a given economic magnitude upon all the other magnitudes.

Such econometric models are not a Dutch monopoly. Similar models have been worked out in a great many other countries. However, the Netherlands leads in two respects. It has the oldest tradition in the construction of econometric models, conceived in the thirties by Jan Tinbergen, and it was the first country to make practical use of them in the formulation of governmental policies.

Macroeconomic models of the econometricians represent the structure of an economic system in a fashion entirely different from input-output models we have dealt with in Chapter 7. They are not interested in accounting for transactions between firms, industries, and final buyers. They want to be able to predict, on the basis of the past record, what will be the numerical value of various broad key magnitudes of the system, such as the volume of consumer spending, investment expenditures, incomes, tax revenues, employment, imports, exports, or the general price level. More exactly, econometric models try to forecast, first of all, what these outcomes will be on the basis of what has been happening in the most recent past and what is known to be planned (e.g., known changes in tax rates, government transfer payments, and other government spending). If the forecast shows the outcomes to be out of line with what policy makers consider as their objective (e.g., full employment), econometricians want to be able to tell the policy makers what needs to be done to the instrumental variables in order to forestall the undesirable and to make the desirable happen.

The technique of econometric models consists in linking up various variables of the economic system mathematically into functional equations. These have to make theoretical and practical sense in terms of economic relationships. Thus, it makes sense to write an equation which says that consumption expenditure next quarter will be a function of after-tax wages in this quarter, disposable nonwage income (dividends, social security benefits, etc.), the amount of money people have in the bank, and the past general trend in consumer expenditure. It is then possible to evaluate the strength of these functional relationships on the basis of past statistical data and to attach a numerical coefficient to each of the variables which are supposed to determine consumption. The result may be an equation of the following kind.[2]

$$C = 0.68L^B_{-\frac{1}{4}} + 0.15Z^B_{-\frac{3}{4}} + 0.43\Delta pc + 0.08c^r - 0.19C_{-1} - 0.76$$

This reads as follows: In the period for which the estimate is calculated, the probable percentage change in the value of consumer expenditure over the preceding period will be obtained by adding up 68 percent of the change in disposable labor income one quarter earlier, 15 percent of the change in disposable nonlabor income three quarters earlier, 43 percent of the change in the consumer price index, and 8 percent of the change in the volume of demand and time deposits; this sum will be further adjusted by subtracting 19 percent of last year's change in the volume of consumption and a constant equal to 76 points. Similar equations can be set up for other key variables, such as investments, profits, wage incomes, etc. The choice of the exact form given to these functional relationships is guided by a combination of theoretical insights, hunches, and experimenting with various correlation possibilities as to the best statistical fit. (There are still

[2] United Nations, *Macro-economic Models for Planning and Policy Making*, Geneva, 1967, p. 38.

other types of equations, some of which merely serve to make sure that forecasted variables add up to totals they are supposed to add up to; these are the "definitional equations.")

In the equation given as example, consumption is being explained as determined by the variables on the right-hand side. In other equations, it is consumption that may appear on the right-hand side among variables explaining other magnitudes. In this manner, the set of model equations captures the interdependence of all the various variables: their effects in one direction, feedback reactions in the opposite direction, i.e., the pattern of mutual interactions of the elements.

For policy-making purposes, it is necessary to rearrange the structural model we have just sketched out in an important way. One has to sort out the variables into two groups. Economic variables that are given from the past, or can be fixed by policy makers because they are under their control, and therefore can also be known, form the group of *lagged endogenous* and *exogenous variables*. Variables whose future values are unknown, because they will emerge as "consequence" of the lagged endogenous and exogenous variables, through processes expressed in the functional relationships, form the group of *endogenous variables*. In terms of our Figure 10-1, "instrumental variables" will be found among those in the exogenous group, and "target variables" in the endogenous group.

Having sorted out variables according to these two categories, the econometrician rearranges the relationships expressed by the structural model in such a way that endogenous variables will appear only on the left-hand side of the equations as the unknowns, and be "explained," or determined, by a functional relationship to the lagged endogenous and exogenous variables, all of which will appear on the right-hand side. Each of the latter explanatory variables will have a coefficient expressing the relative strength of its impact upon the given endogenous variable. These coefficients are called impact multipliers, and the equations are called reduced-form equations. In Figure 10-2 we present an arrow diagram which helps us visualize the relationships expressed by the reduced form of the econometric model.

In the latter portion of Chapter 7, we have explained how an uncompensated change in demand causes reverberations throughout a given capitalist market system. Now, with the help of the econometric model, we can estimate empirically how large will be the outcome of these reverberations caused by a given uncompensated change in an exogenous variable. The quantitative estimate gives us then a handle on policy. Thus, we can pick from the various reduced-form equations an exogenous variable—say government expenditure—and see what its coefficients, i.e., impact multipliers, are with respect to the various endogenous variables. In simple words, this will tell us what a given change in government spending will do to consumption spending, investments, exports, the GNP, etc. Table 10-1 shows us a concrete example of such an estimate. Let us assume the policy makers are unhappy with the forecast of target variables yielded by the prediction model. With the help of the impact multipliers they can calculate by how much government expenditure (or other exogenous instrumental variable)

Figure 10-2 Structure of functional relationships in an aggregative econometric model.

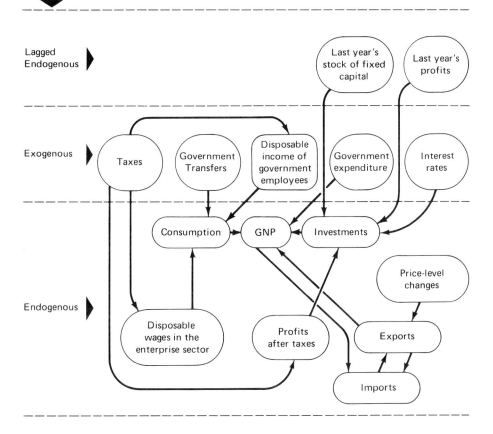

should be corrected in order to obtain the desired results in reality. The quantitative estimate serves as a guide. It reduces the uncertainties that go with decisions of the shooting-from-the-hip kind.

Table 10-1 Short-Term Effects of 100-Guilder Increase in Government Expenditure

Impact on:	
Private consumption	+5
Private investments	+6
Exports	−43
Net exports (exports minus imports)	−104
Unemployment (in percent)	−0.04
Wage level (in percent)	+0.07
Price level of consumption (in percent)	+0.10

Source: B. Hickman (ed.), *Quantitative Planning of Economic Policy,* Brookings, Washington, 1969, p. 139.

Tying Up Policies into the Plan

With the benefit of the CPB's thinking, the government makes its final policy decisions. In practice, this may mean, for example, putting into operation public investment projects which are on the shelf or, on the contrary, curtailing them if aggregate spending is to be kept within bounds. These final decisions are then incorporated into the CPB econometric model, and a revised final forecast is worked out and published, early in the year, as the *central economic plan*. The plan serves as an orientation device. Its function is purely *indicative*. Therefore, in contrast to Soviet-type plans, there is no question of its implementation or execution, since economic units of the market sector maintain their freedom of action.

The process of policy making is, of course, considerably more complex. The CPB supplements its econometric work with information from other sources, e.g., surveys of current investment plans. There is also a detailed input-output model which the CPB keeps up to date and uses as a check on the results obtained from the macromodel. Government officials keep informally in constant touch with the CPB, tapping each other for information and advice on a continuous basis.

The mutual-consultation and social-cooperation spirit of policy making is particularly evident in the role played by the *Social and Economic Council*. This is the most influential official advisory board of the government. It has been repeatedly summoned to advise the government before all major decisions in matters of social and economic policy. It is a tripartite body consisting of forty-five members appointed by employers' associations, trade unions, and the government. It has distinguished itself in the past by the ability to subordinate group interests to expert opinion and willingness to accept social compromise. Besides the policy-making machinery of the government, there is, of course, also the Central Bank (Nederlandsche Bank), which, while listening to the CPB, follows its own counsel in regulating the supply of money.

In principle, the Dutch approach to policy making is undoubtedly a highly rational one. This general statement is in no way invalidated by the fact that the actual record of Dutch stabilization policies is far from perfect. The economy underwent marked recessions in 1952 and 1958, and abnormal bouts of inflation in 1964–1965 and from 1969 on. Comparatively speaking, the degree of instability was not among the worst, but neither was it among the best, as one might be entitled to expect from the advertised virtues of Dutch policy planning. Was it because of the exceptional "openness" of the Dutch economy, which exports about one-half of its national output and is exposed to shocks from that side of foreign trade? Contrary to what one might expect, foreign trade has been remarkably stable. Hence, the responsibility has to be laid on the door of domestic policy measures.

It has been admitted that, a few times, policy measures were indeed badly timed, or their effect badly gauged, so that, instead of being stabilizing, they contributed to instability. Thus, the recession of 1952 was caused by policies restricting domestic aggregate demand; they were intended to slow down the demand for imports and to stimulate exports—in other words, to safeguard the balance-of-payments equilibrium. Shrinking back from the results, the government switched to expansionary policies which were intensified in 1955–1956, when the economy was already expanding under its own steam. The unnecessary stimulus just added to inflationary pressures. In 1958, another reversal—again because of balance-of-payments considerations—produced another recession.

However, after that, the mistakes of 1955–1956 were not repeated. Thus, we might think of these policy episodes as reflecting a learning process: making mistakes is an important part of learning. It should also be mentioned that the CPB econometric model in use before 1961 was not as good as the one introduced in 1961, which had the advantage of being based on more recent data and was being constantly refined. It has proved its merit, for example, in another major policy episode, of which Dutch planners are proud, in connection with the revaluation of the German mark in 1961. At that time, the government had to estimate on short notice the effects of German revaluation upon Dutch exports and imports. The value of the guilder had to be adjusted so as to forestall excessive demand for Dutch goods on the part of Germany—a task that was carried off with admirable precision.

On the other hand, the inflationary period after 1968 cannot be blamed on the policy makers; rather, it illustrates the political and social constraints under which policy makers operate. In the postwar years and throughout the fifties, the Netherlands was famous for its ability to keep wage and price developments under better control than most other countries. Credit for the successful application of what is called "incomes policy" (see Chapter 11) went to the responsible attitude of labor and business, and the active role of government in wage bargaining. "Responsible" refers, in this connection, to the priority of keeping the cost of Dutch goods down in order to foster Dutch exports. However, success in this respect was at the root of subsequent failure: demand stimulated by exports led to chronic labor shortages. Under the pressures of the labor market situation, the complex institutional framework of disciplined incomes policy exploded in two installments, in 1963 and 1967. From then on, Holland joined all the other European countries where control of inflation got out of hand as a by-product of full-employment prosperity.

SWEDEN: THE FACTOR-MOBILITY APPROACH

As far as fiscal and monetary stabilization policies in general are concerned, Sweden does not differ greatly from other countries practicing aggregate-demand management. If there is anything special about Sweden, it is the fact that it discovered the wisdom of using taxation and government spending for stabilization purposes so early, namely, in the thirties. Between 1933 and 1937, while most other countries were still pledging allegiance to the dogma that balancing the budget was the only sound fiscal policy, with unfortunate consequences for their economies, the Swedes were already switching to the notion of expansionary deficit financing.

The originality of the Swedish system today lies in two directions: in the use of instruments which tend to regulate the flow of investment spending, and in actively helping the unemployed find jobs. Both aspects deserve closer examination.

Stabilizing Investment

Private investment spending has been notoriously the most volatile component of private expenditure. Theoretically speaking, fiscal policy may try to compensate for the ups and downs in private investments by varying the volume of public spending in the opposite direction. Or else the government may use various instruments to *smooth out the flow of private investment spending in the first place, which would make compensatory fiscal action superfluous*. The Swedish policy makers have tried both approaches, with a progressively greater reliance upon the latter.

The government budget contains on the expenditure side several items which can be brought into play as the state of the economy demands. There is a 10 percent *reserve on capital expenditures*, available to the Ministry of Finance for speeding up public investment projects. Another element is the so-called *emergency budget*, which could be activated at short notice in a recession. It refers to funds appropriated to standby investment projects for which blueprints are kept in a continuously updated reserve. The authority over the emergency-budget investments is annually delegated by the parliament to the *Labor Market Board*, an institution of central importance in the regulation of investments altogether.[3] It so happens that there has been no need to use the emergency budget in the postwar era. The blueprints on reserve have been regularly passed up to normal public investment planning, while investment control was achieved by other means, i.e., by controlling housing construction and other private investments.

Control of housing construction for anticyclical purposes can be effective, but it may hurt housing. The instruments at the government's disposal have been quite powerful: public subsidies and loans to housing, and the number of building permits issued. In the years 1947–1951, the government allowed housing construction to decline by 25 percent, in order to slow down aggregate demand. Unfortunately, this policy contributed to a housing shortage, particularly in the southern urban areas toward which the economic center of gravity was just then shifting. After this experience, the government never again chose to cut housing to dampen demand.

For ironing out fluctuations in private investment outside housing, Sweden developed in the fifties an original technique which has proved its merit since. It is known as the *investment reserve*. It operates on the same principle as flood control: When the flow is high, water gets intercepted behind a dam; when the flow falls off, water is released from the reservoir. The flow in this case is retained corporate profits, an important source of investible funds. The technique works as follows: Companies are invited to set aside up to 40 percent of their profits before taxes as a fund earmarked for eventual investment spending. The inducement consists in the fact that, on this portion of their profits, companies pay no

---

[3] The Labor Market Board is one of the so-called autonomous agencies which form part of the Swedish governmental organization. Its supervisory board and the director are appointed by the government from among the nominees of the most powerful organized interest groups, i.e., the employers' associations and trade unions. It was originally designed for the implementation of manpower policies, hence the name. However, in the course of time, its functions expanded to cover an important segment of stabilization policies in general.

profits tax, which amounts to 40 to 50 percent of profits. The catch is that, in return, they have to give up their right to choose freely as to when, and at what rate, the money is to be released. That, the Labor Market Board decides. However, what the specific investment projects are, is up to the firms. (The government has a supplementary tool for influencing general investment activity in the form of an investment tax. A temporary imposition of this tax, such as that in 1951–1952, 1955–1957, and 1967, has a noticeable postponement effect upon investments. This helps to reduce their bunching and spreads them out more evenly over time.)

Active Manpower Policy

The topic of this section is a reminder that Keynesian demand management is not a surefire remedy against any kind of unemployment. Only to the extent that unemployment is due to a decline of spending, a simple return of spending to the previous level is all that is required: the flow of spending fills the old channels and draws labor back into the same old economic shell. However, insofar as unemployment is the result of structural changes in the economy, it may not be enough. Manipulating the volume of demand in general cannot of itself absorb labor which was released because of drying up of demand for a specific article, technological change, or geographic shifts of economic activity. This kind of *structural unemployment* can be absorbed only if labor is capable of moving and has the skills required in vacancies created by compensatory increases in demand.

From the point of view of the individual, structural changes strike at random. Adjustment carries a cost which may be quite heavy or even prohibitive. If a skill suddenly becomes obsolete, it is like having the investment in a durable asset destroyed by a natural disaster. To take care of the costs of adjustment from public funds is equivalent to paying insurance benefits in cases of insurable risks. There is an extra justification in this instance: It is in everyone's selfish interest to return the structurally unemployed to a productive activity where they would earn their upkeep again and contribute to the financing of public expenditures and investments. It is not a matter of charity.

This is the rationale of the Swedish so-called active manpower policy, which explains a good deal why unemployment has been persistently so much lower than, for example, in the United States: Sweden has kept in check the structural component in unemployment figures. The Swedish Labor Market Board, armed with the most recent statistics on available labor supplies and vacancies, and supplemented by a network of labor exchanges, provides the following services: vocational guidance, vocational rehabilitation, training and moving allowances, and others. The extent of such aid has been quite considerable. At certain periods, the number of participants in job retraining programs was as high as 3 percent of the labor force (1968–1969). Policies that help labor move to jobs have been supplemented by measures bringing jobs to labor, in the form of emergency public works. Thus, this entire aspect of stabilization policies may be characterized as the *factor-mobility approach*, in contrast to approaches that would rely on demand management alone.

National-Budget Planning

Returning to macroeconomic stabilization policies, we have to inquire into the information framework that serves as basis of policy decisions. Somewhat surprisingly, Swedish forecasting techniques have been rather primitive in comparison with the Dutch one, though not necessarily less serviceable. As far as policy makers are concerned, Erik Lundberg's words still hold: "There is so far in Sweden very little of Dutch econometric courage in finding a system of responses, a model to be used for forecasting purposes."[4] Reliance is placed mainly on surveys of investment plans, consultations, and independent estimates provided by various research institutes (such as Agricultural Marketing Board, Industrial Institute for Economic Research, etc.). The formal framework is provided by the so-called *national budget*. National budgets—a concept and name of Norwegian origin—are nothing but ex ante estimates of the national-product accounts. In principle, the estimates are made independently from the supply side and the demand side. On the supply or sources side, an estimate is made of the volume of domestic production (by considering prospective increases in labor force and labor productivity) and of imports. On the demand or uses side, we find estimates of aggregate demand by the usual components: public and private consumption, public and private investments, change in inventories, and exports. The work of consolidation of piecemeal estimates is done by the Planning Commission, but the result represents a plan only in the sense of providing nonbinding guidance for governmental and business decisions.

How well did the Swedish system perform in attaining its policy objectives? Judged by the level of employment, performance has been among the best. Unemployment varied from 1 percent in boom periods to 3 percent in slowdowns, and the gap between potential and actual output "hardly ever exceeded two percent (as compared with around 10 percent for the United States in 1958 and 1960–61)."[5] On the side of price-level control, Sweden has been less successful, though, by European standards, inflation rates have by no means been out of the ordinary.

The difficulties with controlling inflation in Sweden have a general illustrative value. One part of the difficulties has to do with *correct dosing* of policy measures. Low tolerance for unemployment means that, in a slowdown, even a small dose of expansionary measures very quickly brings the economy back to its full-capacity potential. From there on, they tend to generate for a while excess demand with its inflationary pulls on prices, before the policy can be reversed. The fact that Swedish forecasts have repeatedly underestimated the spontaneous growth of production only contributed to repeated overdosing of economic stimulation.

The second difficulty refers to the problem of *correct timing* of expansionary measures. For correct timing in a high-employment economy, annual forecasts are too crude as guides to action. A much more up-to-date, continuous observa-

---

[4] E. Lundberg, *Instability and Economic Growth*, Yale, New Haven, Conn., 1968, p. 212.
[5] Ibid., p. 202.

tion of business conditions is needed. So far, with the best of efforts—here Sweden is no exceptional case—it has been impossible to eliminate the so-called *recognition lag*. By the time a recessionary spell is recognized, economic conditions may be improving again. Add to this another time lag, the *impact lag*, between the moment expansionary measures are adopted and when they begin to have impact, and it becomes comprehensible why expansionary policies may easily come on top of an autonomous expansion, or last longer than necessary, and thus generate inflation.

FRANCE: GENERALIZED MARKET RESEARCH

French approach to economic coordination has two faces. On the one hand, there is the highly logical and orderly concept of *indicative planning*, which presumably welds economic activities into a smooth and coherent process. On the other hand, there is a pragmatic sequence of the usual fiscal and monetary policies, alternating between expansionary measures in times of slackening aggregate demand and restrictive measures in times of advancing inflation. We shall pay our greatest attention to the first aspect, as it raises a number of interesting issues. The traditional demand management seems to have been much less systematic, and prone to dramatic turnabouts which we shall briefly review toward the end.

Macrostability through Microregulation

Traditional demand management lets the market take care of microeconomic coordination and concentrates only on the adjustment of larger aggregates. It works on the assumption that the market can handle reasonably well detail adjustments between demand and supply concerning specific commodities. Should there appear a residual discrepancy between aggregate supply possibilities and aggregate demand, this is when, and only when, aggregate demand management steps in. It corrects only the volume of large blocks of demand spending, not their internal composition. In essence, this is Hayek all over again, tempered by the teachings of Keynes.

An entirely different position with respect to coordination is possible. One can take the partial discrepancies of the microeconomic order much more seriously. One can view them as signs of a basic incapacity of the market to achieve an acceptable degree of coordination. One can emphasize the danger of errors when individual firms decide on their investment and production plans, each acting in its narrow horizon, with a limited view of what others are doing and where the economy is going. Unable to perceive the complex of economic interdependencies, firms cannot see what their market prospects are and how they affect them by their own actions. The logical policy conclusion, then, is to give firms a helping hand and clear the fog of uncertainty around them. Let participants come out with the partial forecasts for their firms or sectors; confront them with each other; discover inconsistencies between their forecasts, adjust them to each other. Finally, combine them into a coherent, internally consistent scenario—a plan for the economy as a whole. If firms then allow their decisions to be guided by the coordinated sectoral forecasts, errors and local disturbances will be minimized, and residual discrepancies between aggregates will be prevented from ever even appearing.

This is the approach which was tried by the French. It does not lack cogency. Its merits were persuasively argued by French economists and planners whose eloquence contributed greatly to the widespread popularity of their conception during the sixties. It should be noted, however, that the sectoral coordination techniques applied in France have been in the service of another overriding policy objective, namely, a chosen rate of economic growth. In the Dutch or Swedish models, full-employment stabilization policies are regarded as primary goals, and a certain rate of growth then automatically emerges ex post facto as a by-product. In France, a desirable rate of growth is defined in advance, and in the planning process a pattern of coordination—especially in investment—is promoted, such as to achieve the set growth target. (More on this aspect in Chapter 12.)

The Indicative Plan

How do the French coordination techniques work in practice? How can the *Commissariat Général au Plan* know what the market does not know, or know it better? Has the formal establishment of plans been really essential, or at least helpful, to the successful operation of the market?

Let us take the problem of information resources first. No, the national planning staff does not produce its forecasts in an ivory tower on the basis of past paper data alone. We have seen that not even the planners in a Soviet-type CPE can manage without information from enterprises. The idea of French planning is that the market will know better what it needs to know if its notions are checked and supplemented by what the planners know. The process is one of cooperation between the business community and the planners. The French like to describe it as *concertation*, and their system as *économie concertée*.

Formally, we might think of the process as stages in a progressive filling in of an input-output table. The contribution of the professional planning staff consists in the knowledge of the actual input-output pattern realized in the past. Further, they are able to forecast the overall structure of final demand and labor supply on the basis of trends, inquiries, and econometric studies. Finally, they know how to construct a full new input-output table projecting the future state of the economy, given the structure of final demand and certain assumptions about technology, productivity, and capital/output ratios.

The representatives of the business community supply their own private partial views of the future development of their markets and of technological change in their individual branches. They act through the institution of *modernization commissions*, which are the crucial working part of the planning setup. The task of the planning office is to provide the modernization commissions with preliminary "growth sketches" of the economy and their particular sectors, and then to work at the integration and reconciliation of the forecasting material supplied by business and digested by the staff of the commissions.

The final product coming out of the process is a prospective *input-output picture of the economy* for the *terminal year of the plan period*, lasting usually five years. (This is an important point: French plans have been medium-term target plans, meant to guide business allocation strategy, in contrast to Dutch short-term forecasts, serving short-term stabilization purposes.)

At one time, the favorite topic of discussion was the issue of compulsion and voluntary adherence in the implementation of the plan. The pure philosophy of French planning held to the view that the plans do not need to be enforced by any exogenous instruments. Since they were constructed in close consultation with the decision-making agents of the economy and on the basis of their own forecasts, they were said to be *self-fulfilling*. They amounted to a *generalized market research* for and by business, and individual firms had an interest in letting themselves be guided by these forecasts. The term coined to render the voluntary nature of the exercise was *indicative planning* (in contrast to *imperative planning* of the Soviet type).

Skeptics were quick to point to the use by the government of certain power-ful instruments in the interest of plan fulfillment. The preferred instrument was credit rationing. The closely supervised governmental credit institutions were instructed to discriminate in favor of investment projects conforming to the plan. Furthermore, subsidies and selective tax alleviations were applied in the same sense, and a large core of investments undertaken by the nationalized sector of industry was treated as a mandatory segment of the indicative plan. There is no doubt about the compelling force of these instruments. It was conceded even by Pierre Massé, the most articulate interpreter of French planning, when he pro-posed the euphemism *active planning*—less than imperative, but more than indic-ative. However, the heaviest use of the active instruments fell into the period of the fifties, and it has tapered off since the late sixties.

Another favorite issue of controversy used to be the effect of French plan-ning upon *competition*. Contrary to what one may think at first blush, possibilities of competitive behavior are not improved if firms have more economic informa-tion about each other's plans. Competition requires a certain degree of informa-tional privacy, and therefore uncertainty about the intentions of one's rivals and one's own chances of success. If the economy grows increasingly more *transpar-ent*, and private forecasts become generally available through the procedures of French-type planning, firms are tempted to coordinate their plans with each other. The probable result is some form of *collusion* or *cartelization*. As the com-petitive drive is blunted, the system loses dynamic vitality.

This view is contradicted by close observers of the French economy who claim that the fear of cartelization is based on the outdated experience with prewar cartels, reacting to the Great Depression by restrictive agreements. Thus, Stephen S. Cohen interprets the situation as follows:

> The component of the planning process circumscribed by the *économie concertée* is a system of cartels. But they are cartels with a difference. The goals are expansionist and modernizing, not restrictive and protectionist. And the state is an active, initiat-ing partner, not a distant policeman. Its role is to create structures of cooperation and through them to guide the economy towards expansion and modernization.[6]

[6] Stephen S. Cohen, "From Causation to Decision: Planning as Politics," *American Economic Review*, vol. 60, no. 2, May 1970, p. 181.

The arguments and counterarguments show how difficult it is to apply theoretical principles straightforwardly to concrete economies. It seems warranted to conclude that what is good for one country is not necessarily what is needed in another. While the competitive order may have proved whatever merits it has in countries such as the United States, West Germany, Switzerland, and others, French-type planning procedures worked well as a substitute for the dynamism of competition in a country where competitive business spirit was traditionally weak and government intervention strong and willingly accepted.[7] However, partisans of competition might derive comfort from the fact that the state has been increasingly trying also to enlist forces of competition, e.g., by systematically reducing foreign-trade barriers and exposing domestic firms to competitive imports. Furthermore, the growth of multinational companies on French soil may also have contributed to a permanent change of the traditional complacent business climate.

Finally, some critics have questioned the need of sectoral forecasts and indicative targets for achieving coordination without hitches. The actual record lends strong support to this view. Vera Lutz has shown that actual production of individual industries has, in most cases, been far above or below the sectoral forecasts of the plan.[8] Hence, the forecasts could not have been very helpful as practical guides. V. Lutz carried the criticism still further, claiming that useful sectoral forecasts are, in the nature of the case, altogether impossible. First of all, forecasts of individual firms, which are aggregated into the sectoral forecasts, are necessarily of different quality, some reasonably good, others hardly more than wild guesses. The quality of an aggregated sectoral forecast cannot but suffer from its poor components. More serious, a five-year forecast cannot banish uncertainty due to unforeseen changes. To adapt to these changes, firms have to rely on flexible short-run market-adjustment processes, which are not amenable to any ex ante planning.

Critical analysis along these lines is undoubtedly correct. However, advocates of French planning methods might still save their case by shifting the ground of their defense. They may emphasize simply the *pedagogic value* of the planning procedures. So they do not lead to precision forecasts. But they have taught French executives to think in terms of forward-looking growth-oriented business planning. And with the progress of time, as this "training" became assimilated, planners have been relaxing their earlier attitude concerning the importance of sectoral target forecasts.

We shall now interrupt the account of the French planning system; it will be resumed again in Chapter 12 from the point of view of its role in promoting growth.

Instability under Demand Management

France joined the club of countries practicing demand management by "traditional" methods of fiscal and monetary policies in 1963, the year of the historic

---

[7] John Sheahan, *An Introduction to the French Economy*, Merrill, Columbus, Ohio, 1969, pp. 1–7 and 75.

[8] Vera Lutz, *Central Planning for the Market Economy*, Longmans, London, 1969, esp. pp. 67–95 and graphs on pp. 102–104.

"stabilization plan." Until then, throughout the postwar period, neither fiscal nor monetary operations were used as economic levers. Budget deficits had to make up for the inefficiencies of the taxation system and for the erosion of government revenues by chronic inflation. Money supply and volume of credit were geared to the needs of financing the level of activities foreseen by the plans. There were no slumps either in investment activity that would call for a Swedish-type policy of compensatory investments, or in government spending. Inflation was cheerfully taken in stride. Were French exports endangered because of rising French prices? The government simply devalued the franc. This lowered the prices of French goods for their customers abroad, despite inflation raging inside the country. And it raised prices of foreign goods to the French, reducing their appetite for imports, quite aside from direct import controls which also were in force.

The reasons for the turnabout in 1963 seem to have been the necessity to discontinue foreign-trade controls, and political aversion to devaluations. Foreign-trade controls became incompatible with free-trade contractual agreements between France and the other members of the European Common Market (see Chapter 15). Besides, opening the French economy to the competition of foreign imports began to be welcomed as a spur to domestic business. Devaluations (i.e., a "weak" franc) came to be considered bad for French international prestige—it was the era of President de Gaulle.

The *stabilization program of 1963* initiated a period of standard macroeconomic demand management by means of fiscal and monetary instruments. With it came the problem of short-term forecasting and proper timing, as well as dosing of stabilization measures. We met these issues in the Swedish and Dutch cases and are forewarned that stabilization policy can also create instability. Thus, the 1963 plan of fiscal and monetary restraint succeeded in checking inflation through 1965, but restrictive policy lasted too long. It overshot the target and brought about a recessionary slowdown in 1967. A controlled return toward expansion got out of control in consequence of the explosive events—student riots and general strike—of May 1968. A large wage increase and renewed inflation were part of the price paid for social appeasement, leading eventually to another devaluation of the franc in August 1969. After this turbulent episode, policy makers found themselves once more, as in 1963, at a new start of a more orderly macroeconomic management of demand and price movements. The experience since then has been one of varying fortunes in the fight with inflation, as in most other Western European countries.

UNITED STATES: GROPING TOWARD A STAND

From the preceding accounts we have learned that policy makers have to grapple with two kinds of difficulties with timing their policy measures. Diagnosis often limps behind the changing state of the economy. This is the *recognition lag*, which makes information always a little bit obsolete. And then there is the delay between the time a policy measure is adopted and the time it begins to have effect upon economic activity. This is the *impact lag*. The illustrative value of this section is in demonstrating a third kind of delay, the *decision lag*, which refers to the time that elapses after the economic situation had been diagnosed (already with a lag) and before the appropriate policy measures are adopted. This delay has to do with the fact that those who diagnose the state of the economy, namely, professional economists, are not the same as those who are in charge of writing and signing the prescription, namely, the politicians. (It also can happen that professionals who diagnose the economy correctly are not the same as those who advise the politicians. Politicians can always choose advisers whose professional views suit their lay notions.)

It is conceivable for stabilization policies to become strictly a matter of technical judgment. A chosen group of economic professionals could receive a general mandate to do whatever they deem necessary to keep the economy on its full-employment path. In that case, the decision lag would presumably be quite short. Why is it that such a professionalization of economic policy has so far not been realized anywhere? Even in Holland or Sweden, where the process of taking politics out of economic policy has gone the furthest, professionals are formally kept in an advisory position. The reason is that different policy measures affect various social and economic interest groups differently. They are perceived differently by groups holding contrary beliefs, opinions, and prejudices. Hence, their political representatives tend to guard jealously the right of final decision. The consequence is delays. While the economy suffers, politicians bargain, lobby, procrastinate, hesitate, deliberate, and obstruct. If they reach a decision, they reach it after long meanderings through the political labyrinth. And, because of that, the decision may be wrong, besides being late.

The Law Is There

On the face of it, the United States government has been under legal obligation to promote full employment ever since the adoption, in 1946, of the *Employment Act*. However, a close reading of the act reveals that its weasel-word formulation allows political forces ample room for time-consuming struggles over conflicting objectives and policy measures. Its opening statement says: "It is the continuing policy and responsibility of the Federal Government to use all practicable means consistent with its needs and other essential considerations of national policy with the assistance and cooperation of industry, agriculture, labor, and State and local governments, to coordinate and utilize all its plans, functions, and resources for the purpose of creating and maintaining, in a manner calculated to foster and promote free competitive enterprise and the general welfare, conditions under which there will be afforded useful employment for those able, willing and seeking to work, and to promote maximum employment, production, and purchasing power." One analyst, Edwards S. Flash, Jr., characterized this piece of legislation as being simultaneously of the "moral gesture" and "pass-the-buck" variety.[9]

---

[9] Edward S. Flash, Jr., *Economic Advice and Presidential Leadership: The Council of Economic Advisers*, Columbia, New York, 1965, p. 297. On the same page Flash quotes Wayne A. R. Leys: " 'Moral gesture' legislation amounts to an instruction to do nothing specific but most of the 'pass-the-buck' legislation is an instruction to resolve the conflict between groups who want definite but rival standards to be legalized." (From "Ethics and Administrative Discretion," *Public Administration Review*, vol. III, Winter 1943, p. 14.)

The same act established the *Council of Economic Advisers*. This body was charged with making policy recommendations to the President but otherwise its status was not clearly specified. What use would be made of it depended on the personalities and philosophies of successive Presidents and the chosen Council members. In any case, the Council had never any executive power of its own. Its fate was to remain just one of a plurality of agencies furnishing advice and wielding portions of executive power of their own, such as the Treasury Department, Bureau of the Budget, the Congress, organs of the Federal Reserve System, and others. Each of these held views and objectives of its own, and even if they did not necessarily act at cross-purposes, neither has there been a systematic coordination of their activities or an agreement on priorities and on reconciliation of various policy objectives. Economic policy that did emerge was necessarily a result of the interplay of many such forces.

The political process affects primarily the application of fiscal instruments—taxation, government borrowing, and spending. Monetary policy instruments have been largely off limits to politicians. Through a curious quirk of the legislation, monetary authorities, i.e., top organs of the Federal Reserve System, have been almost entirely free to keep their own counsel. Actual policy is therefore made up of the relatively ponderous fiscal measures and the relatively supple monetary measures, whereby the monetary measures can support, moderate, or sabotage the effects of the fiscal ones. Since we are using the case of the United States to illustrate the *decision lag*, we shall concentrate on the fiscal-policy area. There, the decision lag has been due regularly to hesitancy or unwillingness to use fiscal operations as an instrument in demand management. The unwillingness can be ascribed, in turn, to a lack of understanding of how these instruments work on the part of political decision makers, in other words, to what in polite society is called a cultural lag.

The Theory Is There

An economically unsophisticated mind thinks of the government budget as if it were the same thing as the budget of an individual. If one cannot cover current expenditures from current income, one has to borrow. That means mortgaging future income, which is why one tries not to borrow if one can help it. Applying these notions to the government budget is called "fiscal orthodoxy." That amounts to insisting on the principle that government spending should be financed from ordinary revenues, i.e., primarily from taxation, and railing against deficit financing, i.e., against raising revenues through borrowing from banks or the public, as being contrary to fiscal integrity.

If the policy objective is to keep economic activity close to full employment, the above principles are worse than useless. If they were applied consequently in time of need, they would create more unemployment instead of less, besides missing out on their own narrow objective, the balanced budget.

To demonstrate that, let us assume the time of need arises because of a recession. This is also the time when government revenues fall because the tax base (i.e., aggregate income) falls, and a budget deficit is likely to appear. Such deficit is not the fault of fiscal management but an automatic consequence of economic circumstances. However, fiscal orthodoxy considers it a responsibility of the government to keep spending and tax revenues in balance.

The simpleminded course ordered by orthodox principles would require either to increase the rate of taxation or to cut spending, or both, so that the government would "live within its means" again. The hitch is that orthodoxy forgot all about the links which connect changes in taxation and government spending to changes in national income, and national income back again to tax revenues. Reduction in private spending (caused by increased tax rates) or cuts in government spending would act as an autonomous shock that, triggering the multiplier mechanism, would send the overall level of production and incomes tumbling down. Since incomes serve as the tax base, the revenues may also fall short of the figure needed to close the budget deficit. The deficit could easily increase further. The gain in revenues expected from higher tax *rates* might be nullified by the loss in revenues due to the shrinking tax *base*.

The problem with orthodoxy is this: It refuses to recognize that fiscal operations, besides their primary function, having to do with the supply of governmental output, have also a secondary instrumental function with respect to the state of the economy, by virtue of their links to aggregate demand. This instrumental function cannot be exorcised. Hence, in fiscal management, every decision on government spending and taxation must be examined with respect to the question: "What will it do to aggregate spending?"

The Politicians Waver

The history of American policy making over the last forty-odd years may be read as a progressive but slow abandonment of orthodoxy and acceptance of the modern principles of "functional finance," to use Abba P. Lerner's expression (see Chapter 6). As Herbert Stein has demonstrated, orthodox principles of government finance were never carried out, during the period in question, to their ultimate disastrous consequences.[10] However, neither can one say that they received mere lip service. The last orthodox attempt to balance the budget in a depression by raising tax rates was undertaken by the Hoover administration in 1932. Nonetheless, until 1963, orthodox ideas remained a potent inhibiting factor that prevented Presidents, officials, and politicians from seeing the economic issue clearly and acting upon it.

During the prewar New Deal era, fiscal instruments were used hesitantly and often inconsistently. Anticyclical spending on public works was accepted in principle but remained limited in scope. The fear was that a deliberate policy of deficit spending would undermine "business confidence" and incentives to invest, as if a healthy state of aggregate demand were not the prime condition. At the same time, the Revenue Act of 1935 did exactly that by raising tax rates on incomes of potential investors. Finally, a sharp reduction of the government deficit in 1937, while some 14 percent of the labor force were still unemployed,

---

[10] Herbert Stein, *The Fiscal Revolution in America*, The University of Chicago Press, Chicago, 1969.

contributed to turn a promising recovery into a new recession. Ironically, the main reasons were the jump in revenue from the newly introduced social security taxes and the discontinued payments of veterans' benefits.

In the postwar period, the economics profession was almost universally converted to the principles of "functional finance," and even important business groups, such as the Committee for Economic Development, incorporated them into their policy recommendations as early as 1947. Despite the emerging professional consensus, fiscal management continued to be haphazard in its effects upon the economy. In particular, sudden cuts in military expenditures after 1946 and 1953 (after the Korean war), not having been offset by any compensatory actions, played a role in the recessions of 1948–1949 and 1953–1954. During the Eisenhower administration, budgetary transactions could be used for stabilization purposes at least partially. Significantly, deficits during recessions began to be tolerated in fact, even though deplored in official speeches.

The triumph that was sounded in 1963 for modern fiscal-policy ideas turned out to have been premature. That was the time when, after an extensive public discussion and ideological conversion of President Kennedy, the Congress enacted the one celebrated tax cut which made it possible for the economic expansion, started in 1961, to continue, for a record period of nine years, without serious interruptions, until 1970.[11] This practical demonstration of what demand management can accomplish seemed to have opened an era of full-employment policies conducted as an accepted routine, with fiscal operations an accepted instrument forever after.

We said the triumph was premature. The hopes were killed by an upsurge of inflation after 1966–1967 and a decision of the Nixon administration in 1970 to use demand management in reverse, i.e., to moderate aggregate demand, even at the cost of unemployment, in the hope of slowing down inflation. The policy has lasted well into the midseventies.

The years after 1970 signify a severe relapse to attitudes typical of the years before 1963. United States policy makers then also had inhibitions about pursuing expansionist policies too vigorously, for fear of stimulating inflation. This was independent of and in addition to the ideological prejudices. It was related to the responsibilities assumed by the United States in the international monetary system after World War II (see Chapter 15). Unlike France, the United States was not free to devalue the dollar when payments abroad exceeded payments by foreigners to the United States. The dollar was the key reserve currency, and therefore technically unable to vary its exchange rate with respect to other currencies. As United States payments abroad have chronically exceeded payments in the opposite direction, the United States was under pressure to work toward controlling its international payments by other means than devaluations. One was to go slow about full-employment policies, in order to keep prices stable and

[11] The average length of previous postwar expansions was three years. The importance of the 1963 cut in tax rates was in having eliminated the so-called fiscal drag. Until then, tax rates were set so steep that fiscal revenues tended to rise above the level of expenditures before the economy even reached full employment. The resulting budget surplus acted as a drag upon expansions.

exports up, and at the same time not to stimulate too much domestic demand for imports. This was a constraint which operated in a much more pronounced fashion in the case of Great Britain (see below).

We are inclined to see in this inflation constraint only a contributing factor to the long-term ideological and political decision lag. It is the latter which is the main explanation why the country failed to develop a reliable machinery for the pursuit of full employment. The cost to the economy has been as substantial as it was unnecessary. Thus, potential output lost annually over the period from 1950 to 1964 may be put at about 5 percent of actual GNP. In comparative terms, while a number of Western European countries have managed to keep their rate of unemployment systematically below 2 percent, the United States averaged 4.5 percent between 1950 and 1960, and reached close to 9.0 percent in 1975. This may be a reason for self-congratulation if one thinks of the 1930–1938 average of about 18 percent (25 percent maximum), but not if one looks at countries with a mature approach to macroeconomic policies.

WEST GERMANY: KEYNES IN THE LAND OF HAYEK

For West Germany, the turn to mature stabilization policies came in 1967. The dawn of Keynesianism, as one may call it, set in during the political change of guard a year earlier when the Christian Democratic regime of Ludwig Erhard was replaced by a coalition regime whose moving spirit in economic matters became the Social Democratic minister, Prof. Karl Schiller. He is the author of the motto we put at the head of this chapter—"As much competition as possible, as much planning as necessary"—which he also expressed, in a more technical language, as "self-regulation in microrelations and global steering in macrorelations." The principle, as we know by now, has a wide applicability.

The core of the 1967 legislation was a higher version of the "fiscal revolution" which occurred in 1963 in the United States. In the pure spirit of "functional finance," the government was empowered to vary (within specified limits) the rate of borrowing to finance public expenditures and the rate of income and corporate taxes. Furthermore, in boom periods, the federal and state governments were to sterilize temporarily a portion of revenues in an anticyclical reserve fund with the central bank, to be released when contraction threatened. (We recognize here, in the area of fiscal management, the principle of the Swedish investment reserve.) Variation of rules for depreciation allowances was another device made available for stabilization purposes. Finally, the federal government was charged with working out annual projections of the economy, budget plans for five years ahead (annually "rolled forward"), and an investment program with a priority scale of projects. The professionalism of policy making was to be enhanced by the establishment of a Council for Anti-Cyclical Policy and the tapping of academic advice on the part of the Council of Experts (in existence since 1963). The success of stabilization policies depended henceforth entirely on the art of policy makers to use the panoply of instruments made available by the 1967 law.

The Dilemmas of the "Erhard Era"

The preceding period provides an interesting illustration of a rather special case: a capitalist market system adhering fully to fiscal orthodoxy, relying only on monetary instruments, putting price stability above full employment, being successful with respect to both, and finally, seeing monetary instruments lose all effectiveness in consequence of its very successes.

Postwar reconstruction of the West German economy—the famous "German economic miracle"—took place under the sign of a doctrine known under its official public-relations title as *soziale Marktwirtschaft*, in free translation, the "socially responsible market economy." It was a practical offshoot of theoretical economic liberalism represented by the so-called Freiburg school, whose major protagonists have been Friedrich A. Hayek, Walter Eucken, Wilhelm Röpke, Alfred Müller-Armack, and others. The doctrine combined a reliance upon forces of free market competition with limited government intervention of a special kind. Economic policy was geared almost single-mindedly to the core task of reconstruction: to a stimulation of savings and investments, of profit-seeking entrepreneurship, and of exports needed to finance purchases of necessary inputs from abroad. The instruments were tax exemptions, subsidies, and an informal incomes policy that kept wages from rising too fast.

Price stability was a subsidiary objective—it assisted the propensity to save and encouraged exports by keeping German prices attractive. If this be demand management, it was a policy of stimulation of foreign demand for German goods and of domestic investments, the latter being rather part of supply management, i.e., of capacity expansion. Besides, the bias in favor of price stability is also explainable by the traumatic memories of the German hyperinflation of 1923–1924. Only monetary instruments were regarded as admissible. Fiscal policy was altogether shut out because a rigid balanced-budget rule was incorporated into the country's constitution.

Up to 1958, monetary policy was successful in maintaining price stability and supporting economic expansion led by exports and investments, which helped the progressive absorption of about 10 million postwar immigrants expelled from Poland and Czechoslovakia. The rule of restricting bank credit and raising interest rates as soon as prices showed a tendency to rise did slow down the rate of growth twice (in 1952–1953 and 1956–1958), but it was not so severe as to cause true recessions.

After 1958, an entirely different set of problems appeared. Successes in the foreign-trade area deprived monetary policy of its earlier effectiveness. The economy had closed up on its full-capacity potential, and at the same time currencies had become freely convertible. The consequences of the changed situation became linked in the following chain: (1) restrictive monetary policy keeps the domestic price level stable; (2) German exports soar relative to imports, and export surpluses appear; (3) earnings of foreign currencies earned through export surpluses are converted by German exporters into marks, and this adds to the domestic supply of money; (4) in a full-employment situation, this puts upward pressure on prices—one begins to speak of "imported inflation"; (5) monetary

authorities attempt to stem this pressure by restricting credit supply and raising
interest rates; (6) raised interest rates attract foreigners to buy German marks
and invest, or deposit them, in Germany for the sake of higher earnings, thus
adding to the domestic money supply further; (7) monetary authorities apply
restrictive measures with even greater severity, to the point of reducing aggregate
spending and squashing expansion. However, inflation-generating increases of
the money supply continue through the mechanism under (4) and (6). Monetary
policy then becomes powerless to control the price level as before and, in addition, threatens to produce unemployment which is not tolerable any more.

Such, in essence, were the monetary-policy dilemmas in the three periods
when the rate of expansion fell, around 1957–1958, 1962, and 1966. The last
episode of monetary restrictions was compounded by the classic sequence produced by a faithful application of fiscal orthodoxy in times of budgetary deficits,
as described in the section on the United States. The country, accustomed to
annual growth rates in the 4 to 8 percent range, had zero growth in 1967, the year
of the fundamental change of style in stabilization policies. The ground had been
well prepared.

The Record So Far

The 1967 change of style did not produce perfect full-employment stability and
complete absence of inflation. That could not be a realistic standard of performance, considering the concrete world circumstances in the first half of the seventies. However, it is possible to claim that the pre-1967 system could not have
handled the stabilization problem at all. Stabilization policy gained considerably
in flexibility and capacity of "fine tuning." The recovery from the 1967 slump
was aided by the activation in two installments of public contingency investment
programs (1967 and 1968), and continued expansion was sustained. However,
fiscal stimulation was reduced as soon as it was apparent that demand had regained its own momentum. In the years 1971 and 1972, when West Germany had
to cope with inflationary pressures due to extraordinary inflows of foreign currencies (attracted, among other things, because of expected up-valuation of the
mark), monetary authorities could concentrate on problems connected with foreign-exchange rates, e.g., inhibit inflows of foreign currencies by reducing the
discount (from 5 percent in October 1971 to 3 percent in February 1972), while
fiscal instruments throttled or stimulated domestic demand according to short-
term changes in business conditions. In the following years, it was possible to
follow successfully a restrictive monetary policy to counteract inflationary pressures, and at the same time an expansionary fiscal policy to counter shocks
administered to aggregate demand by events beyond government control (rise in
oil prices, slump in exports).

The 1967 Law for Promoting Stability and Growth (the *Stabilisierungsgesetz*)
was characterized by many as "one of the most perfectly worked-out legal devices for demand management in existence."[12] It seems fair to admit that Ger-

---

[12] Wolfgang Kasper, in Emil Claassen and Pascal Salin (eds.), *Stabilization Policies in Interdependent Economies*, North-Holland Publishing Company, Amsterdam, 1972, p. 274.

man handling of the tools provided by the law—the fiscal and monetary policy mix—has been professionally very competent.

GREAT BRITAIN: STOP-GO IN THE LAND OF KEYNES

Curiously, in Keynes's own native country, stabilization policies have been relatively least successful. Great Britain of the fifties and sixties presents a case where, in the words of one of its foremost analysts, "budgetary and monetary policy failed to be stabilizing, and must on the contrary be regarded as having been positively destabilizing."[13] However, the reason was not that "no one is prophet in his own land." Rather, it was due to a conspiracy of circumstances clamping policies associated with the name of Keynes within rather narrow limits. It can be argued that British governments could have done something about those circumstances instead of submitting to them more or less meekly. Nevertheless, they did submit to them, and in so doing they provided us with an opportunity to study the working of macroeconomic coordination under conditions of *low growth rates* and a *chronic disequilibrium in the balance of payments*.

What does balance-of-payments equilibrium mean? Putting it crudely, payments made by foreigners for British exports and acquisition of various assets in Britain (which normally means that foreign currencies have to be converted into British pounds) ought to match payments made by the British for imports from abroad and acquisition of various assets abroad (for which purposes pounds are converted to foreign currencies). If these two payment flows do not match, the British balance of payments is said to be in disequilibrium. It is in deficit if outpayments from Britain exceed payments to Britain. This is brought about most often by an excess of imports over exports.

The British balance of payments has been continuously in danger of such a deficit. The deficit tended to appear regularly, and unfortunately, at a particular stage of general business conditions, namely, during expansions. There is no mystery about why this should be so. As British domestic demand grows, demand for imported goods surges faster than foreign demand for British exports. Demand for British exports is largely independent of the domestic situation in Britain. It depends on foreign needs for British goods, and these have been growing relatively slowly. For one thing, British exports have been heavy on the side of traditional slow-demand articles and light on the side of modern growth items. Further, British exports have become relatively expensive compared to exports of countries with higher growth rates of productivity than Britain. And, to the extent that foreign demand has been sensitive to the domestic situation in Britain, price increases, which tend to go with expansions and approach of full employment, have been no help. Against this steadiness of exports, demand for imported goods goes up fast and far for every increase in domestic incomes. It has been highly income-elastic.

We know how the French used to deal with this kind of issue in the years

[13] J. C. R. Dow, *The Management of the British Economy: 1945–1960*, Cambridge University Press, London, 1964, p. 384.

before 1963: They concentrated on steady domestic expansion, let prices rise, and resorted to devaluations of the franc in order to keep the price of French exports in terms of foreign currencies low, no matter what was happening to the price level domestically. Devaluations of the franc, making foreign currencies more expensive to the French, made also foreign goods more expensive to them, which put a damper on imports.

Great Britain resorted only twice to a devaluation of the pound in the course of the postwar years, in 1949 and in 1967, and each time it was an event. In the intervening years, British governments have consistently preferred an alternative solution, namely, to slow down the rate of domestic economic activity. This would cut down the demand for imports, and protect exports by reducing the risk of an inflationary price rise. Part of the operation would be an increase in domestic interest rates, preventing pounds from seeking higher returns abroad and making foreign investments in British securities more attractive. Thus, equilibrium in the balance of payments would be eventually restored.

Once the balance of payments began to show a surplus, the government would again take courage and press the fiscal and monetary levers in the sense toward expansion, whereupon the cycle would be repeated. This is how the stop-go phenomenon in British demand management came about.

The "stop" periods have been closely associated with balance-of-payments crises in 1951, 1955, 1957, 1960–1961, 1964–1965, and 1967. Why was it precisely Great Britain, among Western European countries, that had a balance of payments always on the verge of a deficit?

Some blame the fact that the exchange rate of the pound was initially set too high and remained too high even after the devaluation of 1949. Norman Macrae, the deputy editor of the London *Economist*, writes:

> After all, when the pattern of world exchange rates had last been fixed in 1949, at least four of the main industrial powers of the world (Japan, Germany, France and Italy) were still largely war-destroyed. The two big industrial powers who were not war-destroyed, America and Britain, were therefore bound to find within the next twelve years or so that their exchange rates were too high relative at least to the currencies of Japan and Germany. Even if Britain had followed a brilliant economic policy . . . (which was far from being the case), the relative strengthening of the economies of Japan and Germany in that period, was almost bound to be greater than the relative strengthening of Britain's economy; in 1949 Japan and Germany had nowhere to go but up.[14]

The argument is highly plausible and is supported by the eventual resort to devaluation in 1967 and further pound depreciation in 1972. However, still other aspects of the British situation have made the problem worse. The balance-of-payments constraint was aggravated by the additional constraint of the *relatively slow growth of the productive potential and factor productivity*. The interaction of the various elements at play is quite complex and not always clear. However, the basic set of interdependencies can be easily explained.

---

[14] Norman Macrae, "Whatever Happened to British Planning?" in Daniel Bell and Irving Kristol (eds.), *Capitalism Today*, Basic Books, New York, 1970, p. 141.

Let us place ourselves again in an expansion phase. Since it usually starts from a rate of unemployment which is relatively low, though high enough to be unacceptable to the British (i.e., about 2 percent), the state of full employment is reached very quickly. As economic activity approaches the full-capacity ceiling, customary cost-push pressures of wages and prices set in and raise the price level. This hampers exports and saps the balance-of-payments equilibrium.

If the productive potential—the supply capacity of the economy—grew fast, the state of inflationary pressures would be reached later. Expansion of demand would proceed while the full-capacity ceiling would be fast receding upward at the same time. Unfortunately, British economy has grown relatively slowly in the postwar period, and growth-promoting policies either were nonexistent or were frustrated by the short-run impact of expansions upon the balance of payments. The effect of relatively low growth rates of labor productivity upon the price of British goods in international competition, and upon exports, was mentioned earlier.

The British case is in many respects the reverse of the West German one. Germany has "suffered" from a chronic tendency to balance-of-payments surpluses. The reasons were: initial high rate of unemployment, strict control of inflation made that much easier, high rates of investment and productivity increases, export-promoting policies, high growth rates led by increases in foreign demand, and an undervalued exchange rate of the mark making German articles chronically a good buy.

If one were to judge British stabilization policies by the degree of resource utilization alone, one would have to agree with C. D. Cohen: "Simply in terms of unemployment aims . . . , governments have been extraordinarily successful—beyond the wildest dreams of the 1944 White Paper or the authors of the Beveridge report."[15] Until 1970, unemployment rarely exceeded the 2 percent mark.

*   *   *

The British case, which concludes our series of illustrations, thus raises a new important issue: Is demand management doing an adequate job if it defines its goal only in static terms of full employment? Instruments of aggregate demand management affect simultaneously the composition of demand. The composition of demand implies choices about the growth orientation of the economy. Therefore, demand-management policies are simultaneously growth or anti-growth policies. The subject matter is overflowing the confines of this chapter and moving the discussion forward to Chapter 12, which deals with the topic of growth performance.

In the previous illustrations, we drew mainly on empirical material of two decades, the fifties and sixties. At the start we posed the issue as economic system versus the system's "drivers," its managers and guardians. The conclusion now would appear to be that market capitalism is a viable system provided it is subject

[15] C. D. Cohen, *British Economic Policy: 1960–1969*, Butterworth, London, 1971, p. 38. (The two cited documents are the Magna Charta of Keynesian principles in macroeconomic management.)

to competent overall management which keeps it on a straight full-employment course. The twenty or more years of experience have shown that business cycles of prewar experience *can* be made obsolete.

Did the seventies come to shake this conclusion again? In our account, we have repeatedly had a brush with the issue of inflation. It appeared to be a by-product of full-employment policies. In the years 1973–1975, capitalist market economies have experienced recessions more severe than any that have been registered in the postwar era. They were due to reactions of policy makers to rates of inflation which seemed to be getting out of control. Is this to be a new permanent unmanageability, a stop-go, marking the managed variety of market capitalism? Chapter 11, which covers the question of inflation, does not give a yes-no answer, but the comparative analysis does suggest where the solutions might lie.

BIBLIOGRAPHY

Kirschen, E. S. (ed.): *Economic Policies Compared: West and East*, vol. 1, *General Theory*; vol. 2, *National and International Experiences*, North-Holland Publishing Company, Amsterdam, and American Elsevier, New York, 1974, 1975.

Hickman, Bert G. (ed.): *Quantitative Planning of Economic Policy*, Brookings, Washington, 1965.

Fox, K. A., J. K. Sengupta, and E. Thorbecke: *The Theory of Quantitative Economic Policy*, North-Holland Publishing Company, Amsterdam, 1973.

Lundberg, Erik: *Instability and Economic Growth*, Yale, New Haven, Conn., 1968.

Denton, Geoffrey, Murray Forsyth, and Malcolm Maclennan, *Economic Planning and Policies in Britain, France and Germany*, G. Allen, London, 1968.

Shonfield, Andrew: *Modern Capitalism: The Changing Balance of Public and Private Power*, Oxford University Press, New York, 1965.

"Planning for Full Employment," *The Annals*, American Academy of Political and Social Science, vol. 418, March 1975.

Abert, James Goodyear: *Economic Policy and Planning in the Netherlands: 1950–1965*, Yale, New Haven, Conn., 1969.

Lindbeck, Assar: *Swedish Economic Policy*, University of California Press, Berkeley, 1974.

———: "Theories and Problems in Swedish Economic Policy in the Post-War Period," *American Economic Review*, vol. 58, no. 3, part 2, supplement, June 1968, pp. 1–87.

Snavely, William P.: "Macroeconomic Institutional Innovation: Some Observations from the Swedish Experience," *Journal of Economic Issues*, vol. 6, no. 4, December 1972, pp. 27–60.

Martin, Andrew: "Is Democratic Control of Capitalist Economies Possible?" (United States, Sweden, Great Britain), in Leon N. Lindberg et al. (eds.): *Stress and Contradiction in Modern Capitalism*, Lexington Books, D. C. Heath and Company, Lexington, Mass., 1975, pp. 13–56.

Cohen, Stephen S.: *Modern Capitalist Planning: The French Model*, Harvard, Cambridge, Mass., 1969 (bibliography).

Liggins, David: *National Economic Planning in France*, Lexington Books, D. C. Heath and Company, Lexington, Mass., 1975.

Bornstein, Morris (ed.): *Economic Planning, East and West*, Ballinger, Cambridge, Mass., 1975.

Dow, J. C. R.: *The Management of the British Economy: 1945–60*, Cambridge University Press, London 1964.

Cohen, C. D.: *British Economic Policy: 1960–69,* Butterworth, London, 1971.

Caves, Richard E. (ed.): *Britain's Economic Prospects,* Brookings, Washington, 1968.

Cairncross, Sir Alec (ed.): *Britain's Economic Prospects Reconsidered,* G. Allen, London, 1971.

Chapter 11

Income Distribution
and Inflation

Although I do not wish them to, let prices continue to rise if it is necessary for our civilization to live and for us to be spared unemployment and dictatorship.

René Maury

. . . society should aim to ameliorate, and certainly not to compound the flaws of the universe. It cannot stop rain, but it does manufacture umbrellas.

Arthur M. Okun

It may seem strange to lump together two topics which, on the face of it, are only incidentally related. The strange feeling will go away as soon as the reader realizes that the relationship is not just incidental but intimate. Distribution of income, as well as wealth, is what inflation is mainly about. General increase in the price level and excessive growth of the money supply are surface technicalities. They do not explain the underlying social purpose of inflation which is for social groups to slug it out without seeming to (i.e., in a civilized manner) concerning the share of national income each of them shall receive.

Nevertheless, income distribution and inflation still are two topics. One concerns the pattern of income inequalities, i.e., a state. The other concerns a process through which the given state can be challenged and simultaneously protected. Therefore, the discussion calls for a split-level organization. We shall devote the first part of the chapter to the problem of comparing and evaluating economic systems from the static point of view of income distribution: the slippery question of establishing a standard of reference, and the fragmentary statistical evidence.

The second part of the chapter will explain why inflation should be considered a form of social struggle over income shares; how it can be controlled by *incomes policies;* how incomes policies have fared in economic systems of various countries. We shall give special attention to the form incomes policy takes under the centrally administered system of state capitalism, which will take us into the broader area of monetary controls in CPEs of the Soviet type, and into explaining the phenomenon of "suppressed inflation."

IS EQUALITY THE CORRECT STANDARD?

We need a standard of performance with respect to income distribution so that we could say which of the observed size distributions of income are better and which are worse. The correct theoretical definition of the optimal income distributions is easy: "Given a certain volume of aggregate income, that income distribution is best which maximizes the utility of all participants taken together." It is easy, but it also is empty. It could come straight from the Delphian oracle.

It does not improve matters if one specifies further, still in the abstract theoretical vein, that under optimal income distribution every participant should derive the same marginal utility from a dollar's worth of income, because if for some people the marginal utility of their income were lower than for others, total utility could be increased by shifting some dollars from the former to the latter. The utility loss to the former would be less than the utility gain to the latter, and there would be a net gain in overall utility. How incontrovertibly true, except that we cannot tell how to observe, measure, and compare such incommensurate private experiences as marginal utilities of income.[1] Hence, we cannot know from whom to take and to whom to give. Economists are the first ones to point this out, so as to warn people against jumping from the abstract definition to egalitarian policy conclusions. The definition of optimal income thus amounts to an insipid intellectual game.

Go Ask the Philosopher

Economists have no objection if anyone chooses income equality as the standard of what is optimal or desirable. Many are themselves in favor of equality. But most of them will say they cannot supply any strictly economic arguments in support of the egalitarian position. The justification will have to be found in morality, sense of justice, fairness, solidarity, need for social cohesion, there-but-for-the-grace-of-God-go-I and similar attitudes. Income-distribution standards are a matter of subjective value judgments, or politics. Such has been the fairly wide consensus in the economics profession.

A few economists did make an attempt to provide the income-equality standard with a theoretical underpinning that would get along without ethical value

---

[1] A rare exception to this standard assumption appears to be C. W. Churchman. See his article "On the Intercomparison of Utilities," in Sherman Roy Krupp (ed.), *The Structure of Economic Science,* Prentice-Hall, Englewood Cliffs, N. J., 1966, pp. 243–256.

judgments. There is A. P. Lerner's probabilistic argument, which has not been very well received, but is still interesting. According to Lerner one does not need to know, or measure, people's actual marginal utilities of income. It is enough to demonstrate logically that a decline in aggregate utility is more *probable* with every move away from equality than the other way around, and the case for equality is safe.[2]

Another intriguing idea is to treat the rule of income equality as a form of insurance against the chance factors which prevent an individual from earning better than substandard income. In the words of Richard Zeckenhauser, who suggested it, "society should establish a mechanism that insures against unfavorable outcomes in the lottery of genetic inheritance, against the possibility that they will have low capabilities and little opportunity to earn in a competitive factor market."[3] There exist other egalitarian arguments which try hard to build on subjective value judgments, some of considerable subtlety.[4]

Inequality May Be Good for Us

Curiously, while most economists would claim that there are no solid economic arguments for income equality, many have ready economic arguments in support of income inequality. This goes also for economists who, in principle, are in favor of income equality, but in practice find enough reasons to water down the principle and emerge with recommendations of some degree of inequality.

The reasons speaking in favor of inequality are based on the assumption that unequal incomes make the total pie to be divided larger than it would be under the rule of equality, and that it also would grow faster from one baking period to the next. Income inequality is assumed to act as an incentive. It motivates people to do their best to get into the highest income slot they can. And since a correlation is assumed between income level and productive contribution, the urge to earn the highest possible income acts at the same time as a spur to make the highest productive contribution one is capable of.

Some reasoning of this sort is necessary to make sense of the idea that income inequality is beneficial for productivity, efficiency, and volume of output. If the reasoning is valid, then it may be rational to give up the goal of equal sharing for the sake of a larger total to be shared. The question is: How valid is it?

Nibbling at the Incentive Hypothesis

Income distribution is one of the subjects that generate much controversy, besides occasioning a good deal of hypocrisy, because it is so difficult to get an analytic handle on the problems it poses. First of all, incomes are a very heteroge-

---

[2] A. P. Lerner, *The Economics of Control,* Macmillan, New York, 1946, pp. 28–32.

[3] In U. S. Congress, Joint Economic Committee, *The Analysis and Evaluation of Public Expenditures, The PPB System,* vol. 1, 1969, p. 159.

[4] See, for example, contributions by Kenneth Boulding and Martin Bronfenbrenner in *The Annals of the American Academy of Political and Social Sciences,* vol. 409, subtitled *Income Inequality,* September 1973.

neous mixture of different types of incomes earned under different situations. To some of them, the inequality-as-incentive hypothesis clearly does not apply. Incomes based on usufruct claims to inherited wealth—land, securities, stock—are as far removed from personal productive contribution of the recipients as anything.

Some incomes, or their portion, should be treated as economic rent, i.e., payment to a factor of production whose services would be forthcoming in any case, even if the reward were lower. In that case, the amount that is above the necessary minimum also lacks any incentive function.

Some incomes contain elements of monopoly; they are maintained at high level by keeping access to the occupation limited or by creating patterns of cartelized behavior. Sometimes, these occupational cartels are formal and overt—see bar associations setting the level of legal fees—but sometimes they are difficult to identify as such. They may be based on informal codes of behavior of an occupational group, and be hallowed by tradition or custom. Reverse cases of discrimination against members of different social groups also exist. In that case it may be low pay, i.e., the danger of losing the opportunity of earning even that little, which acts as a powerful incentive to work hard.

When speaking of incentives, we are often mixing up entirely different incentive situations. Incentives to move to areas of higher rewards are part of the issue of allocation signals and efficiency in the allocation of labor. Occupational areas of chronically higher rewards would then be a symptom of inefficiency in allocation. The speedier the adjustments in allocation, the lower would have to be the income differentials. Besides, job vacancies and discharges represent a most powerful mechanism of allocation, so that having wide wage differentials on top of it may be superfluous from the point of view of efficiency in labor allocation. Differentiation of earnings within a job category ("incentive schemes," "payment by results," piece-rate wages) is still another aspect of association between income and productive contribution, a valid one, but normally of small importance for the overall distribution of incomes.

The incentive function of incomes of active entrepreneurs and managers, associated with profits, is of a totally different order. There, personal incomes are directly derived from an economic category which has a central position as indicator of efficiency in allocation, within the framework of a market-capitalist price system. Society benefits if the allocational instructions of the profit indicator are obeyed. Hence, as long as motivational systems based on inner-directed professional ethics (such as postulated in Lange's model) are not clearly on the horizon, society may wish to make peace with seeing organizers of economic activities give themselves a preferential treatment, somewhat along the biblical "Thou shalt not muzzle the ox that treadeth out the corn."

Which Spread Is Best?

The armchair musings of the preceding section could go on, now making the incentive arguments about inequality look pretty ridiculous, now conceding their validity in the setting of present-day economic and social systems. To the extent that we accept the arguments as valid, what is the optimum degree of inequality that societies should tolerate, or aim for? It is questionable whether one can even define it theoretically, let alone express it numerically. No advocate of "that certain degree" of inequality ever committed himself to a precise figure. Neither shall we, but we do want to suggest a few definite pointers concerning comparative evaluation, before we go over the statistical record.

The Less Inequality the Better   Let us first of all drop all pretense at a scientifically grounded standard of optimal income distribution. Further, let us put aside the reservations we may have about the incentive function of inequality, and accept that some degree of inequality is needed. Let us then follow the convention, broadly shared by economists and laypersons, which intimates that, if inequality be necessary, it should not be pushed any further than necessary. Keynes expressed this attitude as follows:

> There are valuable human activities which require the motive of money-making . . . for their full fruition. . . . But it is not necessary for the stimulation of these activities and the satisfaction of these proclivities that the game be played for such high stakes as at present. Much lower stakes will serve the purpose equally well, as soon the players are accustomed to them.[5]

If this convention is applied to comparisons of economic systems, it leads to the following rule of thumb: *If two systems are performing equally well in terms of productive efficiency (factor productivity) and growth efficiency, the one with greater income equality is to be judged superior.* If one system displays greater income inequality than another, but is also characterized by greater productive efficiency, it will not be offhand judged inferior.

Inefficiency Shall Not Be Automatically Blamed on Too Much Equality   We recall the account of inefficiencies in allocation under Soviet-type CPEs given in Chapter 9. As we shall see, the CPEs also display a relatively high degree of income equality. Outside observers, as well as insiders, have frequently drawn the conclusion that CPEs have been paying for excessively egalitarian income distribution in the form of low productivity and reluctance to assume responsibilities necessary for better performance. However, this seems to be fallacious reasoning. We have seen that the inefficiencies that exist have been due to the impersonal characteristics of the CPEs. They are therefore not amenable to improvement by individual participants' trying harder. Hence, higher remuneration would be pointless, unless the basic characteristics of the allocation system were changed simultaneously. The incentive power of income differentials cannot be evaluated in isolation. One has to read them with reference to the allocation system of which they are a part. As a telling counterexample, let us take underdeveloped precapitalist formations which often display extremely steep income inequalities.

---

[5] J. M. Keynes, *The General Theory of Employment Interests and Money,* Harcourt, Brace, New York, 1936, p. 374.

However, no greater productive efficiency ensues. This is because the high in-comes are not geared to any participation in the productive process. They are merely a reflection of the taxing powers of the rich and powerful.

Income Differentials in Light of Savings and Taxation Methods No one should draw any conclusions about income differentials before checking the ways in which the economic systems under comparison raise savings to finance investments and taxes to finance government spending. Market-capitalist systems have relatively wide income differentials, but then they count to a significant degree, though not exclusively by far, on voluntary savings from the richer people's personal incomes, and on revenues from progressive income taxation. State-capitalist systems run along the CPE lines, reformed or classic, keep their rich relatively poorer, but then they rely on voluntary savings and income taxes hardly at all. The bulk of savings and tax revenues is raised by a combination of taxes levied on profits and indirect sales taxes (turnover taxes) levied on retail sales of consumer goods. In other words, instead of paying out incomes as per-sonal incomes and then collecting from them savings and taxes, the CPE state does not bother with these circuitous methods of market capitalism; it withholds a large portion of finance earmarked as savings and fiscal revenue at the source, i.e., at the enterprise level, and pays out personal incomes shorn of these amounts. The method contributes to an apparent income equality. (To correct for these distortions, we would have to compare income distributions net of income taxes and net of personal savings, but we have very few data to do that.)

We May Have the Wrong Figures, Anyway Statistically speaking, there is more equality in the world than meets the eye. Usually, statistics on income distribution give us snapshot pictures of differences in incomes received by indi-vidual units (earners or families) in a given year. How would it change matters if one plotted incomes received over people's lifetimes? Most likely it would make for greater equality.

Let us assume that the typical person passes through an occupational career whose movement is from the modest income of a beginner to a substantially higher income in later years. Naturally, the annual average of the person's life-time income will then be closer to the middle of the range than to the income received at either extreme. It is thus conceivable to have steep income inequality in any given year and absolute equality of lifetime incomes. This is presumably the direction of the effect of reward systems in which promotion and pay raises are largely a matter of seniority, such as the Japanese wage system, but it oper-ates in other economies as well. Some individuals may be stuck in the same income bracket throughout their life, but to the extent that others move upward, the effect is to make for a lifetime income distribution more egalitarian than any observed at a point in time (see Figure 11-1).

Incidentally, income inequality over one's occupational life history has an incentive effect of its own. It is of a somewhat different order from the incentive aspects of occupational income differences discussed above, which are the ones usually talked about. However, it may be by far the most potent sanction spur-

Figure 11-1 Income distribution at one point in time, contrasted with hypothetical distributions of lifetime incomes.

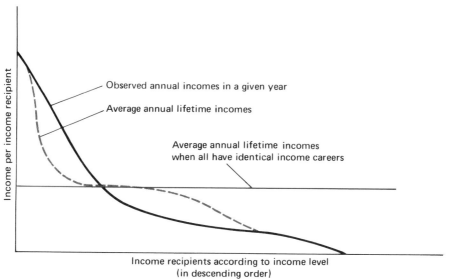

ring people to do well in their chosen profession, to prove themselves, and to increase their qualification. In other words, this is the aspect which definitely does contribute to productive efficiency. Unfortunately, it is also the least studied and statistically documented dimension of the distribution of incomes. The following survey can therefore deal only with point-in-time distribution patterns.

VAGUE DATA FOR VAGUE COMPARISONS

As it is, available comparative data on income distribution patterns leave much to be desired. Countries do not collect statistics according to a common formula. One always has to ask whether one looks at incomes before or after taxes, whether transfers, incomes from part-time work and from profits are included, whether the distribution refers to individual incomes or family incomes, and how complete the coverage is (agriculture and incomes of women are sometimes missing).

We have chosen two collections of data which have a definite indicative value, although their authors had to struggle with statistics to bring them as close as possible to a common denominator, and neither of them is very up-to-date. Fortunately, information on income-distribution patterns does not become obsolete very quickly. The patterns change very slowly, and it is improbable that the change would affect the relative standing of countries with respect to the degree of inequality.

Telling It with Percentile Ratios

The method of presentation in Figures 11-3 and 11-4 needs a preliminary note of explanation. In Figure 11-1, which shows an imaginary pattern of income distribution, we have plotted along the horizontal axis the total number of income receivers. Looking at the diagram, we can tell, for every given income level, how many income receivers were getting more and how many were getting less than that amount. In Figure 11-2, we have plotted, on the horizontal axis, the same total number of income receivers, only in percentage terms. It is clear that the income receivers are arranged in descending order, the poorer the further to the right one goes.

It is now possible to pinpoint certain income levels by specifying what percentage of income receivers fall above or under a given income level. There is an income level of which one can say that 50 percent of income receivers receive more than that, and 50 percent less. Someone just at the boundary between these two halves of the population could be receiving that level of income, which is then called the *median income.* Similarly, 5 percent—the richest 5 percent—of the number of income receivers will be getting more, and 95 percent less than a certain income level, which is then called the *fifth percentile income.* And 5 percent—the poorest section—of income receivers will be receiving less, and the luckier 95 percent more than a certain rather low income figure, the *ninety-fifth percentile income.* Following the same principle, one can identify the *tenth* and the *ninetieth percentile incomes;* the *twenty-fifth* and the *seventy-fifth percentile incomes;* and any other. All these relationships are shown in Figure 11-2.

There is a purpose in choosing these percentile incomes by pairs, symmetrically, one on the high side of the income range and the other on the low side. By comparing the high with the low percentile income, one gets an impression of the

Figure 11-2 Some measures of inequality in income distribution.

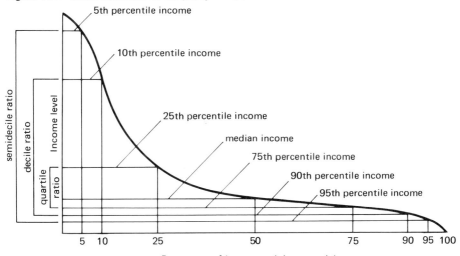

Percentage of income recipients receiving
the given percentile income or more

The various percentile ratios indicated on the left are ratios of the upper income level to the lower income level in every given pair of percentile incomes (e.g., the semidecile ratio is the ratio of the fifth percentile income to the ninety-fifth percentile income).

relative spread between incomes: how many times richer are the rich than the poor, in a given pair of percentile income levels. In other words, one can express the tenth percentile income level as a ratio, as a multiple, of the ninetieth percentile income. This is called the *decile ratio.*

Similarly, the fifth percentile income as multiple of the ninety-fifth percentile income gives us the *semidecile ratio,* and the twenty-fifth percentile income as multiple of the seventy-fifth percentile income gives us the *quartile ratio.* It is also possible to show the spread between incomes by expressing the percentile incomes in the upper and lower reaches as multiples of the median income. These ratios have no special names. All these measures are utilized in Figures 11-3 and 11-4. The percentile income in the denominator of the given ratio is always made equal to 1; when the various percentile incomes are related to the median income, the median income is made equal to 100.

Inequality in Wages and Salaries

The diagram in Figure 11-3 is based on data in Table 11-1. The twenty-five countries are arranged in five groups identified by Roman numerals. Every line connects the values of the fifth, tenth, and seventy-fifth percentile incomes expressed as percentages of the median income ($= 100$). The lines refer always to the country with the steepest income differences in its group (in terms of the spread between the fifth percentile and the median income). In Table 11-1, it is always listed as last in its group. For group I, both the upper and lower boundaries are shown within which the data for the four countries fall.

The sample of countries is relatively large, but that advantage is diminished by the coverage of incomes which leaves out agriculture, women, and property incomes. With this limitation in mind, what is the most striking impression conveyed by the data? It is the fact that what separates the highest-inequality from the low-inequality countries is not so much a matter of differences in economic systems as of stages in economic development. Underdeveloped countries and countries with a relatively large share of their labor force in agriculture have much steeper wage-and-salary differentials than the more-developed and advanced countries. Degree of equality apparently increases with economic development.

Within the more-developed group, countries having market-capitalist systems are interspersed with countries operating under the Soviet-type CPE model. It is remarkable to find New Zealand and Australia in the same group with Hungary and Czechoslovakia, and Poland, as well as Yugoslavia, in the group of market-capitalist countries having the next-steeper wage-and-salary differentials.

Market-Capitalist and Soviet-Type Inequalities

To provide a clearer picture of relative inequalities in the communist and noncommunist countries, we are reproducing the results of an important investigation undertaken by Peter Wiles with the assistance of S. Markowski (see Figure 11-4). The method of measurement has been explained. The data refer to distri-

Figure 11-3 Patterns of inequality in income distribution.

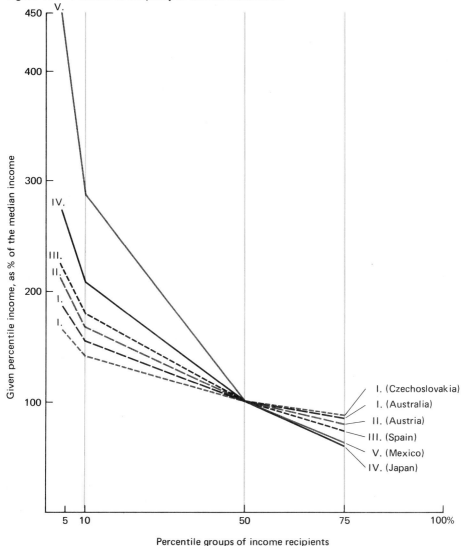

Percentile groups of income recipients

Source: Harold Lydall, *The Structure of Earnings,* Clarendon Press, Oxford, 1968, p. 153.

bution of household incomes per head, which is a broader coverage than that of the earlier statistics. Soviet data are an exception: They exclude incomes of collective-farm peasants. If included, they would surely raise the measured degree of inequality, which is surprisingly high as is, especially in comparison with other countries of the communist area.

On the evidence of these data one might be ready to conclude that, except

**Table 11-1   Measures of Inequality of Before-Tax Money
Wages and Salaries of Full-Time Males in Nonagricultural
Industries, Twenty-five Countries**

| Country and year | Percentage of median income received by specified percentile | | |
	P_5 (1)	P_{10} (2)	P_{75} (3)
Group I			
Czechoslovakia, 1964	165	145	85
New Zealand, 1960–1961	178	150	83
Hungary, 1964	180	155	83
Australia, 1959–1960	185	157	84
Group II			
Denmark, 1956	200	160	82
United Kingdom, 1960–1961	200	162	80
Sweden, 1959	200	165	78
Yugoslavia, 1963	200	166	80
Poland, 1960	200	170	76
Germany (F.R.), 1957	205	165	77
Canada, 1960–1961	205	166	79
Belgium, 1964	206	164	82
United States, 1959	206	167	75
Austria, 1957	210	170	80
Group III			
Netherlands, 1959	215	175	70
Argentina, 1961	215	175	75
Spain, 1964	220	180	75
Group IV			
Finland, 1960	250	200	73
France, 1963	280	205	73
Japan, 1955	270	211	64
Group V			
Brazil, 1953	380	250	—
India, 1958–1959	400	300	65
Ceylon, 1963	400	300	—
Chile, 1964	400	300	—
Mexico, 1960	450	280	65

Source: Irving B. Kravis, "A World of Unequal Incomes," *The Annals of
the American Academy of Political and Social Sciences,* vol. 409, September
1973, p. 69.

for the Soviet Union, communist economic systems have performed better in
respect to income equality than Western market capitalism. However, we have
already issued a warning against mechanically placing income distributions under the two types of systems side by side, without inquiring into the question of
taxation techniques and methods of raising savings for investment finance. As we
explained, under the CPEs, incomes are distributed to households net of amounts
which, under market capitalism, first flow through the channel of household
incomes before they are returned to the enterprise sector as personal savings or
collected as income or property taxes by the government. This makes automati-

Figure 11-4 Selected measures of income inequality in some Western and some Eastern European economies.

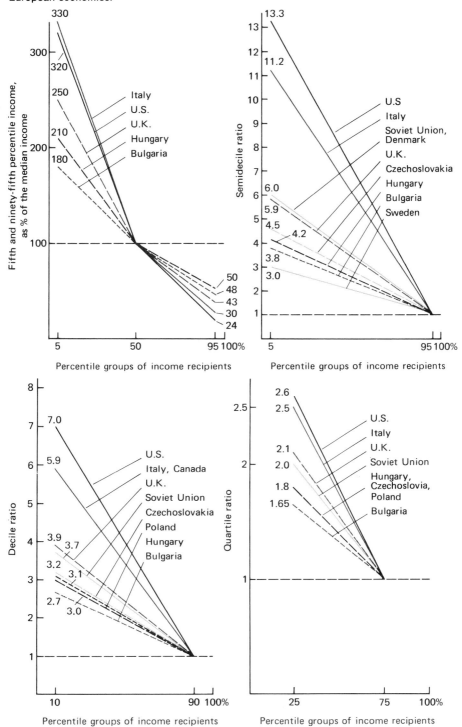

Source: Peter Wiles, *Distribution of Income East and West,* North-Holland Publishing Company, Amsterdam, 1974, pp. xiv and 48, and "Recent Data on Soviet Income Distribution," in NATO, Directorate of Economic Affairs, *Economic Aspects of Life in the USSR,* Brussels, 1975, p. 122.

cally for greater equality in distributed incomes under the CPEs, a fact which has under these conditions no clear meaning either with respect to welfare or to justice.

Let us give this matter some more thought. There is the fact that, under state capitalism of the Soviet type, savings can be withheld by the state in the manner of tax withholding by the employer, as practiced almost everywhere. Only, in contrast to ordinary tax withholding, state capitalism does not give any account of what the amount of personal incomes would have been if savings had not been withheld. This is a purely institutional arrangement, but it changes the concept of personal incomes entirely from one system to the next.

To understand the difference, it is helpful to recall the interpretation of state capitalism as a modified extension of the capitalist corporation (Chapter 3). State capitalism eliminates the usufruct rights of individual suppliers of savings (corporate stock- and bondholders). The system's caretakers do not have to worry about any share of earned enterprise revenues to be paid out as dividends. There are no dividends, no personal incomes from profits, and no other property incomes either. The equivalent of all such revenues can be devoted to finance investments and government spending. To this we may add the proceeds of the turnover tax, the hidden sales tax on consumer goods sold in retail, which also serves to finance investments and government spending. (Note, however, that the equivalent of the turnover tax *does* form part of distributed personal incomes.)

The sum of finance originating (1) in undistributed revenues at the enterprise level and (2) in taxed-away labor revenues in the form of the turnover tax at the retail level forms the bulk of savings covering investments and those budget revenues that cover noninvestment purposes. We call these two categories together the nonconsumption uses and their finance. Since none of these flows is under control of citizens directly, or their representatives indirectly, it is customary to speak in these instances of *forced saving,* though one might speak in the same breath of forced taxation, too.

What is the upshot, in real economic terms, of these institutional differences concerning the way income flows, generated through the sales of output, are channeled to their various destinations at the point of final expenditures? To our mind, it is the comparatively high rate of investments in the CPE systems. Whereas the share of investments in the GNP of most Western systems has been, typically, within the 20 to 25 percent range, in Eastern European CPEs it has attained, at times and in some countries, close to 40 percent, and a 25 to 35 percent range has been typical.

Besides investment shares being high, the forced-saving method seems to be associated with wasteful practices in the utilization of the investment funds. This can be seen, among others things, in the relatively low "growth mileage" the CPE systems have been able to obtain from their high investments. As we shall see in Chapter 12, the growth performance of an economic system is a complex matter. But, while we are discussing techniques of income allocation, it is a good moment to remark on the consequences of the forced-saving method for efficiency. Under market capitalism, firms have to compete for investible funds, offer interest payments, satisfy stockholders, and offer an image of credible investment projects. This creates a climate conducive to careful calculation, economizing, and responsible planning. Under forced saving, investible funds are obtained easily and cheaply. And—easy come, easy go.

As for the incentive function of income differentials, the data in Figure 11-4 suggest some interesting conclusions which happen to play into the hands of those who do not believe too strongly in the beneficial effects of inequality. For one, the Eastern European countries for which data are given have more equality than the Soviet Union, but they are economically not more inefficient, rather to the contrary. And then, as if to vindicate Keynes and put other economic systems, East and West, to shame, there lurks in the background the case of Sweden (and even more of Australia): as efficient as any, but in the lead of egalitarian income distribution. If there is a trade-off between equality and efficiency, it cannot be very strong. Other features of economic systems probably matter more as far as efficiency is concerned. In that case, societies can afford to look at the income-distribution problem from the point of view of welfare and equity without excessive concern for the collapse of incentives.

*   *   *

We have said what we thought worth saying on patterns of income distribution viewed statistically, and we are now shifting to the second cluster of topics. These deal with the ways by which participants in different systems try to change or preserve the given pattern, and the ways by which governments try to control and regulate the contest. We start with a short remark on the process by which governments themselves redistribute incomes in a pacific manner.

ORDERLY INCOME REDISTRIBUTION: THE WELFARE STATE

Governmental give and take—or rather take and give—is apt to change the distribution pattern of incomes. Direct income taxes (including social security contributions) and transfer payments to households (social security benefits, family allowances, welfare payments, pensions, etc.) convert incomes earned into personal disposable incomes. Depending on the incidence of taxes and tax rates, and the distribution of benefits, disposable incomes may be distributed differently than were incomes when originally earned.

Offhand, one is inclined to expect greater equality. This expectation seems to be based on the progressivity of income-tax rates—higher incomes being taxed in most countries more heavily than low ones—as well as on the notion that transfer payments benefit people in the low income brackets more than the rich. While this is, on the whole, not incorrect, to get a full picture, one has to look also at the incidence of other kinds of taxes (indirect sales taxes, which reduce the progression of overall taxation; capital-gains and other taxes, which do the same by cushioning the impact of high income-tax rates on the rich, etc.), as well as at the complete actual distributional effects of governmental services enjoyed without charge (public education, air transport subsidization, etc.).

These effects work often in contrary directions and are very difficult to measure. It is not surprising to see researchers wind up their estimates on a sadly inconclusive note. Thus, in a UN study we read these final lines:

> It seems legitimate to conclude that for the bulk of the population the pattern of primary income distribution is only slightly modified by government action. Structural changes—such as the falling share of agriculture in manpower distribution, and the reduction in self-employment generally—have probably had a more important influence on dispersion of final household incomes than government policies. One reason for this may be that the reduction of inequality (except at the extremes) has not recently been a significant objective of policy. Another reason may be that the combined effects on income distribution of the various forms of government action are rarely regarded as integrated parts of a single policy.[6]

The last sentence sounds a warning against misunderstanding the subtitle to this section. "Orderly" is not supposed to signify "coherent." It refers only to the fact that the income-distribution effects considered above are based on formal policies. They are the result of legislative and administrative procedures, not of haphazard acts of social groups, which are to be examined next.

PUSH AND SHOVE OF THE INFLATIONARY PROCESS

Inflation is usually *defined* as increase in the general level of prices over time. In the market-capitalist context, it is usually *explained* in one of three ways: (1) it is a consequence of some increase in spending to which the production sector cannot respond by immediately supplying the corresponding extra volume of goods at prevailing prices (*demand pull*); (2) it is the result of a deliberate increase in prices charged by firms for their goods, or in wages demanded by labor and followed by an increase in prices of goods (*wage-price push*); (3) it is a combination of the first two kinds of events which necessarily interact, one spilling over into the other: Increase in spending, pulling up prices in the first round, provokes labor into trying to push up wages, and firms into pushing up their prices in the next round, in order to make up for the decline in real incomes due to the first-round price increases; autonomous increases in wages or prices become naturally increases in spending from wages and profits. Demand pull and wage-price push feed each other. As a fourth element, which keeps inflation going once it has started, are expectations that it will continue; these make participants want to raise their prices and wages to protect their incomes ahead of time, whereby the very act of protection brings about the feared event, i.e., continued inflation.

The pure case of wage- or price-push inflation—case number 2—obviously is aimed at a change in the distribution of incomes. Increase in wages (in general or of a particular segment of labor), while prices and other things (such as productivity) are unchanged, means reduction of profits. Increase in prices, while money wages and other things are unchanged, means an increase in profits and a reduction of the purchasing power of money wages, i.e., a reduction of real wages. To counter an increase in wages, profit recipients raise prices of products. To protect

[6] United Nations, *Incomes in Postwar Europe,* Geneva, 1967, chap. 6, p. 41.

themselves against price increases, wage and salary earners demand increases in wages and salaries. This is the simple meaning of the familiar phrase, the "wage-price spiral."

However, the pure case of a demand-pull inflation—case number 1—will, as a rule, also quickly turn into a series of moves and countermoves which involve income adjustments, so that the inflationary process becomes indistinguishable from the one caused by a scramble over income shares, even though the initial impetus was different.

In our summary treatment of the inflation theories, we are distinguishing between the *original impetus* and the *inflationary process* itself. The impetus may be of either kind—the demand pull or the wage-price push/demand pull spiral. The underlying social-economic significance of the process turns around the concern of individual participants and social groups not to be shortchanged as far as their real-income share is concerned. In the scramble, some may not play a defensive game but, on the contrary, try aggressively to get ahead of others.

Why the Appeal to the Visible Hand?

The visible hand is always implicated in the inflationary process, if we include central monetary authorities among its agencies. Even if the government wished to practice a hands-off policy and let the inflationary process run its course, monetary authorities would have to regulate the supply of money so that it would keep up with the inflating nominal sum of payments that would need to be made. An increase in the supply of money will ordinarily also accompany a demand-pull impetus that may start the inflationary process rolling. For instance, an increase in government spending will have less of an inflationary impact, even under conditions of full employment, if the money comes from increased taxation or lending by the public from current incomes; it *will* have inflationary impact if the money is freshly created for that purpose by the banking system.

The topic of this section and the next cries for brushing up on our recollection of the classic money equation. Expressed in that equation is the necessary relationship between the sum of payments made in buying an economy's final output and the amount of monetary instruments needed for making these payments. The sum of payments made in a given period is obtained by multiplying the number of physical units of every good or service sold, q_i, by their unit prices p_i and adding up these multiplication products (i.e., $\Sigma\, q_i p_i$). As far as the required amount of monetary instruments M is concerned, it need not be equal to the sum of payments, $\Sigma\, q_i p_i$, because a given unit of money can be used in payment several times over, in the course of the given period. The number of times a unit of money is so used, on the average, is called velocity of circulation, V. The stock of money in existence, multiplied by the velocity of circulation, yields the nominal amount of payments that stock of money can perform. The complete equation then reads

$$\Sigma q_i p_i \;=\; MV$$

The value of V is, for various reasons, relatively constant (2.5 to 3 for the United

States). Therefore, if the term p_i goes up because of the inflationary process, it is ordinarily accompanied by an increase in M. This reflects the permissive, passive, accommodating role of monetary authorities under a hands-off policy.

Usually, however, the visible hand is called upon to do something active and energetic about inflation. The number of economists who keep their voices nonhysterical in inflationary periods, urging society to master the art of "living with inflation," is relatively small.[7] They do have a valid point in emphasizing that the rise in the general price level does not in itself signify a decline in the available output, only a conflict over its distribution. If the choice is to fight inflation by demand-management methods involving unemployment, they opt for inflation because unemployment signifies a shortfall in the available output, a much more palpable loss than the nuisance of inflation. However, even these cool-headed economists favor policies that keep the rate of inflation within limits.

The reason is that, beyond a certain limit, inflation becomes more than just a nuisance and begins to affect, after all, production levels and, beyond that, social stability, especially if it accelerates out of control into a hyperinflation. (There is a built-in tendency for the rate of inflation to accelerate when inflationary expectations lead firms to raise their prices and labor unions their wage demands in order to beat other price makers to it.) The list of dangers can be made alarmingly long. They include export difficulties, confusion in accounting and business calculations, weakening of the propensity to save and to invest, and especially spreading demoralization due to imagined or actual hardships faced by people unable to adjust their prices or incomes. In reference to high-inflation countries of Latin America, H. A. Turner describes the approach to the critical threshold as follows:

> . . . Institutional mechanisms involved can no longer function adequately—partly because of the time they take (major legislative regulations or industrial negotiations can hardly take place more often than annually), partly because it becomes quite impossible to predict what prices will be within the term of the settlement, or even to establish what the current price level actually is: "index-watching" and acrimonious dispute over the meaning and accuracy of the monthly price-indices are obsessional preoccupations in these economies. . . . Industrial and social conflict increases, there are demonstrations against the authorities, even spontaneous "unofficial," "unconstitutional" or illegal strikes as workers attempt to obtain "interim" pay increases to maintain their standards of living, and so on.[8]

Hence, governments see it as their responsibility to stem the inflationary process, even though in some cases it is a question of expiating the guilt of having given the original demand-pull impetus.

Demand Pull in Reverse

Whether it is to expiate the guilt of having started an inflationary process or to stem one which is not of government's doing, governments sometimes apply

---

[7] See, for example, James Tobin and Leonard Ross, "Living with Inflation," *The New York Review of Books,* May 6, 1971, or René Maury, *La Société d'inflation,* Editions du Seuil, Paris, 1973, from which the motto of this chapter was taken.

[8] Dudley Jackson, H. A. Turner, and Frank Wilkinson, *Do Trade Unions Cause Inflation?* Cambridge University Press, London, 1972, pp. 34–35.

policies which reflect a short-circuit kind of reasoning. If inflation was started by a demand-pull effect of increased spending, doesn't it stand to reason that one must reduce or moderate spending in order to stop inflation? There is a variant of the same proposition: If price-and-wage inflation requires an increased supply of money to service the increased nominal amount of payments, then if one simply denied the economy that increase in the stock of money, inflation would be made impossible. Under both variants, the policy recipe calls for reversing the demand pull, i.e., engineering a *demand squeeze*. The instruments available for this exercise of demand management are downward pressure upon government spending and upon the supply of money (i.e., upon the volume of credit for credit-financed spending, public or private).

Unfortunately, economic processes are not all, or not always, reversible. If demand pull pulls up prices, it does not necessarily follow that a demand squeeze will do the opposite. The assumed symmetry in both directions may not exist. If prices are rigid in face of sluggish or falling demand, then all that such demand management achieves is to reduce the quantity element in the expression $\Sigma\ q_i p_i$ on the left-hand side of the money equation. In other words, it causes a recession without coming to grips with inflation. The result is the familiar phenomenon of recent years, first noticed in 1958–1959 in the United States, of "stagflation," i.e., stagnation and inflation combined.

The conclusion is that, under these circumstances, the trade-off between the rate of change in the price level and the rate of employment (the famous Phillips-curve relationship) is not valid. One does not buy greater price stability by paying the price of greater unemployment, except at such catastrophic levels of unemployment which are politically not acceptable (i.e., society will not stand for them).

Thus, it is extremely important to understand that the social mechanism of changing, or protecting, one's relative income share can operate independently of the state of aggregate demand. It is possible to have a contest about income distribution even when the aggregate income available for distribution is less than the full-employment level, and even when it is declining. The strength of autonomous upward changes in wages and prices—case number 2—swamps the downward pressures coming from the demand side. Even if money supply tries to act restrictively, the spillover from the wage-price push into demand pull keeps feeding price-wage increases, instead of eliciting increased supply of physical quantities and increased employment.

Do governments in market-capitalist systems have any alternatives when they wish to control inflation? Let us think of inflation for a second just as a special example of a much more general phenomenon. Whenever there is a situation of scarcity without accepted workable rules of how the limited supply is to be distributed, the result is a stampede. A popular-band concert with free admission and no iron-clad arrangement for waiting lines means a mob scene. Inflation means a breakdown of accepted rules governing income distribution. The existing pattern is challenged, either with respect to income differentials between wage and salary earners, or with respect to the relative shares of labor incomes and profits, or both. Social groups are, so to speak, jumping the economic police barriers. To stop the nervousness and the panic about will-there-be-enough-left-for-me, some kind of "income rationing" seems to be the obvious remedy. There exist techniques to that effect. They go under the name of *incomes policies.*

INCOMES POLICIES WESTERN STYLE

The above-mentioned "incomes rationing," or perhaps some arbitration of income-distribution conflicts, that is called for must be adapted to the situation of increasing total of incomes and increasing labor productivity. Increasing labor productivity spells the possibility of labor incomes and property incomes both growing in real terms without constantly threatening to encroach upon each other's share.

To fix in our mind clearly the basic relationships which are involved, and which are of key importance to all subsequent discussion, let us set up a few elementary formulas. The share of money wages W in the total money value of output or incomes Y is the ratio of the two magnitudes. The numerator and the denominator can both be divided by total employment L without changing the value of the ratio. This operation reveals that the ratio is the same as the ratio of wages per worker W/L to the value of output per worker Y/L. The last expression happens to be a formula for average labor productivity. The equality of the two ratios reads

$$\frac{W}{Y} = \frac{W/L}{Y/L}$$

and implies that, if wage per worker grows at the same rate as output per worker (i.e., labor productivity), the relative share of wages W in total incomes Y remains constant and the share of profits consequently also remains constant. If money wages grew faster than labor productivity, the share of profits could be safeguarded only if prices of products were raised enough to cut the purchasing power of money wages down, so that *real* wages would again grow only as fast as labor productivity.

The message of the above formula is the centerpiece of contemporary price-stabilization policies: "Noninflationary wage increases are those that keep pace with increases in labor productivity." The silent part of the message is that the share of profits is to be treated as untouchable, and price increases as legitimate, if meant to safeguard the profit share in the face of wage increases in excess of the increase of labor productivity.

Another way of translating the message is to say that, if the visible hand succeeds in holding wage increases down to increases in labor productivity, wage costs per unit of output (unit wage costs) will stay constant. In that case, firms have no reason and no pretext to raise their prices. Since the direct controlling pressure is upon wage incomes, one speaks of "*incomes* policies," even though the aim is stabilization of the *price* level.

Conventional wisdom holds that, wherever they were tried, incomes policies have been a failure. We shall qualify that conclusion after a survey of some concrete postwar experiences with incomes policies. In the meantime, let us introduce the survey with a speculative remark. In spite of past disappointments, income policies are likely to be kept on the agenda or on the back burner, and tried again, until they will eventually be made to work. Their lasting attractiveness is in the fact that, by influencing wages and price setting directly, they avoid the unreliable alternative course—downward pressure on spending, which risks causing unemployment without containing prices and wages.

It is convenient to distinguish between three broad approaches to truce making in the inflationary free-for-all. Two are of a voluntary nature: the *guidelines* approach and the *national-bargain* approach. The third one is *statutory,* i.e., imposed by administrative and price controls through official ceilings to the permissible rates of change, or temporary freezes. In practice, the distinctions can become fuzzy, especially if a government switches from one approach to another over time.

Wage-Price Guidelines: United States 1962–1967

The guidelines episode in the United States is a good starting point. The principles then formulated gave the issue precise shape. They apply to incomes policies in general and illuminate clearly some of their built-in difficulties.

The central idea was the one mentioned earlier: Money wages should rise at no higher rate than average growth of labor productivity in the economy. This assumes (arithmetically at least) that unit labor costs will remain constant, at the average, and firms will have no cost-push reason for raising their prices. In consequence, the average price level will also remain constant. Wage earners will benefit by productivity increases because, with prices stable, the rise in money wages will be identical with the rise in real wages. Nonwage incomes will equally benefit, and their share will not experience any squeeze that might disturb their recipients.

These crystal-clear rules must undergo a first set of complications as soon as one peers behind the "averages" of increases in money wages and productivity. What about the sectors where labor productivity increases more slowly than the national average, or not at all, say, in barbershops and other services? There, raising money wages at the rate set by the guidelines will pinch the nonwage incomes unless prices are raised. Let them be raised, said the guidelines. Such price rises will be compensated for elsewhere, namely, in sectors where productivity increases faster than the average. There, prices will have to fall. Above-average increase in labor productivity will lead to an above-average decline in unit labor costs. If prices were allowed to remain fixed, these sectors would show an extraordinary increase in the level and share of nonwage incomes. Hence, above-average productivity gains must be passed on to society in the form of reduced prices.

Thus, the guidelines formula manages to take care of these complications and solve them perfectly—on paper. In application, there appear difficulties. First, there is an understandable recalcitrance of firms to price reductions. In consequence, abnormal profits do have a chance to appear in sectors with above-average productivity increases. These sectors then become the areas of least resistance against wage pressures, as well as their obvious targets. If workers elsewhere follow suit, in order not to slip behind in the scale of interindustry wage differentials, they create a cost-push pressure upon prices in their sectors.

Further, the government may simultaneously pursue a policy of reducing income differences, or allowing wage differentials to arise in response to market demand, i.e., to labor shortages. These objectives may easily work against price stabilization. Finally, since wage-price guidelines are, by definition, only indicative, any abnormal and conspicuous wage gains flouting the guidelines will discredit the entire idea and bring back the old every-man-for-himself atmosphere.

All these circumstances, plus one, conspired to undermine this worthy undertaking and led to its abandonment in 1967. It received its last blow in the form of an injection of excess government spending for increased military needs in the Vietnam war. In rejecting the recommendation of the economic advisers to raise taxes (which would have reduced private spending and made room for a noninflationary increase of governmental expenditure), the administration invited an inflationary development.

The years 1972–1974 saw a return to incomes policies but not to the guidelines approach. No simple formula can describe the mixture and succession of the following principal elements: temporary general freezing of wages and prices; selective supervision of wage increases in individual firms and collective bargaining agreements in reference to a standard rate of increase set up as a goal (not unlike a guidepost); temporary selective price freezes; attempts to involve labor and management in a tripartite cooperative agency with the government (suggesting the national-bargain approach). In the end, monetary authorities and the administration concentrated on demand management, hoping that a sustained demand squeeze would squeeze out inflationary expectations. It did to some extent, but it also raised the official rate of unemployment into the neighborhood of 8 percent, creating a situation of scarcity amidst potential plenty.

National Bargains

Implied in the national-bargain approach are also guidelines of the sort just described: numerical targets, expressed as percentage rate of wage and price changes, and as far as possible consistent with the assumed future values of other variables in the economic system. It is the procedures and the identity of participants which are different. *Guidelines* are the voice of the government from above. *National bargain* is an agreement reached between top organs of labor unions and employers' associations, with the government engaged heavily in some cases, and in others almost absent—just a supplier of statistical data.

The Exemplary Dutch   For years—until 1963—the Dutch case served as a classic example of a successful incomes policy of the type in which wage movements and price stability are carefully managed, in the interest of national prosperity, by the government-labor-business triangle. It was a living proof that it can be done. The collapse of the harmony and discipline in the sixties was then used as proof that, after all, it cannot be done, not even in the Netherlands. However, a more fruitful point of view suggests itself: Was it perhaps that, in view of changing circumstances, the early *forms* of incomes policy had outlived their usefulness, and could it be that they may yet have to be rediscovered and adapted to current needs?

It has been observed that incomes policies in general tend to be successfully introduced in periods of national emergencies. They are willingly accepted in wartime or—the less dramatic instance—during balance-of-payments crises. Circumstances surrounding the successful phase of Dutch incomes policies amounted to an emergency of a different order. Postwar reconstruction of a ravaged economy, adaptation to the loss of a colonial empire, excess supply of labor, need to industrialize and to earn the country's way in foreign trade—such were the factors which made for easy acceptance of wage restraint. Andrew Shonfield pointed out a certain similarity with the traditional case for protecting infant industries: "Only in this instance, instead of providing shelter for these industries at home by means of a high tariff wall, it was to be supplied by putting an artificially low ceiling on wages and holding it there by decree."[9] Labor did not object because future job supply was at stake.

It appears that social consensus is by far the most important prerequisite of an effective incomes policy of this type. It is more important than the institutional concentration of authority which is needed in agreements of a national scope—needed to keep sectional interests in line and to enforce the top-level agreements. In the Netherlands, this concentration was provided by the postwar Foundation of Labor, a bipartite negotiation forum established by the three Dutch national labor federations and three employers' associations. The government was also involved. It issued official guidelines and tried to have them accepted and observed through a Board of Mediators, as well as through the advice of the Social and Economic Council. Despite considerable enforcement powers of the mediators—they could, for instance, declare out-of-step collective contracts null and void—the observance grew progressively weaker as the consensus petered out. And it had petered out because of an accumulation of new factors: inequities in the structure of wages, the lag of Dutch real incomes behind those of neighboring countries, local rigidities disregarding conditions of the labor market, and the general shortage of labor supply requiring injections of foreign labor from southern Europe.

Between 1959 and 1963 and after, the government tried to apply a more differentiated wage-price formula, somewhat similar to the United States guideposts. then to lean more heavily on prices, to shift responsibility for enforcement upon labor and business (as in Sweden), and to introduce temporary price and wage freezes—a development too involved to be related blow by blow. It became obvious that, for a while, restraint went out of fashion, as in most other countries of Western market capitalism, especially after the tumultuous year 1968, so that orderly incomes policies became inoperative.

Trying Too Much at a Time in Sweden   The Swedish approach, which keeps the government as much as possible in the background, has been characterized as a "privately operated incomes policy." The private parties to the "national wage

---

[9] A. Shonfield, *Modern Capitalism,* Oxford University Press, New York, 1965, p. 212.

bargain" have been the highly centralized, not to say authoritarian, Confederation of Swedish Trade Unions (LO) and the Swedish Employers' Confederation (SAF). This desire to keep the government out of industrial relations, which dates from prewar days, seems to end up in stricter controls than if the government were in. It brings to mind the French saying concerning a character named Gribouille, who jumps into water to protect himself from the rain. The price of autonomy has been renunciation of freedom of action: a self-imposed discipline and, in turn, the need to police or placate the respective constituent members—unions, workers, and employers—with responsibility for failure added as an extra fine.

As with United States guideposts and the Dutch system, one of the major sources of relative failure has been the difficulty of tackling price stabilization and at the same time changes in the structure of earnings by different industrial categories or income brackets. Swedish labor unions have prided themselves on their policy of "wage solidarity," which means, to put it simply, special attention to low-wage categories for the sake of greater equality. This introduces an element of wage increases independent of productivity changes, which starts further upward wage-price movements rippling through the economy.

Before we trace out some of these destabilizing consequences, we want to spotlight a dynamic connection between wage movements and productivity which must not be left out of account because it is of major general importance. Conventionally, productivity increases are treated most of the time as something attributable to changes in the technology of production, stimulated by competition, but unaffected by wage movements. This is not the full story. Wage pressures, too, can be a factor contributing actively to the progress in productivity. *By squeezing profit margins, wage raises prod entrepreneurs to adopt innovations which would reduce unit labor costs, i.e., raise labor productivity.* This reflex is the stronger the more difficult it is for firms to raise prices as a means of protecting profit margins. Thus, labor does not just share in an exogenously given growth of output per worker. Labor promotes this growth, up to a point, by wage demands which motivate managements to make it happen!

In Sweden, this situation has apparently prevailed in industries exposed to foreign competition. At home, they have been under pressure to match prices of imports. Industries working for exports have had to more than match prices of competitive foreign goods abroad. The only avenue open to safeguard profits while granting wage raises determined by domestic pressures has been growth of productivity. Noninflationary wage increases in these "exposed sectors" are then, curiously, at the origin of inflationary ripples. Labor in the so-called sheltered domestic industries wants the same wage increases. However, there, with less exposure to pressures of foreign competition, incentives to increase productivity have been weaker, and freedom to raise prices correspondingly stronger. It goes without saying that this effect has been even more pronounced in sectors where productivity cannot grow much in any case, incentives or no incentives.

Wage increases are linked to further wage increases through still another mechanism, that of a vigorous process of structural change. Policy of wage solidarity hits particularly hard firms in declining industries where productivity lags and prices are dampened by sluggish demand. This is where wage increases squeeze profits, as well as firms, out of existence. In the meantime, unfilled vacancies multiply in the growth industries which post wage increases to attract workers.

Deviations from wage rates agreed upon in the national bargain are due further to the phenomenon of wage drift and, allied to it, to the backlash against the policy of wage solidarity on the part of various categories of wage earners (and especially white collar workers), intent on preserving the old pattern of wage differentials. Wage drift has been usually linked to the prevalence of piecework in Swedish industry—a method of remuneration offering ample opportunities for shop-level bargaining between the individual worker and the immediate supervisor, the foreman.[10] In the antiequality backlash, the better-paid categories clamor for raises parallel to those arranged for the bottom categories. This frustrates the original purpose of reducing inequality and gives an upward push to the average rate of wage increases.

This survey of difficulties encountered in the implementation of incomes policies applies not only to Sweden but to other countries of market capitalism as well. It concentrates on internal social mechanisms. It leaves out of account inflationary shocks from the expenditures side and country-to-country transmission of price increases through the foreign-trade sector (see below) which further complicate the interaction of inflationary forces and frustrate the ambitions of incomes policies.

Toward a "Social Contract"?   By way of glimpses from a speeding train, we shall now sample a few salient features of incomes policies elsewhere. Norway, Finland, and Denmark have set up, in the course of the sixties, an institutional framework similar to the Dutch model. At its core have been centralized wage negotiations conducted with a view to the scope of attainable wage increases and their likely effect on the economy. West Germany has relied on triangular consultations between its so-called *Sozialpartner,* and on the persuasive power of an extragovernmental Council of Economic Experts, staffed by independent academicians, which has been issuing its periodic guidance reports of nonbinding nature ever since 1965. Without any rigid formal framework, the German method of *concertation* has achieved, comparatively speaking, remarkable results in stabilization. In France, a country with a poorly developed system of collective bargaining, the government has worked mainly through controlling the movement of prices and thus, indirectly, the movement of wages. However, it had to condone periodic spurts of inflation and sanction upward wage adjustments, particularly in moments of political stress, most conspicuously during the general strike in May 1968. (That earthquake was calmed by a 13 to 14 percent wage increase granted on the basis of a central tripartite agreement.)

Great Britain has a checkered history of short-lived experiments with one or another type of incomes policy, sometimes successful, but mostly not: voluntary wage freezes, statutory wage and price controls, exhortation through guidelines,

[10] See William Brown, *Piecework Bargaining,* Heinemann, London, 1973.

and finally, in 1974, a voluntary "social contract" between the government and the unions concerning wage restraint.[11] In contrast to Germany or the Scandinavian countries, Britain has often been held up as an example of unions exercising their power in a socially irresponsible manner. Inflationary effects of wage pressures in England are a phenomenon too complex to be adequately explained by charging union irresponsibility. However, it has been true that the organizational structure of British unions—high degree of decentralization, fragmentation into craft unions—is an obstacle to making the global point of view prevail. This is why the commitments of the union confederation, the Trade Union Congress (TUC), have been so difficult to make binding upon the innumerable member organizations. Nevertheless, the idea of a social contract is, and will remain, at the heart of any incomes policy in a democratic setting.

Did Incomes Policies Really Fail?

Judged by perfectionist standards, incomes policies have been a failure. Nowhere did they succeed in stabilizing the price level by holding average wage increases to the average growth of labor productivity. However, there is a world of difference between the 2.5 to 6 percent annual rates of inflation experienced by advanced market-capitalist economies in the fifties and sixties and the 25 to 35 percent rate typical for some of the Latin American countries. The difference is that, in the advanced systems of market capitalism, the principles of incomes policies, even when not implemented in a formal way and even when disobeyed, have become, so to speak, part of social conscience. Besides the principles of demand management, concerns with wage, price, and productivity developments have been permanently entered on the normal agenda of the visible hand.

Lowering one's eyesight, one encounters a less-than-perfectionist yardstick in the concept of the "equilibrium rate of inflation." Considering the continuous conspiracy of minor and not so minor destabilizing influences that are at work in systems of mature market capitalism, perfect price stability would be a miracle. We mentioned some of these influences in the preceding account: pressures on prices in sectors of below-average increases in productivity under average or above-average increases in wages; above-average wage increases meant to reduce inequality; imitative wage demands meant to maintain existing inequality; the "wage drift." These are joined by strong secular forces tending to expand aggregate demand at a faster rate than the economy's capacity to deliver: increasing spending through the government sector and credit-financed private spending, stimulated by advertising. The popular phrase "revolution of rising expectations" refers to these trends in spending. Finally, under full-employment demand management, demand continues to press against capacity, which then tends to create supply bottlenecks here and there, and with them price and wage increases. When the participants get used to a certain rate of inflation, when they learn to anticipate it and to adjust their plans accordingly, without exacerbating unduly the push-and-shove of competing claims, one may be content with the pragmatic

---

[11] For a quick, informative survey, see *The Economist*, Mar. 29, 1975, pp. 92–93.

notion of an equilibrium rate of inflation and use it as a yardstick of performance.

In the first half of the seventies, the rate of inflation in advanced market-capitalist countries underwent a marked acceleration. Was that perhaps a conclusive demonstration of the failure of incomes policies? The fact that prices and wages shot up then is often seen as evidence that business, government, and the union "establishment" were unable to cope with increased militancy of rank-and-file employees. This element was undoubtedly present. In that respect the authority behind incomes policies was clearly not strong enough. However, inflation of the seventies had an additional set of powerful and unprecedented causes which neither incomes policies nor domestic demand management could deal with.

First of all, it was a period of readjustment in the exchange rate of national currencies, forced upon other countries by the devaluation of the United States dollar in 1971. This meant an initial rise in dollar prices of goods imported to the United States and fall in the prices paid by foreigners for goods coming from the United States. This stimulated demand for American goods, which was booming anyway, and eventually pushed their prices up, especially after the massive buying of wheat by the Soviet Union in 1972–1973. Finally, in 1973–1974, there came out of the blue a quadrupling of oil prices by the cartel of oil-exporting countries (OPEC). Underneath all this, the familiar struggle-for-income-shares mechanism continued to operate throughout the period, dammed in by various incomes policies and demand restrictions, but at a higher general price level than would have been the case without these exceptional circumstances.

To conclude on a general note, even if one feels forced to admit that incomes policies have thoroughly failed, does it follow that society may just as well drop the idea? If there is no other effective way of keeping the contest over income distribution more or less orderly, shouldn't perhaps the correct conclusion be that market-capitalist systems have no choice but to try again, and try to do better?

INCOMES POLICY UNDER A SOVIET-TYPE CPE

Officially, in Soviet-type economies inflation does not exist. We shall demonstrate that, actually, inflation has not been a stranger to the CPEs, even though it has been dissimulated in various ways, or manifested itself indirectly in the symptoms of the so-called repressed inflation. However, to evaluate the inflationary phenomenon under a CPE properly, one also has to understand its meaning in the broad social and political context, a perspective we have not bothered about until now.

We would get trapped in a false comparative framework if we stuck to the assumption that inflation is, in all respects, an unmitigated evil. The argument sails past the true meaning of the issue if it is conducted at the level of no-they-don't-have and yes-they-do-have inflation. In those terms, if one has demonstrated that CPEs do have inflations, all one has done is to cut official claims down to size. One has shown that Soviet-type economies are, on the point of inflation, not so different from everyone else.

The issue appears in a different light if one realizes that inflation, in the Western market-capitalist context, is a by-product of free bargaining over wages and salaries and, via the question of profits, part of a mute and confused social debate over the share of investments in total output. If inflation is successfully moderated, it is a sign of the social conflicts becoming less chaotic and bitter. On the other hand, if inflation is banished under the CPEs of the Soviet type, it is merely a sign that the free play of social conflicts had been successfully stamped out. From this vantage point, the existence of the inflation problem is a symptom of something good, if one considers as good the freedom of social groups to defend their interests. Elimination of the inflation problem would then have the opposite significance.

We shall proceed by first explaining why, on formal grounds, there should not be any inflation in Soviet-type systems. We shall then ask why there has been inflation after all, and what form it has taken.

Checks on Inflation

In a perfect overall economic plan of the Soviet type, planned flows of commodities are supposed to be matched by corresponding planned flows of money. Individual commodities are priced at fixed prices. These are determined outside the selling enterprise by price-setting authorities. On that account alone, an upward movement of prices should be out of the question.

As an extra precaution against upward pressure on prices from the spending side, financial planning sees to it that spenders should not have independent control over purchasing power which would be in excess of "legal" spending on quantities of goods, at fixed prices, as foreseen by the overall plan and by the production plans of individual enterprises. Without freely spendable money, they are in no position to bid up prices of goods which might be in short supply.

This control over spending power is exercised by the banking system along two separate money circuits: the noncash circuit and the cash circuit. The noncash circuit consists of deposits of bank money, not convertible into cash, on the bank accounts of individual enterprises and government units ("budgetary organizations"). The amounts of these deposits are determined by the planned volume of payments for material inputs to which a given firm is entitled by virtue of its production plan.

The source of deposits on enterprise bank accounts is mainly bank credit, repayable from the firm's sales receipts. Receipts come from deposits transferred to the seller's account from the accounts of its customer firms, but they are quickly withdrawn by the bank from the enterprise account in repayment of earlier credits granted, taxes due, and other charges. New money which the enterprise needs for the next round of payments for inputs comes again from a fresh grant of bank credit.

In this manner, the firm can never put its hands on any liquid money which it might use for spending at its discretion. It can never call the money in its account its own: it is always owed to the bank. All receipts go to repay the outstanding credit so that fresh credit can be granted, and so on, in constantly revolving rounds.

The cash circuit is an offshoot of the noncash circuit. A portion of bank deposits in a firm's account *is* convertible into circulating currency, namely, the portion meant for the payment of wages. It is planned quite parallel to noncash payments for material inputs: for quantities one substitutes the planned number of employees of various "grades," and for fixed prices one substitutes centrally determined wage rates. The arithmetic product of the two yields the so-called wage fund. Wages paid out in cash by enterprises and other organizations return to the state bank after they have been spent on consumer goods. Part of this flow makes a detour through the free market for farm products but eventually most of it ends up in retail shops which deposit their daily take with the bank. This completes the cash circuit. (When retail shops pay for goods delivered from manufacturing enterprises, they pay again in noncash funds.)

Equilibrium in the cash circuit is maintained by the planners' trying to balance the value of consumer goods produced with aggregate disposable incomes, the bulk of which is the aggregate wage bill. If disposable income and consumer goods are exchanged for each other as expected, the population is left with no appreciable amounts of cash purchasing power, and what there is, is expected to be absorbed by personal savings accounts. If all these magnitudes balance out, no excess liquidity ever comes to exert pressure on the fixed prices of consumer goods.

Inflation Despite the Checks on Inflation

Let us make a distinction between observed *signs* of inflation and the underlying inflationary *situation*. An inflationary situation exists when aggregate spending is greater than the physical volume the economy can supply at preexisting prices. Observed manifestations of this imbalance can be of different sorts. If prices are free to increase to restore financial equality between the volume of spending and the market value of goods sold (the $\Sigma q_i p_i$ and the MV side of the money equation), we speak of *open* inflation. If prices are not free to move (because, for instance, they are fixed by decree), then it is the volume of actual spending that has to adjust. It is kept below the volume of desired potential spending. What cannot be spent—because the goods are simply not there—is kept in the spenders' pockets. It is added to their liquid money holdings (cash balances). This involuntary increase in cash balances (i.e., fall in velocity V) is, then, one of the observable manifestations of the inflationary situations.[12] There are others, as we shall see. Since prices are not allowed to rise openly, this case is called *repressed* inflation.

That a chronic inflationary situation should have been the rule in Soviet-type economies is not surprising. It has been due to the habit of "pressure planning" discussed in Chapter 9, and it is nothing but the sellers' market put differently. It boils down to saying that financial plans, i.e., planned flows of spending, usually do not match—i.e., exceed—the feasible counterflows of commodities at fixed prices. One can speak quite rightly of excess demand, even though it is not

---

[12] "Repressed inflation" is another way of describing the "disequilibrium system" in financing wartime military expenditures, discussed in Chap. 8.

a spontaneously formed market demand but demand built into the economic plans and expressed in their planned targets.

Excess demand in the noncash circuit is generated by funds earmarked for planned spending by the government on goods and services, and by enterprises on material inputs. Excess demand in the cash circuit is mainly due to the discrepancy between the amount of wages paid out and the volume of consumer goods supplied. To be more precise, one should say: consumer goods in the composition and of the quality actually demanded since there may be enough consumer goods by physical volume, but of the wrong sort or of unsatisfactory quality. Accumulation of inventories of unsalable products, a perennial problem in Soviet-type economies, amounts to a shortfall in the supply of goods that are effectively in demand.

The inflationary gap in the cash circuit is being pulled open from two sides: deficit in the goods supply and a tendency to exceed the projected wage fund. Deficits in consumer goods are easily explained by the unwritten scale of importance. Consumer goods happen to have a low priority rating so that, in case of strain on resources, which is always, their plans tend to be underfulfilled. But why is there a tendency to overpayment of wages in spite of financial controls over the wage fund?

In a situation of tight labor supply and periods of rush alternating with standing around while waiting for deliveries of material, enterprises are hard pressed to find discreet ways of granting wage raises in order to get things done. For instance, they may reclassify workers into higher categories. Wage drift in piecework operations is not unknown in Soviet-type economies either. And the bank may be willing to give in somewhat on wage payments for the sake of the fulfillment of plans.[13] As a result, average money earnings have been rising consistently more than planned.

There Is No Hiding a Repressed Inflation

What have been the observable symptoms of the inflationary situation in Soviet-type systems? There has been a mixture of signs indicating repressed inflation, as well as of effective price increases which define open inflation. Insofar as prices actually charged have been kept in line with officially fixed prices, all that which is typical for repressed inflations in market economies becomes noticeable: queues—real ones and in the form of waiting lists for cars and apartments; vain inquiries about unavailable merchandise; disappearance of goods from official stocks into the black market; rudeness toward customers; and unusual accumulation of savings.

---

[13] However, there is no comparison between the degree of financial control and discipline in the Soviet Union today and the money flood of the thirties. Then, there was almost no limit to money wage increases. What enterprises paid out in wages, the retail market mopped up through jacked-up prices. The consumer price level increased roughly ten-fold from 1928 to 1940, while the average annual wage increased somewhat more than five-fold. Between 1940 and 1948, wages doubled and prices somewhat more than doubled. Consumer prices increased to a considerable extent by raising of the rate of the turnover tax, while wholesale price increases lagged behind. Thus, Soviet inflation of the thirties was at the origin of the two-tier price system described in Chap. 9.

Price increases, manifestations of open inflation, assume peculiar forms when supposedly prices are fixed and inflation is repressed. The device frequently employed has been to put a high-grade label on a low-grade article and to sell it at the official price of the high-grade one. Another ploy has been to make a minor alteration in a standard article, which would make it eligible for special individualized pricing outside the standard price lists. Finally, there is the tendency toward quality deterioration: the price remains fixed but there is less of a good behind it.

All this remains unrecorded in the statistical series which work with official list prices only. As for undisguised price increases, only those in the nonregulated farm market, where peasants sell their produce directly and freely, are registered in statistics. Price movements in the farm market have been a telltale indirect indicator of the rate of inflation: in the Soviet Union the ratio of farm market prices to the official retail-price level changed from 1.05 in 1950 to 1.6 in 1972. What escapes statistics, but surely not the awareness of the public, is prices charged by persons selling their services on illegal free markets, such as plumbers and other essential trades, connected mainly with household maintenance and construction, for which the planned sector does not provide adequately.

Inflationary symptoms in the noncash circuit take similar forms. Enterprises circumvent official price lists by producing "nonstandard" items which need to be priced individually, or by faking them. Bribes of one form or another, offered for the sake of obtaining bottleneck articles, also amount to an effective price rise. Finally, funds earmarked for spending on investment projects remain periodically unspent at the end of a period. And even though they do not accrue to the enterprises—they are not transferable from one planning period to the next (except in some of the reformed systems)—they are the equivalent of the involuntary accumulation of personal savings by the household sector.

If There Were No Inflation—So?

If there is effective inflation under Soviet-type systems, spenders are of course worse off than they would be if their money incomes were what they are (or what they are planned to be) but goods were forthcoming, at constant prices, in the corresponding volume. However, even then the absence of inflation would not have the same significance as in capitalist market economies. It would only mean that central economic controls over real production flows, as well as over financial flows, have been successful in conforming to the will of the planners. To the extent that the will of the planners conflicts with the preferences of society and its members, society would not gain anything by stable prices.

Seen as part of the general system of administrative planning, control of money flows and prices contributes to the enforcement of planners' preferences. Is disposable income being kept down to the planned volume of consumption? That spells success in neutralizing all direct and spontaneous expression of people's preferences concerning their share in national income, which is not exactly a success for the citizens. Its obverse is the high proportion of nonconsumption uses of the national product, especially that extraordinarily high proportion of investments (between 30 and 40 percent of GNP).

In one sense, strict control of wage payments deprives the CPEs of one valuable stimulus of productivity increases. In the section on Swedish incomes policies, we explained how, up to a point, industrial management tends to respond to wage pressures by intensifying its cost-cutting innovation efforts. Cost cutting is nothing but the financial side of raising productivity. Thus, efficient maintenance of discipline in wage payments appears, in a close-up view, as one special aspect of the systemic inefficiencies of the CPEs.

*   *   *

As with full employment stabilization, credit for relative price stability must go to those who are responsible for the formulation and implementation of policies, rather than to economic systems as such. At the same time, lower rates of inflation signify better performance only if, in all other relevant respects, the systems under comparison perform equally well. Otherwise, comparative evaluation must take into account difficult trade-offs.

Traditionally, the major trade-off seemed to be between price stability and unemployment: either high rates of employment with inflation, or unemployment with price stability. However, with the phenomenon of "stagflation," that simple trade-off lost its former relevance. Policy makers in different systems could be compared on the basis of speed of adaptation to that fact: How tenaciously do they cling to the costly methods of administering demand squeeze which has limited effectiveness; how creative and enterprising are they in devising new and better forms of incomes policies?

As for comparisons between market-capitalist systems and the CPEs of the Soviet type, they can be meaningful only in reference to the full political and social context. The apparent mildness of open inflation in Soviet-area economies is, in Marxian terms, a sign of suppressed class conflict. Its openness in Western economies is a sign of free class struggle in action. Whenever it becomes virulent, it indicates low morale of capitalist employers: instead of putting up a bold front to wage demands and arguing out the economically feasible limits of real-wage increases, they give in to union pressures by granting unrealistic money wage increases. Then, through the back-door gambit of price increases, they shear their real purchasing power down to feasible rates.

Nonetheless, despite its many adverse effects, inflation is misleadingly compared to a sickness. Rather, being a form and symptom of open social conflict, conducted under political freedom, it can also be seen as a sign of systemic vitality. This seems to be the meaning of the motto by René Maury which opened this chapter.

BIBLIOGRAPHY

The Annals of the American Academy of Political and Social Sciences, vol. 209, subtitled *Income Inequality,* September 1973.

Lydall, Harold: *The Structure of Earnings,* Clarendon, Oxford, 1968.

Marchal, Jean, and Bernard Ducros (eds.): *The Distribution of National Income,* Macmillan, London, and St. Martin's, New York, 1968.

Okun, Arthur M.: *Equality and Efficiency: The Big Tradeoff,* Brookings, Washington, 1975.

Pen, Jan: *Income Distribution,* Allen Lane, The Penguin Press, London, 1971.

Wiles, Peter: *Distribution of Income East and West,* North-Holland Publishing Company, Amsterdam, 1974.

Jain, Shail (The World Bank): *Size Distribution of Income: A Compilation of Data,* Johns Hopkins, Baltimore, 1976.

Haberler, Gottfried, Michael Parkin, and Henry Smith: *Inflation and the Unions,* The Institute of Economic Affairs, London, 1972.

Jackson, Dudley, H. A. Turner, and Frank Wilkinson: *Do Trade Unions Cause Inflation?* Cambridge University Press, London, 1972.

Zawadzki, K. K. F.: *The Economics of Inflationary Processes,* Weidenfeld and Nicolson, London, 1965.

Galenson, Walter (ed.): *Incomes Policy: What Can We Learn from Europe?* New York State School of Industrial and Labor Relations, Ithaca, N. Y., 1973.

Hein, John: *Aspects of Incomes Policies Abroad,* The Conference Board, Inc., New York, 1972.

Sheahan, John: *The Wage-Price Guideposts,* Brookings, Washington, 1967.

Ulman, Lloyd, and Robert J. Flanagan: *Wage Restraint: A Study of Incomes Policies in Western Europe,* University of California Press, Berkeley, 1971.

Wootton, Barbara: *Incomes Policy: An Inquest and a Proposal,* Davis-Poynter, London, 1974.

Grossman, Gregory (ed.): *Money and Plan,* University of California Press, Berkeley, 1968 (chaps. by A. Brzeski and J. M. Montias, pp. 17–56).

Hodgman, Donald R.: "Soviet Monetary Controls through the Banking System" (and F. D. Holzman's "Comment") in Gregory Grossman (ed.): *Value and Plan,* University of California Press, Berkeley, 1960, pp. 105–131.

Holzman, Franklyn D.: "Financing Soviet Economic Development," in National Bureau of Economic Research (ed.), *Capital Formation and Economic Growth,* Princeton University Press, Princeton, N. J., 1955.

Laulan, Yves (ed.): *Banking, Money and Credit in Eastern Europe,* NATO Information Service, Brussels, 1973.

Montias, J. M.: "Inflation and Growth: The Experience of Eastern Europe," in W. Baer, and I. Kerstenetsky (eds.), *Inflation and Growth in Latin America,* Irwin, Homewood, Ill., 1964.

Growth Performance

Grow, industry, grow, grow, grow!
Harmony and sincerity!
Matsushita Electric!

From a Japanese company anthem

Fast progress curves . . . are, to some extent, accidents of economic history, because those growth rates are, on mathematical grounds, absolutely impossible to be extended indefinitely.

René Dumont

Since the late sixties, economic growth has been receiving an increasingly bad press. This was a remarkable turnabout, coming after two decades of intense concern with growth rates and growth-conscious policies. Enthusiasm with "growthmanship" cooled off as a result of the realization that there are limits to available natural resources, that growth tends to spoil the environment, and that population cannot continue increasing indefinitely without making the earth un-inhabitable. Professor Kenneth Boulding issued a call to abandon the mentality of a "cowboy economy" unconcerned with limits of any sort, in favor of attitudes suited to a "spaceship economy" dominated by acute awareness of limits and of the need to husband resources. The notion of "zero growth" gained popularity and came to be advocated not only for population numbers but for economic output as well.

290

In view of this disenchantment with growth, is it still legitimate to count growth rates among the positive performance criteria of economic systems? Were growth to stop, what about the latecomers to economic development? What about the poor within advanced economies? Are they supposed to stay, economically, where they are?

Besides, speaking of growth, does increasing output necessarily imply a proportional devouring of limited resources? It has been observed that, as output grows, the relative share of material-intensive production declines and that of labor-intensive services increases. We may easily envisage continuing growth with stable levels of material output and forever-expanding volume of personal services (education, science, entertainment, and human care of all types).

What if we broaden our notion of economic outcome regarding growth to include gains in available leisure time? In that case, we shall hardly ever tire of growth. Of course, it will not be growth of material output as such but of output per worker, i.e., growth of labor productivity. Gains in labor productivity will, however, not be used for expanding the marketed output of goods and services while continuing to work the same number of hours and days. They will be used to cut the number of working hours and days, while stabilizing the volume of marketed goods and services, or to achieve some combination of increasing leisure as well as output, as has been the historical case with capitalism.

While taking due notice of valid objections to a single-minded and simple-minded glorification of growth, we shall therefore continue in the tradition of treating growth performance as a valuable characteristic of economic systems. This still leaves us with the task of clarifying what we mean by growth performance and how we propose to measure it so as to be able to make meaningful comparisons.

HOW DO WE MEASURE GROWTH PERFORMANCE?

From the outset, we have to reject as unsuitable for our purposes the statistically observed overall growth rates of national output or income of individual countries. We called them earlier "crude growth rates" (see Chapter 5), to indicate that they were unanalyzed and did not permit an examination of the role played by the economic system in achieving growth. For one thing, they are the result of many circumstances specific to the situation of a given country for which the system is not responsible. Further, they do not provide any information at what cost they were achieved, e.g., what amount of inputs was used. However, this piece of information is essential for judging growth efficiency.

The Part of Growing Labor Force Output can grow for a number of reasons, not all of which are reasons of performance efficiency. Thus, if output of a given country's economy grows because the economy adds more workers to its labor force, growth amounts to a mere widening of the economy. One needs to visualize the additional workers together with additional capacities (equipment, etc.) growing in proportion to their numbers, in order to have a perfect analogy with the process of blowing up photography. Such enlargement of the economy is as little a sign of performance efficiency as doubling the crop by doubling the seed and the sown area.

The implication is that, if a country exhibits low crude growth rates, it is not necessarily a sign of poor performance. They may be due to low rates in the population growth. Ireland's rate of growth, between 1950 and 1969, 2.5 percent annually, was the worst among Western European countries, but it does not look all that bad if one takes into account that labor force was annually declining by 0.7 percent.

For our purposes, it seems reasonable to regard the growth of employment as independent of the economic system. The system should not be credited for growth rates insofar as they were obtained simply by enlarging the labor force. Changes in the volume of employment are one of the major circumstances specific to the situation of individual countries, unrelated to their systems. Such differences may be due to a number of accidents of history and geography. Changes in labor force have to do with changes in population. These are influenced, besides the basic local parameters of birth and death rates, by temporary or permanent migration. Charles Kindleberger drew attention to the relationship between high postwar growth rates in certain Western European countries and the extraordinary influx of population and manpower.[1] This was the case of West Germany, which experienced an enormous infusion of population expelled from Eastern European countries and then opened the borders to millions of "guest workers" from Yugoslavia, Italy, and Turkey. A similar open-door policy was followed by Switzerland, the Netherlands, and to some extent France.

The association of growth of output with the growth of the labor force does not mean that growing labor force by itself causes growth. It contributes to growth only under conditions of self-sustained economic expansion, i.e., in the environment of advanced capitalist economies (private or state), which provide additional manpower with complementary equipment (capital). Under conditions of an insufficient expansion of work opportunities in new capacities, growing supply of labor would merely swell chronic unemployment (i.e., economic overpopulation).

Changes in the labor force may also be influenced by shifts in the age composition of the population and labor participation rates. Some countries may go through a period of high natural additions to the labor force because strong contingents reach the working age (e.g., as a consequence of an earlier "baby boom"), or the other way around (e.g., as a consequence of periods of low birthrates or demographic catastrophes, such as wars). Or else the labor force may be swelled by the influx from categories not gainfully employed, such as housewives, which raises the labor participation rate. In the Soviet Union, for instance, participation of women in the labor force increased from around 30 to 35 percent in the thirties to 54 percent in the seventies—an exceptional case as far as both speed and extent of the change are concerned (except for some other Eastern

---

[1] Charles Kindleberger, *Europe's Postwar Growth,* Harvard, Cambridge, Mass., 1967, chap. 2.

European countries). The phenomenon has been due to the pressures of organized labor recruitment, as well as to low real wages of male family heads. In that respect, labor supply is, after all, not quite independent of the character of the economic system.

Growth of Labor Productivity   In the preceding section, we made the important distinction between mere enlargement of an economy and that aspect of economic growth which needs to be considered when one wants to speak of growth performance. We see it as a mere enlargement of the economy if output grows at the same rate as the labor force and the stock of capital. If output grows faster than the volume of either of the two production factors, then one can begin to discuss economic performance.

In the case of growth, the notion of performance refers to the change of productive efficiency over time. In devising measures of efficiency—and that applies to any area—one sets up a ratio of the outcome in question to the quantity of ingredients responsible for the outcome (miles covered to gallons of gasoline burned). Working out the division, which is implied in the ratio, one ends up with a measure signaling the quantity (size, extent, or value) of the outcome per *one* unit of an ingredient (miles per gallon) or combination of ingredients.

Productive efficiency in the economic sense is to be understood as volume of output per unit of a factor of production. Volume of output per worker measures productive efficiency with respect to factor labor; it is called *labor productivity*. To make things more precise, one adds a time dimension to indicate the duration of the worker's activity, and calculates output per worker-day, worker-year, etc.

Volume of output per unit of capital measures productive efficiency of the stock of producer goods. In this form, it is exactly parallel to the notion of labor productivity. It amounts to the *productivity of physical capital* being equivalent to the output/capital ratio. Higher values of this ratio mean higher capital productivity. However, it has become customary in this case to use as measure the reciprocal of this ratio. This reciprocal is called the capital/output ratio. Naturally, in this case, the lower its value the better. We shall come back to this measure shortly, after first taking up the labor-productivity aspect.

So far, the definitions have referred to a single period. Performance with respect to growth can be judged by observing how the value of the labor-productivity measure changes from one period to the next. *Dynamic efficiency* will be reflected in the speed of this change. The higher the rate of growth of labor productivity, the better is the system's performance with respect to dynamic efficiency—provided all other things are equal.

That this all-other-things-being-equal condition is hardly ever fulfilled makes for a great deal of uncertainty in comparing rates of growth of labor productivity. Table 12-1 provides a general survey of intercountry comparisons.

In contrast to the growth of labor force as such, differences in the rate of growth of labor productivity can, with some reason, be ascribed to the systemic characteristics of national economies. They reflect the ability of the systems to

Table 12-1   Average Annual Rates of Growth of Output (GNP), Labor Force, and Labor Productivity in Selected Countries

	GNP	Labor force	Labor productivity
Western Europe (1950–1969)			
West Germany	6.2	1.2	5.0
Italy	5.4	0.4	5.0
France	5.0	0.4	4.6
Austria	5.0	0.1	5.0
Netherlands	5.0	1.1	3.9
Finland	4.4	0.9	3.5
Switzerland	4.2	1.6	2.5
Norway	4.1	0.3	3.7
Sweden	4.1	0.3	3.8
Denmark	4.0	1.1	2.8
Belgium	3.5	0.4	3.1
United Kingdom	2.7	0.5	2.2
Ireland	2.5	−0.7	3.2
Southern Europe (1950–1959)			
Greece	6.0	0.9	5.0
Portugal	5.1	0.2	4.9
Spain	6.1	0.8	5.3
Yugoslavia	6.2	0.8	5.4
United States (1950–1959)	3.7	1.4	2.3
Japan (1955–1968)	10.1	1.5	8.6
Eastern Europe (1950–1967)			
Bulgaria	5.9	—	—
East Germany	5.2	1.2	4.0
Romania	5.0	—	5.0
Hungary	4.0	0.8	3.2
Czechoslovakia	3.3	0.8	2.5
Poland	3.1	—	2.6
Soviet Union (1950–1972)			
1950–1958	7.1	1.7	5.3
1958–1965	5.3	1.7	3.5
1965–1972	5.1	1.8	3.3

Sources: United Nations, *The European Economy from the 1950's to the 1970's,* New York, 1972, p. 6. U.S. Congress, Joint Economic Committee, *Economic Developments in Countries of Eastern Europe,* 1970, pp. 47 and 63. Stanley H. Cohn, "Analysis of the Soviet Growth Models," in M. Bornstein and D. Fussfeld, *The Soviet Economy: A Book of Readings,* Irwin, Homewood, Ill., 1974, p. 249. Hisao Kanamor, "What Makes Japan's Economic Growth High?" *Japanese Economic Studies,* vol. 1, no. 1, Fall 1972, pp. 36 and 47.

equip labor with more instrumental producer goods and to generate and absorb innovations in the methods of production, in other words, technological progress. However, there exist enough circumstances having nothing to do with the systemic characteristics of individual economies, which also make for differences in the change of labor productivity. These have to be taken into account before one allows oneself to be thrilled by one country's performance and depressed by another's.

Differences in growth of labor productivity may be associated with mere differences in the stage of economic development. In the early stages, overall labor productivity is enhanced by shifts in employment from low-productivity branches (agriculture) into high-productivity branches (manufacturing). In later stages, as the share of both agriculture and manufacturing in total output declines, we encounter a reverse effect: overall productivity is slowed down by the increased weight of the service sector, where increases in labor productivity are slow or nonexistent. This consideration takes some of the glitter off the figures for Italy, Greece, Spain, Yugoslavia, or Romania, and makes the relatively poor performance of the United Kingdom or the United States more understandable.

Furthermore, latecomers to the process of industrialization tend to benefit from technological advances of the more-developed countries. Countries such as Japan and Russia, but also France, etc., were able to "borrow" up-to-date technology en bloc, without having to devote costly resources and years of work to original research and development as the trailblazers had to.

Differences in growth of labor productivity may also be due to greater opportunities for *economies of scale* offered by the enlargement of the economy in large countries. Growth may also reduce gains in labor productivity if it leads to the exhaustion of low-cost supplies of natural resources and resort to less attractive reserves (low-grade ores, less-accessible minerals, etc.). On the other hand, some countries may have an easier time making productivity gains if they are well endowed in resources for which there is expanding demand.

Capital Efficiency

A paragraph was devoted in the preceding section to the definition of productivity of the stock of producer goods. It is only natural to expect that the measure of dynamic efficiency would, in this case, be simply analogous to the rate of growth of labor productivity. In principle, this is correct. In the ratio of output to labor force, one would merely substitute the stock-of-capital figure for labor force and calculate the value of output per one dollar's worth of capital. One would do this for a series of years and then calculate at what percentage rate this indicator of capital productivity was growing.

Unfortunately, figures on the stock of capital and its growth are very difficult to obtain, at least not for a sufficiently large number of countries. This is mainly because of difficulties with statistical measurement and data collection. The next-best solution is then to resort to substitute measures. The rate at which stock of capital grows is reflected in the share of investments in the national product. The faster it grows, the higher must be the percentage share of investments in GNP. This is a most handily obtainable statistic, and it serves therefore as an element in a widely used measure of capital efficiency, the "incremental capital/output ratio."

The value of the incremental capital/output ratio (the ICOR of United Nations statistics) can be obtained either from absolute or from relative figures. This is obvious from the equivalence of the following formulas:

$$\text{ICOR} = \frac{I}{\Delta\text{GNP}} = \frac{I/\text{GNP}}{\Delta\text{GNP}/\text{GNP}}$$

which reads

$$\frac{\text{Dollar value of investments}}{\text{Increase in this year's GNP}\atop\text{over last year's GNP}} = \frac{\text{percentage share of}\atop\text{investments in GNP}}{\text{percentage rate of increase}\atop\text{of GNP over last year's GNP}}$$

To understand the relationship of this measure to capital productivity, one only has to realize that the value of current investments I contains the net value of new producer goods that are added to the past stock of capital (ΔK). The ICOR suggests an answer to the following question: "How much additional capital did it take to obtain one dollar's worth of additional output?" or "What percent of GNP had to be devoted to the production of investment goods in order to obtain 1 percent rate of growth of GNP?"

Efficiency in the use of capital pays off in the form of less need to save for the sake of a given rate of growth, and a correspondingly higher share of consumption that does not have to be sacrificed. A selective survey of comparative growth performance in the light of the ICOR indicator is given in Table 12-2. Information of the first two columns is rendered graphically in Figure 12-1. If we follow a horizontal line at a certain level of GNP growth rate, we can read off countries according to decreasing level of performance, in terms of their dynamic capital efficiency, from left to right.

Total Factor Productivity

By distinguishing between growth of the labor force and growth of labor productivity, we have set the stage for the analysis of observed *crude* growth rates according to two separate sets of sources contributing to growth.

Any observed rate of output growth can be decomposed into two parts, one of which is accounted for by the increase in labor force, and the other by the increase of labor productivity. Nothing can be more simple. However, one can also take into account, side by side with labor, the physical volume of capital which is at labor's disposal. Let us assume, for a start, that the proportion of capital to labor does not change, even as the labor force grows. We speak of the capital/labor ratio being constant, in which case one can think of homogeneous units, each made up of one worker and the average volume of capital per worker. The rate of output growth can then be decomposed into one part which equals the rate of increase of the number of such "worker-capital units," and the remainder which corresponds to the rate of increase in productivity of labor and capital combined. The latter is the concept of *total factor productivity*.

Table 12-2   Capital Growth Efficiency Data for Selected Countries and Periods

Country	Average annual rate of growth of GNP (1950/52–1967/69)	Investment share (av. for 1950–1969)	Incremental capital/output ratio	
			1950–1959	1960–1969
1. Italy	5.4	22.1	2.8	3.0
2. West Germany	6.2	27.0	2.3	4.3
3. France	5.0	23.7	3.3	3.6
4. Netherlands	5.0	26.0	3.9	4.1
5. Austria	5.0	26.2	3.3	5.3
6. Belgium	3.5	22.4	4.9	3.9
7. Denmark	4.0	21.0	4.3	4.1
8. Sweden	4.1	24.4	4.8	4.4
9. Finland	4.4	27.3	4.7	4.9
10. United Kingdom	2.7	17.5	5.0	5.4
11. Norway	4.1	32.0	7.7	5.5
12. Greece	6.0	23.1	2.5	3.4
13. Portugal	5.1	18.8	3.0	2.6
14. Spain	6.1	22.6	3.6	2.5
15. United States	3.7	18.9	4.8	3.1
16. Japan	10.0	30.0+	1.5	1.0
Eastern Europe (1950–1967)				
17. Czechoslovakia	3.2	35		
18. Hungary	4.0	35		
19. Poland	5.1	32		
20. Soviet Union				
1950–1958	7.1	25		
1958–1967	5.5	30		

Sources: United Nations, *The European Economy from the 1950's to the 1970's,* part 1, *Economic Survey of Europe in 1971,* New York, 1972, pp. 12 and 14. U.S. Congress, Joint Economic Committee, *Economic Developments in Countries of Eastern Europe,* 1970, pp. 52 and 59.

If, under these assumptions, output grows at the same rate as labor and capital, we can write equalities of the following sort (p.a. = per annum):

$$\begin{array}{ccc} 2 \text{ percent p.a.} & = \quad 2 \text{ percent p.a.} & = \quad 2 \text{ percent p.a.} \\ \text{growth rate of output} & = \text{growth rate of labor} & = \text{growth rate of capital} \end{array}$$

or, alternatively,

$$\begin{array}{cc} 2 \text{ percent p.a.} & = 2 \text{ percent p.a.} \\ \text{growth rate of output} & = \text{growth rate of the number of} \\ & \text{labor-capital units} \end{array}$$

If there is nothing more to growth than that, we have a pure case of a mere

Figure 12-1   Relationship between investment shares and growth rates of output in selected countries.

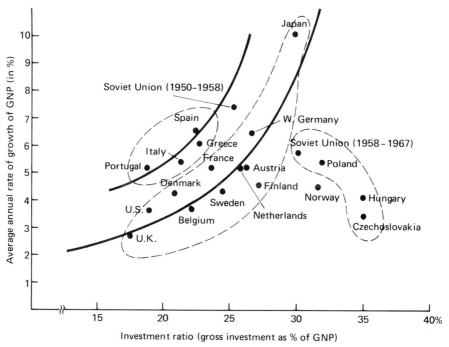

Note: Freehand trend lines are fitted to a group of less developed and a group of more advanced Western countries, as indicated by broken lines.
Source: Table 12-2.

progressive *enlargement* of the economy we spoke of earlier. Eastern European economists have been referring to this case as the *extensive type of growth.*

If output grows faster than the combined volume of labor and capital, then we know there has also been growth of total factor productivity. Since it is obtained as the arithmetic difference between the growth rate of output and the growth rate of the volume of labor and capital combined, it is often simply called the *residual.* If labor and capital did not grow at all while output grew, such growth of output could then be ascribed only to the increase in total factor productivity. Eastern European economists would then speak of a pure case of the *intensive type of growth.*

The residual serves as indicator of progress in productive efficiency quite analogous to the growth rate of labor productivity, except that it is more subtle. If labor and capital grow at identical rates, but slower than output, the subtlety is not needed. In that case, labor productivity, capital productivity, and total factor productivity all grow also at identical rates. It is when labor and capital grow at different rates, one slower, the other faster, that one starts looking for a measure indicating the rate of change in productive efficiency with respect to both factors combined.

There is a small but important technical point to be cleared up. How does one construct a homogeneous worker-capital unit when capital grows faster than labor, as is ordinarily the case? This implies that the capital/labor ratio increases. Labor tends to be equipped with a progressively larger volume of producer goods. Therefore, one cannot equate the "extensive" part of output growth indifferently to either growth of labor or growth of capital, as we did in the equalities set up above.

One solves the difficulty by calculating a *weighted average of the growth rates of labor and capital.* (As weights, one uses the relative shares in total national income of labor incomes and property incomes, on grounds of theoretical considerations that would take us too far afield.) It is then also possible to show the growth rate of output in a three-way decomposition, according to the growth contribution of labor, capital, and total factor productivity, which is done below in Table 12-3. The figures in columns 2 and 3 are growth rates of labor and capital, multiplied respectively by the income shares of labor and capital in national income. The sum of the figures in columns 2 and 3 for a given country is the weighted average rate of growth of the volume of labor and capital combined.

Returning to the question of subtlety, which makes total factor productivity superior to the indicator of labor productivity, the issue can be put as follows. Growth of total factor productivity corrects for that part of cost of growth which has the form of capital accumulation. It makes a difference whether a given increase in labor productivity is obtained thanks to a larger or smaller proportion of resources being devoted to the production of new producer goods. If an eco-

Table 12-3 Contribution of Factor Inputs and Their Productivity to Economic Growth in Selected Countries (1950–1962)

	(1)	(2)	(3)	(4)	(5)
		Part of growth rate attributable to growth of			
Country	Growth rate of national income	Labor	Capital	Total factor productivity (residual)	(4) as percent of (1)
1. France	4.92	0.45	0.79	3.68	75
2. Italy	5.96	0.96	0.70	4.30	72
3. Norway	3.45	0.15	0.89	2.41	70
4. Belgium	3.20	0.76	0.41	2.03	63
5. West Germany	7.26	1.37	1.41	4.48	62
6. Japan (1955–1968)	10.1	1.31	2.72	6.1	60
7. Netherlands	4.73	0.87	1.04	2.82	60
8. United Kingdom	2.29	0.60	0.51	1.18	52
9. United States	3.32	1.12	0.83	1.37	41
10. Soviet Union	6.3	1.33	3.15	1.82	29

Sources: E. F. Denison, *Why Growth Rates Differ,* Brookings, Washington, 1967, p. 192. Hisao Kanamor, "What Makes Japan's Economic Growth High?" *Japanese Economic Studies,* vol. 1, no. 1, Fall 1972, p. 47. U.S. Congress, Joint Economic Committee, *New Directions in the Soviet Economy,* 1966, p. 212.

nomic system obtains the same growth of labor productivity as another, but does so without a heavy increase in the capital/labor ratio, it is dynamically more efficient because it saves on capital, relatively speaking. It will show in a higher value of the "residual."

However, total factor productivity reflects also increases in efficiency due to other reasons than progress in the engineering sense. It lumps together results of many disparate sources of growth, some related to the economic system, some not: improvements in the education and skills of labor, intensification of work, changing technical efficiency of capital equipment, organization of production, economies of scale, and other factors mentioned in connection with our earlier examination of crude growth rates. It has a catchall character. We may repeat what we said apropos labor productivity: "Changes in total factor productivity reflect the ability of the economic system to absorb technological innovations and take advantage of all other opportunities of improving efficiency in the use of factors of production, independently of the growth in their sheer volume." In that broad sense the measure is of immense value. While increases in working time and capital accumulation indicate increases in the sacrifice of physical effort, increases in factor productivity indicate the contribution of inventiveness, intelligence, and creativity. They show the part of the brain over brawn.

In Table 12-3 we have assembled what we believe is the most significant available evidence on the comparative growth performance of the country systems, and for the periods shown. We have explained the meanings of the main figures a few paragraphs earlier. The central column of data is column 4, showing the growth rates of total factor productivity. However, the countries are arranged in a descending order according to the values of indicator column 5, which calls for a word of explanation.

We have treated the growth of the labor force throughout as an exogenous fact having nothing to do with the systemic aspects of national economies. We have separated the part played in the growth of output by the increase in the mere volume of labor and capital from the part played by the increase in factor productivity. It would appear that we have finally succeeded in isolating the growth rate of total factor productivity, a measure which can stand by itself, being independent of the growth in volume of the two basic production factors. This conclusion is premature.

If one pushes the examination of total factor productivity a little further, one soon discovers that its growth is not all that independent from the growth rates of labor and capital. For one thing, the rate of technological progress is, to a large extent, linked to the rate of capital accumulation. It is "embodied" in the technological parameters of new items of equipment. Therefore, higher rates of capital accumulation mean faster rejuvenation of the stock of capital, and that means greater opportunities for modernization and technical progress.

Furthermore, the rate of capital accumulation is, in turn, not independent of the rate of growth of labor. True, the rate of capital accumulation is not rigidly dictated by growth of labor, but it is kept by it within certain limits. Up to a point, the stock of capital can grow faster than the labor force. As mentioned before, the average volume of capital equipment per worker tends to grow. There is such a thing as substitution of capital for labor—backhoes for spades, walkie-talkies for messengers, automation. However, in any given period, there are technical limits to the feasible substitution of capital for labor.

To that extent, the rate of capital accumulation depends only on how many more workers are entering the labor force, waiting to be equipped with fixed producer goods. Thus, the higher the growth rate of labor, the higher is the growth of capital justified by it, and the higher can be the rate of growth of productivity which is carried into the economy on the back of new and technologically up-to-date capital.

As in the case of crude growth rates, in the case of growth of total factor productivity, too, we want to eliminate the contributing effect of how fast labor force happens to grow. The simplest way of accomplishing it is to calculate the *proportion of the growth rate of total factor productivity in the growth rate of output.* This proportion, in percentage terms, is what we list in column 5 of Table 12-3. It shows the relative extent to which the country systems rely on growth of combined factor productivity, rather than on more workers or higher rates of investment, in making output grow over time.

*   *   *

In the following account of important country cases and broad comparisons between groups of countries with different systems we shall have occasion to refer to many of the comparative measures of dynamic efficiency explained in the first part of the chapter. The purpose of the concrete case studies is to illuminate specific instances of growth performance, high or poor, by relating them to their institutional setting and economic environment.

FRANCE: PLANNING FOR GROWTH

Among Western-type systems of market capitalism, a sustained growth rate of GNP equal to 5 percent p.a. or more came to be regarded as excellent. And so it was, considering that the long-term growth rate of most industrialized nations up to the fifties and sixties ranged from about 1.5 to 4 percent p.a. Not counting Japan and the less-developed group of southern Europe, there were five growth leaders in postwar industrialized Europe. France was one of them. It was outdistanced by West Germany (6.2 percent p.a. in the two decades between 1950 and 1969), which benefited by exceptionally high increases in the labor force, and by Italy (5.4 percent), which—being less developed—had considerably greater opportunities of shifting labor from poor agriculture to modern manufacturing. France, Austria, and the Netherlands all grew by 5 percent p.a. on the average.

What makes it inviting to single out France for special examination is its system of planning and policies geared explicitly to the objective of growth. This is not to say that advanced capitalism needs French-style planning in order to grow fast. The other growth leaders managed without. The French case, amply studied and publicized, just happens to be well suited for studying the ingredients of growth as they were made visible by deliberate systemic measures.

As for the actual merits of French planning, opinions differ. American economists have tended to downgrade its importance for growth. Stephen S. Cohen suggests "it has been at a minimum, decorative, at a maximum, indirectly influential." Stanislaw H. Wellisz calls it "an excellent patent medicine" where "we should not ask whether the medicine does good or whether it harms the patient, because the unshaken belief in its efficacy is an essential condition for the medicine's success." Charles Kindleberger stresses the practical empiricism of planners in action, in contrast to the abstract formalism of official accounts of planning. Professor Kindleberger's view seems to be the soundest. The formal elaboration of plans and forecasts was not useless. It provided a general reference framework for the application of practical measures and activities, though in the end it was the latter that mattered most.

Even more basic than any particular measures was probably the change in attitudes of decision makers, for which planning frequently receives the credit. The prewar sluggishness of the French economy was often blamed on the psychological traits of the typical French entrepreneur: conservative, overcautious, concerned with saving for his family's security rather than with investment for expansion, preferring accommodations with other firms in industrial *ententes* (cartels) to aggressive competition, and tending to protect, in the last consequences, the least fit. Economic stagnation due to restrictive practices, labeled "malthusianism," was accepted fatalistically as a permanent fixture of the French situation. Thus, the emergence of dynamic executives and entrepreneurs in the fifties struck observers as a dramatic reversal in need of an explanation. There developed a mystique about the mobilizing power of planning which seemed to inspire and animate from the top the economic "establishment" below.

However, this may be misplacing the true source of the change. "Institutions are outgrowths of underlying facts," as Professor Kindleberger reminds us. The underlying facts that changed the economic atmosphere were of many kinds: There was a striking increase in fertility after the war—preference for more children—heavily aided by generous family allowances; there was a desire to make up for the humiliations of the French defeat in 1939 and occupation; consumer aspirations, formerly dominated by meat, wine, and handcrafted luxury items, shifted toward consumer durables; reform of graduate economic and administrative training replaced the emphasis on status-conferring Education with capital "E" by a pragmatic, problem-solving orientation; postwar political changes made room, in the government, for the so-called technocratic element, overshadowed in the past by the practitioners of politics by eloquence. All these changes tended to converge and express themselves in a desire for expansion. The Planning Commission became its supreme spokesman and instrument, the Plan its symbol.

However, the picture would not be complete if we did not mention one external stimulus to the adoption of planning provided by the Marshall Plan. To secure maximum effectiveness in the use of United States aid, recipient governments were asked to draw up a systematic allocation plan to direct the flow of investment funds—one of the earliest practical exercises in planning encouraged, paradoxically, by the no-plan economy of the United States.

Leaving generalities aside and getting down to specific contributions of planning to growth, we shall discuss, first, the formal design of plans insofar as it is related to the pursuit of growth, and then turn to the nitty-gritty content of planning: active consultation, growth-promoting policy measures, and the stimulus of foreign trade. We are now picking up the thread of the French system left hanging in Chapter 10.

The overriding concern with growth is evident from the fact that the process of formulating the plan opens with the choice of a target rate of growth. The target rate of growth, projected for four years ahead, is the backbone around which the rest of the plan is built. The rate of growth is chosen in regard of projected availabilities of labor and assumed rates of labor productivity.

Given the target rate of growth, a number of requirements automatically follow. One extrapolates the volume of GNP for the terminal year of the plan and determines what volume of investments will be needed to bring about the desired increment in output and the assumed increases in labor productivity. The volume of investments can be calculated with the help of the incremental capital/output ratios obtained from past statistics. Then one subtracts from the total GNP the volume of investments and the estimated amount of government spending. The remainder corresponds to the aggregate figure for private consumption. Should this last figure turn out too low, the planners will reduce the original tentative target rate of growth. This will reduce the volume of required investments so as to allow for a larger volume of private consumption. In other words, the aim is *not* the absolutely highest rate of growth that is feasible but as high a rate as is compatible with other social objectives, of which increases in private consumption are among the most prominent.

Having established the magnitudes for the major components of GNP, planners work backward to reconstruct the supply side: the pattern of interindustry deliveries and investment requirements by industrial branches, from which the projected final demands would emerge. For this, they break down the final-demand aggregates into detailed components, such as different groups of consumer goods making up the total of consumers' spending. Coefficients of total input requirements per unit of specific types of final demand (known from past statistical investigations) make it possible to calculate a projected input-output table corresponding to the projected volume and structure of the target GNP. Partial capital-output coefficients for individual branches permit calculation of branch requirements of investments, and thus to provide a detailed breakdown of the global investment volume.

The amount of detailed industry studies, projections, and other aspects of the planned development is, of course, much larger than that. In particular, import requirements and estimated demand for exports have to be worked in, as well as major financial flows (fiscal revenues, transfers, savings), real-wage development, and implications for general price movements. However, the numerical projections described in the previous two paragraphs serve as the frame of reference for the flesh-and-blood content of planning, which has been the practice of vigorous and continuous consultations between the planning officials and industrial executives.

The preliminary stages of plan preparation fall in the competence of the Planning Commission (*Commissariat du Plan*), working hand in hand with the Ministry of Finance (its Service of Economic and Financial Studies, SEEF) and other statistical and research organs. Consultation, or—as the French prefer to call it—*concertation,* takes place within the twenty-plus so-called *Modernization Commissions* organized by major industrial branches. Representatives of industry—and that means mainly big business firms—bring along their own expansion and investment programs. The planning officials offer their own kind of expert advice based on their view of the whole, its projected dynamics, and insight into the interdependence of branches. They are also able to suggest possibilities of technological innovations and, in general, encourage expansionist moods and intentions.

It is hard to know with absolute certainty how strong the influence of planning organs upon actual decisions of firms has been. There are some grounds for skepticism. Even among the largest firms (those with more than 1,000 employees, which include a mere fifth of total employment), only between one-third and one-half declare letting the plan influence their investment decisions "imperceptibly," and another two-fifths slightly. However, theirs may be the strategically most important ones in the sense that they pull significant portions of the economy with them.

Pierre Massé, one of the most prominent French planners, recalls from his days as executive of the national electric company what a shock it was to have been confronted at one time with a planners' objective of power supply twice as high as the company was planning, basing its thinking as it did on the prewar maximum. It seems that the widespread impression of the stimulating power of planning cannot be entirely wrong.

The importance of formal planning techniques should not, however, be overrated. What matters most is their impact on the real sources of productivity, on technological progress, and their coupling with policies fostering innovation. On that count, French postwar performance has been outstanding. The rate of growth of total factor productivity was one of the highest among advanced industrial countries—close to 4 percent per year. In certain periods (such as 1955–1962) and excluding certain cases (such as that of Italy or Japan with its large shifts from agriculture to industry), it was the highest of all. This was a remarkable change, considering that, between 1913 and 1949, the rate was only about 1 percent. Growth of total factor productivity after the war accounted consistently for about 75 to 80 percent of the overall growth of GNP, a larger proportion than anywhere else.

The technological upsurge was a result of a combination of factors, each of a different order (attitudes, psychology, institutions, policies, international environment). They reinforced each other cumulatively. We have mentioned already the novel dynamics in the mentality of bureau-technocrats, to which should be added the fresh spirit of youngish entrepreneurs and executives. Eager to "make their country move again," they organized, in the early fifties, a number of much-heralded "productivity missions" to the United States. They followed them up with a wave of purchasing industrial patents abroad. The annual sum spent on foreign patents quintupled between 1953 and 1965 (an average annual increase of 11 percent). In this, France was part of the general process of technological catching up in postwar Europe and Japan. The influx of innovations of foreign origin has continued even after French activity in research and development began to yield its own substantial contribution—another general European phenomenon.

There is wide agreement about the stimulating influence of foreign economic relations upon the behavior of French business. Two distinct periods mark French policies toward foreign trade: the first one protectionist (up to 1958), the second increasingly liberal and culminating in an almost complete opening up of the economy to foreign imports in 1968. Curiously, policies of both stages contributed to growth, each in its own way.

The protectionist stage meant a strict control of imports through the usual array of instruments—licensing of imports, rationing of foreign exchange needed to pay for them, tariffs, etc. This, together with an uninhibited resort to devaluation of the French currency whenever needed, saved the country from a stop-go pattern of the British kind. As explained in Chapter 10, balance-of-payments difficulties were not allowed to interfere with growth policies.

In the period of liberalized trade, we discover an entirely different effect upon the domestic economic system. The influx of cheaper or more interesting goods from abroad woke up French firms to the need of innovations, cost cutting, and concentration on articles promising to give French producers a competitive advantage. If there continued to be informal agreements between firms, they were not of the restrictionist and price-upholding type characterizing cartels, but rather agreements about who shall specialize in what in order to aid competitiveness and expansion of French firms with respect to international trade. The midsixties were also the time of a wave of spectacular mergers among a number of industry giants, encouraged by the government. Increased specialization, taking advantage of economies of scale, enlarged exchanges with foreign countries—these were the beneficial effects of the European Common Market for France.

The French growth performance must therefore not be seen in isolation as a single-handed feat of one nation. It has been in important ways a matter of transmission of accomplishments between countries, especially if we take the effects of trade upon competition together with the imports of advanced technology through patents. However, credit is due to the properties of the French postwar economic system for the ability to respond to stimuli from abroad in a constructive way.

JAPAN: A GROWTH MIRACLE EXPLAINED

No other country's economy ever grew as fast as that of postwar Japan. The average rate of growth was about 10 percent per year throughout the fifties and sixties. This is twice as fast as the best growth rates typical of industrialized Western Europe. Japan's performance was watched with gasping admiration, as was that of West Germany, the other defeated country parading its growth prosperity before the eyes of stagnating victors, such as Britain. Until the public grew accustomed to the fact, one used to speak of the twin "economic miracles" of Germany and Japan. Without detracting from the real accomplishments, we shall proceed to take the growth performance of Japan apart analytically and wipe the supernatural tinge off the hyperbole.

We shall first enumerate the major factors and circumstances whose intertwined interactions resulted in the spectacular crude growth rates. References to other countries will help us keep the subject in comparatist perspective.

1 Japanese labor force increased faster than in most other countries—almost 2 percent per year.

2 The stock of fixed capital, equipping the growing labor force, grew faster than elsewhere—by more than 10 percent per year. (The usual observed growth rates fall between 2.5 and 5 percent. In Western Europe, only in Germany did growth reach more than 6 percent, and only in the Soviet Union as much as 9 to 10 percent.) The corollary of the fast expansion of capital equipment has been the exceptionally high investment ratio: the share of gross fixed investment in GNP has been consistently higher than 30 percent. (The usually observed shares in Western industrial countries fall between 18 and 25 percent of GNP. The exceptions are Norway with a ratio of 32 percent, Yugoslavia, and some of the countries of the Soviet area where the postwar ratio has risen far above 30 percent.) This is all the more remarkable as it happened in a country of still low levels of output and consumption per capita (about two-thirds of West Germany and less than 40 percent of the United States), and under a regime of largely voluntary supply of savings.

3 Total factor productivity, covering technological progress and other efficiency factors, advanced by more than 6 percent per year. (We recall that the French rate, one of the highest among Western industrialized countries, has been close to 4 percent; that of Italy and Germany was between 4 and 5 percent, and that of the Soviet Union, 1.6 percent and falling.)

The foregoing three elements represent the result of a statistical analysis of the crude rate of growth. The remaining are factors of the institutional and circumstantial order, usually cited in overall discussions of the Japanese growth phenomenon:

4 Ample supply of voluntary savings feeding the investment drive
5 Quality of entrepreneurship
6 The role of exports
7 Minimal military expenditures
8 The role of government as catalyst in the competition—coordination syndrome of business behavior
9 Presence of "planning" of sorts

Each of these factors requires further comments.

In the general section of this chapter, we put great emphasis on the idea that dynamic efficiency of economic systems is properly reflected in the growth of factor productivity, rather than in the growth of the volume of factors labor and capital. We stand by this proposition. However, if we are interested in a country's superiority in crude growth rates, we may wish to know why labor supply grew faster and especially what made it possible to raise the volume of capital faster than elsewhere. This has nothing to do with the dynamic *efficiency* of the economic system. As on similar earlier occasions, we may rather want to speak of the *effectiveness* of the system in raising the volume of productive resources, and inquire which properties make one system in that sense more effective than another.

What astonishes in the case of Japan is the exceptionally high rates of investment achieved, in contrast to Soviet-type economies, without recourse to any forced-saving methods. Investments have been financed to an exceptionally high degree from funds originating in personal savings deposited with financial intermediaries and passed on as loans to business firms. As we have seen in Chapter 11, in Soviet-type economies investment finance is dominated by methods of coercive taxation.

What explains the high individual propensity to save of the Japanese, who tend to put aside about 20 percent of their disposable income? (The rate is 12 percent for West Germany, 7 percent for the United States.) It is usually pointed out that the absence of a strong social security system forces individuals to rely on personal savings for old age and emergencies. The system of wage payment which includes twice-a-year substantial bonuses may also be a factor: current spending is adjusted to the basic compensation while a large proportion of the bonuses is saved. At the same time, the disparity between the fast growth of output per man and the slower growth of real wages provided room for profit expansion and increasing business savings from profits.

The other side of the coin is the willingness to use the generated savings for investment purposes. Behind that willingness lies the fascinating story of the postwar emergence of dynamic business executives for whom the sweeping purge of the prewar and wartime decision-making personnel made room. In investment behavior, they displayed a "will to expand" not tempered by fear of overinvestment and cautious calculations of expected profitability typical, say, of American business. This amounts to investing *ahead of demand,* in which case firms operate for a while below optimal-capacity levels, or duplicate facilities.

Considering the high global investment ratio, it is surprising—again in contrast to the Soviet case—that the Japanese incremental capital/output ratio should have been by far the lowest in the world—1.5 in the fifties and falling below 1 in the sixties. (The usually encountered magnitudes fall between 3.5 and 6.) The secret is to be sought in the incorporation of the latest technology in the large net additions to capacity, intensity and efficiency of its utilization by the work force, and also in the concentration of investments in areas characterized by relatively low branch capital/output ratios, namely, manufacturing. Branches of high capital/output ratios, such as residential housing, transportation, and social overhead, have been relatively neglected. (The same has been true of Soviet investment strategy since the thirties, in contrast to Western Europe and North America.)

The mention of technology brings up the issue of opportunities enjoyed by latecomers to economic development, and ability to make good use of them. Borrowing of foreign technological innovations, supplemented by domestic advances, has been a widespread feature in the postwar growth of capitalist economies, but nowhere was it more deliberate and less uninhibited than in Japan. Up to 1961, the amount of royalties paid for patents and licenses grew by more than 30 percent annually, and after that by more than 7 percent. However, the real forte of Japanese entrepreneurship and engineering has been in the ability to improve the imported innovations and adapt them to the needs of demand in new markets of which it is difficult to say whether they were discovered or created.

The new markets were to a large extent foreign export markets. Japanese exports grew about one-third faster than Japanese total output, and more than twice as fast as the volume of world trade. The share of Japanese goods in world trade increased correspondingly, and led the London *Economist* to compare Japanese economy to a "hosepipe squirting a jet of exports on to the world."

The question has often been raised whether Japan was not a classic example of "export-pulled growth." If this were the case, it would have to mean that it was *demand* for Japanese goods which played the role of an exogenous factor, while the economy only responded. In that simple sense trade definitely has not been an "engine of growth" for Japan. It was rather the reverse: Growth of productivity and technological innovations, particularly in manufacturing, created conditions to which foreign buyers responded by expanding their demand. However, there was a deliberate active strategy behind the export drive. In order to grow, Japan had to promote exports and export-oriented industries. It needed the export earnings to pay for the ever-increasing need of raw materials and fuels from abroad, i.e., essentials in which the country is notoriously poor. Growth of exports was therefore a prerequisite as well as a consequence of the overall growth performance.

In assessing the role of the government as the conductor and promoter of economic growth, one is led to think again of the French mix of indicative planning, business-government consultation, and the stimulus of governmental incentives and controls. The elements are the same, but their importance in the mix is different, and the flavor is distinctly Japanese.

The influence of indicative planning is very difficult to define, even more difficult than in France. Japanese planners never aspired at operational guidance of the economy. If the purpose was to enhance growth-consciousness through the "announcement effect" of projected growth rates, Japanese planners were the moderators and business executives were the pacemakers: realized growth rates have been, as a rule, up to twice as high as the announced projections! This is true even of the famous "Doubling National Income Plan 1961–1970," which asked for a 7.2 percent growth rate, a goal believed overly ambitious at the time of its promulgation.

Government's contribution is not to be sought in formal planning, but in its concentrated effort to foster the real sources of growth—investments and technology—without worrying about any specific targets to be attained, and as a result merrily overshooting the target figures issued by the Economic Planning Agency. The key institution guiding these efforts has been the MITI—Ministry of International Trade and Industry. Major areas under its influence or control have been the regulation of access to imported technology; regulation of the volume of investments by firms and by branches; sponsorship of cartel-type arrangements, mergers, and limitation of the number of firms in a given branch; and promotion of exports.

However, to explain the mode of operation of the MITI, one must put aside the customary notion of governmental authority impinging upon business from above and down the slopes of the power pyramid. This is rarely a truthful image anyway, but least of all for Japan, where the symbiotic interpenetration of business and government defies orderly description. According to William W. Lockwood, one of the foremost specialists on Japanese economy,

> the metaphor that comes to mind is a typical Japanese web of influences and pressures interweaving through government and business. . . . Business is somewhat shielded from government dictation by inter-agency and inter-group tensions. . . . The hand of government is everywhere in evidence, despite its limited statutory powers. The Ministries engage in an extraordinary amount of consultation, advice, persuasion, and threat. The industrial bureaus of M.I.T.I. proliferate sectoral targets and plans; they confer, they tinker, they exhort. This is the "economics by admonition" to a degree inconceivable in Washington or London. Business makes few major decisions without consulting the appropriate governmental authority; the same is true in reverse. . . . On fundamentals both businessmen and bureaucrats are in sufficient agreement to avoid the kind of stalemate that often befuddles policy in the United States.[2]

Even though this sketch of the Japanese growth performance cannot possibly be a complete account, one more factor favoring Japan has to be mentioned, and that is the absence of a heavy defense burden. In the words of Robert Guillain, "Japan runs in the race of international competition carrying as little weight as possible, while all its rivals are heavily loaded."[3] Military expenditures in Japan of the sixties were less than 1 percent of GNP. (The rate was around 9 to 10 percent for the United States, the Soviet Union, and China; and between 4 and 7 percent for the next rank of powers.) There was that much more room for devoting resources to civilian investments and for concentrating research and development expenditures on production rather than on military technology. Some observers go beyond the aspect of simple resource availabilities. They believe the postwar economic drive replaced Japan's earlier imperialist aspirations, and energies thus released came to benefit economic growth.

---

[2] William W. Lockwood (ed.), *The State and Economic Enterprise in Japan,* Princeton University Press, Princeton, N.J., 1965, p. 503.
[3] Robert Guillain, *The Japanese Challenge,* Lippincott, Philadelphia, 1970, p. 203.

GREAT BRITAIN: SCLEROSIS?

Going over the titles of publications dealing with Britain's postwar economic affairs can be a frightfully depressing pastime. Take some typical book titles: *Why England Sleeps* (John Cockcroft), *The Stagnant Society* (Michael Shanks), or *Can Britain Survive* (D. E. Bland and K. W. Watkins). Titles of articles do not sound a bit more cheerful: "Is the British Sickness Curable?" (*Fortune,* May 1974), "Why Nothing Works in Britain" (*Business Week,* Feb. 10, 1975). The subtitle to this section can be added to the collection. It all turns around the fact that, among advanced economies, the postwar British growth rates of output, labor productivity, and total factor productivity have been at the bottom of the list.

For the sake of the argument, one could try out on Britain the hypothesis, touched upon in Chapter 5, that the nation simply has not had a strong preference for growth. If so, then low growth rates would appear as something deliberately chosen and could not be judged as inferior. The perceptibly more humane and leisurely style of life, observed and enjoyed by visitors from faster-growing countries, might support that hypothesis. However, public discussions; one or two governmental attempts in 1964 and 1966 at planning for growth; and, by international standards, extraordinary wage pressures of the early seventies speak another language. The country *would* prefer a higher rate of growth of living standards, and of production which makes them possible.

There have been attempts to explain and excuse poor growth performance in Britain on objective grounds. Nicholas Kaldor pointed out that Britain, having been the oldest pioneer of industrial development, had long ago exhausted that source of growth which consists in labor transfers from agriculture to industry. Another favorite explanation has been the alternation between expansionary and deflationary phases in aggregate demand management, the stop-go phenomenon. It has been seen as unavoidable insofar as it was due to the concern for equilibrium in the balance of payments. This concern, in turn, was imperative because of the role of the pound as international reserve currency, and British responsibility for keeping the foreign-exchange rate of the pound steady. The stop-go alternation is said to have kept undermining the confidence of business in long-term prospects, which is necessary for dynamic investment planning.

However, if one traces the interdependence between some of these seemingly unmovable obstacles to growth and the rest of the economic system, they turn out to be consequences, and not causes, of slow growth. For instance, on the face of it, balance-of-payments equilibrium does not allow the pursuit of sustained expansions because expansions make demand for imports go steeply up, which leads to balance-of-payments deficits. At closer range, it turns out that expanding demand would not have to spill over into demand for imports, or not so fast, if domestic supply capacity were growing steadily, ahead of demand, and were responsive to it. Higher growth rates of productivity would also have kept the price of British exports competitive with exports of high-growth countries, which would have protected the balance of payments on the exports flank. Hence, slow growth has to be explained by other causes than objective obstacles.

Economic growth is a matter for analysis in economic terms. However, economic variables are only proximate causes. Besides, they can be putty in the hands of policy makers. The case histories of France and Japan have shown that search for understanding constantly pulls us to other levels of explanation of sociological and psychological order. They may sometimes come close to sounding like folk wisdom, which does not deprive them of validity if the observations are well taken.

We need to realize that concern with economic growth is a new thing which made its appearance only after the war (the Soviet Union excepted). Until then, growth just happened as a natural characteristic of the capitalist system. It was not promoted. It has often been remarked that the fastest postwar rates of growth were those of countries that suffered defeat or large-scale destructions. The connection between the two facts is seen in terms of opportunities for massive modernization, offered by the necessity of wholesale reconstruction of the productive apparatus. However, there may also be a connection at the level of political sociology. The change of political regimes in Japan, Germany, and France allowed a new generation of civil servants of a new type to enter the governments and put constructive ideas, hatched during the war, to work. The absence of any long-range growth perspective in Britain may be due to the fact that its elites had not been shaken up in a similar way.

We get on somewhat slippery ground if we start psychologizing and interpreting national behavior in terms of categories applicable to individuals. However, postwar attitudes, expressed in policies, do suggest something similar to lassitude: greater concern with security and income distribution, preference for rearrangements of the old rather than for active creation of the new. Maybe it is the trait of quiet self-assurance in the British character, the not-having-to-prove-anything-to-the-world, which is not favorable to growth. Attempts to get to the psychological bottom of things are just a way of finding a common denominator to the various idiosyncrasies in British economic behavior. These can be summarized under the twin topics of *quality of management* and *industrial relations.*

A number of surveys conducted over the years have revealed certain characteristics of industrial management which go far to account for below-par business practices. There has been a bias against professional schooling and training in recruitment, in favor of prestige-school graduates who are basically educated amateurs and, in the words of Richard E. Caves, "tend to retain the civil service as their model and settle into a trustee role of gentlemanly responsibility that hardly conduces to rapid innovation."[4] The durability of family firms, operating under complacent family management, works in the same direction. There has been little interfirm mobility of managerial personnel, and too much cartel mentality with accompanying restrictive practices which began to be broken down only in the sixties under the impact of antitrust legislation.

There is no dearth of anecdotal evidence concerning the lack of innovative

---

[4] Richard E. Caves and Associates, *Britain's Economic Prospects,* Brookings, Washington, 1968, p. 303.

ventures, slowness in responding to demand and in grasping new opportunities, even "when they appear right in their own backyard," as *Business Week* put it in reporting on North Sea oil exploitation:

> While companies in Norway, the Netherlands, and France make rigs and other gear for offshore oil drilling, only one British company is making rigs. And that is American owned.[5]

While Japan operated regularly at about 80 percent capacity, because it grew so fast ahead of demand, "lack of plant capacity is . . . one reason for the notoriously poor performance of British companies in meeting deadlines on deliveries to foreign customers. The result is shrinking foreign markets."[6]

Some of these difficulties are due to the anarchy in industrial relations. Frequent wildcat strikes by small groups of British workers can disrupt production and delivery schedules in ways which are beyond the control of management of individual firms. At the root is the system of fragmented, craft-oriented unions, plant-by-plant bargaining, and endless jurisdictional disputes. On the other hand, Britain is also the country which originated the system of *productivity bargaining,* linking wage increases to union cooperation in cost cutting—an incomes policy on the microscale. This would rather point to enlightened attitudes on both the management and the union sides.

However, productivity bargaining did not become sufficiently widespread to create a spurt of productivity for the economy as a whole. It may well be that it could not have done that in any case. Indeed, the entire conception, which tries to make labor coresponsible for productivity increases, may be still another symptom of management not being fully up to its tasks.

In Chapter 11, in connection with Swedish incomes policies, we discussed the positive effect upon productivity increases which may come from plain ordinary wage demands. The effect works through the urge to safeguard profits in the face of the increased price of labor services. Increase in the wage per worker motivates management to compensate for it by doing something that would increase output per worker and keep unit costs down. Technological innovation is the obvious answer. Naturally, this by-product of wage pressures presupposes a management capable and willing to respond to wage demands in this described manner. If management is too soft in negotiating with labor and too lethargic in matters of innovations, then the transmission gear, which would translate wage pressures into productivity increases, is missing. Wage pressures then simply puff out into price inflation. The fact that, in Britain, inflation reached the highest rates among advanced market-capitalist countries—about 25 to 30 percent in 1974–1975—is therefore also to be seen as part of the slow-growth syndrome.

SOVIET-TYPE GROWTH

As we pointed out earlier, there is a connection between advances in total factor productivity and the growth rate of the capital stock. The British case conforms

---

[5] *Business Week,* July 27, 1974.
[6] *Business Week,* Feb. 10, 1975.

to the assumption that, the lower the investment share in the GNP and the slower the growth of capital, the narrower is the channel through which embodied technological progress can flow into the economy. With a low investment share (around 17 percent), the British growth of total factor productivity has kept at a slow rate of 1.18 percent per year (1950–1962; see Table 12-3). The striking characteristic of Soviet-style growth has been an even slower growth of total factor productivity (down to 0.9 percent in the period 1958–1967, from 2.4 percent in 1950–1958),[7] despite the extraordinarily high investment shares (above 30 percent).

The significance of this fact is easy to grasp by merely inspecting the relevant figures. In one of the early discussions of this topic, Michael Boretsky chose this simple method to demonstrate relative growth performance of the Soviet Union and Italy.[8] The comparison was made with Italy, to avoid the custom of comparing the semiadvanced Soviet economy with the most advanced industrialized countries of the West. Between 1950 and 1962, Italy and the Soviet Union achieved very similar crude growth rates. But at what "costs," in terms of increases in labor and capital inputs? A tabulation of average annual percentage growth rates shows the following:

	GNP	Labor	Fixed capital
Soviet Union	6.3	1.9	10.5
Italy	6.1	1.5	3.6

The conclusion can be stated this way: If the Soviet Union had been improving the efficiency of its labor and capital stock at the same rate as Italy, considering how fast it was adding to its labor force and capital stock, its growth rate could have been about twice as high.

The most systematic comparative study of the growth performance of Soviet-type economies as a group with Western-type market-capitalist economies as a group was undertaken by Abram Bergson.[9] In this study, Bergson took care to downplay, in the comparisons, the influence that stage of economic development has upon growth performance. In Figures 12-2 and 12-3, observations in terms of the measure of growth performance on the vertical axis are plotted against a measure standing for the stage of economic development (i.e., real income per head). This makes it easy to see how countries, similar with respect to their level of economic development, compare with respect to growth performance. One traces a vertical line at a given value of real income per head (such

---

[7] Abram Bergson, "Future Growth Strategy for the Soviet Economy," *The ACES Bulletin* (Association for Comparative Economic Studies), vol. 14, no. 1, Spring 1972, p. 4.

[8] See U.S. Congress, Joint Economic Committee, *New Directions in the Soviet Economy,* part II-A, 1966, pp. 213–215.

[9] Abram Bergson, "Development under Two Systems: Comparative Productivity Growth since 1950," *World Politics,* vol. 23, no. 4, July 1971, pp. 579–617.

Figure 12-2 Rate of growth of GNP per worker, 1955–1967, and real national income per worker, 1960, COMECON and OECD countries.

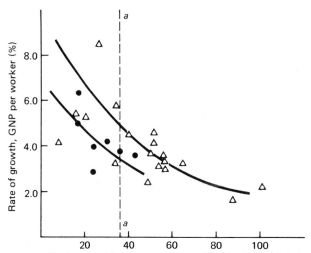

Real national income per worker, 1960 (as % of U.S.A.)

● COMECON (group B of the text)

△ OECD (group A)

Source: Abram Bergson, "Development under Two Systems: Comparative Productivity Growth since 1950," *World Politics,* vol. 23, no. 4, July 1971, p. 573. (Reproduced by the author's permission.)

as *aa* in the two figures), and reads off the values of the growth-performance indicator for countries whose dots fall on, or close to, that vertical line. If observations for countries belonging to group A fall systematically above observations for countries in group B, one is as close as one will ever get to a documented conclusion about the comparative merit of the two types of systems in regard to growth performance.

The message of both figures, which summarize the main part of Bergson's findings, is loud and clear: Market-capitalist systems of the West have been more efficient in achieving their growth rates than systems organized according to the CPE model. Market-capitalist rates of growth of labor productivity have been generally higher for any level of economic development (Figure 12-2). And market-capitalist rates of growth of labor productivity have been obtained at lower cost in terms of resources devoted to investment, as reflected in lower values of the ratio of investment share to growth of labor productivity (Figure 12-3). Trend lines were fitted freehand to the data of each of the country groups, in order to bring out more clearly the central tendency of their respective performance records.

These findings concerning dynamic efficiency dovetail with the conclusions of Chapter 9 on the low rating of CPEs in matters of static efficiency. However, the causes that have been holding back dynamic efficiency are not entirely the same as those interfering with static efficiency. They have to do mainly with obstacles standing in the way of technological progress.

Figure 12-3 Ratio of gross fixed investment share in GNP to rate of growth of GNP per worker, 1955–1967; and real national income per worker, COMECON and OECD countries.

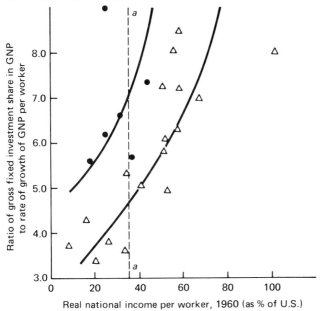

● COMECON countries

△ Countries of the OECD

Low values of the ratio on the vertical scale signify relatively better performance than high values: the higher the rate of growth of labor productivity (denominator) and the lower the share of investments in GNP (numerator), the better the performance.

Source: Abram Bergson, "Development under Two Systems: Comparative Productivity Growth since 1950," *World Politics,* vol. 23, no. 4, July 1971, p. 601. (Reproduced by the author's permission.)

Technological progress means supply of inventions and ability to turn them into technical innovations. With respect to both phases, the CPEs of the Soviet sphere have done worse in comparison with Western-type market capitalism. They have generated technical inventions at a slower rate, they have delayed borrowing more-advanced technology from abroad much too long, and as far as practical adoption of innovations is concerned, the system has lacked a built-in mechanism for the introduction of inventions into industry. In Evsey D. Domar's words, "If anything, the system has developed an automatic device for the rejection of such inventions, or at least for a long delay in their acceptance."[10]

The "automatic device" mentioned by Domar is the array of incentives that makes executives in the CPEs prefer old routine technologies which had been "mastered," as the Russian phrase goes, to the uncertainties, adventures, and interruptions of the innovative effort. The result has been the pervasive anti-innovation bias of Soviet-type systems, noted in Chapter 9. Even if novel ideas

[10] Evsey D. Domar, *American Economic Review,* vol. 59, no. 2, May 1969, p. 45.

and processes are available, enterprises tend—using another idiomatic phrase—to "put them away into the long drawer." The systemic element which is missing is either competition or an inner-directed concern for technical progress.

The reluctance to innovate is frequently given the justification that the output of research and development institutes is too far removed from the needs of "praxis." This has amounted to more than a phony excuse, judging by available information on the ways production of ideas has been organized. The governments have been rather lavish as far as financial and personnel appropriations to scientific and project design institutes are concerned. However, these institutes have always been somewhat insulated from the world of factories.

Offhand, one would expect centralization to be more advantageous to research and development than dispersion. One thinks of resources being allocated methodically so as to avoid duplications of effort and to attack each project in maximum force. But that is a fallacy. Interestingly, inventive activities thrive on dispersion, duplication of effort, cross-pollination between disciplines, and on nobody having a corner on a particular project. This is because chance plays such an important role in discoveries, and so does rivalry. Besides, manufacturing needs to keep a backlog of alternative technical solutions, so as to be able to adapt quickly to unforeseen changes.[11]

Borrowing of technology from the advanced industrial West was hampered, for a while, by Stalin's information wall and the now forgotten Russians-invented-everything-first propaganda theme. However, even when borrowing of technology was "in," it did not bring the same results as, for instance, in postwar France or Japan. This was, among other reasons, because borrowing did not take the form of a continuous stream of licenses purchased from abroad. It took the form of acquiring actual foreign articles and using them as prototypes for duplication at home.

This principle was followed from the start in the early thirties, during the first Five-Year Plans, then repeated during the wartime lend-lease shipments, and again to some extent in the course of trade expansion with the West, begun in the late sixties.[12] This trade-expansion drive, which centers on imports of modern technology-intensive products, makes great sense from the Soviet point of view if one considers the hidden implications of the Soviet-style growth pattern for the future.

The credit for bringing these implications to public attention goes again to A. Bergson. As he has shown, when capital stock grows at a substantially higher rate than output (because of slow growth in total factor productivity), there comes a point where a painful choice must be made. Either the planners must

---

[11] See Robert W. Campbell, "Problems of Technical Progress in the USSR," in M. Bornstein and D. Fussfeld (eds.), *The Soviet Economy: A Book of Readings,* 4th ed., Irwin, Homewood, Ill., 1974, pp. 348–364.

[12] For empirical documentation of the role Western technology played in Soviet development, see Antony Sutton, *Western Technology and Soviet Economic Development, 1917 to 1930,* Hoover Institution, Stanford, Calif., 1968, and *Western Technology and Soviet Economic Development, 1930 to 1945,* Hoover Institution, Stanford, Calif., 1971.

keep raising the investment share in GNP at the expense of consumption, armaments, and other government spending, in order to maintain the rate of growth of output (see Figure 12-4); or else they keep the investment share more or less steady and reconcile themselves to declining rates of growth of output.

Pulling up the growth rate of total factor productivity is the one and only way out of this dilemma. If that rate can be increased, then the stock of capital does not have to grow so fast, and the claim of investments upon national output is reduced, leaving that much more for consumption, armaments, etc. Such is the background of the intensified interest of the Soviet Union in importing Western technology.

*   *   *

We avoided some of the major pitfalls of discussions about growth by focusing on comparisons of productivity increases, rather than on crude growth rates. René Dumont's statement, used as motto to this chapter, is perfectly valid with respect to material production. There, the exponential curve must sooner or later flatten out and turn into an S curve, implying saturation and stabilization. It is not valid with respect to increases in factor productivity. It is these which permit us to envisage further progressive reductions of working time in the future and the development of entirely new life-styles.

In the selection of illustrative cases, we have come repeatedly across the fact of technology borrowing or, as it is usually called nowadays, the *international diffusion of technology*. We noted earlier (in the section on growth of labor productivity) the advantage enjoyed by latecomers to economic development in being able to incorporate the trailblazers' accumulated results of technological progress into their systems. This catching-up process contributes to a comparatively faster growth of factor productivity of the latecomers, at least in the short run.

Lately, concern has been expressed here and there about the apparent decline in the ability of trailblazers, in particular of the United States, to generate technological progress at their accustomed rate.[13] Charles Kindleberger would drop hints at some kind of "climacteric" in the economic life of nations,[14] but the slippage in technological leadership appears less dire if one considers some of its objective causes. In the catching-up process, there comes a point when the erstwhile imitator starts having original ideas. The pupil becomes able to generate a backflow of technology to the leader of yesterday. This has been increasingly the case, especially with respect to Japan.

Another factor has been the territorial diffusion of technology carried out in connection with the spread of multinational companies. It was pointed out by

---

[13] For example, Michael Boretsky, "Trends in U.S. Technology: A Political Economist's View," *American Scientist,* vol. 63, no. 1, January–February 1975, pp. 70–82; "The Breakdown of U.S. Innovation," *Business Week,* Feb. 16, 1976.

[14] Charles P. Kindleberger, "An American Economic Climacteric?" *Challenge,* vol. 17, no. 1, January–February 1974, pp. 35–44.

Figure 12-4 The problem of "extensive growth" of the Soviet type.

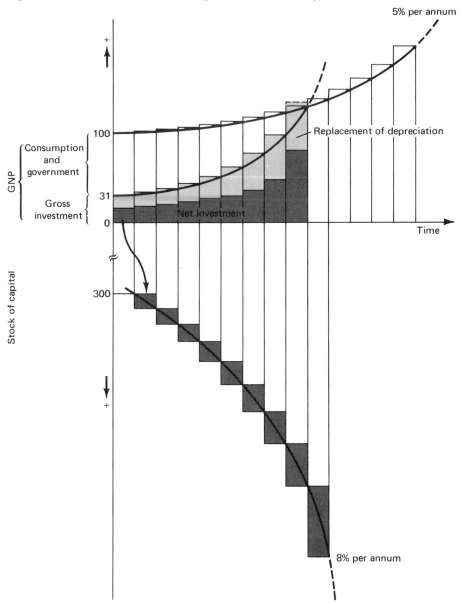

If a given rate of growth of GNP requires a higher rate of growth of the capital stock, sooner or later the entire GNP will have to be devoted to investments. Investment requirements can be lowered either by accepting a lower rate of growth of GNP or by raising the rate of growth of total factor productivity (see text).

Source: Based on Abram Bergson, "Future Growth Strategy for the Soviet Economy," *The ACES Bulletin* (Association for Comparative Economic Studies), vol. 14, no. 1, Spring 1972, pp. 2–13.

Harvey Brooks, Chairman of the Committee on Science and Public Policy of the National Academy of Sciences, that the

> scientific system is increasingly international, so that the very concept of national superiority in science or technology is obsolescent. It will be harder and harder to tell who is "ahead" or "behind" as frontier science is conducted in multinational institutions . . . and as technology is introduced and diffused by international corporations that will become truly multinational and identify less with particular home countries.[15]

As for the declining percentage share of research and development expenditure in the GNP of the United States—it has fallen from more than 3 percent in the early sixties to 2.4 percent in 1973—one should think of the character of such activities as *social overhead*. This means that they need not vary forever in proportion with total output, in order to maintain their effectiveness. If other countries simultaneously increase their shares of research and development expenditures, could one not see it as a more equitable distribution of the research and development burden among the advanced countries of market capitalism that can afford it?

BIBLIOGRAPHY

Nadiri, M. Ishaq: "Some Approaches to the Theory and Measurement of Total Factor Productivity: A Survey," *Journal of Economic Literature,* vol. 8, no. 4, December 1970, pp. 1137–1177.

Dennison, Edward F.: *Why Growth Rates Differ: Postwar Experience in Nine Western Countries,* Brookings, Washington, 1967.

Kindleberger, Charles P.: *Europe's Postwar Growth: The Role of Labor Supply,* Harvard, Cambridge, Mass., 1967.

United Nations: *Some Factors in Economic Growth in Europe during the 1950s,* part 2, *Economic Survey of Europe in 1961,* Geneva, 1964.

———: *The European Economy from the 1950s to the 1970s,* part 1, *Economic Survey of Europe in 1971,* New York, 1972.

Carré, Jean Jacques, Paul Dubois, and Edmond Malinvaud: *French Economic Growth,* Stanford University Press, Stanford, Calif., 1975.

Ohkawa, Kazushi, and Henry Rosovsky: *Japanese Economic Growth,* Stanford University Press, Stanford, Calif., 1973.

Ozawa, Terutomo: *Japan's Technological Challenge to the West, 1950–1974: Motivation and Accomplishment,* M.I.T., Cambridge, Mass., 1974.

Kanamori, Hisai: "What Makes Japan's Economic Growth Rate High?" in *Japanese Economic Studies,* vol. 1, no. 1, Fall 1972, pp. 31–48.

Henderson, P. D. (ed.): *Economic Growth in Britain,* Weidenfeld and Nicolson, London, 1966.

Mills, John: *Growth and Welfare: A New Policy for Britain,* Martin Robertson, London, 1972.

Shanks, Michael: *The Stagnant Society,* rev. ed., Penguin, Harmondsworth, England, 1972.

---

[15] Harvey Brooks, "What's Happening to the U.S. Lead in Technology?" *Harvard Business Review,* vol. 50, no. 3, May–June 1972, p. 118.

Kaldor, Nicholas: *Causes of the Slow Rate of Economic Growth of the United Kingdom,* Cambridge University Press, London, 1966.

Bergson, Abram (ed.): *Soviet Economic Growth,* Row, Peterson, Evanston, Ill., 1953.

Cohn, Stanley: *Economic Development in the Soviet Union,* Heath, Lexington, Mass., 1969.

NATO: *Prospects for Soviet Economic Growth in the 1970s,* NATO Information Service, Brussels, 1971.

Bergson, Abram: "Development under Two Systems: Comparative Productivity Growth since 1950," *World Politics,* vol. 23, no. 4, July 1971, pp. 579–617.

Alton, Thad P.: "Economic Structure and Growth in Eastern Europe," in U.S. Congress, Joint Economic Committee: *Economic Developments in Countries of Eastern Europe,* 1970, pp. 41–67.

Janossy, Ferenc: *The End of the Economic Miracle: Appearance and Realization in Economic Development,* International Arts and Sciences Press, White Plains, N.Y., 1971.

Goldman, Josef, and Karel Kouba: *Economic Growth in Czechoslovakia,* International Arts and Sciences Press, White Plains, N.Y., 1969.

Horvat, Branko: *Business Cycles in Yugoslavia,* International Arts and Sciences Press, White Plains, N.Y., 1971.

Bajt, Alexander: "Investment Cycles in European Socialist Economies: A Review Article," in *Journal of Economic Literature,* vol. 9, no. 1, March 1971, pp. 53–63.

Morphology
of the Industrial
Enterprise Sector

The capital is there, and so is capitalism. The waning factor is the capitalist.

Adolf A. Berle, Jr.

Morphology is the descriptive study of shapes and structures. What shapes and structures are there to be described when we think of the production sector outside agriculture and government proper? The basic *technical unit* may be a plant, a mine, a workshop, a store, a farm, a school, a hospital, a railroad. The basic *economic unit* is an enterprise or a firm—a legal administrative entity which may coincide with one single technical unit or encompass a number of them. The shapes and structures in question refer to the organizational patterns formed by technical units within firms, and by firms with each other. The size distribution of basic units is another pattern which morphology is concerned with.

ESCALATION OF ECONOMIES OF SCALE

We have just finished discussing growth performance in the aggregate. Before we proceed, it ought to be clearly realized that morphological patterns in the production sector, and their changes, are the microeconomic side of macroeconomic growth. If employment, stock of capital, and their productivity grow in the aggregate, it means they must grow, on the average, per individual production unit, too. (We leave aside the arithmetic possibility of growth through adding more and more units of the same size, which is economically irrelevant.)

Relative Concentration

When we say "on the average," we allow for the possibility of some units expanding faster than others, new extra-large units being founded, and some of the small ones disappearing, either through effective liquidation or through merging with one another. All this does not *have* to happen—individual units could conceivably grow in unison—but this is what *does* happen, thanks mainly to the play of chance and competition, as we have shown in Chapter 8 (section on "Monopolistic Behavior"). As a result, *economic concentration* tends to increase in the course of economic growth: expanding volume and proportion of output are being produced by a declining number of large units.

When we say "units," we are being vague as to whether we mean technical units or economic units, i.e., firms. The truth of the matter is that we mean both. At each stage, growth is accompanied by expansion, up to a point, of the technical units of production. This is where technological economies of scale come in, as source of productivity increases, engendering in turn qualitative innovations in technological processes.

Beyond the point at which profitable expansion of the *technical* units stops, expansion of the *economic* unit takes over. The economic unit, the firm, expands in terms of the value of assets under its control. This value grows from within, thanks to the reinvestment of profits generated by the firm, and thanks to additions of fresh investable funds from outside the firm. The physical shape of productive assets, whose value expands, takes the form of stringing on newly founded *additional technical units,* not necessarily of the same type or in the same production line. Alternatively, or simultaneously, increase in firm size occurs by *independent firms merging* and forming superfirms.

Types of Integration

The morphological patterns that emerge in this process of expansion soon come to resemble complex molecules of organic compounds.[1] When production units grow new ones, or combine into superfirms, the market connection between them is eliminated at some level of decision making, even if they retain a degree of operational autonomy. We speak of their *integration.* There are three basic types of integration, depending on whether the firms were originally in a competitive relationship, in a supplier-customer relationship, or neither of the two. *Horizontal integration* takes place when the merging firms belong to the same industry or product line. Under *vertical integration* a firm combines with the suppliers of

---

[1] It may be instructive, at the next visit to the reference library, to leaf through the latest volumes of *Directory of Corporate Affiliations,* National Register Publishing Co., Inc., Skokie, Ill., or *Who Owns Whom* (Continental edition or U.K. edition), O. W. Roskill and Co. (Reports) Ltd., London.

inputs ("upstream integration") or with its customers ("downstream" or "forward integration"). In other words, vertical mergers link up firms along an axis of raw material–processing–distribution. Finally, there are combinations where the character of the firms' specialization does not matter at all. The reason for bringing them hodgepodge under the roof of a single organization is to centralize investment decisions and to orchestrate their expansion strategies. This last case is known as *conglomerate mergers*.

In popular literature, the chemistry of firm integration and expansion is often presented as a crude control-grabbing drive. This may be a correct description if one observes the process at the level of personal motives and psychological processes of the decision makers. It is a world inhabited by speculators buying and selling entire firms; magnates organizing mergers, instigating corporate takeovers, building economic empires, and losing them again; adventurers animated by greed for wealth and thirst for power.[2] Academic economists prefer to look past these features and to search for the presence of the invisible hand which safeguards the interest of society in economizing resources, i.e., reducing costs and raising productivity.

Economic Rationale of Integration

The concept which tries to make economic sense of the luxuriating organizational molecules is *economies of management*. This is analogous to the technological economies of scale. The idea behind both concepts is that, as far as scale of units is concerned, its optimum should be governed by the scale of the largest indivisible factor. Complementary factors ought to be applied in such quantities as needed to assure a "full load" of the indivisible factor.

In the case of managerial decision making, running a single plant may just not be enough of a load for a management capable of handling more, especially if managerial capacity keeps outgrowing its limits thanks to innovations of all sorts which widen its *control span*. In other words, management itself ends up in the role of the indivisible factor in need of being fully utilized.

To be realistic, we have to stop thinking of management as if it were one large swarm of administrative activities. Management consists of many functional layers of decisions of different types. They differ by their respective control span. At the lower end, the control span of a workshop supervisor is very narrow. Technical management has a control span which encompasses a plant. Other aspects of management have a still wider span which allows technical production units to be recast into a higher-order configuration of economic units, i.e., firms.

Economic management of firms thus becomes differentiated and articulated into hierarchic patterns. Narrow-span management functions stay confined to the plant, division, or subsidiary. Wider-span functions split off and move to the administrative headquarters of the firm. Subordinate units may retain their identity as independent accounting units, e.g., as "profit centers," such as the largely

---

[2] See Robert Sobel, *The Age of Giant Corporations,* Greenwood Press, Westport, Conn., 1972, pp. 195–209.

autonomous product divisions of the modern multidivisional corporation. The wide-span functions which are reserved to the headquarters comprise, typically, monitoring the performance of subordinate units, raising and allocating finances, making major investment decisions, and evolving strategies for further expansion.

Another way of interpreting the same process is to see it as a replacement of market relationships, which relate firms to each other externally by direct administrative methods which make the former market relations internal to the larger unit of consolidated firms.

The economic rationale, especially as far as consolidation of firms into superfirms is concerned, is found in the reduction of costs associated with market transactions before consolidation takes place. These costs may be information costs, haggling over terms of sale, policing contracts, living in uncertainty about time and quality of shipments, etc. The advantage of consolidation theoretically evaporates when, with increasing scale, the marginal cost of direct coordination methods becomes greater than the "transaction costs" associated with market dealing.[3] This is the time to start thinking of breaking up consolidated units, decentralizing, subcontracting, and for overextended parent companies to divest themselves of some of their holdings.

The Size of Units, West and East

The discussion so far has dealt with the more or less spontaneous processes observable under Western market capitalism. In Chapter 8 (section "Through Competition to Concentration") we noted a few basic facts about the degree of relative concentration. Here we want to ask whether there are any significant size differences of production units between different economic systems. In countries of Western-type market capitalism, the absolute size of production units and firms (in terms of employment) increases with the absolute size of the market (represented by the GNP). Contrary to what one would expect, it matters much less how far advanced a given country is in terms of level of technology (as reflected by output per worker). Countries with a larger GNP are also the ones which have a relatively greater number of multiestablishment firms (United States, Japan, West Germany, France). Small-size GNP usually goes hand in hand with the predominance of single-plant firms.[4] In Figure 13-1, a handy graph devised by French statisticians is reproduced, showing the relative size of the average establishment in seven countries. (It is expressed by the slope of straight lines connecting the origin with the coordinate point of the number and total employment of establishments.)

Under state capitalism of the Soviet type, the size of plants, establishments,

---

[3] This line of analysis was started by Professor Ronald H. Coase in his classic article "The Nature of the Firm," *Economica,* November 1937, vol. 4, pp. 386–405; reprinted in George J. Stigler and Kenneth E. Boulding (eds.), *Readings in Price Theory,* Irwin, Homewood, Ill., 1952, pp. 331–351.

[4] These observations draw on comparative computations undertaken by Frederic L. Pryor. See his *Property and Industrial Organization in Communist and Capitalist Nations,* Indiana University Press, Bloomington, 1973, chaps. 5 and 6.

Figure 13-1 Indicators of the degree of concentration and average size of establishments in manufacturing, selected countries.

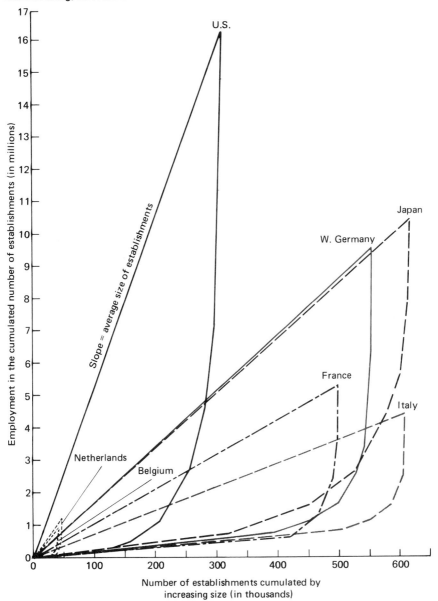

Source: *Les Collections de l'I.N.S.E.E.*, E 1, p. 17, reproduced in Yves Morvan, *La concentration de l'industrie en France*, Librairie Armand Colin, Paris, 1972, p. 198.

and enterprises is decided by administrative fiat, not by a spontaneous economic process. It has been typical for Eastern European economies to organize the industrial sector in extraordinarily large plant establishments and enterprises.

According to Frederic L. Pryor's estimates, their plant establishments are two to four times as large as they would be in a comparable Western market-size setting.[5] Enterprises are, on the average, four to sixteen times as large; those of Czechoslovakia and Hungary are among the largest in the world.[6]

Preference for large *plant* design reflects the planners' unsophisticated belief in technical economies of scale. In occasional self-critical moods, the Soviet regime deplored what has been called "gigantomania," without ever seriously revising the practice. The Soviet preference for mammoth plants draws attention to a negative corollary of economies of scale, namely, to cost of transportation. As unit cost of production declines with increasing scale of plant, unit cost of transportation may be rising. Therefore, when deciding on the scale of plant, one should go by the delivered-cost schedule and choose that scale at which the delivered cost is lowest, even if one could save on unit production costs by choosing a larger plant (see Figure 13-2). This reasoning is particularly compelling in the case of bulky products with high transportation costs and a geographically dispersed raw-material base (e.g., cement).[7]

As for the enormous size of *enterprises* in Soviet-type systems, one might wish to explain it in terms of administrative economies of scale, parallel to economies of management under market capitalism. The parallel is unfortunately not very close. First of all, under the classic version of the CPE, which determined the size of enterprises, there was no question of weighing the relative cost of management by administrative methods against that of market relationships. Virtually all that would have been interenterprise market relationships were internalized by the central planning system. Second, insofar as large enterprises mean that the center can deal directly with a small number of units only, the administrative effort thus saved is dumped into the lap of the large enterprises that still have to deal with their subdivisions.

Soviet "gigantomania" may be seen as a continuation of one part of the prerevolutionary legacy. Industrial projects constructed in czarist days, under heavy participation of Western companies, were the largest of their time. The Soviet era followed in that tradition. On the other hand, czarist legacy of small-scale enterprises in trade and handicrafts was firmly rejected, not only because they were private but also because they were believed to be uneconomical. The elimination of the small workshop and store, which took place in the Soviet Union in the late twenties, was reenacted in the rest of Eastern Europe in the late forties. Under the latest economic reforms, in Hungary, Czechoslovakia, and Poland, the petty private enterprise sector was partially resurrected in acknowledgment of its economic advantages.

What are the economic advantages of the small enterprise that would explain its capacity of survival under market capitalism? Considering the powerful

[5] Pryor, ibid., p. 162.
[6] Ibid., pp. 190–193.
[7] Leon Smolinski, "The Scale of Soviet Industrial Establishments," *American Economic Review*, vol. 52, no. 2, May 1962, pp. 138–148; Alan Abouchar, *Soviet Planning and Spatial Efficiency: The Prewar Cement Industry*, Indiana University Press, Bloomington, 1971.

Figure 13-2 Optimum plant size and transportation costs.

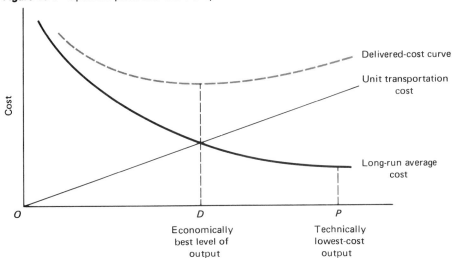

The long-run average cost curve indicates the range of alternative plant sizes in terms of output capacity. The more production is concentrated in large-size plants, the higher are unit transportation costs of inputs and output. If it were not for transportation costs, the optimal size would be one of capacity *OP* (lowest point of the average cost schedule). Taking the cost of transportation into account means summing up vertically average cost and transportation cost for every size plant. The resulting delivered-cost schedule indicates that a smaller size plant of capacity *OD*, which is technically less efficient, may be more efficient economically.

tendency toward concentration, it seems puzzling how small firms survive at all. Marx, who was among the first to incorporate the tendency toward concentration into his model of capitalist growth, envisaged a theoretical extreme where "the entire social capital was united in the hands of either a single capitalist or a single capitalist company."[8] However, even he noted the existence of "counteracting tendencies, which have a continuous decentralizing effect,"[9] whereby "the increase of each functioning capital is thwarted by the formation of new and the subdivision of old capitals."[10] Nonetheless, it is difficult to believe that today's corporate colossuses could not displace or absorb the small-firm sector overnight, if they so wished. Since they do not, there must be a reason.

There seems to be more than one major reason, as there is more than one type of small business. Using terms and distinctions proposed by Robert T. Averitt in his lively portrait of the United States dual economy, the sector of small-scale "periphery firms" is made up of the following: (1) *free agents*, filling the interstices of the industrial system left by the large "center firms," either in small-scale manufacturing, services, or distribution; (2) *satellites* of the large center

---

[8] K. Marx, *Capital*, vol. I, p. 627. This extreme situation seems to fit Soviet-type state capitalism rather well.

[9] Ibid., vol. III, p. 246.

[10] Ibid., vol. I, p. 625.

firms acting as their subcontractors (such as machine-tool firms) or licensed distributors (such as gasoline stations); and (3) the *loyal opposition,* capable maverick firms, existing under the protective umbrella of oligopoly pricing practiced by the large companies.[11]

Small firms may specialize in custom-made or individualized articles, in small-batch production, or in services where quality of personal contact with customers is essential. Large firms keep out of such activities, which do not lend themselves to large-scale methods of mass production and marketing. The case of "satellites" is somewhat different. The large firm may prefer subcontracting or leasing ("franchising") certain portions of otherwise-integrated activities because direct supervision methods are inefficient. Turning over such functions to a quasi-independent entrepreneur means letting his self-interest do the supervising. In addition, he gets to bear the risk of failure and effects of recessions. The large firm may even earn interest if it supplies the satellite with equipment or merchandise on credit.

This approach to the study of the size distribution of firms represents a valuable supplement to the starkly quantitative analysis of data. It traces various interdependencies and complementarities not only between firms of different sizes but also of different ownership models. In Chapters 3 and 4, dealing with the classification of systems, we remarked at several places on the fact that concrete economic systems of national economies are regularly composites of several types of systemic models. The suggestion contained in Averitt's approach is to study actual country systems in ways analogous to those of the biologist who studies communities of different organisms forming symbiotic ecosystems in nature, i.e., as live, interdependent, and interacting structures.

*   *   *

The process of concentration, as well as the emergence of complex structures of integrated or otherwise consolidated production units, has occurred under two basic legal forms of the firm: the *private capitalist corporation* and the so-called *public enterprise.* In the remaining part of the chapter, we shall be dealing with these two types of what fundamentally amounts to a capitalist firm, according to our nomenclature developed earlier. The first section on the modern corporation is of a more or less general order. It serves to supplement what has already been said about the subject in Chapter 3. The section on public enterprise contrasts two divergent conceptions of nationalized industries, a staid one and a vibrant one, with the help of the example of Britain and Italy. The case of Japanese organizational structures is a study of tensions between cartel-mindedness, competitive spirit, and rival organs of the state, each sponsoring one of these attitudes. The section on Soviet problems with devising a proper administrative structure for a CPE is in a class by itself. It provides a unique opportunity to illuminate a general issue, namely, the difference between the natural structure of

---

[11] Robert T. Averitt, *The Dual Economy,* Norton, New York, 1968, pp. 86–103.

economic relationships and the formalistic administrative framework into which they are supposed to fit.

MODERN CAPITALIST CORPORATION

The story of corporate law in different countries is an edifying illustration of how powerful the legal subsystem can be in stimulating or holding back economic development. The effects of legal limitations of the guild system (see Chapter 4) are well known. They had been an incubus on the development of the capitalist firm in the early stages. In later stages, further increase in the scale of capitalist operations was again either retarded or advanced, depending on the existence of legal forms that permitted escape from the confines of individual proprietorship. The corporate form was it.

A Historical Flashback

This form of enterprise had the advantage of not being financially limited to the investible resources of one or a few persons. Innumerable individual savings are pooled to create funds large enough to finance undertakings on a scale which no single individual, no matter how rich, could support. It is therefore surprising to learn how long it took for capitalism to obtain legal recognition of what came to be considered as "one of the most important achievements of modern industrial society."

There were reasons for the delay. Legal obstacles reflected society's initial distrust of an organizational form which seemed to lend itself too easily to swindle and speculation. In England, the Bubble Act of 1720 was enacted in the wake of speculative scandals involving some early joint-stock companies; it retarded their development for at least a century. As late as 1826, the *Times* of London could scorn "corporate bodies" as a definitely inferior form of conducting business, compared to individual enterpreneurs.[12] In France, the development of the corporate form suffered a setback around the same time as in England, and for similar reasons, although there, the slow headway made by the corporate form is also attributed to the French preference for organizational forms based on the strength of kinship ties. In the United States, the corporation had a fifty-year head start over Europe because of its popularity, based on the resemblance of its statutes to political forms of democracy.[13] Thus, every country had its own special history of the corporation, as well as of its imperfect substitutes and predecessors, such as unincorporated joint-stock companies, partnerships, *Kommanditgesellschaften,* etc.

The most important element in the "invention" of the corporation was the concept of *limited liability*. It quieted the shareholders' fears of putting small

[12] Bishop Carleton Hunt, *The Development of the Business Corporation in England: 1800–1867,* Harvard, Cambridge, Mass., pp. 3–13. See also Dudley Dillard, *Economic Development of the North Atlantic Community,* Prentice-Hall, Englewood Cliffs, N.J., 1967, pp. 159–161, 369–374, and 388–389 (bibliography).

[13] Oscar Handlin and Mary F. Handlin, "Origins of the American Business Corporation," *The Journal of Economic History,* vol. 5, no. 1, May 1945, pp. 1–23.

parcels of savings at the disposal of strangers. The fears were understandable as long as shareholders were held responsible for the debts of the undertaking "to their last shilling and last acre," as was the case under "unlimited liability."[14] Such an apparently minor change in the legal sphere removed a major hurdle in the path of capitalist accumulation.

A Matter of Perception

Once it obtained a green light from the legislative side, the capitalist corporation developed into the central economic institution of market capitalism. It has been viewed with gasping admiration, it has been used as a scapegoat for every ill of contemporary society, it has rarely been treated with cool detachment. Robin Marris sees it, in the tradition of Max Weber, as a "bureaucratic organization [which] has developed as a means of large scale cooperation and is thus an impressive expression of human rationality. In effect, it is *the* great human achievement."[15]

At the other end of the spectrum, Jeremy Rifkin provides an illustration of the extreme radical perception: "The corporate giants have violated our sacred rights to life, liberty and the pursuit of happiness by denying us adequate access to the means to sustain life. . . . An economic system whose character is thus marked by every act that may define an absolute tyranny is unfit to claim the loyalty and allegiance of a free and democratic people."[16]

Marx's interesting view of the corporation as one of the "transitional forms from the capitalist mode of production to the associated one"[17] has already been noted in Chapter 3 (section on "Production Cooperatives, Communes, Socialism"). It is in that tradition of seeing the corporation as an open-ended form that Adolf A. Berle, Jr., points to its potentialities: "As an instrument, our [corporate] system is obviously capable of doing anything the American public consensus really wishes it to do."[18]

The multiplicity of views is mirrored in the enormous literature on the subject. It includes muckraking collections or horror stories; insiders' observations of the ways of corporate management à la Peter Drucker; antiseptic treatises in the formal analytic vein, exemplified by Oliver W. Williamson and Robin Marris; elder-statesman writings pondering the social and cultural significance of the corporate phenomenon; econometric studies of the kind pioneered by F. Modigliani; and broad popular generalizations of the J. K. Galbraith brand.

Analytic Pointers

There is no way of summarizing this richesse of approaches, impressions, and

[14] This is what distinguishes an unincorporated joint-stock company from an incorporated one. The "incorporation" consists in the grant of a charter on the part of public authorities. It is a kind of license guaranteeing the trustworthiness of the founders. Further stipulations, such as "public disclosure" of information concerning the officers, certain aspects of finances, and others, merely amplify and bolster the basic guarantee.

[15] Robin Marris (ed.), *The Corporate Society,* Macmillan, London, 1974, p. 241.

[16] *The New York Times,* May 26, 1975.

[17] K. Marx, *Capital,* vol. III, p. 387.

[18] Adolf A. Berle, Jr., *The American Economic Review,* Harcourt, Brace & World, New York, 1963, p. 7.

findings. We shall limit ourselves to highlighting the major aspects of the corporate system, most of which this literature brought to public attention. In conclusion, we shall draw a few comparisons between the United States and some of the European countries.

(1) The modern corporation represents a phase in the development of the capitalist firm from its patriarchal origins to fully collectivized forms. It is not an expression of individual private property; it possesses important features of socialized ownership (broad ownership of shares, public disclosure of information, management of human groups). However, the issue of managerial accountability (accountable to whom—stockholders, consumers, the "public," the firm as such?) remains muddled, thus keeping the corporation within the confines of capitalism and this side of "socialization." It can be analyzed as a specimen of a large profit-oriented bureaucratic organization, operating within significant market and legal constraints.

(2) The life span of a typical corporation is not limited to the life cycle of an individual or that of a particular product: it is "immortal." In the end it cannot even be liquidated through bankruptcy. Once too many people depend on a company for their livelihood, business failure becomes socially unacceptable. Besides, its assets may be too vast or too specialized to find private buyers at liquidation. The state is called upon to come to the rescue of such ailing giants; this means that they are less exposed to the disciplining sanctions of the market, similar to enterprises under central administrative planning.[19] The corporate system experiences an infusion of state-capitalist characteristics.

(3) The progressive independence of the capitalist firm from a specific individual or product line has its corollary in the organizational scheme of the corporation. In the terms proposed by O. E. Williamson, the U-form (unitary form) evolves into the M-form (multidivision form).[20] Under the U-form regime, the chief executive is at the hub of functional divisions (manufacturing, sales, finance, engineering, etc.). These divisions report to the chief executive, who coordinates their activities. This type of organization is satisfactory as long as the firm is of small or moderate size, and its product line is simple. As it grows and its products multiply, functional divisions become overburdened; there is loss of efficiency in information flows and coordination. The overhead cost of functional divisions is spread indiscriminately over too many products, making the determination of specific costs very imprecise. The time comes to redraw the organization chart: the unitary company is broken up into divisions, each in charge of a specific product line, and with its own set of technical, marketing, financial, and other functional organs. Each product division becomes a "quasi-firm" generating its own profits (or losses) as an objective gauge of its success. The divisions represent separate "profit centers." The "headquarters" retains the authority of collecting the profits, redistributing them among divisions, supplementing them

[19] "When Companies Get Too Big to Fail," *Business Week,* Jan. 27, 1975, p. 16.

[20] Oliver E. Williamson, "Managerial Discretion, Organization Form, and the Multi-division Hypothesis," in R. Marris (ed.), *The Corporate Economy,* Harvard, Cambridge, Mass., 1971, pp. 343–386.

with additional finance, and making strategic decisions about the expansion and direction of the product divisions.

(4) The single concept which underlies the change of organizational forms is diversification. The principle of diversifying product lines within the company is repeated, at a higher level, whenever companies from different industrial branches join to form conglomerates as discussed earlier. When a company branches out beyond the borders of its country of origin, to become a "multinational company" (see Chapter 15), the organizational principle tying the foreign subsidiaries with the headquarters is again the same: the M-form.

(5) The consequence (or purpose) of diversification is the spreading of risk (which contributes to the long-term survival of the company) and internalization of the investment process. With diversification, corporate activities resemble more and more smaller-scale replicas of the economy itself. If partial failure occurs in one spot, funds can be channeled there to heal the breach. In making basic allocations of investment funds, managers have direct access to internally generated accounting data and estimates of divisions, which is an advantage compared to investments made by autonomous and narrowly specialized units, having to guess the comparative advantage of investment opportunities.

(6) The major issues concerning the corporation, which are unresolved and in a state of flux, center on the problem of its accountability: how are corporate decision makers in the sphere of entrepreneurship and management selected; what are their legitimate objectives; what are their actual objectives; what do they "owe" to the various segments of society affected by their decisions (stockholders, employees, local communities, environmentalists, consumers, cultural interests of society, domestic and foreign political interests of the state and society, and possibly others); by what rules are they supposed to reconcile conflicting interests?

At one time, economic research liked to choose, from among these issues, the question of whether corporations follow the rules of "profit maximization," "satisficing," growth of sales, growth of assets, or some judicious combination of different objectives. For certain purposes, the carefully balanced answer given by Professor Neil W. Chamberlain can be entirely satisfactory:

> [The firm] is pursuing a number of simultaneously held objectives . . . all more or less systematically related, the achievement of which is in turn dependent on attaining some given rate of return on assets of given or growing magnitude. It is the way in which profit envelops and makes possible a stream of objectives which led to its characterization here as a "portmanteau" goal, along with growth.[21]

However, it is clear that this barely scratches the surface of the problems involved.

The European Corporation

There is nothing strikingly special to be said about the character of the corporation in Europe, except for one lag and one lead over its American counterpart.

The lagging aspect is organization and methods of management. There has

---

[21] Neil W. Chamberlain, *Private and Public Planning*, McGraw-Hill, New York, 1965, p. 23.

been a lag in the conversion from individual or family ownership to joint-stock companies,[22] in the conversion of joint-stock companies from the U-form to the M-form, a lag in shifting the focus of attention from the production aspect to marketing and innovation, and a lag in changing the internal style of management. As for the last aspect, modern corporate management has been undergoing a continuous (and some say revolutionary) shift in the principles and practice of management. The change points from the old-fashioned, authoritarian command pyramid to something much more fluid, and also more efficient. The new style is best described as task-oriented cybernetic teamwork. Its basic principle is emphasis on the cooperative-division-of-labor side of the firm, on the so-called systems-analytic approach to problem solving, and on the concept of "continuum of information and responsibility" among participants within the firm, as well as responsiveness to the broad cultural and political environment of the firm.[23]

As for the lead, it also concerns the internal structure of relationships between participants within the firm. This refers to various formulas establishing workers' (or employees') representation (and/or participation) in corporate management. From the pioneering introduction in 1952 of "codetermination" in West German companies, the idea has been spreading to France (late sixties), England (midseventies), and other countries, to say nothing of the Yugoslav formula of "workers' management," formally introduced as early as 1950. This issue will be discussed in greater depth in Chapter 17.

One more point ought to be mentioned here, namely, attempts at preparing a unified legislation that would establish standard European-company statutes for the countries of the Common Market. Discussions of this desideratum and preparatory work have been taking place since the late sixties,[24] so far inconclusively.

THE PUBLIC-ENTERPRISE SECTOR: MAINLY BRITISH

When one says "mixed economies," one has in mind economies with a significant admixture of firms operated under the authority of the government or of municipal organs. That means all economies of contemporary Western-type capitalism are mixed. There are no pure cases of private-enterprise systems, and perhaps there never were. Indeed, historically, in many instances, the state helped to hatch the private sector by founding enterprises which were later "denationalized," i.e., turned over into private hands (France, Japan, Austria-Hungary, Unit-

---

[22] For instance, see the concise survey of the demise of industrial family dynasties in West Germany, in *The Economist* (London), Jan. 25, 1975, pp. 62–63.

[23] The process of adaptation of the European corporate firm to this challenge posed mainly by the presence of competitive American firms in Europe and their stimulating example, is treated, for example, in H. van der Hass, *The Enterprise in Transition: An Analysis of European and American Practice,* Tavistock Publications, London, 1967. For a useful brief characterization of the new management styles see George E. Berkley, *The Administrative Revolution: Notes on the Passing of Organization Man,* Prentice-Hall, Englewood Cliffs, N.J., 1971.

[24] For a comparative view of the character of company legislation in Europe in the late sixties, see Charles de Hoghton, *The Company, Law, Structure, and Reform in Eleven Countries,* G. Allen, London, 1970.

ed States).[25] In expanding its role as entrepreneur by taking over private enterprise, the state has thus been turning a full circle.

The Extent

The precise extent of public entrepreneurship is difficult to measure because the cutoff line is not clear. There is a gradation in the degree and kind of governmental participation, all the way from activities incorporated into the governmental administrative structure (as the postal service everywhere) to piecemeal intervention in the running of independent private firms (as in the case of regulated utilities, zoning rules, licensing, or rules imposed on the conduct of corporations, such as disclosure of information, accounting for depreciation, etc.). In between are enterprises organized as separate entities in the form of autonomous, or semi-autonomous firms; as joint ventures in partnership with private investors; or as closely watched specialized contractors such as suppliers of military hardware. From the point of view of legal ownership, the state, as a "legal person," may be the direct single owner or may hold shares, all or part, in enterprises organized as joint-stock companies.[26] Financially, such enterprises may be tied in various ways to the governmental budget (through capital grants, loans, subsidies, and collection of profits), or they may be entirely on their own, like any private corporation.[27]

A rough idea of the public sector's relative position in the economies of various countries can be obtained from Table 13-1. The situation under Western-type capitalism has been largely stabilized, even though the British Labour party has made moves in the direction of further nationalizations after winning the fall 1974 elections.[28] Elsewhere there have been minor changes on the fringes, such as the turning over of the German government-owned Volkswagen Werke to private shareholders in 1958, or the establishment of new combinations of teamed-up government-private activities (such as the United States Communications Satellite Corporation, the power companies and Atomic Energy Commission complex, Conrail, the British and Norwegian North Sea oil development enterprises, and others).

In the sample of countries of Table 13-1, the share of public enterprises ranges from one-tenth to one-third of the entire enterprise sector. It seems an

---

[25] David S. Landes, "Japan and Europe: Contrasts in Industrialization," in William W. Lockwood (ed.), *The State and Economic Enterprise in Japan,* Princeton University Press, Princeton, N.J., 1965, pp. 100–106.

[26] A meticulous, though far from dry, comparative account of the legal forms is to be found in W. G. Friedmann and J. F. Garner (eds.), *Government Enterprise,* Columbia, New York, 1970. It covers the United Kingdom, France, Italy, Germany, Sweden, United States, Canada, Australia, Israel, and East Africa.

[27] Logically, activities conducted under the form of nonprofit organizations (private colleges and universities, charitable foundations, etc.) are also public enterprises. They are treated as "private" only because the "public" does not exercise its ownership through the government. They may be lumped together with some of the government-controlled activities under the concept of the "not-for-profit" sector, as in Eli Ginzberg, Dale L. Hiestand, and Beatrice G. Reubens, *The Pluralistic Economy,* McGraw-Hill, New York, 1965.

[28] Nationalizations have been deemphasized, though not renounced, in the Labour party program throughout the sixties, under the leadership of Hugh Gaitskell.

Table 13-1 Proportion of the Public-Enterprise Sector in Selected Economies*
(Various Years)

	West Germany	Japan	Switzerland	United States	France	Sweden	Israel	United Kingdom	Austria	Finland
Total	9	10	11	15	17	20	24	25	31	34
Utilities†	43	20	60	28	83	71	100	70	100	53
Transportation and communication	74	42	63	18	69	53	32	—	78	59
Construction	0	14	6	12	1	12	6	8	4	31
Manufacturing and mining	1	0	1	1	8	4	2	9	25	14

* Percent of the economically active population in publicly owned enterprises and units to the corresponding total for the economy, branch, or sector; included are enterprises owned 50 percent or more by the government.
† Electricity, gas, water sanitation.

Source: Frederic L. Pryor, *Property and Industrial Organization in Communist and Capitalist Nations*, Indiana University Press, Bloomington, 1973, pp. 46–47.

335

economy has to reach at least the French proportion of 17 percent before it starts projecting the image of having a significant public sector.

The Reasons

A large sector of nationalized enterprises is often seen as a legacy of the political swing leftward in the early postwar period: the British Labour victory in 1945, the early French coalition government with Communist participation. The implication is that the degree of public entrepreneurship is simply a matter of political and ideological preferences. For some people it is, but the real origins of extended public enterprise are considerably less exalted, and also more varied.

A clue to the nonideological origins of public enterprise is the fact that it tends to be concentrated in a few chosen sectors: transportation, communication, utilities, fuels (especially coal mining). Each has its own, often composite, rationale: reasons of security and military strategy; large-scale needs for investment finance; exercise of control stemming from political sovereignty (postal service); control of natural monopoly from within (rather than by regulation or antitrust from without); supply of "social overhead," promising to spread benefits throughout the economy (transportation, communications); control of "commanding heights" or "key sectors" (in the sense of industries supplying basic inputs).

The monopoly-control rationale is ironic to the extent that some early public enterprises, many of which are surviving, were themselves meant as state monopolies collecting revenue for the treasuries (e.g., tobacco, salt, matches). The commanding-heights rationale also sounds hollow if it is applied to cases such as the postwar British and French nationalizations of coal mines. In both countries coal happened to be a "sick industry," suffering from decline in demand, chronic underreplacement of capital assets, rising costs, fragmentation into innumerable independent pits, and technological obsolescence. A horizontal merger under the guise of nationalizations appeared to be the only viable remedy. It amounted to more than a "socialization of losses." It produced a recovery similar to that which often follows ordinary mergers, and for similar reasons: shake-up of management, closing of inefficient units, and concentration of resources on the ones kept in operation. The generous supply of funds from the treasury of the state was, of course, essential for the salvage operation to succeed.

Public entrepreneurship has been called upon to remedy an analogous situation in certain portions of the United States railway net (the case of Eastern railroads and Conrail). Cases of individual firms facing bankruptcy and rescued by governmental intervention or nationalization are essentially the same (the British Rolls-Royce in 1971, United States Lockheed, and others). The contrasting example of the French government resisting strong pressures to rescue a losing proposition, as in the case of the watchmaking concern Lip (in 1973), points to a problem raised sharply by *The Economist* for Britain: "Is there, in practice, a policy at all, or does the state merely rush in to save lame ducks? . . . Should the state confine itself to lame ducks? Why lumber public enterprise with whatever is worst . . . ?"[29] The socialization of business risk through bailouts on the part of the state brings into the market-capitalist system an element which recalls strongly the way in which bureaucracy under Soviet-type state capitalism covers up its own mistakes :"A game in which there are no losers puts no premium on good management or good economic policy. . . . The economy will have no built-in discipline, no way of confirming good decisions and revising bad ones."[30]

Comparative Efficiency

The last point brings up a central issue. How efficient have public enterprises been, in general, compared to the private sector of "mixed economies"? There is a widespread belief that public enterprise is inherently less efficient than a private firm. The excellent reputation earned, for instance, by the Tennessee Valley Administration in the United States does not appear sufficiently conclusive; such cases are usually canceled out, in the public mind, by the example of the United States Post Office or the French telephone service.[31] On the other hand, users of, say, the German Bundesbahn and Trans-European Express trains have few complaints about public enterprise in that sector. From yet another point of view, practices of the British Railways have not always been praised by observers of their performance, though, interestingly, they draw greatest fire when management sets out to apply strict "commercial criteria," such as to require that every single mile of track "pay for itself."[32] French public enterprise is symbolized by Renault automobile works and Electricité de France: Renault held its own in the world competition, and it beat the private Citroën to the competitive game; French alumni of the Ecole Polytechnique, in charge of the power industry, have become world-famous for developing and applying theoretically ingenious methods of pricing and investments in the utility field—one of the few entrepreneurs putting the gospel of marginal-cost pricing to practical use. Thus, piecemeal observations yield a picture which is neither universally somber nor glowing.

Fortunately, in the case of Britain, we now possess a comprehensive evaluation by Richard Pryke, in which statistical evidence supports a passionate defense of the nationalized sector against its detractors.[33] Richard Pryke chose to use growth of sectoral productivity as his major criterion of comparison, and came to the conclusion that, on the average, labor productivity, as well as total factor productivity, grew faster in the public-enterprise sector than in private manufacturing. Moreover, from an international perspective, British nationalized sectors performed, in terms of productivity increases (between 1958 and 1968), as well as

---

[29] *The Economist,* May 10, 1975, p. 39.

[30] John Cobbs in *Business Week,* Jan. 27, 1975, p. 16.

[31] See the discussion of differences as in national attitudes toward public enterprises in Andrew Shonfield, *Modern Capitalism,* Oxford University Press, New York, 1965, pp. 73–76, and 301–307.

[32] Alec Nove, *Efficiency Criteria for Nationalized Industries,* G. Allen, London, 1973, passim. See also the section on cross-subsidization in Chap. 8.

[33] Richard Pryke, *Public Enterprise in Practice,* MacGibbon & Kee, London, 1971.

the same sectors in most other countries, while private manufacturing performed significantly worse.[34]

It may be asked whether other criteria than productivity should not be taken into consideration. One often hears grumbles about public enterprises "operating at a loss." However, relative profitability need not be the most appropriate yardstick, for a number of reasons. Having the function of monopoly control "from within," public enterprises are not free to indulge in monopolistic pricing practices. Governments often try to stem inflation by preventing price increases in sectors over which they have greatest control. Also, public enterprises are expected to assume social responsibilities and take into account externalities which are particularly pervasive in the case of "social overhead" and provision of the economic "infrastructure." Being complementary to private branches, public enterprise may be suffering low returns in its accounts, for the sake of making it possible for the private sector to rake up high profits! In any case, the growth-of-productivity record alone emboldens R. Pryke to state that "ownership matters." In his words, "the relationship between good behaviour and public ownership must henceforth be regarded as one of cause and effect."[35]

The comparative performance of the private sector in Britain, which has its share of responsibility for British economic ills (see Chapters 10 and 12), has put on the agenda the possibility of new forays of state entrepreneurship into the territory of private enterprise. After twenty-five years of relative stability, a new Industry Bill, introduced in 1975, turned nationalizations into an open-ended affair again, but this time with a difference. A proposed National Enterprise Board would be able to buy into private companies without being restricted to any particular industry or to salvaging lame ducks. This might allow for public participation to act as a catalyst of progress. If this were to be the case, we would see Britain adapting to its purposes another country's formula, namely, public entrepreneurship Italian style.

ITALIAN PUBLIC-ENTERPRISE FORMULA

The segment of the Italian public sector which has attracted the greatest attention, the "IRI formula," first of all differs in spirit from all other types of nationalization. French public-sector management impresses observers by its climate of professional technocratic perfectionism. The British one is marked by its "fishbowl" characteristics of incessant public scrutiny, internal audits, commissions of inquiry, and regular detailed reports. The Italian one

> creates a large and varied complex of technical cadres, which are able quickly to exploit new opportunities for industrial investment . . . in a position to pop up, like any other lively entrepreneur, in unexpected places. . . . The public or semi-public enterprise is a gadfly . . . looking for places where private enterprise is soft or where its prices are too high or its profits too large. . . . There is none of the French esprit de corps uniting the great officials of the state, none of the feeling that they ought to

[34] Ibid., pp. 160–165 and table 17, p. 162.
[35] Ibid., p. 445.

have a purpose in common. Instead the "condottiere principle" . . . takes charge.
. . . Individualism seems to have scope to run riot.[36]

One gets an inkling of some intriguing connections which undoubtedly exist between economic behavior, national psyche, and organizational principles. Let us leave it at that, and turn to the last aspect, interesting enough in itself.

There are several major subsystems in the Italian public-enterprise sector: the standard administration of railroads and communications; the national electricity company (ENEL), financially autonomous, established in 1962; and a host of public holding corporations, running and controlling clusters of operating companies via a complex system of shareholding. Of the holding corporations only two stand out: the National Hydrocarbon Board (ENI, Ente nazionale idrocarburi) and the Institute for Industrial Reconstruction (IRI).

ENI has been a phenomenon in a class by itself, especially in 1953–1962, under the legendary leadership of Enrico Mattei, a colorful, strong personality who gave the organization his dynamic imprint. Descendent of a moribund prewar office in charge of oil prospecting, it was established in grand style in 1953, after important natural-gas discoveries in northern Italy. ENI took over a handful of state-controlled companies associated with the extraction and processing of natural gas, but before anyone knew, Mattei transformed it, with a flair for drama, into an industrial empire of oil refineries, pipelines, gas stations, diversifying into other branches, including printing and hotels,[37] and engaged in swap deals with Russia for cheap oil. This business saga prompted A. Shonfield to remark that "it seems nowadays that the bosses of great public enterprises often operate with greater personal freedom of decision than the typical head of the big corporation in private industry."[38]

IRI has had a less personalized history, though the element of individualistic aggressive entrepreneurship of the public-enterprise technostructure is by no means absent. However, the principles on which IRI is run have a more general significance, and perhaps applicability. In contrast to classic nationalizations of the British or French type, which amount to horizontal mergers, IRI is a clear-cut conglomerate. One gets a complete helicopter view of its pluralism by inspecting the large organization chart of IRI inserted at the end of the monograph edited by Stuart Holland.[39] However, it is also demonstrated in the overall degree of state participation in manufacturing. In other European countries, of the total number of public-sector employees, rarely more than 10 percent work in manufacturing; in Italy, 26 percent do.[40] ("IRI is into just about all that moves in Italy: steel, ship-building, engineering, Alfa Romeo, Alitalia, telephones, motor-

[36] A. Shonfield, op. cit., pp. 189, 191, and 196–197.
[37] See M. V. Posner and S. J. Woolf, *Italian Public Enterprise,* Duckworth, London, 1967, pp. 53–56; also ibid., pp. 184–185.
[38] Shonfield, op. cit., p. 185. We may recall, in this connection, Robert Moses of the New York City Port Authority, who was in some ways Mattei's American counterpart in the municipal sphere.
[39] Stuart Holland (ed.), *The State as Entrepreneur,* Weidenfeld and Nicolson, London, 1972.
[40] Estimates of the Centre Européen de l'Entreprise Publique, in *Les entreprises publiques dans la Communauté Economique Européenne,* Donod, Paris, 1967, p. 585. (These figures are not comparable to those in Table 13-1, owing to different definitions.)

ways and God knows what else down to Motta ice-cream," writes *The Economist* of February 8, 1975, in a capsule report.)

The origins of IRI under the prewar fascist regime were as unglamorous as its postwar role was impressive. It was established in 1933 in order to provide state financial assistance to banks and firms pushed toward the brink by the Depression, and in a great number of cases it was forced to take complete possession of chronically insolvent firms. Shonfield calls it "perhaps the most absent-minded act of nationalization in history."[41] The state resigned itself reluctantly to its unwanted charges, and after the war discovered that its position of guardian gave it an opportunity to influence creatively the general course of the economy.

Successes in assisting Italy's postwar economic growth may be traced to three major ingredients: the qualities of the selected managerial personnel; the ample sources of investment finance; and the profit-and-growth-oriented policies of the IRI typical of private conglomerates. The IRI could have done even better if it had not been required by the government to assume other tasks of social importance which impeded its growth. Thus, alleviating the postwar unemployment problem meant keeping unprofitable plants in operation longer than a private owner would, and participating in the regional development of the Italian south meant foregoing more profitable opportunities.

Descriptions of IRI's style of operating give the impression of freewheeling financing of somewhat adventurous undertakings, where a lost gamble in one spot does not matter much because the deficit will be covered by profits earned elsewhere, or by interest-free transfusion of funds from the state treasury. It seems as if one had to qualify considerably the opinions cited earlier about the bad effects upon entrepreneurial efficiency of public assistance to ailing firms. In the Italian context, the "socialization of risk" assumed by public finances has had the result of encouraging daring ventures and thus contributing to the overall dynamism of the economy.

What the nature of this contribution has been is well expressed, in a more technical language, in the following:

> There is an "intra-sectoral" follow-my-leader effect which under low macro-economic growth conditions, operates against enterprise investment, since when the sector-leader stays put, other firms stay with him. But when the state controlled sector leader moves the others also move or risk loss of market share. It is in this sense that the multi-sectoral character of a state enterprise group such as IRI can be employed to reinforce the . . . potential of partial state ownership of the means of production.[42]

There can hardly be a better explanation of the function of "catalyst" in the context of an economic system. As a rationale of nationalizations, it has supplanted the worn-out catchwords of the past, such as "key sectors" or "commanding heights," and inspired other countries to adopt and adapt the IRI formula.[43]

---

[41] Shonfield, op. cit., p. 179.

[42] Holland, op. cit., p. 21.

[43] For a survey of these attempts in Britain (up to about 1970), such as France, Canada, Australia, Sweden, and West Germany, see ibid., pp. 242–265.

JAPAN: FROM *ZAIBATSU* TO *KEIRETSU*

The morphology of Japanese industry is a special phenomenon, but not so special as to call for new analytic concepts. The organizational form of the dominant firms is the corporation. It was imported from the West, together with capitalist technology and under governmental auspices, during the Meiji industrialization era after 1868.

Antitrust Imposed

The extraordinary thing about the prewar corporation in Japan was the extent to which it was used as an instrument of highly personalized control over vast economic empires by a small number of entrepreneurial families (the Big Four, six medium big ones, about twenty in all). In contrast to the Krupps or the Rockefellers, who were satisfied with dominating a single industry, the Mitsuis, Mitsubishis, Sumitomos, Furukawas, etc., held sway over hierarchic structures of companies straddling many different branches. Their "empires" were diversified conglomerates, or combines, with elements of horizontal as well as vertical integration, known by the name of *zaibatsus* (meaning "financial cliques"). Each *zaibatsu* had a center of command, a holding company (fully owned by the family), which held a portfolio of shares in operating subsidiaries. Some of these in turn owned shares in further layers of subsidiaries. Some had strategic functions: Banks supplied loans to member companies, and through loans controlled their activities; trading companies acted as cartel-type agencies in charge of centralized buying and selling. The ties between operating companies were reinforced by interlocking directorates; centrally appointed executives owned anachronistic feudal obedience to the family at the top, their fealty sealed by formal loyalty oaths.

This hierarchical structure was the core of Japan's industrial system at the time of the surrender in 1945. Because of its role in supporting and executing Japan's prewar policies of imperial expansion and aggression, the American command found it logical to dismantle the *zaibatsu* system and purge its top personnel. There never was a case of collusion and concentration of economic power more perfect upon which to let loose American instincts of antitrust.

The antitrust operation of the occupation days had several lasting results: It eliminated the top families from any significant role in the combines; it dispersed shareholding widely, and thus instituted at a single stroke the modern split between ownership of corporate assets and their control; it produced a shake-up in management. Furthermore, the holding-company device was permanently outlawed. Some operating companies were broken up under the Deconcentration Law of 1947, and all companies were expected to be on their own from then on. The Anti-Monopoly Law, enacted also in 1947, established a Fair Trade Commission to keep a watchful eye on any future attempts at reconsolidation, collusion, cartels, takeovers, and other transgressions against competition.

Antitrust Diluted

However, the domestic organizational structures proved resilient to radical change. Antitrust policy amounts to setting up the law against powerful tendencies of an economic and technological nature. In Japan, antitrust law of distinctly foreign and doctrinaire inspiration was confronted, in addition, by domestic cultural patterns, dominant governmental ideology, and exigencies of the economic situation. During the 1950s, the independent companies, former members of the busted *zaibatsus,* found the old trails and paths to each other. The prewar patterns reappeared, but they reappeared with significant differences.

After Japan regained its sovereignty, and even before, the antitrust legislation was punctured through permissive amendments (1949 and 1953) and new laws (1952), legitimizing cartels, mergers, interlocking directorates, and resale price maintenance—always with the proviso that "competition would not be substantially restricted." (Recall the escape clauses, allowing "good cartels," in European and Common Market antitrust legislation.) It was not possible to jettison antitrust entirely. Public opposition and protests of the Socialist party (as in 1957 and 1962) prevented that. However, the government found ways, as we shall see, to accomplish by the back door what it had failed to obtain by the front door. Large and powerful conglomerates, cartel agreements, and noted horizontal mergers became again a thoroughly familiar sight.

Old Patterns Reconstituted

One significant difference with the past has been that the ties linking companies into company clusters have been largely of an informal kind, except for outright mergers. The links grew from functional association rather than from the imposition of a formal table of organization. They were not based on stock ownership, or hierarchy of managerial authority, as they are in Western conglomerates or multidivisional companies.

One instance of functional association has been through the supply of finance. During the period of reconstruction, while investment demand was heavy and cash flow a trickle, banks (which had come through the deconcentration program virtually intact) were the lenders of first resort. They tended to give preferential treatment to the firms which used to belong to the same combine. As internal financing picked up, companies became more independent, but often, to finance major new projects, several companies had to pool their resources in joint ventures—another functional interfirm tie. There also were trading companies acting to strengthen the ties based on exclusive buying and selling between former combine members, which helped their integration.

However, banks and trading companies have not played any strong inward coordinating role. They have been more after diversification in their own spheres. Real, though informal, coordination has been the job of regular council meetings of the different companies' top executives—the "presidents' clubs." This is where information is exchanged and some "indicative coordination" takes place. For instance, it may concern financial help to member companies in trouble, or admission of new companies into the orbit of the group.[44] The new "headless" combines have been obviously in search of some substitute coordinating organ.

---

[44] See an informative account on the Sumitomo ways in *Business Week,* Mar. 31, 1975, pp. 43–48.

It is not that the new type of associations, called *keiretsu* or *guruupu,* have been yearning for the strong authority of former top holding companies. The postwar groups resemble loose *confederations* of independent enterprises, i.e., groupings without a strong central executive. The postwar climate of economic expansion favored the spirit of autonomy and self-direction among individual companies. If there were a felt need for some kind of coordination, the concern was to avoid excessive duplication and cutthroat competition among the growth leaders, not to supplant competition by the comfort of restrictive cartels.

The Japanese blend of toughness and tactfulness in competition was captured by W. W. Lockwood as follows:

> Vigorous rivalry to build new plants and stake out positions in new fields has generated an investment boom reminiscent of an armaments race. Leading groups spread out their commitments from one sector to another in interlacing patterns of investment that appear often to disregard market limitations. . . . Relations among rival firms in large-scale industry are characterized on the one hand by keen competition, which is qualified by much consultation, back-stage collusion, price leadership and other such restraints, on the other.[45]

Despite the insights into the market prospects provided by such contacts, there has been a tendency toward periodic overinvestment. It provided the government with a legitimate reason to intervene by imposing a degree of cartelization "through the back door."

The Visible Right Hand Fighting the Left Hand

Governmental promotion of cartels (and mergers) provides another qualifying footnote to the stereotype image of Japan as a harmonious beehive. It is a story of a three-way conflict which has pitted against each other the powerful establishment of the MITI (Ministry of International Trade and Industry), the FTC (the Fair Trade Commission, the antitrust watchdog), and business. The governmental bureaucracy generally has been imbued with a sense of mission and responsibility for the country's economic achievements. Its philosophy, strongly recalling that of the French *économie concertée,* was well expressed in a 1962 statement by Morozumi Yoshihiko, an MITI official: "In place of the strife under freedom and the compulsion under controls, it is possible to have a 'consent economy.' "[46]

The consent MITI most wished to obtain (or exact) concerned coordination and discipline in cutbacks of production during recessions and in investment plans during expansions. (Such cyclical movement was superimposed upon the generally high growth trend in the 1950s and 1960s.) For this, the FTC had to be either mollified or circumvented. The MITI has used interoffice memoranda to move FTC toward greater leniency in granting approvals of cartel agreements

[45] William W. Lockwood, "Japan's 'New Capitalism,' " in Lockwood (ed.), *The State and Economic Enterprise in Japan,* pp. 495–498. See also M. Y. Yoshino, *Japan's Managerial System,* M.I.T., Cambridge, Mass., 1968, p. 136.

[46] Quoted in Eleanor M. Hadley, *Antitrust in Japan,* Princeton University Press, Princeton, N.J., 1970, p. 398.

and mergers. As FTC was found not sufficiently cooperative, the MITI developed a technique of so-called advice cartels. By acting as a discreet initiator and coordinator, MITI made administrative arrangements which were legally unassailable. Interestingly, when FTC protested, the MITI discontinued the practice, whereupon the FTC did what MITI had wanted by facilitating the formation of "depression cartels." FTC was bowing to the pressure of circumstances. The years in question, 1964–1965, were recession years, and cartels have traditionally been "offsprings of recessions."[47]

Two other exigencies of the economic situation helped undermine the influence of antitrust. One was the relaxation of foreign trade controls in the early 1960s (a consequence of Japan's joining the OECD and the International Monetary Fund). The other was progressive liberalization of restrictions on the entry of foreign capital. Both were perceived as a challenge.[48] The response to the first one was a push toward mergers; a strong belief in efficiency through bigness has been part of the governmental ideology.[49] The response to the second one was increased cross-ownership of stock among companies, intended as a protection against foreign takeovers. Both reactions have worked toward increased concentration and consolidation of interfirm ties.

What about the business vertex of the triangle? The MITI-sponsored cartelization and the rearguard actions to safeguard competition, led by the FTC, have both been resented by the business community. This seems schizophrenic. As we have seen, Japanese business is a priori neither against competition nor against cartel agreements and consolidations. The explanation seems to lie in the mentality of postwar management. With *zaibatsu* holding companies gone, the management teams of individual companies gained in stature and tasted the pleasures of independence and sovereignty. They have resented the extent of authority which MITI has tried to arrogate to itself. (They seem to be more tolerant of the Anti-Monopoly Law administration. It has less clout.) If there is to be restraint of competition, they would prefer it to be their own doing. If closer ties and mergers are needed, it should be on their initiative. Thus, MITI felt forced to resort, on a number of occasions, to real arm twisting. For instance, it cut foreign-exchange allocation for essential raw-materials imports to recalcitrant companies, until they complied with the "advice" of the MITI "advice cartel."

On balance, however, business seems to be sufficiently dependent on governmental favors and goodwill for its executives to prefer to be autonomous with circumspection and to camouflage conflict in traditional Japanese ways: polite

---

[47] The FTC signaled a new counterattack in early 1975 by publishing a detailed report on the concentration of economic power. (*The New York Times,* Feb. 10, 1975.)

[48] See Yoshino, op. cit., chap. 6, pp. 162–195.

[49] The two conspicuous mergers concerned three large Mitsubishi companies in 1964 and two automobile companies, Nissan and Prince, in 1965 (see Kozo Yamamura, *Economic Policy in Postwar Japan,* University of California Press, Berkeley, 1967, pp. 83–84). Note parallel developments in Europe about the same time, described in Philip Siekman, "Europe's Love Affair with Bigness," *Fortune,* March 1970, reprinted in J. M. Samuels (ed.), *Readings on Mergers and Takeovers,* Elek, London, 1972, pp. 248–264, esp. the chart on the consolidation in British computer and automobile industries, pp. 250–251.

indirection, accommodation here, quiet fait accompli there, and saving everyone's face. Moreover, the influence of the state on the economy is not exhausted with the question of antitrust. The role of the state as direct entrepreneur is limited to transportation, communications, and some banking. Otherwise, the government participates in private entrepreneurial decisions, and influences them, without anyone's being able to tell how far or deep the state's communication lines penetrate.

In some cases, the government's visible hand *is* visible: some industries are openly regulated (utilities, mining, cotton textiles, machine industry, and electronics); exports, imports, and domestic investments are openly assisted (and controlled) by credits from the Export-Import Bank, Japan Development Bank, and a host of institutions supporting small business. State influence is more disguised in organs designed for two-way consultations between business and government, such as the Industrial Structure Council with its numerous committees and sub-committees (reminiscent of the French "modernization commissions"), or the Japan External Trade Organization (JETRO), with threads always leading to the MITI. One cannot do better than get a sense of the government's preeminence from the following characterization:

> Japan is a country of paradox. A vigorous private enterprise system in which the state has only marginal economic activity coexists with official supervision of business activity. No other private enterprise economy approaches the same degree of government control of business. But most of this control is expressed not in legal enactments, but in administrative action, or in even less definable "guidance" and "persuasion."[50]

THE SOVIET SCENE: TOWARD A "SOCIALIST CORPORATION"?

The problems Soviet-area economies have been having with industrial organization go back to the original wish of the Stalinist state to rule the economy pervasively with a visible (and iron) hand. Its failure is most instructive. It has become a textbook example of the need to adjust organization to the natural character of economic relationships, and of the absurdity of trying it the other way around.

National Economy as a Single Enterprise

The Stalinist model of centralized planning rested on the notion that the administrative center of the economy needs as much information on the operating units as possible, and ought to direct them by instructions as specific as possible.

The first concession to reality may be seen in the subdivision of each ministry into a number of administrative boards in charge of narrower industrial subsectors. We shall refer to these boards as *glavki* (singular *glavk*), which has been their name in the Soviet Union. In principle, the administrative link led from the *glavk* straight to the enterprise, even though in a large country such as the Soviet

---

[50] Business International, *Japan,* Briefing Paper, Japanese Roundtable, New York, 1965, p. 5, quoted in Hadley, op. cit., p. 390.

Union an important proportion of enterprises was connected to the All-Union *glavk* and ministry via the *glavki* and ministries of individual republics. Also, an enterprise was not necessarily an atom; it could be a molecule made up of plants or could be vertically integrated with other enterprises into a *kombinat*, or horizontally into a *trust*. The second concession has to do with the necessity to aggregate detailed information somewhere on the way up from the enterprise to the ministry, and further, to the central-planning office. We shall return to this later.

Speaking in Western organizational terms, the Stalinist scheme resembled a countrywide combine: a three-tier set of holding companies at the top (Council of Ministers, ministries, and their *glavki*), administering horizontally integrated sets of enterprises at the bottom. The "integration" consisted in their administrative subordination to a *glavk*. On the face of it, horizontal integration of enterprises, i.e., segmentations of economic administration by industries, made sense. In reality—it never was a reality. The neat administrative partitions fell victim to the force of economic circumstances.

We recall from Chapter 9 the discussion of the "elusiveness of consistency" in the assignment of output targets and their allocation as inputs. Inconsistencies in the detail of planned figures have produced a chronic climate of uncertainty about deliveries. This has been the major factor behind the tendency of enterprises, *glavki*, and ministries to try to become self-sufficient. Self-sufficiency always implies diversification. Instead of staying specialized, a production unit bent on self-sufficiency moves toward vertically integrated production. It tries to bring under one roof, namely its own, capacities supplying inputs. Chemical industry goes into producing its own transportation equipment, electricity, instruments, machine tools; the synthetic-fibers industry constructs its own chemical plants, and so on.[51] The arrangement is more costly (e.g., because of short production runs), but at least it can be counted on. In the extreme case, each *glavk* or ministry would re-create a miniature national economy in its own bailiwick. In this way, the administrative "turfs" of *glavki* and ministries looked more and more like vertical conglomerates. Believers in the personal guilt of executives never ran out of opportunities to denounce empire building and departmentalism.

Another source of inefficiency has been associated with the meandering of information flows through the enterprise-ministerial structure. In a capitalist market economy, a firm knows more or less what its needs will be and tries to place its orders well in advance. If shortages develop, it makes a few telephone calls to see who could make a stopgap shipment at short notice. The information flows are lateral—from firm to firm—and direct. In the Stalinist ministerial structure, the *glavk* and the ministry have to secure basic deliveries for their enterprises by dealing on their behalf with other *glavki* and ministries and getting their

---

[51] See Barry M. Richman, *Soviet Management,* Prentice-Hall, Englewood Cliffs, N.J., 1965, pp. 27–29; Michael Ellman, "The Consistency of Soviet Plans," *Scottish Journal of Political Economy,* vol. XVI, no. 1, February 1969, pp. 50–74 (table 2), reprinted in M. Bornstein and D. Fusfeld (eds), *The Soviet Economy: A Book of Readings,* 4th ed., Irwin, Homewood, Ill., 1974, pp. 62–82.

prospective needs worked into the central allocation scheme of the planning office (material balances). When shortages develop, enterprises have to involve their *glavki* again in order to arrange for emergency shipments with their opposite numbers who supervise the suppliers. As everyone is working at full capacity, or says he is, and the superior organs have no precise idea of how their enterprises stand, it is not easy to get through the barrier of "sorry, out of the question." If informal self-help on the part of enterprises does not help, dislocations due to supply bottlenecks take time to disappear. This vertical flow of information along the administrative ladder, required to arrange for lateral transactions, is one of the main sources of informational inefficiencies in the system.

Isomorphism

Robert W. Campbell has dealt with these issues theoretically by using the concept of isomorphism between the structure of production relationships, the organizational structure, and the structure of outcomes desired. "Isomorphism" means a state in which shapes of structures fit each other snugly, as glove and hand.[52] Taking the Soviet case as point of departure, Professor Campbell arrived at the general conclusion that "there is some basic incompatibility between the structure of production relationships in reality and a hierarchical administrative structure."[53] If one tries to visualize relationships between different aspects of interacting economic units (such as geographic location, input-output relationships, or personal ties), one will observe *overlapping network patterns*, not hierarchies. Enterprises integrate and reconcile these networks in the shape of concrete modules. They represent the nodes from which emanate the decisions governing purposeful activities. There is no simple way in which a distant superior administrative organ could substitute for this integrating function of basic economic units, placed as they are at the intersection of all the networks of relevant relationships. This is the fundamental reason why centralization and administrative pyramids are not fit to handle economic processes efficiently. They are not isomorphic.

The Advent of Middle-Layer Organs: Associations

Soviet industry grew up under the Stalinist model of ministerial administration, which was introduced in 1932. Its dysfunctional features were never a secret, but the situation was never clearly defined and confronted. Lingering crisis was accepted as a permanent way of life. In contrast, when the model was exported to other Eastern European countries and installed under the supervision of Soviet experts (around 1950), it created sudden chaos, or at least intolerable conditions. No sooner was it introduced than reforms were contemplated. As far as industrial

---

[52] Flouting of isomorphism can be illustrated by the divergence between the formalistic pattern of asphalted walks on college campuses and the natural paths students tread across the lawn. (The Stony Brook campus of the New York State University is said to be a counterexample: Students were allowed to trace their paths first and only then was asphalt put on top.)

[53] R. W. Campbell, "On the Theory of Economic Administration," in Henry Rosovsky (ed.), *Industrialization in Two Systems: Essays in Honor of Alexander Gerschenkron,* Wiley, New York, 1966, p. 195.

organization is concerned, the major feature everywhere was the abolition of the ministerial system of operational management. The local equivalents of Soviet *glavki* were abolished. Their authority devolved upon entirely new organs. Unlike *glavki,* these were not part of the governmental administrative apparatus proper, but *were integrated with the enterprises they were supposed to head.* Ministries, stripped of *glavki,* were expected to be relieved of the tasks connected with the detailed running of enterprises, and to concentrate on major policy questions: broad coordination, and especially the long-term structural and technological development of the branches. We shall call these intermediate organs *associations,* according to the East German, Polish, and Bulgarian (and later Soviet) usage, though elsewhere they were given other names. But everywhere they were presented as the dawn of economic decentralization.

However, one cannot tell the character of these associations from their place in the organization table alone. Their role depends entirely on their specific rights and duties, and on the character of all accompanying measures, i.e., on the over-all direction of the reform. For one thing, it is necessary to make a distinction between two kinds of decentralization: *administrative decentralization,* where the top organs delegate supervisory tasks to lower ones but do not grant them any autonomy, and *decision-making decentralization,* where associations and enterprises receive a greater leeway to make decisions on their own. Under administrative decentralization one merely decentralizes the implementation of centralism. Associations act as mere "transmission belts," very much like the former *glavki.* Under decentralization of decision making, associations acquire a certain amount of independence; they play the role of "administrative cartels."[54] However, the "cartel role" may, in turn, mean different things, depending on how authority is distributed between the center and the association on one hand, and between the association and its enterprises on the other. As for the latter, the association may lord it over the enterprises and treat them as subsidiaries in a prewar *zaibatsu*-type combine; or it may act as their agent and perform certain services on their behalf and for their benefit. Associations may also represent a cross between the transmission-belt and the administrative-cartel types.

To find which particular formula applies, we have to be much more specific as to which country and which period we are talking about. A clue to the character of the association is the nature of the economic reform in each particular case. In Chapter 9, we made a rough distinction between tame, halfway-house, and radical reforms. As one may expect, the transmission-belt function of associations fits into the tame reforms. Associations of the administrative-cartel type go hand in hand with halfway-house and radical reforms. The less products are allocated centrally and the fewer investment decisions are reserved to the center, the greater is the autonomy of associations. The greater the reliance on the market, the more weight enterprises have within the association-enterprise complex. Thus, we find transmission-belt associations in East Germany (1958–1964) and Czechoslovakia (1958–1967), crossbreeds of transmission-belt and administrative-cartel types in East Germany (from 1964 on), Poland, Bulgaria, and Roma-

---

[54] The term was suggested by Pryor, op. cit., p. 225.

nia; administrative-cartel types, leaning toward the enterprise-agent function, in Czechoslovakia (1967–1974) and Hungary (from 1968 on).[55] There have been reversals toward greater transmission-belt functions in East Germany from 1969–1970 on, and in Czechoslovakia from about 1972 on, and others may be under way elsewhere.

What exactly are the administrative-cartel functions of associations? The major ones may include any combination of the following: market research (domestic and foreign); development of new products; promotion and introduction of new technologies; research and development; major investment projects; allocation of investment funds and reallocation of profits among enterprises of the given set; mergers among enterprises within their jurisdiction; coordination of joint investment projects undertaken by groups of enterprises; long-range projections; and structural revamping of the given sector.

As time progressed, especially from the end of the 1960s on, the latest wave of technological innovations made planners acutely aware of its implications for industrial organization and management; the need to think in terms of broad innovative strategies, asset formation, and organization, and to outgrow the mentality of "petty tutelage." This trend superseded the call for market competition between autonomous enterprises. Thinking shifted toward "strategic management from a higher standpoint." Thus, reversals toward greater transmission-belt functions mentioned before, as well as the Soviet 1973 reform to be discussed shortly, also reflect this change in thinking. The trend points toward a strengthening of the role of associations.

Soviet Regional Organization Interlude

Turning now to the Soviet Union, we have to mention the organizational system which was in force from 1957 to 1964, and turned out to be a passing episode: the organization of industry into a system of regional Councils of National Economy (the *sovnarkhozy*), based on the territorial principle. *Sovnarkhozy* replaced the *glavki* for a while as the intermediate tier of organization between ministries and enterprises. The economic rationale of this sweeping change follows from the critique of the Stalinist ministerial model. If ministries tended toward carving up the economy into self-sufficient ministerial empires, it was hoped that large territorial units would reverse the tendency. Enterprises would be integrated into natural interdependent networks based on geographic proximity.

The catch of the scheme was that, here too, territorial administrative units depended on other units for supplies and, in turn, were required to "export" to them. Under the usual conditions of pressure planning, sellers' market, and shortages, the question again arose: "Who is going to get priority?" And in the territorial system the answer was: "Enterprises of our *sovnarkhoz* come first." In this way, ministerial empire building was replaced by local patriotism of the *sovnarkhozy*.[56]

[55] For an approximate survey, see ibid., pp. 226–227.

[56] Oleg Hoeffding, "The Soviet Industrial Reorganization of 1957," *American Economic Review*, vol. 49, no. 2, May, 1959, pp. 65–77, and Michael Kaser, "The Reorganization of Soviet Industry and Its Effects on Decision Making," in G. Grossman (ed.), *Value and Plan*, University of California Press, Berkeley, 1960, pp. 213–244.

However, the political overtones in the territorial reorganization of 1956 may have been more important than the economic rationale. Under the Soviet regime, the party apparatus and the state bureaucracy have traditionally coexisted in a chronic state of tension. Khrushchev, who was promoting the prerogatives of the party, apparently used the reorganization as means to clip the power of ministries and place industry under tighter control of the Communist party apparatus.[57] Territorial units under *sovnarkhozy* had nothing to do with organic "economic regions" of Soviet geographers. They did correspond to territorial party units. There was more isomorphism between the networks of industrial organization and political party organization than any other kind.

This interpretation is consistent with the fact that, in 1964, as soon as Khrushchev was ousted from power, the *sovnarkhoz* system was scrapped and the ministerial system reinstated. The change was accompanied by a series of reform measures which did not significantly alter the pre-1958 role of ministries, though enterprises did see their authority increase somewhat. However, that stage is now also becoming part of history. In 1973, the government announced a new, thorough reorganization of potentially great significance, to be completed by 1976.

The Latest Scheme: Soviet Conglomerates

The linchpin of the 1973 reorganization is the association. The new Soviet association is not supposed to be an administrative organ presiding over enterprises as separate organizational entities. The novelty consists in its being the result of a true merger of a set of enterprises, based on the principles of product relatedness and geographic proximity. Enterprises lose their independent identities. They are demoted to the status of subsidiaries, divisions, branches, or simply plants, to be managed at close quarters by one of them designated as the head enterprise.[58]

The reorganization seems to be complying, to a degree, with the principles of isomorphism. Thus, it does not insist on applying blindly the principle of horizontal integration which would forbid having a heterogeneous collection of industrial activities in one association. The enterprises to be merged are, as a rule, diversified for reasons already explained. The merger is expected to keep the diversification (i.e., the vertically related plants), but to rationalize it: eliminate duplications and consolidate production runs through greater specialization. For example, instead of having each enterprise run its own workshop whittling away at a multiplicity of standard spare parts, one piece at a time, one workshop will now be able to take care of one type of spare part for the entire association. Cases of pure horizontal mergers are not excluded but may apply only to producers of select items (such as ball bearings), organized across the entire country (in all-Union associations), or across large republic associations.

---

[57] See P. J. D. Wiles, *The Political Economy of Communism,* Harvard, Cambridge, Mass., 1964, pp. 42–43 and 159–163; Jerry F. Hough, *The Soviet Prefects: The Local Party Organs in Industrial Decision-making,* Harvard, Cambridge, Mass., 1969, pp. 104, 108, and 189–191.

[58] This account draws heavily on the analysis by Leon Smolinski in *Survey,* vol. 20, no. 1, Winter 1974, pp. 24–35. See also Alice C. Gorlin, "The Soviet Economic Associations," *Soviet Studies,* vol. 26, no. 1, January 1974, pp. 3–27.

The association will have its own research and development facilities. Gone will be the days when centralized institutes thought up fancy and impractical innovations, at a leisurely pace and at a safe distance from factory halls. Furthermore, the association will receive material allocations in bulk for all its units: a great simplification for the central handling of material balances, and increased room for flexible maneuvering within the association.

Soviet spokesmen have been rather frank about the source of their inspiration. Thus, the economist G. Popov, vaunting the progressive character of the associations, compares them to a multidivisional capitalist corporation which "has become the basic unit of production in all advanced industrial countries, thus reflecting the needs of the scientific revolution and of modern technology."[59] One specific aspect of the multidivisional form deserves a few concluding comments. We mean the financial character of the divisions as independent profit centers.

To be a profit center spells, in Russian, "to work by the *khozraschot*," which is the system of economic and financial accountability described in Chapter 9. Accounting for "cost of goods produced" on the one hand, and sales revenues, plus changes in inventories, on the other, brings out the difference as either positive profit or negative loss. No matter how imperfect the price system, the financial outcome is a reflection of overall performance. Even if profit comparisons between different enterprises are of limited significance, one can at least check realized profits against figures programmed in the enterprise plan, and one can follow the profit movement over time.

Units which do not work by *khozraschot* turn over all their revenues (if they have any) to the appropriate part of the state budget and have their expenditures fully covered from the same source. Their performance is not reflected in any financial outcome. It is natural for, say, the Ministry of Justice to be financed according to the latter "budget system." However, if the same practice is followed by those administrative units which participate in operational economic management, or effectively are management, it has far-reaching implications. As L. Smolinski put it:

> A *glavk,* a ministry, let alone a Gosplan bore no legal or financial responsibility for the consequences of their often ill-informed orders and unfeasible plans. . . . Economic accountability and financial responsibility stopped for all practical purposes at the level of a production unit: a factory, a mine. There was thus a sharp separation between the economic base, i.e., the sphere of production, and the administrative superstructure erected upon it: the former had the responsibilities, the latter the rights.[60]

The 1973 reorganization promises to change all that. Associations, in contrast to the earlier *glavki,* are being put on the *khozraschot.* This means that they have to

---

[59] *Voprosy ekonomiki,* no. 12, 1971, p. 103, quoted by Smolinski, op. cit., p. 31. It should be noted, however, that the Soviets had discovered the virtues of mergers earlier. A number of them were undertaken more or less as isolated pilot projects, under the name of "firmy" or "associations" since the early sixties, during the *sovnarkhoz* and ministerial-system eras.

[60] Smolinski, op. cit., p. 24.

pay their way from internal sources generated by enterprises and are responsible for the payment of what amounts to business profit taxes by the combine as a whole. The association's headquarters are thus involved in the profit performance of their subsidiaries, including the need for internal cash flow for investment purposes, and for the funding of a number of "incentive funds," among them the fund out of which managerial compensations are paid.

* * *

In examining the morphological aspects of the industrial sector under various systems, we have done almost entirely without the conventional concepts of centralization and decentralization. Our preferred concept has been *articulation:* articulation of productive activities into organizational units; corresponding articulation of various components of entrepreneurial decisions; and the relation between organizational articulation and the structure of decision making from the point of view of the "control span" of decisions. It is the same approach that marks the companion chapter on agriculture which follows next.

BIBLIOGRAPHY

Scherer, F. M.: *Industrial Market Structure and Economic Performance,* Rand McNally, Chicago, 1970.

Williamson, Oliver E.: *Markets and Hierarchies: Analysis and Antitrust Implications,* Free Press, New York, 1975 (bibliography).

Pryor, Frederic L.: *Property and Industrial Organization in Communist and Capitalist Nations,* Indiana University Press, Bloomington, 1973.

Averitt, Robert T.: *The Dual Economy: The Dynamics of American Industry Structure,* Norton, New York, 1968.

Silverman, David: *The Theory of Organizations,* Heinemann, London, 1970.

Preston, Lee E.: "Corporation and Society: The Search for a Paradigm," *Journal of Economic Literature,* vol. 13, no. 2, June 1975, pp. 434–453 (bibliography).

Bander, Edward J. (ed.): *The Corporation in a Democratic Society,* H. W. Wilson, New York, 1975 (bibliography).

Marris, Robin: *The Economic Theory of "Managerial" Capitalism,* Free Press, New York, 1964.

——— (ed.): *The Corporate Society,* Macmillan, London, 1974.

de Hoghton, Charles: *The Company,* G. Allen, London, 1970.

Granick, David: *Managerial Comparisons of Four Developed Countries: France, Britain, United States, and Russia,* M.I.T., Cambridge, Mass., 1972.

Silberston, Aubrey, and Francis Seton (eds.): *Industrial Management: East and West,* Praeger, New York, 1973.

van der Haas, H.: *The Enterprise in Transition: An Analysis of European and American Practice,* Tavistock Publications, London, 1967.

Weston, J. Fred (ed.): *Large Corporations in a Changing Society,* New York University Press, New York, 1975.

Chamberlain, Neil W.: *The Limits of Corporate Responsibility,* Basic Books, New York, 1973.

Aaronovitch, Sam, and Malcolm C. Sawyer: *Big Business: Theoretical and Empirical Aspects of Concentration and Mergers in the United Kingdom,* Holmes and Meier, New York, 1975.

Friedmann, W. G., and J. F. Garner (eds.): *Government Enterprise: A Comparative Study,* Columbia, New York, 1970.

Hanson, A. H. (ed.): *Nationalization: A Book of Readings,* G. Allen, London, 1963.

Pryke, Richard: *Public Enterprise in Practice: The British Experience of Nationalization over Two Decades,* MacGibbon and Kee, London, 1971.

Tivey, Leonard: *The Nationalized Industries since 1960,* Alden, Oxford, 1973.

Nove, Alec: *Efficiency Criteria for Nationalized Industries,* G. Allen, London, 1973.

Posner, M. V., and S. J. Woolf: *Italian Public Enterprise,* Duckworth, London, 1967.

Holland, Stuart (ed.): *The State as Entrepreneur,* Weidenfeld and Nicholson, London, 1972.

Broadbridge, Seymour: *Industrial Dualism in Japan,* Aldine, Chicago, 1966.

Lockwood, William W. (ed.): *The State and Economic Enterprise in Japan: Essays in the Political Economy of Growth,* Princeton University Press, Princeton, N.J., 1965.

Hadley, Eleanor M.: *Antitrust in Japan,* Princeton University Press, N.J., 1970.

Yoshino, M. Y.: *Japan's Managerial System: Tradition and Innovation,* M.I.T., Cambridge, Mass., 1968.

Dimock, M. E., *The Japanese Technocracy,* Walker, New York, 1968.

Roberts, John G.: *Mitsui: Three Centuries of Japanese Business,* Weatherhill, New York, 1973.

Gorlin, Alice C.: "The Soviet Economic Associations," *Soviet Studies,* vol. 26, no. 1, January 1974, pp. 3–27.

Smolinski, Leon: "Toward a Socialist Corporation: Soviet Industrial Reorganization of 1973," *Survey,* vol. 20, no. 1, Winter 1974, pp. 24–35.

Chapter 14

Styles in Agriculture

Whether farms are owned by their operators or by private landlords or by land trusts may be a source of convenience or inconvenience to operators, but society at large will not have to make the choice for them. Whether there are family farms or factories in the fields will affect productivity too little for society to object to the choices which are the farmers' own.

Folke Dovring

One would normally not think of picking a specific industry, say, chemicals, for special examination when the subject is to compare entire economic systems. Why single out agriculture? Agriculture deserves special treatment because it plays a particular role in economic development and growth. Also, a unique set of problems is associated with its institutional arrangements. The interplay between economic role and systemic features makes agriculture one of the most absorbing fields of comparative studies.

In advanced economies, agricultural employment declines absolutely and the relative share of agriculture in a growing total output dwindles. It is therefore easy to forget that agriculture is, after all, the primordial sector. The rich spectrum of modern specialized industries developed through a process of splitting off from a single multipurpose sector, centered on agriculture. Developed agriculture depends, to be sure, on other industries for supplies of inputs, but other industries depend on agriculture in a much more fundamental way. Their workers depend on agriculture for the most essential of essentials—"the farmer is the man who feeds them all," as the song says. If it had not been for the productivity of farming proper, differentiation of the economy into specialized sectors would not have been possible. Manufacturing and other sectors could break loose from agriculture only when agriculture became productive enough to provide for the nonfarm population.

ECONOMIC DEVELOPMENT AND AGRICULTURE

This "feeding function" consists, technically speaking, in the *transfer of the marketable agricultural surplus to those active in other sectors*, who themselves are emigrants from the agricultural population, at least originally. This is one of the key topics in development economics, especially in the analysis of the so-called takeoff into industrialization and sustained growth. Here, in the comparative study of systems, we are interested in the institutional side of this transfer. Through what organizational instruments is it accomplished? Which systemic features impede the process? Do farmers trade away their surplus voluntarily? Is it being pried out of their hands under compulsion? What do they get in return? Modalities differ greatly from one economic system to another, and solutions adopted in the early stages of development usually leave deep traces in later systemic arrangements.

Pressures upon agricultural institutions to adapt do not cease with the attainment of a degree of industrialization permitting sustained growth. Once the "takeoff" is successfully achieved, the problem of the initial transfer of surplus resources from agriculture (food and labor) recedes into the background. This is when general growth of productivity and its differential effects upon individual economic sectors come to the fore. As a rule, agriculture loses ground. Relative prices and income per head fall with respect to other sectors. Agriculture is pushed to adapt: Reduce the number of participants ("rural exodus") and continue raising productivity. All this creates new pressures for change in the systemic arrangements: land tenure, size of farm units, type of integration with nonfarm activities. Why should this be the fate of agriculture?

The main reason is the fact that, as productivity throughout the economy progresses and total output grows, demand for agricultural output increases more slowly than demand for other products. This empirical observation is a reflection of the so-called Engel's law. It simply states that, as real incomes increase, the relative saturation comes earlier for foodstuffs than for other types of goods. In other words, the income elasticity of the demand for food is smaller than 1 and declining: for every given percentage increase in income (in the denominator) the percentage increase in the demand for food (in the numerator) is smaller. The consequence of this tendency for relative incomes in agriculture is demonstrated, in a simple way, in the twin diagrams of Figure 14-1.

Why is there so much social and political stress associated with the adapta-

Figure 14-1 Agriculture and manufacturing: interaction of income elasticity of demand, productivity increases, and changes in gross and net revenue.

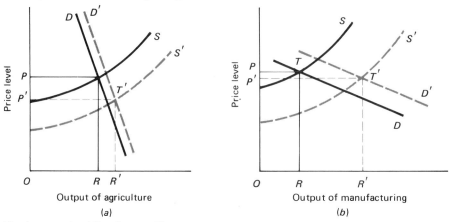

Output of agriculture

(a)

Output of manufacturing

(b)

The two panels of the diagram illustrate the effect of shifts in demand upon total revenue in agriculture and in manufacturing. Demand for agricultural output is relatively inelastic and shifts proportionately less than demand for manufactured articles (Engel's law). In both industries the supply schedule is assumed to fall more or less equally, thanks to cost-cutting improvements in production techniques, i.e., increases in factor productivity.

The shift from one equilibrium situation to another produces an increase in total revenue in manufacturing. Total revenue in agriculture increases less, or may even decline, because the market will not absorb the output capacity of farms except at drastically lowered prices.

If we assume that population and labor force in agriculture do not change much in the given time span, then wage per worker and income per head will have stagnated compared with the possibilities open in manufacturing. To raise income per head in agriculture at a rate similar to that in manufacturing, agriculture must raise productivity by laborsaving methods and displaced labor must be enabled to seek their fortune in manufacturing.

tion of institutional arrangements in agriculture? Generally, one can say that allocation and reallocation of factors of production in agriculture chafe against a combination of rigidities of a particular sort. On the one hand, the basic production factor, land, is in relatively fixed supply and is parceled out among individual owners or collectives according to some legal code or convention. These legal arrangements originate in past stratification patterns and relative power of social and political groups. Reallocation of landholdings in favor of some owners can take place only at the expense of others. Should the reallocation of land become desirable for purposes of economic development or a more equitable income distribution (which may be a matter of survival for some strata of the agricultural population), it is often blocked by the inertia of existing structures of ownership and the resistance of vested interests. Hence the endless historical series of forcible attempts at changing the ownership structure, through violent takeovers or rebellions by the interested parties themselves, through governmental "revolutions from above," or deliberate peaceful land reforms.

On the other hand, the human factor in agriculture tends to resist pressures and inducements which might make for the abandonment of agricultural activities. The reasons are psychological (peasant agriculture has often been characterized as a "way of life" rather than a mere occupation), but also economic: alternative opportunities for both labor and entrepreneurship trained in agriculture are few, and the costs of retraining are high. Sometimes an ideological element is added: A stable peasantry is seen as a mainstay of conservatism—the source of the "strength of the nation," and protected on political grounds.

MORPHOLOGY OF THE AGRICULTURAL SECTOR

Agricultural institutions facing the challenge of economic forces and policy objectives: this is the major theme of this chapter. However, before we deal with illustrative case histories, let us restate this theme. Systemic and morphological aspects of agriculture may be conveniently dealt with under three major topics: size of production units; forms of land tenure and ownership rights; and integration of farm units with related sectors. (Methods of transferring resources from agriculture to other sectors will be treated separately.) Let us briefly examine each aspect in turn.

Size of Farm Units

By "size" we shall mean land area per farm. This meaning is not at all obvious. "Size" may also refer to other dimensions of the production unit: stock of capital, employment, or output capacity as measured, e.g., by value of sales. Size of farms in terms of area is of special interest because of the important, though elusive, notion of "optimal farm size."

It is with respect to some such notion that we judge certain distributions of farms by size as inefficient or inequitable. A given country's agricultural system may contain too many suboptimal farms, insufficient to provide a livelihood for the households of the operators and to keep them fully employed. Or it may be slanted toward excessively large units which create problems of inefficiency, mainly because the tasks of coordination and supervision of farmhands swell beyond the capacity of management. Some economic systems contain both kinds of inefficiencies side by side (see later references to Latin America and the Soviet Union).

How is the optimal farm size to be defined? It would be wrong to look for a definition in terms of some absolute number of hectares per farm. For one thing, different crops or livestock products require different amounts of land per unit of output, e.g., wheat versus chicken. Typical farm size also varies according to the rural density of population which determines the local land/labor ratio. Countries of old settlement and high population density tend to have small units (farms smaller than 2 hectares represent about 70 percent of all farms in Japan and 85 percent in South Korea; for Europe outside the Soviet area the average is about 5 hectares per farm, ranging from less than 3 hectares in Yugoslavia and Italy to 14 hectares and more in Denmark and the United Kingdom). In contrast, countries of relatively recent settlement have predominantly large farm units (two-thirds of United States farms are of the 50- to 500-hectare size, two-thirds of

Canadian farms have from 100 to 500 hectares, 88 percent of Australian farms have more than 200 hectares).[1]

Absolute farm size by itself is not enough to enlighten us about productive efficiency. In countries of a low land/labor ratio the relative scarcity of land may be made up for by intensive cultivation, resulting in agricultural systems characterized by *high yields per hectare*. In countries with high land/labor ratios, scarcity of labor may be made up for by application of laborsaving machinery. The result is the so-called extensive farming with low land yields and *high labor productivity*. The diagrams in Figure 14-2 provide a convenient way of obtaining at a glance a comparative picture of these different types of agriculture.

The definition of a farm optimum therefore has to be flexible. In the words of Theodore W. Schultz, the Chicago agricultural economist, "The critical question is not one of scale but of factor proportionality." In other words, the amount of factors that can be varied by small increments (such as land and other variable inputs) should be as large as necessary to keep any indivisible factor—one that comes only in lump units—fully occupied. It may come as a surprise to learn that empirical application of this principle of factor allocation came to favor, according to prevailing opinion of Western economists, a family farm: the optimal scale is the one which fits the managerial control span of a farm household. "Management," in this case, is the indivisible factor. However, one must add that the factor-proportionality argument is usually compounded by considerations of the farm operator's incentives.

Because of recurrent controversies on the subject, it is worthwhile to spell out the theoretical reasoning used to explain the superiority of family farms observed empirically. For a number of reasons, technological economies of scale tend to be exhausted at a much earlier point in agriculture than in manufacturing. Most material inputs vary in proportion with the cultivated area. They represent constant cost to scale. In contrast to that, transportation costs rise with distance from the farm center. Efficiency of management declines with size because of the difficulty of maintaining a uniformly intimate knowledge of soil, crop, and weather conditions. If wage labor is to be used, cost of supervision goes up with area because it is hard to check on performance "over the hill."

Furthermore, division of labor has fewer opportunities in agriculture. In manufacturing, scale may be enlarged by having successive operations performed side by side by specialized teams of workers in a continuous process. On a given area in agriculture, successive operations have to be performed in sequence under the dictate of an immutable sequence of biological processes. *The duration of the production cycle cannot be compressed by a greater division of labor*. Seasonality of work prevents the steady employment of a large work force. Thus, a variety of technical reasons, besides the built-in self-interest of the farm household (which eliminates the cost of supervision) and limits of the control span (informational and managerial diseconomies), give a decisive edge to the family farm over scale

---

[1] United Nations, Food and Agricultural Organization, *Report on the 1960 World Census of Agriculture*, Rome, 1971, pp. 51–54. (The metric unit of 1 hectare is equivalent to 2.47 acres.)

Figure 14-2 Differences in technical aspects of different types of agricultural systems.

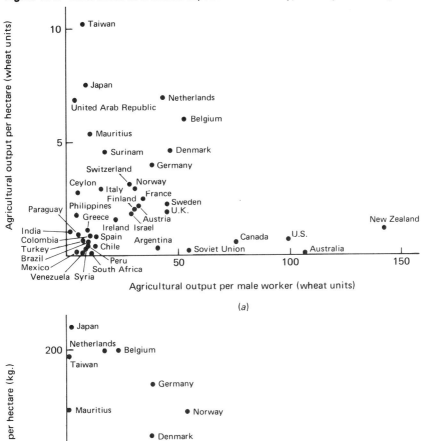

(a)

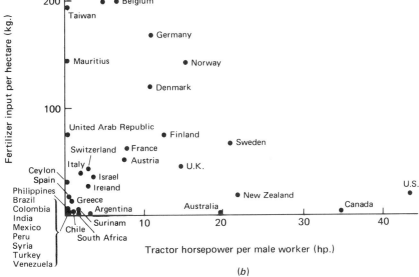

(b)

Panel a: International comparison of agricultural output per male worker and output per hectare of agricultural land (around 1960). Panel b: International comparison of tractor horsepower per male worker and of fertilizer input per hectare of agricultural land (around 1960). Tractor power per worker is associated with the level of labor productivity. Application of fertilizers is associated with agricultural yields, i.e., productivity of land.

Source: Yujiro Hayami and Vernon W. Ruttan, *Agricultural Development: An International Perspective*, Johns Hopkins, Baltimore, 1971, pp. 71–72 (observation for the Soviet Union inserted by us). Copyright © 1971 by The Johns Hopkins Press. All rights reserved.

units achieved by other types of organization. This does not mean that the absolute size of an optimal farm cannot increase over time as technological progress enables a farm household to handle efficiently an increasingly larger area.

Why does the technological factor not determine the optimal size with an iron necessity? Offhand, one would expect modern farm machinery to make the family farm obsolete. However, many elements of technological progress in agriculture are independent of scale (e.g., seed and breed improvements). Tractors come in all sizes. And insofar as some technical operations can be performed more efficiently on larger units than the family farm, they can always be separated out and taken care of through cooperative arrangements, all the way from communal breeding bulls and machine cooperatives to government-sponsored irrigation works and agricultural research. Thus, it is possible to articulate institutional arrangements so as to reap technological advantages of scale available for each partial operation, while the family farm remains at the hub of the system.

In conclusion, let us say a few words on the size distribution of farms within a given agricultural system. For this purpose, farms are sometimes classified according to how many family units they could support. Subfamily farms are those whose area is too small to support a two-worker family under income levels and technology prevailing in the family-farm sector of the particular country. This kind of classification does not have the same significance for different countries. Thus, in Western Europe (except for Italy, Spain, and Portugal) subfamily farms typically belong to part-time farmers whose main income source is outside agriculture proper.[2] In contrast, for other areas such as Latin America, this type of farm distribution means much more because agriculture is the only source of livelihood for most operators of subfamily farms. In some countries, up to 90 percent of all farm units are of the subfamily size (as in Ecuador, Guatemala, or Peru), and a small number of underutilized large estates ("latifundia") cover 50 to 85 percent of the land.[3] Various characteristics of this distribution model make it a chronic cause of rural poverty and economic stagnation. As we shall see, the Soviet agricultural system—despite vast differences in the general environment—presents some surprising analogies to that of Latin America, private plots of Soviet farm workers being a version of subfamily farm units.

Tenure and Ownership Rights

In dealing with the tenure aspect we shall once more make use of our classification of ownership models developed in Chapter 3. The pertinent point is the possibility of splitting the actual custody (disposition or operational rights) from the legal ownership title. They can be vested in different subjects, and the usufruct may be divided up between them according to a variety of rules. The one who tills the land need not be the one who owns it. The one who reaps income from the land need not be the one who tills it.

---

[2] See, for instance, data for West Germany in United Nations, Food and Agricultural Organization, op. cit., pp. 83–84.

[3] See Solon L. Barraclough and Arthur L. Domike, "Agrarian Structure in Seven Latin American Countries," *Land Economics*, vol. XLII, no. 4, November 1966, pp. 391–424, reprinted in Rodolfo Stavenhagen (ed.), *Agrarian Problems and Peasant Movements in Latin America*, Doubleday, Garden City, N.Y., 1970, pp. 41–94.

Another pertinent point is the relationship between those who perform managerial and entrepreneurial functions and those who supply labor services. The two functions may be assumed jointly by one person (or a group), or they may be exercised by different classes. The state may interfere. It may modify the legal ownership patterns, participate in managerial decisions and operations, and share in the usufruct. Combinations of these various possibilities appear in actual agricultural-tenure models of the contemporary scene.

There are two basic models of agricultural land tenure: the *owner-operated farm* and the *capitalist farm*, i.e., an estate operated on account of the owner (by the owner or through appointed staff) with the help of hired wage labor. All other types are mostly modifications of the two basic ones.

The owner-operated farm may be an individual family farm—a *freehold* or homestead—prevalent in the United States, Japan, Poland, Yugoslavia, and most of Western Europe. Such farmers may also supplement their holdings by leasing land from other landowners. In the extreme, they may farm only leased land as *tenants*. They are then, technically, noncapitalist entrepreneurs running agricultural production units without being landowners. This system is widely encountered in advanced economies, such as Great Britain, as well as underdeveloped ones, such as India.

The owner-operator may also be a larger group, such as an internally organized collective. The archetype of this communal model is the Israeli *kibbutz*. Finally, a combination of these two modalities, individual owner-operated farms and collective farming, is represented by various cooperative arrangements of a number of independent family farms. Their voluntary association permits them to undertake some decisions or technical-economic operations in common, while most of the actual cultivation of the land is done in family-size units. This is the general formula for *agricultural cooperatives*.

The *capitalist model* is exemplified by farms in mostly tropical plantation economies or by the agricultural corporation in certain areas of the United States. This is the private-ownership variant of the capitalist farm. The *state-capitalist variant* exists mainly in the form of state farms in the Soviet Union, Eastern European countries of the Soviet sphere, and China. The "absentee owner"—the state—delegates most managerial tasks to appointed farm directors, while labor is supplied by hired wage workers.

Certain *hybrid ownership combinations* of great practical importance pose analytic difficulties. Thus, there may exist a curious economic interdependence between large estates and the subfamily farm sector. At the same time, there may be discrepancies between legal fiction and social reality. We are thinking mainly of the Latin American *haciendas* with the attached sub-subsistence family units, and the Soviet-type collective farms with their private-plot sector.

In the Latin American environment, large estates (latifundia or *haciendas*) appear formally as capitalist units using wage labor, and the small subfamily units (minifundia) as the sector of independent, mostly owner-operated or tenant-operated family farms. However, the system bears heavy traces of its basically feudal origins. Originally, minifarms were functionally a part of the large estates. They were holdings of the aboriginal population burdened by the authority of the conquerors with specified labor obligations vis-à-vis the estates (essentially forced labor or *corvée*); or they were remnants of former freeholds of Spanish settlers and Indians, portions of which were absorbed by the estates; or, finally, they were parcels of estate land ceded by the landlords to individual farmers as tenants in exchange for a portion of the harvest (sharecropping) or for work on the estate (peonage or "service tenancy"). The peasants usually received certain benefits in kind from the estate, e.g., grazing rights on pasture land.

Many of these arrangements survived even after land reforms had promoted private ownership of the small farms and changed the form of compensation for work on estates into wages. What has not changed is the insufficiency of the income derived from the private-plot cultivation, as well as of wages from work on the estates, from the point of view of the small peasant's subsistence needs. Subfamily farm operators could not survive if they did not turn into hired hands part of the time. At the same time, the estate could not operate if it were not for the labor supplied by the small peasants. This symbiotic interdependence is well expressed by the term *latifundio-minifundio complex.*

Despite the formal presence of wage labor (which normally defines the capitalist relationship), the large estate of this sort does not quite fit the capitalist model of the firm. The missing element is the capitalist entrepreneur. Landlords are typically not interested in maximizing profits and reinvesting them for the sake of expanding output and cutting costs under market-competitive pressures. They are classic *rentiers* who view their asset land as a mere source of personal income allowing them to live luxuriously away from farms run indolently by salaried managers. The latifundio-minifundio complex is a model of its own kind.

With all due respect to many substantial differences, the same is true of the *Soviet-type collective farm* (*kolkhoz*). Formally, it is a cooperative, constituted by collective-farm peasants as members, though without any alienable ownership rights to a share of the property. Effectively, it is a combination of a large estate managed by the *kolkhoz* bureaucracy (chairman and his administrative, technical, and supervisory assistants), and small private plots reserved for individual cultivation by peasant households. The actual absentee owner of the *kolkhoz* estate again is the state. The state exercises its substantive ownership rights by remote control through the supervisor—the *kolkhoz* chairman—by making important decisions for him, and regulating the manner in which the state secures its share in the usufruct of the land. The *kolkhoz* rank-and-file member is effectively a part-time worker on the estate and part-time private-plot operator. Since the state is interested in maximizing its share of the usufruct, it is considerably easier to interpret the collective farm as a particular incarnation of the capitalist model than the Latin American *hacienda* with its semifeudal features.

Agriculture and Related Sectors: Integration versus Subordination

There are activities which are part of the business of farming but, unlike the raising of crops or livestock, need not be performed by farm operators themselves. The commercial side of agriculture is one such activity: buying inputs, selling outputs, obtaining credit. Similarly, there is no clear demarcation line at which processing of agricultural output on the farm must stop and specialized firms must take over, as for instance in the case of processing milk into marketed grades and other dairy products.

The relationship between farm units proper and closely associated nonfarm activities is an important issue. Once such activities are organized in specialized firms outside the agricultural sector proper, the question arises: Who has control over them? They may be run under the control of associated farmers, or else under the control of nonfarm entrepreneurs (or agencies) acting in their own interest. If it is the farmers who create and control such specialized establishments, we speak of vertical integration of farming with adjoining activities. In the contrary case there is a clear separation of sectors. The boundary may then easily become an economic battlefront where farm and nonfarm interests clash and the possibility of exploitation arises.

Vertical integration of farming with related activities usually takes the form of agricultural cooperatives, parallel to those which assume certain technical functions of farming on behalf of the member farms. In some ways, agricultural cooperatives are to the farmer what labor unions are to workers. They represent a response of an atomistic sector, composed of numerous competing units, to the threat of monopolistic exploitation. Wherever a monopoly of buyers (usually called monopsony) faces a fragmented group of sellers each acting on his own, the sellers lose. A few wholesale dealers are apt to pay farmers, who are in competition with each other, lowest possible prices. The "terms of trade" turn against competitive agriculture. This effect of monopsony is then added to the other, more basic, price-depressing effects which were discussed earlier (recall Figure 14-1 again), unless farmers manage to overcome their bargaining disadvantage by creating their own countermonopoly of sellers through marketing cooperatives.

The defense against price exploitation is also the driving motive behind purchasing cooperatives buying inputs in bulk, cooperative credit institutions, and processing plants such as mills or dairies. The home of the cooperative movement has been Scandinavia, the Netherlands, and generally Western and Central Europe, whence it has been spreading in all directions. Historically, the impetus toward cooperative associations was given toward the end of the last century by the influx of cheap agricultural products from overseas.

Where farmers' self-help through cooperatives is weak or missing, it may be substituted for by *governmental protection*. Policies designed to support farm prices, import duties on agricultural products, subsidies, and supply of credit to agriculture are meant to shelter the farm sector against some of the ravages of uncontrolled economic forces, as the cooperatives would. On the other hand, there are agricultural systems where the state assumes the control of marketing and other farm-related activities in order to squeeze the agricultural sector to the utmost. This has been the case in Soviet-type systems where the state procurement agencies have traditionally dictated prices and delivery quotas of farm products, and state-controlled machine-tractor stations have for decades taken care of mechanized farm operations at their discretion and for unilaterally imposed fees.

Vertical integration may occasionally proceed in the opposite direction: The manufacturing sector engaged in processing agricultural products may try to turn farms into subordinate production units and fit them into its own plans. For instance, a tire-manufacturing company may take possession of rubber plantations. A step in the same direction has been so-called *contract farming*. It would be wrong to assume that the farmer is necessarily a victim of such arrangements. From his point of view, there may be less risk and uncertainty in supplying a specific customer according to a prearranged contract than in producing for an anonymous market and suffering, for instance, the vagaries of excess aggregate supply and collapsing prices.

TRANSFER OF RESOURCES FROM AGRICULTURE: SYSTEMIC VARIANTS

In the opening of this chapter we mentioned the crucial role played by agriculture in economic development. In the early stages of industrialization agriculture has to bear the brunt of supplying the basic ingredients for laying the ground of manufacturing capacities. It has to release workers for the new industrial construction sites (including infrastructure, such as railroads) and supply food to sustain them while they build the groundwork of industry in the form of nonconsumable investment goods. The transfer of foodstuffs is thus necessarily a one-way transaction. The nonfarm sector, still in the construction stage, is not yet ready to furnish agriculture in return either with consumer goods or with productivity-enhancing farm inputs. *The food supplies amount effectively to the supply of saving*, i.e., the amount of farm output left over after farm home consumption is satisfied. The counterpart of this saving in real terms is the real investment in new industrial capacity. This is the stark formula of the developmental takeoff reduced to its essentials.

The transfer of resources from agriculture may assume different institutional forms, more or less direct, or devious. The most transparent method is the one where a portion of farm output is physically taken away by those who are in charge of organizing the developmental effort, i.e., typically, governmental bureaucracy. The confiscated output is distributed to workers in the industrial-investment sector, recruited by force, appeal, or promise of better wages. Stalinist methods applied in the Soviet Union after forced collectivization of agriculture around 1929–1932 followed this model most closely. Obligatory deliveries of farm output to state procurement agencies, paid for at nominal prices, amounted to an involuntary tribute extracted from agriculture, i.e., an agricultural tax in kind. Labor transfers, too, were obtained through methods marked by naked compulsion.

A more devious procedure consists in the imposition of money taxes upon farmers' income or, as indirect sales taxes, upon items farmers buy. Such tax obligations then force farmers to increase their market sales. They need to raise money from which to pay the agricultural tax or buy taxed items. Marketed foodstuffs are then bought by workers of the industrial sector with their wages, paid out of taxes originally collected from farms. Thus, the circle is closed. (Alternatively, the foodstuffs may be exported abroad in exchange for imports of machinery.) This method was used systematically in Russia during the czarist stage of rapid industrialization in the last decade of the nineteenth century, by Count Witte, the Minister of Finance. It was also applied in Japan throughout the industrialization period of the Meiji era after 1868.

Finally, we come to the most discreet form which develops spontaneously in cases where industrialization proceeds through private initiative of capitalist entrepreneurs.

We may borrow for this case an expression coined by Wynn F. Owen and call it the "Mills-Marshallian model." Professor Owen explains its hidden mechanism as follows:[4] An agricultural sector made up of numerous market-oriented family farms is under constant competitive pressure to adopt all available cost-cutting technological innovations. However, competitive conditions ensure that any profits that accrue to innovators are quickly competed away. In contrast, the nonfarm sector contains enough elements of monopoly—as explained in the previous section—to be able to protect its profit margins. Therefore, in a sense, a portion of profits that might have been earned by agriculture is realized in the nonfarm sector. The nonfarm sector benefits by being able to buy inputs from the farm at low relative prices and to hold on longer to its profits enhanced by its own cost-reducing innovations. The difference between profits agriculture might earn and actually does earn[5] effectively amounts to a tax on farms. It is collected informally by the nonfarm sector and used as a source of finance for the expansion of its own capacities. The mechanism of transfer is dissimulated by the fact that no tax is overtly charged. It is reflected only in the low per capita income in agriculture compared to manufacturing. This differential stimulates further innovations on the farm (the "treadmill effect") and simultaneously induces labor to leave agriculture to seek employment in the expanding sector of manufacturing, which pays better wages.

What about the cases where industrialization has trouble starting? It is often the special character of the agricultural system, especially land tenure, which is responsible for the difficulty of effecting the transfer of saving and labor from agriculture. Flagrant examples are many Latin American countries or India. There the landlords have too much political power to allow the appropriate taxation to be enacted; the market orientation of their farms is of the passive "satisficing," not "maximizing," sort; and there is not enough taste for entrepreneurship either in the government or the society to impose any of the possible models for the transfer of resources.

So far we have presented the issue without paying much attention to possible variations in agricultural output per person while the transfer of resources takes

---

[4] Wynn F. Owen, "Double Developmental Squeeze on Agriculture," *American Economic Review*, vol. 56, March 1966, pp. 43–70.

[5] For instance, the net balance of profits for all United States farms taken together may be zero or even negative. See ibid., p. 56.

place. This is an extremely important aspect which represents one more trait according to which agricultural systems differ. The "stark formula" of the developmental role of agriculture, stated at the beginning of this section, is easy to adapt to deal with such cases.

Its impact upon agriculture will be softened if agricultural productivity of labor and land is sufficiently enhanced to guarantee farmers increasing incomes while they are asked to contribute resources to development.

Growth of productivity in agriculture has its source, to a large degree, in research and development of new techniques, varieties of seed, chemistry of soil and its fertility, irrigation works, reduction of harvest losses, etc. This set of activities is beyond the means of individual farms. Private firms cannot be expected to enter the field because farmers have not the means to pay for such services before they put them to use. The actual returns from their application lie in the future, and long-term credit is not easily available to them.

Whether such activities are undertaken depends in practice primarily on the attitude of governments. If they are ignored or neglected, the "developmental squeeze" upon agriculture can be very hard indeed. It means that the shifts in employment and the imposition of the food tribute can only count on a relatively fixed volume of agricultural output. The farm population cannot enjoy any immediate reward from the developmental effort such as rising consumption per capita. Hence social frictions, resort to compulsion, and discontent. This was the experience of Russia under the above-mentioned Witte system at the end of the last century, and again, in an exacerbated form, under the Stalinist system, from the thirties on to the fifties.

Prominent examples of the opposite approach have been Japan and the United States. American agricultural research in land-grant colleges, established by the government in 1863, and dissemination of advances in knowledge through agents of the extension service have a well-deserved reputation. They were emulated in Japan throughout the Meiji industrialization drive. Interestingly, in both cases progress in technical knowledge, made freely available as a public good, was eagerly absorbed by family farms operating within the Mills-Marshallian model. As a result, increasing agricultural productivity and output helped from their side to attenuate the pains of the industrialization process. Industrialization could proceed parallel to the development of agriculture, rather than at its expense. This was made easier by the fact that the nonfarm sector devoted part of the emerging capacity immediately to supplying agriculture in return with new productivity-stimulating inputs (chemicals, machinery). Agriculture was able to pay for them thanks to that very productivity increase which such inputs made possible. If there ever was a case to which one could apply the Chinese Communist slogan of the fifties—"walking on both feet" (to wit, agriculture and industry)—it is the United States and Japan.

The developmental transfer of resources from agricultural occupations merges imperceptibly into a continuous shift in the allocation of resources as *development* becomes routine *growth* of the developed economy. The major manifestation of this process is the pressure upon labor to leave agriculture. The systemic forms of this exodus may again differ, depending on how the occupational transfer is managed. Are people left to their own devices, even if it means eking out a pitiful existence in marginal conditions of rural poverty or urban ghettos? Is the exodus deliberately slowed down through support programs of agricultural incomes (such as subsidies or price controls), charged to the account of society at large? At more advanced stages of development, the problem of adjustment is aggravated by the dearth of job alternatives for farmers and farmhands. *Agricultural policies then turn out to be actually manpower policies.* The character of the economic system is then shaped by the extent to which society assumes responsibility for some of the human costs of growing productivity and changing occupational structure, i.e., the costs of retraining, relocation, and re-adaptation.

FAMILY FARM SYSTEMS

The United States, Western Europe, and Japan were chosen to illustrate agricultural systems based on family farms. As we saw earlier in the chapter, they are wide apart with respect to average area per farm, but they have one trait in common: unequal distribution of farms by size.

Concentration, or Consolidation and Leveling?

In family farm systems, the degree of inequality of holdings has been incomparably lower than in Latin American agriculture. Only in Portugal and Spain have there been similarities to the Latin American type. Furthermore, differences in the size of holdings have, on the whole, been declining throughout our century.[6] The reason has been the decrease in the proportion and size of the large-estate holdings. To some extent it was spontaneous. Often it was brought about by agrarian reforms bent on redistributing land. The exceptions were England, Sweden, and Belgium, where—especially in England—the average size of the upper 20 percent of farms has kept growing.

The general trend had another corollary: *disappearance of farms using hired labor.* The pure family farm became more and more typical. This means that landownership has tended to be spread more evenly over the agricultural area. However, inequality in land distribution has remained serious enough to leave at least one-half of farms with less land than a family could handle efficiently.

Thus, the unequal size distribution of farms corresponds nowadays to a split-level division. With an allowance for in-between situations, there are two types of family farms. On the one hand, there is the large or good-sized business farm, market-oriented, using inputs purchased from the manufacturing sector, and responsible for the bulk of marketed agricultural produce. (Typically, 10 percent of farm units supply 40 to 50 percent of marketings.) Such a farm behaves and is perceived as a quasi-capitalist enterprise: though using little hired

[6] For a comprehensive comparative survey of the European situation, see Folke Dovring, *Land and Labor in Europe in the Twentieth Century*, 3d rev. ed., Martinus Nijhoff, The Hague, 1965, chap. 3, pp. 113–155.

labor or none, it is run for the operator's profit. On the other hand, there is the farm short of land, run by traditional methods, selling little, and yielding a sub-standard livelihood to the owner. If proper cost accounts were kept, the farm would show losses eating into the owner's personal income.

The present state of "land rationing" is the result of a centuries-long evolu-tion of the peasant freehold from feudal forms of dependency or through settle-ment of virgin land. The small-farm sector developed in function of a number of unrelated variables: relative power of large-estate owners and the multitude of peasants; policies of land reforms and land allocation in areas of recent settle-ment; density of population; topography of the terrain; type of crops; degree of fragmentation owing to different laws of inheritance.

Whatever the origins of the extent of land-starved units, they now present an economic and social problem: that of efficiency and that of equitable (even if not egalitarian) distribution of assets and incomes. Offhand, it would seem helpful to redistribute the land, to take from the large units and give to the small ones. This would certainly be in the spirit of most antifeudal land reforms of the nineteenth century and those enacted after the First World War, when the objective was to provide more employment on land for rural masses. Unfortunately, under pres-ent conditions, such a simple approach is obsolete.

What is it that changed? The astonishing fact is that farms at the upper end of the size distribution, though large relative to the rest, cannot be considered as outsized any more. They tend to be "just right" in light of available technologies as they developed since the Second World War. Thus, there is not much room for redistribution of land that would not cut into the size of viable farms, i.e., farms large enough to provide the operator with a standard of living appropriate to the country in which he lives. As a matter of plain arithmetic, the only alternative is consolidation of small farms into larger viable units and transfer of redundant labor to other occupations.

In some ways, this has been happening spontaneously. Small farmers have been turning increasingly into part-time farmers, supplementing their farm in-come by off-farm employment. Almost one-half of income of the farm popula-tion in the United States comes from nonfarm sources, and 35 percent of farms count as part-time units. The percentage is 32 percent in Holland, 68 percent in Austria, 79 percent in Japan, and 93 percent in Switzerland. At the same time, farms somewhat below the limit of viability have been trying to acquire more land. While small units have been disappearing almost everywhere,[7] the average size of farms has been growing.

However, the adjustment of farms toward larger size has been very slow, slower in Western Europe and Japan than in the United States. Rigidity of farm-ing structures and obstacles to the amalgamation and enlargement of holdings have been too great. Therefore, in some countries, the governments stepped in with instruments promoting agrarian reforms, new style. Since 1960, France has

[7] Between 1960 and 1970, the number of United States farms with less than $10,000 sales per year declined by one-third.

set up semipublic nonprofit corporations buying up land and reselling it with a view to farm enlargement (the SAFER—Societies of Land Management and Rural Establishments). A parallel organization formed in 1962—the FASASA (Fund of Social Action for the Structural Adjustment of Agriculture)—acts to make it easier for farming people to leave agriculture.[8]

From the human point of view, one-family farms notoriously make the farmer a prisoner of his work, especially where livestock is concerned. In that respect, new developments offer interesting remedies. In some countries (Sweden, Holland, France), group farming began to be promoted in recent years, an arrangement under which working time can be budgeted more conveniently (shorter workdays through shift work, alternate free weekends, vacations, sick time). Thus, the traditional individualistic family-farm model is being modified by flexible organization arrangements and may be modified further by individual farm operators learning to form joint management teams. Modern agronomic and commercial knowledge, required for efficient running of a farm, has become too large for a single farmer's head. Thus, economies of scale in agriculture come nowadays from an unexpected side: not from production technology in the physical engineering sense, but from the side of available techniques of management in the knowledge sense. They are now coming to play the role of the indivisible factor, demanding a team of more than one individual to be exploited to the hilt, on correspondingly larger farm areas.

Incomes Policies and Supply Management

Public assistance has been too timid so far to speed up appreciably the spontaneous upward adjustment in farm sizes. Incomes in agriculture have therefore continued to lag behind other sectors,[9] and governments have considered it necessary to protect the slowly responding farm sector or, more precisely, its nonviable portion, from the full impact of market forces. However, the devices used have generally helped farmers who did not need help, while the nonviable ones went without the type of help needed to take them out of agriculture.

Specific national schemes for sheltering the farm sector differ in technical detail, but they usually boil down to some kind of administered price setting (farm-price supports, price guarantees, subsidies, and import tariffs). Unfortunately, the higher-than-competitive prices act as an inducement to expand quantities supplied, a propensity agriculture can ill afford, given its inelastic demand conditions. In consequence, the price guarantors are led either to buy up the surpluses themselves or to resort to "supply management."

History of farm-price supports is full of absurd examples where governments find themselves at one time or another managing unmanageable stockpiles of butter (as in the United Sates and Western Europe) or rice (as in Japan), or

---

[8] See Pierre Coulomb, "Land Policy in France," in David McEntire and Danilo Agostini (eds.), *Toward Modern Land Policies*, University of Padua, Padua, 1971, pp. 79–103.

[9] Farmers in the United States still earn barely three-fourths as much (including their off-farm income) as nonfarmers, though in 1940 the proportion was only one-third. See U.S. Department of Agriculture, *Farm Income Situation*, 1969, p. 50.

processing grapes and sugar beets into alcohol and mixing it with gasoline (as in France). Alternatively, supply management is entrusted to voluntary "marketing boards" of cooperative farmers' organizations or through the imposition of quotas limiting the sown area (as in the case of the United States "soil bank" of the years 1956–1962, followed by various cropland conversion or adjustment programs from 1963 on).

Fortunately, spontaneous arrangements between farmers and their first-line customers in the so-called agribusiness mitigate the need for official intervention. In the case of sugar beets and tobacco, refineries and tobacco companies have pioneered stabilizing *contract farming*. The nature of traditional farming is thus undergoing profound changes through the influence of so-called vertical integrators from among manufacturing companies. In Sweden, for instance, the FINDUS corporation controls 80 percent of the production of frozen and preserved foods, and organizes the supply conditions of crops on the part of individual farm units.[10] The farm becomes a subcontractor whose activities and efficiency are supervised by the "forward link" in a vertically integrated chain of formally separate operations.

Despite temporizing of governmental policies, family-farm agriculture is in a state of flux, and we should be prepared for further far-reaching changes and reforms.[11] The process which has been under way has also important sociological and cultural aspects. Frequently one comes across citations of Karl Marx's views on the "idiocy of rural life" and the anticipated dissolution of the contrast between agriculture and industry.[12] We have been witnessing this transformation taking place at an accelerated rate during the postwar decades, not only in the migration toward urban centers, in the "straddlers" with one foot in the farm and the other out, but, interestingly enough, in the style of life and consumption patterns of the rural population, its exposure to information of all kinds, and its manner of going about the farm business.

Does Corporate Farming Have a Future?

In this connection, mention ought to be made of another expectation of Marx (and others besides him) which did not materialize: the increasing concentration of land in large units and their conversion into capitalist firms employing wage labor, in analogy with the march of events in industry. Many of the reasons why agriculture followed a different path have been touched upon in the earlier general discussion. They have been repeatedly brought to bear upon the question,

---

[10] Similar schemes where the processing sector participates intimately in the management of farms were described in the literature. See, for instance, Jean Valarche on Swiss animal-food industries and Joseph LeBihan on the French case in Ugo Papi and Charles Nunn (eds.), *Economic Problems of Agriculture in Industrial Societies*, St. Martin's, New York, 1969, pp. 325–356.

[11] A useful survey of issues related to this section is to be found in United Nations, Food and Agricultural Organization, *Agricultural Adjustment in Developed Countries*, Rome, 1972.

[12] "Capitalist production completely tears asunder the old bond of union which held together agriculture and manufacture in their infancy. But at the same time it creates the material conditions for a higher synthesis in the future, viz., the union of agriculture and industry on the basis of the more perfected forms they have each acquired during their temporary separation." K. Marx, *Capital*, vol. I, p. 505.

raised in recent years, particularly in the United States, whether there is a future in agriculture for the capitalist corporation. Concern about a possible corporate takeover of American agriculture arose in response to the increasing number of farming corporations in the sixties.

A closer look at the few existing surveys reveals that corporations represent only about 1 percent of all farm units and 7 percent of all farmland. However, of this 1 percent, an overwhelming majority are family farms disguised as corporations, mainly for tax purposes, so that nonfamily corporations might account for only 0.2 percent of all farms and 2 percent of sales—barely a respectable bridgehead.[13] Typically, they specialize in livestock, poultry and eggs, vegetables and fruit for canning or processing. These are types of production where integration of farming with processing and coordination with consumer demand are clearly indicated, especially if capital requirements are high. Here, "factory farms" run on corporate principles, expert in mobilizing finance, have a definite advantage over family units.

One can speculate whether farm corporations are the wave of the future or will remain confined to a few advantageous niches. The prospect of a general amalgamation of farms under corporate auspices is not very likely. Agriculture is not a growth industry and rates of return will remain unattractive; merging land which is split into numerous holdings is an incomparably more difficult task than merging a few firms elsewhere;[14] economies of scale are limited, and seasonality of operations creates difficulties for hiring wage labor. However, whether a corporate takeover is or is not in the cards, there need be no reason for alarm either way. Folke Dovring's statement, used as motto to this chapter, may be suggesting the most reasonable attitude toward this issue, and toward the issue of farm tenure generally.[15]

SOVIET-TYPE AGRICULTURAL SYSTEMS

In England, it took several centuries for landholdings of individual farm operators and rural communities to be expropriated and consolidated into large estates, and for the bulk of peasantry to be converted into hired farmhands.[16] In the Soviet Union and other countries that followed the Soviet example, an analogous change was telescoped into a few years. In both cases, the result was a

[13] William H. Scofield, "Agricultural Corporation Today," in the National Farm Institute, *Corporate Farming and the Family Farm*, The Iowa State University Press, Ames, 1970, p. 17. See also A. Gordon Ball and Earl O. Heady, *Size, Structure, and Future of Farms*, The Iowa State University Press, Ames, 1972, chaps. 15 and 16, pp. 270–313 (bibliography); Philip M. Raup, "Corporate Farming in the United States," *Journal of Economic History*, vol. XXXIII, March 1973, pp. 274–298; Dan Cordtz, "Corporate Farming: A Tough Row to Hoe," *Fortune*, August 1972.

[14] "If a cotton manufacturer had to acquire 1000 hectares for every $250,000 worth of sales of yarn, there would not be many large cotton spinners." (United Nations, Food and Agricultural Organization, *Agricultural Adjustment in Developed Countries*, p. 92.)

[15] The statement is taken from Folke Dovring, "Variants and Invariants in Comparative Agricultural Systems," *American Journal of Agricultural Economics*, vol. 51, December 1969, p. 1272.

[16] For a compact survey and bibliography, see Dudley Dillard, *Economic Development of the North Atlantic Community*, Prentice-Hall, Englewood Cliffs, N.J., chap. 8, pp. 129–149.

certain form of capitalist structure. In the Soviet case, it is important not to be misled by the socialist label. To recall our (and classical Marxian) definition, capitalism is a system where entrepreneurial controls of productive assets are concentrated in the hands of one social group, while labor is supplied by propertyless wage earners. In the Soviet variant, the general model of capitalist organization in agriculture is, of course, modified by special features. These are periodically subject to reforms and adaptations which do not touch the substance. Folke Dovring's relaxed attitude toward arrangements in agriculture is not for political authorities in Soviet-type systems. They have been treating their basic model with doctrinaire rigidity as *the* model of "socialist" agriculture.

Thwarted Family-Farm Development

Russia and the Soviet Union started twice on the way of developing in the direction of a viable family-farm system, the first time in the wake of the revolution of 1905. Under the stewardship of Prime Minister Stolypin the road was opened for peasants to pull out from the archaic bonds of the village commune (the *mir* described in Chapter 3), and to become private proprietors with hereditary land tenure. "Wager on the strong," the motto of Stolypin's reform, expressed the confidence that private property with its incentives would release the initiative of the more dynamic elements among the peasants and lead them, as well as agriculture, to prosperity. A program of consolidation of old Russia's badly fragmented field strips rounded out these promising reforms. They were interrupted most unfortunately by the First World War before they could bear fruit.[17]

The second beginning dates from the twenties. The revolutionary year 1917 witnessed the onset of a spontaneous partition, on the part of peasants, of lands owned by the nobility, the Church, and the Crown. The event was sanctioned by the Bolshevik government, at first with the proviso that peasants could not operate rented land or use hired hands. These prohibitions were lifted only in 1925. Despite a certain reserve and lip service to socialized forms, official policy toward the peasantry seemed to be consonant, for a while, with recommendations associated with the name of one of the Bolshevik leaders, Bukharin: easing the tax burden, creating incentives to expand production and to save, and thus providing a solid base for further industrialization. Bukharin expressed the spirit of the program (then shared by Stalin) by borrowing a phrase from a nineteenth-century French bourgeois politician and addressing it to Russian peasants: "Enrich yourself!"[18]

This course came to an abrupt end toward the close of the twenties. A

---

[17] For two contrasting appraisals of Stolypin's reforms see W. E. Mosse, "Stolypin's Villages," *The Slavonic and East European Review*, vol. 43, no. 101, June 1965, pp. 257–274, and George L. Yancy, "The Concept of the Stolypin Land Reform," *Slavic Review*, vol. 23, no. 2, June 1964, pp. 275–293.

[18] Until that time, Bolsheviks seemed to follow rather faithfully Marx's strictures against forced collectivization, contained in remarks such as this: ". . . The proletariat must adopt measures, in its governing role, that immediately improve the situation of the peasants, in other words that gain him for the revolution; . . . it must not upset him, for instance, by proclaiming the abolition of the right of inheritance or the abolition of his property. . . ." [Karl Marx and Friedrich Engels, *Werke*, vol. 18, Dietz Verlag, Berlin, 1969, p. 633 (our translation).]

combination of economic circumstances and ill-conceived governmental measures created a crisis in grain marketing, which was perceived and denounced as a sabotage inspired by well-to-do peasants (the *kulaks*).[19] Under Stalin's orders, the government resorted to force. Between 1929 and 1933, the bulk of peasant holdings was merged into large-scale collective farms and state farms, under traumatic conditions resembling a pogrom.[20] Slaughter of livestock, especially horses, disastrous famine of 1932–1933, and loss of human lives estimated at about 6 million[21] were among the major social costs of the collectivization enterprise. Other costs will be brought out in the systemic analysis of the institutions and major agricultural policies.

Modalities of Soviet-Type Land Tenure

Distinction has to be made between the "collective farm" and the "state farm" sectors. In form, a collective farm (*kolkhoz*) resembles a producer cooperative. It has—as most Soviet institutions do—the outer trappings of democratic organs and procedures. A general meeting of members (or their representatives) elects the chairman, as well as members of the executive management board and the auditing commission. At the brigade level—a brigade is a *kolkhoz* subdivision— the brigade meeting ratifies some decisions and elects a council, as well as representatives to the general meeting. Along the lines of executive authority, however, the "brigadier" (divisional manager or foreman) is responsible to the chairman, not to the *kolkhoz* members under him.

The state farm (*sovkhoz*) is an openly authoritarian structure like any industrial enterprise, with a director at the helm and employing outright wage labor. Collective-farm members are, in form, not wage workers. Their compensation is formally treated as a share in the farm's disposable revenue, i.e., as a kind of dividend.[22]

However, both types of organization are enmeshed in a network of party and state controls which tend to wash out formal differences. Besides, the trend has been to make the *kolkhoz* members' compensation similar to wage payments and grant them the coverage by social old-age insurance (which they did not have until 1966). Still, the state-farm organization is held to be a superior form. In the fifties and sixties, side by side with the amalgamation of *kolkhoz* farms into giant

[19] For a critical analysis of the thesis that the Soviet government was forced by necessity to adopt collectivization, see Jerzy Karcz, "Thoughts on the Grain Problem," *Soviet Studies*, vol. XVIII, April 1967, pp. 399–431. For a classic account of the period, see Moshe Lewin, *Russian Peasants and Soviet Power*, G. Allen, London, 1968.

[20] For an account of the operation, based on authentic Soviet secret documents, see Merle Fainsod, *Smolensk under Soviet Rule*, Random House, New York, 1963, chaps. 12–15.

[21] See Frank Lorimer, *The Population of the Soviet Union*, League of Nations, Geneva, 1946, pp. 108–110 and 133–137.

[22] Collective-farm peasants have been therefore described in Western literature fittingly as "residual claimants," entitled to pay after the claim of the state purchasing agencies and the farm's "indivisible fund" (for investments and social purposes) have been satisfied. Furthermore *kolkhozniks* differ from modern wage labor, which has been free to move, by being tied to their *kolkhoz*. Before 1975, they were not even entitled to internal passports, an instrument controlling the movement of urban population. For a concise picture of conditions in Soviet agriculture, see Robert Conquest (ed.), *Agricultural Workers in the U.S.S.R.*, Praeger, New York, 1969.

units, a large number were converted to state farms.[23] Newly established units, such as those of the plow-up campaign of "virgin lands" in Kazakhstan (1954–1958), were exclusively state farms. On occasion, the possibility of an eventual conversion of all collective farms is held out.

If the essence of capitalism lies in the social separation of workers from material means of production, the designers of the Soviet agricultural model underscored that separation by spatially keeping agricultural machinery away from collective farms, in the so-called machine-tractor stations (MTS). Through monopolizing mechanized operations, these organs controlled the execution of plans and checked on the volume of harvests and on procurement of marketing quotas. This arrangement lasted until 1958, when, as part of a comprehensive reform, collective farms—by then consolidated into vast units—had the MTS machinery thrust upon them and were asked to pay for it. This was another feature which brought the *kolkhoz* organization closer to that of state farms. State farms controlled the use of their own machine stock from the start.

To complete the roundup of Soviet-type land tenure, we now turn to the sector of minifarms—the so-called *private plots*—cultivated by households of collective-farm members, state-farm workers, and other employees from outside agriculture. Privately operated holdings may appear as a foreign body in the scheme of "socialized" agriculture. Never too enchanted by such anomaly, Soviet authorities have been blowing hot and cold in their direction. However, they have been in no position to abolish them. Such an act would be a blow to the entire agricultural structure. Not only do the 50-odd million private plots, smaller than 1 acre each, contribute an indispensable part of total output. *From an area amounting to a mere 3 percent of all agricultural land, they have been supplying about one-third of total production* (mainly potatoes, vegetables, fruit, milk, meat, and eggs). Two-thirds of that is consumed on the farm and the rest is marketed.

Beyond that, success in the collectivized sector itself depends directly on the peasants' privilege to operate their plots. For instance, the *kolkhoznik* has an incentive to harvest *kolkhoz* hay only if he can count on receiving a portion to feed his livestock. Reviewing a major work on this subject, Arthur W. Wright characterized the relationship between the owner-operated and state-capitalist components as follows:

> The kolkhoz economy is a symbiosis, not merely a coexistence, of collective and private farming. As with the lichen, in which the alga provides food for the fungus but depends on the fungus for water, the collective farms provide fodder and other inputs for the peasants' private plots but depend on the plots to produce livestock and labor-intensive crops. Moreover, the income from the plots is not an insignificant supplement to the low real incomes the peasants earn from collective work. . . . The fungus may be repulsive but the alga cannot live without it.[24]

---

[23] See Robert C. Stuart, *The Collective Farm in Soviet Agriculture*, Heath, Lexington, Mass., 1972, pp. 48 and 54–59. This work gives the most recent comprehensive account of the subject.

[24] Arthur W. Wright in *Problems of Communism*, vol. 24, no. 1, January–February 1975, p. 53. (The work reviewed is Karl-Eugen Wädekin, *The Private Sector in Soviet Agriculture*, University of California Press, Berkeley, 1973.) For a lively literary account, see the story of Fyodor Abramov, *The New Life: A Day on a Collective Farm*, Grove Press, Inc., New York, 1963.

Headaches with Incentives

The problem of work incentives on collective farms has yet to be properly solved. Modest steps forward were made in the sixties when *kolkhozniks* began to be paid cash advances at regular intervals. This reduced considerably the uncertainty as to the value of their forthcoming reward. Under the earlier *trudoden* system, abandoned in 1968, the *kolkhoz* member would cumulate points throughout the year, in the form of "labor-day" units of work done; these would then be re-deemed, in cash or in kind, at the end of the agricultural year when one learned the absolute value of the residual income available for distribution. However, the main difficulty with incentives has to do with the fact that the connection be-tween effort and reward remains very tenuous. Supervision has to do the job of incentives, but considering the scale of Soviet farms, supervision cannot be very effective.

Soviet preference for large-scale farm units has always provoked much head shaking on the part of outside observers. In the words of Lazar Volin, "confusion of the largest with the optimum size has long dominated Soviet policy." The present degree of land concentration in giant units is the result of a long and persistent campaign of collective-farm amalgamation. In the course of twenty years since 1950, the number of farms fell by 70 percent, and the average size grew, through fusions, from about 500 hectares to over 2,800 hectares. State farms, larger by tradition, have reached an average size of 6,700 hectares' arable land. (United States average is about 150 hectares.)

Even though these expanses are subdivided into smaller units—brigades of different types, livestock-raising *fermy*, and work-team "links"—these are still too unwieldy. A brigade of today may be the size of a single *kolkhoz* of 1950. This explains why there has been a string of proposals and pilot experiments simulat-ing what comes naturally in owner-operated farms: personal involvement in effi-cient farm work. Time and again the idea has been broached to transform the lowest organizational unit, the *zveno* (literally "link," i.e., a work gang or squad), into a semipermanent arrangement. A tract of land, with implements, would be entrusted to a group of households for exploitation on their own account. How-ever, so far the idea has not made much headway against ideological fears of "a lapse into property-owning."

Overall Management of Agriculture

Work incentives are, in any case, a minor detail in view of more serious matters, such as the structure and quality of higher-level managerial decision making and of overall agricultural policies. Output decisions have been largely made above the farm level, at higher tiers of the administrative hierarchy, and communicated to the farms via local state and party organs at the *raion* (district) level. Domina-tion from above took the indirect form of procurement quotas, and the direct form of planned targets as to sown areas, size of herds, plus a multiplicity of other indicators. Comprehensive direct command planning was formally abol-ished in 1955, but interference from above never completely stopped.

Interference could conceivably be beneficial, as it has been under Western-type contract farming, insofar as it stimulates innovation and productivity. In the

Soviet case, interference has been more of an antistimulant. *Kolkhoz* management was never free to search for best choices of crops and techniques in accordance with local soil and climatic conditions. For the supply of farm inputs it has passively depended on rations allocated by organs of material distributions (since 1961, the *Selkhoztechnika*). As for mechanized operations, it used to be at the mercy of machine-tractor stations and their convenience in scheduling and quality of work.[25]

Above all, Soviet agriculture was repeatedly subject to monomaniacal campaigns in which a chosen program was imposed on all farms across the board as a panacea: the grass rotation scheme in the forties; Khrushchev's corn program after 1955; the plowing up of grasslands after 1961; and other more localized programs.[26] It is difficult to judge the overall quality of managers in Soviet agriculture, but to the extent that appointments go to professionals, they have not been given enough autonomy to prove their mettle.

Until the late sixties, Soviet overall strategy toward agriculture followed three main tacks: (1) concentrating investments in laborsaving machinery, so as to free enough labor for growing industry; (2) securing self-sufficiency in food supplies; (3) trying to obtain the requisite increases in yields per hectare with a minimum commitment of inputs and income incentives for the peasants. The result has been a modest rate of increase in yields and output, too modest to secure self-sufficiency. Unable to stock up on reserve large enough to fill in deficits caused by crop failures (such as in 1962, 1972, and 1975), the country became dependent on periodic emergency grain imports from overseas.

A corollary of this strategy has been a chronic preoccupation with methods of procurement of the marketed agricultural surplus. Between 1928 and 1970, volume of grain marketings almost quadrupled while grain output increased only 2 to 2.4 times (marketings almost doubled in the first ten years after collectivization started, while output remained constant). Ragnar Nurkse was on the mark with his pun: "The collective farm is not only a form of collective organization; it is above all an instrument of collection." The parallel massive transfer of labor from farms to rural areas was only partly due to farm mechanization; the disparity of living conditions in agriculture and in industry did the rest.[27] In fact, the pull of the town has been too strong, especially on sturdy young men. They have been leaving in droves. Except for supervisory personnel, agriculture has become the province of women and the elderly. This explains why the regime has found it necessary to regulate the outflow to some extent, using methods of mobility control as feudal landlords did in times past.

---

[25] This gave rise to complaints about the so-called double management, though "multiple management" would have been a better term. After the abolition of the MTS system, *kolkhozes* continued having similar troubles with their own internal specialized tractor brigades.

[26] See, for example, Lazar Volin, *A Century of Russian Agriculture*, Harvard, Cambridge, Mass., 1970, pp. 312–320, 330–343.

[27] See David W. Bronson and Constance B. Krueger, "The Revolution in Soviet Farm Household Income, 1953–1967," in James R. Millar (ed.), *The Soviet Rural Community*, University of Illinois Press, Urbana, 1971.

No one would deny that the Soviet system has been crudely effective in extracting marketed surpluses from the agricultural sector. However, observers have been increasingly coming to the conclusion that higher surpluses might have been obtained at lower cost under a different set of institutions and policies. The fact that peasants receive relatively low incomes conceals from view the full cost of farm mechanization and the lost opportunity of obtaining higher increases in resource productivity had one focused more on yields per hectare. "The great revolution in agricultural yields and techniques which occurred in most advanced countries . . . has bypassed the Soviet Union," writes Erich Strauss.[28] While market economies have suffered headaches on account of agricultural surpluses, Soviet-type systems dread deficits. In Western systems, terms of trade tend to move against agriculture, to the benefit of the nonfarm sector; in Soviet-type systems farm output tends to grow more costly relative to manufactured articles. Robert W. Campbell, speaking for many others, closes his survey of these issues on a rather definite note: "It is difficult to escape the conclusion that collectivization was a colossal policy blunder that did little to enhance growth."[29]

Replicas, Recoils, and Variants

Most Eastern European countries under Soviet domination had the Soviet model foisted upon them in the late forties and early fifties. The choice was made for them by local Communist governments. Yugoslavia and Poland were exceptions. Yugoslavia reversed its collectivization program after 1951–1952, and Poland gave up its halfhearted attempts by 1956, not to regret the decision ever since.[30] China, under no direct pressure from Moscow, began to introduce the Soviet collectivization model in 1956. This came after a few years' interlude of private family farming, as it emerged from the land reform of 1950. However, the peasants had barely begun to adjust to the Soviet model when it was superseded, in 1958, by a radical Chinese variant, namely, the system of agricultural "communes."

The Chinese Model   The wholesale introduction of the commune system in 1958 coincided with the short-lived attempt at accelerated industrialization, known as the Great Leap Forward (see Chapter 9, section on "The Chinese Variant"). Indeed, it was an integral part of that policy. As A. L. Erisman put it,

---

[28] Erich Strauss, *Soviet Agriculture in Perspective*, Praeger, New York, 1969, p. 299.

[29] Robert W. Campbell, *The Soviet-Type Economies*, Houghton Mifflin, Boston, 1974, p. 75. It has become customary to contrast the treatment of agriculture under the Soviet system with that of the Japanese model of "concurrent growth" of agriculture and industry. See Kazushi Ohkawa, Bruce F. Johnston, and Hironitsu Kaneda (eds.), *Agriculture and Economic Growth: Japan's Experience*, University of Tokyo Press, 1969, esp. chap. 3.

[30] From prewar to 1968, value added per person employed in agriculture increased, in real terms, as follows: about 2.5 times in Poland and Yugoslavia and only about 1.5 times in countries with "socialized" agriculture. (It tripled in Western Europe.) See Gregor Lazarcik's calculations in U.S. Congress, Joint Economic Committee, *Economic Developments in Countries of Eastern Europe*, 1970, pp. 463–524, and *Reorientation and Commercial Relations of the Economies of Eastern Europe*, 1974, pp. 328–393.

"the leap rested on the questionable belief that a doubling of an already stern workpace would generate the heretofore elusive agriculture surpluses, thereby bringing industrialization several decades closer."[31] Productivity was to be raised by methods of direct exhortation and supervision ("nonmaterial incentives"). Private plots were abolished, communal facilities introduced, structures based on family ties undermined. This frontal assault of utopian authoritarian collectivism upon rural society was a failure. After a series of bad harvests, China abandoned the crude Stalinist soak-the-peasant industrialization strategy. From 1962 on, the regime turned more to Bukharinist precepts of paying greater attention to agriculture and adopted a balanced-growth strategy (see above).

The institutional modifications of the vast unwieldy commune were geared to that purpose.[32] Its organizational structure was better articulated, rather than decentralized: functions of different type and scope were assigned to organs at different tiers of the hierarchy—at the top level of the *commune*, at the intermediate level of the *brigade*, at the level of *production teams*, and at the level of *households* raising pigs, poultry, and vegetables on their resurrected private plots.

The most important element in this arrangement became the production team, specializing mainly in grain crops. The team is a grouping of twenty to forty households. It has at its disposal a certain area of land and its own equipment. It operates within the framework of production plans handed down by the brigade organs, but implements them on the basis of its own internal decisions and by doing its own accounting and distribution of rewards according to a point system analogous to the earlier Soviet *trudoden* (see above). It does not seem incorrect to interpret the team as the Soviet experimental *zveno* ("link"), universally applied.

It is important to add that the commune system is not just an organization of production units but assumes also functions of local government (education, administration, taxation, internal security, etc.). Furthermore, it promotes the development of rural industries complementing and supplementing agricultural activities, a policy not different, in principle, from what the Israeli *kibbutzim* have been doing (see below). However, one must never lose sight of the fact that, in the Chinese case, it is the Communist party which provides the organizational backbone that holds the system together.

Postscript on Cuba   Cuba presents a special variant of the Soviet model. Sugar plantations (about 70 percent of cultivated land) are run along state-farm lines, and the remaining private sector is subject to close planning through state agricultural organizations and procurement agencies (from 1968 on).[33]

---

[31] Alva Lewis Erisman, "China: Agriculture in the 1970's," in U.S. Congress, Joint Economic Committee, *China: A Reassessment of the Economy*, 1975, p. 33.

[32] See Frederick W. Crook, "The Commune System in the People's Republic of China, 1963–74," in ibid., pp. 366–410.

[33] See Carmelo Mesa-Lago, *Cuba in the 1970's*, University of New Mexico Press, Albuquerque, 1974, pp. 89–92.

MEXICAN DUALISM: *EJIDO* COLLECTIVISM AND BUSINESS FARMING

Agrarian reforms always mean redistribution of land, usually in favor of the small peasants or the landless. The goal is greater equity. However, countries set on economic development must also weigh the effect of land reforms on growth of agricultural efficiency and productivity. In principle, the two objectives are not incompatible. In practice, they may easily clash, as they do, for instance, if redistribution of land leads to the creation of suboptimal units. Some output and future productivity potential are then sacrificed for the sake of stilling the peasants' "land hunger." The payoff in social and political stability, in itself a developmental asset, may be well worth the sacrifice, at least in the short run. However, in the long run, growth of productivity is what matters most. Mexico is an interesting example of a country which has been trying to pursue both objectives side by side.

Mexico is known as the "land of the *ejido*," a system of semicollective, semiprivate land tenure of an original type. However, such a label can be misleading since Mexico is just as much—if not more—a country of private family farms. Besides, the formal land-tenure criterion is altogether irrelevant if one views the Mexican agricultural system functionally. From that point of view, it consists of the *subsistence sector*, made up of subfamily *ejido* plots and private minifundios, and a *commercial market-oriented sector*, made up of a certain number of progressive *ejido* units and dynamic private farms.

The proportion of the *ejido* sector to the private one is very roughly 50-50 percent in terms of land and number of farms. The place of the commercial sector (which includes both private and some *ejido* units) with respect to the subsistence sector is indicated by the fact that *only some 4 percent farm units are responsible for four-fifths of total agricultural output* and *almost all gains in output and productivity*. Thus, broadly speaking, *ejidos* are designed to fulfill the land-distribution objectives, while productivist goals are being promoted unsentimentally within the compass of a select portion of the private-farm sector.

The contemporary *ejido* is a product of the *Mexican revolution of the years 1910–1920*. That protracted political upheaval was ignited by the accumulated discontent of rural landless masses (more than 90 percent of all households), languishing under a system where some 8,000 big landlords (*hacendados*) owned almost all land. This was a historically unique degree of inequality and land concentration. With peasant war raging in the countryside, revolutionary legislation of 1915 and 1917 provided for an orderly restitution to village communities of a portion of *hacienda* landholdings, in the form of communal *ejido* grants.

What type of farm the *ejido* was supposed to be came to be settled only in 1925. It was to have some collectivist features: the primary recipient of the land grant was to be the village; a portion of the land was to be *held in common*, and some operations were to be financed from a common fund (such as provision of wells, irrigation, and machinery). However, at the village level *ejido* organs (a three-person commissariat, supervised by a board of vigilance) were charged with distributing *the divisible portion* of the grant among *ejido* members for individual cultivation. This is far from turning the *ejidatarios* into genuine private owners. For better or for worse, their rights have remained strictly circumscribed. *Ejido* plots must not be sold, rented, or used as collateral for mortgage loans. They are forfeited if the operator fails to work them for two years.

These limitations were intended as a protection of the *ejido* cultivators against themselves, i.e., against losing the land, as they surely would if they succumbed to the temptation of selling out or borrowing improvidently. On the other hand, the same rules have also prevented them from enlarging their holdings into more efficient units through renting supplementary plots. They have made them ineligible for mortgage loans to finance improvements. As a result, the typical *ejido* peasant is bogged down in hard work with meager results.

The government has apparently perceived the *ejido* population as being hopelessly passive, illiterate, often alcoholic, hence not worth the resources which might actually change these conditions. E. N. Simpson subtitled his 1937 classic work on the subject *Mexico's Way Out*, an unobtrusive play on words, *ejido* having the same etymological origin as the English "exit."[34] However, the policy of Mexican administrations that came after that of the *ejido*-promoting President Cárdenas (1934–1940) has been to treat the *ejido* increasingly as a rural welfare institution: it provides peasants with enough livelihood and security to prevent the agricultural surplus population from invading the urban areas which are not ready to receive them. From a "way out" the *ejido* was turned into a dead-end track.

In contrast, the commercial portion of the private sector has been receiving the bulk of public support: investment in irrigation works, buildup of a transportation network, technical advice, and credit supply. The discrimination in favor of the well-to-do private family farm is clear from the legal limits of the holdings: about 6 to 10 hectares per *ejido* plot, as against 100 to 300 hectares per private farm, and closing the eyes when the size is exceeded through semilegal devices. One can hear the echo of Stolypin's 1906 policy of "wager on the strong" and Bukharin's recommendation of the twenties to stimulate production by appealing to the Russian *kulak* to "get rich."

In the meantime, the *ejido* is subject to the pulls of economic forces and bursting the dams imposed by legal statutes. *Ejido* plots are being surreptitiously consolidated around the better placed units. *Ejido* land is being leased while the renters prefer to work for wages. The model of internal democracy in *ejido* affairs is being corrupted by the bossism of local strongmen and a tangle of bureaucratic interference on the part of national organs. Insofar as higher authorities do pay attention to the economic advancement of the *ejido* in certain regions suitable for commercial crops—about 15 percent *ejido* units do receive credit from the Ejido Bank—they have to pay the price of a certain loss of autonomy: the lending organs take over important managerial functions for the sake of efficiency and

---

[34] Eyler N. Simpson, *The Ejido: Mexico's Way Out*, The University of North Carolina Press, Chapel Hill, 1937. (The term was transplanted to Mexico by the conquerors from Spain, where it meant an area of communal grounds off a town's gates.)

quality control, and the *ejidos* are reduced to the execution of tasks planned within the framework of larger operations.

The future of the *ejido* remains a subject of controversy. Partisans of the "socialist" solution continue to advocate strengthening the collectivist features and the conversion of farms to the model of the fully collectivized *ejido*. At the same time, population pressures strengthen the argument favoring further redistribution of private land to the *ejidos*. Mexico has one of the highest rates of population growth in the world (3.6 percent per annum compared to about 1.3 percent in the more developed countries of the world). The industrialization process is too slow to absorb these increments; landless masses again grow in numbers in the backwater regions of Mexico, while the commercial sector spurts ahead with the help of laborsaving, mechanized techniques.

COLLECTIVIST FARMING IN ISRAEL

The Israeli *kibbutz* has often been used as proof that a socialist utopia is possible here and now. This is partly due to a certain amount of mythology about this unique type of farm organization. However, the distance between myth and reality *is* rather small, especially as far as the internal structure of social relationships is concerned. The ruling principles of a *kibbutz* (which means "group" in Hebrew) are self-government; maximum participation of members in management organs; rotation in office; egalitarian system of income distribution (even for retired members); self-motivation rather than material incentives; "self-labor" (which translates as distaste for using hired help); communal health insurance and financing of education. Food is taken free in communal dining halls. Child rearing rests on an interesting combination of parental nurture with life in peer-group quarters under supervision and guidance by nonparental authority. *Kibbutz* is an integrated "way of life" at least as much as traditional peasantry used to be.

What about the skepticism which distrusts the possibility of freely creating new human institutions by an act of will, according to some a priori normative ideal? The *kibbutz* economy seems to fly in the face of it. Starting with the first experiments in 1909, it was a creation of Jewish settlers animated by the spirit of democratic socialism, and it did prove its viability. Still, the question remains whether it could be duplicated or generalized, or whether it owes its success to a very special combination of circumstances. For one thing, it was not an experimental "escape into utopia" on the part of people disenchanted with modern living. It was a work of pioneers for whom it was a practical instrument of survival. Shared beliefs and moral values, rooted in old traditions, made for strong social cohesion. And it has benefited from constant support of the community at large and the state.

The *kibbutz* economy enjoys a reputation out of all proportion to the numbers involved. Less than 3 percent of the population live on about 230 *kibbutz* farms (around 350 persons per farm on the average), constituting roughly one-third of the agricultural sector in terms of employment, land, and output. Postwar expansion of agriculture took mostly the form of new private farms (in citrus and other fruit growing) or individual farms associated in cooperative organizations or villages, the so-called *moshavim* (singular *moshav*). One might easily begin to wonder whether the apparently static *kibbutz* sector is not being artificially maintained as a national monument.

It is probably correct to say that *kibbutzim* are economically not as efficient as they theoretically might be. As in Western Europe or Japan, agricultural incomes in Israel are protected by price supports, subsidies, and import tariffs, at the inevitable cost of price distortions, but with the important benefit of self-sufficiency. Overproduction is kept in check through effective planning of crops and marketing quotas. It could well be that *kibbutzim*, by heavily investing in laborsaving machinery instead of hiring extra labor, contributed to unemployment during the years of mass influx of unskilled immigrants. Clinging to the principle of mixed farming, they resisted specialization far too long. However, on balance, the *kibbutz* has earned its upkeep in a businesslike fashion; it became increasingly a source of remarkable low-cost productivity increases and proved flexible by adapting to the changing station of agriculture in a growth economy.

In principle, this adaptation requires, as we have seen, that labor should be leaving agriculture as labor productivity increases. This would spell a progressive loss of population and atrophy of *kibbutz* communes. However, they have been successfully warding off this fate by choosing diversification instead of labor exodus. In consequence, the *kibbutz* economy ceased to be purely a farming enterprise; it includes more and more manufacturing plants, founded on *kibbutz* territory. They now supply more than 30 percent of *kibbutz* income. It is easiest for the *kibbutzim* to diversify into small-scale light industry (plastics, metalwork, food processing, electronic equipment). It seems most compatible with the *kibbutz* structure. However, ventures into manufacturing put the old, established *kibbutz* principles to a severe test. Division of labor in industry seems to bring forth a hierarchy of functions and a permanent specialization distinguishing the technician from the unskilled. The expansionist nature of the industrial enterprise has generated a greater demand for labor than the *kibbutz* farm sector could supply.

Today, wage labor amounts to some 55 percent of the *kibbutz* industrial labor force. The full-fledged *kibbutz* members thus become, in breach of their principles and against their intentions, employers and exploiters of hired workers. The antagonism implied by this formal relationship is softened around the edges by the application of traditional *kibbutz* values, as well as those of "industrial democracy" prevailing in a large portion of the urban industrial sector. However, life in the industrial plant of a *kibbutz* is not quite the same as life on the farm, which reinforces the suspicion that, after all, the *kibbutz* farm model could not be replicated at will.

BIBLIOGRAPHY

Mellor, J. W.: *The Economics of Agricultural Production*, Cornell, Ithaca, N.Y., 1966.
Hayami, Yujiro, and Vernon W. Ruttan: *Agricultural Development: An International Perspective*, Johns Hopkins, Baltimore, 1971.

Johnston, Bruce F., and Peter Kilby: *Agriculture and Structural Transformation*, Oxford University Press, New York, 1975.

Eicher, Carl, and Lawrence Witt (eds.): *Agriculture in Economic Development*, McGraw-Hill, New York, 1964.

Dovring, Folke: *Land and Labor in Europe in the Twentieth Century*, 3d rev. ed., Martinus Nijhoff, The Hague, 1965.

Papi, Ugo, and Charles Nunn (eds.): *Economic Problems of Agriculture in Industrial Societies*, St. Martin's, New York, 1969.

McEntire, David, and Danilo Agostini (eds.): *Toward Modern Land Policies*, University of Padua, Padua, 1971.

United Nations, Food and Agricultural Organization: *Agricultural Adjustment in Developed Countries*, Rome, 1972.

National Farm Institute: *Corporate Farming and the Family Farm*, The Iowa State University Press, Ames, 1970.

Ball, A. Gordon, and Earl O. Heady: *Size, Structure, and Future of Farms*, The Iowa State University Press, Ames, 1972.

Dovring, Folke: "Variants and Invariants in Comparative Agricultural Systems," *American Journal of Agricultural Economics*, vol. 51, December 1969, pp. 1263–1283.

Karcz, Jerzy F.: "An Organizational Model of Command Farming," in Morris Bornstein (ed.): *Comparative Economic Systems: Models and Cases*, 3d ed., Irwin, Homewood, Ill., 1974, pp. 291–312.

———— (ed.): *Soviet and East European Agriculture*, University of California Press, Berkeley, 1967.

Stuart, Robert C.: *The Collective Farm in Soviet Agriculture*, Heath, Lexington, Mass., 1972.

Millar, James R. (ed.): *The Soviet Rural Community*, University of Illinois Press, Urbana, 1971.

Miller, Robert F.: *One Hundred Thousand Tractors: The MTS and the Development of Controls in Soviet Agriculture*, Harvard, Cambridge, Mass., 1970.

Wädekin, Karl-Eugen: *The Private Sector in Soviet Agriculture*, University of California Press, Berkeley, 1973.

Stavenhagen, Rodolfo (ed.): *Agrarian Problems and Peasant Movements in Latin America*, Anchor Books, Doubleday & Company, Inc., Garden City, N.Y., 1970.

Hansen, Roger D.: *Mexican Economic Development: The Roots of Rapid Growth*, National Planning Association, Washington, 1971.

Barkai, Haim: "The Kibbutz as Social Institution," *Dissent*, Spring 1972, pp. 354–370.

Curtis, Michael, and Mordecai S. Chertoff (eds.): *Israel: Social Structure and Change*, Transaction Books, Brunswick, N.J., 1973.

Ogura, Takekazu (ed.): *Agricultural Development in Modern Japan*, Fuji Publishing Co., Tokyo, 1966.

World Agricultural Economics and Rural Sociology Abstracts, Commonwealth Bureau of Agricultural Economics, Oxford.

Chapter 15

Styles in
Foreign Transactions

*The bourgeoisie has through its exploitation of the world-market given a cosmopolitan charac-
ter to production and consumption in every country. To the great chagrin of Reactionists, it has
drawn from under the feet of industry the national ground on which it stood. . . . In place of
the old local and national seclusion and self-sufficiency, we have . . . universal interdependence
of nations. . . . National one-sidedness and narrow-mindedness become more and more impossible. . . .*

Karl Marx

Through foreign transactions, national economic systems become linked up into
an interconnected world system. Taken in isolation, each system appeared to
form a single whole. In the world context, each turns out to be a part interacting
with other parts of a larger entity. In the world economic system, market-capitalist, state-capitalist, as well as precapitalist national systems come together. They
interact to mutual advantage; they injure each other. They make cooperative
arrangements; they clash. We need a simple leading idea under which to subsume
the crowd of topics that belong here.

   Fortunately, there is such an idea: that of division of labor or, as modern
authors prefer to call it, specialization. The economic merit of specialization lies

in its ability to reduce overall unit production costs. Putting it differently, it is able to increase the output yield from available resources, even when production methods do not progress at all. Of course, in most instances, production methods do advance, thanks to the very introduction of specialization. However, to demonstrate the advantages of international specialization, one usually abstracts from all dynamic technological change which it may foster. This brings out the basic principle all the clearer. Since it underlies all optimality considerations in international trade, we cannot pass it by without a quick restatement. The principle is known as that of comparative advantage.

COMPARATIVE ADVANTAGE

One can grasp the principle of comparative advantage best by starting with a country's production-possibilities frontier (see Chapter 5, Figure 5-1). The graph in Figure 15-1, panel *a*, shows all the possible combinations of food and machines a country called Ruritania might be able to produce. As long as it remains a closed system, it can consume only one food-machines combination chosen from this range. Confined to its own resources, it might change its output mix, for instance, from A to A'. To produce an extra m amount of machines, it has to "pay" by giving up a b amount of food.

To advance the argument, one can state that the country would obviously be better off if, by giving up a b amount of food, it could get in return more than m machines, e.g., $m + n$ machines. It would then enjoy the food-machines combination T, which lies outside its attainable set of production possibilities. Is there a practical way of making T ever come true? Yes, there is, and the magic wand is international trade. All that Ruritania needs is to find another country willing to supply machines in exchange for food in the proportion equal to $(m + n)/b$. Of course, such a country (let its name be Vulcania) would have to find advantage in such an exchange, too. That means that the amount b of food, received for the export of $m + n$ machines, would have to be more than the amount of food Vulcania could secure domestically by shifting resources domestically from producing $m + n$ machines toward the production of food.

In Figure 15-1, panel *b*, Ruritania's production-possibilities frontier meets an upside-down production-possibilities frontier of Vulcania. Without trade, Vulcania would have to make do with options such as those between A and A''. A reorientation of production from machines to food, to the tune of $m + n$ machines given up, would gain her only an amount c of food. With trade, $m + n$ machines produced and exported would gain her an amount b of food, which is considerably more than c. Thus, Ruritania's specialization in food and Vulcania's specialization in machines, each exporting the excess above and over its domestic use to its trade partner, benefit both. *Each makes for the other what it can make relatively cheaper than the other—this is what the principle of comparative advantage boils down to.*

Panel *b* of Figure 15-1 shows very clearly that apportioning production between the two countries in a manner which includes the possibility of trade yields

Figure 15-1   Comparative advantage and international trade.

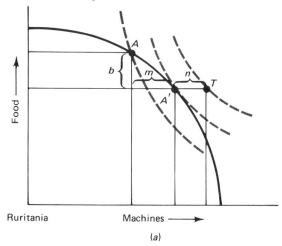

(a)

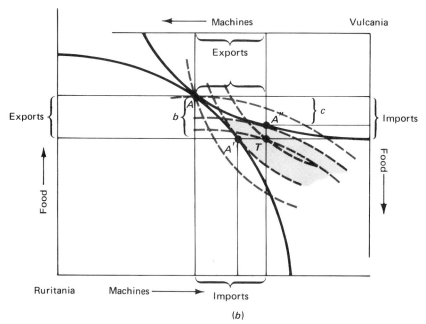

(b)

For the benefit of readers familiar with the device of social-indifference curves, a set of such curves has been drawn for each of the trading countries. Points A' and A'' represent optimal output combinations attainable to each country without trade: the production-possibilities curve is tangent to an indifference curve, the highest attainable. At point T, each country attains a still higher indifference curve, thanks to the availability of output combinations obtained through trade.

a larger amount of combined output (*T*) than if each country had to rely on its own resources (*A'* plus *A''*). *This fortunate opportunity prevails any time that, and to the extent that, the ratio of production costs of a pair of commodities in one country is different from the ratio in the other country.* The interesting part is that it does not matter whether there is an absolute difference in the level of real production costs (factor productivity) between the two countries, or how large the gap is. Ruritania may be an underdeveloped country, with high unit labor costs, and Vulcania a developed one, but the propositions following from the principle of comparative advantage would still hold.

The trading pattern and the ensuing composition of consumption by the two countries need not be exactly *T*, and the exchange ratio ("terms of trade") need not be (*m* + *n*)/*b*. Much depends on demand conditions in the trading countries. Not all of them need to benefit equally from trading, some may impose terms of trade favorable to them through greater bargaining power. The specific content of trade also matters greatly, especially if we want to know whether it promotes development or decadence, construction or conspicuous consumption (whiskey or vocational training? gold-plated Cadillacs or machinery?). However, with "normal" goods, the benefit-from-trade proposition applies to any result where *T* falls within the shaded area of panel *b*.

The rest of international-trade theory is an enormously elaborate structure growing out of the insight into the principle of comparative advantage and specialization. The theory contains qualifications and amplifications of the principle, but never its denial. We shall refer to some of these extensions in passing. Those in need of further theoretical edification will have to consult specialized textbooks.

Pure theory of international trade has established an impregnable case against nations' goals to be economically self-sufficient. Free movement of goods, labor, and capital across political frontiers is essential to maximizing welfare *within* each. Why, in that case, do governments not all embrace the free-trade doctrine? Why have the gods of autarchy not been toppled a long time ago, and for good?

It would seem natural that all countries would wish to buy cheapest no matter from whom, but there also are countertendencies seeking to prevent that. Obviously, the rival tendencies come from rival interest groups. The automatic reflex may actually be the autarchic one. It is trade liberalization that calls for deliberate effort. Whatever the case may be, the unifying theme in the examination of styles in foreign transactions is this: "Does a given economic system promote specialization via free movement of goods and factors of production, or does it impose inhibiting or prohibiting restrictions upon their mobility?"

INSULATION, DISINTEGRATION, AND INTEGRATION UNDER MARKET-CAPITALIST SYSTEMS

If goods and production factors were freely mobile, they would tend to distribute economic activities into certain geographic patterns. These would be determined by cost-price-profitability criteria of the market. *Market-capitalist systems of individual countries would be fully integrated if location of economic activities had the same pattern as would prevail if political boundaries did not exist.* If they are not fully integrated, if it takes effort to open them up to international exchange, it means that the more or less closed state carries, in the perception of governments, some worthwhile benefits.

Autarchy and Protectionism

Among the major reasons for trade restriction one has to distinguish between the goal of autarchy and the goal of protectionism. In both cases the intention is to restrict imports. However, the motivation is not the same. Pursuit of autarchy is a policy of import substitution. One tries to expand domestic supply capacities in order not to have to import any goods. Policy of protectionism aims at sheltering existing domestic capacities against cheaper imports. It is a policy of preventing imports from substituting themselves for domestic supply. Autarchy starts with given imports and cuts them down by expanding domestic supply. Protectionism starts with domestic capacity as given and prevents imports from growing, displacing domestic capacity in the process.

In both cases, costs of production are higher and total availabilities lower than they would be under free trade. Hitler knew what he was saying when, proclaiming his autarchic Four-Year Plan (1936–1940), he demanded its execution "without regard to cost." However, geographic distribution of modern raw materials happens to be such that complete autarchy is not an attainable goal even for the largest of countries. Hitler's famous attempt of pursuing autarchy amounted in reality to concentrating for a short while on the rubber and fuel bottleneck, while preparing a quick "lightning-speed" war (*Blitzkrieg*). After the conquest of Europe, west and east of Germany, there lay the prospect of self-sufficiency in an entirely different sense from autarchy, i.e., in the sense of natural *low trade dependence*. Obviously, the larger a given territory, the less need is there to trade with abroad. No deliberate policy of trade restriction is then needed.[1]

Protectionism is meant to protect specific industries from the free play of comparative advantage. Protectionist measures artificially raise the relative opportunity cost of foreign goods that one otherwise would import in place of domestic production. Such policy has the same rationale as government measures mitigating competition within the country: preventing the cost of social disruption which accompanies economic adjustment. The country pays by not having a certain extra volume of goods available for use. The protected industry is freed from competitive pressures that would otherwise force it to keep up with world production standards, or to outdo them.

---

[1] See Berenice A. Carroll, *Design for Total War*, Mouton, The Hague, 1968, pp. 102–105 and 128–129. It follows that the percentage share of foreign-trade turnover (imports plus exports) in national product is not a sufficient indicator of the country's foreign-trade *policy*. The percentage tends to be naturally low for large countries, such as the United States or the Soviet Union (about 9 and 5 percent, respectively), and high for small countries, such as the Netherlands (80 percent). Also, less-developed countries tend to be less involved in foreign trade, other things being equal.

It is easy to point the finger at vested interests that ask for protection. However, the social-disruption argument deserves to be properly weighed. Thus, United States attempts at protecting its textile industry against Japanese competition were also meant to stabilize employment opportunities in the South, an area in which the textile industry had just recently relocated from the North. On the other hand, one has to be on guard against specious arguments for protection. A favorite ploy is to claim protection in the interest of national security, which is, in essence, an autarchy argument. For instance, the American watch industry claims that the country needs its special engineering capacity and highly skilled labor as reserve for the case of war, and citizens should therefore pay for it by not buying cheaper civilian watches made abroad.

Balance-of-Payments Worries

So far we have dealt with those obstacles to free, market-determined specialization which had their source in microeconomic, i.e., partial, considerations. Another set of obstacles originates in macroeconomic adjustment problems. The relevant macroeconomic aggregates are (1) total exports and imports of goods and services, (2) total value of other types of domestic assets acquired by foreigners, and of foreign assets acquired by nationals of a given country, and (3) the value of the two-way financial payments connected with transactions under (1) and (2), i.e., for goods and services ("on current account"), as well as other types of assets ("capital flows"). The aggregates under (1) are those which enter the *balance of trade*. Aggregates under (3) make up the *balance of payments*.

Behind the obstacles to integration we are about to discuss, there is usually some self-centered attitude of national systems toward adjustments in the area of foreign transactions. A given country may even have several mutually inconsistent attitudes, which only adds to confusion about policies.

What Is to Be Balanced? Whatever its degree of integration, the world system of international transactions requires that residents of every country "raise" enough means of payment to cover their payments for imported goods and services, as well as for the acquisition of "other assets" located abroad (equity ownership in firms abroad, foreign securities, holdings of foreign currencies, evidences of loans made to foreigners, etc.). The simplest way of raising this money is by exporting goods and services. If exports bring in more money than is needed to pay for imports, the country has enough left to pay for "other assets." (It can also keep such earnings unspent.) If export revenues fall short of the amounts needed to pay for imports, such a country has to "sell" some "other assets," besides goods and services. It either has to borrow, which means paying provisionally with private IOUs (e.g., promissory notes) or government securities; or it has to let foreign investors buy up some domestic assets, or let them finance new investment projects. There is still a third sweet possibility: that of obtaining international purchasing power, or part of imports, free, as a gift from another country or an international agency.

A country's total foreign transactions are not properly adjusted in two cases: (1) if the country accumulates a larger stock of international money than it finds convenient to hold, because it consistently receives more from abroad than it spends abroad; and (2), the reverse case, if the country receives from abroad consistently less than it wishes to spend there, which means that it has to dip deeper and deeper into its holdings of international money until they threaten to be depleted. There exist different methods of balancing the two opposite flows of payments experienced by a given country. The question is which of them are helpful to the international integration of national economies as defined earlier and which are not.

And How?   The list of possible methods is short. (1) One can let the price of the domestic currency go up or down, as necessary, to equilibrate the two opposite flows of foreign transactions. For instance, one "lets the pound float." The price in question is the amount of foreign money foreigners must pay to obtain one unit of the domestic currency, or one such unit's worth of goods; conversely, it is the amount of foreign money, or the equivalent quantity of foreign goods, that domestic residents obtain for one unit of their domestic currency. This is the method of flexible exchange rates. (2) One can try to adjust the level of foreign transactions by changing the level of domestic activity. (3) One can influence, by more or less direct orders, or indirect manipulation, various components of foreign transactions—stretch them or cut them to size.

Which Method Is Best for Integration?   We shall examine the methods in mixed order.

Method 2   From the point of view of international integration, the second method can be dismissed out of hand because it injures the domestic economy and its foreign partners all at once. The idea behind it is that lowering the level of domestic activity will lower the demand for imports and that the accompanying fall in prices and interest rates will stimulate foreign demand for goods and other payment flows from abroad, which is what is needed to wipe out a balance-of-payments deficit. This method, often called "deflating the economy," is like trying to wag the dog in order to adjust the position of its tail. The method works against export interests of other countries, and it also works against full-employment stabilization at home—two counts against optimality. Furthermore, as we have seen in the case of Britain (Chapters 10 and 12), it injures domestic export capabilities in the long run. That tends to perpetuate the balance-of-payments problem. By slowing down growth and capital accumulation, deflation slows down productivity increases. That makes it easier for competitors in other countries to steal the show. They are better able to offer lower prices and make it harder for the deflating country to sell its goods abroad.

Method 3   The third method is also anti-integrationist, insofar as it artificially blocks imports and acquisition of other assets, in order to keep them down to the level of revenues from abroad, i.e., to earnings from exports primarily. It operates with quantitative restrictions (import quotas or prohibitions, rationing of foreign exchange) and import tariffs. These are often assisted, from the other end, by export subsidies. It also uses measures impeding capital outflow, e.g.,

investments abroad. The effect is the same as under protection of specific industries against competition from abroad. This is one anti-integrationist aspect.

There is another disintegrating effect which is worse. It occurs when country
A faces a decline in export revenues from abroad and suddenly decides to clamp
down on imports. The decline of export revenues may be due to some other
country B having a domestic recession, and therefore reducing its demand for
foreign goods, too. If country A responds by deliberately reducing its demand
from country B, it only makes things worse for everybody. We discussed this
process of amplification of recessions toward the end of Chapter 7, as the international transmission of business fluctuations.

Method 1   At long last we turn to the first method of adjusting the flow of
payments between countries: raising or lowering the exchange rates of currencies.
First, a review of some elementary technicalities. The basic economic significance
of exchange-rate variation is this: There is a definite link between the exchange
rate of a country's currency (say, dollars) and the volume of payments made or
received by that country.

From the point of view of foreigners, *the exchange rate between the dollar and
other currencies determines the price level of all exportables* coming from the
United States, as the foreigners see it. Depending on how many marks a German
has to pay for a dollar determines how high the dollar prices of American goods
will appear to him, and how much he will want to spend on imports from America. Symmetrically, depending on how much an American has to pay for a mark,
he will tend to spend more or less on German goods.

As long as the exchange rate is such that it generates a greater supply of
dollars (reflecting the wish of Americans to shop abroad) than the volume of
dollars demanded (reflecting the wish of foreigners to "buy American"), the dollar volume of American outpayments will exceed the dollar volume of American
revenues from abroad. The American balance of payments will not be in equilibrium, and neither will the dollar exchange rate. (In this particular example we
would say that the dollar is "overvalued," i.e., too expensive from the point of
view of foreigners, while foreign currencies are too cheap from the point of view
of dollar holders, compared to a situation of equilibrium in foreign-exchange
rates.)

The actual method of determining exchange rates and influencing payment
flows comes in two variants. In one, the job is done through unsupervised demand-and-supply forces in the markets for importable and exportable goods,
capital assets, and currencies as such. This is what is meant by *"freely floating"
exchange rates.* In the other variant, exchange rates are fixed by administrative
fiat, either on the basis of some international agreement or by unilateral decision
of a government. We speak of *"fixed"* or *"pegged" exchange rates.* (They may be
fixed with respect to each other or by reference to some common denominator,
such as gold or a major currency, or both.)

Returning to the main question, as to which method of payments adjustment
is most suitable to integration, offhand it would seem that the *"free float" method*
is the one. It does not distort relative prices or artificially inhibit transactions.

Unfortunately, integration may take place way off production possibilities. If recession should start spreading from one country through decline of demand for other countries' exports, there will be less demand for other countries' currencies, and their foreign-exchange price will fall. Theoretically, this should push demand for those countries' exports up again. However, this "price effect" is ordinarily too slow and too weak. It is swamped by the "income effect": Decline of exports contracts incomes in the exporting countries, and this in turn contracts their demand for imports, which hits back that country's exports and incomes where the recession originated. If this is integration, it is a case of being chained together in a common fall.

We are left with *fixed exchange rates*. Unfortunately, not even that regime contains any automatic mechanism that would prevent countries from pulling each other down the slippery recession slope. On the contrary, it may serve as the tool of policies contributing to an international decline.

There was a short time when leaders of capitalist systems thought they could manipulate exchange rates to protect their countries against the epidemics of economic contraction. During the Great Depression of the thirties, as export demand collapsed, countries attempted to make their exports attractive by depreciating their currencies so drastically as to turn their goods into a bargain no one could refuse, while at the same time curbing their demand for competitive imports in the hope that other countries would bear the brunt of reduced foreign demand. To make doubly sure, protective tariff walls against imports were raised and other restrictions, discussed earlier under method number 2, were imposed. All these measures together were properly dubbed "beggar-my-neighbor" policy. The scheme naturally backfired. A victim country could refuse the export bargains of the depreciating country and retaliate in kind by a depreciation and a tariff wall of its own.[2] This is precisely what happened, with all countries worse off than before.

Nevertheless, these considerations do not in any way condemn either of the two methods of adjusting payment flows by adjusting exchange rates. Exchange rates of national currencies are part and parcel of a world price system. Exchange rates *interlock national price systems by providing a code for translating prices from one national currency into another, and thus making comparison shopping possible.* Therefore, all the nice things that were said in general about the allocative function of prices in Chapters 5 and 8 apply just as much to currency exchange rates. However, as we have repeatedly stressed, the allocative virtues of the price system can come into their own only when full employment is secured.

Therefore, if we wish to uphold integration of national economic systems as a prerequisite of maximizing welfare, we have to say clearly we mean integration under conditions of full employment. National components of the world system must pursue full-employment policies, and pursue them through measures which do not injure one another. In one word, integration requires policy harmonization: trading together while growing and prospering together.

---

[2] The chain of retaliatory depreciation was started by England in 1931, followed by Japan, United States, Switzerland, Belgium, Netherlands, and others.

EUROPEAN INTEGRATION STEP BY STEP

The showpiece of modern integration efforts, the European Economic Community, is a large-scale replica of a stage gone through by individual countries in the process of economic nation building. Before national economies were formed, it was necessary to pull down a maze of barriers to trade: tolls, duties, fees, prohibitions, hard-to-convert local currencies, all that which used to separate towns, provinces, and ministates from each other. Germany, as it was known before the postwar partition, arose in 1871 on the economic foundations of integrated commerce between forty-odd independent states. The process started in 1828 and was carried forward until 1871, by an interstate association called simply the Customs Union (*Zollverein*). United States were united, among other means, by abolishing state currencies and levies on commerce between states. The French Revolution, too, had to put an end to economic particularism of provinces to create a unified framework for the national economy. As a rule, political and economic unification went hand in hand. Sometimes it was politics and sometimes economics that took the lead.

The European Economic Community (EEC) came into being in 1958 through a treaty concluded in Rome by West Germany, France, Italy, Belgium, the Netherlands, and Luxembourg. Since then, it has attracted Great Britain, Denmark, and Ireland. Great Britain and Denmark had been on the periphery, until 1973, belonging to another industrial customs union of the "Outer Seven," called the European Free Trade Association (EFTA). The EEC superseded or absorbed a number of partial integrationist predecessors, such as the Benelux Economic Union, consisting of Belgium, the Netherlands, and Luxembourg ("Bene" since 1921, Benelux since 1948), and the European Coal and Steel Community (1951).

The EEC was conceived from the start as a formal framework with an evolving content. The evolution was envisaged to proceed by stages: abolition of tariff duties between member states (customs union); abolition of impediments to free movement of labor and capital investments; establishment of common policies (especially with respect to antitrust, agriculture, and regional development); unification of taxation systems; and harmonization of stabilization policies. The final goal has been a complete economic union with common currency, central economic institutions, and eventually a common governmental structure.

Considering the heritage of national rivalries, kept alive from 1958 into the seventies by the Gaullist regime in France, and considering many protectionist interests, the process is well under way. The customs-union stage was completed by 1968. By the same time, a common agricultural policy (CAP) was evolved with respect to tariffs, prices, and subsidies, and is being broadened into a policy of global structural adjustment. Under the post-1973 regime of free floating of exchange rates, the continental members of the EEC decided to manage the free float in common, by maintaining stable exchange rates with respect to each other—a preview of what would characterize a common currency.[3] Thus, the

---

[3] The movement of exchange rates of individual currencies being constricted within a narrow wiggly band of an upper and lower limit, the resulting graph gave rise to nicknaming this policy "the snake." France, incidentally, defected from the agreement in 1976.

EEC has been more than "viable," and more than just a "qualified success," though the final achievements, especially the political union, may require some dramatic jolt of events to jell.

EUROPEAN INTEGRATION
AND WORLD INTEGRATION OVERLAP

European integration efforts developed in the postwar climate of economic cooperation among market-capitalist economies. Effort was needed to overcome sources of inherent tension and conflict. National economies, having absorbed the particularism of their regions and provinces, have in turn been particularist with respect to other national economies. The European integration project had enough trouble casting away particularism of its members in relation to each other. It could not rid itself instantly of its particularism with respect to the world system; neither could any other member of the world trading and investing community. We shall find traces of this fact in all three aspects of the world integration process we are about to review.

International Monetary Arrangements

The dominant concern of postwar agreements among Western capitalist countries was to prevent a repetition of the egoistic, as well as myopic stratagems of the thirties. Beggar-my-neighbor policies were never to be repeated again. The Bretton Woods regime of managed exchange rates, and its history from 1944 to 1971, are too complex to summarize adequately in the space available here. We shall confine ourselves to outlining first its major intent and then the nature of the system's central contradiction, which spelled its abandonment between 1971 and 1973.

Just as prices of commodities need not change nervously with every momentary shift of the demand-and-supply intersection, neither do prices of national currencies. Exchange rates of national currencies may even be particularly well suited to be treated as "administered prices." Fixed exchange rates should be beneficial to business planning and trade. They would eliminate one important source of uncertainty. The fixity would by definition preclude aggressive currency devaluations.

Outpayments of a country could, of course, exceed its revenues from abroad, i.e., the currency in question could be in excess supply, even under fixed exchange rates. In that case, the excess supply would be bought up on the foreign-exchange market by the country's central bank, using its reserve of international means of payment. Alternatively, the central bank could temporarily draw upon an international currency reserve maintained by the International Monetary Fund. This would sustain the fixed exchange rate. If a currency turned out to be chronically in excess supply (the case of a "fundamental disequilibrium"), only then would it be permissible to lower its price (devalue). Devaluation would then curb imports as well as other transactions making for that currency's outflow, and stimulate transactions bringing in revenue from abroad—in other words, work toward a payments equilibrium.

The system worked reasonably well for some fifteen-odd years until a flaw developed. The flaw was not suspected at the start, and it worsened in the course of the sixties. It was due to the original choice of the currency to serve as international means of payment, namely, the United States dollar, which was formally "backed" by its convertibility into gold. Or, rather, it was due to what happened to it in the course of years.

The key fact about the dollar as international-reserve currency was that it, too, could appear in excess supply. Should United States payments abroad be higher than its payment revenues from abroad, a balance-of-payments deficit would develop. There would be an excess supply of dollars. This is precisely what came to be a chronic state of the balance of payments of the United States.

If it had been any other currency, the remedy would have been devaluation. However, the dollar could not be devalued because, by international agreement, its price was firmly fixed in terms of gold and all other currencies. Hence, deficits in the United States balance of payments appeared abroad as accumulations of dollar holdings that were to remain permanently expatriated.

As long as other countries were short of international reserves (and most of them were after the war), and eager to buy American goods, they did not mind this accumulation of dollars due to the excess of American payments abroad. It was only after their need of dollar holdings was saturated that grumbles began to be heard.

The fatal contradiction of the system was due to two incompatible attitudes on the part of the other countries, held simultaneously. On the one hand, they objected to the persistent balance-of-payments deficit of the United States. It swelled their dollar holdings. It permitted the United States to finance acquisitions of goods and other assets abroad beyond what the country earned through exports. The automatic counterpart of United States deficits was other countries' balance-of-payments surpluses. However, while other countries complained about American deficits, they grew fond of their own surpluses! They liked them for two reasons. Vigorous exports were beneficial to their export-oriented industries, as well as to domestic stabilization policies. Furthermore, it conferred to their monetary units the status of "strong currencies." This was a strictly psychological advantage, valued for reasons of political prestige.

Insofar as other countries were genuinely unhappy with the size of their dollar holdings, they could have done two things: (1) Nothing would have been easier than to revalue their currencies upward. This is the reverse of devaluation. It would have put a brake on *their* exports and stimulated exports of the United States. This they were reluctant to do out of regard for their export industries. (2) Or else they could have converted their unwanted dollars into gold. This they *were* doing up to a point (especially France). But there were limits to buying gold for dollars. There was the absolute limit set by the size of the United States gold reserve, and there was United States effective power to simply "shut the gold window" or, after all, devalue the dollar unilaterally, should the stock of gold fall too low. Thus, other countries hesitated to push gold purchases too far, so as not to provoke the United States into a devaluation. The situation was thoroughly ambiguous, as the other countries could not decide which to hate more—the malady or the cure.

Finally, the United States solved these ambivalences for its partners. First the United States suspended dollar convertibility into gold (1968) and then, by a series of maneuvers, forced an upward revaluation of Western Europe's and Japan's currencies (1971). Since then, the monetary regime has been a mixture of free float and intermittent management of exchange rates by monetary authorities to mitigate fluctuation.

Whether integration was helped or harmed by these developments cannot be said with certainty. There appeared other powerful factors which, during the early seventies conspired to undermine the integration efforts and to create confusion in foreign transactions. Inflation started to advance at sharply different rates in different countries. Attempts to combat inflation by means of a demand squeeze led to recessions which spread and burst across boundaries. Substantial portions of earnings from exports were swallowed up by the quadrupled prices of oil imports, at the expense of previous imports from other trade partners. Domestic spending on other items than gasoline and oil was also hurt by the increase in oil prices. This, and the reduction of imports, compounded the depressing effects of anti-inflation policies. It was a time of stress. It tested the ability of capitalist market economies to discover new and more powerful devices to coordinate national policies, as well as economic strategies capable of coping with events resembling economic warfare.

GATT

A customs union means ordinarily abolition of tariffs between its members and maintenance of a common tariff wall with respect to the world outside. Hence, the integration effect on the inside, which promotes trade, is countered by an opposite outward effect which inhibits trade with outsiders. The EEC was meant to be such a customs union. However, in the case of the EEC, both the outsiders and the insiders had committed themselves soon after the war, long before the founding of the EEC customs union, to rules leading to an *overall* progressive removal of trade restrictions, and discrimination, by adhering to the General Agreement on Tariffs and Trade (GATT).

Periodic international conferences, conducted under the aegis of this organization, have negotiated a substantial dismantling of trade barriers carried over from the prewar era. Of particular fame are the achievements of the conference known as the Kennedy Round (1963–1967), which succeeded in reducing tariffs by an overall 35 percent. GATT has also been helpful in solving trade disputes among member states. Thus, while the EEC was removing tariffs within, tariffs were simultaneously being lowered with respect to the outside.

Nevertheless, violations of GATT rules were occurring repeatedly, and protectionism has not been banned for good. This applies in particular to EEC import tariffs intended to keep out agricultural products; American import surcharge of 10 percent introduced temporarily in 1971 (as part of the strategy

forcing a realignment of exchange rates; see above); and the barely averted introduction in 1970 of a highly protectionist trade bill in the United States.

Multinational Enterprise

In discussing the doctrine of comparative advantage, we hinted vaguely at the
connection between trade, economic development, and growth. The illustrative
pair of goods in Figure 15-1—food and machinery—was meant to be suggestive.
If traded goods include machinery, such machinery becomes part of the real
capital accumulation (investment) of the importing country. Such additions to
the stock of producer goods are likely to expand the set of production possibilities as the curve of that name shifts outward. The importing country is capable of
offering more goods to foreign customers. It can also buy more from them. Thus,
international trade becomes intertwined with economic development and growth
which, in turn, fosters further trade.

How Do Factors of Production Move?   The important point is that, in this
case, international trade in goods simultaneously amounts to international movement of factors of production. Machinery is an example: It is a component of
real capital. *Transfers of factors of production* serve the integration of national
economic systems in a dramatically new sense. They supplement integration
through trade as such. They *raise the productivity of those production factors (in this
case labor and natural resources) which are tied to the territory of the importing
country*. This does not invalidate the principle of comparative advantage. It just
increases the level of production possibilities while changing their pattern in the
process.

International movement of production factors tends specifically toward the
creation of more advantageous geographic patterns of economic activities. It
tends to create patterns that would emerge if there were no national boundaries.
Movement of factors of production is a practical answer to the following question of allocation: "Can one produce more goods with factors of production
where they are now, or can one obtain more output by moving some of the
factors of production elsewhere?"

A prime example of integration through moving production factors is *labor
migration* from overpopulated countries to empty lands of new agricultural settle-
ment. Another one is migration of underemployed labor to countries which tend
to accumulate capital faster than warranted by the rate of growth of their own
domestic labor force. This was the case of migrations from Eastern and Southern
Europe to the United States before World War I; from Turkey, Yugoslavia, Italy,
and Portugal to West Germany, Holland, France, and Switzerland, from the
fifties to early seventies. In all these cases, improvement of factor proportions has
been a source and integral aspect of economic growth—sometimes of creating
entirely new national economies on virgin soil.

However, movement of labor between established national communities
may carry a cost of adaptation. The newcomers often suffer. The host population
is not necessarily enchanted either. It seems easier to move material items of

capital equipment toward areas of ample labor supply, than the other way around. This is unavoidable in any case if the factor determining location consists of immobile natural resources, such as mineral wealth or climate. Frequently, to be of any good, imported capital equipment needs to be accompanied by still another production factor: management and entrepreneurship. Transfusion of management and entrepreneurship often has it in its power alone to raise the productivity of resources glued to the spot.

How Does Multinational Enterprise Come In?

The multinational enterprise has come to serve as the major organizational vehicle for the aforementioned international transfers of production factors. A multinational enterprise (M-E) is an integrated combination of corporate firms, operating in different countries and unified by a decision-making center, i.e., a *parent company*. Constituent firms, which are subsidiaries of the parent company, may be integrated vertically, horizontally, or as conglomerates (see Chapter 13). The stock ownership may be concentrated in the hands of nationals of one country, or it, too, may be dispersed. One is used to thinking of foreign operations of market capitalist corporations mainly as a matter of "direct foreign investment." This corresponds to an outflow of funds for the acquisition of assets situated abroad (such as stock, i.e., ownership equity in a foreign affiliate or subsidiary established by a parent company elsewhere). The intention is assumed to be to keep the assets under remote control by the investor and to milk them for profit.

The profit motive is undoubtedly present, as in any capitalist venture. However, earning of profits is a secondary, i.e., a derived, fact. The primary fact is the production of commodities whose sale generates those profits, as well as incomes earned by employees. There was a reason why we let this section be preceded by a general economic discussion of international factor transfers. We wanted to see the discussion of the M-E embedded in a somewhat more fundamental context than profit making. That context is the overall expansion of production possibilities through the footloose movement of production factors.

One may think of a foreign operation of an M-E to start with a parent company providing its affiliate abroad with an amount of funds. These funds could be spent primarily on equipment imported from the country of the parent company. That would involve, in real terms, an international transfer of physical factor inputs. This is what we have discussed above in connection with trade in machinery; except that in this case the machinery would be paid for by funds originating in the country of the parent company.

However, the funds could just as easily be converted into foreign currency and spent on equipment produced and purchased locally; on labor hired locally; or on acquiring an entire foreign firm already in existence. In that case, the only international transfer of production factors would consist in the managerial staff dispatched abroad. Such a "transaction" is not registered in any foreign-trade statistics, although it has a definite economic value. It consists in the stock of knowledge, organizational skills, entrepreneurial spirit of initiative and discovery of business opportunities, all of which are embodied in the individuals composing the managerial personnel.

In addition, management may come equipped with licensing agreements, enabling them to use the parent company's patents, i.e., with a supply of technology. Once the operation is set up, it acquires a life of its own. The M-E firms produce output, sell it, pay wages, generate profits, pay taxes, distribute dividends, raise additional funds through borrowing on premises or in the home country, found additional capacities, close old ones, and so on.

This, in a nutshell, is the essence of foreign operations of parent companies turning multinational. As a rule, they are subject to a central command which adopts a general strategy guiding the individual operations from a global point of view. When this happens, a remarkable chain of consequences sets in. The production process, as well as the marketing network, undergoes a remodeling within the complex of the multinational enterprise. Division of labor between individual affiliates is overhauled. The headquarters reassign among them specialized phases of the manufacturing process and assembly of components into the final product. Marketing may also be redesigned. Affiliates are put in charge of selling products of their sister affiliates in their geographic area, offering a full "product line."

In a national multidivision company, such transfers of components and products would be part of internal transactions between divisions within the same firm and the same country. Between affiliates of an M-E, such transfers become part of the international trade. The principle of comparative advantage then applies to these transfers both in their quality as transactions between affiliates and in their quality as part of the trade flows between countries in which the affiliates are located.

There is a host of further consequences. Research and development become somewhat decentralized as affiliates take advantage of their closeness to markets. The initial advantage ordinarily lies in superior technology and management. Usually it is associated with some new growth product. It is then amplified by increased specialization and research effort. Foreign national companies are exposed to increased pressures of competition. These indigenous companies try to enlist public-opinion makers and their governments in a protectionist drive against the intruders. Multinational enterprise finds itself in a crosscurrent of contradictory judgments and policies.[4]

World Economic Integration through the M-E   The multinational enterprise has contributed enormously to the integration of national economies into a worldwide system. By 1970, the M-E sector supplied about one-sixth of total world production. Over the previous twenty years, its output grew by 9 percent a year, or double the typical rate of national GNPs. The M-E firms have been the "leading links" in the growth process and diffusion of technology. They are today's spearhead in the continuing process of geographic consolidation of economic spaces enclosed, until recently, in narrow horizons, into progressively larger ones. As Judd Polk put it:

[4] For a capsule survey, see *The Economist*, Jan. 24, 1976, pp. 68–69, and *Business Week*, July 14, 1975, pp. 64–95.

In earlier stages they were the city companies whose more economic operations under bigger-market techniques pressured the neighborhood company, and later the national companies with similar advantages over smaller, less broadly developed local and regional suppliers. The existence of the large international company reflects larger international markets with efficient communications.[5]

To tie up this section with the earlier ones, it remains to be pointed out that the spread and surge of the M-E was duly assisted by postwar international monetary arrangements and trade-promoting measures. The regime of fixed exchange rates and free convertibility mimicked the characteristics of a single national currency. It facilitated cost-price calculations and payment flows, irrespective of their geographic location. The fact that the dollar has served as basic international means of payment, up to 1970 officially, since then *via facti*, made it easier for United States companies to finance their direct foreign investments.[6] Finally, reduction of trade barriers was beneficial, too, though not without paradox. To the extent that protective tariffs have been kept up, that, too, encouraged the spread of the M-E. Such tariffs have meant that a company producing an article in the United States faced the prospect of having to sell it, for instance, in the EEC, with a European import duty slapped on to the price. It has appeared more sensible to "slip under the tariff barrier" and establish a manufacturing facility within the EEC territory. Competition was then strictly on the basis of cost and quality, without the encumbrance of the import duty. Furthermore, shipments between the parent company and the affiliate could always be priced artificially low, so as to neutralize the effect of the foreign import duty.[7]

SOVIET-STYLE FOREIGN TRANSACTIONS

Economic systems of the Soviet area have engaged in foreign transactions under a set of rules and institutional arrangements which are in many ways the opposite of the sphere of market capitalism. Ponderous, awkward, full of peculiar hurdles—such is the process by which trade flows are determined and adjusted in the East. At the same time, for more than fifteen years, we have been witnessing laborious efforts of Soviet-bloc countries to use trade to better advantage, similar to that enjoyed by market capitalism, without ever seriously considering fundamental change in the rules.

Institutional Peculiarities

The first striking difference between the two worlds of capitalism is in who does the trading. The classic Soviet style is not to allow domestic enterprises or individuals to shop abroad for imports, or, in the case of producers of exportables, to

---

[5] Judd Polk, "The New International Production," *World Development*, vol. 1, no. 5, May 1973, p. 20.

[6] Direct foreign investments tended to add to United States balance-of-payments deficits. On the other hand, insofar as they meant stimulation of net exports and repatriation of profits from foreign operations, these investments helped reduce the deficit, a feature which made them appear desirable.

[7] This technique is so-called transfer pricing.

search for foreign customers. Domestic enterprises are blocked off from their counterparts in other countries by a number of specialized import and export organizations of the Ministry of Foreign Trade. These monopolize all contacts and transactions with the outside world. Like giant bureaucratic trading posts, they assemble in their hands exportable commodities produced domestically to sell them abroad, and they purchase foreign-made commodities to resell, or rather to allocate them, among domestic users.

How do these foreign-trade organizations know what to buy? How do they find out what is available for exports, and from whom? They are simply told by ministries of the various production sectors. These central ministries represent one extra layer of mediators inserted between foreign firms and domestic enterprises who ultimately supply the exported or use the imported goods. Foreign-trade organizations are in charge of implementing specific portions of material balances, as these emerge from the planning process, namely, their import and export components (see Table 9-2, in Chapter 9). These components constitute what is known as the "foreign-trade plan." To the extent that enterprises succeed in making their wishes known, in the course of the planning process, ministries speak for them. In that sense, foreign-trade organizations are basically passive agents. They implement orders of the foreign-trade plan, which interlocks with the overall system of material balances.

However, while the foreign-trade plan is being formulated from the side of production ministries and the central-planning office, the Ministry of Foreign Trade has an important say. Someone has to coordinate domestic import demand with availabilities from specific foreign countries, as well as domestic supply of exportables with the demand of foreign countries. Also, someone has to make sure that earnings from exports are sufficient to pay for the import needs, and to arrange for credit financing if they are not. This is the task of the Ministry of Foreign Trade. It negotiates agreements about trade flows with foreign-trade ministries of the other Soviet-bloc countries, or supervises dealings of its specialized foreign-trade organizations with individual firms in countries outside the Soviet bloc.

To assure an overall balance in payments, the Ministry of Foreign Trade prefers to follow the primitive rule of securing a balance with every individual country. This is the rule of *bilateralism*: essentially, barter deals between pairs of countries. These overall deals are negotiated through bilateral intercountry trade agreements, long-term (general) and annual (very specified).

An automatic corollary of bilateral balancing of trade is currency inconvertibility. Currencies of Soviet-bloc countries are practically inconvertible into other currencies. They cannot be accumulated as part of foreign-exchange holdings abroad. No one would want to hold them, anyway. They do not represent a general liquid purchasing power, enabling its holders to buy Soviet-bloc merchandise at will. Only when accompanied by a Soviet-bloc export contract do they become usable, and then only as a unit of account in which transactions are quoted. Thus, there is no foreign exchange market for Soviet-bloc currencies, and exchange rates are fixed administratively at more or less arbitrarily chosen levels. They have no influence on trade volumes whatsoever.

Further Peculiarities and Economic Efficiency

Foreign trade cannot be used very effectively for improving allocation of resources if the trading countries have no domestic prices reflecting relative scarcities with reasonable accuracy. This lack makes it extremely difficult to answer the basic issue of comparative advantage: "Does the country get more from abroad in return for its exports than it would if it dropped the production of particular exportables, and instead produced at home what it had been importing?" This lack of guidance through prices has been characteristic for foreign-trade decisions of Soviet-type systems, but until recently they did not seem to be giving much thought to this standard benefit-from-trade aspect of the matter.

Soviet-bloc countries did, though, consider it necessary to conduct their bilateral barter deals as sales and purchases accompanied by money flows. This is why goods had to have *some* price tags. However, domestic prices were found unusable for the purpose. The helter-skelter pattern of relative "wholesale prices" in each individual bloc country, owing to different incidence of arbitrary profit (or loss) rates, has completely obliterated the underlying (but unknown) differences in relative costs. Hence, since the early fifties, the countries in question had recourse to an artificial set of prices, constructed on the basis of market-capitalist "world prices" of some past bench-mark year.[8] These prices have never reflected the relative cost-and-demand relationships within the bloc. In fact, they rather ran in the opposite direction, but then they were not meant to be used as guides to decisions. Foreign-trade prices were just accounting prices used to give semblance of money transactions to international barter.

What, then, does determine the content of trade of Soviet-bloc economies? We mentioned the fact that import-export plans are derived from planned material balances. This and knowing something about the planners' mentality give us a clue.

There are three basic types of attitudes toward foreign trade. First, the liberal one: "Buy abroad whatever is cheaper there than at home, and sell abroad whatever commands a higher price there than at home." Second, the mercantilist one: "Export, export! Import only if you absolutely have to." Mercantilists of the seventeenth century valued export surpluses for the sake of the gold they would bring in.[9] The third type of attitude is expressed in the rule to import as little as possible, but also to export as little as possible, certainly not more than necessary to plan for the unavoidable imports. It is this last mentality of autarchic inspiration which has colored Soviet-bloc policies.

Such "trade aversion," as Alan Brown calls this autarchic impulse, is usually explained by planners' preference for having to deal with an easier-to-organize closed economy rather than with an open one. "The primitive planner," in E. A. Hewett's words,

---

[8] See Edward A. Hewett, *Foreign Trade Prices in the Council for Mutual Economic Assistance*, Cambridge University Press, London, 1974.

[9] By analogy, contemporary countries with persistent export surpluses, but reluctant to correct the exchange rate of their undervalued currency upward (such as West Germany and Japan in the sixties), have sometimes been accused of "neo-mercantilism."

is frightened of foreign trade, showing almost total concern for the uncertainty associated with it and almost no concern for the potential gains from trade. Therefore, he consistently gives precedence to the inefficient domestic firm under his (apparent) control over the efficient foreign firm outside his control. Planning is a search for consistency using material balances; hardcore imports are a disgusting fact of life.[10]

The motive of self-sufficiency for military reasons, and as protection against economic fluctuations in the market-capitalist world, has also played a role.

These basic attitudes have been somewhat modified by considerations of various orders. Thus, the preference for a closed economy was ignored in early postwar Soviet demand for high imports from the outlying industrially more advanced satellites. We shall discuss that below in the section on imperialism. Other modifications have been associated with the phenomenon of "trade proclivity" of the smaller bloc countries (another term coined by A. Brown). This was caused, paradoxically, by the early attempts at autarchic ("trade averse") import-substitution development policies. All this will come under discussion in the section on COMECON integration, together with the progressive awakening to opportunities based on comparative advantage. There has been an increasing concern with terms of trade, i.e., with the amount of goods exported compared to the amount of imported goods received in return, which is a rough indicator of comparative advantage.

COMECON INTEGRATION EFFORTS

Nothing could be more misleading than to accept at face value the frequently drawn parallel between the European Economic Community and the Soviet-bloc Council of Mutual Economic Assistance (CMEA), known also under its popular name as COMECON. Despite the similarity of economic systems of the COMECON countries—or perhaps just because of it—the degree of integration within that organization has been incomparably lower than anywhere in the market-capitalist sphere.

Barriers to trade and factor movements have mostly not been of the customary sort, such as tariffs. Rather, they have been built into the bilateral trade contracts. These play effectively the role of direct quantitative controls. Currency regulations and inconvertibility also place limitations upon trade. The contrast between the state of integration of the two areas can be roughly gauged by their involvement in foreign trade. In the case of the EEC, its share in world trade in 1970 was 2.2 times as high as its share in the world's industrial output. The proportion was only 0.7 in the case of COMECON without the U.S.S.R. and 0.33 with the U.S.S.R. included.[11]

The state of relative nonintegration of the Soviet bloc has to be traced back to Stalin's political decision to prevent all spontaneous attempts of satellite states

[10] Hewett, op. cit., p. 124.

[11] Z. M. Fallenbuchl, "Comecon Integration," *Problems of Communism*, vol. 22, March–April 1973, p. 30.

at forming federations, and to thwart some early ideas of areawide coordination of economic development. Stalin's preferred way was to keep the satellites isolated from each other and to deal with each of them separately. Consequently, the less-developed countries of the area were encouraged to embark upon rapid industrialization plans, trying to duplicate the Soviet example. The advanced countries (Czechoslovakia, East Germany) served at the beginning as engines of these every-man-for-himself industrialization strategies, receiving raw materials and foodstuffs for their investment goods.

However, what at the beginning looked like a sensible integration of complementary economies disappeared surprisingly fast. The reason was that each industrializer adopted an import-substitution strategy. Every developing country in the area strove for a capacity to produce a full line of manufactures parallel to each other. As a result, several very similar new national industrial complexes appeared side by side. They were duplicates of each other, all eager to unload exportable surpluses abroad, but none needing to import what the others wanted to export. When it was realized what happened, COMECON countries began to hold conferences, belatedly negotiating specialization agreements, and to coordinate investment plans so as to prevent a repetition in the future.

At the same time, another structural problem developed. With emphasis on manufacturing branches, exporters of raw materials increased their domestic raw-material consumption, while forgetting to expand the supply capacity sufficiently. As a result, a chronic shortage of raw materials began to plague the area, accompanied by a relative surfeit of manufactures, especially machinery. It is important to make clear that the surfeit concerned ordinary, or even substandard, machinery, such as could be expected from countries not exactly on the forefront of technological progress, deprived of advantages of large-scale production, sheltered from pressures of competition, and laboring under the anti-innovation and antiquality biases of the incentive systems (see Chapter 9). Side by side with this kind of plenty, there has been hunger for high-quality machine tools.

Next to defects in industrial specialization, the foreign-trade pulls and stresses between member states can be traced to this structural imbalance in the supply of raw materials and machinery. The raw material exporters were placed in an excellent bargaining position. On the one hand, they could force their trade partners to buy their third-rate machine articles by making it a condition for receiving raw-material shipments. On the other hand, they could divert part of their raw materials to the West in order to finance purchases of superior manufactures from the West, rather than making do forever with inferior COMECON merchandise. Romania and Poland, in that order, were in the best position to exploit the possibility of such partial *trade reorientation*. The more industrialized countries in the bloc found this road closed: their manufactures have not been good enough to find easy markets in the West. These basic facts are essential for understanding the character and structure of economic power relations, i.e., the nature of Soviet economic domination, which we shall examine in the next section.[12]

TYPES OF ECONOMIC IMPERIALISM COMPARED: EAST VERSUS WEST

It has been customary in many quarters to identify modern economic imperialism exclusively with advanced market capitalism. If the phenomenon often stays unrecognized in its Soviet variant, it is either because the observer wears ideological blinkers or has been misled by differences in form. Let us therefore proceed by establishing in what respects the Soviet case is similar to the market-capitalist case, and where they differ.

Traditional Market-Capitalist Type

The basic feature of any imperialism is inequality of power between countries. Thanks to such disparity, the dominant country is able to obtain from the weaker one involuntary favors. These favors consist usually in some transfer of wealth or income from the weaker country to the dominant one.[13] Under market capitalism, such favors are typically connected with the extension of the radius of operation of firms whose home is in the imperial metropolis to the territory of the weaker country.

In the process, the economy of the dominated country, the "colony," usually undergoes a structural transformation. The new structure is geared to the economic objectives of the franchised firms from the imperial metropolis. The objectives may differ: to secure a dependable supply of raw materials; to create a captive market for exports from the metropolis; to utilize a favorable constellation of local cost factors for establishing subsidiaries; and others. The changed structure may be irreversible. That means that a state of dependence is created for the colony. It becomes dependent on the continuation of conditions which have brought the structural change about. The economic-dependence effect solidifies the power of the metropolis further.

All this sounds very negative, but the outcome of market-capitalist imperialism is usually ambiguous or, in any case, not a priori worse than real alternatives available to the colony. If it were not so, why would many politically sovereign underdeveloped countries try to submit to such structural transformations voluntarily? Why would they court foreign firms and entice them to invest in their territory? But even if the transformation is not voluntary, the colony may

---

[12] For useful surveys, see Hertha W. Heiss, "The Council for Mutual Economic Assistance—Developments since the Mid-1960's," in U.S. Congress, Joint Economic Committee, *Economic Developments in Countries of Eastern Europe*, 1970, pp. 528–542, and Zbigniew M. Fallenbuchl, "East European Integration: Comecon," in U.S. Congress, Joint Economic Committee, *Reorientation and Commercial Relations of the Economies of Eastern Europe*, 1974, pp. 79–136.

[13] See Melvin W. Reder, "An Economic Theory of Imperialism," in Paul A. David and Melvin W. Keder (eds.), *Nations and Households in Economic Growth*, Academic, New York, 1974, pp. 147–171.

benefit economically: if there is a transfer of production factors, such as discussed in the section on multinational enterprise, productivity of local factors is raised. Inflow of foreign capital is a supplement to the usually meager investments available through domestic saving. It becomes an ingredient of economic development. It may not be the best development path imaginable; it need not correspond to balanced growth of academic blueprints; but it is not stagnation. And, especially, it is not the kind of development under which the burden of capital accumulation falls exclusively on domestic savings obtainable only at the expense of domestic consumption.

It is, of course, also "exploitation"—insofar as all capitalism is. *Capitalist profits repatriated to the metropolis represent the colonial tribute, the transfer of income, which defines economic imperialism. However, it is a transfer coming from an increment to national income, which had been produced thanks to the very act of imperialist investments.* It would not even exist, or would be much smaller, if it were not for that foreign investment. Besides, the major part of the new income thus created remains anyway in the colony: the wage part; the tax on profits; and the reinvested portion of profits.[14]

Incidentally, Marx's view of economic imperialism is of considerable interest, in this connection. Marx has been usually invoked as the patron of anti-Western nationalist opponents of foreign capital investments in the Third World. In reality, Marx "endorsed" in his writings the fact of capitalist global expansion, which he interpreted as a progressive phase of economic development. Just as he praised, in the *Communist Manifesto*, the bourgeoisie for having "rescued a considerable part of the population from the idiocy of rural life," he also noted in its favor that "it has made barbarian and semi-barbarian countries dependent on the civilized ones, nations of peasants on nations of bourgeois, the East on the West." The civilizing mission of capitalism in its worldwide spread, in spite of the accompanying pains of adjustment due to the shattering of traditional society, was a recurrent theme in Marx's writings, especially in his comments on the British rule in India.[15]

Soviet-Style Economic Imperialism

Soviet economic imperialism differs from the Western type in one crucial aspect: The Soviet Union does not practice net capital exports in the direction of countries it dominates. It does not add from its own resources to the capital stock of the client states. If anything, it has forced them to add to its own stock, or to increase their domestic capital accumulation in order to satisfy Soviet foreign-trade requirements. In contrast to Western imperialism, emanating from advanced industrial countries, Soviet imperialism has been the imperialism of a

---

[14] On the topic of costs and benefits of direct foreign investments in less-developed countries, see chap. 25 in Franklin R. Root, *International Trade and Investment*, 3d ed., South-Western Publishing Company, Cincinnati, 1973, pp. 611–652. See also, P. T. Bauer, "Western Guilt and Third World Poverty," *Commentary*, vol. 61, no. 1, January 1976, pp. 31–38.

[15] See Shlomo Avineri (ed.), *Marx on Colonialism and Modernization*, Doubleday, Garden City, N.Y., 1968. A lucid understanding of Marx's point of view is also reflected in Bill Warren, "Imperialism and Capitalist Industrialization," *New Left Review*, no. 81, September–October 1973, pp. 3–44.

large semideveloped economy, thirsting for capital. The structural changes in the dominated countries, their degree of irreversibility, the colonial tribute, and the state of dependence in consequence have also had a different character.

To understand the issues properly, it is necessary to tell the story of Soviet economic domination by overlapping historical stages. Up to the midfifties, an identifiable net transfer of output flowed in the direction of the Soviet Union from the Eastern and Central European area. It amounted, it so happens, to the value of the postwar grant from the United States to Western Europe, known as Marshall Plan aid.[16] This tribute pure and simple was due mainly to war reparations from East Germany.

The next overlapping stage began in the late forties. It amounted to the enforcement of new economic structures in the satellite countries. The instrument was the system of bilateral agreements. They contained large orders of commodities on the part of the satellites, particularly the more advanced ones. These were supposed to become vast industrial workshops for processing Soviet raw materials into finished manufacturing products, and exporting these back to the Soviet Union. Forced industrialization of the less-developed countries, mentioned in the preceding section, was part of a scheme of achieving areawide self-sufficiency. The colonial tribute was of two kinds. It took the form of diversion of resources from potential consumption to the extraordinarily high investments (see Chapter 12), as well as of the enforced sacrifice of opportunities of economic integration with the West.[17] Almost overnight, Soviet policy created a system of "imperial preferences" which diverted most of the former westward flow of trade inward,[18] a dramatic turnabout, without precedent except for times of war.

The third phase coincides with the emergence of the areawide imbalance between the supply of raw materials and manufactures. As explained earlier, the scarcity of raw materials increased the bargaining power of the raw-material suppliers, which means the Soviet Union in particular. However, the piquancy of the situation consists in the Soviet Union's not being free to exploit its power fully, and becoming, economically at least, something of a loser vis-à-vis the satellites. It is now the Soviet Union which has to forgo the opportunity of switching its exports, primarily of oil and natural gas, from the satellite markets to the West, in exchange for highly coveted technology-intensive products, unob-

[16] See Paul Marer, "Soviet Economic Policy in Eastern Europe," in U.S. Congress, Joint Economic Committee, *Reorientation and Commercial Relations of the Economies of Eastern Europe*, 1974, p. 138–145. Our account draws heavily on this study, as well as on his paper "Has Eastern Europe Become a Liability to the Soviet Union–the Economic Aspects," in Charles Gati (ed.), *The International Politics of Eastern Europe*, Praeger, New York, 1976.

[17] Whereas before the war trade of the Eastern European area with the Soviet Union was insignificant, it rose to about one-third of the total trade from the fifties on. Trade of Eastern European countries with each other rose from one-fourth before the war to about three-fourths of their total trade.

[18] The term "imperial preferences" refers to a preferential treatment of trade between an imperial metropolis and its dependent colonies, intended to keep outsiders out of the imperial market. The British system of 1932 is the most prominent example. The Japanese Great East Asia Co-Prosperity Sphere of prewar times is another one. In the case of the COMECON, however, it is more a case of insiders being kept from trading with the outside.

tainable from the satellites. If it did so, it would create an areawide recession and quite possibly political turmoil. This is a risk it does not want to run.

Nevertheless, the Soviet Union did make the satellite economies feel its increased bargaining clout. For over a decade, Soviet representatives have been hinting that the use of artificial "world prices" in intrabloc trade put the Soviet Union at a disadvantage. They made raw materials relatively cheap and manufactured goods expensive, although the raw materials have been in short supply compared to manufactures. The Soviet Union—a net exporter of raw materials—had to pay with more goods for its imports of manufactures than it felt was fair. For reasons that are not clear, Moscow hesitated to push the issue, until the worldwide quadrupling of oil prices in early 1974 provided an opportunity. After that, it proceeded to negotiate with the bloc countries price increases of oil (somewhat more than doubling them) as well as of other raw materials. Exporters of manufactures have also found themselves under increasing pressure to improve quality and technical design of their articles, under the penalty of being bypassed in favor of Western sources.

However, potentially the most significant effort has been directed by Moscow toward satellite participation in new investment projects, designed to expand the COMECON energy and raw-material base. Joint financing of investment projects in the area is nothing new in relations between individual satellite countries, though it has remained sporadic. What is new is the emphasis, since 1971,[19] on satellite contribution to projects situated primarily on Soviet soil (pipelines, steel mills, etc.). The participation is in the form of cheap long-term credits or, more exactly, "barter over time": satellites deliver machinery and installments now and get a flow of output from the facility when it is finished—the same formula as in the case of some of the contemplated Soviet-Western pipeline deals.

As far as the logic of Soviet imperialism is concerned—its insatiable appetite for capital—this type of transaction is by far the most suitable and conforms to tradition. It is only location and purpose that have changed with time. In the fifties, the satellites were forced to undertake investments desired by the Soviet Union on their territory; in the seventies, on that of the metropolis itself. Then it was heavy industry, armaments, and machine building; now it is fuels and raw materials.

It has been repeatedly submitted, as a hypothesis, that the system of client states has progressively turned into an economic liability for the Soviet Union. "Annex in haste, subsidize at leisure" is the wry comment by Peter Wiles. It could well be that the Soviet Union loses, on balance, by not being free to reorient its trade at will toward the West, or to improve the COMECON terms of trade as harshly as for instance the international oil cartel did. If the Soviet Union were really incurring a net economic loss, one would have to infer from its behavior that the political and strategic value of its empire is well worth stopping short of the degree of economic pressures which is within its power.

---

[19] In that year, the COMECON adopted a far-reaching Complex Program for Intensifying and Improving Cooperation and for Developing Socialist Economic Integration.

FOREIGN TRANSACTIONS BETWEEN ADVERSARIES

Benefits from trade, a basic assumption underlying all our previous discussions, acquire an entirely new color when the trading countries are political enemies and potential belligerents. "Love thy enemy" is a noble maxim, but does it mean that an arms dealer ought to sell ammunition to a robber who will use it on the spot, or to offer food if the robber is faint? Analysis is easy as long as traded assets have positive utility to the buyers, without any adverse effects upon the sellers. The matter becomes more complicated when the "good" sold to a buyer can become in the buyer's hands, from the point of view of the seller, a dangerous or even lethal nuisance.

Today, it is widely taken from granted that rational policy consists in preventing an adversary from being able to import arms, as well as militarily significant "strategic material." Economic blockade, or denial of strategic exports to the enemy, does not seem to require elaborate justification. The reasonableness of United States and Western European embargo on strategic goods, at the height of East-West tensions (up to about 1954), has in general not been questioned. The embargo rested on a multiplicity of legislative acts: U.S. Export Control Act (1949), the Battle Act (1952), the Johnson Act (1964), Trading with the Enemy Act (1950). For Europe and Japan, the lists of prohibitions and limitations were the work of the Coordinating Committee (COCOM) of the Consultative Group of NATO.[20] When relations between the Soviet Union and the West began to be perceived as "relaxation of tensions," it seemed logical to relax about the embargo, too. The list was progressively cut down to a hard core of items of undisputable military significance. Otherwise there was no reason, according to common sense, why trading should not be allowed to expand as far as it would go.

What may be rational in trade relations with an adversary according to common sense may appear less self-evident under closer scrutiny. Unfortunately, different analysts have been arriving at diametrically opposite conclusions. To a layperson, this can be quite disconcerting since they all seem to be equally sophisticated and sincere. Does it increase Western security and chances of lasting peace if one dilutes further and further the notion of strategic items and promotes trade relations by all means? Or would it perhaps be better, on the contrary, to extend the notion of strategic items and limit trade as much as possible? Or limit it judiciously? And what would "judiciously" mean? Let us therefore analyze the competing analyses.

The Trade-Denial School

Under conditions of twentieth-century warfare, foreshadowed by the American Civil War, hostilities are not carried out by limited engagements of limited ar-

---

[20] See Nicolas Spulber, "East-West Trade and the Paradoxes of the Strategic Embargo," in Alan A. Brown and Egon Neuberger, *International Trade and Central Planning*, University of California Press, Berkeley, 1968, pp. 104–129; also U.S. Senate, Committee on Foreign Relations, *A Background Study on East-West Trade*, 1965, pp. 38–44.

mies. The full human, moral, and productive potential of adversaries matters for the outcome on the battlefields. It would therefore seem to follow that all goods available to an adversary through foreign trade are to be considered as more or less strategic products. Indeed, it is plausible to argue that consumer goods, expecially food, have greater military significance than anything else. Food supply through foreign trade, especially if it prevents a drastic consumption decline in the country of an adversary regime, helps preserve the loyalty of the population which is an essential component of a credible capacity to wage war.

The school of thought which argues in favor of a maximum trade denial to the adversary bases the argument, implicitly or explicitly, on the assumption that what the adversary gives in return for imported goods is not of equivalent benefit value to the opposite side. It might be equivalent in strictly commercial terms. Without some reasonable commercial quid pro quo there could not be any trade to begin with. However, this is not the point.

It is the suspicion of belligerent intentions harbored by the adversary which changes the net balance of benefits. Insofar as these suspicions have a foundation in observed behavior, even if only in terms of probabilities, and perhaps only in terms of the use of threats rather than actual shooting war, *the benefit accruing to the adversary contains a negative value for the opposite side, which has to be subtracted from the commercial benefit of goods, or promissory notes, supplied by the adversary.*

Under such conditions, denying trade to the adversary means depriving him of the net benefits he hopes to derive from imports. He then has to obtain whatever it is he covets at the higher opportunity cost given by his own domestic production possibilities. He may be forced to shift resources from munitions to fertilizer plants, if he wants to secure dependable levels of agricultural production. He may have to do his own research-and-development homework if he wants to have computers and other technology-intensive articles. He may have to divert resources from armaments to large-diameter pipelines if he wants to exploit his faraway oil and natural-gas fields.

In each illustrative case it is assumed that domestic output forgone by the adversary in such an enforced process of import substitution would be more valuable to him than the output he is willing to export (e.g., caviar). The trade-denial strategy means letting the adversary stew in his own domestic cost relations. Of course, similar losses accrue to the other side, but there, the full cost-benefit analysis says, they are being erased by not having to face the consequences of the presumed increments to the economic and military power of the adversary.

The Judicious-Use-of-Trade School

This approach sees the costs and benefits of trading with the adversary in just about the same light as the trade-denial school, but it draws different practical conclusions. This is because its advocates have been able to cite not only the inequality of benefits derived from trade but also the potentially superior bargaining power of that side which needs the trade less. They would like to see this bargaining power utilized. The adversary gets his imports cheap, they imply. The market price understates the true benefit of the imports to him, especially if he is able to play Western competitors against each other, time his purchases smartly, or obtain low-interest credits. Also, the import demand of the adversary tends to be more inelastic, especially in times of pressing need owing to bad harvests.

The idea promoted by this school is to *use the concealed superiority in bargaining power in order to improve Western terms of trade*, i.e., to raise the asking price above the commercial market prices. Preferably, the supplement to the market price should have a form which would tend to reduce the dangerous nuisance value of Western goods once in the hands of the adversary. *Most logically, the supplement should be in the form of suitable political concessions* that would contribute to a progressive change in the political character of the adversary, until he would cease being an adversary and trade with him could be evaluated in terms of normal criteria.

The Full-Steam-Ahead Trading School

This school, which has been the most influential of the three approaches, concentrates almost exclusively on the private commercial benefits of trading with the adversary. If it brings in political considerations at all, they are based on an entirely different reading of the long-term intentions of the adversary, or of the influence expanding trade contacts will have upon his intentions, character, and international behavior.

The private-benefit side, which is of interest to individual capitalist firms working for exports, is obviously not an adequate basis for judging the social costs and benefits of trading with the adversary. The supporting political arguments are the ones that count most. Of these arguments, the reasoning which focuses on increasing interdependence of the trading partners is the most persuasive. *If autarchy enhances the ability to wage war, then economic interdependence, i.e., dependence of the adversary on imports from the other side, decreases it.* He is then motivated to behave peacefully in order to secure the flow of imports he needs. In contrast, trade denial forces the adversary to become self-sufficient through autarchic policies, which increase his war-making capability.

The supporting cast of minor arguments is intellectually and logically somewhat less respectable: "If we do not sell, then our competitors in other countries will" (whereas at issue is whether anybody should); the cost inflicted on the adversary by trade denial is minor anyway (which detracts from the question of principle to the estimate of specific magnitudes, and generally amounts to a guess or an assertion); and trade in itself is a road to peace by bringing people together (a non sequitur which ignores the highly controlled circumstances under which East-West contacts take place, so that trading may easily create the image of peacefulness rather than its substance).

Which School Is Right?

This issue, which is a matter of principle, must be carefully distinguished from the question as to which approach is the easiest to follow. As for practical feasibility, the full-steam-ahead school has been carrying the day. Trade has been denied by Western countries less and less, and a "judicious use of trade" was attempted, in a certain sense, only in 1974, when the United States Congress voted the so-called Jackson-Vanik amendment to the Trade Bill. This piece of legislation linked the political issue of free emigration to the issue of granting lowest possible import tariffs (the so-called most-favored-nation clause) and long-term official credits to Soviet-area countries.

As far as validity of the three sets of arguments is concerned, each tendency has its own appeal depending on one's reading of the political nature of the conflict, its historic significance, and the long-range goals of the adversaries. This is *the* area of decision making under uncertainty if there ever was one, and the final advantage will go to the side whose strategists are more astute in predicting the most probable future scenarios under alternative courses of action. This would seem to call for much greater subtlety of political analysis than has been displayed in the West in the course of the controversy on trade. Since it is the full-steam-ahead tendency which has been in vogue, it is convenient to give special attention to its underlying rationale.

As far as private benefits from exports to the Soviet Union are concerned, it must be pointed out that they have been covered, to a significant degree by low-interest private and government credits. There just happens not to be a naturally strong demand for Soviet goods in the West which could pay for Soviet imports. The technicalities of financing exports to the Soviet Union raise the question to what extent they resemble, in effect, unilateral economic aid rather than hard-nosed business deals. To decide that question would call for a closely documented examination.[21]

As for the validity of the political side of the rationale, it hinges on how reliable are the beneficial effects of the trade-induced economic interdependence between the adversaries. The economic-interdependence argument can be X-rayed from two different directions. We have to inquire whether the interdependence is permanent or reversible, or to what degree, for each side taken separately. And we have to ask whether hostile intentions are not compatible after all with economic dependence of the adversary on foreign imports, be they reversible or not.

To come to any conclusions about reversibility or durability of economic interdependence through trade, it is necessary to examine the specific character of major individual transactions. Thus, in the barter deals concerning "Western pipelines now, Soviet oil and gas later," the issue appears as follows: Once Western pipelines and oil rigs are delivered, Soviet dependence stops and Western dependence begins. As for imports of Western high-technology equipment, they can be stopped any time without disrupting the adversary's economy.

---

[21] See Paul Marer, "Indebtedness, Credit Policies, and New Sources of Financing," in Carl H. McMillan (ed.), *Changing Perspectives in East-West Commerce*, Heath, Lexington, Mass., 1975, pp. 125–148; also John T. Farrell, "Soviet Payments Problems in Trade with the West," in U.S. Congress, Joint Economic Committee, *Soviet Economic Prospects for the Seventies*, 1973, pp. 690–696.

Dependence on spare parts is reduced if Western imports are used as proto-types for the Soviet Union's own production. Long-term credits strengthen the hand of the borrower because the lender is dependent on their voluntary repay-ment. The only really serious dependence exists in the case of stopgap imports of Western grains in times of periodic bad harvests. And that dependence may be progressively reduced with the help of new fertilizer plants imported from the West. Thus, the permanence of trade interdependence is very much in question.

Besides, dependence on Western imports need not exclude hostile acts in the military and diplomatic spheres. One cannot properly judge the peace-promoting potential of East-West trade if one ignores the fact that hostilities, short of world-war dimensions, can continue side by side with trade expansion. Trade may be used to project the image of peaceful intentions for the benefit of those suscepti-ble to it, to soften up their defenses. The threat implied by military capabilities, and smaller peripheral shooting wars by proxy, may be used as means of political intimidation against those susceptible. Trade would then have to be interpreted as part of a double-barreled international strategy. While contributing to an at-mosphere of accommodation, it would also have to be seen as contributing mate-rially to making the power threats more believable.

There also exist crude guideposts for analysis, such as Lenin's serious joke to the effect that capitalists would compete with each other to sell communists the rope on which to be hanged, not much different from Count Witte writing in a memorandum to the czar in 1886:

> Why should these countries lend us capital? They simply build up for themselves a more dangerous rival for the future. However, we should pray that their blindness will continue for as long as possible.[22]

However, one can also dismiss such references as cute historical anecdotes, if one is so inclined. On the other hand, if the rationale underlying the full-steam-ahead school is found wanting, this would automatically raise the persuasiveness of the two other schools.

*   *   *

The survey of styles in foreign transactions concludes a long series of chap-ters (7 through 15) which dealt with aspects of economic systems amenable to comparative analysis by means of standard theoretical tools. Even though it was found necessary, once in a while, to reach for political, sociological, or psycholog-ical concepts outside the narrow toolbox of straight economics, this was only incidental. With the remaining three chapters on consumers' and workers' sover-eignty, and on the future of economic systems, we are entering a sphere where the approach from the cultural and historical side becomes preponderant.

---

[22] Cited in Herbert E. Meyer, "Why That Soviet Buying Spree Won't Last," *Fortune*, January 1975, p. 97.

BIBLIOGRAPHY

Kenen, Peter B. (ed.): *International Trade and Finance: Frontiers for Research*, Cambridge University Press, New York, 1976.

Knorr, Klaus: *The Power of Nations: The Political Economy of International Relations*, Basic Books, New York, 1975.

Bergsten, Fred C.: *Dilemmas of the Dollar: The Economics and Politics of United States International Monetary Policy*, New York University Press, New York, 1976.

Hudec, Robert E.: *The GATT Legal System and World Trade Diplomacy*, Praeger, New York, 1975.

Balassa, Bela (ed.): *European Economic Integration*, American Elsevier, New York, 1975.

Denton, G. R. (ed.): *Economic Integration in Europe*, Weidenfeld and Nicolson, London, 1969.

Hoepli, Nancy L. (ed.): *The Common Market*, H. W. Wilson, New York, 1975 (bibliography).

Shonfield, Andrew (ed.): *International Economic Relations of the Western World, 1959–1971*, vol. 1: A. Shonfield et al., *Politics and Trade;* vol. 2: Susan Strange, *International Monetary Relations,* Oxford University Press, New York, 1976.

Baldwin, Robert E.: "International Trade in Inputs and Outputs," *American Economic Review*, vol. 60, no. 2, May 1970, pp. 430–440.

Hymer, Stephen: "The Efficiency (Contradictions) of Multinational Corporations," *American Economic Review*, vol. 60, no. 2, May 1970, pp. 441–448.

Dunning, John H.: *The Multinational Enterprise*, Praeger, New York, 1971.

"The Multinational Corporation," *The Annals* (American Academy of Political and Social Science), vol. 403, September 1972.

Kindleberger, Charles P.: *American Business Abroad*, Yale, New Haven, Conn., 1969.

―――― (ed.): *The International Corporation*, M.I.T., Cambridge, Mass., 1970.

Parry, T. G.: "The International Firm and National Economic Policy: A Survey of Some Issues," *The Economic Journal*, vol. 83, no. 332, December 1973, pp. 1201–1221 (bibliography).

Said, Abdul A., and Luiz R. Simmons (eds.): *The New Sovereigns: Multinational Corporations as World Powers*, Prentice-Hall, Englewood Cliffs, N.J., 1975.

Wiles, P. J. D.: *Communist International Economics*, Praeger, New York, 1968.

Brown, Alan A., and Egon Neuberger (eds.): *International Trade and Central Planning*, University of California Press, Berkeley, 1968.

Holzman, Franklyn D.: *Foreign Trade under Central Planning*, Harvard, Cambridge, Mass., 1974.

Hewett, Edward A.: *Foreign Trade Prices in the Council for Mutual Economic Assistance*, Cambridge University Press, London, 1974.

Fallenbuchl, Zbigniew M.: "East European Integration: Comecon," in U.S. Congress, Joint Economic Committee: *Reorientation and Commercial Relations of the Economies of Eastern Europe*, 1974, pp. 79–134.

Marer, Paul: "Soviet Economic Policy in Eastern Europe," *Reorientation and Commercial Relations of the Economies of Eastern Europe*, 1974, pp. 135–163.

Hirschman, Albert O.: *National Power and the Structure of Foreign Trade*, University of California Press, Berkeley, 1945.

Wolfe, Martin: *The Economic Causes of Imperialism*, Wiley, New York, 1972.

Boulding, Kenneth E., and Tapan Mukerjee (eds.): *Economic Imperialism: A Book of Readings*, The University of Michigan Press, Ann Arbor, 1972.

Cohen, Benjamin J.: *The Question of Imperialism: The Political Economy of Dominance and Dependence*, Basic Books, New York, 1973.

Nove, A.: "East-West Trade," in Paul A. Samuelson (ed.): *International Economic Relations*, St. Martin's, New York, 1969, pp. 100–120; Imre Vajda, "The Problems of East-West Trade," in ibid., pp. 121–133; and comments by J. Bénard, Evsey D. Domar, John Michael Montias, and Michael Kaser in ibid., pp. 134–154.

McMillan, Carl H. (ed.): *Changing Perspectives in East-West Commerce*, Heath, Lexington, Mass., 1975.

U.S. Senate, Committee on Foreign Relations: *East-West Trade: A Compilation of Views of Businessmen, Bankers, and Academic Experts*, 1964 (esp. Robert W. Campbell, pp. 230–233, and Gregory Grossman, pp. 245–249).

————: *A Background Study on East-West Trade*, 1965.

U.S. Senate: *East-West Trade, Hearings before the Subcommittee on International Finance of the Committee on Banking and Currency*, parts 1, 2, and 3, 1968.

Wolf, Thomas A.: *U.S. East-West Trade Policy*, Heath, Lexington, Mass., 1973.

Goldman, Marshall I.: *Détente and Dollars: Doing Business with the Soviets*, Basic Books, New York, 1975.

Chapter 16

Consumers' Sovereignty

Yet, the fact is that information always gravitates from a giant information industry or from a governmental organization, while little of it is feedback from the general mass of consumers. Not until the ever-increasing flow of information is established in genuine two-way traffic patterns can society change basically from what it is now. . . .

Yujiro Hayashi

Gone are the times when people genuinely believed that production took place unequivocally for the consumers' sake. Under Soviet-type CPEs, there never even were such times. Daily experience has taught the population that, as consumers, they have been the object of a not-so-benign neglect in the scheme of planners' preferences. Under market-capitalist systems, the folklore of popular slogans did sustain the belief in consumers' sovereignty for quite a while: the customer was said to be the boss, to be always right, and the customer's satisfaction to be the highest law for business whose agents always "tried harder." Over the years, consumers have grown more skeptical even there, what with all the signs of "built-in obsolescence," the hard sell of advertising, and frequent disappearance of perfectly satisfactory items from production programs.

Infractions of the principle of consumers' sovereignty are not the privilege of any one system. However, as we shall see, they are of an entirely different sort, as well as degree, under market capitalism on the one hand and state capitalism of the Soviet type on the other. Before we examine these differences, we have to analyze more closely the concept of consumers' sovereignty itself.

THE CONCEPT ANALYZED

Consumers' sovereignty is a frankly normative concept. Indeed, it reigns supreme over and above other normative concepts of welfare economics because they all presuppose it. Consumers should and have to be sovereign; they have to be autonomous, self-determined, free, and of their own making, to generate an objectively given set of preferences to which the production sector would cater.

At first blush, it is not clear why there should be any problem. The concept of consumers' sovereignty deals with the character of the relationship between consumers on the one hand and production activities on the other. It is natural to think of the production sector as providing the means, while the obvious end resides in satisfying consumer needs, tastes, preferences, and the demand based on them. It seems strange to have to consider the possibility of the production sector having any interest in limiting consumers' sovereignty. What purposes of its own would it want to pursue in depriving consumers of their autonomy and in manipulating them? In that respect, to be suspicious of governments does apparently not seem particularly strange. One is not all that astonished to find governments influencing certain portions of consumers' preferences, or even suppressing these completely if they happen to clash with preferences of the group in power, which is the normal case in despotic regimes.

However, before we analyze cases where consumers' sovereignty is violated, we must ask ourselves whether the standard notion of independently given consumer tastes makes any sense. Can tastes be really autonomous, free, self-determined? Can they be formed by cultural values existing outside the sphere of the economic system? And if they cannot, where do legitimate influences upon consumers' tastes stop? Where does violation of their sovereignty begin?

Consumption-Production Dialogue

To imagine consumers' preferences to be formed in one airtight compartment of the social system, and production activities to take place in another, is a distortion of reality which, in the study of economic systems, cannot be taken seriously, not even for a moment. Only in fairy tales can capricious kings or princesses make fantastic demands in total disregard of production possibilities, whereupon supernatural powers naturally have to intervene to take care of the supply side. Custom-made production, articles made to order, the case of the "bespoke overcoat"—these come closest to the idea of consumer tastes hatched in isolation and served by a passively obedient production sector. However, even there the production sector provides correctives, suggests modifications, in one word, enters into a dialogue with the consumer.

On the other hand, the production sector never has an absolute power to force upon consumers articles of its own arbitrary choosing. Even in the case of anonymous mass markets, production units do not offer just any kind of commodities at random, to await the verdict of the sales record and then, through elimination, to narrow the set of produced commodities down to those which are acceptable to consumers.

First of all, decision makers on the production side are not complete strangers to the world of consumers' needs and tastes. When they do not organize production, they are consumers themselves. Second, in a competitive growth economy, producers keep scanning the horizon for unsatisfied wants. There is a constant effort to detect latent demand, even without any initiative on the consumers' part.

However, there also is a legitimate place for the production sector to actively shape or create consumers' wants by proposing new products or innovative adaptations of old ones. It is in the course of productive activities that economic systems discover new alternatives, new ways of satisfying human wants, or possibilities to satisfy wants which could not even exist before the possibility of having them, and satisfying them, had been discovered in the course of productive activities. It is entirely misleading to think of consumer wants as entering the scene to confront the production sector already made up, backstage, somewhere in the sphere of culture and psychology. The point is that the production sector, too, is an active part of culture and social psychology.

It would mean limiting the concept unduly if we were to think that consumers' sovereignty can be fully realized if and only if consumers form their tastes entirely on their own. By offering innovations to the consumers, the production sector widens the range of items upon which they can exercise their sovereignty. To pass up these opportunities for the sake of some pristine state of inner-directed consumer preferences would restrict their scope. It would keep consumers from widening their horizons in ways which only a dialogue with the production sector can open.

When the initiative comes from the production side, the mechanism through which consumers' sovereignty is exercised is *consumers' free choice*. Producers put forward the candidate commodities, consumers "vote" in the market with their dollars. Consumers' free choice is a necessary condition of consumers' sovereignty. Is it a sufficient condition? If it is not sufficient, how are we supposed to visualize the case where consumers' free choice does exist but consumers' sovereignty is restricted?

Information Is Power

Communication between consumers and the production sector can be in the nature of a true dialogue only if it is a dialogue between equals. In a dialogue situation, equality hinges on both parties having equal access to relevant information. If the initial distribution of knowledge is unequal, equality hinges on the parties providing each other with full and true information, without any reservations.

What about the possibility of withholding, distorting, or "packaging" information to which the less-informed party does not have direct access? This is precisely where the problem begins. In such a case, the danger appears that the consumers will become objects of manipulation by virtue of not being adequately informed. Thus, *the question of information supply is one focal point in examining the performance of economic systems with respect to consumers' sovereignty.* (The second focal point, which we shall take up later, is the question of the *compliance mechanism.* Assuming consumers do possess adequate information on which to base their preferences, there still remains the question whether the production sector is being made to comply with their wishes.)

Why would decision makers on the production side ever want to withhold, distort, or package information directed at the consumer? Can one think of any plausible reasons? Of course, the existence of a motive is not in itself proof of the deed. However, if one can tell which characteristics of the economic system might make it advantageous for the production sector to manipulate the supply of information, one is alerted to watch out for cases where such manipulation actually exists. One is not so easily taken in.

Under market capitalism, the system appears bent primarily upon stimulating consumer demand beyond the rate at which it would grow if left alone. This is one powerful source of motivation which is behind practices attempting to manipulate the supply of information, and thereby consumers' sovereignty. Under Soviet-type state capitalism, the opposite motive seems to predominate: to rein in consumer demand below the rate at which it would tend to grow spontaneously. In both cases, there also is interference with the formation of tastes and the structure of consumer demand, different under each system. We shall first concentrate on the market-capitalist case.

CONSUMERS' SOVEREIGNTY UNDER MARKET CAPITALISM

At their earlier historical stages, market-capitalist systems may have been also biased toward limiting, naively and unwittingly, consumers' demand. This was when wages were still looked upon primarily as a major element of production costs. Hence, they were kept low. Their role as source of demand was not yet fully understood. Besides, as long as labor productivity was low, generating profits, and thereby internal investment funds, depended much more directly on keeping wages low.

In later stages of market capitalism, adequate effective demand became the dominant concern. This does not mean that capitalist entrepreneurs and managers stopped worrying about wage increases entirely, but they did become more sophisticated about the demand-generating aspect of wages, as we have seen in the section on incomes policies in Chapter 11. *Market-capitalist systems began to behave as if obsessed by the vision of a declining marginal propensity to consume.*

Universal salesmanship, subliminal whispers of "hidden persuaders," overt hawking, and advertising have spread throughout the social space, reminding people relentlessly not to stop spending, not to stop buying. It has appeared as if the system's capacity to supply an ever-increasing volume of output were chronically outrunning the pace at which people would spontaneously wish to increase their demand, at least given the pattern of income distribution generated by the very same system. In this macroeconomic dimension, what we shall summarily label "advertising" has become a loose form of general business-made demand management.

Motivation to manipulate information has also a microeconomic dimension. Supply of information is a major element in interfirm competition. If handled astutely, it can substantially modify the rule which says "the best shall win."

Advertising and Consumers' Sovereignty

Under market-capitalist systems, the issue of consumers' sovereignty, consumption-production dialogue, and information supply can be conveniently narrowed down tó the problem of advertising. Stating it bluntly, does advertising restrict consumers' sovereignty below the attainable degree, and if so, in what way?

Modalities of Information Supply   To gain some perspective, let us consider a number of different methods by which consumers acquire information. Four basic methods are available to that end: (1) *personal search*, which requires on-the-spot inspecting, window shopping, browsing, comparing notes with other consumers, etc.; (2) *delegated search*, which may consist in the provision of consumer information by public agencies, consumer cooperatives, and similar groups; (3) *commercially supplied information*, which covers specialized testing organizations and information periodicals (such as *Consumer Reports*), but also inserts features in the daily press or to interior decorators, physicians, etc.; (4) *supply of information by suppliers of the goods themselves* (hawking, sales talks, advertising).

Under any one of these methods, consumers have to evaluate the information and have the final say in deciding what to buy. Their freedom of choice is not violated, even if it takes some doing to shake off the effects, say, of the advertising hypnosis. It is the quality of information they have to evaluate which is not the same under each of the four methods.

Interestingly, one cannot automatically rate as the highest the method of personal search. Direct personal experience seems to recommend itself naturally because it is so trustworthy and individualized. Unfortunately, personal information gathering stops being dependable as soon as products become somewhat more intricate or less accessible to inspection before delivery. In this case, it takes lengthy testing procedures by specialists to arrive at a good judgment, and even that may be difficult.

This brings home the realization that information is not a free good. It has to be produced at a cost. The cost increases if one wants to make informed comparisons between a number of available products or to explore unavailable potentialities. This is why it pays the individual consumer to delegate the job to specialists. Whether the specialists should be employed by private firms, voluntary associations, or public bodies is a subsidiary question. A good case can be made in favor of assigning this task to governmental agencies: consumer information has a pronounced character of a public good. In the case of suppliers of services, particularly where risks from inferior quality of goods or suppliers of personal services are high, the pertinent information may take the form of professional testing and licensing, as in the case of physicians or barbers, or state-organized inspection, as in the case of food or drugs. This speaks in favor of methods (2) and (3). We are left with method 4, which waits to be evaluated.

Demerits of Advertising   Advertising messages have so saturated the culture of market-capitalist countries that the phenomenon has become almost immune to objective analysis. Advertising seems indispensable. Many people could not even conceive of an economic system where consumer information would be provided exclusively by other means. Nevertheless, an unprejudiced examination of the advertising method may make it easier to envisage such a system, at least in theory.

The analysis must start with the realization that information about commodities is itself a product which, under the advertising system, is being supplied by the same units that supply the commodities. This may seem natural since they are the ones who know about them best. It also seems natural that they should have the right to let the world know about what they have to offer. Still, all advertising information is self-serving. It comes from an interested party, and this fact ought to give us pause. The party may be honest or not, but the testimony remains suspect. On this point, Nicholas Kaldor administered the advertising method the most damanging critical blow when he wrote: "In the world of commodities the 'authors' write their own reviews."[1]

The purpose of advertising, which is to persuade, twists and colors the information further. It is "packaged" in a pleasing way. It is wrapped around by irrelevancies which have nothing to do with the objective characteristics of the advertised items. Long on irrelevancies, it is all too often seriously short on facts. Hence, the public feels the need of supplementing or checking advertising information by some of the other methods, which means incurring the cost of obtaining information twice.

Besides the intrinsic bias and flawed content of advertising messages, the economic form under which they are being supplied impinges upon the principle of freedom of choice. Freedom of choice cannot be exercised if the person who pays has no way of refusing the deal. This happens, for instance, when the buyer is forced to buy an unwanted item as a condition for obtaining a wanted one. We have encountered this type of transaction under the name of *tie-in sales*.

The notion of tie-in sales applies to advertising messages because their price is included in the price of articles which are being advertised. You cannot buy a deodorant without paying at the same time for the commercials which are going to persuade you and others to keep buying it. It is a take-it-or-leave-it deal, a

---

[1] N. Kaldor, "Economic Aspects of Advertising," in *Essays on Value and Distribution*, Free Press, New York, 1960, p. 104.

disguised tie-in sale. It is disguised because the price tag of the commercial is not made explicit in the supermarket price, and because the *direct* buyer of the commercial appears to be the manufacturer. However, the ultimate payer is the consumer himself.

If advertising messages are financed through tie-in sales, they are also being distributed in the form of *tie-in supply*: they are delivered, in one package, with other items or services which are normally of primary interest to the consumer, such as news information or entertainment. In fact, payment for the advertising message hidden in the price of the merchandise is simultaneously payment, in whole or in part, for the entertainment program, newspaper, or other items to which the advertising information may be attached. This is the secret of our receiving television programs "free" and newspapers or periodicals below actual cost. They have been paid for, or subsidized, through the sale of other merchandise.

One may interpret this set of operations in a still different way. We have identified, in the price of commodities, a portion which serves to cover the cost of producing the advertising message, as well as the related items (newspapers, television programs, etc.) which take the ads and commercials piggyback to the public. This portion of the price may be viewed as a *hidden sales tax*: imposed and collected by the business firm, it is then spent as a kind of privately controlled fiscal revenue on items treated and distributed as public goods.

What is disturbing about that aspect of the matter is the absence of any formal controls by the public over the imposition of such a quasi tax and its use. Such controls are, in principle, the mechanism by which consumers exercise their sovereignty with respect to government-supplied goods, i.e., in the area of what may be called *citizens' sovereignty*. Without such controls, the method of raising revenue that ends up financing ads, commercials, and a host of other extremely important items can be rightfully likened to "taxation without representation."

The effects of this financing tangle reach still deeper. Burdening ordinary media of communication with the hawking function affects the character of the main communication itself. Intellectual and artistic production, or even mere entertainment, may become subject to extraneous considerations emanating from the sphere of interests of the advertiser.

There is the obvious conflict which may arise between not wanting to alienate a source of advertising revenue and wanting to sustain the autonomy and integrity of the journalist or artists. There are also less obvious effects which have to do with the desire to reach the widest possible audiences. Popularity of a show or a magazine in this quantitative sense is obviously in the interest of the firms that use them as advertising vehicles. However, that is not necessarily in the best social interest.

A case can be made for exempting intellectual and artistic production from the type of success criteria which apply to the marketplace (which would call for a suitable institutional framework insulated from the world of other commodities). Creativity implies challenge of what is popular and accepted. In this particular sphere, a certain amount of tension or even antagonism between "supply" and the public has to be expected, tolerated, and even promoted. It is unpopularity which may act as leaven, and popularity as check on progress. By drawing intellectual and artistic production into the sphere of marketing, advertising has an impact upon culture of which one is hardly aware.

The effects of advertising could be pursued in their ramifications further and further. In a mild way, society has attempted to intervene, through the government's visible hand, to regulate some of the aspects of advertising. It moderates its external aesthetic effects by protecting certain zones against its spread; it checks on certain aspects of its veracity; it even tries to compensate for some of its effect by obligatory counteradvertising ("Cigarette smoking may be dangerous to your health"). And not in every country of market capitalism are broadcasting and television operated privately and financed from advertising revenue.

These regulatory measures appear marginal compared to a radical reorganization in the supply of consumer information which is theoretically conceivable but, as a practical proposition, is as yet out of the question. It is conceivable to provide all consumer information separately from all other articles, services, and information; to make it available only to those who need it and when they need it; to put the supply of information on a professional basis and make it strictly informative; to provide the suppliers of commodities with an opportunity to tell their own story, but in standardized form, absolutely equal for all suppliers, so as to prevent information supply from creating particular monopoly positions, and to keep out irrelevant packaging of information.

A reform of that scope would probably involve an overhaul of relative prices of many articles and services, and introduction of new methods of financing the "media." Putting the supply of consumer information on an impartial and objective footing could not but benefit consumers' sovereignty and save significantly on resources. Although public regulation of capitalist business has been acceptable in many other respects, such as antitrust, there seems to be no imminent danger of serious intervention in the sphere of consumer information. Nonetheless, this is what would have to happen if consumers' sovereignty were to be fully realized.

The Problem of the Compliance Mechanism   We have covered that class of infringements of consumers' sovereignty which derives from the production sector having a measure of control over the supply of information. We still have to consider a related category of infringements which occur when the production sector has the power to determine *the scope of options* available to consumers, and a reason to use that power irrespective of what the consumers might think about the scope of options offered. If consumers' free choice, exercised through market purchases, is like voting, the issue that is under discussion now is consumers' influence on the nomination of candidates.

Compared to the stream of information welling from the production sector in the direction of consumers, communication in the opposite direction amounts to a trickle. Consumers are restricted basically to a sign language consisting of a single sign—a nod. The production sector does the active propositioning; consumers signal their acceptance through buying, or their refusal through not buying. As for the content and extent of options offered, consumers have to rely on the self-interest of the production sector to read their minds correctly. Are there any important instances where self-interest would lead the production sector to ignore or to override consumers' wishes?

The worst enemy of a capitalist firm or industry is stagnant or declining demand. The danger that demand for an article would stagnate comes at that stage of a product's life cycle when the novelty has worn off, the money-backed need is saturated, and demand settles down to the level of replacement requirements. Two major factors tend to hold replacement demand down: *durability of an article* and *stability of tastes*. With respect to either case, it is within the power of the production sector to do something that would keep replacement demand up. Physical durability of articles can be made purposefully shorter than need be, and their usefulness viewed from the side of psychic satisfaction can also be deliberately reduced.

These actions can be fully effective in imposing a supply-determined range of options only if the production sector acts in unison, and to the extent it does. This does not call for deliberate collusion or conspiracy. It is enough if restrictive manipulation of options becomes so accepted as a standard of behavior that it would not occur to anyone that things could be done in a different way. Annual car-model changes and periodic fashion changes in clothing and other areas are typical examples. At one stroke, fashion changes make previous years' purchases obsolete, at least for a significant segment of consumers, and stimulate replacement purchases.

The paradox of such business policies is that, while engineering change, they actually are at the service of preventing change in the pattern of consumer expenditures overall. If replacement purchases are being deliberately kept above the level toward which they would tend naturally, it means that consumers are deprived of the option either to enrich their repertory of spending, or to let their spending reach a plateau and, e.g., expand their leisure time instead.

The degree to which the production sector restricts consumers' options without consulting them cannot be measured. It is impossible to "prove" in a universally convincing way that the system has a restrictive effect of this sort. We find ourselves in a terrain where cultural and moral values of the observers determine the range of facts they see, and how they perceive them. It is our contention that contemporary market-capitalist systems subject consumers to significant limitations, not always easily discernible, which prevent them from asserting their free will vis-à-vis the production sector.

CONSUMER STATUS IN CENTRALLY PLANNED ECONOMIES

Once in a while one comes across the following characterization of Stalinist command planning: Stalin treated bread as an intermediate input and steel as the actual final good. There is plentiful evidence, anecdotal as well as statistical, to support this characterization.

Bread stands for consumption in general. Insofar as it has been viewed as an input, the objective has certainly not been to maximize it. However, since consumption levels and political loyalty of the population are linked, consumption could not be kept at a subsistence minimum either. The operational rule has rather been: "If there is room for consumption increases, let it be increased, provided the planners' first-priority objectives in investments and armaments are satisfied."

Sovereignty as to the Consumption Share

Our focus in the section on market capitalism was the problem of autonomy in the formation of consumers' preferences, and their authority with respect to production decisions. Consumption was considered from the point of view of its structure. However, one may also apply the concept of consumers' sovereignty to the relative share of consumption in the national product and, by the same token, to the entire composition of aggregate output by final use. This leads to the question: "Is the percentage share of civilian consumption in total output what members of society want it to be?"

We did not dare tackle this problem above because of its complexity under the system of market capitalism. It is difficult to say how society would apportion its total income between civilian consumption, public consumption, and saving if (1) all incomes were distributed among the members of society, (2) all saving came from personal incomes, and (3) members of society were acquainted with the probable consequences of alternative global saving decisions. As it is, saving and investment decisions are the outcome of innumerable acts of individuals and institutions in the sector of government, banking, and other enterprises. We do not know whether these spontaneous outcomes conform to what members of society would desire if they were confronted with this major allocation decision directly.

As for centrally planned economies, we know that the consumption/investment decision for the economy as a whole is definitely in the hands of the planners. We know further that the share of consumption in total output is lower than in market-capitalist economies, and that there has been a tendency for this share to continue to fall. Personal consumption share in GNP of the Soviet and Eastern European economies has been in the range of 44 to 55 percent, whereas in market-capitalist economies the share has typically fallen between 55 and 65 percent. In three Eastern European countries for which the computations have been done, the percentage share of personal consumption in GNP developed over the years as follows:[2]

	1950	1967
Czechoslovakia	52.7	44.1
Hungary	55.8	50.6
Poland	59.6	51.2

[2] Thad P. Alton, "Economic Structure and Growth in Eastern Europe," in U.S. Congress, Joint Economic Committee, *Economic Developments in Countries of Eastern Europe*, 1970, p. 59.

In market-capitalist economies, the share of personal consumption has been steady. This means that consumers have been increasing their consumption levels at the same rate as the total output was growing. If we recall the principle of incomes policies in Western Europe from Chapter 11, this behavior of consumption shadows the relative constancy in the distribution of incomes between wages and profits.

If we make the assumption that consumers everywhere prefer a higher share of consumption to a lower one, and a steady share to a declining one, we may conclude that consumers' sovereignty has been considerably weaker under Soviet-type CPEs than under Western-type market capitalism. If we were to attach great importance to the pressures of selling efforts on the part of market-capitalist businesses, we would have to rephrase the conclusion: Whereas under market capitalism consumers have to protect their sovereignty against a system that wants them to spend more and more, under Soviet-type CPEs they have to assert their demands against a system whose policy it has been to keep consumption down.

Sovereignty as to the Consumption Basket

Under the classic form of the CPE, the production sector has a position of the exclusive supplier. Consumers face a single complex of state monopolies offering them a range of products determined by the judgment of the planning administration. How can consumers' preferences, under these conditions, make themselves be heard at all? Is the consumer totally at the mercy of the interplay between the subjective conscience of state-appointed administrators and the incentive system under which they operate? In principle, this is how it is. Whenever the doors are closed to alternative sources of supply, consumers are in danger of getting to feel the ugliest traits of monopolistic behavior. However, total neglect of the consumer also has its cost for the state as monopolist. It is this cost which provides the the consumer with a modicum of protection.

The strongest motive prodding the political leadership, which stands behind and above economic planners, to try and meet part of consumers' preferences is the desire to avoid situations where discontent would turn into open social protest. Experience has shown that economic grievances tend to function as a rallying point for accumulated political frustrations. Revolts and upheavals which took place in 1953 in East Germany and Czechoslovakia, in 1962 in a number of provincial cities of the Soviet Union, and in 1970 in Poland, were triggered by economic grievances. Whenever political revolts were suppressed by force, or were simply feared, Communist regimes used concessions in the area of consumption as a pacification measure: in the Soviet Union after the death of Stalin in 1953, after the Hungarian revolt in 1956, and after the invasion of Czechoslovakia in 1968.[3]

There exist also purely economic reasons which counsel against disregarding

[3] See Chap. 5, quote at footnote 12.

consumers' demand. Material incentives in the form of wages, salaries, and bonuses are blunted if these incomes cannot be spent on commodities that consumers find acceptable. Under the classic form of the CPEs, where the incentive system rested on the fulfillment of the gross value of *output* rather than on the volume of *sales*, it happened periodically that consumer-goods industries would supply the retail trade with unsalable articles. If the volume of consumer goods was planned to correspond to the volume of personal disposable incomes, such boycott of unwanted articles found its reflection in unplanned increases of saving deposits. Such increases in private liquid balances were always viewed with apprehension. This "overhang of purchasing power," as they were called, weakened the urge to work (reflected in absenteeism) and threatened to spill over into black-market spending, thus diverting resources from the planned objectives.

Meeting consumers' demand has also been in the sectoral interest of retail-trade establishments. Accumulation of unsalable inventories naturally hurt the retail managers. Unfulfilled sales plans mean unearned managerial bonuses in retail trade. They also mean bad marks for failure to fulfill the financial plan: Unfulfilled sales plans leave retail stores short of liquidity and force them to turn to the state bank for unplanned credit.

However, under the classic CPE, there was little that retail trade could do. The missing element was some automatic transmission mechanism, linking the incentive arising at the retail-trade level to production decisions. For long periods manufacturing enterprises could shrug off protests of the retail sector and ignore complaints aired in published letters to the editor by referring simply to their assigned production plans. As long as the level of unsold inventories did not reach a certain "emergency threshold" in the aggregate, nothing was done to remedy the situation. Only after the critical level had been reached, i.e., when the top leadership became alarmed, was there a chance of remedial action.

In the Soviet Union such an emergency threshold of inventory accumulation seems to have been reached around 1963–1964. Around that time, unsold and unsalable inventories of consumers' goods reached a cumulative total of over 12 billion rubles, which amounted to over 7 percent of the 1964 value of GNP. This was the result of an inventory accumulation growing three times as fast, between 1959 and 1964, as retail sales.[4] At this point the leadership began to treat the situation as an intolerable scandal and to look seriously for underlying causes. Economic reforms of the CPEs, which introduced certain elements of the market mechanism (see Chapter 9), were also a response to the phenomenon of consumers' boycott.

The phenomenon is nothing else but a case of consumers' sovereignty asserting itself through passive resistance. Nonetheless, it would be wrong to conclude that consumers' sovereignty has come into its own if everything that the planners put on the market is sold without any leftovers. The case of the consumer-goods

[4] See Marshall I. Goldman, "The Reluctant Consumer and Economic Fluctuations in the Soviet Union," *Journal of Political Economy*, vol. 73, no. 4.

market under the CPEs is a perfect illustration of free consumers' choice coexisting with a faint ability of consumers to influence the range and quality of items on the menu from which they choose.

Consumers' Free Choice—Planners' Sovereignty

In capitalist market economies, the influence of consumers on the composition of the menu is not perfect, as we have seen. However, consumers do have considerable power over the proportions in which different articles are forthcoming. Firms respond directly and quickly to the movement of inventories of individual items, which reflects both consumers' preferences and relative profitability of the merchandise. Under a CPE, there may be occasionally an accumulation of inventories in the aggregate which calls for adjustment. However, in principle, *consumer goods can be offered in an assortment and in proportions of the planners' choosing, and still be bought up by consumers of their own free will.* How is that possible?

The technique by which the two independent sets of choices are reconciled is extremely simple. Consumers have, of course, their own demand schedules. Planners supply consumer goods in planned quantities. That means the supply "curves" for any planning period are vertical lines. They are pure specimens of inelastic supply. Ideally, from the planners' point of view, prices of consumer goods are fixed at the level at which the vertical supply lines intersect with consumers' demand schedules. This principle assures that quantities offered will also be sold. Such an "ideal" set of prices corresponds to the notion of *market clearing prices.*

Figure 16-1 Consumers' free choice without consumers' sovereignty in Soviet-type retail markets.

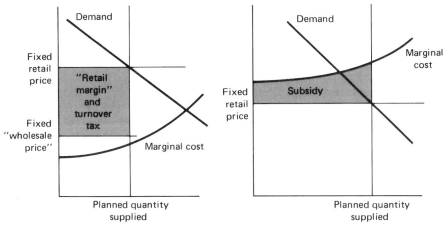

There is no ordinary supply schedule: quantity supplied according to plan is of the perfectly inelastic sort. Consumers regulate their purchases in accordance with their demand schedules and fixed retail prices. If retail prices are fixed at a level corresponding to the intersection of the demand schedule and the quantity supplied according to plan, the market is cleared. Such a market-clearing price is not an equilibrium price in the ordinary sense.

It is important to realize that *these "market clearing prices" are not the same thing as market clearing prices which are at the same time "equilibrium prices"* that would emerge in free markets through the interaction of demand and supply. The point is that planners' vertical supply lines and planners' fixed prices are totally independent of production costs incurred in manufacturing the consumer goods. Each article of consumption has, of course, its own objective cost schedule at some particular level and of a particular shape. However, the market clearing price may have to be fixed far above or below the cost. If it is above cost, the excess revenue is collected in the form of the turnover tax. If it is below, the manufacturing enterprise receives a subsidy to cover the difference. These relationships are summarized visually in Figure 16-1.

It can happen, of course, that the price setters miss the point of intersection between demand and the vertical supply line for a particular good. If the fixed price is higher than it should be, there appears an unsold quantity—a phenomenon we discussed above in connection with consumers' boycott. If the price is too low, there will appear lines, backlog of applications for apartments and cars, vain inquiries in shops, attempts to obtain the article by offering a higher price, etc. Unlike accumulation of inventories, none of these so-called queuing phenomena, the costs of which are borne by the consumers, have by themselves the power to induce planners to change the assortment. They work only insofar as the planners feel they cannot risk the consequences of discontent which similar shortages provoke.

The relative weakness of consumers' sovereignty with respect to the structure of consumption can be gauged very roughly by certain striking differences between consumption patterns under market capitalism and under the CPEs. For one thing, the proportion of food tends to be relatively high under the CPEs, and the proportion of personal services and housing relatively low, both in financial and in real terms. To the extent that information about the outside world penetrates political barriers, the mere availability of certain articles abroad acts as a substitute for competition. Under the impact of a kind of keeping-up-with-the-Joneses effect, planners tend to introduce them too (e.g., cars, blue jeans, tape recorders). This applies least of all to cultural goods, the content of which is severely limited by ideological preferences of the regimes in power.

However, basically, it has remained characteristic for Soviet-type CPEs to treat consumers' sovereignty as a principle antagonistic to consumption planning. There have been sporadic instances, such as Khrushchev's declaration of his credo in "goulash socialism," where consumers were at least verbally deferred to. The spirit in which consumption patterns have been normally shaped by planners in these despotic systems can best be described as paternalistic surveillance. A candid statement from a Czechoslovak economic journal illustrates this attitude:

> In practice, we often discuss shortcomings in the recognition of the population's needs, particularly through market research. . . . The weakness of this approach consists in overrating market research as if it were the decisive factor in providing satisfaction of society's needs. A conception of this sort would mean *respecting spon-*

taneity in the development of production and consumption and an insufficient application of the principle of planning.[5]

*   *   *

This completes our manifold examination of the issue of consumers' sovereignty and of its status under the two variants of capitalism. It has laid bare the fallacies of the idea that consumers' sovereignty is adequately taken care of either by the market principle of "voting with dollars" or by that which says "planners know best." At the same time, we have tried to steer clear of the opposite extreme, which sees total enslavement of the consumer to the production sector under one or the other system.

We have emphasized throughout the key importance of information, i.e., the concrete forms through which it reaches the consumers, and, along with that, the importance of the compliance mechanism through which the production sector is supposed to be made to serve them. In the course of the discussion it became apparent that, under market capitalism, consumers have to cope primarily with the problem of manipulative information, whereas under the CPEs it is the compliance mechanism which leaves much to be desired.

As for consumers' power to influence supply in the category of public goods and services, and the choice of persons in charge of determining its specific content and quality, we refer the reader to what was said on the subject in Chapter 8 (section on government failure).

Finally, one more issue that has been left untouched should be mentioned for the record. We did not properly investigate the nature of social and psychological processes which are at the origin of the formation of consumers' preferences. This would have led us to many a perplexing question such as: "When can consumers' preferences be said to be truly their own? What about subconscious forces, compulsive drives, etc., whereby it is not the consumers who are sovereign but the desires by which they are dominated, so that they do not *really* want what they overtly demand?"

In our field, it might be legitimate to ask: "To what extent does the character of a given economic system help consumers gain insight into their own motivations and promote their autonomy? To what extent does it obstruct such insight and, instead, exploit the subconscious, irrational part of their personalities?" Most economists would say all this belongs in the domain of psychology and philosophy. They may be right, but we should at least be aware that these problems exist and that they impinge upon the criterion of consumers' sovereignty in a most fundamental way.

---

[5] *Ekonomicky casopis*, vol. 11, no. 1, 1963 (our italics). An even more explicit restatement of this policy principle appeared in the Soviet journal *Planovoe Khoziaistvo*, January 1975, under the signature of A. Smirnov, a high official of the State Planning Agency: "One-sided orientation toward satisfaction of consumer demands, especially when it is not followed by the necessary indoctrination, is fraught with the danger of spreading social 'ills' such as individualism, egotism and greed or, on the contrary, dependency." (See the report in *The New York Times*, January 30, 1975.)

BIBLIOGRAPHY

Scitovsky, Tibor: "On the Principle of Consumers' Sovereignty," *American Economic Review*, vol. 52, no. 2, May 1962, pp. 262–268.

Rothenberg, Jerome: "Consumers' Sovereignty Revisited and the Hospitability of Freedom of Choice," *American Economic Review*, vol. 52, no. 2, May 1962, pp. 269–283.

Fisher, Franklin M., Zvi Griliches, and Carl Kaysen: "The Cost of Automobile Model Changes since 1949," *American Economic Review*, vol. 52, no. 2, May 1962, pp. 259–261.

Gintis, Herbert: "Consumer Behavior and the Concept of Sovereignty: Explanations of Social Decay," *American Economic Review*, vol. 62, no. 2, May 1972, pp. 267–287.

Kaldor, Nicholas: "The Economic Aspects of Advertising," in *Essays on Value and Distribution*, Free Press, New York, 1960, pp. 96–140.

Hanson, Philip: *Advertising and Socialism: The Nature and Extent of Consumer Advertising in the Soviet Union, Poland, Hungary, and Yugoslavia*, Macmillan, London, 1974.

Chapter 17

Workers' Sovereignty

When . . . capital is converted into the property of all members of society, personal property is not thereby transformed into social property. It is only the social character of the property that is changed. It loses its class character.

Karl Marx

Before we get into any particulars on the subject of workers' sovereignty, it is essential to go back to Chapter 5 and reread the section bearing the corresponding subtitle. Having done that, we may proceed.

When we first introduced the concept of workers' sovereignty, we dealt with it from the point of view of a single person at work. We asked: "How do individual workers experience their productive activities and their status? What is the quality of that subjective experience? How do they perceive the pleasurable and the not-so-pleasurable sides of their work? Do they have any control over their working conditions which determines the balance between the disutility and utility sides, between costs and benefits, between drudgery and satisfaction, which appear to be normally associated with work activity?"

Still as part of the chapter opening, we want to enlarge that individualistic point of view by a triple set of supplementary comments.

A Moving Target   We shall not assume any absolute standard of some pure 100 percent workers' sovereignty either to have been anywhere realized or to be immediately attainable. We shall think in terms of *relative degrees* of workers' sovereignty, situated between the extremes of forced labor camps (or slavery) and teamwork in a democratically organized commune. Even at the latter extreme, workers' sovereignty must be seen as a matter of dynamic accommodation between the human agent and given constraints of the work situation. A "perfect state" of workers' sovereignty is understood as something humanity may be approaching asymptotically. In the process, the technical nature of work continuously changes, and the characteristics of people as workers are being transformed as well.

Pushing against Constraints   There is a triple layer of constraints in a work situation to which human agents must adapt and, while adapting, assert their interest in relaxing and otherwise modifying the constraints: (1) the basic necessity to work which cannot be shirked, except for the fact that the upper limit of the length of the working day (or week or year) is flexible; (2) technology of production which requires a certain adaptation of the human agent (training, specific physical and mental effort), but can also be adapted to the needs of the worker as a physiological organism, and as a spiritual and emotional being; (3) social organization of functions and activities constituting the work process. The organizational pattern may be imposed by the technological features of the work process, or by the ownership character of the economic system. It may also contain "arbitrary" elements which have nothing to do either with technology or with the type of ownership but may be a matter of cultural tradition, individual psychological quirks of participants, legal prescriptions, etc.

If we confine ourselves to modern industrial capitalism, be it run by individual bosses, corporations, or the state, one thing stands out: Almost all constraints communicate themselves to the human agents through instructions, rules, demands, and commands voiced by some other human agents. Constraints of an objective technical nature, constraints of social, legal, or arbitrary nature, they all reach the awareness of the worker through the voice of personnel whose role is to act as their representatives. In consequence, when we speak of workers' sovereignty, we are not concerned with the situation of any and all participants active in the production process, at least not in the first round. We are concerned with those who face the constraints transmitted through the decision-making power of their superiors. It is with respect to the category of subordinates that the problem of control over working conditions (i.e., workers' sovereignty) arises because they are the ones who obviously do not fully possess it. Hence, the field of action where workers' sovereignty is being pursued, contested, and stepwise resolved is the sphere of rights between the executive and supervisory personnel on the one hand, and the subordinate employees on the other.[1]

---

[1] It is clear that, under complex division of labor and delegation of supervisory tasks, one and the same person may appear simultaneously in both categories, as a superior and a subordinate.

Economic System at Stake   From Chapter 3 we recall that status of labor was one of the criteria used to classify economic systems by type of ownership. Status of labor was defined by the scope and combinations of substantive rights involving the actual use of material productive assets and of labor itself. Wage labor (implying capitalist ownership relations) was defined by the exclusion of workers from the substantive rights over material production assets, and their repeated temporary submission to the command of those who did wield those rights.

Now that we have arrived at the topic of workers' sovereignty, we are once more dealing with the pattern of rights in controlling the use of material means of production and labor. Workers' sovereignty affects, in the first instance, the scope of concrete rights of the employer with respect to the use of hired wage labor: how long the employer is entitled to use it; at what degree of intensity; under what provisions for the workers' safety; and so on. *Through the use of hired labor power, employers effectively, though indirectly, use the material production assets they own.*

From all this, there follows an important conclusion. As workers confront the will of employers and their delegates; as they push against the constraint of the employers' rights; and as they try to assert their own will, powered by their interest in adapting the working conditions to their needs, the substantive content of ownership relations is being modified. The detailed pattern of substantive ownership rights shifts and is regrouped. Hence, *what changes in the process is the ownership character of the economic system itself.*

The change in question is not a change at the surface of the system, such as might be the replacement of private capitalists or corporate executives by a state-appointed economic bureaucracy, which is how change from private capitalist to public ownership is usually understood. Workers' sovereignty, as it is conceived here, refers to fundamental changes at the very core of the social organization of the production process. (This is how one might transcribe and interpret, in modern idiom, the passage from the *Communist Manifesto* used as motto to this chapter.)

This concludes the last of the three supplementary sets of introductory comments. We shall elaborate on their themes in the course of the exposition and in our concluding remarks.

*   *   *

The exposition is organized as follows. First we explain the unique character of transactions in the labor market, which provides the economic and social rationale of special labor-market institutions, such as labor unions and labor legislation. We then survey several basic types of institutions organizing labor. We use "authentic unionism" as the point of reference and define its relationship to the concept of "employees' representation" and "participation in management." Having clarified the conceptual framework, we then illustrate the issues by means of a selection of experiences: unionism as such; the Japanese variant;

codetermination of the West German kind and other participation-in-management schemes; workers' self-management of the Yugoslav variety; and totalitarian pseudo unions of the fascist and Soviet type. We conclude with one more look at the dynamics of strivings for workers' sovereignty and its perspective.

PECULIARITIES OF THE LABOR MARKET

Selling and buying labor services of wage workers is unlike any other category of market transactions involving commodities. First of all, the transaction is basically a *renting agreement* involving the use of human beings. Second, the individual supplier of labor services for hire is generally, in the nature of the case, in an *inferior position* vis-à-vis the buyer.

Workers for Rent   In what sense is a labor contract a renting agreement? As in other contracts of that kind, the sellers place an asset they own at the temporary disposal of another party, against the payment of a rental fee. The asset happens to be the worker's capacity to work, which is embodied in the worker's person. The rental is called, in this instance, the wage.

The problematic part of all rental contracts stems from the fact that the owner of the asset temporarily loses control over it. While it is in the hands of the temporary user, the owner is out of the picture. The owner therefore runs the risk of getting the asset back, at the end of the contract, in a deplorable state—unless there exist sanctions such as will hold the user to acceptable standards of behavior. This is why rental contracts often require a deposit and the possibility of legal redress, should the damage to the asset exceed "normal wear and tear."

In the case of the labor contract, such precautionary stipulations concern the full sweep of working conditions. If limits are not specified, the employer might be led, under pressure of competition, to utilize hired labor so ruthlessly as to return the worker to private status half dead of fatigue, health injured, life expectation shortened. This is why wage and work hours are only a small part of what constitutes price and quantity in the labor market, and why so much else needs to be specified.

Society at large, too, may be interested in supervising the utilization of labor by capitalist employers, be it on grounds of prevailing morality, public health, family protection, and demographic concerns, or perhaps just to make sure there would be enough able-bodied army recruits. This is the foundation of governmental intervention through protective labor legislation regulating the employment of women and children, hours of work, hygienic conditions, etc.

Inferior Bargaining Power   Under other than capitalist institutions, suppliers of labor services may be kept in an inferior position by means of naked power. This may consist in the ability of the superiors to threaten personal injury: incarceration, denial of necessities, corporal punishment, death. If work is performed under such blackmail, we speak of forced labor. Slavery, serfdom, labor camps are familiar examples of such naked compulsion.

In contrast to forced labor, inferiority of free wage labor under capitalist institutions is due to a special kind of situation of job-offer monopoly, or rather monopsony, since the employer offering jobs is a buyer. This arises when the worker has no alternatives to accepting conditions of work as determined by the party that controls the access to the workplace. The worker either submits or does not get the opportunity to work. No naked or legal force compels the worker to submit, only force of circumstances: the necessity to earn income. This situation typifies the model of capitalism where workers are barred from access to means of production by legislation concerning ownership. They can combine their labor services with the complementary factors of production only if they pass the hurdle of concluding a labor contract with the custodians of material production assets.

The worker's inferiority is reinforced because of the character of the "merchandise" itself: its extreme perishability, plus the urgency of the need to sell because wage, which is the "price" in this instance, is also personal income, i.e., a daily necessity.[2] "Perishability" means, in this instance, that labor services, like services in general, cannot be stored. Workers cannot hold back while selling their "article," waiting for an "improved market," or hoping to recoup at least part of its value later, should the market not improve. Labor hours which workers do not sell today are gone forever. Those whose need is most urgent are in a worse position than those who can wait.

Other circumstances still contribute to the bargaining inferiority of labor. If workers act individually and compete for jobs, they can be maneuvered into underselling one another. ("If you don't like the conditions, there are plenty of others waiting to take the job.") An employer of a certain size usually dominates the labor market in a locality. Even if alternative job opportunities do exist elsewhere, individual workers can usually ill afford the cost of searching and moving, and are thus put even more at the mercy of the local company's monopsony power.

Taking all these aspects of the labor market together, it follows that the odds are heavily against workers as long as they bargain individually. Bargaining is not the word. The contract degenerates into a take-it-or-leave-it ultimatum.[3]

To transform labor-market transactions into bona fide contracts, it is therefore necessary to assure that the bargaining power of the sellers and buyers, i.e., workers and employers, be equalized. Labor contract can become a true contract only if the relative weakness of workers acting individually is in some way compensated for. Collective organization—unionization—is a means toward achieving just that. It helps eliminate the disadvantages of competition in a situation where many competing sellers confront a single buyer. And even though it can-

---

[2] To express this aspect, one should draw the household supply curve of labor with an inelastic (steep to vertical) portion, reflecting the underlying demand for income: the amount of labor supplied—or, rather, of employment sought—is unchanged even when the wage offered falls. Indeed, at lowest wages, the supply curve may have a negative slope: if the wage falls far enough, the number of labor hours offered increases, as households try to uphold total income. (See Fig. 17-1.)

[3] Jurists have a special term for this kind of agreement under duress: "contract of adhesion."

Figure 17-1 Some complexities of the labor-supply schedule.

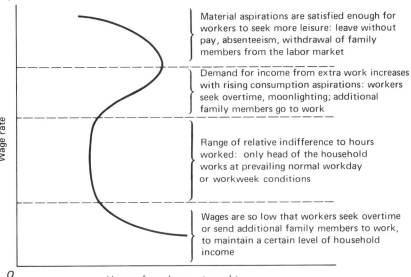

Material aspirations are satisfied enough for workers to seek more leisure: leave without pay, absenteeism, withdrawal of family members from the labor market

Demand for income from extra work increases with rising consumption aspirations: workers seek overtime, moonlighting; additional family members go to work

Range of relative indifference to hours worked: only head of the household works at prevailing normal workday or workweek conditions

Wages are so low that workers seek overtime or send additional family members to work, to maintain a certain level of household income

Wage rate

O   *Hours of employment sought*

not do away with the "perishability" of labor services, through the stratagem of strike it can make their withholding costly to the buyer, too.

It is up to the state to provide, through the political and legislative process, a suitable framework for this category of economic transactions. We have seen, in Chapter 11, which dealt with inflation, that the bargaining power of labor may on occasion outbalance that of employers. It is not excluded for unionized workers to overreach themselves in given concrete situations. However, as a matter of principle, the above is the economic rationale of modern institutional arrangements surrounding transactions in the labor market.

AUTHENTIC UNIONS AND OTHER ARRANGEMENTS

We cannot even begin to summarize the vast amount of information on the historical emergence of labor unionism; related social struggles and ideologies; legislation regulating labor relations; the content, strategy, and techniques of collective bargaining. Neither can we do full justice to intersystem comparisons, which is our main business. We can later pinpoint a few of the more striking variations which distinguish union organizations in some major country systems of market capitalism from one another. Our main object here is to define the fundamental distinction common to all free unionism under market capitalism, without which the deep contrast with institutions organizing labor relations under Soviet-type state capitalism, fascism, and capitalist paternalism cannot be grasped.

If we leave aside the organizationally shapeless stage of early capitalist labor markets studded with paralyzing prohibitions, injunctions, and elements of forced labor, there have been three basic types of institutions organizing labor under capitalism generally:

(1) *Authentic labor unions* are taken to mean organizational instruments for representing workers' interests vis-à-vis capitalist entrepreneurs or the state, or simply employers of any kind. They are created by labor, they act on behalf of their members, and they are responsible to them. Their essential characteristic is autonomy, i.e., independence from employers and the government.

(2) *Company unions* are set up to organize workers in the interest and at the initiative of the employer. They grant labor advantages at the discretion of the employer, with the intent of preempting the function of authentic unions and keeping labor-relation problems under the employer's unilateral control. In practice, this type of organization may not be very important any more, but for conceptual clarification it is essential to keep it on the list.

(3) *State-sponsored, government-controlled unions* monopolize the right to organize labor "from above." They act as adjuncts of economic management. Like company unions, they may assume selected prolabor activities, but use them as a form of social bribes subordinated to the stimulation of work effort and labor discipline, which is their major purpose.

The distinction between authentic unions and other types of labor organizations is based on the character of the ultimate source of authority. Is it the workers to whom the union organization is responsible? Or is it the employer? Or the state? In authentic unions, authority and representation flow from the membership upward. They are organs representing the interests of labor vis-à-vis the employer and the state. Company unions and state-controlled unions do not necessarily *ignore* workers' interests. In their own way, they also take them into account. However, they do not *represent* them. To the extent that they do meet workers' interests, the concessions or satisfactions are *granted* from above, either under pressure or on the basis of their own judgment as to what is good for the workers. The expression which describes the nature of the relationship toward the workers in the latter instance is *paternalism.*

If we speak of authentic unions in the above sense, we do thereby not imply that unions have to conform to some standard of shining perfection to qualify for inclusion in that category. Their way of representing labor's interests may fall short of the mark. They may choose a wide or narrow range of issues to deal with. They may be unable to balance the interest of a particular category of workers, which can encroach upon the interests of another one, with the general interests of labor as a whole. They may be too submissive or too ferocious, to the point at which one can begin to speak of self-inflicted wounds.

Internal democracy of unions may also be far from ideal, especially in view of the need for stable and professionalized bureaucratic organizations, which may develop special interests of their own within the union setup. Authentic unions may be in tow of incongruous political or ideological tendencies. Whatever failings can be cited against them, they do not unmake their authenticity as long as they fit under the criterion of being interest organizations of labor alone.

Scope of Action   Authentic unions speak for a range of labor interests whose delimitation is not given a priori. It is often assumed that there is a sphere of "legitimate" labor interests and a sphere of "management prerogatives" upon which unions have no right to encroach. However, in any situation which involves a conflict of opposing interests, and therefore of their expression in the form of rights, there is no objectively given line at which they could be once and for all reconciled. There are temporary accommodations and compromises. There is never a final equilibrium.

The rights of management consist in directing the activities of hired labor in function of the economic objectives of the firm, and in determining the working conditions correspondingly. The rights of labor consist in protecting the individuals at work against a manner of use that would injure their interest in their physical and mental well-being, security of employment, level of reward, and leisure time. Profit maximization, which calls forth cost minimization and stimulation of output per worker, is clearly an objective which, in its practical consequences, grates against the above-mentioned labor interests. Both sets of rights are legitimate, in function of the given economic system. How can they be balanced against each other? As Marx put it, in a similar context: "Between equal rights force decides." [4]

Force, in this case, is to be understood as bargaining power, not as physical violence, or not necessarily as that. It is beyond our purview to retrace the historical development of the organizational, ideological, and juridical forms through which labor's bargaining power was exercised at various times and in various places. We just need to note that everything which today is widely accepted as of legitimate concern to labor unions or legislation used to fall in the sphere of untouchable managerial prerogatives. Thus, history itself demonstrates the open-ended nature of the accommodation between the interests of labor and those of management which gives voice to the constraints inherent in the economic system. [5]

Labor interests naturally extend beyond factory gates. There are many aspects of social existence which affect labor directly or indirectly: education, transportation, housing policies, full-employment and price-stabilization policies, foreign-trade policies, taxation, decisions in the field of international affairs, etc. Representation of these labor interests needs to extend to the political level, and the organizational forms and modes of action need to be articulated to suit the different purposes. Workers' sovereignty merges, in that respect, with consumers' and citizens' sovereignty. Accommodation of rights, insofar as they conflict with those of other groups in society, takes place through the political process of

---

[4] K. Marx, *Capital*, vol. I, p. 235.

[5] See Neil W. Chamberlain, *The Union Challenge to Management Control*, Archon/Shoe String, Hamden, Conn., 1967, esp. chap. 7, pp. 158–170. The point of view of labor is well expressed in the following quote from another source: "You have complete freedom to run your plant any way you like—so long as you run it yourself. But if you want employees to help you run it, you can have them only on terms which are acceptable to *them* as well as to you." (Alfred Kuhn, *Labor: Institutions and Economics*, 2d ed., Harcourt, Brace & World, New York, 1967, p. 87.)

decision making. Aside from this remark, this side of workers' sovereignty will not be treated here (see Chapter 9).

Workers' Control   Influence of labor upon its conditions of work, exercised through authentic unionism, is what workers' sovereignty is about. This process of asserting labor's interests by confronting them with the rights of management is known under still other expressions. Marx's concept of the emancipation of workers, or more exactly, self-emancipation of the proletariat, certainly covers the same set of phenomena. They are also part of what is usually meant by "industrial democracy" or "workers' control."

It is perhaps useful to dwell on this last expression somewhat. Terminology in the field of labor relations has not been completely standardized. Some concepts suffer from a relatively loose usage, and "workers' control" is one of them. What the term evokes in the popular mind is something on the order of "workers' taking over of the factories." For our purposes, it is important to establish a precise distinction between this idea and workers' control. "Workers' taking over of the factories" corresponds more to the notion of *workers' management.* There exists a spectrum of arrangements whereby representatives of the staff of employees in a firm receive the right to join the top decision-making bodies. These arrangements correspond to what is known as workers' (or employees') *participation in management.* As for the term "workers' control," we reserve it to mean exclusively *effective influence of workers upon the determination of their working conditions, from the point of view of their interests as workers.*[6]

The above terminological distinctions will allow us to deal in the rest of the chapter with the complexities of the following situations and problems: (1) existence and expansion of workers' control in the absence of any direct participation in management or full workers' management; (2) existence of workers' management, or participation in management, without there being any necessary connection with workers' control (in the above sense); and, finally, (3) the possibility of labor's using organs and institutions of workers' management for the purposes and objectives of workers' control.

Of a different order from authentic unionism, other types of labor organizations, or workers' management and participation in management, are organs of *employees' representation* which may be established by law, and organs falling under the term *joint consultation.* What distinguishes these types of arrangements from the previous ones is that their purpose is precisely circumscribed, i.e., not open-ended, and that they are generally established by an enactment "from above," on the initiative of either the state or the employer. Even though they do deal with matters of interest to the workers, they are not membership organiza-

---

[6] To our knowledge, these distinctions were formally established, for the first time, in a French journal, in a series of articles by Paul Barton (pseud.), esp. "Workers' Control of Industry," *Saturne,* vol. 3, no. 15, October–November 1957, pp. 27–39, and "Dynamics of Workers' Control," *Saturne,* vol. 4, no. 18, April–May 1958, pp. 21–30. (English translations are available upon request from the author of the present text.)

tions, nor are they in the proper sense workers' interest organizations. Analysis of concrete cases is often made difficult by the fact that elements, characterizing one or another type of precisely defined arrangements in the area of labor and industrial relations, often intermingle, as will become apparent in the synoptic surveys below. However, keeping in mind distinctions developed in this section should be helpful in telling what exactly it is that intermingles.

VARIETIES OF UNION EXPERIENCE

Much of the standard literature in the field of labor relations appears overloaded with organizational data, procedural aspects, and legal information. It all presumably makes sense to specialists who can see substantive significance behind these technicalities. The lay public tends to be puzzled, and often bored, by what looks like many reference handbooks with running commentary. We shall try to sidestep these difficulties of exposition by keeping the comparative survey that follows on a fairly general level.

The process by which workers protect the attained degree of their sovereignty through labor unions, as well as expand it further, is called *labor bargaining*. The articulation of labor bargaining reflects, more or less, the structure of labor interests. We shall describe this structure in terms of a rough classification of interests by layers, four in all, in a descending order of generality.

The top layer extends beyond the sphere of union-type bargaining proper. In this category, we find interests concerning regulation of aggregate economic activity, social security insurance, and all kinds of general economic and political matters indicated earlier. Of special importance is workers' interest in the character of the political regime itself, namely, in democracy, and in a favorable general legislative framework within which concrete organizational activity and labor bargaining can unfold. Some of these "general class interests" of labor, as Marx would have called them, may be exclusive to labor, but many are ordinarily shared by other social groups.

Second, in the sphere of union bargaining proper we find, first, the more specialized interests common to workers belonging to a given industry, or a group of firms, insofar as they can be formulated in appropriately general terms. Next below, as third layer, exist concrete interests in working conditions which are specific to a company, a plant, or a workshop. Finally, at the bottom, there are particular interests pertaining to a single individual, or small group, and to particular situations as they arise in the course of production activities on the shop floor.

To each of these four categories of interests there corresponds a level and mode of activity: national level, where the object is to influence government policies and legislation, or to bargain with nationwide organs representing employers; industrywide or companywide (multiplant) bargaining; bargaining at plant or shop level; and direct bargaining by individuals "on the job."

This basic four-tier structure is complicated by a number of sectional interests which also need to be accommodated by the bargaining structure. One is the category of concerns common to individual professional subgroups of labor (crafts, office workers, even lower management employees), which cut across different industries. Another kind of differentiation reflects variations due to the character of the employer (private firms, nonprofit institutions, public bodies, unions themselves). Still other distinct categories of interest follow regional and ethnic lines as, for example, in the case of immigrant workers and various minority groups. We shall have to ignore such complications to keep the main lines of the exposition clear and simple.

Bargaining structures under different national systems of market capitalism vary greatly in the institutional implementation of the basic paradigm outlined above, as well as in the relative strength (or even existence) of bargaining at all four levels. Besides, the situation has been in considerable flux since the early seventies, and calls for continuous updating.

As for the category of "common class interests," it has been characteristic that unions in the Western European systems let sympathizing political parties handle them through their influence upon legislation and government. Whereas in the United States unions have acted through selective support of favored political candidates at election time, and through lobbying for specific legislation during their tenure, the British system has been based on a close personal and financial association between the union organization and the Labour party. In France and Italy, three major union confederations have run more or less parallel to three political-ideological groups—the Communists, Christian Democrats, and Democratic Socialists—although the trend has been toward a greater separation of unions from political parties, in the interest of coordinated action among the union confederations. In the Netherlands, the three-way split between Catholic, Protestant, and Socialist unions mirrors the pronounced cultural-religious divisions of society. In Belgium, union pluralism is simplified to only two major confederations, one Socialist and one Christian.

In a number of countries, unions have been coopted as consultants into high-level decision making by the administrative machinery of the government, side by side with representatives of business. This has been true of some of the top-level planning organs in France and the Netherlands, though inclusion of French unions has always been considered more as a matter of courtesy than substance. The strongest forms of government-party-union collaboration at the top have apparently existed in Sweden, where the blue-collar union confederation has always considered itself as a wing and organ of Social Democrats, the perennial governing party.

The inclusion of the top union bureaucracy in national policy-making bodies tends to be welcome (or resented) as a sign that labor has "made it" in capitalist society. However, it is important that observers be aware of the basic ambiguity of such a position, which will be encountered again in the context of "participation in management." "Having a say" carries the danger of labor representatives being possibly saddled with sharing responsibility for decisions which, though necessary from the point of view of society, could be undermining the position of union autonomy. The problem is a difficult one.[7] Here it needs to be pointed out only so as to illustrate a controversial question of broad and rather fundamental significance: *Is it useful, from the perspective of workers' sovereignty and its objectives, that labor representatives join decision-making bodies to defend workers' interests "from within" mixed organs at higher levels of authority? Or should they consistently stick to the position of an autonomous bargaining party that deals with other organs of authority in society "from without"?*

As a general rule, unions are at their strongest at the middle-level of bargaining. Industrywide bargaining on minimum-wage rates and other basic provisions of the collective contracts, in a national or regional framework, with a union federation of the given industry on one side and a symmetrical body representing employers on the other, has been the standard model. It is in the way the middle-level bargains have been articulated with the specific situation at the firm, plant, and shop levels that differences come in.

The United States system has been famous for having its center of gravity in bargaining at the plant level and in a strong and active network of shop stewards, in close touch with members, fulfilling a vital function in handling day-to-day conflicts, demands, and grievances. The state of labor relations has, of course, never stood still. What took decades to accomplish may undergo perceptible backsliding under the challenge of changes in the general economic situation, new technology, and modern techniques of management.

As for the last factor, authoritarian confrontation has been giving way to psychological engineering of human relations, job-enrichment schemes, redesign of work, etc. Such changes have been productivity-oriented, but they also were a response to labor protest, as well as part of never-ending attempts to eliminate the raison d'être of autonomous union activity by "keeping workers happy." In other words, they may be interpreted as a modern insidious form of the company-union philosophy. Nonetheless, American unionism still seems to have a lead over European unionism as far as its organizational backbone in the plant and shop is concerned.

The problem for European unionism has been how to fill the void at the bottom level of the bargaining structure. In some countries, such as England and recently Italy, the role of the shop steward has gained prominence thanks to spontaneous developments. It has been observed that union leadership often harbors misgivings concerning activism of workers' shop-level representatives, who escape union control and centralized organizational discipline. However, earlier antagonism (as displayed, for instance, toward the British shop-steward

---

[7] The issue came under fierce discussion, for example, in the United States during World War II in connection with the "no-strike pledge" of most unions and the rejection of the pledge by the miners.

movement after World War I) has been progressively replaced by acceptance and even promotion. Interestingly, where unionism is heavily preoccupied with the programmatic formulation of doctrines and formulas of global social transformation (as in France, for example), attention to pragmatic shop-level bargaining activity has been traditionally quite weak. Whatever the reason may be for a weak union presence at the shop level, governments and legislatures have often filled the vacancy by setting up some officially sanctioned organs of employees' representation, with strictly defined and limited competences. We shall survey this type of arrangement, which sometimes shades over into participation schemes, after inserting a "special feature" concerning unionism: the case of Japan.

THE SPIRIT OF JAPANESE UNIONISM

The same physical laws are valid throughout the universe, but their manifestations vary from one celestial body to another. There is no reason to expect the same economic system—market capitalism—to produce identical forms of labor-capitalist relations from one country to the next. As Ronald Dore put it so colorfully, "The stirring and spicing and baking process of industrialization may [be] the same . . . , but if you start off with a different culture dough you end up with a different cake."[8] Nonetheless, peculiarities as striking as those of Japanese conditions make them appear as from another planet. In a number of respects, they must seem like the capitalists' dream come true. All the things executives in the West and in the Soviet area struggle for so laboriously, with tricks and treats and with limited success, seem to be a matter of course in a Japanese enterprise: no strikes to speak of, low labor turnover, low absenteeism, punctual and hard-working labor force, discipline, and compliance with orders. In Japan, they are said to come naturally, as a by-product of internalized cultural values which happen to suit the capitalist system just perfectly. Labor unions, while by no means a tool of management, and unmistakably fitting our definition of authentic unionism, have been supportive of the aims of the enterprise in a measure unrivaled anywhere else.

The internalized cultural values in question have been usually summarized in the concept of *paternalism*. The term means that family relationships serve as a model of social organization for other groups which are not based on kinship, such as the management-employees complex of a capitalist firm. The class relationship between management and the workers is perceived as if it were just another instance, or variation, of the ties between father and child. The divisions which set them apart and against each other, and which are not denied, are heavily overlaid by a sense of belonging to a common group, as if it were a family.

It needs to be specified what type of family. The cultural model in question is not of the patriarchal father-tyrant kind but rather of the reciprocal-rights-and-

---

[8] Ronald Dore, *British Factory—Japanese Factory*, G. Allen, London, 1973, p. 375.

duties kind, typical for feudal relationships, where paternal authority is tempered by benevolence and responsibility for the children's well-being. Projected into the capitalist enterprise, loyalty and obedience, which result in industrial peace and efficiency, have their counterpart in the firm's assuming a great number of obligations toward the employees. These go far beyond the fringe-benefits category customary in the West and have earned the Japanese labor-relations system the title of "welfare corporatism."

However, it would be all too superficial to view the postwar state of labor relations in Japan simply as a direct emanation of national cultural values. If it were that, then Japanese capitalism would have adopted its present ways with labor from the start. Actually, the system passed through a prolonged stage during which paternalism had displayed mainly its despotic face, and even through a short totalitarian interlude. The benevolent side developed and grew through a historical process where social and economic forces played their usual part, as everywhere else. Exceptional only was the influence of American policies during the postwar occupation period.

A full-scale historical account would have to start with the pathetic attempts at establishing unions of skilled crafts, organized at the turn of the century and up to the twenties. These have left no practical traces unless we attribute to tradition the fact that national federations have had, then as well as now, a tendency to embrace rigid political doctrines. This, however, is of little real import as far as union effectiveness is concerned. The present state emerged through the confluence of two independent sets of events: increasing influence of a home-grown benevolent paternalist management philosophy and a shift of seismic proportions in the relationship of forces between labor and management which occurred under the impact of occupation after World War II.

Benevolent paternalism of Japan brings to mind Robert Owen and his nineteenth-century enlightened reformism in managerial practices, or the "Lowell factory system" in the early Massachusetts textile industry, which tried to combine the notion of wage labor with that of a young ladies' boarding school. The popularity of such approaches in Japan, on steady increase from the early twenties, has been due to a combination of factors among which not the least important was the insight that the carrot was more powerful than the stick. The textile industry was the original pacesetter. "This is perhaps not surprising," writes Ronald Dore. "Adolescent girls are more likely to stimulate paternal proclivities in tough employers than adult male engineering workers."[9] However, it took a crisis in recruitment, caused by abominable working conditions and depletion of rural labor supply, "before the profit motive sought the support of such magnanimous instincts."[10] In other words, social and economic circumstances turned out to be the factor that determined which component of cultural values was utilized by the system as the most serviceable to its ends.

Besides its welfare features, the full-blown Japanese model is characterized

[9] Dore, op. cit., p. 394.
[10] Loc. cit.

by the following: Companies recruit "raw labor" straight from the school benches rather than trained labor of specific skills from a labor market. Companies provide the finishing vocational training on their own, according to their specifications, and when their labor demand changes in structure, redundant employees are not fired to be later rehired from the outside, but are reassigned internally. The enterprise provides a "lifetime employment" and assumes internally the burden of unemployment benefits when business is slow. The wage bill is part of the fixed cost, not variable cost, as under European and American conditions. (This, besides heavy reliance on credit finance, is what makes Japanese firms dependent on a steady expansion course of the economy and rather vulnerable to bankruptcies in a true slump, as in 1975.)

The wage system is strongly marked by the principle of seniority, which overshadows that of skill differentials. However, wage rates do contain an element of payment by results (piecework) and a merit element which is administered by the supervisory personnel (mainly foremen). Part of employees' compensation is received in the form of twice-a-year bonuses. Unrelated to work performance as they are, they recall the notion of employees' profit sharing.

"Lifetime employment," wages according to length of service, profit sharing, job-related welfare benefits, "extracurricular" social activities—all these features of the benevolent style of management helped turn the enterprise into something of a self-contained community. The shape and style of postwar unionism has reflected this fact. A Japanese union is an enterprise union. Let us recall the full four-tier paradigm of labor bargaining: whereas European labor had the problem of filling in the lowest tier at enterprise level, in Japan it is the one which is most complete, whereas the middle and upper ones are rudimentary.

In its earlier stages, up to the thirties, Japanese unionism could never penetrate inside the enterprise, so strong was the capitalists' opposition. And outside the enterprise, industrywide bargaining withered because of the waning power of skilled craftsmen, on which the unions were based. Skilled labor was being superseded by the masses of semiskilled operatives of modern industry.

The sudden postwar eruption of enterprise unionism on the industrial scene was made possible by a total collapse of morale on the side of capitalists and executives, compromised by their support of the wartime regime. American occupation policies made a positive contribution by encouraging labor unionism. This direct intervention of one system in the structure of another was all the more extraordinary as labor unionism had, after fierce struggles, barely gained full legitimacy on American soil during the thirties. Ten years later, it was being exported to Japan as a mainstay of democracy.

Labor bargaining at the enterprise level is of a narrower scope than elsewhere; it is mainly about wage increases and safety. It also is milder in manner, which creates an impression of weakness. To some extent, this is due to the management style which takes a number of issues from the bargaining agenda by taking care of them in the first place. Further, the lines of confrontation are not as sharply drawn as in a Western context. There is a stronger identification of a stable labor force of regulars with the objectives of the firm. The link between success or failure of the firm and the interests of its employees is more direct and palpable than with a rootless and fluctuating labor force. Hence, joint consultation committees, which concern themselves with production matters, have greater reality in Japan than, say, in England. Labor conflicts are generally rounded off around the edges. Class-conscious confrontation, which is part of the official trade-union ideology, is in practice tempered by the moral climate of Japanese society and the we-are-in-the-same-boat spirit of the Japanese firm.

Is the Japanese model of labor relations an Asiatic antique, i.e., a local cultural deviation from a pattern set by Western capitalism? Is the blend in which benevolent management practices and deeply rooted social values predominate going to cede the place to the classic pattern of a more pronounced antagonism of interests? Ronald Dore points out in his informative book that the reverse may be taking place. The search for new cooperative modes in European economies we are about to discuss may be seen as an attempt at introducing a Japanese solution to Europe.

EMPLOYEES' REPRESENTATION
AND PARTICIPATION IN MANAGEMENT

Employees' representation usually takes the form of some elective *works councils*, introduced by legislation, whose function is to be consulted by management on matters, specifically enumerated, which concern the personnel of an enterprise. On the face of it, in introducing such arrangements from above, the state is meeting the demands for industrial democracy part of the way. At closer examination, the meaning of these organs is not without a certain ambiguity.

By regulating the form and content of relations between employers and employees, the state aims at containing industrial conflict. Intervention of this kind is meant to provide a routine channel of communication between management and employees so as to anticipate grievances and prevent trouble. However, it also does something else. It spirits off a portion of issues from the field of competence of unions, especially those that pertain to plant and shop-level interests, and entrusts them to consultative organs of very circumscribed effective power. Although consultation may be difficult to distinguish from bargaining, the point is that organs of employees' representation cannot back up whatever negotiating they engage in by any overt instruments of pressure, the prototype of which is the strike.

From this point of view, introduction of organs of employees' representation can be interpreted as a sociopolitical maneuver having an ulterior purpose, namely, to banish authentic unions from the scene at the plant and shop levels. This is how a number of observers, including union representatives, have perceived the issue.

Codetermination Mainly West German   Employees' representation is one of the two elements of so-called codetermination *(Mitbestimmung)* of the West German type, the other one being participation in management, which we shall discuss separately.

Symptomatic for the spirit of West German arrangements is the title of the law which introduced, in 1952, works councils into enterprises and plants: the Act on the Enterprise Constitution. It indicates the desire to substitute the idea of constitutionality, i.e., of a process based on binding legal norms, for unpredictable power confrontations between management and employees' interests. This is why works councils have been forbidden to resort to traditional weapons of class conflict. Consultation, negotiation, mediation, and arbitration, conducted in the interest of "the welfare of the employees and the enterprise"—these are the sanctioned methods of solving, and especially preventing, industrial disputes. The competence of works councils is confined to matters such as forms and principles of wage-rate determination; working time; overtime; dismissals and other personnel changes; physical working conditions; bonuses, premiums, and fringe benefits.

Basic (minimum) wage rates are reserved to industrywide negotiations by the unions, which are entitled to back them up with strikes. The right to strike itself, though, is carefully regulated by law, which defines what is a "socially legitimate" action and what is not. (Politcally motivated strikes, for instance, are outlawed as not being legitimate.) It is only logical that a hierarchy of powerful and respected labor courts should be an essential complement of this system of cooperative labor relations. Their verdicts fulfill the role of arbitration which, in United States conditions, is mostly voluntary and unsystematic.

Works councils also have the right of access to management's economic information concerning the enterprise. Disclosure of information does not seem to make for much effective influence upon managerial decisions, but this, in any case, is a side issue, as far as works councils are concerned. It is part of that aspect of codetermination which falls under other provisions, namely those concerning participation in management (see below).

The institution of works councils, in West Germany and elsewhere, has been traditionally of concern to labor unions. This may be taken as a practical indication of their ambiguous position, situated as they are at the intersection of interests pursued by the government, management, unions, and still other groups, such as radical activists.[11] The tension that results can be gauged by unionist tendencies either to distrust and ignore works councils or to influence them to the point of absorption into the union structure. In West Germany, unions maintain their influence by means of their right to nominate the candidates to positions on works councils and through continuous communication.[12] Effective union control has apparently superseded the influence of works councils in Belgium, Austria, and Italy. Unions dominate works councils in the Scandinavian countries and are somewhat aloof in France and the Netherlands.[13]

---

[11] See, for example, the dissection of the situation in Belgium by Marc-Henri Janne and Guy Spitaels in Solomon Barkin (ed.), *Worker Militancy and Its Consequences, 1965–75,* Praeger, New York, 1975, pp. 185–186.

[12] See the study by Joachim Bergmann and Walther Müller-Jentsch in ibid., pp. 248–251.

[13] However, a word of caution is necessary. It is difficult for an outside observer to determine precisely the actual state of the relationship of forces in each case. Insiders who are in the know rarely publish the results of their experiences, and those who do publish are all too often outside observers or ideologues. An attitude of suspended judgment is generally advisable.

Participation in Management   This type of arrangement ordinarily refers to the presence of representatives of labor on higher decision-making bodies, such as boards of directors or supervisors heading capitalist companies. Their prototype has been the participation-in-management provisions of West German codetermination laws. Since 1952, codetermination law covering the steel and coal industries required half the members of supervisory boards *(Aufsichtsrat)* to be labor representatives. Elsewhere, "labor directors" were allocated one-third of the seats, but in 1976 the proportion was raised to one-half in companies with over 2,000 employees, irrespective of industry.[14]

In the midseventies, the West German prototype began to spread to other European countries. The one-third version has been closely imitated in Austria (1974) and, somewhat less closely, in Norway (1973). In Denmark, two labor representatives were added to the company boards of directors in 1974. A special participatory arrangement was enacted in the Netherlands. By 1975, participation in management had been placed on the agenda in Sweden, Great Britain, and France, and in the organs of the European Economic Community. There, participation-in-management provisions have been under consideration to be included in the so-called European company statutes, intended to apply to units of multinational companies operating in Europe. The idea was also picked up in Japan.

How is one to evaluate the phenomenon from the point of view of the objectives of workers' sovereignty or control? Offhand, nothing could be more obvious than to regard participation in management as a higher degree of workers' sovereignty, compared to that attainable by the bargaining methods of authentic unionism. Workers' self-management would then be the apex. However, what is so striking about the attitudes of concerned parties toward participation in management, and should make us think again, is that the dividing line between opposition and support runs across the capitalist management, as well as labor circles.

Thus, most business people in the United States, Switzerland, or Japan would not hear of labor participation in management, but it leaves labor and its representatives just as cold in the United States, in France, and to an important extent in Great Britain. On the other hand, there are unionists who, even if they do not see in it total salvation, find participation in management worth pursuing. German business leaders, who should know after a quarter of a century of practical experience, have no complaints. And there is an increasing number of business executives who display an attitude of sophisticated statesmanship, intimating: "Why scuffle with them if you can coopt them?" What conclusions can be drawn from this confusing picture?

A Beachhead or a Trap?   To get a handle on the issue, let us recall the meaning of the concept of workers' sovereignty, or control, we have been working with. At its heart has been the ability of labor to influence working conditions so as to protect and assert the interest of workers in their well-being. Now, it is

---

[14] Special provisions govern the selection to the crucial position of board chairman.

undoubtedly correct that workers' interests will in some ways be affected, directly or indirectly, at all levels of decision making that emanate from management running an enterprise. We also know that the actual content of managerial decisions in a given enterprise is determined not only by what management might wish to do, but also by what it can do or has to do, in view of the "state of the world," putting it as generally as possible. That covers the state of the enterprise inherited from the past; the global character of the economic system that binds individual enterprises together; decisions of other enterprises, the government, and other countries; the overall economic situation.

These are the constraints which, at every moment, limit the range of alternatives open to the management of an individual enterprise with respect to the major categories of managerial decisions: production programs; decisions to expand, retrench, diversify, relocate, or liquidate; allocation of internally generated funds; tapping of external sources of finance; introducing major technological innovations. If, in any given concrete instance, there is only one option available, or if there are several options, each of equal impact on workers' interests, then it clearly does not matter who makes the decision and whether labor representatives are in on it. The problem arises only when, among several alternatives, some are on balance more favorable to workers' interests than others. The question then is: "Will the presence of labor representatives in the decision-making bodies in such cases be a guarantee that workers' interests are safeguarded?"

On that central issue, the answer is neither clear nor simple. Labor advocates of labor participation in management assume this to be so naturally. They may be taking too lightly the possibility of labor representatives agreeing with the management point of view, either because of insufficient professional training or because of the sway of the view from the top. At the level of managerial commanding heights the way issues are perceived is different than from the shop-floor perspective. Advocates of labor participation on the business and management side seem to be hoping just for this possibility that labor representatives will agree with the management point of view.

In a survey of attitudes it was noted that British and Italian employers have been pressing for union "codetermination," i.e., assumption by unions of management responsibilities, as a "means of gaining labor peace," "last resort to reduce the number of industrial disputes," and "to defuse worker militance by pulling unions under the corporate umbrella."[15] The counterpart to this has been the philosophy of those unions which fear the problem of "divided loyalties" of labor representatives' "wearing two hats." It is illustrated, in the same source, by a simple statement of an American labor official: "You must be on one side or the other to maximize your effectiveness."[15]

On the other hand, it is equally undeniable that participation in management provides an avenue for bringing the point of view of labor interests to bear upon high-level managerial decisions, especially when the issues are of the clear-and-present-danger sort. If West German experience is an indication, it suggests that

[15] *Business Week,* July 14, 1975, p. 133.

labor representatives raise their voices when job security and other issues close to their heart are at stake. Otherwise, it was found by special inquiries, codetermination never prevented business projects, initiated by the management, from being carried out. A survey of such surveys concludes:

> The review of various decision-making areas shows that the employee representatives do (or can) make use of [codetermination] only to safeguard the immediate interests of the employees with regard to employment security. Planning, investment, restructuring, mergers, dividend payments, etc., are left to the management and can meet with the consent of labor if the "social interests are taken into account." [16]

In other words, participation in management seems to be meaningful if it carries into supervisory organs the process of labor bargaining.

From an organ of comanagement at the top, participation in management thus turns, in substance, into a supplementary instrument of workers' control "from below." This backstairs mode of extending the striving for workers' sovereignty cannot, in the nature of the case, take the overt form of full-fledged bargaining. Neither can it be backed up by the most effective means of pressure as collective bargaining by unions can. In that respect, it shares the weaknesses of works councils as organs of employees' representation.

SELF-MANAGEMENT: THE YUGOSLAV FIRM

If participation in management under corporate capitalism is cursed by ambiguities, would full governance by workers dissolve them? Or would it, on the contrary, lead to their exacerbation?

What is a priori certain, even in a hypothetical or utopian model of genuine workers' self-management, is that the dualism of perspectives would persist. This dualism is rooted in the antinomy of the two sets of functions and interests. Managerial functions, representing the economic and institutional interests of the firm, are at one pole. Employees' interests as workers remain at the other. In a technical sense, the functions of managers and employees surely are complementary. A cooperative meeting of wills in some form is unavoidable for the economic process to go on. However, in the structure of interests, where specific concerns of employees for their personal well-being come in as the relevant variable, there is always potential conflict, no matter who is in charge of the managerial tasks.

It is in this framework that we shall outline the Yugoslav system of self-management by "workers' councils" and explain its nature and problems. The point of view adopted here diverges considerably from the widespread conventional approach, which is to treat the institution as a matter of "workers gaining access to levers of command." Rather, it consists in *seeing workers as wage earners, with all the interests and problems of hired labor, and, in addition, being drawn into involvement with managerial tasks and responsibilities.*

Thus, the Yugoslav model is analyzed not so much as a variety of "social-

---

[16] W. Albeda (ed.), *Industrial Democracy in Three West European Countries,* Rotterdam University Press, 1973, p. 32.

ism," which is the official Yugoslav stylization, but in the context of other varieties of wage earners' involvement in managerial concerns for the economic successes of the firm. The smudging of the distinction between the two sets of roles, functions, and interests has been present, as we have seen, as an element of Japanese industrial relations and in European schemes of participation in management. However, it has not been entirely foreign to nonparticipatory models of capitalist industrial relations either. Stock ownership by employees of capitalist corporations is one variety. Profit sharing is another. Every once in a while, the press reports on isolated cases of firms being brought under the administration, or some form of ownership or coownership, by their employees.[17] Regularly, observers cluck their tongues at the sudden increase of work effort that usually results. This raises the important question whether workers' interests are better served when workers turn into their own supervisors, or when they force management indirectly, by their demands, to invest and innovate.[18] In all these varieties of arrangements we come across problems that arise when the system, to speak with Marx, makes "the associated labourers into their own capitalists."[19]

Charts and Social Realities   To understand the character of the Yugoslav model, several things have to be kept in mind. One is that it did not come into being as a result of demands or aspirations of labor. It was introduced in 1950, two years after the historical break with the Soviet Union, by the Titoist regime as an organizational formula intended to differentiate the Yugoslav system from Soviet-type economic etatism. Until this day, workers' councils are treated as anathema in all countries of the Soviet bloc. The enmity is probably due more to the fact that they have become a symbol of national independence than to any reasons of substance. Workers' councils have not undermined the power of the ruling party, and they have been elevated to the position of an official dogma, just as Soviet-type arrangements have in the Soviet area. As David Granick puts it, "Self-management is one of the great 'myths' of Yugoslav society, and as such it is immune to attack from within the system."

Another important point is that, under the Yugoslav system, workers do not actually manage the firms they work for; neither do employees' representatives, delegated to a Yugoslav firm's workers' council, take direct care of managerial duties. In periodic workers' council meetings, *they participate in the selection of the general director and four other members of the operational management board.* They have a final say in a few key classes of decisions, such as allocation of profits between investments and employees' supplementary compensation; allocating enterprise earnings to a housing fund; fixing wage rates for different job categories; and setting policy on labor discipline, working conditions, and hiring and

---

[17] For example, the case of South Bend Lathe in Indiana; see "The Saving of SBL," *Newsweek*, Sept. 1, 1975.

[18] This links up with our discussion of sources of growth in Chap. 12 (the brawn-versus-brain theme centering on growth of total factor productivity), and the connection between wage pressures and technological progress in Chap. 11 (sections "Trying Too Much at a Time in Sweden" and "If There Were No Inflation—So?").

[19] K. Marx, *Capital*, vol. III, p. 440.

firing. Workers' councils also approve production plans and transactions involving the sale or purchase of capital equipment. Self-management therefore amounts to employees' delegates intervening selectively and intermittently in management, which is exercised by professional executives.

Analysis of the Yugoslav model must deal with a task similar to that encountered in the analysis of the capitalist corporation. It ought to penetrate beneath the image projected by the letter of formal statutes, and discover the true lines of authority, delimitation of decision-making rights, and relationships of power. In that respect, an extreme view holds that self-management is a sham. Employees' meetings are likened to stockholders' meetings in their relative lack of influence on the composition of workers' councils. Workers' councils are seen as a counterpart of boards of supervisors in the corporate model with a two-tier executive: though not entirely without influence, they serve mainly to legitimize the exercise of real executive power which is in the hands of professional managers, members of what Milovan Djilas calls the "new class," the upstart heir of private capitalist entrepreneurs.

It would be futile to try and argue away sociological realities which do favor the predominance of the managerial elite. The predominance of managers follows from their central function as organizers and coordinators, and the necessary professional qualifications. It is enhanced by managers' greater durability. They are elected for at least four years, compared to the two-year rotation rule of unpaid members of workers' councils who in any case have little time to devote to their tasks. Furthermore, like the bourgeoisie in its heyday, Yugoslav executives form an overlapping part of the local and national political elite. This means extraneous backing, although, under Yugoslav political conditions, it can also mean that their heads roll when a political purge strikes (as in winter 1972–1973), without workers' councils being in the least consulted, which says something about their real status in the system as a whole.

Nonetheless, it would be equally wrong to be blind to the way workers' councils do effectively constrain the freedom of decision of the management boards. When it comes to certain major issues, the voice of employees' representatives has to be heeded, or at least taken into account. As far as strictly technocratic decisions are concerned, sociological inquiries have confirmed the same indifference of the rank-and-file and workers' representatives as in Western instances of participation in management. The activists in workers' councils tend to belong to the middle echelons of management, who use workers' councils as a stepping-stone in their careers. Workers' representatives on the councils revive only when an issue affects workers' well-being directly: distribution of apartments, allocation of bonuses between departments of the factory, hygienic installations, and—above all—distribution of profits as supplementary pay. In other words, self-management comes to life when it becomes a vehicle for substitute labor bargaining.[20]

[20] See Josip Obradovic, "Workers' Participation: Who Participates?" *Industrial Relations,* vol. 14, no. 1, February 1975, pp. 32–44. The analogy with the experience of Western European participation in management is remarkable. See quote at footnote 16 above.

Allocation of Profits: Plow Back or Distribute? The zone of conflict between what portion of corporate profits should be paid out as dividends and what portion should be reinvested is a well-known feature of corporate capitalism and cause of headaches for its executives. It has its analogy in the life of Yugoslav firms, except that the beneficiaries of distributed profits work on the premises, whereas stockholders receiving dividends are far away and dispersed.

Analysts of the Yugoslav system usually combine the examination of the formal ways in which workers' compensation is determined with the consequences for the pattern of resource allocation. In the present account, we shall follow the established custom.

Yugoslav rules of the game channel the pressure of workers' interests toward the question of the level of employees' compensation in a given enterprise, and the portion of reinvested profits. Employees of a Yugoslav firm receive their compensation in two parts: a wage part determined according to usual capitalist principles of "payment by results" and a share in net revenue made available for distribution (equivalent to capitalist profit sharing or dividend).

Obviously, firms of varying efficiency differ in their ability to pay high or low compensation, and that goes for wages as well as profit shares. This runs counter to the idea of "same wage for same work," a principle one would expect to meet in a system that sports the socialist label. It also is one of the rules of optimal allocation of resources. It means, furthermore, that employees are made financially responsible for the past history and entrepreneurial decisions of the firm they happen to work in, although both are beyond their personal control and competence. The resulting income differentials are both inequitable and economically irrational.

Equalization of labor incomes could be approached through labor mobility, but the necessary corrective mechanism is very weak. The rules of the game create barriers to entry of labor into rich firms and industries, and favor maintenance of inefficient firms for the sake of not destroying local employment opportunities. This is because the work force in rich firms tends to oppose new hirings for fear of having to share distributed profits with greater numbers. As early as 1958, Benjamin Ward was able to predict such behavior, on the basis of abstract theorizing about a firm whose objective is maximization of income per worker.[21] (The bare elements of his analysis are shown in Figure 17-2.) That labor pressure has been effective, in this respect, was strikingly confirmed after reforms in 1965, after autonomy of workers' councils had been enhanced. Growth of employment immediately fell by two-thirds.[22] The corollary has been two-fold: in prosperous firms, wrong factor proportions (relative understaffing of existing equipment); elsewhere, unemployment and continued operation of substandard firms artificially shielded from bankruptcy.

[21] Benjamin Ward, "The Firm in Illyria: Market Syndicalism," *American Economic Review*, vol. 43, no. 4, September 1958, pp. 566–589, and his book *The Socialist Economy*, Random House, New York, 1968, chaps. 8–10. See also Evsey Domar, "On Collective Farms and Producer Cooperatives," *American Economic Review*, vol. 56, no. 4, September 1966, pp. 734–757.

[22] See David Granick, *Enterprise Guidance in Eastern Europe*, Princeton University Press, Princeton, N.J., table 12-3, p. 392.

Figure 17-2 Employment restrictions in a firm under workers' self-management.

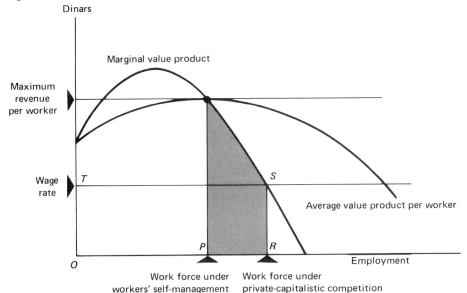

A profit-maximizing firm under competition will employ a number of workers equal to *OR* and earn a profit volume corresponding to the area bounded by the marginal-value-product curve and the line *TS*. A firm maximizing revenue per worker will tend to employ only a number of workers equal to *OP* because at that number the average value product per worker (equivalent to revenue per worker) is the highest.

The rules stipulate further that the undistributed portion of profits be used for autofinancing of the firm's investments. Employees having been put into the role of entrepreneurs are, like the classical capitalist, torn by having to decide how much of profits is to be distributed and how much saved and reinvested. In a passage examining this allocation decision by the capitalist, Marx quotes Goethe's *Faust*:

> Two souls, alas, do dwell within his breast;
> The one is ever parting from the other.[23]

What makes the decision all the more painful for Yugoslav labor is the fact that workers' usufruct rights in profits are contingent upon their employment in a given firm. They cannot take them along when they change jobs. Therefore, reinvestment of profits they agree to today will raise productivity and incomes in the future when they will perhaps not be around any more. Hence, their interest in plowing profits back into investments is weakened. They prefer naturally to see the greatest possible portion of profits being distributed here and now. Their situation resembles that of a tenant farmer, reluctant to invest when unsure whether the lease will be renewed, or of a distant stockholder interested mainly in current high dividends.

[23] K. Marx, *Capital,* vol. I, p. 593.

Self-management organs are the forum where Yugoslav employees make their personal interests count, much more directly than capitalist stockholders can in their stockholders' meetings, or by getting rid of their shares. The substitute-bargaining aspect comes clearly to the fore in that the conflict of interests becomes polarized between the management board and those who represent the employees' interest in the workers' council. The "accumulationist" point of view is often backed up by banking institutions that make long-term loans conditional upon a certain quota of reinvested profit, as well as by competitive pressures from other firms—Yugoslavia has a genuine competitive market economy—quite apart from vaguer arguments concerning healthy development of the firm and general social interest. All this militates against profits being completely eaten up, but employees' pressures have been strong enough to make the share of reinvested profits less than management would like to see, especially after the 1965 reforms.[24]

Beyond the Yugoslav Model   Irrationalities of the Yugoslav system from the point of view of resource allocation and income distribution have been examined critically by Jaroslav Vanek. His merit is to have proposed arrangements in the financial rules of the game that would do away with the decisions outlined above, while retaining the organizational features of self-management.[25] What is missing in Vanek's general model, which corrects for the economic deficiencies of the Yugoslav empirical case, is an appreciation of the problems arising from the antithetic nature of managerial and labor interests.

The questions that need to be faced are as follows: Assuming there is an area of actual or potential conflict between, on the one hand, the interests of the firm as an economic entity in its own right, represented by management, and, on the other hand, its employees in their performance of concrete work, how can the latter interests be best protected? By unitary organs of self-management? By a dual organizational structure allowing for an explicit confrontation of interests where they conflict, and their accommodation through open bargaining?

Managing a firm and at the same time representing workers' interests from a single pole of self-management would dispense with unions. Interest conflicts would then become internal to self-management organs. There is no way of telling what the outcome would be in each particular case. Would managerial interests dominate at the expense of workers' interests? Would some kind of workers' council paternalism emerge, attempting a harmonization of interests from above? Would a polarity emerge within the organs of self-management, such as we chose to call "substitute bargaining"?

Yugoslav experience suggests that the practical outcome tends to be a mixture of all three possibilities, with emphasis shifting from case to case according to local conditions. We can guess that this has not been adequate from the point of view of labor interests, in view of sporadic spontaneous strike activity, noticed

[24] See Granick, op. cit., pp. 392–393.
[25] See Chap. 6 (section on Vanek's "Participatory Economy"); also J. Vanek (ed.), *Self-Management: Economic Liberation of Man*, Penguin, Harmondsworth, England, 1975, esp. pp. 445–455.

since the late sixties, which has often pitted workers against decisions endorsed or taken by workers' councils.

Yugoslav experience suggests further that self-management is not up to the task of proper ventilation and resolution of conflicts even if the system maintains a shadowy official organization of trade unions whose functions with respect to bargaining on behalf of labor are not clearly defined. Yugoslav unions are never found in the unequivocal role of a representative organization of labor interests. They occupy a murky area of ill-defined subsidiary functions, somewhere between those of a local social-welfare bureau and a handmaiden of management. Strikes, though, have been legal, in contrast to Soviet-area systems (see below), but trade-union officers have not been sure whether to side with the strikers or to pacify them. In most reported cases they have done the latter.

All this seems to point to the necessity, from the perspective of workers' sovereignty, to maintain an organizational dualism, even under systems of workers' self-management. The need for a specialized organ representing workers' interests is the greater the less the real weight of workers' interests in self-management organs. However, even if workers should dominate self-management organs as fully as possible, duality of point of view would not thereby disappear. In that case, too, workers' interest representation through union organizations, serving workers' control from below, would be needed.

This conception, not as yet tested in practice, was formulated in a simple and lucid statement, issued by Hungarian democratic labor union circles in the course of the revolution of 1956. The revolutionary program then also demanded the establishment of workers' councils, but with a difference. It saw clearly the distinction between managerial and labor interests, even after the supersession of private capitalism and Soviet-type bureaucratic nationalizations by a regime of self-management. The text in question reads:

> Not even the most perfect and most democratic decree concerning the workers' councils will ensure the right to strike. . . . The workers' councils fill the role of the enterprises' business management. The right to strike, on the other hand, is the peculiar form of the protection of interests, a trade union activity. . . .
>
> We want the workers, through the workers' councils, to be masters of the enterprises, in actual practice. . . . The world, however, has never seen a master who has assured the right to strike—whether a capitalist master or any kind. However, it is important that the master, the owner of the enterprise, even if it be the workers themselves, be controlled by an organ whose primary task is to protect the workers' interests. This is the mission of the trade union.[26]

---

[26] *Nepakarat* (Budapest), Nov. 24, 1956. This warning against regarding labor participation in management, self-management, or nationalizations as a substitute for workers' control through union action animates also the writings of Hugh A. Clegg—for example, his *Industrial Democracy and Nationalization,* Blackwell, Oxford, 1951, and *A New Approach to Industrial Democracy,* Blackwell, Oxford, 1960. For a critique, see Paul Blumberg, *Industrial Democracy: The Sociology of Participation,* Constable, London, 1968, pp. 139–152, reprinted in J. Vanek (ed.), op cit., pp. 77–89. (However, even the critical P. Blumberg is aware of the problem at hand, as he writes: "Any trade union, then, which seeks active participation in management, must carefully *isolate* its trade union functions from its managerial functions, and in this way the autonomy of each can be protected." Vanek, p. 89.)

TOTALITARIAN PSEUDO UNIONS

The character of institutions organizing labor (rather than labor organizations) in totalitarian systems is best explained in reference to the triangle labor, employers, and the state (or government).

Under private market capitalism, the state has a separate existence apart from interest groups which make up the capitalist social structure. This is not to say it stands necessarily above the battle. Its actions may be biased. The state may heavily favor entrepreneurial interests, as it did in the formative period of capitalism, and often still to a considerable extent does. However, the historical course of social conflicts and the growth of labor power have increasingly maneuvered the state into a more neutral role, that of an organ legislating rules according to which conflicts of interest are to be played out. The state becomes an umpire, mediator, or arbitrator. Such has been the modern trend. It has been supported and reinforced by attempts at establishing international standards of conduct, especially in the legislative area, through the International Labor Office in Geneva.

This development has meant that what formerly amounted to employers' private dictatorships internal to capitalist firms has been progressively replaced by general civil legislation administered by the state. Labor relations took more and more the form of a freely negotiated contract between organized labor and employers.

Soviet-Type Model of Labor Relations

What happens when private entrepreneurs and corporate executives are evicted from their social positions and replaced throughout by appointees of the state, i.e., when the state becomes the universal employer? It means that the tripartite structure of relationships—employers, labor, state—is reduced to a duality: on one side the state-employer, a two-headed creature, and on the other side labor. The consequence is that all the organized power of the state, its administrative and coercive machinery, accrues at one stroke to the state as employer. Whereas state power had limited the powers of the employer as long as the latter was a private capitalist, it is at the employer's disposal as soon as the employer is the very same state. The danger from the point of view of workers' sovereignty is that the position of labor may be immediately weakened.

Theoretically, the position of labor could also be immensely strengthened. Reference in this section is primarily to Soviet-type systems (including China and Cuba), and there the official ideology holds such theoretical possibility to be a fact. The state is presented as a revolutionary workers' state (instrument of the "dictatorship of the proletariat," exercised through the Communist party), the capitalist component is eliminated, and the entire system is interpreted as one large case of nationwide workers' self-management.

Putting this central dogma aside as a matter of ideological self-stylization, one is led to examine sociological realities and the specific content of legislation. One discovers the existence of a complex bureaucratic power structure and a legislation which, through its concrete provisions, puts extremely severe limitations upon the scope of permissible activities of labor and citizenry alike. There continue to exist labor unions under that name, but they are a shell whose content was redefined so as to make them useful as instruments of constraints.

A Transmission Belt   To the usual concept of authentic unions as organizations representing labor interests, Soviet-type systems oppose, in their part of the world, the concept of unions as a "transmission belt" between the party and the mass of "toilers." What are those "belts" supposed to transmit? The sense of obligation to fulfill the tasks of the economic plans, to raise labor productivity, to strengthen labor discipline, to organize labor competition, to participate in raising piece-rate norms, and to engage in other output-enhancing activities. Subordinate to these tasks are functions of safety inspection and attention to hygienic conditions. Trade unions usually administer health-insurance benefits, distribution of tickets to cultural programs, and admissions to vacation resorts to meritorious workers. In a version of "joint consultation," union representatives and engineers are expected to meet periodically in so-called production conferences. Wage rates are not a subject of bargaining, being set centrally, under formal assistance of top union officials.

Officially, the notion of bargaining is not applicable in any case. Since the state declares itself to be a workers' state and "socialist managers" are its appointees, and "toilers" themselves, labor would be bargaining with labor, an obvious logical contradiction. Labor relations are construed in strictly cooperative terms. Thus, in annual documents called "collective contracts," enterprise management and labor force make a mutual pledge as to the fulfillment of the economic plan, specifying concrete measures to be adopted to that end by each partner. The pledge is as solemn as it is unenforceable. To all appearances, it is an extra set of rivets securing the assignment of production targets, but its formalism suggests it also is just one of the many kinds of mock activities meant to keep people occupied in the system's predetermined grooves.

Strikes are outlawed. They are considered sabotage. Selection of union officers follows the usual totalitarian formula: Member meetings confirm by vote single slates of candidates nominated backstage under the auspices of the party organization. Soviet-type unions organize workers, rather than workers organizing unions. They act mainly as auxiliaries of the state as employer.

Labor Protection—within Limits   This particular formal framework, which makes little allowance for the possibility of conflicting interests, does not necessarily indicate that legislation regulating working conditions is oppressive down the line. Surely, there exist severe restrictions upon the freedom to choose and change jobs—labor books (and internal passports in the Soviet Union) are among the instruments controlling mobility. A range of penalties has been available for the enforcement of labor discipline: pillorying by "comrades' courts" in the plant, reduction of pay, corrective labor colonies.

These elements of compulsion have existed side by side with prescriptions which are entirely consonant with the concept of protective labor legislation elsewhere. There has been progressive improvement, especially in comparison with draconian rules of the Soviets in force between the late thirties and midfifties (e.g., incarceration for repeated lateness). However, the real point is that, should such protective legislation interfere with the fulfillment of production targets, it is apt to be easily disregarded under the motto "The plan is the supreme law."

Even though *group* interests are off limits, disregard of labor legislation and other prescriptions provides a formal legal ground for complaints *by individuals.* Such disputes have been handled, in the Soviet Union, by labor dispute commissions. These are mixed management-union organs, instituted in 1957, and there has been the possibility to appeal their verdicts to courts. Outside this channel for grievances, labor demands have made themselves felt informally, e.g., through individual bargaining on the job between workers and foremen who have the power to fix the actual rate of pay and other conditions of work. As a result, Soviet-type economies have been prone to the phenomenon of *wage drift,* which means "a rise in the effective rate of pay . . . brought about by arrangements outside the control of the recognized procedures for scheduling wage rates," to use the handy definition of Phelps-Brown. Hence the recurrent campaigns to revise work norms upward, in order to regain the terrain lost through wage drift (see Chapter 11).

Authentic Unionism in the Wings   Below the officially sanctioned principles of labor relations, and quite close to the surface, there lie in wait labor's aspirations to convert the regimes' pseudo unions into unions of the authentic kind. As a sign of the permanent instability of labor relations, the history of Soviet-area countries has been punctuated by spontaneous workers' revolts—East Germany and Czechoslovakia of 1953, Poland and Hungary of 1956, Soviet Union of 1962, just to mention the major cases. Unionist aspirations are ready to erupt at the first opportunity supplied by a political crisis, as during the Polish October of 1956 or in Czechoslovakia's Prague Spring of 1968, or to precipitate such a crisis, as in the Polish December of 1970.

The call for a reconstitution of authentic unionism is sometimes coupled with demands for self-management through workers' councils. From a historical point of view it is important to note that workers' control through factory committees had been a powerful element in the revolutionary convulsions after the October Revolution of 1917, soon to be incorporated into the official trade-union structure, and subdued. A similar sequence was reenacted after the Second World War in Czechoslovakia. The demand for workers' control (in the sense of self-management) was resurrected, and then suppressed, in Poland and Hungary in 1956, as well as, once more, in 1968 in Czechoslovakia.

Postscript on China and Cuba   It has frequently been claimed by partisans of Cuban and Chinese communism that labor relations have been qualitatively different there from those prevailing under Soviet-area systems. At the center of this view has been the assertion that revolutionary consciousness has become the inner-directed motivating force of labor. Labor interests have, in any case, been defended by the government, said to represent workers, which removes all basis for conflicts and confrontation of interests.

An on-the-spot verification of this state of affairs has been difficult. Obstacles to direct inquiries have been such as to create a prima facie suspicion that one is dealing with ideological formulas of the same family as the official stylized interpretations of Soviet-type systems. Effective insulation of the working class from the outside world betrays a patronizing attitude of the government vis-à-vis the workers it allegedly represents. It shows a lack of confidence in their loyalty, as if exposure to outside information would endanger internally nurtured attitudes.

Significant events, or aspects of society, about which knowledge does transpire, do not suggest a state of affairs of basically different order from that of the Soviet type (e.g., mass compulsory work assignments to Chinese "rural areas," strikes and factory disturbances in certain regions of China in 1975). As for the character and functions of the union organization in China, as well as Cuba, they are substantially identical with those discussed in this section, even though particular techniques of persuasion and control discussed in this section may be different.[27]

Fascist and Soviet-Type Unions: A Family Resemblance?

In conclusion, let us raise the question of affinity between Soviet-type unions and their equivalent under fascism. Both types have one feature in common: They deprive labor of the legal possibility to organize autonomously for the defense of its interests. The room which elsewhere belongs to authentic unions is occupied by pseudo unions organized from above under the supervision of the totalitarian state and party. Freedom to organize, freedom of expression, right to withhold labor services through strikes, free choice of jobs and employers are all gone. Industrial relations lose, in consequence, the character of a contract and acquire the character of compulsion, all the way down to forced labor.

However, there are differences. Fascist regimes of historical experience did not rattle at the social foundations of the market-capitalist system (although nationalization of industry was part of Hitler's early program before the conquest of power). The private capitalist class was left in its place, and even though political allegiance to the regime was a requirement, its operational and organizational rights were only partly modified (see Chapter 4). They were understood to be necessary for the economic system to provide the political regime with the material means enabling it to pursue its goals. In other words, the state's power was used to tip the power relations between labor and entrepreneurs in favor of the entrepreneurs.

The attitude of Soviet-type regimes toward the managerial class of nationalized enterprises under state capitalism is somewhat more complex. On balance,

---

[27] See Charles Hoffman, *The Chinese Worker,* State University of New York Press, Albany, 1974, pp. 123–150; Carmelo Mesa-Lago, *Cuba in the 1970's,* University of New Mexico Press, Albuquerque, 1974, pp. 80–89.

managers have the preponderance of rights enabling them to keep labor in its place. However, they are, in turn, a social group which the totalitarian system also wishes to keep in its place, like all other social groups. The union organization, therefore, serves as one of the checks and balances neutralizing the aspirations of managers who might wish to consolidate themselves as a social interest group in its own right. (Such balancing of social groups against each other is one of the ruling principles of systems bequeathed by Stalin.) As little authenticity as Soviet-type unions possess, they are expected to counteract management power by their presence, and also by serving as a separate channel of internal intelligence. (The head of Soviet trade unions until 1975, Shepilov, served previously as head of the secret police.)

The ideological rationale of fascist and Soviet-type unions is not the same either. In the case of Nazi Germany, labor's place in society was defined in terms of communality and allegiance to the mystic union constituting the nation, a conception which admits of no cleavages between class-oriented interests. The organizational principle was that of "leadership." Officers were instituted from above and were expected to be obeyed unquestioningly. In the Soviet-type setup, class interests are verbally obliterated by the assertion that classes have been abolished by virtue of the fact that private entrepreneurs have been eliminated. Conflicts are admitted only in the sense of "horizontal" frictions between "non-antagonistic social groups," and as far as industrial relations are concerned, only as a matter of personal transgressions of individuals against the established socialist legality. The pretense of classless unity is driven home by letting state-appointed management personnel function in the roles of employers and union members at the same time. In fact, however, the "leadership" principle permeates the organization of unions, too (under the label of "democratic centralism"), but—in contrast to fascist ideology, which proclaims it openly and proudly—it is dissimulated: decision-making organs act formally as collective boards and are staffed by methods simulating democratic procedures. Instead of stark orders, enforcement of decisions is expected to be done through "persuasion." Despite basic family resemblance, the differences are sufficiently important to make the Soviet-style unionism appear much "softer" and not entirely immune to being infiltrated by attitudes of authentic unionism from below.

*   *   *

With all its social, political, and humanistic connotations, the degree of workers' sovereignty is, at bottom, an economic criterion of performance: it aims at reducing the cost of productive activities borne by people at work, and increasing their benefits. This category of cost has many dimensions. It involves the working individuals' comfort, health, life expectation, possibility to enjoy their leisure time (they cannot if it is all spent on recuperating from work), and insurance protection against the risk of unforeseen events. It also involves spiritual discomfort that may come from certain ways of organizing productive activities and being variously fitted into hierarchies of power and command.

Striving for greater workers' sovereignty amounts to making these costs explicit and letting them count in the labor bargain and contract. Workers' sovereignty can be said to have attained its goal if the cost side of work is brought down to some objectively unavoidable level. Since this is a forever-moving target, the striving for workers' sovereignty is an open-ended process.

Work under conditions of modern technology has become a cooperative affair: a network of interdependent and complementary activities, a matter of division of labor in a technical sense. Under the capitalist system, private, state, or other, this structure of relationships based on technical requirements of cooperative work has developed while being simultaneously overlaid by a pattern of power relations which are extraneous to it. These relations are at the source of psychic disutilities—alienation—which strivings for workers' sovereignty aim to reduce and eventually eliminate. Stripped of these nonessential aspects of power relations, the work process should then yield its potential of pleasure and satisfaction that is characteristic for group activities conducted in the spirit of teamwork.

We have compared a number of institutional and organizational forms by which the strivings for workers' sovereignty are being pursued, or impeded, under economic systems of different countries. It is not clear how one could measure quantitatively the relative effectiveness of the various institutional arrangements—authentic unionism, participation in management, combinations of unionism and participation in management, self-management, etc. We had to base the comparative evaluation on qualitative analysis and circumstantial evidence of diverse sorts.

Proceeding in that manner, we tried to avoid accepting at face value popular or officially projected images of the various organizational formulas. Keeping an eye on the objectives of workers' sovereignty, we focused the analysis on the effects upon actual working conditions and human status of labor at the workplace itself. The consequence of this "bias" has been to give their due to union-type activities fueled by concerns and pressures "from below," and to point out certain ambiguities, which are frequently overlooked, in schemes of participation in management and self-management. Given this set of criteria, the interpretation of so-called unions under the totalitarian variant of state capitalism has been preordained.

BIBLIOGRAPHY

Somers, Gerald R. (ed.): *The Next Twenty-Five Years of Industrial Relations,* Industrial Relations Research Association, Madison, Wis., 1973.

Chamberlain, Neil W.: *The Union Challenge to Management Control,* Archon/Shoe String, Hamden, Conn., 1967.

Derber, Milton: *The American Idea of Industrial Democracy: 1865–1965,* The University of Illinois Press, Champaign, 1970.

Blauner, Robert: *Alienation and Freedom,* The University of Chicago Press, Chicago, 1964.

Jenkins, David: *Job Power: Blue and White Collar Democracy,* Doubleday, New York, 1973.

Blumberg, Paul: *Industrial Democracy: The Sociology of Participation,* Constable, London, 1968.

Clegg, H. A.: *A New Approach to Industrial Democracy*, Blackwell, Oxford, 1960.

Barkin, Solomon (ed.): *Worker Militancy and Its Consequences, 1965–75*, Praeger, New York, 1975 (Great Britain, Italy, the Netherlands, Belgium, Sweden, German Federal Republic, France, Canada, United States).

Albeda, W. (ed.): *Participation in Management: Industrial Democracy in Three West European Countries*, Rotterdam University Press, Rotterdam, 1973.

Vanek, Jaroslav (ed.): *Self-Management: Economic Liberation of Man*, Penguin, Harmondsworth, England, 1975 (bibliography).

Abegglen, James C.: *Management and Worker: The Japanese Solution*, Harper & Row, New York, 1973.

Ballon, Robert J. (ed.): *The Japanese Employee*, Sophia-Tuttle, Tokyo, 1969.

Dore, Ronald: *British Factory—Japanese Factory: The Origins of National Diversity in Industrial Relations*, G. Allen, London, 1973.

Harari, Ehud: *The Politics of Labor Legislation in Japan: National-International Interaction*, University of California Press, Berkeley, 1973.

Levine, Solomon B.: *Industrial Relations in Postwar Japan*, The University of Illinois Press, Urbana, 1958.

Okochi, Kazou, Bernard Karsh, and Solomon B. Levine (eds.): *Workers and Employers in Japan: The Japanese Employment Relations System*, University of Tokyo Press, Tokyo, 1973.

Broekmeyer, M. J. (ed.): *Yugoslav Workers' Selfmanagement*, D. Reidel Publishing Company, Dordrecht, Holland, 1970.

Vanek, Jan: *The Economics of Workers' Management: A Yugoslav Case Study*, G. Allen, London, 1972.

Granick, David: *Enterprise Guidance in Eastern Europe: A Comparison of Four Socialist Economies*, Princeton University Press, Princeton, N.J., 1975, chaps. 11–13 (Yugoslavia).

Horvat, Branko, Mihailo Markovic, and Rudi Supek (eds.): *Self-Governing Socialism: A Reader*, International Arts and Sciences Press, White Plains, N.Y., 1975.

Zukin, Sharon: *Beyond Marx and Tito: Theory and Practice in Yugoslav Socialism*, Cambridge University Press, New York, 1975.

Conquest, Robert (ed.): *Industrial Workers in the U.S.S.R.*, Bodley Head, London, 1967.

Barton, Paul: "The Current Status of the Soviet Worker," in Abraham Brumberg (ed.): *Russia under Khrushchev*, Praeger, New York, 1962, pp. 263–279.

————: "Role of the State in Russian Trade Unions," *New Politics*, vol. 2, no. 1, Fall 1962, pp. 120–127.

Bunyan, James: *The Origin of Forced Labor in the Soviet State, 1917–1921: Documents and Materials*, Johns Hopkins, Baltimore, 1967.

Turin, S. P.: *From Peter the Great to Lenin: A History of the Russian Labor Movement with Special Reference to Trade Unionism*, A. M. Kelley, Publishers, New York, 1968.

Sorenson, Jay B.: *The Life and Death of Soviet Trade Unionism, 1917–1928*, Atherton, New York, 1969.

Brown, Emily Clark: *Soviet Trade Unions and Labor Relations*, Harvard, Cambridge, Mass., 1966.

McAuley, Mary: *Labour Disputes in Soviet Russia, 1957–1965*, Clarendon Press, Oxford, 1969.

Hoffman, Charles: *The Chinese Worker*, State University of New York Press, Albany, 1974.

Chapter 18

Change and Succession
of Economic Systems

Future is hope, and the gift of time was given to man out of kindness, so that he might live in expectation.

Thomas Mann

Of one thing we may be fairly certain: None of today's economic systems will stay the way we have known them. In fact, while studying the systems, we could not help making comparisons in the midst of their changing. We have had to follow each of them on their development through time for some stretch of the way, usually spanning two decades or so, even though our organizing principle has been to compare systems synchronically, not historically. Have we learned enough to be able to say anything useful about what makes for internal change of economic systems, and what direction that change is likely to take in the future?

To deal with these questions in a truly adequate manner, one would have to work from a full-fledged study of the historical emergence, development, and decline of economic systems, as well as of their complete or partial displacement by new ones. That vast task is beyond the scope of this book, as well as of our field (although both the book and the field are part of the task). As it is, we have to assume some knowledge of economic history beyond the hints interspersed in

Chapter 3 and elsewhere throughout the book. We shall further reduce the subject of this chapter to manageable proportions by considering, as far as the more distant past is concerned, mainly the emergence and development of modern capitalism. As for the future, we set ourselves no particular limit.

The outline of topics of these concluding remarks is extremely simple. We devote the first and longest section to the problem of how to visualize the process of systemic change. We then survey some of the major current tendencies at work, and finish with a tentative outlook on possible future developments.

THE MAINSPRING(S) OF CHANGE

The issue around which we shall be circling in this section can be expressed as follows: Do economic systems emerge and change, and are they supplanted or transformed through some automatism of impersonal forces, or are the changes a matter of human choice?

Humans as Technical Innovators

Many readers will recall the opening footage of Stanley Kubrick's *2001: A Space Odyssey,* where technical progress is telescoped into the sequence that first shows man apes fooling around with gravity by throwing bones into the air, and then switches abruptly to the picture of a spaceship floating majestically on its way to the moon. The technological element of economic systems is subject to change which is clearly synonymous with change due to the creativity of the human species, an attribute which is a constant source of wonderment to the human species itself. It represents the perpetual current of creative innovations in humanity's methods of production and their products, in its style of life, and ultimately in the character and aspirations of human beings themselves.

There is no discernible mechanism that governs the process of change at the technical level. Creativity is the very opposite of mechanical automaticity. Of course, it needs to be understood as a collective process. Activity of the individual genius or inventor is always embedded in the heritage of the past and supported by the state of the arts and sciences of the day. There also is an impersonal cumulative effect that enhances the rate of technical creativity with every advance, and with increasing numbers participating. And, of course, there is special interaction between the socioeconomic organization of the system and its technical element, to which we shall come back. However, technical achievements are humanity's own creation; they are not in themselves an alien force, cheap philosophizing to the contrary and Frankenstein-monster cartoons notwithstanding.

Humans as Organizers

Can one interpret organizational and institutional change of systems in the same way? Are organizational forms of production units, allocation of resources, and distribution of products also creative inventions and innovations like the technical ones?

In one sense, the answer must be yes. Participants who have provided the impetus to institutional change have always been acting individuals. More, they have been *activists:* persons with initiative, organizers able to exercise leadership or power over others, inventors, explorers, outsiders, nonconformists, challengers, and adventurers.

People of this stripe were the ones who opened up the routes of medieval commerce. Through market centers, they provided the nodes around which the owner-operated system of trades and crafts crystallized. Indirectly, they became agents of the dissolution of the feudal manorial economy and creators of the historical underbrush out of which capitalism arose. One could speak in the same vein of the early entrepreneurs who chose to organize economic activities in the mode of the capitalist firm, and who received their share of glorification in Schumpeter's work. True, they could not proceed without finding real opportunities to do so, opportunities provided by the confluence of a number of circumstances making it possible for that "historical precipitate" of capitalism to appear.[1] Nonetheless, it was their personal drive, their ruthless creativity and creative ruthlessness, that was the moving force of change that "produced" the capitalist system.

Innovative individuals were also behind the drive for the acceptance and legalization of the capitalist corporation (see Chapter 13). The development of the multidivisional form of corporate organization, which has proved to be the most flexible framework for economic activities in today's world, is associated with particular individuals.[2]

Thus, in the sense indicated above, the organizational and institutional dimension of economic systems has also been of human origin, just like the technical dimension. However, this simple formulation is not entirely satisfactory when we raise questions about the process of systemic change. The matter of "authorship" looks different in the case of "creation" of social institutions and in the case of individual acts.

Spontaneous Features of Systemic Change

Surely, the behavior of economic systems *is* the behavior of their individual participants. It is the aggregate of their acts and interactions. However, the *social resultant* of all the individual acts and interactions may acquire its own special set of characteristics which cannot be derived from the isolated individual acts. The social whole is more than the sum of its parts.

As we pass from the perspective of the acting individual participant to the perspective of the economic system as a whole, the question of systemic change appears in a new light. There is a new and different aspect to the control of individual participants over their acting. In the preceding section, we looked at the creative organizing function of the key dynamic individuals *insofar as they were in control* of activities through which they contributed to the working of the existing or emerging economic system. Now we have to consider *limits to their*

---

[1] The expression is Manning Nash's; see his *Primitive and Peasant Economic Systems,* Chandler, San Francisco, 1966, p. 30.

[2] See Alfred D. Chandler, *Strategy and Structure,* Doubleday, New York, 1962.

discretionary control which have their origin in the behavioral characteristics of the economic system as a whole.

As economic system, which in its totality is one of the social resultants of individuals acting, tends to assume an objective existence of a sort that is experienced by the participants who compose it as an exogenous force. It seems to have a life of its own. It has features that have not been willed by any of its participants who find themselves under their coercive power.

This is particularly true of the capitalist system. Preceding systems were, more or less, aggregates made up of relatively small juxtaposed units. They were decomposable. The weight of the discretionary control of individual participating units, relative to the system as a whole, was therefore greater, although technical mastery over nature and ability to satisfy human needs were smaller. In contrast, capitalism integrates individual units much more tightly. The formation of a universal market and extreme specialization makes everything interdependent. This explains the increased power of general characteristics of the system over its individual units. Hence the image of human cogs, or the idea of people enacting roles according to a script prepared by the system.

We show an awareness of this relationship between human participants and the institutional setting each time we use such words as "economic mechanism" or "dynamics of the economic system." In a similar sense, Marx spoke occasionally of capitalism as an "automaton" where, for instance, "competition makes the immanent laws of capitalist production to be felt by each individual capitalist, as external coercive laws."[3] We think of economic systems having an impersonal inner dynamics (or lack thereof), which controls or constrains the behavior of individual units. Nowhere is the grasp of the mechanical, autonomous, impersonal behavior of economic systems better exemplified than in theoretical models of economic fluctuations and growth. From that point of view, it may well be true that economic systems are made up of humans, but they are not "man-made" in the sense of being the result of purposeful acts. Insofar as their features produce effects contrary to society's interests, the Frankenstein analogy becomes appropriate.

When we discuss such autonomous characteristics of economic systems, we have in mind their *spontaneous tendencies* which cannot be linked to any conscious intentions and deliberate decisions of the participants. Hence, they are not under their control. Let us give some illustrations.

The major unintended effect of economic systems is their very success or failure. Which spontaneous tendency is responsible for the fact that, historically, economic systems are superseded, or eclipsed, by other ones? The *appearance* of new institutional and organizational forms can be understood as a matter of chance opportunities (confluence of circumstances) and personal initiatives. Their *survival, spread, and eventual domination* needs to be explained in terms of what makes for their superior viability. The decisive factor appears to be greater economic efficiency. It is higher productivity which leads to an absolute and

---

[3] K. Marx, *Capital,* vol. I, p. 592.

relative increase of income and wealth of participants in the particular system, their greater power and prestige, their eventual dominant position in society, and imitation by others.

This was true of the feudal manorial system of serfdom with respect to medieval slavery. It was true of the owner-operated system of urban crafts and trades and tenancy or freehold in agriculture with respect to feudal serfdom. And it was true of the system of capitalist enterprise with respect to the owner-operated system of petty producers. The organizational dimension of systems thus appears, historically, as part of the perpetual stream of technological innovation in the broadest sense. As Marx puts it, "a certain mode of production, or industrial stage, is always combined with a certain mode of co-operation, or social stage, and this mode of co-operation is itself a 'productive force.' "[4] It is not farfetched to interpret the historical succession of economic systems as a societywide technical competition of old and new systems with one another.

Part of this process is the equally unintended interaction between technology in the narrow sense and the social technique of organizing economic functions. Certain engineering inventions need an appropriate social organization before they yield their full productive potential. Machines existed before capitalism without leading to any industrial revolution. On the other hand, as the social scale of economic organizations increases, it generates new ideas in the realm of engineering innovations. Changes in the two dimensions of economic systems, the socioeconomic one and the engineering-technical one, thus reinforce each other.[5]

Let us also mention here certain unintended effects of the collective behavior of participants upon the behavior of systems in their macroeconomic dimension, or rather, more narrowly, on the behavior of market capitalism. What we have primarily in mind is labor's demands for higher wages, shorter hours, and improved working conditions. These, at least, are labor's direct objectives. Indirectly, however, they evoke responses on the part of the system's managers which raise labor productivity and cut costs. Thus, struggles concerning income levels and income distribution are transformed into pressures pushing, alongside competition, for technological innovations. Furthermore, continuous wage pressures contribute to economic stabilization of the system, insofar as they counteract the tendency of aggregate demand to slip behind the volume of full-employment output.

Among the most serious spontaneous tendencies, or unintended characteristics of the capitalist system which are contrary to the interests of its participants, we may simply refer to those sections of Chapter 7 which dealt with destabilizing cumulative mechanisms pulling the system away from its full-employment path. On the other hand, the wage and profit system, coupled with competition, leads

---

[4] K. Marx, *The German Ideology,* in R. Tucker (ed.), *The Marx-Engels Reader,* Norton, New York, 1971, p. 121.

[5] For an engrossing account of this interaction between systemic organization and technology, see chaps. 13 ("Co-operation"), 14 ("Division of Labour and Manufacture"), and 15 ("Machinery and Modern Industry") in K. Marx, *Capital,* vol. I, pp. 322–427.

to a spontaneous quasi-automatic tendency toward positive capital accumulation and growth, as well as toward the expansion of the system beyond the boundary of countries of its origin.

Lack of control over the "spontaneous" characteristics of the capitalist system, or any system, by participants taken individually seems to imply *the possibility of supraindividual control.* Let us consider it next. Supraindividual control means decisions emanating from some center of power, or authority, which lead to a pattern of individual behavior different from the one the system would generate if it evolved only under the impact of its spontaneous characteristics. Intervention of supraindividual control thus represents another factor of systemic change, and an extraordinarily important one at that.

Systemic Change by Deliberate Intervention

It is, of course, the old analytic urge to disentangle which makes us distinguish change due to spontaneous characteristics of a system from change attributable to conscious, deliberate, voluntarist intervention of a supraindividual order. In reality, the effects of all factors we have been discussing merge into one set of real events we actually observe. The present distinction harks back to the one we have been repeatedly led to make throughout the book, namely, between behavior of the "economic system as such" on the one hand and "policies" on the other. Here, basically the same distinction is extended to the very *creation of and changes in economic systems* in the most general sense.

The center of authority from which supraindividual intervention most frequently emanates is the state. We are thus back again at the notion of the visible hand, this time, first, in its role of demiurge: creator, promoter, and helping agent in the formation of economic systems. Second, we shall examine its ability to produce change *in* a given system.

It is often not sufficiently appreciated how much the development of capitalism owes to the early support by governmental measures. This was so even in the case of England, where the emergence of capitalism comes closest to the image of spontaneous combustion. The state was called upon to facilitate the transformation of agricultural tenure to suit the needs of capitalist enterprise; to set maximum wage rates; repeal legislation trammeling capitalist entrepreneurs in their wish to be full masters in their houses.

If supraindividual intervention played an active role in the country where modern capitalism was born, it was doubly and triply true of countries where it had to be bred by design. "In the beginning there was England. And contentment vanished from the world." These are the opening words of an article by Joseph Berliner,[6] dealing with the "other-directed," imitative development of countries that came after and needed, to a less or greater degree, the initiative of governments for launching capitalist forms of enterprise.[7]

---

[6] Joseph Berliner, "The Economics of Overtaking and Surpassing," in Henry Rosovsky (ed.), *Industrialization in the Two Systems,* Wiley, New York, 1966, p. 159.

[7] See Chap. 13, section on "The Public Enterprise Sector: Mainly British"; footnote 25, same section.

As a minimum, the state provided protection of "infant industries" through import tariffs. At the intermediate degree of intervention, the state orchestrated a coherent set of measures with a view to promoting accelerated industrialization via implantation of capitalist institutions and forms of organization. Prominent examples are the Russian industrialization effort at the end of the last century, especially under Minister of Finance S. Witte, and Japanese modernization of the Meiji era after 1868. As a maximum, the state may completely assume the role of the collective capitalist entrepreneur, not as a surrogate but as the real thing. This is the pattern of a number of underdeveloped countries, mainly those following the example of the Soviet model, such as China or Cuba.

Marx, whose observations are naturally most handy when one discusses historic changes of economic systems, took notice of this voluntarist element in systemic change. The modalities of supraindividual intervention employ, according to him, "the power of the state, the concentrated and organized force of society, to hasten, hothouse fashion, the process of transformation of the feudal mode of production into the capitalist mode, and to shorten the transition. Force is the midwife of every old society pregnant with a new one. It is itself an economic power."[8]

State power of the absolutist kind is in a position even to supplant an existing system by a new one invented entirely at the drawing boards of governmental planning bureaus, as happened in the Soviet Union after 1929. Reforms of the CPEs discussed in Chapter 9 have been of the same order, and so were the successive metamorphoses of the Yugoslav system. Wholesale transformations of economic systems may also be the consequence of military conquest or extension of political influence to the point where it is capable of imposing imitation, as happened in the Eastern European area after World War II. Under those conditions, it may also happen that an inferior system replaces a superior one. We are free to regard that as an anomaly, a temporary deviation from the historical trend mentioned earlier. If Marx spoke of force as "midwife" of economic systems, we must add that it can act also as an abortionist.

Besides playing a role in the demise and instauration of entire systems, supraindividual intervention is capable of *changing the behavior of a given system* "from within," without pulling down its entire institutional scaffolding. Such changes may not be as dramatic as the wholesale ones, but they need not be insignificant. Their real consequences may even be revolutionary, if we do not insist on narrowing the meaning of the word to one-shot violent upheavals and rather emphasize the "depth" and direction of the change in question.

Some of the more spectacular interventions of the visible hand, suitable to serve as illustration, include the state assuming responsibility for an orderly supply of money. State-assisted development of central banking, and an increasingly sophisticated control of it, have represented an important step eliminating one source of spontaneous instability in the behavior of the market-capitalist system. A similar change, making for greater stability of the system, has been a by-

[8] K. Marx, *Capital,* vol. I, p. 751.

product of the introduction of unemployment insurance and other income-sustaining measures known under the generic name of "automatic stabilizers."

There is no need to enumerate painstakingly all the other types of systemic change effected by the visible hand. Full-employment stabilization policies; promotion of economic growth; incomes policies; antitrust; international economic integration measures—they all have been dealt with throughout the text in the appropriate chapters. What may be of some interest in this context is to give a once-over to a set of questions concerning the identity of the beneficiary, or beneficiaries, of systemic changes of this sort. Is their purpose to "save capitalism" and protect it against revolutionary change? Do they amount to superficial cosmetics? Or do they alter the system in some fundamental way?

It was fashionable at one time to debate such questions in connection with policies amounting to a practical application of Keynesian economics, and even though the phrasing was more likely to lead to sterile scholastic disputation than to scholarly elucidation, the issues raised were not unimportant. For the sake of orderly discussion, it is useful to separate the question "Who benefits?" from the question "How superficial, or how revolutionary, is the change?"

Beneficiaries of Change

As to the matter of beneficiaries, there surely is a category of measures and changes introduced by the visible hand which benefit some social groups at the expense of other social groups. More specifically, in the market-capitalist environment, primary beneficiaries may be the key decision makers of the system, the "capitalists," as they are frequently referred to. Examples abound in matters of taxation or redistribution of incomes through subsidization of articles used or consumed mainly by the rich. "Class bias" of the visible hand may also work in favor of the capitalists in their performance of economic functions that impinge upon the well-being of workers, consumers, or citizens as residents or users of the environment. In the state-capitalist environment of the Soviet type, the class bias of the state has an even more pronounced tilt in favor of the layer of the system's executives, as shown in the corresponding sections of Chapters 16 and 17, concerning consumers' and workers' sovereignty.

However, the visible hand may also engineer changes that modify the spontaneous tendencies of the system in ways forcing adaptation on the part of capitalists. Even though, in the end, they need not suffer in any real sense of the word, at first such changes tend to be perceived as striking at their interests and benefiting other groups, e.g., workers.

In those instances, the state does not act as a simple "committee for managing the common affairs of the whole bourgeoisie," as Marx put it in the *Communist Manifesto.*[9] The state becomes the agent of other group interests, or even of general interests of society's members, transcending their narrower perspective as members of divergent social groups or classes. It is interesting to note that Marx,

---

[9] See Tucker (ed.), op. cit., p. 337.

as theoretician of the process of systemic change, had a very clear conception of this other role of the state. Thus, he interpreted measures shortening the working day as "effected by the State to prevent the coining of children's blood into capital,"[10] and he referred to the early British factory legislation as *"that first conscious and methodical reaction of society against the spontaneously developed form of the process of production."*[11] By way of extrapolation, a large part of modern governmental policies intervening in the working of market capitalism, as they developed from modest beginnings in the first half of the nineteenth century, fits easily into this category of change. It amounts to a certain degree or aspect of *mastery* of society over uncontrolled forces originating with its economic organization.

Cosmetic versus Fundamental Change

As for the "depth" or "shallowness" of deliberately introduced changes, it would seem that analytic understanding is not well served by ill-defined terms such as "radical," "conservative," "reformist," "revolutionary," and the like. What is needed is not so much to devise a better, more operational *vocabulary*, as to revise the conventional *basic approach* to the issue of systemic transformation of capitalism, which, incidentally, is widely (and unconsciously) shared alike by many of the conservative opponents and radical advocates of profound change.

Two things are involved in such a revision of the basic approach. First, one has to ask specifically at which "level" of the system, with respect to which systemic aspect, a given change is taking place. Second, one has to be clear in one's mind about the normative state of the system, or the projected normative model, against which one tries to evaluate a given change.

A given change may concern the macroeconomic behavior of the system (measures affecting stability or growth); decision making in resource allocation insofar as it leads to certain patterns in the composition of output (information supply, incentives, rules and regulations, sanctions); patterns of decision-making rights involving material assets or human participants; methods of selecting people for various decision-making functions. These are major examples of systemic levels, or aspects at which changes occur. And, of course, one needs to study the paths by which change at one level may induce changes at other levels of the system.

The issue of an explicit normative bench mark takes us back to the topics discussed systematically in Chapters 5 and 6. A normative bench mark is needed to enable us to say whether we consider a given change desirable or odious, progressive or retrograde.

Once the problem is laid out in our minds in this methodical manner, the evaluation of a given change from the point of view of its "depth" becomes much more meaningful. Our attention is less likely to be diverted by the spectacularity

---

[10] K. Marx, *Capital,* vol. I, p. 271.
[11] Ibid., p. 480 (our italics).

aspect—whether a change is mild or drastic. We are likely to focus more on whether it takes place at a level which matters to us most, and whether it is in the right direction.

To give a clear-cut illustration: Widespread nationalization measures in Eastern Europe after World War II amounted undoubtedly to an extremely drastic change in methods by which people have been selected for various decision-making functions. An entire social class was removed by social surgery. Taken in isolation, such an act might seem desirable from the point of view of those who favor socialization of ownership. However, at the level of patterns of decision-making rights involving material assets and human participants, the accompanying changes were nil, mild, or drastic, but in any case not in the direction of greater workers' sovereignty, and therefore retrograde.

In contrast, apparently minor changes of the superficial and "reformist" sort, such as improvements in working conditions, shortening of working time, and wage increases, as well as institutional instruments by which they have been achieved ("authentic unionism," protective labor legislation, etc.), meant substantial change not only in the performance of the system with respect to workers' sovereignty (see Chapter 17), but also in its stability and productive efficiency. It still is a capitalist system, but with a difference: with a greater degree of *social* control than has been the case, for instance, under Soviet-type state capitalism, where it is the state, not society, that has wide discretionary control, on the state's own behalf, of both the economic system *and* society.

The words "it still is a capitalist system" naturally bring up the question of the fundamental transformation of the capitalist system, i.e., its disappearance. Assuming that the system, as we know it, is not likely to be eternal, is it the cumulative effect of partial deliberate changes that might result in the postulated fundamental transformation? Or is it conditional upon some drastic changes of a different, "revolutionary" order?

Throughout this book, we have preferred the imagery of organic processes in order to convey the character of what happens in the economic subsystem of society. As we now think of the historical transformation of socioeconomic systems, the organic paradigm is particularly appropriate. It helps us keep in mind the aspect of organic continuity of social structures, and the impossibility of accelerating arbitrarily processes of organic change. The process of organic transformation of an economic system is, at every phase, a matter of transition: elements and characteristics destined to disappear coexist with sprouts of those promising to unfold in the future. Prefigurations anticipating tomorrow's structures are present within the old cells that decay. Phraseology that opposes slow organic transformation via partial interventions to revolutionary change represents a linguistic block hampering the comprehension of the issue.

To go beyond these broad hints would lead us to a critical examination of the entire vast socialist literature dealing with the problem of transition from capitalism to socialism, an undertaking which is obviously out of the question. However, merely to indicate what direction such a review might take, let us point out that the beginning was made by no less an authority on the subject than Karl Marx. One is apt to be surprised, unless one is closely acquainted with his writings, to learn that he was actually highly critical of conventional revolutionary conceptions which would advocate drastic action at the expense of substantive changes in the right direction. Thus, he complained for instance about French Proudhonist radicals of his day in the following terms: "They reject all action which is *revolutionary,* i.e., which issues from the class struggle itself; all concentrated social movement, hence also one that can assert its goals by *political* means (as, e.g., shortening *by law* of the working day)."[12]

It should be clear from this pointer what the effect upon conventional evaluation of concrete systemic changes would be if one proceeded from the vantage point of a general conception that sees the revolutionary transformation of capitalism as an organic process rather than as some kind of violent overthrow. The pointer indicates the need to learn how to differentiate strictly between outer form and inner substance, revolutionary appearances and reactionary content, or radical progressive content and nonradical form.

CONTEMPORARY TENDENCIES

We mentioned a short while ago that, in the process of organic change, future structures are concealed, as a potentiality, in structures that precede them and from which they unfold. Is it possible today to identify such anticipations of the future likely to unfold from contemporary economic systems? We shall try. We shall compress into a few paragraphs a review of what currently seem to be the most conspicuous trends of Western market capitalism, and the state of "arrested change" under state capitalism of the Soviet sphere.

Internationalization

In the second half of the sixties, the Western public's imagination was caught, and rightly, by the increasing scope and importance of operations conducted by the so-called multinational enterprises (see Chapter 15). By 1970, the share of production originating with this "internationalized" sector reached 15 percent of total world output. If the trends observable until then continued, that share would come to about one-half of total world output some fifty years later.[13] In terms of systemic organization, this development has meant a territorial spread of the system of corporate capitalism and increasing entanglement of national economies into the world market moving products as well as factors of production and technology.

Side by side with this "globalization" and its integrative tendencies, internationalization of a different kind has been on the increase. It has been taking place at the level of coordination of economic activities and joint exploitation of resources: use of communication satellites; joint management of the rolling stock of national railroad systems; electric power grids; joint development of innovations (the British-French development of the supersonic airplane; efforts to develop a Western European computer industry); etc. National governments have

---

[12] K. Marx, Letter to Kugelmann, Oct. 9, 1866 (our translation, italics in the original).
[13] See Judd Polk, "The New International Production," *World Development,* vol. 1, no. 5, May 1973, p. 17.

been further propelled toward attempts at international coordination by the existence of economic resources beyond the pale of national sovereignties, as in the
cases of ocean fishing and seabed exploitation. (Space may come next.)

Finally, there has been growing awareness of the need to coordinate national
macroeconomic stabilization policies and management of the money supply,
both of national currencies and of international liquidity. In the midseventies,
many of the problems of international coordination in this area have been handled through temporary makeshift arrangements, in expectation of a political
consensus that would lead to adoption of more permanent solutions.

Shifts in Patterns of Decision-making Rights

We have dealt with some of the most-talked-about trends in Chapter 17. The
shifting patterns discussed there concerned the demarcation of managerial prerogatives against the rights of labor and labor representatives to be in on decisions touching upon their interests. Various schemes of workers' participation in
management have been experimented with, and in a number of countries also
implemented, side by side with consolidation of traditional forms of unionist
activity.

These innovations seem to be part of a more general trend which consists in
the progressive dilution of personal power that used to belong to top participants
in the executive structure of capitalism. Beginnings have been made to dilute it in
other quarters, too. People's interests in the preservation or restoration of the
natural environment; in the quality and safety of products; in upholding certain
standards of morality and legality in decisions of corporate executives—these
and others found their advocates in individuals, voluntary associations, and legislatures. Although the movement is far from having matured—it has not gone
beyond disconnected forays concerned with this or that ill—it does represent
another strand in the attempts of society to increase the scope of its mastery over
the system's working, in this case over its external effects (see Chapter 8).

State Capitalism of the Soviet Sphere:
"Arrested Change"

Trying to identify trends of change under the CPEs poses a special problem
because the parable of organic change is not quite applicable. Under Western-
type market capitalism, *continuity* of organic change is, of course, accompanied
by *discontinuities* represented by the adoption of new policy measures or legal
enactments. However, ordinarily, there is a close relationship between the *continuous developments* in the socioeconomic sphere, on the one hand, and the *discrete
events* at the level of policy and legislation, on the other. Discrete events either
register and codify changes that have been in progress at the level of continuous
development, or they introduce changes for which the system has been made
ready by its own continuous development. The "readiness" may not be absolute,
in which case the discrete measures will require some effort of adjustment on the
part of the system's participants. However, as long as decision making at the
policy and legislative levels is reasonably democratic, discrepancy between dis-

cretely introduced change and the system's readiness for it cannot be too excessive.

Systemic change is of a different order when the system itself operates by virtue of strict and comprehensive rules imposed by the planners' visible hand. Continuity of spontaneous developments is repressed, change is almost always entirely engineered. "Spontaneous developments" assume the form of accumulation of tensions due to the system's malfunctions. Change appears in the form of discrete jumps, after political authorities become sufficiently alarmed by the consequences of malfunctions, and the power constellation among the leadership becomes favorable to the promulgation of reforms.

Throughout the sixties, and especially from the middle of the decade on, it seemed that Soviet-type CPEs were about to embark upon a thoroughgoing revision of their operating principles. Decentralization, autonomy of enterprise management, subordination of decision making to market forces—these were the most significant elements of change in the most radical economic reforms in Czechoslovakia and Hungary. The Czechoslovak reform was explicitly conceived as an open-ended process of continuous adjustments, oriented toward a system combining eventually a full-fledged market with indicative planning. The Soviet reform of 1964 and parallel reforms in East Germany, Poland, and Bulgaria were more of the tame, administrative kind, but it was felt that in due time they, too, would swing over to the radical, market-oriented reforms.

This expectation has not been fulfilled. What looked like the beginning of a trend turned out to be a series of nonstarters, or flights grounded soon after takeoff. The most radical reforms achieved a great simplification in allocation procedures and a palpable increase in flexibility at enterprise level, but lost the originally announced dynamics. The Soviet reform never got even that far. On the contrary, it appears that it was diverted from the original direction and redefined in the sense of modernizing the technical side of central planning instruments (mathematization and computerization) and creating administrative conglomerates of enterprises (see Chapter 13).

Thus, there has been considerable uncertainty about fundamental systemic changes of state-capitalist economies of the Soviet sphere. Leaving that aside, it is possible to detect a faint symmetry with certain particular trends in Western market capitalism. Thus, there has been a certain degree of internationalization in the management of rail transportation, electric power networks, and joint investment projects. In contrast, there has been little or no movement in the restructuring of decision-making rights that would perceptibly benefit workers', citizens', or consumers' sovereignty.

FUTURE PROSPECTS

Extrapolating current trends far into the future has always been a riskless enterprise: by the time the future arrives, the futurologist is not around any more to receive congratulations on his forecast, or to face the music. So, to escape scorn for indulging in forecasting whimsy without responsibility, we shall ask the reader to accept the concluding remarks strictly as speculation on a few possibilities, with no probabilities attached to any of them.

In the idyllic interlude of the midsixties (between the Cuban missile crisis and the Soviet invasion of Czechoslovakia), while reforms of Soviet-type systems were well under way and Western market capitalism celebrated its achievements in planning for economic growth and stabilization of prosperity, a group of Dutch economists (including Jan Tinbergen) came up with a thought marvelously suited to the climate of coexistence: the *convergence hypothesis.*[14] By drawing superficial parallels between isolated features of economic systems in both East and West, the group concluded there was a discernible though slow tendency for the two sets of systems to become more and more similar. The famous think-piece spawned an entire literature examining its merits, after which it was relegated to the attic to join other passing fads of yesteryears.

Does it mean one should altogether reject the possibility of progressive assimilation of today's contrasting systems to each other? There is no need to do that. However, an effort should be made to imagine scenarios of possible developments that take into account not only abstract tendencies but also the concrete forces of economic, political, and military power within and between today's nation states. Power relations may be the decisive factor to shape the world pattern of systemic change, at least for the next fifty to a hundred years, overshadowing intrinsic tendencies at work within each system considered in isolation.

We accept the higher-productivity rule as a general explanation of success and succession of major economic systems in the historical past. We accept it also as a general hypothesis in contemplating possibilities of the future. Those economic systems whose organization and behavior lead to higher factor productivity increases will tend, in the long run, to displace and supplant systems of inferior productivity performance. This long-run tendency may be set back, or distorted, by conquests, wars, natural or demographic catastrophes, or by hidden systemic flaws, such as, for instance, the absence of a warning mechanism to prevent destruction of the resource base upon which a given system rests. We take such events to represent deviations from the historical trend, even if entire societies count among their victims. If these events had not been mere deviations, humanity in the aggregate would still be in the Stone Age, or not even that far.

Geographic Shifts

Let us now be more specific about the various possible scenarios of the future. Let us start with what might be called the "smooth alternative," favoring tendencies that issue from the side of Western corporation-dominated market capitalism. If they could freely unfold, what would we see? Most probably, in the course of the next half century, a vast territorial expansion of capitalist multinational enterprises in the manufacturing, transportation, and service sectors. These

[14] H. Linnemann, J. P. Pronk, and Jan Tinbergen, "Convergence of Economic Systems in East and West," in Emile Benoit (ed.), *Disarmament and World Economic Interdependence,* Columbia University Press, New York, 1967, pp. 246–260, reprinted in Morris Bornstein (ed.), *Comparative Economic Systems: Models and Cases,* 3d ed., Irwin, Homewood, Ill., 1974, pp. 493–510.

would become better articulated in terms of size, technology, and output by being dovetailed with development plans of the less-developed countries. Corollary development of agriculture would be promoted by internationally organized research, and local land reforms favoring commercial family farming. National governments would learn to reconcile their narrow nationalistic perspective with the acceptance of multinational enterprise.

Soviet-area systems would learn to accept joint investment projects with Western companies (as Yugoslavia has been doing increasingly) and let them introduce Western methods of management. They would unlimber their rigid organizational framework and develop varieties of "socialist corporations," cooperatives, and straight corporations, and decollectivize agriculture. They would relax their foreign-trade regulations and join in the process of universal integration of national economies. Soviet government would progressively grasp the vast economic advantage of peaceful West-East investment flows and free trade over the policy of anticipating gains by means of continued military buildup and territorial expansion of influence or control. The unspoken assumption is, of course, that substantial changes would take place in the Soviet political system, making rational economic decisions possible.

It is easy to contrast the smooth alternative with a hamstrung alternative. That would amount to a simple extension of the process as witnessed so far. The general direction would be the same as under the smooth alternative, except that it would be much slower. All the described tendencies would continue to be hampered by forces of inertia of all sorts. Nationalism would be one of them, and with it the obsolescent prerogatives of the nation state, jealous of the transnational goings and doings of the multinational enterprise. Another one would be the staying power of the Soviet totalitarian system, its archaic and anachronistic conceptions of political and imperial advantage, which its own population and the rest of the Western world find so difficult to handle. Nevertheless, the relative superiority of Western capitalist systems, revealed in specific aspects throughout the earlier chapters, lends them a silent, steady, matter-of-fact capacity to expand, to advance, and to penetrate under their own power, which the forces of inertia may in the end not be able to withstand.

The two scenarios outlined above appear very much like illustrations of Marx's notorious phrase to the effect that "no social order ever perishes before all the productive forces for which there is room in it have developed." The scenarios spell out the worldwide job which seems to be well within the capabilities of Western capitalism. On the other hand, one must not be deterred from also thinking the unthinkable.

One cannot exclude the possibility that future political shifts so reorder the map of the world that a third scenario would be enacted: imposition, in some form, of the Soviet version of the state-capitalist system upon large portions of the West. What such development might exactly entail, and how its significance might be interpreted, say, by a historian writing in the year 2500, is impossible to say. History has known cases where conquerors have destroyed the civilization of the conquered, but then there also were instances where conquerors absorbed the civilization of the conquered and were literally domesticated in the process.

The experience of a conquest, whatever its methods, can hardly be pleasurable for those who undergo it. Those living today cannot be expected to give in passively for the sake of some higher historical tendencies. However, if we place ourselves artificially on a higher historical standpoint, it is conceivable that further extension of Soviet hegemony might lead to a thorough metamorphosis of the system, including its economic subset, and thus to a kind of convergence as a result of force. In the opposite case, convergence by force might mean assimilation of Western systems to the Soviet pattern, or the formation of various hybrid systems, although without the counterweight pull of Western systems the tendency toward hybridization (along, say, the Hungarian-reform pattern) may weaken considerably, or even disappear.

The most catastrophic scenario—a "Dr. Strangelove" kind of end of the world; a carbon-dioxide-induced overheating of the atmosphere and the consequent deluge from melted polar caps; absolute exhaustion of natural resources— would take the problem of systemic change presumably off the agenda altogether, and need not therefore occupy us here.

Control, Mastery, Freedom

In this speculative review of possible images of the future, we have so far concentrated on aspects which have to do with the territorial spread of the major economic systems of today. What about the future of the internal restructuring of rights, decision making, human relations, and the general character of society's life insofar as it is determined by the economic system?

In this respect, our preference is to step out of the narrow technical categories of economics and view the changing shape of economic systems as a phase in the drama of humanity's struggle for mastery over its existence, for the definition of its purposes and of what it wants to become—in a word, for its freedom.

Glancing back at the topics of past chapters, the reader may now realize that this has been their underlying theme all along. Regulating aggregate economic activity so as to avoid the waste of unemployment; promoting growth; pushing for wider rights of labor in the determination of its working conditions; searching for ways to enhance the sovereignty of people as consumers—these and the many other aspects of consciously influencing the operation of economic systems were treated as specific instances of human determination to tame, subdue, regulate, stimulate, modify, and reform, i.e., to control the social forms of economic activities. As for the future, we would expect more of the same.

However, in this respect, the scenario is not so much a mere speculative forecast based on trend projection as it is a *project*, i.e., something society is able to want and must work at to make happen.

With an increasing degree of society's control the economic system is bound to change more and more from a congeries of objective forces to an instrument of freedom. Continued growth of productivity promises to enlarge the time available for freely chosen activity and to make possible new flexible arrangements of our working time. It is also bound to blunt the edge of conflicts over income distribution. In due time, it should also deprive the many socially sterile activities concerned with the management of private wealth of their rationale.

Parallel trends are dormant in state-capitalist systems of the Soviet type. Sooner or later they are likely to awaken, and through a series of social struggles gather enough force to enable the respective societies to participate freely in this universal process of restructuring the economic system of capitalism. We believe this would eventually happen even if the world were forced to pass through the detour of first seeing Soviet state capitalism expand beyond its present borders. It would only mean that the structure of social controls that had developed in the West over the last century would in a number of ways be seriously thrown back, and stages that seemed to have been left behind would have to be recapitulated before the forward march could be resumed again. This would particularly be the case of the organization of labor.

In the back of this basically optimistic long-range outlook there are certain assumptions about human nature and the direction of history which make us reject the image of a permanent totalitarian "black utopia" as human destiny. In a nutshell: Just as, physically, it is human nature to live erect and not crouched, spiritually it is human nature to want to be free, and to strive to be so as long as one is not free. As long as the structure of the economic and social system continues to be felt as oppressive and constraining, it will generate forces striving for emancipation.

We said the future process of restructuring capitalism would involve more of the same tendencies of growing social control we have been able to observe currently. We should elaborate slightly and say—more of the same but better. We would expect new advances in scientific understanding of social and economic processes, greater diffusion of that understanding, and, with better information, a greater involvement of society in articulating its needs and policies to serve those needs.

We would finally expect an overwhelming shift in the structure of economic activities away from material output, whose level would stabilize, toward personal services; and among services toward one particular category of exceptional significance which has been sadly undernourished and underadvertised in the development of capitalism up to the present, namely, education.

The most promising source of future increases in economic welfare is not in a growing volume of material output but in the enhancement of human ability to experience satisfaction. Education—not just schooling, but education in the broadest sense—is the "industry" able to tap that source, by equipping individuals spiritually and intellectually for the pursuit of the deepest satisfactions that matter: in the quality of human relations and in creativity.

*   *   *

That stage in the future development of economic systems of today probably will not be called capitalism any more. The process of progressive restructuring would presumable dissolve the basic relationship of capitalism, which opposes wage labor to the system as such, and to those who staff the system's key posts. If we are correct in thinking that there are no shortcuts permitting society to bypass the slow historical process of cumulative change, the process which consists in the removal by feasible degrees of layers and layers of constraints and impediments to full freedom and humanization of society, then we have another follow-up thought to offer. The postcapitalist system may arrive undramatically, by stealth, without fanfare, without banners, and possibly even without the old ideological labels. However, if it arrives, the fact itself will not remain unnoticed: our descendents will find out by truly feeling at home in society and in the world.

And there will be one more sign to go by: The subject matter of the comparative study of economic systems will have vanished, and become of historical interest only.

BIBLIOGRAPHY

North, Douglas C., and Robert Paul Thomas: "An Economic Theory of the Growth of the Western World," *The Economic History Review,* Second Series, vol. 23, no. 1, 1970, pp. 1–17.

Hicks, Sir John Richard: *Theory of Economic History,* Clarendon Press, Oxford, 1969.

Davis, Lance Edwin, and Douglas C. North: *Institutional Change and American Economic Growth,* Cambridge University Press, London, 1971.

Perlmutter, Howard V.: "The Multinational Firm and the Future," *The Annals,* vol. 403, September 1972, pp. 139–152.

Spulber, Nicolas, and Ira Horowitz: *Quantitative Economic Policy and Planning,* Norton, New York, 1976, chap. 18, "Convergency Theories and Optimal Systems," pp. 367–391.

Bhagwati, Jagdish N. (ed.): *Economics and World Order from the 1970's to the 1990's,* Macmillan, New York, 1972.

Heilbroner, Robert L.: *An Inquiry into the Human Prospect,* with "Second Thoughts" and "What Has Posterity Ever Done for Me?" Norton, New York, 1974, 1975.

Index